Fodor's 2002

W9-BHI-603

New York City

CONTENTS

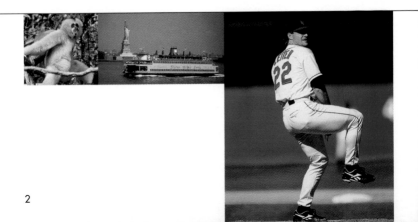

MAPS

Circled letters in text correspond to letters on the photographs. For more information on the sights pictured, turn to the indicated page number Ⓐ▷ on each photograph.

DESTINATION
NEW YORK CITY

It's been called the "greatest city in the world" so many times—usually by its own politicians, its own media figures, its own men and women in the street—that the claim may seem empty. But that slogan takes on new life when inverted: New York is civilization's greatest *world within a city*. It feels as though *everything* is here. It's not, of course, but that's a trifling observation. What truly matters is the overpowering impression that New York gives of being both a mirror and a magnet for all of humanity and all that humanity does. Come and see for yourself: New York is the world's beating heart.

SKYSCRAPERS

Years back, the story goes, a sightseer stood on 5th Avenue ogling the ⒶⒷ**Empire State Building** (1931). After a minute or so he pronounced, deadpan, "It gives the impression of height." Yes, it certainly does. It's no longer the world's tallest building—not even New York's—but it *feels* tall, especially to anyone on the 86th-floor observation deck. Year-round its summit is floodlit in honor of holidays and events. The tallest-building title has also been held by the Ⓔ**Chrysler Building** (1930), a midtown study in Art Deco; downtown's lacy Woolworth Building (1913); and the World Trade Center's twin

Ⓒ▷ 112

Ⓓ 36

Ⓔ 100

towers (1972–73), which anchor Manhattan near the concrete canyons of the Ⓓ**Financial District.** Skyscraper fashions change. Park Avenue's Seagram Building (1958) ushered in an era of large plazas and deep setbacks. The tilted top of the Ⓒ**Citicorp Center** (1977) introduced whimsy to the city skyline, which now includes the Sony Building (1984), scalloped like a Chippendale highboy.

CLASSIC
ARCHITECTURE

For a city so young, New York is home to an impressive number of architectural classics. When you're talking early 20th-century American architecture, it doesn't get any better than this. In the shadow of the gleaming Chrysler Building on 42nd Street near Lexington Avenue, Ⓐ**Grand Central Terminal** sparkles behind 75-ft fluted columns. Step onto its concourse and let yourself be dazzled by the immensity of the space, the human energy, and the zodiac fresco twinkling benignly overhead. Two stone lions guard the Beaux Arts–style New York Public Library immediately to the west, on Fifth Avenue. Marking the foot of the avenue is the ⒟**Washington Arch,** stellar for the people-watching to be had in the park below. Everywhere, blocky high-rises contrast with church spires: St. John the Divine, the world's largest Gothic cathedral, uptown; St. Patrick's Cathedral, opposite Rockefeller Center; St. Mark's-in-the-Bowery, in the East Village; and an emblem of godliness near Wall Street, ⒝**Trinity Church.** Among the small wonders in the vicinity of Trinity are colonnaded Federal Hall, the handsome U.S. Custom House (now housing the Museum of the American Indian), and the exquisite ⒞**Brooklyn Bridge,** one of the world's great spans. Views from its walkway are incredible—across the spiky ship masts at South Street Seaport into the thicket of Manhattan skyscrapers. Make the trip late in the day, when the sun is low and pinkish-gold light coats the cityscape like honey.

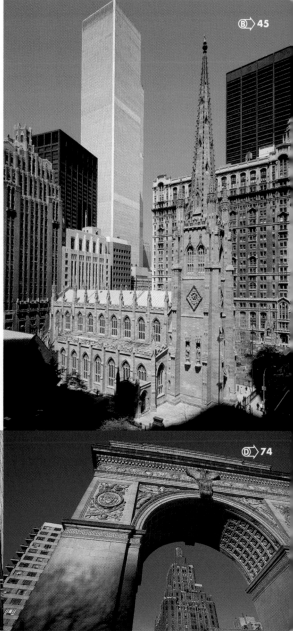

⒝ 45

⒞ 49

⒟ 74

CITY OF IMMIGRANTS

Ⓐ▷ **144**

For many who love New York, this, above all else, is what makes the city special: From the beginning it has opened its doors to those from other lands who would make America their home. For millions in the late 19th and early 20th centuries Ⓓ**Ellis Island** meant landfall. The island's former immigrant-processing center is now a museum, accessible via the same excursion boat that takes you to the Statue of Liberty. Even if your ancestors didn't come through Ellis Island you will be stirred by the exhibits. Many immigrants traveled no farther into the New World than New York. The French, disembarking on the midtown piers, started restaurants right there, on 52nd Street. Italians stopped in Ⓕ**Little Italy,** which is now squeezed by New York's increasingly robust Ⓒ**Chinatown.** Go Chinese for dinner then wrap up your

Ⓑ▷ **446**

Ⓒ▷ **52**

Ⓓ 41

evening with cannolis and espresso. Or step a few blocks uptown to the East Village, or to Little India on Lexington Avenue in the 20s, for an aromatic feast. Farther north, the Irish pubs in Turtle Bay prove that the greening of New York continues: when the city salutes its Irish heritage at the annual Ⓑ**St. Patrick's Day Parade,** many a recent Irish arrival joins in, and the crowd is full of lilting accents. Nowadays many newcomers hail from outside Europe. They season the melting pot at flea markets on the Ⓐ**Upper West Side** and march in Brooklyn's Ⓔ**West Indian American Day Parade.** About the only group that hasn't emigrated to New York yet is extraterrestrials (although some days you wonder).

Ⓔ 448

RISTORANTE PUGLIA RISTORANTE

Est. 1919

Ⓕ 52

Even if some Hollywood renditions of New York cross the line into cliché, there's a lot of truth to the image of the city as elbow-to-elbow and high-voltage, seething with the nervous energy of so many people crowded into so little space. Think about it: Elsewhere in America, pedestrians appear eccentric, if not

Ⓐ 118

NEW YORK
ON THE MOVE

Ⓑ 116

subversive; a gathering of two or three constitutes a throng, perhaps warranting a slow pass by a police cruiser. By contrast, New York is a city of foot traffic, and walking—say, along Ⓑ**5th Avenue**—is often the smartest way to get around, despite the crowds on the sidewalks. Except when stuck in bumper-to-bumper traffic in Ⓒ**Times Square** or elsewhere, New Yorkers keep up a relentlessly brisk pace. Could anyone but a Zen master remain mellow at Ⓐ**F.A.O. Schwarz,** particularly during the Christmas shopping season, or meander languidly through Penn Station, Grand Central, or the subways at rush hour? On a turbulent trading day the floor of the Ⓓ**New York Stock Exchange** is the scene of bellowing and flailing that suggest an aerobics class

Ⓒ 106

in hell. Thank goodness for green spaces like Central Park, Riverside Park, and Brooklyn's Prospect Park, where cars are sometimes banned, and a guy and his dog can own the road if they move fast enough.

For some, what New York is really all about is Stuff, from budget to off-the-charts, from armoires to zippers. Everywhere, the ambience is part of the experience, and stores are stage

374

sets—the elaborate Ralph Lauren mansion, the minimalist Calvin Klein boutique, super-hip NikeTown, endlessly eclectic ABC Carpet & Home. Bookstores are legion, including big names and

SHOPPING

311

wonderful secondhand specialists like the Strand, with 8 miles of books, and alfresco bookstalls. The mother ship of all department stores may be Bloomingdale's, an institution at 59th Street and Lexington Avenue, or maybe Ⓐ**Macy's** in Herald Square, whose famous sign reminds you how big the store is. Jog around it three times, and you can easily cover more than a mile. (Some people cover more ground because they get lost.) Fifth Avenue is home to scattered electronics micro-stores (where haggling is expected),

© 374

© 388

D&G
DOLCE&GABBANA

Lord & Taylor, ©**Saks Fifth Avenue,** and, in its upper reaches around the ®**Plaza Hotel,** to Henry Bendel and Bergdorf Goodman. All of these specialize in clothing—very, very nice clothing, of a type that also hangs in stores along Madison Avenue. Between 60th and 72nd streets this avenue is New York's answer to Beverly Hills' Rodeo Drive, and to Monaco in general. In the rarefied Barneys New York and designer emporiums like Prada, Cerruti, and ®**Dolce & Gabbana,** regulars who shop 'til they drop are apt to be caught by their chauffeurs before they hit the floor. Come to look even if you know you won't buy. Everything is gorgeous, including the people. If your ancestors arrived at Ellis Island they may have shopped on the Lower East Side, specifically on ©**Orchard Street.** The languages on the street are different now, but the feeling is the same. As you admire the Stuff—some of it waving in the breezes outside, some of it in chic shops, and all of it discounted—think of your walk as part of your Ellis Island tour. And while you're philosophizing, keep your eyes peeled for bargains.

© 367

Many people who move to New York bring good kitchen skills and a fondness for cooking. Soon they're eating in restaurants as often as they can afford it. And who can blame them? The variety of cuisines makes the senses reel: You'll find everything

DINING OUT

Ⓐ 285

from great steaks to the freshest of fish, spaetzle to tapas, roti to farofa. For breakfast, go native and start the day with a bagel. Understand, though, that bagel quality varies widely, even in New York: some taste like cardboard, others like heaven. For lunch and dinner, study all the options before you choose. The inventiveness of menus around town is almost novelistic. You might be tempted to play it safe with pasta in an Italian trattoria. But give your adventurous side free rein, and you might end up sampling kimchee at a Korean lunch counter, trying the crispest-ever

Ⓑ 259

© 290

Ⓓ 95

french fries at a Belgian bistro, gobbling a pastrami sandwich on the Lower East Side, perusing the wine list at Ⓑ**Tabla,** or feasting on sea bass in a potato crust or tuna carpaccio at Ⓐ **Daniel.** Tucked into Central Park, ©**Tavern on the Green** occupies a tiny, magical principality of its own, a wonderland of tiny white lights. And, in Chelsea, the Ⓓ**Empire Diner** is a wee-hours stalwart, open 24/7. To create a picnic, seek out Fairway or Zabar's on the Upper West Side, a stone's throw from Central Park, or look up Ⓔ**Balducci's** on 6th Avenue at 9th Street.

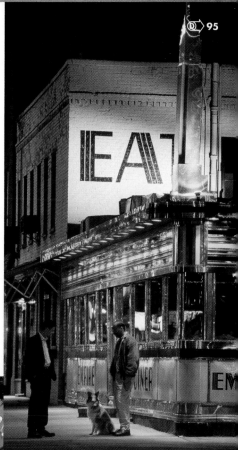

Ⓔ 70

New York's museums span interests from modern armaments—at the Ⓑ*Intrepid Sea-Air-Space Museum,* aboard a giant aircraft carrier—to

MUSEUMS

Ⓐ▷113   Ⓑ▷103

photography, film, and 20th-century painting and design at the Ⓐ**Museum of Modern Art.** Repositories of art are the dominant species of museum, but if the city housed no other museum than the colossal Ⓒ**Metropolitan Museum of Art,** you would sense nothing amiss. You could spend whole years happily roaming its labyrinthine corridors and still not see it all. Weather permitting, go up to the roof garden at sunset for a drink and a nice angle on Central Park. Some museums also distinguish themselves as works of architecture. Marcel Breuer designed the stark, square Whitney Museum of American Art,

Ⓒ▷131

PAINTINGS

and the Ⓔ**Solomon R. Guggenheim Museum** is Manhattan's only building by Frank Lloyd Wright. At the borough's northern tip the Ⓓ**Cloisters** was cleverly assembled from chunks of European monasteries to look like a monastery itself, a perfect showcase for one of the world's best collections of medieval art. Go on a weekday—preferably a rainy one—and you'll have the tranquil garden walkways a bit more to yourself. Equally unusual is the Ⓕ**Frick Collection,** in Henry Clay Frick's fine limestone 5th Avenue mansion. It seems impossible that so many masterpieces of the stature of Holbein the Younger's portrait of Thomas More could have been amassed by just one man. After the Frick there's the Museum of Television and Radio (a treasure). And the American Museum of Natural History (an adventure). And the Lower East Side Tenement Museum. And many more. As a New Yorker might say, "You want museums? We got museums."

Ⓔ 134

Ⓕ 131

THE GREAT WHITE WAY

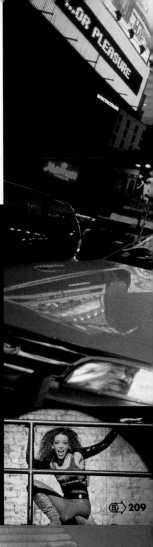

Ⓐ 100

There are places in this world where telling someone to "break a leg" might get you some fractures of your own. Not so in New York City's ⒹTheater District, where theater people wish each other luck in perverse ways. Radiating mainly north and west from Times Square, this is a tight little zone of bright lights and big dreams—the latter belonging to everyone from the well-heeled backers who finance the productions to your bartender, who might have auditioned for the show you just saw. He may have heard the three words actors hate, "We'll call you," but for some the dream comes true. They can quit waiting tables, at least for a while, and tread the boards in style at the ⒶFord Center for the Performing Arts or snag a role in a hit such as ⒷRent or ⒺPhantom of the Opera. Some tickets are

Ⓑ 209

Ⓒ 210

impossible to get unless you plan well in advance—one case in point is ©*The Lion King.* But to see great theater you've only to join the line at the Ⓕ**TKTS** discount ticket booth at 47th Street. Message boards at the head of the line tell you what shows are available that evening; with luck, your first choice won't sell out before you get to the window. Then again, pot luck can be fun. And the price is right. Once you step inside the theater, the magic really begins. Musical, drama, comedy, or revival, a Broadway show will transport you far

beyond the city even as you sit at its very heart. And no moment is more purely New York than when the curtain rises. As the lights go down and the audience hushes, you know without a doubt that you're not in Kansas anymore.

21

OUTDOORS & SPORTS

Ⓐ 74

You may not think of New York as a place of exquisite green spaces. But these are far more plentiful than you might expect—and city dwellers find many ways to enjoy them. The chess tables permanently set up in Ⓐ**Washington Square Park** lure players from all five boroughs; you may be able to get a game. Sign up early enough and, with luck, you can join the more than 30,000 New Yorkers and other runners from all over the world in the Ⓑ**New York City Marathon,** which begins with an epic stampede across the Verrazano-Narrows Bridge. If you're a less competitive runner, don't miss Central Park. Run the 1½-mile reservoir or make the 6-mile circuit on the road, known as the Loop. Or stroll among the park's many landmarks: the

Ⓑ 359

Ⓔ**Sheep Meadow,** which along with the Ⓓ**Lake** is one of the park's loveliest areas; John Lennon's memorial, Strawberry Fields; and the Ⓕ**Wollman Memorial Rink,** where you can take a spin on the ice under the watchful gaze of the Pierre and Plaza hotels. If you just want to watch, head for the basketball court at 3rd Street and 6th

Ⓒ 363

Avenue, which attracts some of the city's best asphalt hoopsters. Or catch the Knicks at Madison Square Garden. Or head out to ©**Yankee Stadium,** where multimillionaires dress up in pinstriped pajamas to entertain you, or to any of the many other big-time sports venues. If you're a fan, the New York area's 10 major-league franchises won't let you down.

E 143   F 144

THE CITY THAT NEVER SLEEPS

Ⓐ▷338

If night is your element, New York is your playground—and not just on Halloween, when the Ⓓ**Greenwich Village Halloween Parade** clogs 6th Avenue with some of the campiest, most outrageous street theater on *any* planet. This event will remind you, in case you'd forgotten, of New York artists' amazing creativity, their talent, and their passion for doing what it takes to make each performance the best. As examples, just watch the Rockettes high-kick at Ⓑ**Radio City Music Hall** or study the ballerinas fouettéing through performances at City Center, the Joyce Theater, or Lincoln Center's American Ballet Theatre or the Ⓒ**New York City Ballet**; the latter is famed for its phenomenal yuletide *Nutcracker.* Afterward, all over the Theater District and around Lincoln Center, restaurants are aclatter with late-night diners and bars are shoulder-to-shoulder and hip-to-hip.

Ⓑ▷114

Ⓒ▷207

You might discuss the marvels you've just seen over expensive martinis and the suavest live piano music at a swank spot like the Carlyle Hotel's Bemelmans Bar. Or go catch a rising star or two at a comedy club. Hit the dance clubs, a rock dive, a cabaret, or a doormanned lounge. Or take in some R&B or salsa. If New York nights have a sound track, though, it's jazz. Walk the streets after dark and you can almost hear it. Settle into a seat at any Manhattan jazz club and you *will* hear it—the Ⓐ**Village Vanguard** is

only one of the greats. Swing by the Royalton or the Ⓔ**Paramount Hotel** in the Theater District, purpose-built to be cool. Bend an elbow here and call it a night, or keep going: Grab a bite, then ride the Staten Island Ferry until dawn. When you start doing the town after dark in New York, you won't want the night to end.

GREAT ITINERARIES

New York in 5 Days

Enjoying everything New York City has to offer during a short trip is more than a challenge, it's an impossibility. The city's riches can seem as overwhelming as they are exhilarating: Whether your bent is sightseeing or shopping, museums or music, New York does indeed have it all. In five days you can see only the best of the best.
☯ So that you don't show up and find your destination closed, shuffle itinerary days around as suggested.

Ⓐ▷ 105

DAY 1
Launch your exploration with a visit to the top of the Empire State Building to take in the entire city in one panoramic glance. Stroll up 5th Avenue past the leonine guardians of the Ⓐ New York Public Library Humanities and Social Sciences Library and step inside to take a look at the gleaming Main Reading Room. Forty-Second Street takes you to the beaux arts Grand Central Terminal, a hub of frenetic activity and architectural wonder. Move on to the Chrysler Building, an Art Deco beauty, and continue east to the United Nations. Make your way back west to Ⓑ Rockefeller Center for more grandeur, then across 5th Avenue to St. Patrick's Cathedral and into Saks Fifth Avenue. The Museum of Modern Art stands a few

blocks away, and to the south Times Square lights up as night falls. Walk down 7th Avenue to take in all the bright sights on your way to a Broadway show.
☯ Don't do this on Wednesday.

DAY 2
Go in search of history via ferry to Ellis Island and the Statue of Liberty. An early start helps you beat the crowds, though it's impossible to visit both in a single morning. When you return, head northeast for a tour through the Wall Street area; on the way you'll pass colonial-era Fraunces Tavern and Trinity Church. Then follow your nose to no-longer-so-fishy South Street Seaport, a great place to shop, have a bite, and soak up New York's seafaring history along with views of the Brooklyn Bridge. Head back past ornate City Hall, the neo-Gothic Woolworth Building (don't miss the splendid gilded lobby) and 18th-century St. Paul's Chapel on your way to the towering World Trade Center, where you can take in the sunset. For dinner, choose among TriBeCa's many restaurants.
☯ This is fine any day.

DAY 3
Fine art and the finer things in life beckon, starting at the magnificent Metropolitan Museum of Art. You could easily spend a whole day here, but tear yourself away and choose between the Guggenheim and the Whitney. If you choose the Solomon R. Guggenheim Museum, the giant spiral filled with 20th-century art, meander over to pricey and chic Madison Avenue afterward and shop your way down to 59th Street. If, instead, you walk southeast from the Met to the modern Whitney Museum of American Art, Bloomingdale's is just a quick southeast jaunt

away. After exploring the museums, find nearby Grand Army Plaza, its western edge graced by The Plaza hotel, across the way from F.A.O. Schwarz. After dinner, hail a hansom cab for a carriage ride in Central Park.
☯ This won't work on Monday, Tuesday, or Thursday, depending on what you want to see.

DAY 4
First thing this morning, head west to the American Museum of Natural History. Take a gander at the dinosaurs and stop by John Lennon's last home, the Dakota apartment building on Central Park West at 72nd Street. Walk into lush, green Central Park itself to see its Shakespeare Garden, Belvedere Castle, Bethesda Fountain, and Wildlife Center (more familiarly known as the Central Park Zoo). After your dose of fresh air, shop 'til you drop along 5th Avenue and 57th Street. Then treat yourself to dinner followed by a performance at Carnegie Hall or Lincoln Center for the Performing Arts.
☯ Do this any day.

DAY 5
Make your way downtown and wander around Chinatown, where you can enjoy a dim sum breakfast or brunch. From here head north to SoHo and NoLita for galleries and the crème de la crème of both shops and restaurants. Next, take a walk on the Lower East Side, a former immigrant enclave where you'll find the Lower East Side Tenement Museum and bargain shopping on Orchard Street. If you haven't eaten by now, hit a café a few blocks away in the happening East Village, home to yet more shopping. Head west from here to see the historic sights and pretty streets of Greenwich Village; a quick stroll north will take

Solomon R. Guggenheim Museum

Metropolitan Museum of Art

Belvedere Castle

American Museum of Natural History

Shakespeare Garden

Roosevelt Island

113

The Dakota

Bethesda Fountain

Whitney Museum of American Art

Central Park

5th Ave.

Madison Ave.

Lincoln Center

Central Park Wildlife Center (Zoo)

Grand Army Plaza

Bloomingdale's

Broadway

Plaza Hotel

59th St.

F.A.O. Schwarz

57th St.

Carnegie Hall

Museum of Modern Art

1st Ave.

7th Ave.

53rd St.

Rockefeller Center

St. Patrick's Cathedral

Saks Fifth Avenue

47th St.

United Nations

Grand Central Terminal

42nd St.

Times Square

Public Library

5th Ave.

Chrysler Building

Empire State Building

34th St.

Herald Square

East River

22nd St.

23rd St.

Madison Square

Flatiron Building

Chelsea

Flatiron District

20th St.

8th Ave.

5th Ave.

Union Square

Greenwich Ave.

Greenwich Village

St. Marks Pl.

8th St.

1st Ave.

Washington Square

East Village

Houston St.

Prince St.

NoLita

SoHo

Greene St.

Broadway

Mott St.

Orchard St.

Lower East Side Tenement Museum

W. Broadway

Canal St.

TriBeCa

Chinatown

Church St.

City Hall

Woolworth Building

Fulton St.

Brooklyn Bridge

World Trade Center

St. Paul's Chapel

South Street Seaport

Trinity Church

Wall Street

Pearl St.

Broadway

Fraunces Tavern

Hudson River

Ferry to Ellis Island and Statue of Liberty

Ellis Island

To Statue of Liberty

you to Chelsea and its galleries, and to the fashionable Flatiron District with its inimitable Flatiron Building. After dark, haunt one of the Village's many jazz clubs or slink into a SoHo or East Village hipster lounge. ⊘ *Don't do this on Monday, Friday, or Saturday; some galleries are closed Sunday.*

If You Have More Time

Take a break from Manhattan with a day trip to Brooklyn, where you'll find the Brooklyn Museum of Art right next to the lush Brooklyn Botanic Garden. Adjacent to the gardens is Prospect Park, which forms the southeastern boundary of the vibrant neighborhood of Park Slope. The Slope's main street, 7th Avenue, is lined with distinctive cafés and shops. For entertainment, see what's happening at the Brooklyn Academy of Music or spend the evening in Brooklyn Heights, strolling the Promenade at sunset. Back in Manhattan, another day sees another side of the city uptown. In Morningside Heights you'll find Riverside Park overlooking the Hudson and the Gothic work-in-progress Cathedral of St. John the Divine, as well as the ivory towers of Columbia University. Come back down to earth in Harlem, whose rich history is documented at the Schomburg Center near the famous Abyssinian Baptist Church. Other landmarks include the legendary ©Apollo Theatre, Striver's Row, the Studio Museum in Harlem, and soul-food restaurants such as Sylvia's.

If You Have 3 Days

An abbreviated visit can give you a tempting taste of the Big Apple. Follow the itineraries for days 1 and 3 above, then zip downtown for your third day. Start early, with a visit to Ellis Island or the Statue of Liberty, and take a quick spin around the Wall Street area and South Street Seaport. Next head northwest to bustling, colorful Chinatown on your way to gallery- and shop-filled SoHo. Cruise through trendier and less expensive NoLita, then up to the East Village. When you've had your fill of funky, walk west to the historic sights and winding streets of Greenwich Village. Stay downtown for dinner in a budget Village eatery or a SoHo hot spot, then dance the night away before you bid the city good-bye.

A Kid's-Eye View of New York

New York City can make a kid's eyes pop and his jaw drop. The playgrounds in Riverside and Central parks are world-class, and just walking down the street can be an adventure for tots and teenagers alike. New York bursts with fantastic activities and sights for kids. Best of all, these stops appeal to adults as well.

DAY 1

Start off with a trip to that perennial favorite, the American Museum of Natural History, to see the genuinely awesome dinosaurs. Afterward take a rumbling ride down to 34th Street on the subway's B line, in the front car for a cool view of the tracks. You'll find all kinds of action in Herald Square,

home of Macy's. Shop if you like, or walk to the nearby Empire State Building. Take in the view and stop in the lobby to purchase a three-day double-decker bus ticket to get around the rest of this itinerary. Ride down to SoHo, location of the New York City Fire Museum and the Children's Museum of the Arts. Adventurous eaters love dinner in colorful Chinatown, where the whole family can play tic-tac-toe with the celebrity chicken in the Mott Street arcade, just off the Bowery.

DAY 2

Greet the day at the World Trade Center and take the elevator trip of your life to the "Top of the World." Back on the ground, catch a free ride across New York Harbor on the Staten Island Ferry past such famous sights as the Statue of Liberty and Ellis Island. The round trip will put you in a suitably nautical mood for a visit to South Street Seaport, which offers food and fun of every description. Next take the double-decker bus up to Rockefeller Center; in winter the ice-skating and Christmas tree are special treats. There's more fun to be had at the nearby Museum of Television and Radio and at the high-tech Sony Wonder Technology Lab in the Sony Building. And no kid's trip to N.Y.C. is complete without a pilgrimage to F.A.O. Schwarz. An evening at a Broadway musical such as *The Lion King* thrills many youngsters. Or see what's on the child-friendly program at the New Victory Theater.

DAY 3

Cruise around Manhattan island this morning on the Circle Line, and when your tour's completed stop by the *Intrepid* Sea-Air-Space Museum. Next take in some of the wild energy of the cleaned-up Times Square. If weather permits, look for more outdoor magic in Central Park. There, check out the Children's Zoo, take a ride on the famous carousel, catch a performance at the marionette theater in the Swedish Cottage, and watch

the miniature boats on the Conservatory Water. If you still have energy to burn, visit the playground near the zoo or near the carousel. Afterward stop in at the Metropolitan Museum of Art to see the Temple of Dendur, the arms and armor, and other fun stuff. As night falls, try one of the special kids' music offerings at Lincoln Center for the Performing Arts or take in a movie on the huge screen at the nearby ⓓ Sony IMAX Theater.

Art Attack!

For art lovers of every taste, there's no place like New York. You have so much to choose from, whether you favor the classic, the experimental, or the outrageous. This itinerary allows you to try a little of everything.

DAY 1

The first stop on every aesthete's schedule should be the Metropolitan Museum of Art. Although you could easily while away whole weeks here, limit yourself to a morning, then head for the many galleries along Madison Avenue between 80th and 70th streets—be sure to stop in at both Gagosian and Knoedler & Co. Don't miss the masterpiece-heavy Frick Collection before strolling east to view the art collections at the Asia Society. In the evening attend a performance at Lincoln Center for the Performing Arts, City Center, or Carnegie Hall. Then catch a cabaret act at Café Carlyle or the Oak Room.

DAY 2

Spend a thoroughly modern morning at the Solomon R. Guggenheim Museum and the Whitney Museum of American Art. With visions of de Kooning and Klee dancing in your head you'll be ready for a visit to the Museum of Modern Art (which closes for renovations starting summer 2002). Spend the rest of the afternoon at the galleries along 57th Street, whose standouts include the

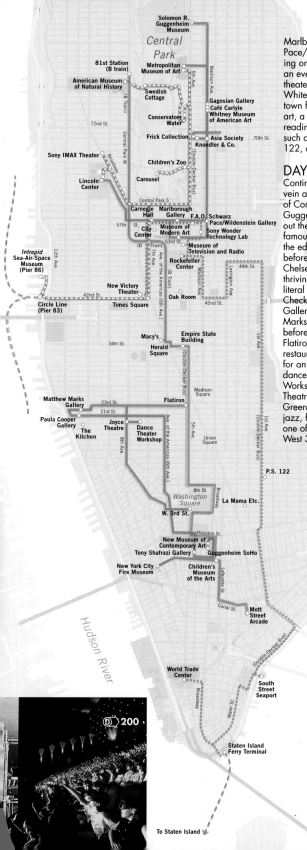

Marlborough Gallery and Pace/Wildenstein. Depending on your inclination, enjoy an evening of dinner and theater along the Great White Way, or taxi downtown for funkier performance art, a play, music, or a reading at a famous venue such as The Kitchen, P.S. 122, or La Mama Etc.

DAY 3

Continue in the downtown vein at SoHo's New Museum of Contemporary Art, and the Guggenheim SoHo. Scope out the neighborhood's rightly famous galleries, including the edgy Tony Shafrazi, before heading up to Chelsea, which has its own thriving gallery scene—and literal warehouses full of art. Check out the Paula Cooper Gallery and the Matthew Marks Gallery, among others, before dinner in one of the Flatiron District's sizzling restaurants. Return to Chelsea for an evening of modern dance at Dance Theater Workshop or the Joyce Theatre. Then head down to Greenwich Village to take in jazz, folk, blues, or rock at one of the many clubs along West 3rd Street.

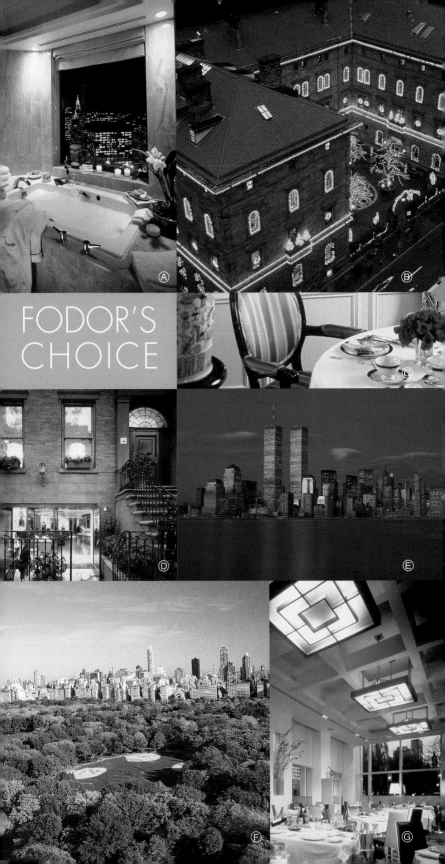

FODOR'S
CHOICE

Even with so many special places in New York City, Fodor's writers and editors have their favorites. Here are a few that stand out.

MOMENTS

The Cloisters at sunset. Nestled in enchanted gardens far above the urban din, the medieval Cloisters are most gorgeous as the sun sets over the Hudson River and the soaring Palisades. ☞ p. 155

New York City Marathon. The city unites in a cheering, breathless mass as thousands of runners dash through the five boroughs to the finish line in Central Park. ☞ p. 359

Romance at the Supper Club. On a Friday or Saturday evening, slip into your white tie or black satin and sip champagne to the strains of a big band. Then take to the dance floor to glide and whirl and hold your sweetheart close. ☞ p. 333

Times Square at night. As daylight wanes, New York's energy seems to concentrate here and erupt in brilliant display. ☞ p. 106

Ⓔ **A walk on the Brooklyn Heights Promenade.** For stunning views of downtown Manhattan and the Brooklyn Bridge nothing beats a stroll along this elegant esplanade, especially in early morning with sun glinting off Wall Street's glass monoliths. ☞ p. 176

PLACES

American Museum of Natural History. Whether you are among the dinosaur fossils, beneath the 94-ft blue whale, or admiring the dioramas depicting human evolution, you can't help but be awed. ☞ p. 148

Brooklyn Botanic Garden. In one of the city's loveliest spots, savor the tranquillity of the Japanese Garden, commune with the Bard in the Shakespeare Garden, or get lost in a profusion of pink at spring's Cherry Blossom Festival. ☞ p. 182

Ⓕ **Central Park.** Dusted with snow or awash in autumn colors, humming with week-end athletes or silent but for the clip-clop of a carriage horse, this oasis offers citified outdoor pleasures and a skyline spiked with sky-scrapers. ☞ p. 134

NoLita. Tiny designer boutiques, velvet-upholstered lounges, and bold new restaurants are popping up all over this tenement neighborhood east of SoHo. This is New York as downtowners think it should be, with nary a chain store nor T-shirt shop in sight. ☞ p. 367

West Village. Historic town houses and hidden courtyards charm one and all along winding, tree-lined lanes—most notably St. Luke's Place and Commerce, Bedford, and Grove streets. ☞ p. 65

DINING

Daniel. Daniel Boulud's grand dining room presents French classics as well as the chef's own brilliant inventions, such as scallops in black tie (dressed with truffles). $$$$ ☞ p. 285

Ⓖ **Jean Georges.** Dramatic picture windows give you a view of Central Park from this sleek, modernist dining room as Jean-Georges Vongerichten casts his culinary spell over some of the most astonishing dishes you'll ever taste. $$$$ ☞ p. 290

Lespinasse. The service is exquisitely refined and Christian Delouvrier's French cuisine marvelously innovative in this gilded dining room. $$$$ ☞ p. 279

Nobu. Reservations are hard to come by at this striking, contemporary Japanese-inspired restaurant, but persevere: flawless sushi and sashimi and Nobu creations like seared black cod with sweet miso are utterly delicious. $$$$ ☞ p. 239

Babbo. This is Italian food as it was meant to be, updated, and after your first bite of the ethereal homemade pasta or tender suckling pig you'll know why critics rave. $$$–$$$$ ☞ p. 250

Gramercy Tavern. If wild Scottish partridge in consommé and fondue of sea urchin and Maine crabmeat sound good, head for this urbanely rustic restaurant. $$$–$$$$ ☞ p. 256

Union Pacific. Exotic ingredients and unusual flavor combinations work beautifully here. Anyone for seared duck liver on pickled green papaya with toasted pistachio oil and tamarind glaze? $$$–$$$$ ☞ p. 259

LODGING

Ⓐ **Four Seasons.** Towering over 57th Street, this I. M. Pei spire houses palatial, sound-proof guest rooms with 10-ft ceilings, English sycamore walk-in closets, and blond-marble baths whose immense tubs fill in 60 seconds. $$$$ ☞ p. 320

Ⓑ **New York Palace.** Sleep amid glamorous deco or traditional Empire-style furnishings. The health club's views of St. Patrick's cathedral are terrific. $$$$ ☞ p. 320

The Carlyle. Everything about this landmark suggests refinement, from the first-rate service to the artfully framed Audubons in the rooms. Bemelmans Bar and Café Carlyle are destinations unto themselves. $$$–$$$$ ☞ p. 326

Ⓒ **The Lowell.** Many rooms and suites have working fireplaces in this gem on a quiet, tree-lined Upper East Side street. The Pembroke Room serves a stunning tea, and the Post House is renowned for steaks. $$$–$$$$ ☞ p. 327

Ⓓ **Inn at Irving Place.** The tea salon of this grand pair of 1830s town houses near Gramercy Park evokes a gentler New York, as do the ornamental fireplaces, four-poster beds, and embroidered linens. $$$ ☞ p. 307

Mercer Hotel. The hotel of the moment for unconventional travelers, this SoHo minimalist is all dark African woods and high-tech light fixtures. The decadent two-person tubs, surrounded by mirrors, steal the show. $$$ ☞ p. 306

1 EXPLORING MANHATTAN

On the next block, a visitor to New York will always find something new to discover uptown and down—world-class museums and ultra-modern galleries, breathtaking skyscrapers, ethnic festivals, historic town houses, vibrant neighborhoods, parks, and gardens. From the Battery in the south to Harlem in the north, this chapter uncovers the essential places to see in each part of Manhattan, as well as worthwhile sights off the tourist track. Be sure to stop and rest along the way so you'll have a chance to observe the fabulous street life that makes this city extraordinary.

Updated by
Karen Deaver,
Margaret
Mittelbach,
and Michael
de Zayas

M**ANHATTAN IS, ABOVE ALL, A WALKER'S CITY.** Along its busy streets there's an endless variety of sights everywhere you go. Attractions, many of them world-famous, crowd close together on this narrow island, and because the city can only grow up, not out, the new simply piles on top of the old. Manhattan's character changes every few blocks, so quaint town houses stand shoulder to shoulder with sleek glass towers, gleaming gourmet supermarkets sit around the corner from dusty thrift shops, and chic bistros inhabit the storefronts of soot-smudged warehouses. Many visitors, beguiled into walking a little farther, then a little farther still, have been startled to stumble upon their trip's most memorable moments.

Our walking tours cover a great deal of ground, yet they only scratch the surface of the city. If you plod dutifully from point to point, nose buried in this book, you'll miss half the fun. Look up at the tops of skyscrapers, and you'll see a riot of mosaics, carvings, and ornaments. Step into the lobby of an architectural landmark and study its features; take a look around to see the real people who work, live, or worship there today. Peep down side streets, even in crowded midtown, and you may find fountains, greenery, and sudden bursts of flowers. Find a bench or ledge on which to perch and take time just to watch the crowd passing by. New York has so many faces that every visitor can discover a different one.

Orientation

The map of Manhattan has a Jekyll-and-Hyde aspect. The rational Dr. Jekyll part prevails above 14th Street, where the streets form a regular grid pattern, imposed in 1811. Numbered streets run east and west (crosstown), while broad avenues, most of them also numbered, run north (uptown) and south (downtown). The chief exceptions are Broadway and the thoroughfares that hug the shores of the Hudson and East rivers. Broadway runs the entire length of Manhattan. At its southernmost end it follows the city's north–south grid; at East 10th Street it turns and runs on a diagonal to West 86th Street, then at a lesser angle until West 107th Street, where it merges with West End Avenue.

Fifth Avenue is the east–west dividing line for street addresses: on either side, addresses begin at 1 where a street intersects 5th Avenue and climb higher in each direction, in regular increments. For example, 1 East 55th Street is just east of 5th Avenue, 99 East 55th Street is at Park (the equivalent of 4th) Avenue, 199 East 55th Street is at 3rd Avenue, and so on; likewise, 1 West 55th Street is just west of 5th Avenue, 99 West 55th Street is at 6th Avenue (also known as Avenue of the Americas), 199 West 55th Street is at 7th Avenue, and so forth. Above 59th Street, where Central Park interrupts the grid, West Side addresses start numbering at Central Park West, an extension of 8th Avenue. Avenue addresses are much less regular, for the numbers begin wherever each avenue begins and increase at different increments. An address at 552 3rd Avenue, for example, will not necessarily be anywhere near 552 2nd Avenue. Even many New Yorkers cannot master the complexities of this system, so they give addresses in terms of intersections: 5th Avenue and 55th Street, for instance, or 55th Street between 9th and 10th Avenues.

Below 14th Street—the area settled before the 1811 grid was decreed—Manhattan streets reflect the disordered personality of Mr. Hyde. They may be aligned with the shoreline, or they may twist along the route of an ancient cow path. Below 14th Street you'll find West 4th Street

Manhattan Neighborhoods

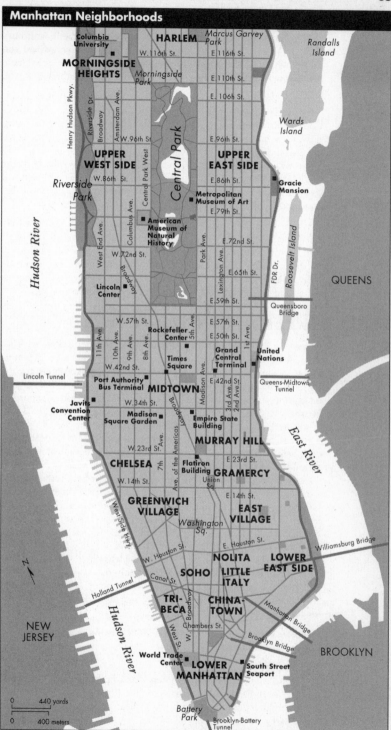

Columbia University
HARLEM
Marcus Garvey Park
Randalls Island
MORNINGSIDE HEIGHTS
W. 116th St.
E. 116th St.
Morningside Park
E. 110th St.
E. 106th St.
Henry Hudson Pkwy.
Riverside Dr.
Amsterdam Ave.
Broadway
W. 96th St.
E. 96th St.
Wards Island
UPPER WEST SIDE
UPPER EAST SIDE
Central Park
W. 86th St.
E. 86th St.
Gracie Mansion
Riverside Park
Central Park West
Columbus Ave.
West End Ave.
Metropolitan Museum of Art
E. 79th St.
American Museum of Natural History
E. 72nd St.
Hudson River
W. 72nd St.
Park Ave.
Lexington Ave.
E. 65th St.
FDR Dr.
Roosevelt Island
QUEENS
Lincoln Center
E. 59th St.
W. 57th St.
E. 57th St.
Queensboro Bridge
Rockefeller Center
E. 50th St.
5th Ave.
Times Square
Grand Central Terminal
United Nations
11th Ave.
10th Ave.
9th Ave.
8th Ave.
W. 42nd St.
E. 42nd St.
3rd Ave.
2nd Ave.
1st Ave.
Lincoln Tunnel
Port Authority Bus Terminal
MIDTOWN
Queens-Midtown Tunnel
Javits Convention Center
W. 34th St.
Madison Square Garden
Empire State Building
Broadway
Madison Ave.
East River
W. 23rd St.
MURRAY HILL
CHELSEA
Flatiron Building
E. 23rd St.
7th Ave. of the Americas
W. 14th St.
Union Sq.
GRAMERCY
E. 14th St.
GREENWICH VILLAGE
EAST VILLAGE
West Side Hwy.
Washington Sq.
W. Houston St.
E. Houston St.
Williamsburg Bridge
NOLITA
LOWER EAST SIDE
SOHO
LITTLE ITALY
Holland Tunnel
Canal St.
TRI-BECA
CHINA-TOWN
Manhattan Bridge
NEW JERSEY
Broadway
West St.
Chambers St.
Brooklyn Bridge
Hudson River
World Trade Center
LOWER MANHATTAN
South Street Seaport
BROOKLYN
N
Battery Park
Brooklyn-Battery Tunnel
0   440 yards
0   400 meters

intersecting West 11th Street, Greenwich Street running roughly parallel to Greenwich Avenue, and Leroy Street turning into St. Luke's Place for one block and then becoming Leroy again. There's an East Broadway and a West Broadway, both of which run north–south and neither of which is an extension of plain old Broadway. Logic won't help you below 14th Street; only a good street map and good directions will.

You may also be confused by the way New Yorkers use *uptown, downtown,* and *midtown.* These terms refer both to locations and to directions. Uptown means north of wherever you are at the moment; downtown means to the south. But uptown, downtown, and midtown are also specific parts of the city. Unfortunately, there is no consensus about where these areas are: Downtown may mean anyplace from the tip of lower Manhattan through Chelsea. Midtown is generally known to be between 34th and 59th streets, although it too can extend beyond those limits.

A similar situation exists with *East Side* and *West Side.* Someone may refer to a location as "on the east side," meaning somewhere east of 5th Avenue. A hotel described as being "on the west side" may be on West 42nd Street. But when New Yorkers speak of the East Side or the West Side, they usually mean the respective areas above 59th Street on either side of Central Park. Be prepared for misunderstandings.

WALL STREET AND THE BATTERY

Island city that it is, much of Manhattan strangely turns its back on the rushing waters that surround it—not so the Battery. From waterside walks in Battery Park, you can look out on the confluence of the Hudson and East River estuaries where bustling seaborne commerce once glutted the harbor that built the "good city of old Manhatto," Herman Melville's moniker from the second chapter of *Moby-Dick.* It was here that the Dutch established the colony of Nieuw Amsterdam in 1625; in 1789 the first capitol building of the United States was built here. The city did not really expand beyond these precincts until the middle of the 19th century. Today this historic heart of New York is experiencing a rebirth as a high-tech district, where recently refitted, super-wired buildings have attracted some of the biggest names in Internet commerce, turning parts of Wall Street into a 24-hour community dubbed Silicon Alley. But for the most part, Wall Street, which is both an actual street and a shorthand name for the vast, powerful financial center that clusters around the New York and American stock exchanges, continues to dominate much of lower Manhattan. Just off the tip of the island as you gaze across the great silvery harbor, however, not far from this powerful center of commerce, are enduring symbols of America: the Statue of Liberty and Ellis Island, port of entry for countless immigrants to a new land.

Numbers in the text correspond to numbers in the margin and on the Lower Manhattan map.

A Good Walk

The immediate vicinity of the Staten Island Ferry Terminal (just outside the South Ferry subway station on the 1 and 9 lines) is a little unsightly, but that doesn't detract from the pleasure of a ride on the **Staten Island Ferry** ①.

Just north of the Staten Island Ferry Terminal, the tall white columns and curved brick front of the 1793 **Shrine of St. Elizabeth Ann Seton at Our Lady of the Rosary** ② are a dignified sight. The house was one of many mansions lining State Street. To the left of the shrine, the verdant **Battery Park** ③, Manhattan's green toe, curves up the west side of the island. It is filled with sculpture and monuments, including the circular **Castle Clinton National Monument** ④. The venerable fort is where you buy tickets for the ferries to the **Statue of Liberty** ⑤ and **Ellis Island** ⑥. From Castle Clinton follow the esplanade lined with rose bushes toward **Bowling Green** ⑦, an oval greensward at the foot of Broadway that in 1733 became New York's first public park. An excellent view up Broadway of the formidable Canyon of Heroes, site of many a ticker-tape parade, can be had from the northern tip of the park. While you're here, duck inside the Cunard Building at 25 Broadway to see the superb ceiling frescoes by Ezra Winter. Now a post office, this Renaissance-style building completed in 1921 once was the booking hall for the great ocean liners owned by Cunard. Across State Street, facing the south side of Bowling Green, is the beaux arts Alexander Hamilton U.S. Custom House, home of the **National Museum of the American Indian** ⑧.

Next follow Whitehall Street down the east side of the American Indian museum. A left turn onto Bridge Street will bring into focus a block of early New York buildings. As you approach Broad Street, the two-tone Georgian **Fraunces Tavern** ⑨ will appear. Across Pearl Street, 85 Broad Street pays homage to urban archaeology with a transparent panel in the sidewalk showing the excavated foundations of the 17th-century Stadt Huys, the Old Dutch City Hall. The course of old Dutch Stone Street is marked in the lobby with a line of brown paving stones.

Head north on Pearl Street to **Hanover Square** ⑩, a quiet tree-lined plaza, then head inland on William Street to the triangular convergence of South William and Beaver streets. On the right, 20 Exchange Place towers and adds street-level interest with weighty art deco doorways depicting the engines of commerce. On the corner to your left is the elegant entrance to the legendary Delmonico's Restaurant. Two blocks farther north, William Street crosses **Wall Street** ⑪, a jaw-dropping display of the money that built Manhattan; the massive arcade of 55 Wall Street, home of the Regent Wall Street hotel, alone speaks volumes.

One block west on Wall Street, where Broad Street becomes Nassau Street, a regal statue of George Washington stands on the steps of the **Federal Hall National Memorial** ⑫. Across the street is an investment bank built by J. P. Morgan in 1913. By building only four stories, Morgan was in effect declaring himself above the pressures of Wall Street real estate values. Now Morgan Guaranty Trust, the building bears pockmarks near the fourth window on the Wall Street side; these were created in 1920 when a bomb that had been placed in a pushcart nearby exploded. The temple-front **New York Stock Exchange** ⑬ is the central shrine of Wall Street (even though its address is officially on Broad Street).

The focal point at the west end of Wall Street is the brownstone **Trinity Church** ⑭. Just north of the church is tiny Thames Street, where a pair of skyscrapers playfully called the Thames Twins—the Trinity and U.S. Realty buildings—display early 20th-century attempts to apply Gothic decoration to skyscrapers. Across the street at 120 Broadway, the 1915 Equitable Building rises 30 stories straight from its base with no setback; its overpowering shadow on the street helped persuade the city government to pass the nation's first zoning law.

Four sculpture installations make for an interesting side tour. The first is on Broadway between Cedar and Liberty streets, where the black-glass HSBC Bank USA (1971) heightens the drama of the red-and-silver Isamu Noguchi sculpture *Cube* in its plaza. Two blocks east, near

Lower Manhattan

CHINATOWN

South Street Seaport

Pier 17
Pier 16

Catherine Slip
Henry St.
Madison St.
St. James Pl.
Mott St.
Mulberry St.
Baxter St.
Hayes Pl.
Worth St.
Hogan Pl.
Pearl St.
Dover St.
Peck Slip
Beekman St.
Fulton Fish Market
Titanic Memorial
Burling Slip
Fletcher St.
Maiden Lane
Pearl St.
Gold St.
Fulton St.

32
30
29
Foley Square
27
28

Lafayette St.
Centre St.
4,5,6
Pace University
Spruce St.
Beekman St.
William St.
Louise Nevelson Plaza
Platt St.
John St.
20

26
J,M,Z
Brooklyn Bridge Walkway

15
Maiden Lane
Chase

Elk St.
31

Old New York Life Insurance Company Headquarters

Federal Plaza

Duane St.
25
24
City Hall Park
Ann St.
23
Park Row

2,3
A,C
J,M,Z

Reade St.
Chambers St.
Broadway
22
N,R
21
Fulton St.
4,5
John St.

Leonard St.
Worth St.
Thomas St.
Murray St.
Church St.
Dey St.
N,R
Cortlandt St.

A,C
West Broadway
16
1,9
Liberty St.
Cedar St.
Thames St.

Chambers St.
1,2,3,9
Warren St.
Park Pl.
Barclay St.
2,3
C,E
World Trade Center

Hudson St.
Vesey St.

Franklin St.
Staple St.
Harrison St.
Jay St.
Greenwich St.

Independence Plaza

West St.
West Side Highway

Cedar St.

Promenade

Stuyvesant High School

Warren St.
Park Pl. W.
Murray St.
North End Ave.
New York Mercantile Exchange
Vesey St.

17
World Financial Center

Hudson River Park

Hoboken Ferry Terminal
North Cove Yacht Harbor

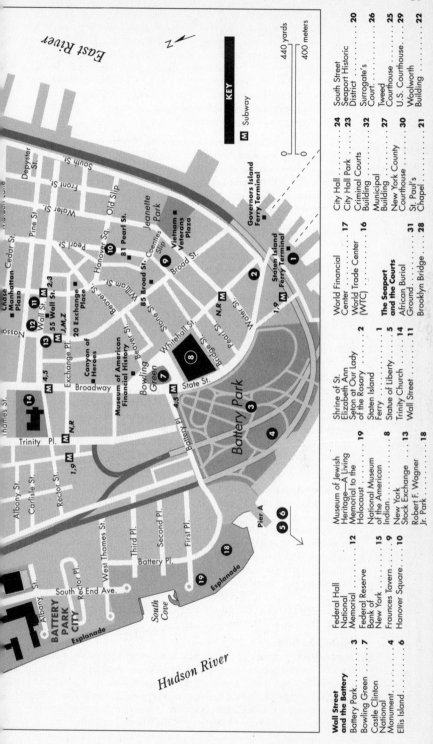

East River

N

KEY

M Subway

440 yards
400 meters

Hudson River

**Wall Street
and the Battery**

Battery Park 3
Bowling Green 7
Castle Clinton
National
Monument 4
Ellis Island 6

Federal Hall
National
Memorial 3
Federal Reserve
Bank of
New York 15
Fraunces Tavern 9
Hanover Square 6

Museum of Jewish
Heritage—A Living
Memorial to the
Holocaust 12
National Museum
of the American
Indian 8
New York
Stock Exchange . . . 10
Robert F. Wagner
Jr. Park 18

Shrine of St.
Elizabeth Ann
Seton at Our Lady
of the Rosary 2
Staten Island
Ferry 1
Statue of Liberty . . . 5
Trinity Church 14
Wall Street 11

World Financial
Center 17
World Trade Center
(WTC) 16

**The Seaport
and the Courts**

African Burial
Ground 31
Brooklyn Bridge . . . 28

City Hall 24
City Hall Park 23
Criminal Courts
Building 32
Municipal
Building 27
New York County
Courthouse 30
St. Paul's
Chapel 28

South Street
Seaport Historic
District 20
Surrogate's
Court. 26
Tweed
Courthouse 25
U.S. Courthouse . . . 29
Woolworth
Building 22

the William Street edge of the plaza surrounding the 65-story Chase Manhattan Bank Building (1960), stands Jean Dubuffet's striking black-and-white *Group of Four Trees*. South of the Dubuffet and slightly inset is another Noguchi installation, a circular sculpture garden with his signature carved stones. Just north of the Chase plaza, where Liberty Street converges with William Street and Maiden Lane under the Federal Reserve Bank, the triangular Louise Nevelson Plaza contains four pieces of her black-welded-steel abstract sculpture: three of moderate size and one 70-footer.

The massive, rusticated **Federal Reserve Bank of New York** ⑮, directly across the street, recalls the Palazzo Strozzi in Florence, Italy and looks the way a bank ought to: solid, imposing, and absolutely impregnable. Walk west back toward Broadway on Maiden Lane, which will turn into Cortlandt Street. There, the **World Trade Center** ⑯ contains New York's tallest buildings.

During the towers' construction more than a million cubic yards of rock and soil were excavated—then moved across West Street to help beget Battery Park City. An impressive feat of urban planning, this complete 92-acre neighborhood houses more than 5,000 residents and 20,000 workers. It is almost like a separate city within the city, with high-rises, town houses, shops, and green squares—though it's not a very exciting place to visit. The pedestrian overpass north of 1 World Trade Center leads to Battery Park City's centerpiece, the **World Financial Center** ⑰, a four-tower complex designed by Cesar Pelli. Just north of the basin is the terminal for ferry service to Hoboken, New Jersey. Beyond the ferry terminal is the south end of Hudson River Park. To the south, a riverside esplanade begins in the residential part of Battery Park City and connects with **Robert F. Wagner Jr. Park** ⑱, home to the **Museum of Jewish Heritage—A Living Memorial to the Holocaust** ⑲. Especially noteworthy among the artwork populating the Esplanade are Ned Smyth's columned plaza with chessboards and the South Cove (a collaborative effort), a curved stage set of wooden piers and a steel-frame lookout quietly reminiscent of Lady Liberty's crown.

TIMING

The Manhattan side of this tour takes most of a day—allow a lot more time to ferry out to the Statue of Liberty and Ellis Island. Visit on a weekday to capture the district's true vitality—but expect to be jostled on the crowded sidewalks if you stand too long, peering at the great buildings that surge skyward on every corner. If you visit on a weekend, on the other hand, you'll feel like a lone explorer in a canyon of buildings. Either way, start early, preferably making the first ferry, to try to beat the crowds to Liberty and Ellis islands. Get tickets by lunchtime if you plan to visit the Stock Exchange, which is open only on weekdays until 4. The best place to end the day is on the Hudson River, watching the sun set.

Sights to See

❸ **Battery Park.** Jutting out as if it were Manhattan's green toe, Battery Park (so named because a battery of 28 cannons was placed along its shore in Colonial days to fend off the British) is built on landfill and has gradually grown over the centuries to its present 22 acres. The park's main structure is **Castle Clinton National Monument**, the takeoff point for ferries to the **Statue of Liberty** and **Ellis Island**. The park is loaded with various other monuments and statues, some impressive, some downright obscure. Starting near the Staten Island Ferry Terminal, head north along the water's edge to the East Coast Memorial, a statue of a fierce eagle that presides over eight granite slabs inscribed with the names of U.S. servicemen who died in the western Atlantic during

World War II. Climb the steps of the East Coast Memorial for a fine view of the main features of **New York Harbor**; from left to right: **Governors Island,** a former Coast Guard installation whose future is somewhat undecided; hilly **Staten Island** in the distance; the **Statue of Liberty,** on Liberty Island; **Ellis Island,** gateway to the New World for generations of immigrants; and the old railway terminal in **Liberty State Park,** on the mainland in Jersey City, New Jersey. On crystal-clear days you can see all the way to Port Elizabeth's cranes, which seem to mimic Lady Liberty's stance. Continue north past a romantic **statue of Giovanni da Verrazano,** the Florentine merchant who in 1524 piloted the ship that first sighted New York and its harbor. The **Verrazano-Narrows Bridge,** between Brooklyn and Staten Island, is visible from here, just beyond Governors Island. It's so long that the curvature of the earth had to be figured into its dimensions. At the park's northernmost edge, Pier A, the last Victorian fireboat pier in the city, was undergoing restoration at press time that would transform the building into a visitor and shopping center. Its clock tower, eected in 1919, was the nation's first World War I memorial. ⊠ *Broadway and Battery Pl.*

❼ Bowling Green. This oval greensward at the foot of Broadway became New York's first public park in 1733. On July 9, 1776, a few hours after citizens learned about the signing of the Declaration of Independence, rioters toppled a statue of British King George III that had occupied the spot for 11 years; much of the statue's lead was melted down into bullets. In 1783, when the occupying British forces fled the city, they defiantly hoisted a Union Jack on a greased, uncleated flagpole so it couldn't be lowered; patriot John Van Arsdale drove his own cleats into the pole to replace the flag with the Stars and Stripes. The copper-top subway entrance here is the original one, built in 1904–05.

☙ ❹ Castle Clinton National Monument. This circular red-stone fortress, built in 1811, first stood on an island 200 ft from shore as a defense for New York Harbor. In 1824 it became Castle Garden, an entertainment and concert facility that reached its zenith in 1850 when more than 6,000 people (the capacity of Radio City Music Hall) attended the U.S. debut of the Swedish Nightingale, Jenny Lind. After landfill connected it to the city, Castle Clinton became, in succession, an immigrant processing center, an aquarium, and now a restored fort, museum, and ticket office for ferries to the **Statue of Liberty** and **Ellis Island.** (The ferry ride is one loop; you can get off at Liberty Island, visit the statue, then reboard any ferry and continue on to Ellis Island, boarding another boat once you have finished exploring the historic immigration facility there.) Inside the old fort are dioramas of lower Manhattan in 1812, 1886, and 1941. Outside the landward entrance is a statue titled *The Immigrants,* at the beginning of a broad mall that leads back across the park. At the other end of the mall stands the **Netherlands Memorial Flagpole,** which depicts Dutch traders offering beads to Native Americans in 1626 for the land on which to establish Fort Amsterdam. Inscriptions describe the event in English and Dutch. ☎ *212/344–7220 for Castle Clinton; 212/269–5755 for ferry information.* ☒ *Castle Clinton free, ferry $7 round-trip.* ☉ *Daily 8:30–5, ferry departures daily every 30 mins 9–3:30 (more departures and extended hrs in summer).*

★ ☙ ❻ Ellis Island. Between 1892 and 1924, approximately 12 million men, women, and children first set foot on U.S. soil at this 27½-acre island's federal immigration facility. In all, by the time Ellis Island closed for good in 1954, it had processed the ancestors of more than 40% of Americans living today. The island's main building, now a national monument, reopened in 1990 as the **Ellis Island Immigration Museum.**

There are more than 30 galleries here with artifacts, photographs, and taped oral histories chronicling the immigrant experience. In the main **Registry Room,** inspectors once attempted to screen out "undesirables"—polygamists, criminals, the utterly destitute, and people suffering from contagious diseases. The cavernous **Great Hall,** where immigrants awaited processing, has gorgeous tile arches by Rafael Guastavino; white-tile dormitory rooms overlook this grand space. The **Railroad Ticket Office** at the back of the main building houses exhibits on the *Peopling of America,* recounting 400 years of immigration history, and *Forced Migration,* focusing on the slave trade. The old kitchen and laundry building has been stabilized rather than restored so you can see what the island's buildings looked like prior to the restoration. There is also a children's visitor center and the **Immigrants' Living Theatre,** where immigrant stories are dramatically presented. Perhaps the most moving exhibit is the **American Immigrant Wall of Honor,** where the names of more than 500,000 immigrant Americans are inscribed along an outdoor promenade overlooking the Statue of Liberty and the Manhattan skyline. The names include Miles Standish, Priscilla Alden, George Washington's grandfather, Irving Berlin—and possibly an ancestor of yours. In 1998 the Supreme Court ruled that about 90% of Ellis Island is in New Jersey. ☎ *212/363–3200 for Ellis Island; 212/883–1986 for Wall of Honor information,* WEB *www.ellisisland.org.* ✉ *Free.* ☉ *Daily 9–5:0 (extended hrs in summer).*

⑫ Federal Hall National Memorial. On the steps of this Greek revival building stands a regal statue, created in 1883, of George Washington, who in 1789 on that site—then also Federal Hall—was sworn in as the nation's first president. Washington's likeness was rendered by noted sculptor and relative of the president, John Quincy Adams Ward. After the capital moved to Philadelphia in 1790, the original Federal Hall became New York's City Hall, then was demolished in 1812 when the present City Hall was completed. The current structure, built as a U.S. Custom House in 1842, was modeled on the Parthenon, a potent symbol for a young nation striving to emulate classic Greek democracy. It's now a museum with exhibits on New York and Wall Street. Guided tours are sometimes available, and you can also pick up brochures that lead you on differently themed self-guided walking tours of downtown. ✉ *26 Wall St., at Nassau St.,* ☎ *212/825–6888.* ✉ *Free.* ☉ *Weekdays 9–5.*

⑮ Federal Reserve Bank of New York. Built in 1924, and enlarged in 1935, this neo-Renaissance structure made of sandstone, limestone, and ironwork goes five levels underground. The gold ingots in the vaults here are worth roughly $140 billion—reputedly a third of the world's gold reserves. Tours of the bank end at the $750,000 visitor center. Its dozen or so interactive computer terminals and displays provide almost as much information as an Economics 101 course—explaining such points as what the Federal Reserve Bank does (besides store gold), what the money supply is, and what causes inflation. ✉ *33 Liberty St., between William and Nassau Sts.,* ☎ *212/720–6130.* ✉ *Free.* ☉ *1-hr tour by advance (at least 1 wk) reservation, weekdays 9:30–2:30.*

☾ ⑨ Fraunces Tavern. Redbrick along one side, cream-color brick along another, the tavern's main building is a stately colonial house with a white-marble portico and coffered frieze, built in 1719 and converted to a tavern in 1762. It was the meeting place for the Sons of Liberty until the Revolutionary War, and in 1783 George Washington delivered a farewell address here to his officers celebrating the British evacuation of New York. Later the building housed some offices of the fledgling U.S. government. Today a museum occupies this historic five-building complex. Fraunces Tavern contains two fully furnished period rooms and other displays of 18th- and 19th-century American history. The museum also offers family programs (such as crafts workshops and a scavenger hunt), lectures, workshops, and concerts. ⊠ *54 Pearl St., at Broad St.,* ☎ *212/425–1778.* ⊠ *$2.* ⊙ *Weekdays 10–4:45.*

NEED A BREAK? The **brick plaza behind 85 Broad Street** is flanked by a variety of small restaurants. Order a take-out meal or snack and eat it out here on the benches, where you can watch busy office workers milling around—and enjoy not being one of them.

⑩ Hanover Square. When the East River ran past present-day Pearl Street, this quiet tree-lined plaza stood on the waterfront and was the city's original printing-house square; on the site of 81 Pearl Street, William Bradford established the first printing press in the colonies. The pirate Captain Kidd lived in the neighborhood, and the Italianate sandstone-fronted **India House** (1851–54), a private club at No. 1, used to house the New York Cotton Exchange.

OFF THE BEATEN PATH **MUSEUM OF AMERICAN FINANCIAL HISTORY –** On the site of Alexander Hamilton's law office (today the Standard Oil Building), this four-room museum displays artifacts of the financial market's history, including vintage ticker-tape machines and ticker tape from "Black Tuesday," October 29, 1929—the worst crash in the stock market's history. ⊠ *26 Broadway, north of Bowling Green,* ☎ *212/908–4110.* ⊠ *$2.* ⊙ *Tues.–Sat. 10–4.*

★ **⑲ Museum of Jewish Heritage—A Living Memorial to the Holocaust.** Housed in a granite hexagon rising 85 ft above **Robert F. Wagner Jr. Park,** just below **Battery Park City,** downtown's newest museum, opened in late 1997 after more than 15 years of planning, pays tribute to the 6 million Jews who perished in the Holocaust. Architect Kevin Roche's Star of David–shape building has three floors of exhibits demonstrating the dynamism of 20th-century Jewish culture. You enter through a captivating multiscreen vestibule, perhaps best described as a storytelling gallery, that provides a context for the artifacts of early 20th-century Jewish life displayed on the first floor: elaborate screens painted by a Budapest butcher for the fall harvest festival of Sukkoth, wedding invitations, and tools used by Jewish tradesmen. Also intriguing is the use of original documentary film footage throughout the museum. *The War Against the Jews,* on the second floor, details the rise of Nazism, the period's anti-Semitism, and the ravages of the Holocaust. A gallery covers the doomed voyage of the *St. Louis,* a ship of German Jewish refugees that crossed the Atlantic twice in 1939 in search of a safe haven. Signs of hope are on display, as well, including a trumpet that Louis Bannet (the "Dutch Louis Armstrong") played for three years in the Auschwitz-Birkenau inmate orchestra, and a pretty blue-and-white check dress sewn in 1945 by Fania Bratt at the newly liberated Dachau concentration camp. The third floor covers postwar Jewish life and is devoted to the theme of Jewish renewal. Another gallery leads to a usually light-filled room lined with southwest-facing windows with a view of the harbor and the Statue of Liberty. In October 2000, ground was broken for a new, four-story east wing, an expansion that will contain a theater, memorial garden, resource center and library, more galleries, and a café, all to be completed by fall of 2003. ⊠ *18 1st Pl., Battery Park City,* ☎ *212/968–1800, web:www.mjhnyc.org.* ⊠ *$7.* ⊙ *Sun.– Wed. 9–5, Thurs. 9–8, Fri. and eve of Jewish holidays 9–3 (extended hrs in summer).*

★ ☺ **⑧ National Museum of the American Indian.** This museum, a branch of the Washington, D.C.–based Smithsonian Institution, is the first of its kind to be dedicated to Native American culture. The cultural heritage of indigenous peoples of the Western hemisphere is documented and explored through well-mounted exhibits, dance performances, lectures, readings, film, and crafts. Native Americans of all backgrounds participate in visiting programs and work at all levels of the staff. George Gustav Heye, a wealthy New Yorker, amassed most of the museum's collection—more than a million artifacts, including pottery, weaving, and basketry from the southwestern United States, painted hides from the Plains Indians of North America, carved jade from the Mexican Olmec and Maya cultures, and contemporary Native American paintings. The museum is in one of lower Manhattan's finest buildings: the ornate beaux arts **Alexander Hamilton U.S. Custom House** (1907). From its base, massive granite columns rise to a pediment topped by a double row of statuary. Daniel Chester French, better known for the sculpture of Lincoln in the Lincoln Memorial in Washington, D.C., carved the lower statues, which symbolize continents (left to right: Asia, the Americas, Europe, Africa). The upper row represents the major trading cities of the world. Inside, the display of white and color marble couldn't be more remarkable. The semicircular side staircases are equally breathtaking. Murals by Reginald Marsh completed in 1934 embellish the oval rotunda. ⊠ *1 Bowling Green, between State and Whitehall Sts.,* ☎ *212/514–3700,* WEB *www.si.edu/nmai.* ☞ *Free.* ☉ *Mon.–Wed. and Fri.–Sun. 10–5, Thurs. 10–8.*

🄯 **New York Stock Exchange (NYSE).** The largest securities exchange in the world, the NYSE nearly bursts from this relatively diminutive neoclassical 1903 building with an august Corinthian entrance—a fitting temple to the almighty dollar. Today's "Big Board" can handle a trillion shares of stock per day; in today's market-obsessed media, how those stocks perform each day is news broadcast around the world. The third-floor interactive education center has a self-guided tour, touch-screen computer terminals, video displays, a 15-minute film detailing the history of the exchange, and live guides to help you interpret the seeming chaos you'll see from the visitors' gallery overlooking the immense (50-ft-high) trading floor. ⊠ *20 Broad St., between Wall St. and Exchange Pl.,* ☎ *212/656–5165.* ☞ *Free tickets distributed beginning at 8:45; come before 1 PM to ensure entrance.* ☉ *Weekdays 9–4:30.*

★ 🄳 **Robert F. Wagner Jr. Park.** The newest addition to the downtown waterfront may be the best of the chain of parks that stretch from **Battery Park** to above the **World Financial Center**. Lawns, walks, gardens, and benches spill right down to the river. Behind these, a brown-brick structure rises two stories to provide river and harbor panoramas. A stream of runners and bladers flows by, making it a toss-up as to which is better: the people-watching or the views of the Statue of Liberty and Ellis Island. ⊠ *Between Battery Pl. and Hudson River.*

❷ **Shrine of St. Elizabeth Ann Seton at Our Lady of the Rosary.** The rectory of the shrine is a redbrick federal-style town house, an example of the mansions that used to line the street, with a distinctive portico shaped to fit the curving street. This house was built in 1793 as the home of the wealthy Watson family; Mother Seton and her family lived here from 1801 until the death of her husband in 1803. She joined the Catholic Church in 1805 and went on to found the Sisters of Charity, the first American order of nuns. In 1975 she became the first American-born saint. Masses are held here daily. ⊠ *7–8 State St., near Whitehall St.,* ☎ *212/269–6865.* ☉ *Weekdays 6:30–5, weekends by appointment.*

★ ☙ ❶ **Staten Island Ferry.** The best transit deal in town is the Staten Island Ferry, a free 20- to 30-minute ride across New York Harbor, which provides great views of the Manhattan skyline, the Statue of Liberty, the Verrazano-Narrows Bridge, and the New Jersey coast. The classic blue-and-orange ferries embark on various schedules: every 15 minutes during rush hours, every 20–30 minutes most other times, and every hour after 11 PM and on weekend mornings. A word of advice, however: the ferry service runs swift, new low-slung craft that ride low in the water and have no outside deck space, so wait for one of the higher, more open old-timers. ⊠ *State and South Sts.,* ☎ *718/390–5253.*

★ ☝ ➎ **Statue of Liberty.** Millions of American immigrants first glimpsed their new land when they laid eyes on the Statue of Liberty, a national monument that still ennobles all those who encounter it. *Liberty Enlightening the World,* as the statue is officially named, was sculpted by Frederic-Auguste Bartholdi and presented in 1886 to the United States as a gift from France. Since then she has become a near-universal symbol of freedom and democracy, standing a proud 152 ft high on top of an 89-ft pedestal (executed by Richard Morris Hunt), on Liberty Island in New York Harbor. Emma Lazarus's sonnet *The New Colossus* ("Give me your tired, your poor, your huddled masses . . .") is inscribed on a bronze plaque attached to the statue's base. Gustav Eiffel designed the statue's iron skeleton. In anticipation of her centennial, Liberty underwent a long-overdue restoration in the mid-'80s and reemerged with great fanfare on July 4, 1986.

The top of the statue is accessible in two ways: an elevator ascends 10 stories to the top of the pedestal, or, if you're in good shape, you can climb 354 steps (the equivalent of a 22-story building) to the crown. (Visitors cannot go up into the torch.) Be forewarned that, in summer, only the first daily ferry load of passengers is allowed to walk up to the crown; come prepared to contend with the heat, both outside waiting in line (where there is no overhead protection) and inside the statue. Other times of the year, the park service occasionally closes off the line to the crown as early as 2. So it's vital to catch an early ferry out of **Castle Clinton National Monument**; the earliest leaves at 9 (times vary seasonally). Exhibits inside illustrate the statue's history, including videos of the view from the crown. There are also life-size models of Lady Liberty's face and foot for the blind to feel and a pleasant outdoor café. ⊠ *Liberty Island,* ☎ *212/363–3200; 212/269–5755 for ferry information,* 🕸 *www.nps.gov/stli/.* 🎫 *Free; ferry $7 round-trip.* ☉ *Daily 9–5:30 (extended hrs in summer).*

➓ **Trinity Church.** The present Trinity Church, the third on this site since an Anglican parish was established here in 1697, was designed in 1846 by Richard Upjohn. It ranked as the city's tallest building for most of the second half of the 19th century. The three huge bronze doors were designed by Richard Morris Hunt to recall Lorenzo Ghiberti's doors for the Baptistery in Florence, Italy. The church's Gothic revival interior is surprisingly light and elegant. On the church's north and south sides is a 2½-acre graveyard: Alexander Hamilton is buried beneath a white-stone pyramid, and a monument commemorates Robert Fulton, the inventor of the steamboat (he's buried in the Livingston family vault, with his wife). A daily tour is offered at 2. ⊠ *74 Trinity Pl. (Broadway at the head of Wall St.),* ☎ *212/602–0800,* 🕸 *www.trinitywallstreet. org.* ☉ *Weekdays 8:30–6, weekends 8:30–4.*

OFF THE
BEATEN PATH

VIETNAM VETERANS MEMORIAL – At this 14-ft-high, 70-ft-long rectangular memorial (1985), moving passages from news dispatches and the letters of servicemen and servicewomen have been etched into a wall of greenish glass. The brick plaza around it is often desolate on weekends. ⊠ *End of Coenties Slip, between Water and South Sts.*

⑪ Wall Street. Named after a wooden wall built across the island in 1653 to defend the Dutch colony against the Native Americans (mostly Algonquins), ⅓-mi-long Wall Street is arguably the most famous thoroughfare in the world—shorthand for the vast, powerful financial community that clusters around the New York and American stock exchanges. "The Street," as it's also widely known, began its financial career with stock traders conducting business along the sidewalks or at tables beneath a sheltering buttonwood tree. Today it's a dizzyingly narrow canyon—look to the east and you'll glimpse a sliver of East River waterfront; look to the west and you'll see the spire of Trinity Church, tightly framed by skyscrapers. For a startlingly clear lesson in the difference between Ionic and Corinthian columns, look at **55 Wall Street**, now the location of the Regent Wall Street hotel. The lower stories were part of an earlier U.S. Custom House, built in 1836–42; it was literally a bullish day on Wall Street when oxen hauled its 16 granite Ionic columns up to the site. When the National City Bank took over the building in 1899, it hired architects McKim, Mead & White to redesign the building and in 1909 added the second tier of columns but made them Corinthian.

⑰ World Financial Center. The four towers of this complex, 34–51 stories high and topped with different geometric shapes, were designed by Cesar Pelli and serve as company headquarters for the likes of American Express, Lehman Brothers, and Dow Jones. Like a giant terrarium, the **Winter Garden** atrium, where gray-and-pink marble steps cascade into a vaulted plaza, shelters 16 giant palm trees. A vast arch window overlooking the Hudson fills the Winter Garden's west facade, and 45 shops and restaurants surround the atrium, which is a great place to beat the summer heat. The center hosts traveling exhibits and performances in and around the atrium and in a nearby gallery. The outdoor plaza right behind the Winter Garden curls around a tidy little yacht basin; take in the view of the Statue of Liberty and read the stirring quotations worked into the iron railings. Or hop aboard one of the **Water Taxi**'s bright yellow boats for a sightseeing tour of the harbor or a quick trip across the Hudson to New Jersey's Liberty State Park (a great place for a picnic). The boats are tied up on the north side of the yacht basin, or you can call (☎ 201/985–8000) for more information.

At the northwest corner of the World Financial Center, the **New York Mercantile Exchange**, opened in 1997, houses the world's largest energy and precious metals market. A ground-floor museum details the history of the exchange; a second-floor gallery with a 150-ft-long window overlooks the trading floors. ⊠ *1 North End Ave., at Vesey St.,* ☎ *212/299–2000.* 🎟 *Free.* ⊙ *Weekdays 9–5.*

At the end of North End Avenue, on the water's edge, is the New York Waterway's terminal for **ferry service** to Hoboken, New Jersey (☎ 800/533–3779), across the Hudson River. It's a $2, eight-minute ride to Frank Sinatra's hometown, with a spectacular view of lower Manhattan. ⊠ *World Financial Center, West St. between Vesey and Liberty Sts.*

★ ⊙ ⑯ World Trade Center (WTC). The mammoth WTC comprises New York's two tallest buildings, the third tallest in the world after Kuala Lumpur's Petronas Towers and the Sears Tower in Chicago. Unlike some of the city's most beloved skyscrapers—the Empire State, the Chrysler, or the Flatiron buildings—the WTC's two 1,350-ft towers, designed by Minoru Yamasaki and built in 1972–73, are more engineering marvel than architectural masterpiece. To some they are an unmitigated design disaster—"totalitarian-modernist monstrosity," complains the *Wall Street Journal*'s Raymond Sokolov; to others their brutalist design and sheer magnitude give them the beauty of modern sculpture, and at night when they're lighted from within, they dominate the Manhattan skyline.

The WTC, though, is much more than its most famous twins: it's a 16-acre, 12-million-square-ft complex resembling a miniature city, with a daytime population of 140,000 (including 40,000 employees and 100,000 business and leisure visitors). The WTC has seven buildings in all, arranged around a plaza modeled after, and larger than, Venice's Piazza San Marco; summer concerts are held on the plaza. Underground is a giant mall with nearly a hundred stores and restaurants and a network of subway and other train stations. A **TKTS** booth sells discount tickets to Broadway and off-Broadway shows in the mezzanine of 2 WTC.

From the **Top of the World,** the 107th-floor glass-enclosed observation deck at 2 World Trade Center, the view potentially extends 55 mi (signs at the ticket window disclose how far you can see that day and whether the outdoor deck is open). The elevator ride alone is worth the price of admission, as you hurl a quarter of a mile into the sky in only 58 seconds. Recent additions to the deck include three helicopter simulation theaters with moving seats and a nightly laser light show. On nice days you can ride up another few floors to the Rooftop Observatory, the world's highest outdoor observation platform. It's offset 25 ft from the edge of the building and surrounded with a barbed-wire electric fence. Notice that planes and helicopters are flying *below* you. ✉ *Ticket booth, 2 World Trade Center, mezzanine level,* ☎ *212/323–2340,* WEB *www.wtcny.com.* 💲 *$13.50.* ☉ *June–Aug., daily 9:30 AM–11:30 PM; Sept.–May, daily 9:30–9:30.*

THE SEAPORT AND THE COURTS

New York's role as a great seaport is easiest to understand downtown, with both the Hudson River and East River waterfronts within walking distance. Although the deeper Hudson River came into its own in the steamship era, the more sheltered waters of the East River saw most of the action in the 19th century, during the age of clipper ships. This era is preserved in the South Street Seaport restoration, centered on Fulton Street between Water Street and the East River. Only a few blocks away you can visit another seat of New York history: the City Hall neighborhood, which includes Manhattan's magisterial court and government buildings.

Numbers in the text correspond to numbers in the margin and on the Lower Manhattan map.

A Good Walk

Begin at the intersection of Water and Fulton streets. Water Street was once the shoreline; the latter thoroughfare was named after the ferry to Brooklyn, which once docked at its foot (the ferry itself was named after its inventor, Robert Fulton [1765–1815]). On the 19th-century landfill across the street is the 11-block **South Street Seaport Historic District** ㉑.

Return to Fulton Street and walk away from the river to Broadway, to **St. Paul's Chapel** ㉑, the oldest (1766) surviving church building in Manhattan. Forking off to the right is Park Row, which was known as Newspaper Row from the mid-19th to early 20th centuries, when most of the city's 20 or so daily newspapers had offices here. In tribute to that past, a statue of Benjamin Franklin (who was, after all, a printer) stands in front of Pace University, farther up on Park Row. Two blocks north on Broadway is one of the finest skyscrapers in the city, the Gothic **Woolworth Building** ㉒, for which Frank Woolworth paid $13 million—in cash.

Between Broadway and Park Row is triangular **City Hall Park** ㉓, originally the town common, which gives way to a slew of government offices. **City Hall** ㉔, built between 1803 and 1812, is unexpectedly modest. Lurking directly behind it is the **Tweed Courthouse** ㉕, named for the notorious politician William Marcy "Boss" Tweed. The small plaza east of Tweed Courthouse is used as a farmers' market on Tuesday and Friday.

Directly opposite the Tweed Courthouse on the north side of Chambers Street incongruously sits an eight-story beaux arts château, the 1911 **Surrogate's Court** ㉖, also called the Hall of Records. Across Centre Street from the château is the city government's first skyscraper, the imposing **Municipal Building** ㉗, built in 1914 by McKim, Mead & White. Just steps south of the Municipal Building, a ramp curves up into the pedestrian walkway over the **Brooklyn Bridge** ㉘. The river-and-four-borough views from the bridge are wondrous.

Foley Square, a name that has become synonymous with the New York court system, opens out north of the Municipal Building. On the right, the orderly progression of the Corinthian colonnades of the **U.S. Courthouse** ㉙ and the **New York County Courthouse** ㉚ is a fitting reflection of the epigraph carved in the latter's frieze: THE TRUE ADMINISTRATION OF JUSTICE IS THE FIRMEST PILLAR OF GOOD GOVERNMENT. Turn to look across Foley Square at Federal Plaza, which sprawls in front of the gridlike skyscraper of the Javits Federal Building. The black-glass box to the left houses the U.S. Court of International Trade. Just south of it, at the corner of Duane and Elk streets, is the site of the **African Burial Ground** ㉛.

Continue north up Centre Street past neoclassical civic office buildings to 100 Centre Street, the **Criminal Courts Building** ㉜, a rather forbidding construction with Art Moderne details. In contrast, the Civil and Municipal Courthouse (1960), across the way at 111 Centre Street, is an uninspired modern cube, although it, too, has held sensational trials. On the west side of this small square, at 60 Lafayette Street, is the slick black-granite Family Court, built in 1975, with its intriguing angular facade.

Turn left onto Leonard Street, which runs just south of the Family Court, and take a look at the ornate Victorian building that runs the length of the block on your left. This is the old New York Life Insurance Company headquarters, an 1870 building that was remodeled and enlarged in 1896 by McKim, Mead & White. The ornate clock tower facing Broadway is occupied by the avant-garde Clocktower Gallery and is used as studio space by artists, who sometimes host exhibitions of their work here. The stretch of Broadway south of here is the subject of what is believed to be the oldest photograph of New York. The picture focuses on a paving project—to eliminate the morass of muddy streets—that took place in 1850.

TIMING
You can easily spend a half day at the Seaport, or longer if you browse in shops. Completing the rest of the walking tour takes about 1½ hours. The real Seaport opens well before the sun rises and clears out not much after, when fishmongers leave to make way for the visitors. Unless you're really interested in wholesale fish, however, you're best off visiting the Seaport when its other attractions are open. Try to do this during the week, so that the government offices will be open, too. Also, consider walking across the Brooklyn Bridge in the late afternoon for dramatic contrasts of light.

Sights to See

③① **African Burial Ground.** This grassy corner is part of the original area used to inter the city's earliest African-Americans—an estimated 20,000 were buried here until the cemetery was closed in 1794. The site was discovered during a 1991 construction project, and by an act of Congress it was made into a National Historic Landmark, dedicated to the people who were enslaved in the city between 1626 and Emancipation Day in New York, July 4, 1827. ✉ *Duane and Elk Sts.*

★ ②⑧ **Brooklyn Bridge.** "A drive-through cathedral" is how the critic James Wolcott describes one of New York's noblest and most recognized landmarks. Spanning the East River, the Brooklyn Bridge connected Manhattan island to the then-independent city of Brooklyn; before its opening, Brooklynites had only the Fulton Street Ferry to shuttle them across the river. John Augustus Roebling—a visionary architect, legendary engineer, metaphysical philosopher, and fervid abolitionist—is said to have first conceived of the bridge on an icy winter's day in 1852, when the frozen river prevented him from getting to Brooklyn. To be sure, he was by no means the first person so inconvenienced, but as a bridge builder, Roebling was perfectly qualified to rectify the matter. Roebling spent the next 30 years designing, raising money for, and building what would be one of the first steel suspension bridges—and what was for several years one of the world's longest. Alas, its construction was fraught with peril. Work began in 1867; two years later Roebling died of gangrene, after a wayward ferry boat rammed his foot while he was at work on a pier. His son, Washington, took over the project and was himself permanently crippled—like many others who worked on the bridge underwater, he suffered from the bends, or decompression sickness. With the help of his wife, Emily, Washington nonetheless saw the bridge's construction through to completion.

The long struggle to build the bridge so captured the imagination of the city that when it opened in 1883 it was promptly crowned the "Eighth Wonder of the World." Its twin Gothic-arch towers, with a span of 1,595½ ft, rise 272 ft from the river below; the bridge's overall length of 6,016 ft made it four times longer than the longest suspension bridge of its day. From roadway to water is about 133 ft, high enough to allow the tallest ships to pass. The roadway is supported by a web of steel cables, hung from the towers and attached to block-long anchorages on either shore.

A walk across the bridge's promenade—a boardwalk elevated above the roadway and shared by pedestrians, in-line skaters, and bicyclists—takes about 40 minutes, from Manhattan's civic center to the heart of Brooklyn Heights; it's well worth traversing for the astounding views. Midtown's jumble of spires looms to the north, to the left of the Manhattan Bridge. Mostly newer skyscrapers crowd lower Manhattan, while the tall ships docked at their feet, at South Street Seaport, appear to have sailed in straight from the 19th century. Governors Island sits forlornly in the middle of the harbor, which sweeps open dramatically toward Lady Liberty and, off in the distance, the Verrazano-Narrows Bridge (its towers are more than twice as tall as those of the Brooklyn Bridge). A word of caution to pedestrians: do obey the lane markings on the promenade—pedestrians on the north side, bicyclists on the south—as the latter often pedal furiously.

②④ **City Hall.** Reflecting not big-city brawn but the classical refinement and civility of Enlightenment Europe, New York's surprisingly decorous City Hall is a diminutive palace with a facade punctuated by arches and columns and a cupola crowned by a statue of Lady Justice. Built between 1803 and 1812, it was originally clad in white marble only on its front and sides, while the back was faced in more modest brownstone because city fathers assumed the city would never grow farther north than this. Limestone now covers all four sides. A sweeping marble double staircase leads from the domed rotunda to the second-floor public rooms. The small, clubby Victorian-style **City Council Chamber** in the east wing has mahogany detailing and ornate gilding; the **Board of Estimate Chamber,** to the west, has colonial paintings and church-pew-style seating; and the **Governor's Room** at the head of the stairs, used for ceremonial events, is filled with historic portraits and furniture, including a writing table that George Washington used in 1789 when New York was the U.S. capital. The **Blue Room,** which was traditionally the mayor's office, is on the ground floor; it is now used for mayoral press conferences.

Although the building looks genteel, the City Hall politicking that goes on there can be rough and tumble. News crews can often be seen jockeying on the front steps, as they attempt to interview city officials, and frequent demonstrations and protests are also staged here. In 1998, City Hall itself was at the center of a controversy, when Mayor Giuliani closed the building to the public for security reasons. It is now open to the public for tours, and there are free interactive video machines located on the main floor that dispense info on City Hall and Lower Manhattan history. ⊠ *City Hall Park,* ☎ *212/788–6865 for tour information.* 🎟 *Free.* ⊙ *Weekdays 9–5; tours at 10, 11, and 2 (reservations required 2 wks in advance).*

㉓ **City Hall Park.** Originally used as a sheep meadow, this green spot was known in Colonial times as the Fields or the Common. It went on to become a graveyard for the impoverished, the site of an almshouse, and then the home of the notorious Bridewell jail before it became a park. Even as a park, the locale was far from peaceful: it hosted hangings, riots, and political demonstrations. A bronze statue of patriot Nathan Hale, who was hanged in 1776 as a spy by the British troops occupying New York City, stands facing City Hall. In conjunction with the 1999 restoration of the park's 19th-century grandeur, archaeologists uncovered human bones, coins, clay pipes, and other remnants of the 17th and 18th centuries. ⊠ *Between Broadway, Park Row, and Chambers St.*

㉜ **Criminal Courts Building.** Fans of crime fiction, whether on television, in the movies, or in novels, may recognize this rather grim art deco tower, which is connected by a skywalk (New York's Bridge of Sighs) to the detention center known as the Tombs. In *The Bonfire of the Vanities,* Tom Wolfe wrote a chilling description of this court's menacing atmosphere. ⊠ *100 Centre St., at Hogan St.*

㉗ **Municipal Building.** Who else but the venerable architecture firm McKim, Mead & White would the city government trust to build its first skyscraper in 1914? The roof section alone is 10 stories high, bristling with towers and peaks and topped by a 25-ft-high gilt statue of Civic Fame. New Yorkers come here to pay parking fines and get marriage licenses (and to get married, in a civil chapel on the second floor). An immense arch straddles Chambers Street (traffic used to flow through here). ⊠ *1 Centre St., at Chambers St.*

㉚ **New York County Courthouse.** With its stately columns, pediments, and 100-ft-wide steps, this 1912 classical temple front is yet another spin-off on Rome's Pantheon. It deviates from its classical parent in its hexagonal rotunda, shaped to fit an irregular plot of land. The 1957 courtroom drama *Twelve Angry Men* was filmed here; the courthouse also hosts thousands of marriages a year. ⊠ *60 Centre St., at Foley Sq.*

㉑ St. Paul's Chapel. The oldest (1766) public building in continuous use in Manhattan, this Episcopal house of worship, built of rough Manhattan brownstone, was modeled on London's St. Martin-in-the-Fields (a columned clock tower and steeple were added in 1794). A prayer service here followed George Washington's inauguration as president; Washington's pew is in the north aisle. The gilded crown adorned with plumes above the pulpit is thought to be the city's only vestige of British rule. In the adjoining cemetery, 18th-century headstones crumble in the shadows of glittering skyscrapers. ⊠ *Broadway and Fulton St.,* ☎ *212/602–0874.* ⊙ *Weekdays 9–3, Sun. 7–3.*

★ ☾ ⓴ **South Street Seaport Historic District.** Had it not been declared a historic district in 1967, this charming, cobblestone corner of New York with the city's largest concentration of early 19th-century commercial buildings would likely have been gobbled up by skyscrapers. In the early 1980s the Rouse Corporation, which had already created Boston's Quincy Market and Baltimore's Harborplace, was hired to restore and adapt the existing buildings, preserving the commercial feel of centuries past. The result is a hybrid of historical district and shopping mall. Many of its streets' 18th-, 19th-, and early 20th-century architectural details re-create the city's historic seafaring era.

At the intersection of Fulton and Water streets, the gateway to the Seaport, stands the *Titanic* **Memorial,** a small white lighthouse that commemorates the sinking of the RMS *Titanic* in 1912. Beyond it, Fulton Street, cobbled in blocks of Belgian granite, turns into a busy pedestrian mall. Just to the left of Fulton, at 211 Water Street, is **Bowne & Co. Stationers,** a reconstructed working 19th-century print shop. Continue down Fulton around to Front Street, which has wonderfully preserved old brick buildings—some dating from the 1700s. On the south side of Fulton Street is the seaport's architectural centerpiece, **Schermerhorn Row,** a redbrick terrace of Georgian- and Federal-style warehouses and countinghouses built in 1811–12. Today the ground floors are occupied by upscale shops, bars, and restaurants, and the **South Street Seaport Museum** (☎ 212/748–8600, ⊙ Apr.–Sept., Fri.–Wed. 10–6, Thurs. 10–8; Oct.–Mar., Wed.–Mon. 10–5), which hosts walking tours, hands-on exhibits, and fantastic creative programs for children, all with a nautical theme. ⊠ *12 Fulton St.,* ☎ *212/732–7678 for events and shopping information,* 🖳 *www.southstreetseaport.com.* 🖳 *$6 (to ships, galleries, walking tours, Maritime Crafts Center, films, and other seaport events).*

Cross South Street, once known as the Street of Ships, under an elevated stretch of the FDR Drive to **Pier 16,** where historic ships are docked, including the *Pioneer,* a 102-ft schooner built in 1885; the *Peking,* the second-largest sailing barque in existence; the iron-hulled *Wavertree;* and the lightship *Ambrose.* The Pier 16 ticket booth provides information and sells tickets to the museum, ships, tours, and exhibits. Pier 16 also hosts frequent concerts and performances, has an ice rink in winter, and is the departure point for various cruises, including the **Seaport Music Cruise** (☎ 212/630–8888; 🖳 $25 and up), featuring jazz and blues, and the Circle Line's (☎ 212/563–3200) **Seaport Liberty Cruise,** a one-hour sightseeing trip (🖳 $12), and "**The Beast,**" a 30-minute speedboat ride out to the Statue of Liberty (🖳 $15).

To the north is **Pier 17,** a multilevel dockside shopping mall featuring standard-issue national chain retailers such as the Gap and Banana Republic, among others. Its weathered-wood rear decks make a splendid spot from which to sit and contemplate the river.

As your nose will surmise, the blocks along South Street north of the museum complex still house a working fish market, which has been in operation since the early 1800s. Hundreds of species of fish—from swordfish to sea urchin roe—are sold by the fishmongers of the **Fulton Fish Market.** Get up early (or stay up late) if you want to see it: the action begins around 3 AM and ends by 8 AM. ☎ 212/748–8590. ✉ *$12.* ☉ *1st and 3rd Thurs. of every month, depending on weather, at 6 AM; tours by reservation only.*

NEED A BREAK?
The cuisine at the fast-food stalls on Pier 17's third-floor **Promenade Food Court** is nonchain eclectic: Pizza on the Pier, Daikichi Sushi, Simply Seafood, and Salad Mania. What's really spectacular is the view from the tables in a glass-walled atrium.

㉖ **Surrogate's Court–Hall of Records.** This 1911 building is the most ornate of the City Hall court trio. In true beaux arts fashion, sculpture and ornament seem to have been added wherever possible to the basic neoclassical structure, yet the overall effect is graceful rather than cluttered. Filmmakers sometimes use its elaborate lobby in opera scenes. A courtroom here was the venue for *Johnson v. Johnson,* where the heirs to the Johnson & Johnson fortune waged their bitter battle. ✉ *31 Chambers St., at Centre St.*

㉕ **Tweed Courthouse.** Under the corrupt management of notorious politician William Marcy "Boss" Tweed (1823–78), this Anglo-Italianate gem, one of the finest designs in the City Hall area, took some $12 million and nine years to build (it was finally finished in 1872, but the ensuing public outrage drove Tweed from office). Although it is imposing, with its columned classical pediment outside and seven-story octagonal rotunda inside, almost none of the boatloads of marble that Tweed had shipped from Europe made their way into this building. Today it houses municipal offices; it has also served as a location for several films, most notably *The Verdict.* ✉ *52 Chambers St., between Broadway and Centre St.*

㉙ **U.S. Courthouse.** Cass Gilbert built this courthouse in 1936, convinced that it complemented the much finer nearby Woolworth Building, which he had designed three decades earlier. Granite steps climb to a massive columned portico; above this rises a 32-story tower topped by a gilded pyramid, not unlike that with which Gilbert crowned the New York Life building uptown. Julius and Ethel Rosenberg were tried for espionage at this courthouse, and hotel queen Leona Helmsley went on trial here for tax-evasion. ✉ *40 Centre St., at Foley Sq.*

★ ㉒ **Woolworth Building.** Called the Cathedral of Commerce, this ornate white terra-cotta edifice was, at 792 ft, the world's tallest building when it opened in 1913. The Woolworth Company (now Venator Group), whose eponymous stores closed in 1997, sold the building and now leases only a few floors. The spectacular **lobby**'s extravagant Gothic-style details include sculptures set into arches in the ceiling; one of them represents an elderly F. W. Woolworth pinching his pennies, while another depicts the architect, Cass Gilbert, cradling in his arms a model of his creation. ✉ *233 Broadway, between Park Pl. and Barclay St.*

LITTLE ITALY AND CHINATOWN

Mulberry Street is the heart of Little Italy; in fact, at this point it's virtually the entire body. In 1932 an estimated 98% of the inhabitants of this area were of Italian birth or heritage, but since then the growth and expansion of Chinatown to the south have encroached on the Italian neighborhood to such an extent that merchants and community leaders of the Little Italy Restoration Association (LIRA) negotiated with Chinatown to let at least Mulberry remain an all-Italian street. More recently, trendy shops and restaurant have sprouted in what were Little Italy's northern reaches, and the area is now known as NoLita.

In the second half of the 19th century, when Italian immigration peaked, the neighborhood stretched from Houston Street to Canal Street and the Bowery to Broadway. During this time Italians founded at least three Italian parishes, including the Church of the Transfiguration (now almost wholly Chinese); they also operated an Italian-language newspaper, *Il Progresso*.

In 1926 immigrants from southern Italy celebrated the first Feast of San Gennaro along Mulberry Street—a 10-day street fair that still takes place every September. Dedicated to the patron saint of Naples, the festival transforms Mulberry Street into a virtual alfresco restaurant, as wall-to-wall vendors sell traditional fried sausages and pastries. Today the festival is one of the few reminders of Little Italy's vibrant history as the neighborhood continues to change. If you want the flavor of a truly Italian neighborhood, visit Arthur Avenue in the Bronx— or rent a video of the Martin Scorsese movie *Mean Streets,* which was filmed in Little Italy in the early 1970s.

Visually exotic, Chinatown is a popular tourist attraction, but it is also a real, vital community where about half the city's population of 300,000 Chinese still lives. Its main businesses are restaurants and garment factories; some 55% of its residents speak little or no English. Historically, Chinatown was divided from Little Italy by Canal Street, the bustling artery that links the Holland Tunnel (to New Jersey) and the Manhattan Bridge (to Brooklyn). However, in recent years an influx of immigrants from the People's Republic of China, Taiwan, and especially Hong Kong has swelled Manhattan's Chinese population, and Hong Kong residents have poured capital into Chinatown real estate. Chinatown now spills over its traditional borders into Little Italy to the north and the formerly Jewish Lower East Side to the east.

The first Chinese immigrants were primarily railroad workers who came from the West in the 1870s to settle in a limited section of the Lower East Side. For nearly a century anti-immigration laws prohibited most men from having their wives and families join them; the neighborhood became known as a "bachelor society," and for years its population remained static. It was not until the end of World War II, when Chinese immigration quotas were increased, that the neighborhood began the expansion that is still taking place today.

Chinatown is now livelier than ever—a thriving marketplace crammed with souvenir shops and restaurants in funky pagoda-style buildings and crowded with pedestrians day and night. From fast-food noodles or dumplings to sumptuous Hunan, Szechuan, Cantonese, Mandarin, and Shanghai feasts, every imaginable type of Chinese cuisine is served here. Sidewalk markets burst with stacks of fresh seafood and strangely shaped fruits and vegetables. Food shops proudly display their wares: if America's motto is "A chicken in every pot," then Chinatown's must be "A roast duck in every window."

A Good Walk

Start your tour at the corner of Mott and Prince streets, among the pricey new boutiques and quaint restaurants that form the chic little neighborhood of NoLita (North of Little Italy). Mulberry, Mott, and Elizabeth streets between Houston and Spring streets are the core of this swiftly gentrifying neighborhood. Hip clothing, design, and secondhand boutiques as well as restaurants and cafés have opened up and down these few blocks, and many new ventures continue to debut, making the area a sort of new SoHo. Although the neighborhood lacks big-draw exploring sights, its unique stores are worth a stop. Among these neighborhood debutantes sits the stately dowager, **St. Patrick's Old Cathedral** ①, the oldest Roman Catholic church in New York City. Tour the church and walk east on Prince Street to **Mulberry Street** ②; then walk south to Broome Street. East of Mulberry Street, the building at 375 Broome Street is known for its sheet-metal cornice that bears the face of a distinguished, albeit anonymous, bearded man.

To see the ornate Renaissance revival former **New York City Police Head-quarters** ③, walk west on Broome Street to Centre Street, and south to Grand Street. Next, head east to the corner of Grand and Mulberry streets and stop to get the lay of the land. Facing north (uptown), on your right you'll see a series of multistory houses from the early 19th century, built long before the great flood of immigration hit this neighborhood between 1890 and 1924. Turn and look south along the east side of Mulberry Street to see Little Italy's trademark railroad-apartment tenement buildings.

On the southeast corner of Grand Street, E. Rossi & Co., established in 1902, is an antiquated little shop that sells housewares, espresso makers, embroidered religious postcards, and jocular Italian T-shirts. Two doors east on Grand Street is Ferrara's, a pastry shop opened in 1892 that ships its creations—cannoli, peasant pie, Italian rum cake—all over the world. Another survivor of the pre-tenement era is the two-story, dormered brick Van Rensselaer House, now Paolucci's Restaurant; built in 1816, it's a prime example of the Italian federal style.

One block south of Grand Street, on the corner of Hester and Mulberry streets, you'll reach the site of what was once Umberto's Clam House, best known as the place where mobster Joey Gallo was munching scungilli in 1973 when he was fatally surprised by a task force of mob hit men. Turn left onto Hester Street to visit yet another Little Italy institution, Puglia, a restaurant where guests sit at long communal tables, sing along with house entertainers, and enjoy southern Italian specialties with quantities of homemade wine. One street west, on Baxter Street about three-quarters of a block toward Canal Street, stands the **San Gennaro Church** ④, which each autumn sponsors Little Italy's keynote event, the annual Feast of San Gennaro.

To reach Chinatown from Little Italy, cross Canal Street at Mulberry Street. A good place to get oriented is the **Museum of Chinese in the Americas** ⑤, in a century-old schoolhouse at the corner of Bayard and Mulberry streets. For a taste of Chinatown-style commercialism, walk one block north to Canal Street, where restaurants and markets abound.

If Chinese food products intrigue you, stop to browse in Kam Man, at 200 Canal Street. In east Chinatown, head to **Mott Street** ⑥, the principal business street of the neighborhood.

Turn right from Canal Street onto Mott Street and walk south three blocks. On the corner of Mott and Mosco streets, you'll find the **Church of the Transfiguration** ⑦, established in 1801. From here turn right from Mott Street onto Mosco Street, proceeding downhill to Mulberry Street, where you'll see **Columbus Park** ⑧. This peaceful spot occupies the area once known as the Five Points, a tough 19th-century slum ruled by Irish gangs.

Across Mott Street from the church is a sign for Pell Street, a narrow lane of wall-to-wall restaurants whose neon signs stretch halfway across the thoroughfare. Midway up Pell is **Doyers Street** ⑨, the site of turn-of-the-20th-century gang wars. At the end of Doyers you'll find the **Bowery** ⑩. Cross the street to **Chatham Square** ⑪, then continue past Park Row onto St. James Place to find two remnants of this neighborhood's pre-Chinatown past. On St. James Place is the **First Shearith Israel graveyard** ⑫, the first Jewish cemetery in the United States. Walk a half block farther, turn left on James Street, and you'll see St. James Church, a stately 1837 Greek revival edifice where Al Smith, who rose from this poor Irish neighborhood to become New York's governor and a 1928 Democratic presidential candidate, once served as altar boy.

Return to Chatham Square once again and walk north up the Bowery to **Confucius Plaza** ⑬, which is graced by a statue of the Chinese sage, beneath which are his words, "The World Is a Commonwealth." Then cross the Bowery back to the west side of the street; at the corner of Pell Street stands 18 Bowery, which is one of Manhattan's oldest homes—a Federal and Georgian structure built in 1785 by meat wholesaler Edward Mooney. Farther north up the Bowery, a younger side of Chinatown is shown at the **Asian American Arts Centre** ⑭, which displays current work by Asian-American artists.

Continue north. At the intersection of the Bowery and Canal Street, a grand arch and colonnade designed by Carrère & Hastings in 1910 mark the entrance to the Manhattan Bridge, which leads to Brooklyn. This corner was once the center of New York's diamond district. Today most jewelry dealers have moved uptown, but you can still find some pretty good deals at jewelers on the Bowery and the north side of Canal Street.

TIMING

Since Little Italy consists of little more than one street, a tour of the area shouldn't take more than one hour. Most attractions are food-related, so plan on visiting around lunchtime. A fun time to visit is during the **San Gennaro Festival,** which runs for two weeks each September, starting the first Thursday after Labor Day. For more information, call the festival information line at 212/768–9320. Come on a weekend to see Chinatown at its liveliest; locals crowd the streets from dawn until dusk, along with a slew of tourists. For a more relaxed experience, opt for a weekday instead. Allowing for stops at the two local museums and a lunch break, a Chinatown tour will take about three additional hours.

Sights to See

Numbers in the text correspond to numbers in the margin and on the Little Italy, Chinatown, SoHo, TriBeCa map.

⑭ **Asian American Arts Centre.** This space has impressive contemporary works by Asian-American artists, annual Chinese folk-art exhibitions during the Chinese New Year, Asian-American dance performances, and videotapes of Asian-American art and events. The center also sells unique art objects from Asia. The entrance is to the right of the McDonald's. ✉ *26 Bowery, between Bayard and Canal Sts.,* ☎ *212/ 233-2154.* ▣ *Free.* ◷ *Tues.–Fri. noon–6, Sat. 4–6.*

⑩ **The Bowery.** Now a commercial thoroughfare lined with stores selling light fixtures and secondhand restaurant equipment, in the 17th century this broad boulevard was a farming area north of the city; its name derives from *bowerij,* the Dutch word for farm. As the city's growing population moved northward, the Bowery became a broad, elegant avenue lined with taverns and theaters. In the late 1800s the placement of an elevated subway line over the Bowery and the proliferation of saloons and brothels led to its demise as an elegant commercial thoroughfare; by the early 20th century it had become infamous as a skid row full of indigents and crime. After 1970 efforts at gentrification had some effect, and some of the neighborhood's indigent population dispersed. Today the Bowery is undergoing further gentrification.

⑪ Chatham Square. Ten streets converge at this labyrinthine intersection, creating pandemonium for cars and a nightmare for pedestrians. A memorial, the **Kim Lau Arch,** honoring Chinese casualties in American wars, stands on an island in the eye of the storm. A statue on the square's eastern edge pays tribute to a Quin Dynasty official named Lin Zexu. Erected in late 1997, the 18-ft, 5-inch-tall granite statue reflects Chinatown's growing population of mainland immigrants and their particular national pride: the Fujianese minister is noted for his role in sparking the Opium War by banning the drug. The base of his statue reads, SAY NO TO DRUGS. On the far end of the square, at the corner of Catherine Street and East Broadway, stands a bank that was built to resemble a pagoda.

❼ Church of the Transfiguration. Built in 1801 as the Zion Episcopal Church, this is an imposing Georgian structure with Gothic windows. It's now a Chinese Catholic church distinguished by its trilingualism: here Mass is said in Cantonese, Mandarin, and English. ⊠ *29 Mott St.,* ☎ *212/962–5157.*

NEED A BREAK?
Right across from the Church of the Transfiguration, at the corner of Mott and Mosco streets, you'll see a red shack, **Cecilia Tam's Hong Kong Egg Cake Company,** where Ms. Tam makes mouthwatering small, round egg cakes for $1 a portion. At 35 Pell Street, off Mott Street, is **May May Chinese Gourmet Bakery** (☎ 212/267–0733), a local favorite, with Chinese pastries, rice dumplings wrapped in banana leaves, yam cakes, and other sweet treats. A colorful flag hangs outside the entrance of the **Chinatown Ice Cream Factory** (⊠ 65 Bayard St., between Mott and Elizabeth Sts., ☎ 212/608–4170), where the flavors range from red bean to litchi to green tea. Prepare to eat your scoop on the run, since there's no seating.

❽ Columbus Park. Mornings bring groups of elderly Chinese practicing the graceful movements of tai chi to this shady, paved space; during afternoons the park's tables fill for heated games of mah-jongg. One hundred years ago the then-swampy area was known as the **Five Points**—after the intersection of Mulberry Street, Anthony (now Worth) Street, Cross (now Park) Street, Orange (now Baxter) Street, and Little Water Street (no longer in existence)—and was notoriously ruled by dangerous Irish gangs. In the 1880s a neighborhood-improvement campaign brought about the park's creation.

⑬ Confucius Plaza. Just north of **Chatham Square,** a bronze statue of Confucius presides before the redbrick high-rise apartment complex named for him. The statue was originally opposed by leftist Chinese immigrants, who considered the sage a reactionary symbol of Old China. ⊠ *Intersection of the Bowery and Division St.*

❾ Doyers Street. The "bloody angle"—a sharp turn halfway down this little alleyway—was the site of turn-of-the-20th-century battles between Chinatown's Hip Sing and On Leon tongs, gangs who fought for control over the local gambling and opium trades. Today the street is among Chinatown's most colorful, lined with tea parlors and barbershops.

⑫ First Shearith Israel graveyard. Consecrated in 1656 by the country's oldest Jewish congregation, this small burial ground bears the remains of Sephardic Jews (of Spanish-Portuguese extraction) who emigrated from Brazil in the mid-17th century. You can peek through the gates here and at the second and third Shearith Israel graveyards in Greenwich Village and Chelsea, respectively. ✉ *55 St. James Pl.*

❻ Mott Street. The main commercial artery of Chinatown, Mott Street has appeared in innumerable movies and television as the street that exemplifies the neighborhood. Chinatown began in the late 1880s when Chinese immigrants (mostly men) settled in tenements in a small area that included the lower portion of Mott Street as well as nearby Pell and Doyer streets. Today the street is often crowded during the day and especially on weekends; it overflows with fish and vegetable markets, restaurants, bakeries, and souvenir shops.

Opened in 1891, **Quong Yuen Shing & Co.** (✉ 32 Mott St.), also known as the Mott Street General Store, is one of Chinatown's oldest curio shops, with porcelain bowls, teapots, and cups for sale. Next door is one of Chinatown's best and oldest bakeries, **Fung Wong** (✉ 30 Mott St.), where you can stock up on almond cookies, sticky rice cakes, sweet egg tarts, roast pork buns, and other goodies. If you've never tried dim sum (Chinese dumplings and other small dishes), now's your chance.

❷ Mulberry Street. Crowded with restaurants, cafés, bakeries, imported-food shops, and souvenir stores, Mulberry Street is where Little Italy lives and breathes. The blocks between Houston and Spring streets fall within the neighborhood of NoLita.

....

NEED A
BREAK?

You can savor cannoli and other sweet treats at **Caffé Roma** (✉ 385 Broome St., at Mulberry St., ☎ 212/226–8413), a traditional neighborhood favorite with wrought-iron chairs and a pressed-tin ceiling.

....

★ ☺ **❺ Museum of Chinese in the Americas (MCA).** In a century-old schoolhouse that once served Italian-American and Chinese-American children, MCA is the first U.S. museum devoted to preserving the history of the Chinese people throughout the western hemisphere. The permanent exhibit—*Where's Home? Chinese in the Americas*—explores the Chinese-American experience through displays of artists' creations, personal and domestic artifacts, and historical documentation. Slippers for binding feet, Chinese musical instruments, a reversible silk gown (circa 1900) worn at a Cantonese opera performance, and antique business signs are some of the unique objects on display; changing exhibits fill a second room. MCA sponsors workshops, walking tours, lectures, and family events. Its archives (open by appointment only) dedicated to Chinese-American history and culture include 2,000 volumes. ✉ *70 Mulberry St., at Bayard St., 2nd floor,* ☎ *212/619–4785,* ⓦⒺⒷ *www.moca-nyc.org.* ✑ *$3.* ☺ *Tues.–Sat. noon–5.*

❸ New York City Police Headquarters. This magnificent Renaissance revival structure with baroque embellishments and a striking dome served as the New York City police headquarters from its construction in 1909 until 1973; in 1988 it was converted into a high-priced condominium complex. Known to New Yorkers today as "240 Centre Street," its big-name residents have included Cindy Crawford, Winona Ryder, and Steffi Graf, among others. ✉ *240 Centre St., between Broome and Grand Sts.*

★ **❶ St. Patrick's Old Cathedral.** The first cornerstone of the original St. Pat's was laid in 1809, making it the oldest Roman Catholic church in the city. It was completed in 1815 and restored following a fire in 1866. The first American cardinal, John McCloskey, received his red hat in this building, and Pierre Toussaint, a former slave, who, as a freed man, donated most of his earnings to the poor, was buried in the graveyard;

he was reburied at St. Patrick's Cathedral on 5th Avenue in 1983, prior to his veneration by Pope John Paul II. ✉ *233 Mott St., between Houston and Prince Sts.,* ☎ *212/226–8075,* WEB *www.oldsaintpatricks. org.*

❹ **San Gennaro Church.** Every autumn San Gennaro Church—officially called the Most Precious Blood Church, National Shrine of San Gennaro—sponsors the Feast of San Gennaro, the biggest event in Little Italy. (The community's other big festival celebrates St. Anthony of Padua in June; the church connected to the festival is at Houston and Sullivan streets, in what is now SoHo.) ✉ *113 Baxter St., near Canal St.*

SOHO AND TRIBECA

Today the names of these two downtown neighborhoods are virtually synonymous with a certain style—an amalgam of black-clad artist-types, young Wall Streeters, expansive loft apartments, chic boutiques, and packed-to-the-gills restaurants. It's all very urban, very cool, very now. Before the 1970s, though, these two areas were virtual wastelands. SoHo (so named because it is the district *South* of *Ho*uston Street, bounded by Lafayette, Canal Street, and 6th Avenue) was regularly referred to as "Hell's Hundred Acres" because of the many fires that raged through the untended warehouses crowding the area. It was saved by two factors: first, preservationists here discovered the world's greatest concentration of cast-iron architecture and fought to prevent demolition; and second, artists discovered the large, cheap, well-lighted spaces that cast-iron buildings provide.

All the rage between 1860 and 1890, cast-iron buildings were popular because they did not require massive walls to bear the weight of the upper stories. Since there was no need for load-bearing walls, these buildings had more interior space and larger windows. They were also versatile, with various architectural elements produced from standardized molds to mimic any style—Italianate, Victorian Gothic, neo-Grecian, to name but a few visible in SoHo. At first it was technically illegal for artists to live in their loft studios, but so many did that eventually the zoning laws were changed to permit residence.

By 1980 SoHo's galleries, trendy shops, and cafés, together with its marvelous cast-iron buildings and vintage Belgian-block pavements (the 19th-century successor to traditional cobblestones), had made SoHo such a desirable area that only the most successful artists could afford it. Seeking similar space, artists moved downtown to another half-abandoned industrial district, for which a new, SoHo-like name was invented: TriBeCa (the *Tri*angle *Be*low *Ca*nal Street, although in effect it goes no farther south than Murray Street and no farther east than West Broadway). The same scenario has played itself out again, and TriBeCa's rising rents are already beyond the means of most artists, who have moved instead to west Chelsea and the Meatpacking District, Long Island City, areas of Brooklyn, or New Jersey. In SoHo, meanwhile, the arrival of large chain stores such as Pottery Barn and J. Crew has given some blocks the feeling of an outdoor suburban shopping mall.

Numbers in the text correspond to numbers in the margin and on the SoHo, TriBeCa, Little Italy, and Chinatown map.

A Good Walk

Starting at Houston (pronounced *how*-ston) Street, walk south down Broadway, stopping at a few of the noteworthy museums between Houston and Prince streets. The **Museum for African Art** ⑮, whose handsome two-story building complements its high-quality exhibits; and the

New Museum of Contemporary Art ⑯, which is exclusively devoted to living artists. The **Guggenheim Museum SoHo** ⑰, which opened in 1992, was downsized in 1999 (a Prada store now occupies the corner of Prince and Broadway) but still maintains a large floor-through gallery upstairs at 572 Broadway. Several art galleries share these blocks as well, most notably at 568 Broadway, which houses 10 galleries and the trendy Armani Exchange store on the ground level.

Just south of Prince Street, 560 Broadway on the east side of the block is another popular exhibit space, home to a dozen or so galleries. Across the street, Ernest Flagg's 1904 Little Singer Building (✉ 561 Broadway) shows the final flower of the cast-iron style, with wrought-iron balconies, terra-cotta panels, and broad expanses of windows. One block south of the Little Singer Building, between Spring and Broome streets, a cluster of lofts that were originally part of the 1897 New Era Building (✉ 495 Broadway) share an Art Nouveau copper mansard. At the northeast corner of Broadway and Broome Street is the **Haughwout Building** ⑱, a restored classic of the cast-iron genre. At the southeast corner of Broadway and Broome Street, the former Mechanics and Traders Bank (✉ 486 Broadway) is a Romanesque and Moorish revival building with half-round brick arches. At the northwest corner of Broadway and Grand Street, the popular Antique Flea Market draws about 100 dealers selling everything from used bicycles to vintage posters and clothing on weekends from 9 to 5.

If you have youngsters in tow, head east on Grand Street two blocks to the **Children's Museum of the Arts** ⑲, where the interactive exhibits provide a welcome respite from SoHo's mostly grown-up pursuits. Farther east, along Mulberry, Mott, and Elizabeth streets, is the district known as NoLita.

Otherwise, walk west on Grand Street three short blocks to discover several of SoHo's better exhibition spaces run by younger and more innovative dealers and artists, which are clustered on the south end of Greene and Wooster streets near Grand Street and Canal streets. You'll find art worth checking out at Deitch Projects (✉ 76 Grand St. and 26 Wooster St.), the Drawing Center (✉ 35 Wooster St.), and Spencer Brownstone (✉ 39 Wooster St.).

From here you may continue north on Wooster Street for Prince Street shops or first head east one block to Greene Street, where cast-iron architecture is at its finest. The block between Canal and Grand streets (✉ 8–34 Greene St.) represents the longest row of cast-iron buildings anywhere. Handsome as they are, these buildings were always commercial, containing stores and light manufacturing firms, principally in the textile trade. (Notice the iron loading docks and the sidewalk vault covers that lead into basement storage areas.) Two standout buildings on Greene Street are the so-called **Queen of Greene Street** ⑳ and the **King of Greene Street** ㉑. Even the lampposts on Greene Street are architectural gems: note their turn-of-the-20th-century bishop's-crook style, adorned with various cast-iron curlicues from their bases to their curved tops.

Greene Street between Prince and Spring streets is notable for the SoHo Building (✉ 104–110 Greene St.); towering 13 stories, it was the neighborhood's tallest building until the SoHo Grand Hotel went up in 1996. At Prince Street, walk one block west to Wooster Street, which, like a few other SoHo streets, still has its original Belgian paving stones. In the blocks between Prince and Spring streets on Wooster Street, shoppers will find a retail paradise. Also in this vicinity is one of Manhattan's finest photography galleries, Howard Green-

60

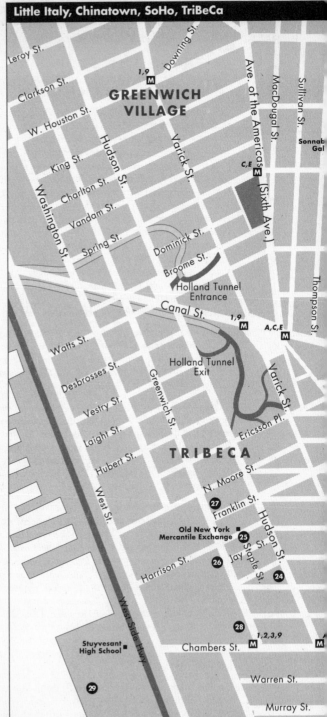

Little Italy, Chinatown, SoHo, TriBeCa

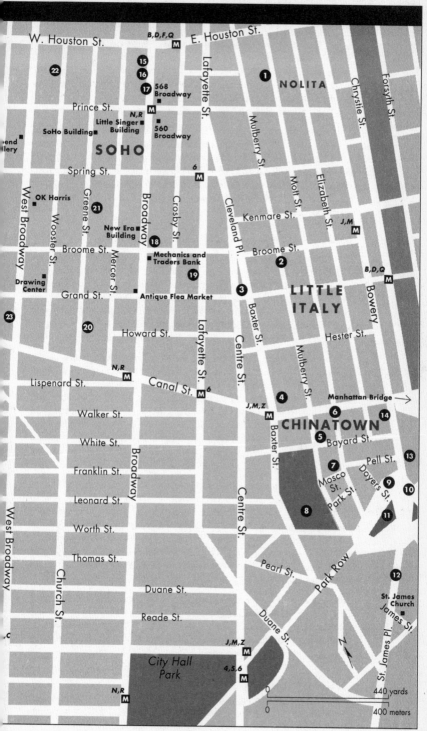

W. Houston St.

B,D,F,Q

E. Houston St.

Lafayette St.

NOLITA

Chrystie St.

Forsyth St.

15
16
17 568
Broadway

Prince St.

N,R

Little Singer
Building

SoHo Building

560
Broadway

Mulberry St.

SOHO

Spring St.

6

22

OK Harris

Greene St.

21

Broadway

Crosby St.

Cleveland Pl.

Kenmare St.

Mott St.

Elizabeth St.

J,M

West Broadway

New Era
Building

18

Broome St.

Mercer St.

Mechanics and
Traders Bank

Broome St.

2

Wooster St.

19

B,D,Q

Drawing
Center

Grand St.

Antique Flea Market

3

**LITTLE
ITALY**

Bowery

23

20

Howard St.

Lafayette St.

Centre St.

Baxter St.

Hester St.

Mulberry St.

Lispenard St.

N,R

Canal St.

6

Manhattan Bridge →

4

Walker St.

Broadway

J,M,Z

CHINATOWN

6

14

White St.

Baxter St.

5

Bayard St.

13

Franklin St.

7

Pell St.

Mosco
St.

Dovers St.

9

10

Leonard St.

Park St.

Worth St.

8

11

Thomas St.

West Broadway

Church St.

12

Duane St.

Pearl St.

Park Row

Reade St.

St. James
Church

Duane St.

James St.

J,M,Z

City Hall
Park

N

St. James Pl.

4,5,6

440 yards

N,R

0

0

400 meters

berg (✉ 120 Wooster St.) and the Dia Center for the Arts' **New York Earth Room** ㉒, a must-see reminder of art from SoHo's early days.

From Wooster Street, continue one block west on Prince Street to SoHo's main shopping drag, West Broadway. Although some big-name galleries such as Castelli and Sonnabend have moved uptown, there are still some holdouts worth seeing, among them, in the block between Prince and Spring streets, Franklin Bowles (✉ 431 W. Broadway) and **Nancy Hoffman** (✉ 429 W. Broadway).

Continue south on West Broadway to the blocks between Spring and Broome streets to one of the area's major art galleries, the immense OK Harris (✉ 383 W. Broadway). Stay on West Broadway on the west side of the street and proceed south; between Grand and Canal streets stands the **SoHo Grand Hotel** ㉓. From here TriBeCa is less than one block away; just follow West Broadway south to Canal Street, the neighborhood's official boundary. Stop to marvel at the life-size iron Statue of Liberty crown rising above the kitschy white-tile entrance to El Teddy's (✉ 219 W. Broadway), a popular Mexican restaurant.

Continuing south on West Broadway to Duane Street, you'll pass Worth Street, once the center of the garment trade and the 19th-century equivalent of today's 7th Avenue. Turn right on Duane Street to Hudson Street and you'll find the calm, shady **Duane Park** ㉔. When you walk one block north on Hudson Street, on the right-hand side you'll see the art deco Western Union Building (✉ 60 Hudson St.), where 19 subtly shaded colors of brick are laid in undulating patterns.

The area to the west (left), near the Hudson River docks, was once the heart of the wholesale food business. Turn off Hudson Street onto quiet Jay Street and pause at narrow **Staple Street** ㉕, whose green pedestrian walkway overhead links two warehouses. Also gaze up Harrison Street toward the ornate old New York Mercantile Exchange. If you continue west on Jay Street, you'll pass the loading docks of a 100-year-old food wholesaler, Bazzini's Nuts and Confections, where an upscale retail shop peddles nuts, coffee beans, and candies; there are also a few tables where you can rest and have a snack.

Jay Street comes to an end at Greenwich Street; just north, at the intersection of Harrison and Greenwich streets, is a surprising row of early 19th-century town houses nestled in the side of **Independence Plaza** ㉖, a huge high-rise apartment complex. Two bocks north on Greenwich Street, at Franklin Street, is the **TriBeCa Film Center** ㉗, owned by Robert De Niro. Two blocks south of Jay Street on Greenwich Street lies 2½-acre **Washington Market Park** ㉘, a landscaped oasis that has great playground equipment for children.

At the corner of the park, turn west on Chambers Street, heading west toward the Hudson River. A five-minute walk will bring you to the overpass across the West Side Highway. Here, behind the huge Stuyvesant High School building, you'll reach the north end of the **Hudson River Park** ㉙, a great place for a stroll.

TIMING

To see SoHo and TriBeCa at their liveliest, visit on a Saturday, when the fashionable crowd is joined by smartly dressed uptowners and suburbanites who come down for a little shopping and gallery hopping. If you want to avoid crowds, take this walk during the week. Keep in mind that most galleries are closed on Sunday and Monday. If you allow time for browsing in a few galleries and museums, as well as a stop for lunch, this tour can easily take up to an entire day.

Sights to See

🖑 **19** **Children's Museum of the Arts.** In a bi-level space in SoHo, children ages 1–10 have the chance to become actively involved in visual and performing arts. ⊠ *182 Lafayette St., between Grand and Broome Sts.,* ☎ *212/274–0986.* ⌑ *$5; Wed. 5–7, pay what you wish.* ☉ *Wed. noon–7, Thurs.–Sun. noon–5.*

24 **Duane Park.** The city bought this calm, shady triangle from Trinity Church in 1797 for $5. Cheese, butter, and egg warehouses have surrounded this oasis for more than 100 years. ⊠ *Bordered by Hudson, Duane, and Staple Sts.*

NEED A
BREAK?

For a real New York story, duck into the **Odeon** (⊠ 145 W. Broadway, ☎ 212/233–0507), an art deco restaurant-bar. With black-and-red banquettes, chrome mirrors, and neon-lighted clocks, this place has a distinctively slick atmosphere. Come for a drink at the bar or a snack anytime from noon to 2 AM.

★ **17** **Guggenheim Museum SoHo.** This downtown branch of the uptown museum has on permanent display Andy Warhol's series of paintings *The Last Supper.* The museum was downsized in 1999 but still occupies space in the landmark 19th-century redbrick structure with its original cast-iron storefronts and detailed cornice. Arata Isozaki designed the stark, loftlike gallery as well as the museum store facing Broadway. ⊠ *575 Broadway, between Prince and Houston Sts.,* ☎ *212/423–3500,* WEB *www.guggenheim.org.* ⌑ *Free.* ☉ *Thurs.–Mon. 11–6.*

NEED A
BREAK?

Diagonally across from the Guggenheim Museum SoHo, **Dean & DeLuca** (⊠ 560 Broadway, at Prince St., ☎ 212/431–1691), the gourmet emporium, brews superb coffee and tea and sells yummy pastries, but it's standing room only.

18 **Haughwout Building.** Nicknamed the Parthenon of Cast Iron, this Venetian palazzo–style structure was built in 1857 to house Eder Haughwout's china and glassware business. Inside, the building once contained the world's first commercial passenger elevator, a steam-powered device invented by Elisha Graves Otis. ⊠ *488 Broadway, at Broome St.*

★ 🖑 **29** **Hudson River Park.** A landscaped oasis with playgrounds, promenades and walkways, handball and basketball courts, and grassy areas, this park on the river at the corner of Chambers and West streets and north of the World Financial Center fills with downtown residents soaking up rays on sunny days. Top-rated by Manhattan children is the playground just south of Vesey Street, where child-size bronze sculptures of people and animals are integrated into the landscape. Be sure not to overlook *The Real World* sculpture garden at its north end, by Tom Otterness, which playfully pokes fun at the area's capitalist ethos. The Stuyvesant High School building (1992) is also at this end of the park; on its north side begins the paved river esplanade that extends to Gansevoort Street in the West Village. The **esplanade** is full of skaters, joggers, and strollers at all hours, and the benches along the path are terrific spots from which to watch the sunset over New Jersey. The park is included in plans for a considerably large riverside green space, which will extend north to 59th Street by 2005. For the latest on the park, visit WEB www.hudsonriverpark.org.

26 **Independence Plaza.** These high-rise towers at the intersection of Greenwich and Harrison streets are the fruit of a pleasant, if somewhat utilitarian, project of the mid-1970s that was supposed to be part of a wave of demolition and construction—until the preservationists stepped in. For several years Independence Plaza remained a middle-class island stranded downtown, far from stores, schools, and neighbors. With TriBeCa's increasingly chic reputation, however, plus the development of Battery Park City to the south, it has become a much more desirable address. The three-story redbrick houses that share Harrison Street with Independence Plaza were moved here from various sites in the neighborhood when, in the early 1970s, the food wholesalers' central market nearby was razed and moved to the Bronx. ⊠ *Greenwich St. between Duane and N. Moore Sts.*

㉑ King of Greene Street. This five-story Renaissance-style 1873 building has a magnificent projecting porch of Corinthian columns and pilasters. Today the King (now painted ivory) houses the M-13 art gallery, Alice's Antiques, and Bennison Fabrics. ⊠ *72–76 Greene St., between Spring and Broome Sts.*

⑮ Museum for African Art. Dedicated to contemporary and traditional African art, this small but expertly conceived museum is housed in a handsome two-story space designed by Maya Lin, who also designed Washington, D.C.'s Vietnam Veterans Memorial. Exhibits may include contemporary sculpture, ceremonial masks, architectural details, costumes, and textiles. The museum store sells African crafts, clothing, and jewelry. ⊠ *593 Broadway, near Houston St.,* ☎ *212/966–1313.* ⊡ *$5.* ⊙ *Tues.–Fri. 10:30–5:30, weekends noon–6.*

⑯ New Museum of Contemporary Art. The avant-garde exhibitions here, all by living artists (many from outside the United States), are often innovative and socially conscious. A 1997 renovation added a second-floor gallery, a well-stocked bookstore, and no-admission-charge exhibition space in the basement devoted to interactive art (all of which can be touched). ⊠ *583 Broadway, between Houston and Prince Sts.,* ☎ *212/219–1222.* ⊡ *$6; free Thurs. 6 PM–8 PM.* ⊙ *Wed. and Sun. noon–6; Thurs., Fri., and Sat. noon–8.*

NEED A
BREAK?   **Space Untitled Espresso Bar** (⊠ 133 Greene St., near W. Houston St., ☎ 212/260–8962) serves coffee, tea, smoothies, sweets, and sandwiches, as well as wine and beer, in a minimalist gallery setting.

㉒ New York Earth Room. Walter de Maria's 1977 avant-garde work consists of 140 tons of gently sculpted soil (22 inches deep) filling 3,600 square ft of space of the Dia Center for the Arts' second-floor gallery. Fans of de Maria's work shouldn't miss his *Broken Kilometer,* just a few blocks away at 393 West Broadway. ⊠ *141 Wooster St., between Houston and Prince Sts.,* ☎ *212/473–8072.* ⊡ *Free.* ⊙ *Jan.–mid-June and mid-Sept.–Dec., Wed.–Sat. noon–3 and 3:30–6.*

OFF THE
BEATEN PATH   **CHARLTON STREET –** The city's longest stretch of redbrick town houses preserved from the 1820s and 1830s runs along the north side of this street, which is west of 6th Avenue and south of West Houston Street and has high stoops, paneled front doors, leaded-glass windows, and narrow dormer windows all intact. While you're here, stroll along the parallel King and Vandam streets for more fine Federal houses. This quiet enclave was once an estate called Richmond Hill, whose various residents included George Washington, John and Abigail Adams, and Aaron Burr.

⑳ Queen of Greene Street. The regal grace of this 1873 cast-iron beauty is exemplified by its dormers, columns, window arches, projecting

HOW TO
USE THIS GUIDE

Great trips begin with great planning, and this guide
makes planning easy. It's packed with everything you
need—insider advice on hotels and restaurants, cool
tools, practical tips, essential maps, and much more.

COOL TOOLS

Fodor's Choice Top picks are marked throughout with a star.

Great Itineraries These tours, planned by Fodor's experts,
give you the skinny on what you can see and do in the time
you have.

Smart Travel Tips A to Z This special section is packed with
important contacts and advice on everything from how to get
around to what to pack.

Good Walks You won't miss a thing if you follow the numbered bullets on our maps.

Need a Break? Looking for a quick bite to eat or a spot to
rest? These sure bets are along the way.

Off the Beaten Path Some lesser-known sights are worth a
detour. We've marked those you should make time for.

POST-IT® FLAGS

Dog-ear no more!

"Post-it" is a registered trademark of 3M.

Favorite restaurants • Essential maps •
Frequently used numbers • Walking tours
• Can't-miss sights • Smart Travel
Tips • Web sites • Top shops • Hot
nightclubs • Addresses • Smart contacts
• Events • Off-the-beaten-path spots •
Favorite restaurants • Essential maps •
Frequently used numbers • Walking
tours • Can't-miss sights • Smart
Travel Tips • Web sites • Top shops • Hot
nightclubs • Addresses • Smart contacts •
Events • Off-the-beaten-path spots • Favorite
restaurants • Essential maps • Frequently
used numbers • Walking tours •

ICONS AND SYMBOLS

Watch for these symbols throughout:

★   Our special recommendations

✕   Restaurant

🏠   Lodging establishment

✕🏠   Lodging establishment whose restaurant warrants a special trip

☺   Good for kids

☞   Sends you to another section of the guide for more information

✉   Address

☎   Telephone number

FAX   Fax number

WEB   Web site

💳   Admission price

🕐   Opening hours

$-$$$$ Lodging and dining price categories, keyed to strategically sited price charts. Check the index for locations.

①❶   Numbers in white and black circles on the maps, in the margins, and within tours correspond to one another.

ON THE WEB

Continue your planning with these useful tools found at **www.fodors.com**, the Web's best source for travel information.

"Rich with resources." —*New York Times*

"Navigation is a cinch." —*Forbes* "Best of the Web" list

"Put together by people bursting with know-how."
—*Sunday Times* (London)

Create a Miniguide Pinpoint hotels, restaurants, and attractions that have what you want at the price you want to pay.

Rants and Raves Find out what readers say about Fodor's picks—or write your own reviews of hotels and restaurants you've just visited.

Travel Talk Post your questions and get answers from fellow travelers, or share your own experiences.

On-Line Booking Find the best prices on airline tickets, rental cars, cruises, or vacations, and book them on the spot.

About our Books Learn about other Fodor's guides to your destination and many others.

Expert Advice and Trip Ideas From what to tip to how to take great photos, from the national parks to Nepal, Fodors.com has suggestions that'll make your trip a breeze. Log on and get informed and inspired.

Smart Resources Check the weather in your destination or convert your currency. Learn the local language or link to the latest event listings. Or consult hundreds of detailed maps—all in one place.

central bays, and Second Empire–style roof. ⊠ *28–30 Greene St., between Grand and Canal Sts.*

㉓ SoHo Grand Hotel. The first major hotel to appear in the area since the 1800s, the 15-story SoHo Grand, which opened in 1996, was designed to pay tribute to the neighborhood's architectural history, particularly the cast-iron historic district. Serving as a "dog bar," a 17th-century French stone basin stands at the hotel's entrance, signaling that pets are welcome. A staircase—made of translucent bottle glass and iron and suspended from the ceiling by two cables—links the entryway with the second-floor 7,000-square-ft lobby, which has 16-ft-high windows and massive stone columns supporting the paneled mercury mirror ceiling. ⊠ *310 W. Broadway, between Canal and Grand Sts.,* ☎ *212/965–3000.*

NEED A BREAK? For a taste of SoHo shabby chic, head for **Scharmann's** (⊠ 386 W. Broadway, between Spring and Broome Sts., ☎ 212/219–2561), where the hip drink tea from gleaming brass pots on oversize couches and mismatched chairs beneath a giant chandelier.

㉕ Staple Street. Little more than an alley, Staple Street was named for the eggs, butter, cheese, and other staple products unloaded here by ships in transit that didn't want to pay duty on any extra cargo. Framed at the end of the alley is the redbrick **New York Mercantile Exchange** (⊠ 6 Harrison St.), with a square corner tower topped by a bulbous roof. On the ground floor is the acclaimed French restaurant Chanterelle.

㉗ TriBeCa Film Center. Robert De Niro created this complex of editing, screening, and production rooms, where Miramax Films, Steven Spielberg, Quincy Jones, and De Niro keep offices. Like many of the other stylish and renovated buildings in this area, it's a former factory, the old Coffee Building. On the ground floor is the TriBeCa Grill restaurant, also owned by Robert De Niro. ⊠ *375 Greenwich St., between Franklin and N. Moore Sts.*

OFF THE BEATEN PATH Particularly if you're visiting on a weekend with the children, it's worth a side trip to the **New York City Fire Museum,** where real firefighters give the tours, and the collection of authentic firefighting tools from the 18th, 19th, and 20th centuries includes hand-pulled and horse-drawn apparatus, engines, sliding poles, uniforms, and fireboat equipment. Guided tours for 12 or more can by made by appointment. ⊠ 278 Spring St., near Varick St., ☎ 212/691–1303. 🎟 $4 (suggested donation); tours $5. ⊙ Tues.–Sun. 10–4.

㉘ Washington Market Park. This much-needed recreation space for TriBeCa was named after the great food market that once sprawled over the area. It is now a green, landscaped stretch with a playground and a gazebo across from a public elementary school. At the corner, a stout little red tower resembles a lighthouse, and iron ship figures are worked into the playground fence—reminders of the neighborhood's long-gone dockside past. ⊠ *Greenwich St. between Chambers and Duane Sts.*

GREENWICH VILLAGE

Greenwich Village, which New Yorkers invariably speak of simply as "the Village," enjoyed a raffish reputation for years. Originally a rural outpost of the city—a haven for New Yorkers during early 19th-century smallpox and yellow fever epidemics—many of its blocks still look somewhat pastoral, with brick town houses and low-rises, tiny green parks and hidden courtyards, and a crazy-quilt pattern of narrow, tree-lined streets (some of which follow long-ago cow paths). In the mid-19th century, however, as the city spread north of 14th Street, the Village became the province of immigrants, bohemians, and students (New York University [NYU], today the nation's largest private university, was planted next to Washington Square in 1831). Its politics were radical and its attitudes tolerant, which is one reason it became a home to such a large lesbian and gay community.

Several generations of writers and artists have lived and worked here: in the 19th century, Henry James, Edgar Allan Poe, Mark Twain, Walt Whitman, and Stephen Crane; at the turn of the 20th century, O. Henry, Edith Wharton, Theodore Dreiser, and Hart Crane; and during the 1920s and '30s, John Dos Passos, Norman Rockwell, Sinclair Lewis, John Reed, Eugene O'Neill, Edward Hopper, and Edna St. Vincent Millay. In the late 1940s and early 1950s, the Abstract Expressionist painters Franz Kline, Jackson Pollock, Mark Rothko, and Willem de Kooning congregated here, as did the Beat writers Jack Kerouac, Allen Ginsberg, and Lawrence Ferlinghetti. The 1960s brought folk musicians and poets, notably Bob Dylan and Peter, Paul, and Mary.

Today, block for block, the Village is still one of the most vibrant parts of the city. Well-heeled professionals occupy high-rent apartments and town houses side by side with bohemian, longtime residents, who pay cheap rents thanks to rent-control laws, as well as NYU students. Locals and visitors rub elbows at dozens of small restaurants, cafés spill out onto sidewalks, and an endless variety of small shops pleases everyone. Except for a few pockets of adult-entertainment shops and divey bars, the Village is as scrubbed as posher neighborhoods.

Numbers in the text correspond to numbers in the margin and on the Greenwich Village, East Village, and the Lower East Side map.

A Good Walk

Begin your tour of Greenwich Village at the foot of 5th Avenue at Washington Memorial Arch in **Washington Square** ①. Most buildings bordering Washington Square belong to NYU. On Washington Square North, between University Place and MacDougal Street, stretches **The Row** ②, two blocks of lovingly preserved Greek revival and federal-style town houses.

If you walk south, through the park, at the corner of Washington Square South and Thompson Street you'll see the square-towered **Judson Memorial Church** ③. One block east, at La Guardia Place, NYU's student center (being rebuilt at press time) is slated to stand on the site of a famous boardinghouse that had once been nicknamed the House of Genius for the talented writers who lived there over the years: Theodore Dreiser, O'Henry, and Eugene O'Neill, among others. Another block east is the hulking red sandstone Bobst Library, built in 1972, which represents an abortive attempt to create a unified campus look for NYU as envisioned by architects Philip Johnson and Richard Foster. At one time plans called for all the Washington Square buildings to be refaced in this red stone; fortunately, the cost proved prohibitive.On the east side of the square, you can take in a contemporary art exhibit at **Grey Art Gallery** ④, housed in NYU's main building.

From Washington Square Arch and the park, cross Washington Square North to the east side of 5th Avenue. On your right, at the northeast corner of Washington Square North and 5th Avenue, is the portico entrance to 7–13 Washington Square North. Beyond the white columns of this entrance is the small, attractive Willy's Garden. A statue of Miguel

Greenwich Village, East Village, and the Lower East Side

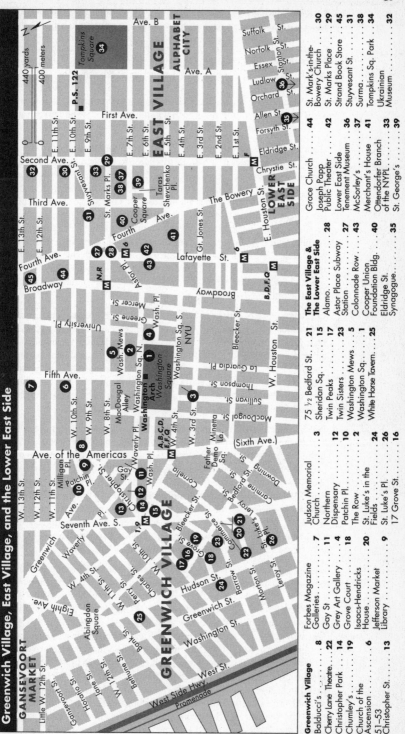

de Cervantes, the author of *Don Quixote,* stands at the far end. The likeness, cast in 1724, was a gift from the mayor of Madrid.

Another half a block north, on the east side of 5th Avenue, is **Washington Mews** ⑤, a cobblestone private street. A similar Village mews, MacDougal Alley, can be found between 8th Street and the square just off MacDougal Street, one block west. Continue up the west side of 5th Avenue; you'll pass the **Church of the Ascension** ⑥, a Gothic revival brownstone building. At 5th Avenue and 12th Street you can stop in the **Forbes Magazine Galleries** ⑦.

Backtrack on 5th Avenue to West 11th Street and turn right to see one of the best examples of a Village town house block. One exception to the 19th-century redbrick town houses here is the modern, angled front window of 18 West 11th Street, usually occupied by a stuffed bear whose outfit changes from day to day. This house was built after the original was destroyed in a 1970 explosion of a basement bomb factory, which had been started by members of the Weathermen, the revolutionary faction of the Students for a Democratic Society. Toward 6th Avenue, behind a low gray-stone wall on the south side of the street, is the Second Shearith Israel graveyard, used by the country's oldest Jewish congregation after the original cemetery in Chinatown and before the one in Chelsea.

On Avenue of the Americas (6th Avenue), turn left to sample the wares at **Balducci's** ⑧, a high-end gourmet food store. Directly opposite, the triangle formed by West 10th Street, 6th Avenue, and Greenwich Avenue originally held a market, a jail, and the magnificent towered courthouse that is now the **Jefferson Market Library** ⑨. Just west of 6th Avenue on 10th Street is the wrought-iron gateway to a tiny courtyard called **Patchin Place** ⑩; around the corner, on 6th Avenue just north of 10th Street, is a similar cul-de-sac, Milligan Place.

Next, proceed to Christopher Street, which veers off from the south end of the library triangle. Christopher Street has long been the symbolic heart of New York's gay and lesbian community. Before you proceed just a few steps, you'll see **Gay Street** ⑪ on your left. Continuing west on Christopher Street, cross Waverly Place, where on your left you'll pass the 1831 brick **Northern Dispensary** ⑫ building. At **51–53 Christopher Street** ⑬, the historic Stonewall riots marked the beginning of the gay rights movement. Across the street is a green triangle named **Christopher Park** ⑭, not to be confused with **Sheridan Square** ⑮, another landscaped triangle to the south.

Across the busy intersection of 7th Avenue South, Christopher Street has many cafés, bars, and stores; several cater to a gay clientele, but all kinds of people traverse the busy sidewalks. Two shops worth a visit are McNulty's Tea and Coffee Co. (✉ 109 Christopher St.), with a large variety of tea and coffee blends, and Li-Lac Chocolate Shop (✉ 120 Christopher St.), a longtime favorite for its homemade chocolate and butter crunch. West of 7th Avenue South, the Village turns into a picture-book town of twisting tree-lined streets, quaint houses, and tiny restaurants. Starting from Sheridan Square west, follow Grove Street past the house where Thomas Paine died (✉ 59 Grove St.)—now the site of Marie's Crisis Cafe—and the onetime home of poet Hart Crane (✉ 45 Grove St.). At this point you'll be close to the intersection of Grove and Bleecker streets. You may now choose to take a leisurely stroll along the portion of Bleecker Street that extends west of 7th Avenue South from Grove Street to Bank Street, heading northwest toward Abingdon Square. This section of Bleecker Street is full of crafts and antiques shops, coffeehouses, and small restaurants.

If you forego Bleecker Street, continue your walk west on Grove Street. The secluded intersection of Grove and Bedford Streets seems to have fallen through a time warp into the 19th century. On the northeast corner stands **17 Grove Street** ⑯, one of the few remaining clapboard structures in Manhattan. Behind it is **Twin Peaks** ⑰, an early 19th-century house that resembles a Swiss chalet. Heading west, Grove Street curves in front of the iron gate of **Grove Court** ⑱, a group of mid-19th-century brick-front residences.

Return to Bedford Street, turn right and walk until you get to No. 86. Behind the unmarked door is **Chumley's** ⑲, a former speakeasy. Continue a couple of blocks farther east to the oldest house in the Village, the **Isaacs-Hendricks House** ⑳. The place next door, **75½ Bedford Street** ㉑, at 9½ ft wide, is New York's narrowest house. Bedford Street intersects Commerce Street, one of the Village's most romantic untrod lanes, and home to the historic **Cherry Lane Theatre** ㉒. Across the street, past the bend in the road, stand two nearly identical brick houses separated by a garden and popularly known as the **Twin Sisters** ㉓.

Turn left from Commerce Street onto Barrow Street, which next intersects with Hudson Street, so named because this was originally the bank of the Hudson River. The block to the northwest is owned by **St. Luke's in the Fields** ㉔. Writer Bret Harte once lived at 487 Hudson Street, at the end of the row. If your feet are getting tired, you can head north on Hudson Street for four blocks and take a rest at the legendary **White Horse Tavern** ㉕, at 11th Street.

Walk south on the promenade and turn right onto Leroy Street. Leroy Street becomes **St. Luke's Place** ㉖, a one-block row of classic 1860s town houses. Across 7th Avenue South, St. Luke's Place becomes Leroy Street again, which terminates in an old Italian neighborhood at Bleecker Street. Because of all the touristy shops and crowds, Bleecker Street between 6th and 7th Avenues seems more vital these days than Little Italy does. For authentic Italian ambience, step into one of the fragrant Italian bakeries, such as A. Zito & Sons (⊠ 259 Bleecker St.) and Rocco's (⊠ 243 Bleecker St.), or look inside the old-style butcher shops, such as Ottomanelli & Sons (⊠ 285 Bleecker St.) and Faicco's (⊠ 260 Bleecker St.). In a town that's fierce about its pizza, some New Yorkers swear by John's Pizzeria (⊠ 278 Bleecker St.), the original in a chain of four branches citywide. Be forewarned, however: no slices; whole pies only.

Head east on Bleecker to Carmine and the Church of Our Lady of Pompeii, where Mother Cabrini, a naturalized Italian immigrant who became the first American saint, often prayed. When you reach Father Demo Square (at Bleecker Street and 6th Avenue), head up 6th Avenue to West 3rd Street and check out the basketball courts, where NBA stars of tomorrow learn their moves and city-style basketball is played in all but the very coldest weather. Return along West 4th Street and note, on the north side of the street, the illustrious Blue Note, where an international crowd lines up to hear jazz greats. At MacDougal Street turn right. The Provincetown Playhouse (⊠ 133 MacDougal St.) premiered many of Eugene O'Neill's plays. Louisa May Alcott wrote *Little Women* while living at 130–132 MacDougal Street. The two houses at 127 and 129 MacDougal Street were built for Aaron Burr in 1829; notice the pineapple newel posts, a symbol of hospitality.

Caffe Reggio (⊠ 119 MacDougal St.) is one of the Village's first coffeehouses, and its interior hasn't changed much since 1927 when it opened. At Minetta Tavern (⊠ 113 MacDougal St.), a venerable Village watering hole, turn right onto Minetta Lane, which leads to narrow Minetta Street, another former speakeasy alley. Both streets follow the course of Minetta Brook, which once flowed through this neighborhood and still bubbles deep beneath the pavement. The foot of Minetta Street returns you to the corner of 6th Avenue and Bleecker Street, the stomping grounds of 1960s-era folksingers (many performed at the now-defunct Folk City, one block north on West 3rd Street). This area still attracts a young crowd—partly because of the proximity of NYU—to its cafés, bars, jazz clubs, coffeehouses, theaters, and cabarets, not to mention its long row of unpretentious ethnic restaurants.

TIMING

Greenwich Village lends itself to a leisurely pace, so allow yourself most of a day to explore its backstreets and stop at shops and cafés.

Sights to See

★ **⑧ Balducci's.** From the vegetable stand of the late Louis Balducci Sr. sprouted this full-service gourmet food store. Along with more than 80 Italian cheeses and 50 kinds of bread, the family-owned enterprise features imported Italian specialties and first-rate take-out foods. ⊠ 424 6th Ave., at 9th St., ☎ 212/673–2600.

㉒ Cherry Lane Theatre. One of the original off-Broadway houses, this 1817 building was converted into a theater in 1923, thanks to Edna St. Vincent Millay and a group of theater artists. Over the years it has hosted American premieres of works by O'Neill, Beckett, Ionesco, Albee, Pinter, and Mamet. The playhouse was modernized in 1996, but it still contains the original audience seats. ⊠ 38 Commerce St., ☎ 212/989–2020.

⑭ Christopher Park. Sometimes mistaken for Sheridan Square, this triangular island has a bronze statue of Civil War general Philip Henry Sheridan and striking sculptures designed by George Segal of a lesbian couple sitting on a bench and gay male partners standing near them, having a conversation. ⊠ Bordered by W. 4th, Grove, and Christopher Sts.

⑲ Chumley's. A speakeasy during the Prohibition era, this still-secret tavern behind an unmarked door on Bedford Street retains its original ambience with oak booths, a fireplace once used by a blacksmith, and subdued lighting. For years Chumley's attracted a literary clientele (John Steinbeck, Ernest Hemingway, Edna Ferber, Simone de Beauvoir, and Jack Kerouac), and the book covers of their publications were proudly displayed (and still appear) on the walls. There's another "secret" entrance in Pamela Court, accessed at 58 Barrow Street around the corner. ⊠ 86 Bedford St., near Barrow St., ☎ 212/675–4449.

⑥ Church of the Ascension. A mural depicting the Ascension of Jesus and stained-glass windows by John LaFarge, as well as a marble altar sculpture by Augustus Saint-Gaudens, are the highlights of this 1841 Gothic revival–style brownstone church designed by Richard Upjohn. In 1844 President John Tyler married Julia Gardiner here. ⊠ 36–38 5th Ave., at 10th St., ☎ 212/254–8620. ☉ Weekdays noon–2 and 5–7, Sun. services 9 and 11.

⑬ 51–53 Christopher Street. On June 27, 1969, a gay bar at this address named the Stonewall Inn was the site of a clash between gay men and women (some in drag) and the New York City police. As the bar's patrons were being forced into police wagons, sympathetic gay onlookers protested and started fighting back, throwing beer bottles and garbage cans. Every June the Stonewall Riots are commemorated around the world with parades and celebrations that honor the gay rights movement. A clothing store now occupies 51; a bar named Stonewall is next door at No. 53.

★ ☺ **❼** **Forbes Magazine Galleries.** The late publisher Malcolm Forbes's idiosyncratic personal collection fills the ground floor of the limestone
Forbes Magazine Building, once the home of Macmillan Publishing.
Exhibits change in the large painting gallery and one of two autograph
galleries, while permanent highlights include U.S. presidential papers,
more than 500 intricate toy boats, 12,000 toy soldiers, and some of
the oldest Monopoly game sets ever made. Perhaps the most memorable permanent display contains exquisite items created by the House
of Fabergé, including 12 jeweled eggs designed for the last of the Russian czars. ✉ *62 5th Ave., at 12th St.,* ☎ *212/206–5548.* ✉ *Free.* ☉
Tues.–Sat. 10–4.

NEED A BREAK?	If you're yearning for a *pain au chocolat* or a madeleine, stop by **Marquet Patisserie** (✉ 15 E. 12th St., ☎ 212/229–9313), a sleek, friendly café that serves irresistible French pastries, great coffee, and satisfying sandwiches, salads, and quiches.

OFF THE BEATEN PATH	**MEATPACKING DISTRICT–** Until recently, this area between the Hudson River and 9th Avenue, from Gansevoort Street to West 14th Street, seemed immune to gentrification due to its rather industrial function and location far west. But since the late 1990s, when the high-fashion shops, fine art galleries, and adorable bakeries moved in, swinging carcasses and their attendant odors seem no longer to be much of a deterrent. Although the overnight beef and poultry movers for which the district is known are still here, as are the transvestites who contribute to the area's fringe character, the seeds of chic have already been sown by ambitious gallery owners, photographers, filmmakers, new-media wunderkinds, and retailers in search of affordable space. Likewise, locals pushed to Manhattan's edges by rising rents in SoHo, TriBeCa, and the East Village have snatched up the large, unfinished warehouses of abandoned meat-processing plants and automotive stores for renovation as residences. The main drag for the rapidly multiplying eateries, galleries, shops, and nightclubs is West 14th Street (at the end of which, near the Hudson, Herman Melville was once a customs inspector). But for a glimpse of the old neighborhood, Gansevoort Market any morning, when otherwise undistinguished warehouse buildings become the meat market for the city's retailers and restaurants. Sides of beef make a fascinating, if not very pretty, sight. The action peaks on weekdays between 5 AM and 9 AM. ✉ *Between 9th Ave. and Hudson River, from Gansevoort St. north to 14th St.*

⓫ **Gay Street.** A curved lane lined with small row houses from circa
1810, one-block-long Gay Street was originally a black neighborhood
and later a strip of speakeasies. In the 1930s this darling thoroughfare
and nearby Christopher Street became famous nationwide when Ruth
McKenney published her somewhat zany autobiographical stories in
The New Yorker, based on what happened when she and her sister moved
to Greenwich Village from Ohio (they appeared in book form as *My
Sister Eileen* in 1938). McKenney wrote in the basement of No. 14.
Also on Gay Street, Howdy Doody was designed in the basement of
No. 12. ✉ *Between Christopher St. and Waverly Pl.*

❹ **Grey Art Gallery.** On the east side of Washington Square, New York
University's main building has a welcoming street-level space with
changing exhibitions usually devoted to contemporary art. ✉ *100
Washington Sq. E,* ☎ *212/998–6780.* ✉ *$2.50 (suggested donation).*
☉ *Tues., Thurs., and Fri. 11–6; Wed. 11–8; Sat. 11–5.*

⓲ **Grove Court.** Built between 1853 and 1854, this enclave of brick-front
town houses was originally intended as apartments for employees at

neighborhood hotels. Grove Court used to be called Mixed Ale Alley because of the residents' propensity to pool beverages brought from work. It now houses a more affluent crowd. ⊠ *10–12 Grove St.*

⑳ Isaacs-Hendricks House. Originally built as a Federal-style wood-frame residence in 1799, this immaculate structure is the oldest remaining such house in Greenwich Village. Its first owner, Joshua Isaacs, a wholesale merchant, lost the farmhouse to creditors; the building then belonged to copper supplier Harmon Hendricks. The village landmark was remodeled twice; it received its brick face in 1836, and the third floor was added in 1928. ⊠ *77 Bedford St., at Commerce St.*

❾ Jefferson Market Library. After Frederick Clarke Withers and Calvert Vaux's magnificent, towered building was constructed in 1877, critics variously termed its hodgepodge of styles Venetian, Victorian, or Italian; Villagers, noting the alternating wide bands of red brick and narrow strips of granite, dubbed it the "lean bacon style." The structure, named after our third president, was built as a courthouse, and over the years it has harbored a number of government agencies (public works, civil defense, census bureau, police academy); it was on the verge of demolition when local activists saved it and turned it into a public library in 1967. Note the fountain at the corner of West 10th Street and 6th Avenue and the seal of The City of New York on the east front; inside are handsome interior doorways and a graceful circular stairway. If the gate is open, visit the flower garden behind the library, a project run by local green thumbs on the former site of a women's prison. ⊠ *425 6th Ave., at 10th St.,* ☎ *212/243–4334.*

❸ Judson Memorial Church. Designed by celebrated architect Stanford White, this Italian Roman-Renaissance church has long attracted a congregation interested in the arts and community activism. Funded by the Astor family and John D. Rockefeller and constructed in 1892, the yellow-brick and limestone building was the brainchild of Edward Judson, who hoped to reach out to the poor immigrants in adjacent Little Italy. The church has stained-glass windows designed by John LaFarge and a 10-story campanile. Inquire at the parish office for weekday access at 243 Thompson St. ⊠ *55 Washington Sq. S, at Thompson St.,* ☎ *212/477–0351.* ☉ *Weekdays 10–6; Sun. service at 11.*

⑫ Northern Dispensary. Constructed in 1831, this triangular Georgian brick building originally served as a clinic for indigent Villagers. Edgar Allan Poe was a frequent patient. In more recent times the structure has housed a dental clinic and a nursing home for AIDS patients. Note that the Dispensary has *one* side on *two* streets (Grove and Christopher streets where they meet) and *two* sides facing *one* street—Waverly Place, which splits in two directions. ⊠ *165 Waverly Pl.*

❿ Patchin Place. This little cul-de-sac off West 10th Street between Greenwich and 6th Avenues has 10 diminutive 1848 row houses. Around the corner on 6th Avenue is a similar dead-end street, **Milligan Place,** consisting of four small homes completed in 1852. The houses in both quiet enclaves were originally built for the waiters (mostly Basques) who worked at 5th Avenue's high-society Brevoort Hotel, long since demolished. Patchin Place later attracted numerous writers, including Theodore Dreiser, e. e. cummings, Jane Bowles, and Djuna Barnes. John Reed and Louise Bryant also lived there. Milligan Place eventually became the address for several playwrights, including Eugene O'Neill.

★ ❷ The Row. Built from 1829 through 1839, this series of beautifully preserved Greek revival town houses along Washington Square North, on the two blocks between University Place and MacDougal Street, once belonged to merchants and bankers, then writers and artists such as

John Dos Passos and Edward Hopper; now the buildings serve as NYU offices and faculty housing. Developers were not so tactful when they demolished 18 Washington Square North, once the home of Henry James's grandmother, which he later used as the setting for his novel *Washington Square*. (Henry himself was born just off the square, in a long-gone house on Washington Place.) The oldest building on the block, 20 Washington Square North, was constructed in 1829 in the Federal style, and with Flemish bond brickwork—alternate bricks inserted with the smaller surface (headers) facing out—which before 1830 was considered the best way to build stable walls. ✉ *1–13 Washington Sq. N, between University Pl. and 5th Ave.; 19–26 Washington Sq. N, between 5th Ave. and MacDougal St.*

★ ㉔ **St. Luke's in the Fields.** The first warden of St. Luke's, which was constructed in 1822 as a country chapel for downtown's Trinity Church, was Clement ("'Twas the Night Before Christmas") Clarke Moore, who figured so largely in Chelsea's history. An unadorned structure of soft-color brick, the chapel was nearly destroyed by fire in 1981, but a flood of donations, many quite small, from residents of the West Village financed restoration of the square central tower. Bret Harte once lived at 487 Hudson Street (today the St. Luke's parish house), at the end of the row. The Barrow Street Garden on the chapel grounds is worth visiting. ✉ *487 Hudson St., between Barrow and Christopher Sts.,* ☎ *212/924–0562.* ☉ *Grounds open Tues.–Sun. 9–dusk, with some exceptions.*

★ ㉖ **St. Luke's Place.** This often peaceful street has 15 classic Italianate brownstone and brick town houses (1852–53), shaded by graceful gingko trees. Novelist Theodore Dreiser wrote *An American Tragedy* at No. 16, and poet Marianne Moore resided at No. 14. Mayor Jimmy Walker (first elected in 1926) lived at No. 6; the lampposts in front are "mayor's lamps," which were sometimes placed in front of the residences of New York mayors. This block is often used as a film location, too: No. 12 was shown as the Huxtables' home on *The Cosby Show* (although the family lived in Brooklyn), and No. 4 was the setting of the Audrey Hepburn movie *Wait Until Dark*. Before 1890 the playground on the south side of the street was a graveyard where, according to legend, the dauphin of France—the lost son of Louis XVI and Marie Antoinette—is buried. ✉ *Between Hudson St. and 7th Ave. S.*

NEED A BREAK? The **Anglers and Writers Café** (✉ 420 Hudson St., at St. Luke's Pl., ☎ 212/675–0810) lives up to its name with bookshelves, fishing tackle, and pictures of Door County, Wisconsin, hung on the walls. It's an ideal spot to linger over a pot of tea and a slice of cake.

⑯ **17 Grove Street.** William Hyde, a prosperous window-sash maker, built this clapboard residence in 1822; a third floor was added in 1870. Hyde added a workshop behind the house in 1833. The building has since served many functions; it housed a brothel during the Civil War. The structure is the Village's largest remaining wood-frame house. ✉ *17 Grove St., at Bedford St.*

㉑ **75½ Bedford Street.** Rising real estate rates inspired the construction of New York City's narrowest house—just 9½ ft wide—in 1873. Built on a lot that was originally a carriage entrance of the **Isaacs-Hendricks House** next door, this sliver of a building has been home to actor John Barrymore and poet Edna St. Vincent Millay, who wrote the Pulitzer Prize–winning *Ballad of the Harp-Weaver* during her tenure here from 1923 to 1924. ✉ *75½ Bedford St., between Commerce and Morton Sts.*

⑮ Sheridan Square. At one time an unused asphalt space, this green triangle was landscaped following an extensive dig by urban archaeologists, who unearthed artifacts dating to the Dutch and Native American eras. ⊠ *Bordered by Washington Pl. and W. 4th, Barrow, and Grove Sts.*

⑰ Twin Peaks. In 1925 financier Otto Kahn gave money to a Village eccentric named Clifford Daily to remodel an 1835 house for artists' use. The building was whimsically altered with stucco, half-timbers, and the addition of a pair of steep roof peaks. The result was something that might be described as an ersatz Swiss chalet. ⊠ *102 Bedford St., between Grove and Christopher Sts.*

㉓ Twin Sisters. These attractive Federal-style brick homes connected by a walled garden were said to have been erected by a sea captain for two daughters who loathed each other. Historical record insists that they were built in 1831 and 1832 by a milkman who needed the two houses and an open courtyard for his work. The striking mansard roofs were added in 1873. ⊠ *39 and 41 Commerce St.*

❺ Washington Mews. This cobblestone private street is lined on one side with the former stables of the houses on The Row on Washington Square North. Writer Walter Lippmann and artist-patron Gertrude Vanderbilt Whitney (founder of the Whitney Museum) once had homes in the mews; today it's mostly owned by NYU. ⊠ *Between 5th Ave. and University Pl.*

★ ☺ **❶ Washington Square.** The physical and spiritual heart of the Village, 9½-acre Washington Square started out as a cemetery, principally for yellow fever victims—an estimated 10,000–22,000 bodies lie below. In the early 1800s it was a parade ground and the site of public executions; bodies dangled from a conspicuous Hanging Elm that still stands at the northwest corner of the square. Made a public park in 1827, the square became the focus of a fashionable residential neighborhood and a center of outdoor activity. Today it's a maelstrom of playful activity, shared by earnest-looking NYU students, Frisbee players, street musicians, skateboarders, jugglers, stand-up comics, joggers, chess players, and bench warmers, watching the grand opera of it all. Two well-equipped and shady playgrounds attract gaggles of youngsters, and dog lovers congregate at the popular dog run. A huge outdoor art fair is held here each spring and fall.

Dominating the square's north end, the triumphal **Washington Memorial Arch** stands at the foot of glorious 5th Avenue. A wooden version of the Washington Arch designed by Stanford White was built in 1889 to commemorate the 100th anniversary of George Washington's presidential inauguration and was originally placed about half a block north of its present location. The arch was reproduced in Tuckahoe marble in 1892, and the statues—*Washington at War* on the left, *Washington at Peace* on the right—were added in 1916 and 1918, respectively. The civilian version of Washington was the work of Alexander Stirling Calder, father of the renowned artist Alexander Calder. Bodybuilder Charles Atlas modeled for *Peace*. ⊠ *5th Ave. between Waverly Pl. and 4th St.*

㉕ White Horse Tavern. Built in 1880, this amiable bar occupies one of the city's few remaining wood-frame structures. Formerly a speakeasy and a seamen's tavern, the White Horse has been popular with artists and writers for decades; its best-known customer was Welsh poet Dylan Thomas, who had a room named for him here after his death in 1953. ⊠ *567 Hudson St., at 11th St.,* ☎ *212/243–9260.*

THE EAST VILLAGE
AND THE LOWER EAST SIDE

The gritty dwellings of the East Village—an area bounded by East 14th Street on the north, 4th Avenue or the Bowery on the west, East Houston Street on the south, and the East River—have housed immigrant families since the mid-1800s, although the cultural composition of those families continues to change. The 1970s brought a counterculture of hippies, experimental artists, writers, and students who benefited from the inexpensive living spaces and the East Village's reputation as a progressive neighborhood. During the 1980s, artists fleeing skyrocketing real estate prices in SoHo brought in their wake new restaurants, shops, and somewhat cleaner streets. Longtime bastions of the arts, such as the Classic Stage Company, La MaMa E.T.C., and St. Mark's-in-the-Bowery Church were joined by newer institutions such as P.S. 122, and several "hot" art galleries opened in narrow East Village storefronts. But the gallery scene here lasted only a couple of years—just long enough to drive up rents substantially on some blocks but not long enough to drive out all the neighborhood's original residents. Today an interesting mix has survived: artistic types and longtime members of various immigrant enclaves, principally Polish, Ukrainian, Slovene, Puerto Rican, and other Latino groups. More recent arrivals come from the Dominican Republic, Japan, and the Philippines, and the neighborhood's traditional gentrification frontier has pushed east from Avenue A to Avenue B. The once impenetrable Alphabet City now seems like a walk in the park, where worthwhile restaurants, stylish bars, and funky shops welcome the avant-garde set.

South of East Houston Street, the Lower East Side (bounded by the Bowery to the west and East Broadway to the south) was, from the mid-19th century to the early 1920s, home to millions of mostly European refugees and Jews seeking a haven from famine, wars, and political repression. It became, in 1870, one of the most densely populated districts in the world. Entire families worked in unregulated sweatshops, mostly in the needle trades, and lived in cold-water railroad tenements. The influx was stemmed following passage of restrictive immigration laws in the 1920s. Some streets, such as Orchard, Essex, Eldridge, Hester, and Norfolk, still retain active reminders of this period, mostly in the form of family-owned shops that date to the 1900s. Recent years have seen the rapid proliferation of new chic boutiques, restaurants, and bars, as artists and young professionals have colonized the streets that also house substantial Hispanic and Chinese communities. The streets of the Lower East Side are a colorful mix of Puerto Rican bodegas, Chinese produce markets, and kosher restaurants, but at night the sidewalks increasingly belong to lounge lizards.

Numbers in the text correspond to numbers in the margin and on the Greenwich Village, East Village, and the Lower East Side map.

A Good Walk

Begin at the intersection of East 8th Street, 4th Avenue, and Astor Place, where you'll see two traffic islands. One of these contains an ornate cast-iron kiosk, a replica of a beaux arts subway entrance, which provides access to the **Astor Place Subway Station** ㉗. On the other traffic island stands the **Alamo** ㉘, a huge black cube.

Go straight east from the Alamo to **St. Marks Place** ㉙, the name given to 8th Street in the East Village. Second Avenue, which St. Marks crosses after one block, was called the Yiddish Rialto in the early part of this century, because at that time eight theaters between Houston and 14th streets presented Yiddish-language productions of musicals, revues, and heart-wrenching melodramas. Two survivors from that period are the Orpheum (⊠ 126 2nd Ave., at 8th St.) and the neo-Moorish Yiddish Arts Theatre, now the multiscreen Village East Cinemas (⊠ 189 2nd Ave., at 12th St.), which has preserved the original ornate ceiling. In front of the Second Avenue Deli (⊠ 156 2nd Ave., at 10th St.), Hollywood-style squares have been embedded in the sidewalk to commemorate Yiddish stage luminaries.

Second Avenue is also home to a neighborhood landmark, **St. Mark's-in-the-Bowery Church** ㉚ on the corner of East 10th Street. From in front of the church, you can take a quiet detour to investigate the facades of handsome redbrick row houses on **Stuyvesant Street** ㉛, which stretches southwest to East 9th Street. If you continue north up 2nd Avenue from St. Mark's-in-the-Bowery, you'll reach the **Ukrainian Museum** ㉜.

Next, walk south on 2nd Avenue to East 9th Street. At 135 2nd Avenue, between East 9th Street and St. Marks Place, is the **Ottendorfer Branch of the New York Public Library** ㉝.Continue east on East 9th Street or St. Marks Place, toward Alphabet City, the area's nickname; here the avenues are named A, B, C, and D. A stroll east on East 9th Street will take you past a number of cafés and small, friendly shops selling designer and vintage clothing, housewares, toys, music, and much more, while St. Marks Place between 1st Avenue and Avenue A is lined with inexpensive cafés catering to a late-night younger crowd.

At the northeast corner of 1st Avenue and East 9th Street stands P.S.122 (⊠ 150 1st Ave.), a former public school building transformed into a complex of spaces for avant-garde entertainment. At Avenue A is **Tompkins Square Park** ㉞, a fairly peaceful spot during the day.

If you walk south on Avenue A past Houston Street, you'll run into the historical Lower East Side, one of Manhattan's most recently gentrified neighborhoods. Today the young and hip now occupy apartments on such streets as Rivington and Clinton, and fashion-furious boutiques such as Shop. (⊠ 105 Stanton St., at Ludlow St.) and TG 170 (⊠ 170 Ludlow St., at Stanton St.) compete with a new generation of Orchard Street shops, a longtime shopping strip. The face of the Orchard Street Garment District has been modernized by boutiques such as Zao (⊠ 175 Orchard St., at Stanton St.), a fusion of clothing, art, homeware design, and an indoor waterfall. The locals turn out to eat and be entertained at Baby Jupiter (⊠ 170 Orchard St., at Stanton St.), The Saint (⊠ 105 Stanton St., at Ludlow St.), and Mercury Lounge (⊠ 217 E. Houston St., at Essex St.), a popular club. But if you look up at the old brick walls of the tenement buildings, here and there you'll see reminders of the old days—the fading signs for defunct Jewish businesses, as well as for a few holdouts that still operate, such as Gertel's Bakery (⊠ 53 Hester St.) and Guss' Lower Eastside Pickle Corp. (⊠ 35 Essex St.). Historic establishments such as Katz's Delicatessen (⊠ 205 E. Houston St., at Ludlow St.), Ratner's Restaurant (⊠ 138 Delancey St., between Norfolk and Suffolk Sts.), and the more upscale Russ & Daughters (⊠ 179 E. Houston St., between Orchard and Allen Sts.) anchor the area firmly in its immigrant past. Two important synagogues, markers of time and tradition, are persevering renovations: the city's oldest synagogue, dating to 1850, the Shul of New York (⊠ 172 Norfolk St., between Stanton and E. Houston Sts.), now the Angel Orensanz Center for the Arts and, farther south, the **Eldridge Street Synagogue** ㉟, once the largest Jewish house of worship. On Orchard Street, the **Lower East Side Tenement Museum** ㊱ brings a bygone era to life.

Head back up into the East Village, to the corner of 1st Avenue and East 6th Street. The entire south side of East 6th Street between 1st and 2nd Avenues belongs to a dozen or more Indian restaurants serving inexpensive subcontinental fare (New Yorkers joke that they all share a single kitchen). Continuing west on East 6th Street, past 2nd Avenue, turn right onto Taras Shevchenko Place (named for the Ukrainian Shakespeare) to East 7th Street and **McSorley's Old Ale House** ㊲. Just west of McSorley's is **Surma, the Ukrainian Shop** ㊳, and across the street is the copper-dome **St. George's Ukrainian Catholic Church** ㊴, whose interior is lit by impressive stained-glass windows.

Across 3rd Avenue, the massive brownstone **Cooper Union Foundation Building** ㊵ houses a tuition-free school for artists, architects, and engineers and overlooks Cooper Square, a large open space. To the south are the offices of the *Village Voice* newspaper (✉ 36 Cooper Sq.). If you're here from Sunday through Thursday, walk south on Cooper Square and turn right on East 4th Street to visit the **Merchant's House Museum** ㊶.

One block west of Cooper Square is Lafayette Street. The long block between East 4th Street and Astor Place contains on its east side a grand Italian Renaissance–style structure housing the New York Shakespeare Festival's **Joseph Papp Public Theater** ㊷; in the 19th century the city's first free public library opened here. Across the street note the imposing marble Corinthian columns fronting **Colonnade Row** ㊸, a stretch of four crumbling 19th-century Greek revival houses. Walking north on Lafayette Street brings you back to Astor Place; heading west brings you to Broadway. To the left (south) is a busy downtown shopping strip, with several clothing shops and chain stores. Above street level the old warehouses here have mostly been converted into residential lofts. North on Broadway from Astor Place lies **Grace Church** ㊹, on the corner of Broadway and East 10th Street, which has a striking marble spire. If you continue north on the same side of the street as the church, you'll pass a few of the many antiques stores in the area. You can end your walk at the popular **Strand Book Store** ㊺, the largest secondhand bookstore in the city and an absolutely necessary stop for anyone who loves to read.

TIMING

Allow about three hours for the walk. If you plan to stop at museums, add one hour, and at least another hour to browse in shops along the way. If you end your walk at the Strand Book Store, you may want to stop somewhere for coffee before perusing the bookshelves, which can easily eat up another hour or more of your time.

Sights to See

㉘ **Alamo.** Created by Bernard Rosenthal in 1967, this massive black cube made of steel was originally part of a temporary citywide exhibit, but it became a permanent installation thanks to a private donor. Balanced on a post, the "Cube," as it is locally known, was one of the first abstract sculptures in New York City to be placed in a public space. ✉ *On traffic island at Astor Pl. and Lafayette St.*

OFF THE BEATEN PATH

ALPHABET CITY– Beyond 1st Avenue, the north–south avenues all labeled with letters, not numbers, give this area its commonly used nickname. Until fairly recently, Alphabet City was a burned-out territory of slums and drug haunts, but some blocks and buildings were gentrified during the height of the East Village art scene in the mid-'80s. The reasonably priced restaurants with their bohemian atmosphere on Avenues A and B, and the cross streets between them, attract a mix of locals and visitors. A close-knit Puerto Rican community lies east of Avenue A, but amid the

Latin shops and groceries Avenue B has become a sort of far-out restaurant row. ⊠ *Alphabet City extends approximately from Ave. A to the East River, between 14th and Houston Sts.*

NEED A
BREAK? **Old Devil Moon** (⊠ 511 E. 12th St., between Aves. A and B, ☎ 212/ 475–4357) is a delightfully snug, dimly lighted hangout with whimsical decor where you can stop for a snack or something more substantial.

㉗ Astor Place Subway Station. At the beginning of this century, almost every Independent Rapid Transit (IRT) subway entrance resembled the ornate cast-iron replica of a beaux arts kiosk that covers the stairway leading to the uptown No. 6 train. In the station itself, authentically reproduced ceramic tiles of beavers, a reference to the fur trade that contributed to John Jacob Astor's fortune, line the walls. Milton Glaser, a Cooper Union graduate, designed the station's attractive abstract murals. ⊠ *On traffic island at E. 8th St. and 4th Ave.*

㊸ Colonnade Row. Marble Corinthian columns front this grand sweep of four Greek revival mansions (originally nine) constructed in 1833, with stonework by Sing Sing penitentiary prisoners. In their time these once-elegant homes served as residences to millionaires John Jacob Astor and Cornelius Vanderbilt until they moved uptown. Writers Washington Irving, William Makepeace Thackeray, and Charles Dickens all stayed here at one time or another; more recently, writer Edmund White lived here. Today three houses are occupied on street level by restaurants, while the northernmost building houses the Astor Place Theatre. ⊠ *428–434 Lafayette St., between Astor Pl. and E. 4th St.*

㊵ Cooper Union Foundation Building. This impressive Italianate eight-story brownstone structure overlooks Cooper Square, a large open space where 3rd and 4th Avenues merge into the Bowery. A statue of industrialist Peter Cooper, by Augustus Saint-Gaudens, presides here. Cooper founded this college in 1859 to provide a forum for public opinion and free technical education for the working class. Abraham Lincoln, Mark Twain, and Susan B. Anthony have all delivered speeches here. The foundation still offers tuition-free education in architecture, art, and engineering. Cooper Union was the first structure to be supported by steel railroad rails—rolled in Cooper's own plant. The Great Hall gallery is open to the public and presents changing exhibitions during the academic year. ⊠ *E. 7th St. to Astor Pl., 4th Ave. to the Bowery at Cooper Sq.,* ☎ *212/353–4200.* ⊡ *Free.* ☉ *Weekdays 11–7, Sat. noon–5.*

★ ㉟ Eldridge Street Synagogue. Today the Congregation K'hal Adath Jeshurun and Anshe Lubz, and once the largest Jewish house of worship, this was the first Orthodox synagogue erected by the large number of Eastern European Jews who settled on the Lower East Side in the mid to late 19th century. The lavish Moorish revival–style building has undergone a major restoration. Inside is an exceptional hand-carved ark of Italian walnut, a sculptured wooden balcony, and enormous brass chandeliers. ⊠ *12 Eldridge St., between Canal and Division Sts.,* ☎ *212/219–0888,* WEB *www.eldridgestreet.org.* ⊡ *$4.* ☉ *Tours Tues. and Thurs. 11:30 and 2:30; Sun. 11–4.*

★ ㊹ Grace Church. Topped by a finely ornamented octagonal marble spire, this Episcopal church, designed for free by James Renwick Jr., has excellent Pre-Raphaelite stained-glass windows. The building—a fine mid-19th-century example of an English Gothic revival church—fronts a small green yard facing Broadway. The church has been the site of many society weddings (including that of P. T. Barnum show member Tom Thumb). ⊠ *802 Broadway, at E. 10th St.,* ☎ *212/254–2000.* ☉ *Weekdays 10–6, Sat. noon–4, Sun. 8:30–1.*

㊷   **Joseph Papp Public Theater.** In 1854 John Jacob Astor opened the city's first free public library in this expansive redbrick and brownstone Italian Renaissance–style building, which was renovated in 1967 as the Public Theater to serve as the New York Shakespeare Festival's permanent home. The theater opened its doors with the popular rock musical *Hair*. Under the leadership of the late Joseph Papp, the Public's five playhouses built a fine reputation for bold and innovative performances; the long-running hit *A Chorus Line* had its first performances here, as have many less commercial plays. Today, director and producer George C. Wolfe heads the Public, which continues to present controversial modern works and imaginative Shakespeare productions. The Public produces the two annual summer productions in Central Park's Delacorte Theater. ☒ *425 Lafayette St., between E. 4th St. and Astor Pl.,* ☎ *212/260–2400.*

㊱   **Lower East Side Tenement Museum.** America's first urban living-history museum preserves and interprets the life of immigrants in New York's Lower East Side. A guided tour (reservations suggested) takes you to a partially restored 1863 tenement building at 97 Orchard Street, where you can view the apartments of Natalie Gumpertz, a German-Jewish dressmaker (dating from 1878); Adolph and Rosaria Baldizzi, Catholic immigrants from Sicily (1935); the Rogarshevsky family from Eastern Europe (1918); and the Confino family, Sephardic Jews from Kastoria, Turkey, which is now part of Greece (1916). The tour through the Confino family apartment is designed for children, who are greeted by a costumed interpreter playing Victoria Confino. The museum also leads historic walking tours around Orchard Street. If you wish to forego the tours, you can watch a free historical slide show as well as a video with interviews of Lower East Side residents past and present. The gallery (free) has changing exhibits relating to Lower East Side history. ☒ *90 Orchard St.,* ☎ *212/431–0233.* ▧ *Tenement tour $9, tenement and Orchard St. walking tours $12.* ☉ *Museum Tues.– Fri. noon–5, weekends 11–5; tenement tours Tues.–Fri. every 30 mins 1–4, weekends every 30 mins 11–4:30; walking tours April–Dec., weekends 1:30 and 2:30. Tours are limited to 15 people.*

㊲   **McSorley's Old Ale House.** One of several pubs that claim to be New York's oldest, this often-crowded saloon attracts many collegiate types enticed by McSorley's own brands of ale. McSorley's asserts that it opened in 1854; it didn't admit women until 1970. The mahogany bar, gas lamps, and potbelly stove all hark back to decades past. Joseph Mitchell immortalized the spot in *The New Yorker*. ☒ *15 E. 7th St., between 2nd and 3rd Aves.,* ☎ *212/473–9148.*

㊶   **Merchant's House Museum.** Built in 1831–32, this redbrick house, combining Federal and Greek revival styles, offers a rare glimpse of family life in the mid-19th century. Retired merchant Seabury Tredwell and his descendants lived here from 1835 right up until it became a museum in 1933. The original furnishings and architectural features remain intact; family memorabilia are also on display. The parlors have 13-ft ceilings with intricate plasterwork, freestanding Ionic columns, a mahogany pocket-door screen, and black-marble fireplaces. Self-guided tour brochures are always available, and guided tours are given on weekends. ☒ *29 E. 4th St., between the Bowery and 2nd Ave.,* ☎ *212/777–1089.* ▧ *$5.* ☉ *Thurs.–Mon. 1–5.*

㉝   **Ottendorfer Branch of the New York Public Library.** Eager to improve the lives of fellow German immigrants then heavily populating the East Village, philanthropists Oswald and Anna Ottendorfer commissioned the construction of this library and adjacent German Dispensary (now Stuyvesant Polyclinic) at 137 2nd Avenue, which was designed by

William Schickel in 1884. The library began as the German-language branch of the Free Circulating Library (hence the words FREIE BIBLIOTHEK UND LESEHALLE on its facade) and eventually it became part of the city's public library system. The Dispensary is among the first buildings in New York to display ornamental terra-cotta, including busts of noted figures in medicine on the exterior. ⊠ *135 2nd Ave., near St. Marks Pl.,* ☎ *212/674–0947.*

㊴ St. George's Ukrainian Catholic Church. Notable for its copper dome and the three brightly colored religious murals on its facade, this ostentatious modern church serves as a central meeting place for the local Ukrainian population. Built in 1977, it took the place of the more modest Greek revival–style St. George's Ruthenian Church. An annual Ukrainian folk festival is held here in the spring. ⊠ *30 E. 7th St., between 2nd and 3rd Aves.,* ☎ *212/674–1615.* ☉ *Daily 7:30–5.*

㉚ St. Mark's-in-the-Bowery Church. A Greek revival steeple and a cast-iron front porch were added to this 1799 fieldstone country church, which occupies the former site of old Dutch governor Peter Stuyvesant's family chapel. St. Mark's is the city's oldest continually used Christian church site (Stuyvesant and Commodore Perry are buried here). Its interior had to be completely restored after a disastrous fire in 1978, and stained-glass windows were added to the balcony in 1982. Over the years St. Mark's has hosted progressive events, mostly in the arts. In the 1920s a forward-thinking pastor injected the Episcopal ritual with Native American chants, Greek folk dancing, and Eastern mantras. William Carlos Williams, Amy Lowell, and Carl Sandburg once read here, and Isadora Duncan, Harry Houdini, and Merce Cunningham also performed here. During the hippie era St. Mark's welcomed avant-garde poets and playwrights, including Sam Shepard. Today dancers, poets, and performance artists cavort in the main sanctuary, where pews have been removed to accommodate them. ⊠ *131 E. 10th St., at 2nd Ave.,* ☎ *212/674–6377.*

NEED A
BREAK?   Bright and bustling 24-hour **Veselka** (⊠ 144 2nd Ave., at 9th St., ☎ 212/228–9682), a longtime East Village favorite, serves muffins, Italian coffee, egg creams, and Ben & Jerry's ice cream alongside good, traditional Ukrainian fare such as borscht, pierogies, and veal goulash.

㉙ St. Marks Place. St. Marks Place, as East 8th Street is called between 3rd Avenue and Avenue A, is the longtime hub of the hip East Village. During the 1950s beatniks such as Allen Ginsberg and Jack Kerouac lived and wrote in the area; the 1960s brought Bill Graham's Fillmore East concerts, the Electric Circus, and hallucinogenic drugs. The black-clad, pink-haired, or shaved-head punks followed, and some remain today. St. Marks Place between 2nd and 3rd avenues is lined with ethnic restaurants, jewelry stalls, and stores selling posters, incense, and curious clothing. The street vendors who line the sidewalks add to the daily bazaarlike atmosphere, although a Gap store dilutes the effect.

At 80 St. Marks Place, near 1st Avenue, is the Pearl Theatre Company, which performs classic plays from around the world. The handprints, footprints, and autographs of such past screen luminaries as Joan Crawford, Ruby Keeler, Joan Blondell, and Myrna Loy are embedded in the sidewalk. At 96–98 St. Marks Place (between 1st Avenue and Avenue A) stands the building that was photographed for the cover of Led Zeppelin's *Physical Graffiti* album. The cafés between 1st Avenue and Avenue A attract customers late into the night.

★ ㊺ **Strand Book Store.** Serious book lovers the world over make pilgrimages to this secondhand book emporium with a stock of some 2 million volumes, including thousands of collector's items (the store's slogan is "Eight Miles of Books"). Opened in 1929 by Ben Bass, the Strand was originally on 4th Avenue's Book Row until it moved in 1956 to its present location on Broadway. Review copies of new books sell for 50% off, and used books are often priced at much less. A separate rare-book room is on the third floor at 826 Broadway, to the immediate north of the main store. ⊠ *828 Broadway, at 12th St.,* ☎ *212/473–1452.* ⊙ *Main store Mon.–Sat. 9:30–10:30, Sun. 11–10:30; rare books Mon.–Sat. 9:30–6:30, Sun. 11–6:30.*

★ ㉛ **Stuyvesant Street.** This block-long thoroughfare, the hypotenuse of two triangles bounded by 2nd and 3rd avenues and East 9th and 10th streets, is unique in Manhattan: it's the oldest street laid out precisely along an east–west axis. (This grid never caught on, and instead a street grid following the island's geographic orientation was adopted.) The area was once Governor Peter Stuyvesant's *bouwerie,* or farm; among the handsome redbrick row houses are the Federal-style **Stuyvesant-Fish House** (⊠ 21 Stuyvesant St.), which was built in 1804 as a wedding gift for a great-great-granddaughter of the governor, and **Renwick Triangle,** an attractive group of carefully restored one- and two-story brick and brownstone residences originally constructed in 1861. In 1998, The George Hecht Viewing Gardens were built at 3rd Avenue and East 9th Street, with one side of the gardens bordering Stuyvesant Street.

㊳ **Surma, the Ukrainian Shop.** The exotic stock at this charming little store includes Ukrainian books, magazines, and greeting cards, as well as musical instruments, painted eggs, and an exhaustive collection of peasant blouses. ⊠ *11 E. 7th St., between 2nd and 3rd Aves.,* ☎ *212/477–0729.*

⟳ ㉞ **Tompkins Square Park.** This leafy spot amid the East Village's crowded tenements is the physical, spiritual, and political heart of the radical East Village. The square takes its name from four-time governor Daniel Tompkins, an avid abolitionist and vice president under James Monroe, who once owned this land from 2nd Avenue to the East River. Its history is long and violent: the 1874 Tompkins Square Riot involved some 7,000 unhappy laborers and 1,600 police. In 1988 riots again broke out, as police followed then-mayor David Dinkins's orders to clear the park of the many homeless who had set up makeshift homes here, and homeless rights and antigentrification activists armed with sticks and bottles fought back. After a yearlong renovation, the park reopened in 1992 with a midnight curfew, still in effect today. The park fills up with locals on clement days year-round, partaking in minipicnics; drum circles; rollerblade basketball; and, for dog owners, a large dog run. East of the park at 151 Avenue B, near East 9th Street, stands an 1849 four-story white-painted brownstone, where renowned jazz musician Charlie Parker lived from 1950 to 1954. ⊠ *Bordered by Aves. A and B and 7th and 10th Sts.*

NEED A BREAK? At the northwest corner of the park is **Life Cafe** (⊠ 343 E. 10th St., at Ave. B, ☎ 212/477–8791), a frequently busy local hangout featured in the hit Broadway musical *Rent.* Two of the city's best Italian pastry shops are nearby. **De Robertis Pasticceria** (⊠ 176 1st Ave., between 10th and 11th Sts., ☎ 212/674–7137) offers exceptional cheesecake and cappuccinos in its original 1904 setting, complete with glistening mosaic tiles. Opened in 1894, the popular **Veniero's Pasticceria** (⊠ 342 E. 11th St., between 1st and 2nd Aves., ☎ 212/674–7264) has rows and rows of fresh cannoli, fruit tarts, cheesecakes, cookies, and other elaborate desserts on display in glass cases; there's a separate café section.

③② **Ukrainian Museum.** Ceramics, jewelry, hundreds of brilliantly colored Easter eggs, and an extensive collection of Ukrainian costumes and textiles are the highlights of this small collection, nurtured by Ukrainian Americans in exile throughout the years of Soviet domination. At press time, the museum was raising money for the construction of new quarters, at 222 East 6th Street. ✉ *203 2nd Ave., between 12th and 13th Sts.,* ☎ *212/228–0110.* 🖾 *$3.* ✆ *Wed.–Sun. 1–5.*

MURRAY HILL, FLATIRON DISTRICT, AND GRAMERCY

As the city grew progressively north throughout the 19th century, one neighborhood after another had its fashionable heyday, only to fade from glory. But three neighborhoods, east of 6th Avenue roughly between 14th and 40th streets, have preserved much of their historic charm: Murray Hill's brownstone mansions and town houses; Madison Square's classic turn-of-the-20th-century skyscrapers; and Gramercy Park's London-like leafy square. And one historic area (which was long forgotten and unfashionable), the Union Square/Flatiron District, has in recent years reemerged as a hot shopping and restaurant neighborhood. These days, it's not the leisure activities but the industries that make the neighborhood sizzle—the Flatiron District is aswarm with new-media technology companies and dot-coms that have usurped the historical buildings for office space, resulting in the area's appropriate "Silicon Alley" appellation, shared with the Wall Street area. Commentary on the new-media explosion can be spotted on billboards, which all seem to sell fast and faster-still Internet service. Despite the distractions, the only must-see along this route is the Empire State Building, the symbol of an older but ever-impressive technology.

Numbers in the text correspond to numbers in the margin and on the Murray Hill, Flatiron District, and Gramercy map.

A Good Walk

Begin on East 36th Street, between Madison and Park avenues, at the **Morgan Library** ①, where old-master drawings, medieval manuscripts, illuminated books, and original music scores are on opulent display. Proceed south on Madison Avenue. At East 35th Street you'll pass the **Church of the Incarnation** ②, a brownstone version of a Gothic chapel. Across the street and taking up the entire next block is the landmark **B. Altman Building/New York Public Library Science, Industry, and Business Library (SIBL).** ③, home of the famous department store from 1906 to 1989 and now the site of the New York Public Library's most high-tech research center.

Head for the corner of 5th Avenue and 34th Street where you can't miss the **Empire State Building** ④, one of the world's best-loved skyscrapers. Walk a block west on 34th Street to 6th Avenue: Before you is Herald Square and across the street is the venerable **Macy's** ⑤ department store. Walk south down Broadway, passing Herald Square's twin at West 32nd Street, Greeley Square. At West 29th Street, head a block east back to 5th Avenue, where you'll find **Marble Collegiate Church** ⑥. East of here, toward Lexington Avenue in the high 20s, is a neighborhood affectionately known as Little India, which has a concentration of Indian restaurants, spice shops, clothing emporiums, as well as Middle Eastern, Indonesian, and Vietnamese restaurants. From Marble Collegiate Church, cross the street and head east on 29th Street to **Church of the Transfiguration** ⑦, known as the Little Church Around the Corner. Continuing south along Madison Avenue, you'll see the **New York Life Insurance Building** ⑧, which occupies the block between East 26th

Murray Hill, Flatiron District, and Gramercy

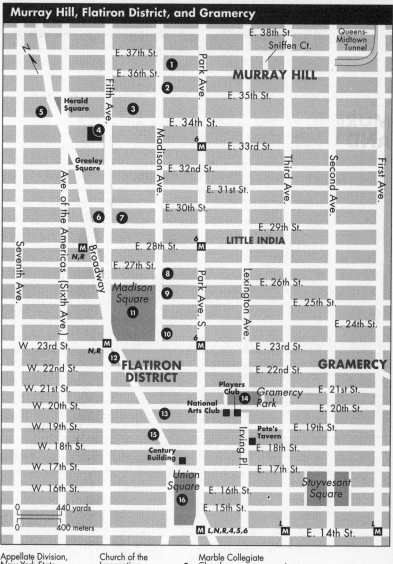

and 27th streets on the east side of Madison, its distinctive gold top visible from afar. The limestone beaux arts courthouse, one block down at East 25th Street, is the **Appellate Division, New York State Supreme Court** ⑨. The **Metropolitan Life Insurance Tower** ⑩, between East 23rd and 24th streets, is another lovely, classically inspired insurance-company tower.

On the west side of Madison Avenue, is **Madison Square** ⑪, one of Manhattan's nicest green pockets. A walk through the square leads to one of New York's most photographed buildings—the Renaissance-style **Flatiron Building** ⑫. This distinguished building has lent its name to the now trendy Flatiron District, which lies to the south between 6th Avenue and Park Avenue South. Continue south on Broadway and turn east on East 20th Street to the **Theodore Roosevelt Birthplace** ⑬. The prettiest part of this residential district, **Gramercy Park** ⑭, lies a block farther east, at the top of Irving Place between East 20th and 21st streets.

Jutting off Gramercy Park to the south is Irving Place, a short street lined with charming row houses, some of them occupied by restaurants. Local legend has it that O. Henry (pseudonym of William Sydney Porter) wrote "The Gift of the Magi" while sitting in the second booth to the right of the door at Pete's Tavern (✉ 129 E. 18th St., at Irving Pl.), which also claims to be the oldest saloon in New York (1864). Both assertions are disputed, but it's still a good spot for a drink in a Gaslight Era atmosphere. O. Henry lived at 55 Irving Place in a building long ago demolished.

Now turn around, head back to Broadway, and turn left. Once again lined with stores—such as Fishs Eddy, a china shop specializing in American "diner"-ware, and ABC Carpet and Home, a multi-level home-decor extravaganza—this section of Broadway was part of *the* most fashionable shopping area in the city during the Gilded Age. Thanks to the Union Square/Flatiron District renaissance, its incredible emporium-style buildings have finally been reoccupied. The old **Arnold Constable Dry Goods Store Building** ⑮, which takes up almost an entire city block, has been taken over by such retailers as Nine West and Victoria's Secret. If you continue down Broadway, it leads to **Union Square** ⑯.

TIMING

Half a day should suffice for this tour. Allow 1½ hours each for the Empire State Building and the Morgan Library. Keep in mind that some office buildings included in the walk are open only during the week. The Union Square Greenmarket, a must-visit, is open all day every Monday, Wednesday, Friday, and Saturday. Before traipsing to the top of the Empire State Building, consider the weather and how it is likely to affect visibility. Sunsets from the observation deck are spectacular, so you may want to end your day there (but be sure to factor in the time you'll spend waiting in line).

Sights to See

❾ **Appellate Division, New York State Supreme Court.** Figures representing "Wisdom" and "Justice" flank the main portal of this imposing Corinthian courthouse, built in 1900, on the east side of Madison Square. Statues of great lawmakers of the past line the roof balustrade, including Moses, Justinian, and Confucius; a statue of Muhammad was removed in the 1950s at the request of local Islamic groups, as Islamic law forbids the representation of humans in sculpture or painting. Inside are exhibitions of New York historical ephemera, murals, and furniture by the Herter Brothers. ✉ *27 Madison Ave., at 25th St. (entrance on 25th St.),* ☎ *212/340–0400.* ☉ *Weekdays 9–5.*

⓯ **Arnold Constable Dry Goods Store Building.** Imagine yourself riding in a shining black carriage drawn by a set of four trotters, and you'll travel back in time to when this section of Broadway was the most fashionable strip of stores in New York. Arnold Constable was the Bloomingdale's of its era. Built 1869–1877 and designed by architect Griffith Thomas, this elegant five-story dry-goods building spans East 19th Street with entrances on both Broadway and 5th Avenue. A double-story mansard roof tops it, white marble covers the Broadway side, and a cast-iron facade hovers over 5th Avenue. Reoccupied by several high-end clothing stores on the street level, this historic building again crackles with business. ✉ *881–887 Broadway, at 19th St.*

✋ ➌ **B. Altman Building/New York Public Library Science, Industry, and Business Library (SIBL).** In 1906, department-store magnate Benjamin Altman gambled that the fashionable shoppers who patronized his store at 6th Avenue and West 18th Street would follow him uptown to large new quarters on 5th Avenue and 34th Street, then a strictly residential street. They indeed came, and other stores followed, but then moved uptown again, to the 50s, leaving this trailblazer behind. In 1996, seven years after the bankruptcy and dismantling of the B. Altman chain, the New York Public Library transferred all scientific, technology, and business materials from its main 42nd Street building to a new state-of-the-art facility here, the **Science, Industry, and Business Library (SIBL).** This is a high-tech library with a sleek grace, which heeds Ruskin's words, "Industry without art is brutality," one of many quotations along the undulant upper wall inside the Madison Avenue lobby. Further demonstrating this philosophy is the artwork displayed within Healy Hall, the 33-ft-high atrium that unites the two floors of SIBL. Downstairs a wall of TVs tuned to business-news stations and electronic ticker tapes beam information and instructions to patrons. Hundreds of computers wired to the Internet and research databases are the library's hottest tickets. ✉ *188 Madison Ave., at 34th St.,* ☎ *212/592–7000.* ☉ *Mon. and Fri. 10–6, Tues. and Thurs. 11–8, Wed. 11–7, Sat. noon–6.*

➋ **Church of the Incarnation.** A brownstone version of a Gothic chapel on the outside, this 1864 Episcopal church has jewel-like stained glass inside that counteracts the building's dour effect. The north aisle's 23rd Psalm Window is by the Tiffany Glass works; the south aisle's two Angel windows, dedicated to infants, are by the 19th-century English writer-designer William Morris. ✉ *205 Madison Ave., at 35th St.,* ☎ *212/689–6350.*

➐ **Church of the Transfiguration.** Known as the Little Church Around the Corner, this Gothic revival church complex (1849–1861) is set back in a shrub-filled New York version of an old English churchyard. It won its memorable nickname in 1870 when other area churches refused to bury actor George Holland, a colleague of well-known thespian Joseph Jefferson. Jefferson was directed to the "little church around the corner" to accomplish the burial, and the Episcopal institution has welcomed literary and theater types ever since. The south transept's stained-glass window, by John LaFarge, depicts 19th-century superstar actor Edwin Booth as Hamlet, his most famous role. ✉ *1 E. 29th St., between 5th and Madison Aves.,* ☎ *212/684–6770.* ☉ *Sun. after 11 AM mass.*

★ ✋ ➍ **Empire State Building.** It may no longer be the world's tallest building (it currently ranks seventh), but it's certainly one of the world's best-loved skyscrapers, its pencil-slim silhouette a symbol for New York City and, perhaps, the 20th century. The skyscraper craze of the 1920s generated a slew of buildings in Manhattan, each outstretching the next in the quest to claim the title of world's tallest building. Developer John Jacob Raskob was no different, asking architect William Lamb, "Bill, how high can you make it so it won't fall down?" The art deco behemoth opened in April 1931 after a mere 13 months of construction; the framework rose at a rate of 4½ stories per week, making the Empire State Building the fastest-rising major skyscraper ever built. Many floors were left completely unfinished, however, so tenants could have them custom-designed. But the depression delayed occupancy, and most of the building remained unfinished and empty, causing critics to deem it the "Empty State Building." The crowning spire was originally designed to dock dirigibles—another example of the period's soaring ambition—but after two failed attempts, the idea was set aside. In 1951 a TV transmittal tower was added to the top, raising the total height to 1,472 ft (its signals reach 8 million television sets in four states). Ever since the 1976 American bicentennial celebration, the top 30 stories have been spotlighted at night with seasonal colors. Today some of the holidays celebrated in lights include: Martin Luther King Jr. Day (red, black, and green); Valentine's Day (red and white); the Fourth of July (red, white, and blue); Columbus Day (red, white, and green); Hanukkah (blue and white); and Christmas (red and green). The building has appeared in more than 100 movies, among them 1933's unforgettable *King Kong* and 1957's *An Affair to Remember,* in which Cary Grant waited impatiently at the top for his rendezvous with Deborah Kerr.

Today about 20,000 people work in the Empire State Building, and more than 3.8 million people visit its observation decks annually. Tickets are sold on the concourse level; on your way up admire the illuminated panels depicting the Seven Wonders of the World—with the Empire State Building brazenly appended as number eight—in the three-story-high marble lobby. If you choose one observatory, make it the 86th (1,050 ft high), which is open to the air and spans the building's circumference; on clear days you can see up to 80 mi. The 102nd-floor deck (1,250 ft high) is smaller, cramped, and glassed in (but if you have time for both, it's fun to compare the views from the different heights). It's worth timing your visit for early or late in the day (morning is the least crowded time), when the sun is low on the horizon and the shadows are deep across the city. But at night the city's lights are dazzling. The French architect Le Corbusier said, "It is a Milky Way come down to earth." Really, both views are a must; one strategy is to go up just before dusk and witness both, as day dims to night. ⊠ *350 5th Ave., at 34th St.,* ☎ *212/736–3100,* WEB *www.esbnyc.com.* ☑ *$6.* ☉ *Daily 9:30 AM–midnight; last elevator up leaves at 11:30 PM.*

The Empire State Building's other major tourist attraction is the **New York Skyride.** A Comedy Central video presentation on the virtues of New York precedes a rough-and-tumble motion-simulator ride above and around some of the city's top attractions, which are projected on a two-story-tall screen. Since it's part helicopter video and part roller-coaster ride, children love it. The ride is not recommended for anyone who has trouble with motion sickness, and pregnant women are not admitted. ☎ *212/279–9777.* ☑ *$11.50; $14 for Skyride and Observatory.* ☉ *Daily 10–10.*

★ ⑫ **Flatiron Building.** When completed in 1902, the Fuller Building, as it was originally known, caused a sensation. Architect Daniel Burnham made ingenious use of the triangular wedge of land and employed a revolutionary steel frame, which allowed for its 20-story, 286-ft height. Covered with a limestone and terra-cotta skin in the Italian Renaissance style, the ship's-bow-like structure, appearing to sail intrepidly up the avenue, was the most popular subject of picture postcards at the turn of the 20th century. Winds invariably swooped down at its 23rd Street tip, billowing up the skirts of women pedestrians on 23rd Street, and local traffic cops had to shoo away male gawkers—coining the phrase "23 skiddoo." ⊠ *175 5th Ave., bordered by 22nd and 23rd Sts., 5th Ave., and Broadway.*

NEED A BREAK?
A good stop for hearty soups or sandwiches on thick, crusty bread is **La Boulangère** (⊠ 49 E. 21st St., between Park Ave. S and Broadway, ☎ 212/475–8772). Or try **Henry's Gourmet Foods** (⊠ 186 5th Ave., at 23rd St., ☎ 212/924–2050) for hot blueberry oatmeal, grilled vegetable sandwiches, and smoothies. On cool days locals take to the marshmallowy hot chocolate at **The City Bakery** (⊠ 3 W. 18th St., between 5th and 6th Aves., ☎ 212/366–1414). Madison and Union squares are both nearby take-out picnic destinations.

⑭ Gramercy Park. In 1831 Samuel B. Ruggles, an intelligent young real estate developer (he graduated from Yale at age 14), bought and drained a tract of what was largely swamp and created a charming park inspired by London's residential squares. Hoping that exclusivity would create demand, the park was preserved for only those who would buy the surrounding lots. Sixty-six of the city's fashionable elite did just that, and no less than golden keys were provided for them to penetrate the park's 8-ft-high cast-iron fence. Although no longer golden, keys are still given only to residents; it is the city's only private park. Passersby can enjoy the carefully maintained landscaping through the wrought-iron fence.

Instead of taxis and traffic—Lexington Avenue ends here, so vehicles rarely venture near—original 19th-century row houses in Greek revival, Italianate, Gothic revival, and Victorian Gothic styles surround the park's south and west sides. In the park stands a statue of actor Edwin Booth playing Hamlet; Booth lived at No. 16, which he purchased in 1888 to serve as the **Players Club**, an association to elevate the then-low status of actors. Stanford White, the architect who renovated the club, was a member, as were many other nonactors. Other members over the years have included Mark Twain (who was once expelled, in error, for nonpayment of dues), John and Lionel Barrymore, Irving Berlin, Winston Churchill, Sir Laurence Olivier, Frank Sinatra, Walter Cronkite, Helen Hayes, and Richard Gere. The Players Club library holds one of the largest theater collections in America.

The **National Arts Club** (⊠ 15 Gramercy Park S) was once the home of Samuel Tilden, a governor of New York and the 1876 Democratic presidential candidate. Calvert Vaux, codesigner of Central Park, remodeled this building in 1884, conjoining two houses and creating a 40-room mansion. Among its Victorian Gothic decorations are medallions outside portraying Goethe, Dante, Milton, and Benjamin Franklin. The club, founded in 1898 to bring together "art lovers and art workers," moved into the mansion in 1906. Early members included Woodrow Wilson and Theodore Roosevelt; Robert Redford and Martin Scorsese are more recent members. While it is a private club (it has about 2,000 members), there are a number of rooms open to the public exhibiting works from member artists.

The austere gray-brown Friends Meeting House at 28 Gramercy Park South (1859) became the **Brotherhood Synagogue** in 1974, and a narrow plaza just east of the synagogue contains a Holocaust memorial. No. **19 Gramercy Park South** (1845) was the home in the 1880s of society doyenne Mrs. Stuyvesant Fish, a fearless iconoclast who shocked

Mrs. Astor and Mrs. Vanderbilt when she reduced the time of formal dinner parties from several hours to 50 minutes, thus ushering in the modern social era. ⊠ *Lexington Ave. between 20th and 21st Sts.*

❺ Macy's. On any given day about 30,000 people walk through the doors of the city's most famous (and the "World's Largest," according to its own boast) department store. Covering a full city block from 6th to 7th Avenues between West 34th and 35th Streets, with 11 floors and over 2 million square ft of selling space, Macy's is a living retail legend. In 1902, half a century after whaling sailor Rowland Hussey Macy established a fancy dry goods store at West 14th Street and 6th Avenue, the store moved to its current Herald Square site. Livestock was sold out of the main floor, but, equipped with the world's first modern escalators, Macy's introduced a new consumer phenomenon: vertical shopping, in which customers were transported from floor to floor of merchandise. You can still ride these magical wooden steps today. Another promotional innovation was the Macy's Thanksgiving Day Parade, which stepped off in 1924. During its first decade, the large helium balloons for which the parade is known nationwide were released into the air and recovered by the public for prizes. Macy's continued to stay ahead of the curve in the 1940's and 1950's, when it sold prefabricated houses, airplanes, and automobiles out of the ninth floor, and when it popularized Scrabble after a Macy's buyer discovered the Brooklyn invention. The store was also the first retailer to promote such products as the Idaho baked potato and colored bath towels. ⊠ *W. 34th St., between 6th and 7th Aves.,* ☎ *212/695–4400,* WEB *www.macys.com.* ☒ *Free.* ☉ *Mon.–Sat. 10–8:30, Sun. 11–7; extended hours Christmas season and sale days.*

. . . .

NEED A   Across from Macy's in the whirlwind intersection of Broadway and Sixth
BREAK?   Avenue, **Herald Square** may seem like an unlikely spot to seek peace.
                But this urban oasis is a testament to New York's new, cleaner image,
                brought about, in part, through private business organizations. Formerly
                a useless cement slab, Herald Square, like its identical twin two blocks
                south, **Greeley Square,** is now a redoubt of trees; flowers; and movable,
                Paris-style tables and chairs. A spacious pedestrian thoroughfare has
                been built around it, along with an attractive period newsstand and—
                talk about a miracle on 34th Street—an automated public bathroom.
                The parks are landscaped and cleaned continually by the 34th Street
                Partnership, which has also done a wonderful job with Bryant Park. The
                monument that features Minerva and a large bell—the two bronze men
                strike the bell on the hour—stood atop the *New York Herald* building, on
                the north end of the square, from 1895 to 1921. The parks are open
                daily, 7–7.

. . . .

⑪ Madison Square. With a picturesque view of some of the city's oldest and most charming skyscrapers (the Flatiron Building, Met Life Insurance Tower, and New York Life Insurance Building), this tree-filled 7-acre park mainly attracts dog owners and office workers, but it's a fine spot for people- or squirrel-watching, relaxing, and picnicking, too. Baseball was invented across the Hudson in Hoboken, New Jersey, but the city's first baseball games were played here circa 1845. On the north end an imposing 1881 statue by Augustus Saint-Gaudens memorializes Civil War naval hero Admiral Farragut. An 1876 statue of Secretary of State William Henry Seward (the Seward of the phrase "Seward's folly"—as Alaska was originally known) sits in the park's southwest corner, though it's rumored the sculptor placed a reproduction of the statesman's head on a likeness of Abraham Lincoln's body. ⊠ *E. 23rd to 26th Sts., between 5th and Madison Aves.*

❻ Marble Collegiate Church. Built in 1854 for the Reformed Protestant Dutch Congregation first organized in 1628 by Peter Minuit, the canny Dutchman who bought Manhattan from the Native Americans for the equivalent of $24, this impressive Romanesque revival church takes its name from the Tuckahoe marble that covers it. Dr. Norman Vincent Peale (*The Power of Positive Thinking*) was pastor here from 1932 to 1984. ✉ *1 W. 29th St., at 5th Ave.,* ☎ *212/686–2770.*

❿ Metropolitan Life Insurance Tower. When it was added in 1909, the 700-ft tower, which re-creates the campanile of St. Mark's in Venice, made this 1893 building the world's tallest. Its clock's four dials are each three stories high, and their minute hands weigh half a ton each; it chimes on the quarter hour. A skywalk over East 24th Street links it to Met Life's North Building. Its art deco loggias have attracted many film crews—the building has appeared in such films as *After Hours, Radio Days,* and *The Fisher King.* ✉ *1 Madison Ave., between 23rd and 24th Sts.*

★ ❶ Morgan Library. One of New York's most patrician museums, the Morgan is a world-class treasury of medieval and Renaissance illuminated manuscripts, old-master drawings and prints, rare books, and autographed literary and musical manuscripts. Many of the crowning achievements produced on paper, from the Middle Ages to the 20th century, are here: letters penned by John Keats and Thomas Jefferson; a summary of the theory of relativity in Einstein's own elegant handwriting; three Gutenberg Bibles; drawings by Dürer, da Vinci, Rubens, Blake, and Rembrandt; the only known manuscript fragment of Milton's "Paradise Lost"; Thoreau's journals; and original manuscripts and letters by Charlotte Brontë, Jane Austen, Thomas Pynchon, and many others. Originally built for the collections of Wall Street baron J. Pierpont (J. P.) Morgan (1837–1913), the museum has at its core a Renaissance-style palazzo, completed in 1906 by McKim, Mead & White, which houses the opulent period rooms of Morgan's original library. The **East Room** (the main library) has dizzying tiers of handsomely bound rare books, letters, and illuminated manuscripts. The **West Room,** Morgan's personal study, contains a remarkable selection of mostly Italian Renaissance furniture, paintings, and other marvels within its red-damask-lined walls.

Changing exhibitions, drawn from the permanent collection, are often highly distinguished. The library shop is within an 1852 Italianate brownstone, once the home of Morgan's son, J. P. "Jack" Morgan Jr., which is connected to the rest of the library by a graceful glass-roof garden court where lunch and afternoon tea are served. Outside on East 36th Street, the sphinx in the right-hand sculptured panel of the original library's facade was rumored to wear the face of architect Charles McKim. Exhibition tours are offered free with admission Tuesday–Friday at noon. ✉ *29 E. 36th St., at Madison Ave.,* ☎ *212/685–0008,* WEB *www.morganlibrary.org.* 🎫 *$8 (suggested donation).* ☉ *Tues.–Fri. 10:30–5, Sat. 10:30–6, Sun. noon–6.*

❽ New York Life Insurance Building. Cass Gilbert, better known for the Woolworth Building, capped this 1928 building with a gilded pyramid that is stunning when lighted at night. The soaring lobby's coffered ceilings and ornate bronze doors are equally grand. P. T. Barnum's Hippodrome (1890–1925) formerly occupied this site, and after that Madison Square Garden, designed by architect and playboy Stanford White. White was shot in the Garden's roof garden by Harry K. Thaw, a partner in White's firm and the jealous husband of actress Evelyn Nesbit, with whom White was purportedly having an affair—a lurid episode more or less accurately depicted in E. L. Doctorow's book *Ragtime.* ✉ *51 Madison Ave., between 26th and 27th Sts.*

SNIFFEN COURT – Just two blocks from the Morgan Library, the 10 Romanesque revival former brick carriage houses that line this easily overlooked cul-de-sac are equal parts Old London and New Orleans. Peer through the locked gate to admire them. ⊠ *150–158 E. 36th St., between Lexington and 3rd Aves.*

⑬ Theodore Roosevelt Birthplace National Historic Site. The 26th U.S. president—the only one from New York City—was born on this site in 1858. The original 1848 brownstone was demolished in 1916, but this Gothic revival replica, built in 1923, is a near-perfect reconstruction of the house where Teddy lived until he was 15 years old. Now administered by the National Park Service, the house has a fascinating collection of Teddyana in five Victorian period rooms. Saturday-afternoon chamber music concerts are offered each fall, winter, and spring. ⊠ *28 E. 20th St., between Broadway and Park Ave. S,* ☎ *212/260-1616.* ⊡ *$2.* ☉ *Wed.–Sun. 9–5; guided tours every hr until 4.*

A vegetarian restaurant in the style of a Japanese teahouse, the **Zen Palate** (⊠ 34 E. Union Square, at 16th St., ☎ 212/614–9291) serves up an innovative culinary experience at moderate prices. Try the sweet yam fries, kale and seaweed salad, or steamed vegetable bun. Table service downstairs is fast-paced; consider carrying out and picnicking in neighboring Union Square, or eat in the more formal upstairs dining room. The restaurant does not serve alcohol, but you can bring your own.

⑯ Union Square. A park, meeting place, outdoor shopping area, and home to some of the city's trendiest restaurants, this pocket of green space is the focus of a bustling residential and shopping neighborhood. Its name—"Union"—originally signified that two main roads—Broadway and 4th Avenue—crossed here, but it took on a different meaning in the late 19th and early 20th centuries, when the square became a rallying spot for labor protests and mass demonstrations; many unions, as well as fringe political parties, moved their headquarters nearby. In fact, the square is full of the statues of former politicians: George Washington (1856, Henry Kirke Brown), Abraham Lincoln (1866, Henry Kirke Brown), the Marquis de Lafayette (1875, Frederic Auguste Bartholdi, who also sculpted the Statue of Liberty), and Gandhi (1986, Kantilal B. Patel), whose likeness, usually wreathed with flowers, stands in the park's southwest corner.

Union Square is at its best on Monday, Wednesday, Friday, and Saturday (8–6), when the largest of the city's 28 **Greenmarkets** brings farmers and food purveyors from all over the Northeast. Crowds of neighborhood residents and workers browse among the stands of fresh produce, flowers and plants, homemade bakery goods, cheeses, cider, New York State wines, and fish and meat. On the north end, the park's 1932 **Pavilion** is flanked by playgrounds and **Luna Park** (☎ 212/475-8464), a trendy open-air restaurant open mid-May through October.

Movie theaters and retail superstores occupy the handsome, restored 19th-century commercial buildings that surround the park. The run of diverse and imaginative architectural styles on the building at 33 Union Square West (the former name, the **Decker Building**, which is visible above the second floor's incised decoration) is, indeed, "fabulous"—it was the home of Andy Warhol's second Factory studio. The redbrick and white-stone **Century Building** (built in 1881, ⊠ 33 E. 17th St.) on the square's north side, is now a Barnes & Noble bookstore, which has preserved the building's original cast-iron columns and other architectural details. The building at 17th Street and Union

Square East, now housing the New York Film Academy and the Union Square Theatre, was the final home of **Tammany Hall**. This organization, famous in its day as a fairly corrupt yet effective political machine, moved here just at the height of its power in 1929, but by 1943 it went bankrupt and had to sell the building. A block south on Union Square East is former U.S. Savings Bank, most recently used as an alternative theater. The southern block is dominated by an abstract timepiece on the exterior wall of the Virgin Records superstore. Stand under the colossal magic wand on the hour for a surprise. You have to be quite clever to read the digital clock made up of 15 changing numbers. A clue: at midnight, all the digits display "0." ⊠ *E. 14th to 17th Sts., between Broadway and Park Ave. S.*

CHELSEA

Like the London district of the same name, New York's Chelsea has preserved its villagelike personality. Both have their quiet nooks where the 19th century seems to live on; both have been havens for artists, writers, and bohemians—New York's notables include Louise Bourgeois and Susan Sontag. New York's Chelsea is catching up to London's upscale real estate, with town house renovations reclaiming side-street blocks. Restored historic cast-iron buildings on 6th Avenue house America's ubiquitous superstore tenants, who have helped revitalize the area. Although 7th, 8th, and 9th Avenues may never equal the shopping mecca of King's Road in London's Chelsea, they have one-of-a-kind boutiques sprinkled among unassuming grocery stores and other remnants of the neighborhood's immigrant past.

Actually, the New York neighborhood was named not after Chelsea itself but after London's Chelsea Royal Hospital, an old soldiers' home. Until the 1830s one family's country estate occupied the area from West 19th to 28th streets and from 8th Avenue west. Then the owner, Clement Clarke Moore, realized the city was moving north and decided to divide his land into lots. With an instinctive gift for urban planning, he dictated a pattern of development that ensured street after street of graceful row houses. A clergyman and classics professor, Moore is probably best known for his 1822 poem "A Visit from St. Nicholas"—"'Twas the night before Christmas. . . ." He composed it while bringing a sleigh full of Christmas treats from lower Manhattan to his Chelsea home.

Today's Chelsea extends west of 5th Avenue from 14th to 29th streets. Eighth Avenue has surpassed Christopher Street in the West Village as New York's gay Main Street: shops, fitness clubs, and restaurants cater to a largely gay clientele. Yet the thriving neighborhood also accommodates a multicultural population that has lived here for decades, as well as a booming arts community west of 10th Avenue. Indeed, for many, Chelsea is synonymous with the galleries of principally contemporary art that pepper its many streets between 10th and 11th Avenues.

Numbers in the text correspond to numbers in the margin and on the Chelsea map.

A Good Walk

Begin on the corner of 6th Avenue and West 18th Street. Sixth Avenue was once known as Ladies' Mile for its concentration of major department stores (also in the late 19th century, elevated tracks cast their shadow along this street). After the stores moved uptown in the early 1900s, the neighborhood declined, and the grand old store buildings stood empty and dilapidated. The 1990s, however, brought a renais-

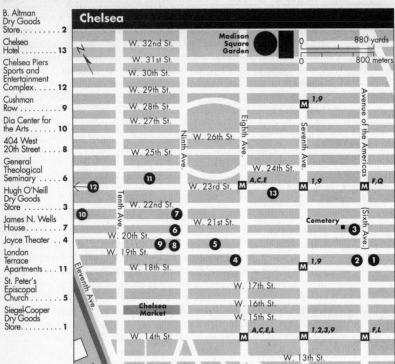

sance to the Flatiron district to the east, and 6th Avenue's grandest buildings once again purvey wares of all kinds. On the east side of the avenue, between West 18th and 19th streets, stands the former
Siegel-Cooper Dry Goods Store ①.

Between West 18th and 19th streets on the west side of the avenue is
the 1877 cast-iron **B. Altman Dry Goods Store** ②, now occupied by
Today's Man. Continue walking north to West 20th Street. The Gothic-
style Church of the Holy Communion, an Episcopal house of worship
dating from 1846, is on the northeast corner of the avenue. To the horror of some preservationists, it was converted into the now popular
Limelight nightclub. On the west side of the avenue between West 20th
and 21st streets stands another former cast-iron retail palace, the **Hugh
O'Neill Dry Goods Store** ③. If you turn left from 6th Avenue onto West
21st Street you'll come upon Third Cemetery of the Spanish & Portuguese Synagogue, Shearith Israel on the south side of the street.
These days it's a rather neglected spot with upset marble gravestones,
adjacent to a parking lot. In use from 1829 to 1851, it is one of three
graveyards created in Manhattan by this congregation.

Weekends, in parking lots cater-cornered on 6th Avenue between West
24th and 26th streets, you'll find the city's longest-running outdoor
flea markets. Branching from 6th Avenue for almost a block in each
direction along West 25th Street are smaller markets and an assortment of antiques shops. While it may not come as a total surprise to
find a terrific floral selection in the Flower District along 6th Avenue
from West 25th to 29th streets, you will be impressed by the trees and
plants on display along the sidewalks.

Continue west to 8th Avenue, where the Chelsea Historic District officially begins. Its residential heart is between West 19th and 23rd Streets,

from 8th to 10th Avenues. To get a quick feel for 8th Avenue, head down to West 19th Street to the art deco **Joyce Theater** ④, primarily a dance venue. Its presence, along with the burgeoning lesbian and gay community here, helped attract many good moderately priced restaurants to 8th Avenue.

On West 20th Street between 8th and 9th Avenues, you'll find the brick parish house, fieldstone church, and rectory of 19th-century **St. Peter's Episcopal Church** ⑤, home of the well-known Atlantic Theater Company. Next, head west on West 20th Street to 9th Avenue; on the west side of the avenue between 20th and 21st streets is the **General Theological Seminary** ⑥, the oldest Episcopal seminary in the United States. A block north at West 21st Street on the northwest corner is the **James N. Wells House** ⑦, once the home of the man who planned Chelsea.

Across the street from the seminary, **404 West 20th Street** ⑧ is the oldest house in the historic district. The residences next door, from 406 to 418 West 20th Street, are called **Cushman Row** ⑨ and are excellent examples of Greek revival town houses. Farther down West 20th Street, stop to look at the fine Italianate houses from Nos. 446 to 450. The arched windows and doorways are hallmarks of this style, which prized circular forms (no doubt because the expense required to build them showed off the owner's wealth). West 22nd Street has a string of handsome old row houses between 9th and 10th Avenues.

Crossing 10th Avenue, you'll pass beneath old elevated train tracks; these form the eastern border to the vital Chelsea gallery scene. Between 10th and 11th Avenues, from West 20th to 29th streets, you can spend an afternoon wandering in and out of ultra-stylish art spaces. A good place to begin is West 22nd Street, home to **Dia Center for the Arts** ⑩, the anchor of Chelsea's renaissance as an art community. Besides West 22nd Street, 21st, 23rd, 24th, and 26th streets also have an ever-growing contingent of galleries large and small, including many relocated from SoHo. East of Dia on West 22nd Street are quite a few galleries, including Matthew Marks Gallery and Pat Hearn Gallery, as well as the ultra-hip Japanese fashion boutique Comme Des Garçons. One block down, on West 21st Street, is a major SoHo transplant, Paula Cooper Gallery. On the corner of West 24th Street and 11th Avenue is another transplant, Gagosian Gallery, one of the city's most influential and respected galleries. Building no. 524 on West 26th Street is home to no fewer than 14 new galleries. Because each gallery keeps its own hours, it's best to call ahead about openings and closings.

From the gallery zone return to 10th Avenue and walk to West 23rd Street. Occupying the entire block between 10th and 9th Avenues and 23rd and 24th streets, the **London Terrace Apartments** ⑪ is a vast 1930 complex containing 1,670 apartments. As you walk along 23rd Street, notice the lions on the arched entrances; from the side they look as if they're snarling, but from the front they have wide grins.

If you walk west on West 23rd Street, crossing the West Side Highway (yes, this highway has red stoplights), you'll come to the mammoth **Chelsea Piers Sports and Entertainment Complex** ⑫, the city's largest sports center. You can also take in views of New Jersey along Chelsea's slice of the Hudson River waterfront from here. If you don't head to the river, continue east on West 23rd Street. During the 1880s and Gay '90s, the street was the heart of the entertainment district, lined with theaters, music halls, and beer gardens. Today it is an undistinguished commercial thoroughfare. Among the relics of its proud past is the **Chelsea Hotel** ⑬.

In three to four hours you can tour Chelsea. Art appreciators should plan to spend the day, however, and take time to browse the galleries and stores and have a leisurely lunch.

Sights to See

② **B. Altman Dry Goods Store.** Built in 1877 with additions in 1887 and 1910, this ornate cast-iron giant originally housed B. Altman Dry Goods until the business moved in 1906 to its imposing quarters at 5th Avenue and 34th Street. ⊠ *621 6th Ave., between 18th and 19th Sts.*

OFF THE
BEATEN PATH

CHELSEA MARKET – In the former Nabisco plant, where the first Oreo cookies were made in 1912, nearly two dozen food wholesalers flank what is possibly the city's longest interior walkway in a single building—from 9th to 10th Avenues. Admire the market's funky industrial design as you take in the delectable scents of the bread, wine, and meats sold here. The Food Network is setting up tent in a glassed-in test kitchen and television studio near the 10th Avenue side, making Chelsea Market a requisite gastronomical stop. ⊠ *75 9th Ave., between 15th and 16th Sts.,* ☎ *212/247–1423.* ☯ *Daily 8–8.*

⑬ **Chelsea Hotel.** Constructed of red brick with lacy wrought-iron balconies and a mansard roof, this pleasingly out-of-place, 11-story neighborhood landmark opened in 1884 as a cooperative apartment house. It became a hotel in 1905, although it has always catered to long-term tenants, with a tradition of broad-mindedness that has attracted many creative types. Its literary roll call of former live-ins includes Mark Twain, Eugene O'Neill, O. Henry, Thomas Wolfe, Tennessee Williams, Vladimir Nabokov, Mary McCarthy, Brendan Behan, Arthur Miller, Dylan Thomas, William S. Burroughs, and Arthur C. Clarke (who wrote the script for *2001: A Space Odyssey* while living here). In 1966 Andy Warhol filmed artist Brigid Polk in her Chelsea Hotel room, the footage eventually became included in *The Chelsea Girls.* More recently the hotel was seen on screen in *I Shot Andy Warhol* (1996) and *Sid and Nancy* (1986), a dramatization of the true-life Chelsea Hotel murder of Nancy Spungen, who was stabbed to death here, allegedly by her boyfriend, drugged punk rocker Sid Vicious. The shabby aura of the hotel is part of its allure. Read the commemorative plaques outside, then check out the eclectic collection of art in the lobby, some donated in lieu of rent by residents down on their luck. In the building's basement, accessible from the street, is the stylish bar Serena. ⊠ *222 W. 23rd St., between 7th and 8th Aves.,* ☎ *212/243–3700.*

 ⑫ **Chelsea Piers Sports and Entertainment Complex.** Beginning in 1910, the Chelsea Piers were the launching point for a new generation of big ocean liners, including the *Lusitania,* the British liner sunk by a German submarine in 1915. And it was here that the *Titanic* was also headed. Decades-long neglect ended with the transformation of the four old buildings along the Hudson River into a 1.7-million-square-ft state-of-the-art sports and recreation facility, providing a huge variety of activities and several restaurants with river views, including the Chelsea Brewing Company, New York State's largest microbrewery. A trip to the Statue of Liberty without the hassle of a long wait can be arranged at the marina via a speed boat, yacht, or combined with a brunch or dinner onboard. ⊠ *Piers 59–62 on the Hudson River from 17th to 23rd Sts.; entrance at 23rd St.,* ☎ *212/336–6666.*

⑨ **Cushman Row.** Built by dry-goods merchant Don Alonzo Cushman, a friend of Clement Clarke Moore, who made a fortune developing Chelsea, this string of homes between 9th and 10th Avenues represents some of the country's most perfect examples of Greek revival town houses. The residences retain such original details as small wreath-encircled attic windows, deeply recessed doorways with brownstone frames, and striking iron balustrades and fences. Pineapples, a traditional symbol of welcome, perch atop the black iron newels in front of Nos. 416 and 418. ⊠ *406–418 W. 20th St., between 9th and 10th Aves.*

★ ⑩ **Dia Center for the Arts.** Dia is more like the Whitney Museum than the scores of Chelsea galleries it has helped draw to the neighborhood. Besides installations by diverse artists on its four floors of space, you might find an exhibit from Dia's permanent collection, which includes creations by Joseph Beuys, Walter De Maria, Dan Flavin, Blinky Palermo, Cy Twombly, Richard Serra, and Andy Warhol. Don't miss a visit to the roof, which has a café and a two-way glass pavilion designed by Dan Graham that invites contemplation of the surrounding cityscape. There is also an annex across the street. ⊠ *548 W. 22nd St., between 10th and 11th Aves.,* ☎ *212/989–5566,* WEB *www.diacenter.org.* ⊠ *$6.* ☺ *Wed.–Sun. noon–6; closed mid June–early Sept..*

NEED A BREAK?

Wild Lily Tea Room (⊠ 511A W. 22nd St., between 10th and 11th Aves., ☎ 212/691–2258) is a tranquil Japanese art-cum-food shop, with an indoor stone koi pool. Teas with poetic names, such as Buddha's Finger and Pink Infusion, are served alongside salads, sandwiches, and desserts. For burgers and shakes, stop at **Empire Diner** (⊠ 210 10th Ave., at 22nd St., ☎ 212/243–2736), a gleaming stainless steel hash house.

⑧ **404 West 20th Street.** The oldest house in the historic district was built between 1829 and 1830 in the Federal style. It still has one clapboard side wall; over the years it acquired a Greek revival doorway and Italianate windows on the parlor floor, and the roof was raised one story. ⊠ *404 W. 20th St., at 9th Ave.*

⑥ **General Theological Seminary.** You'll satisfy the stealth explorer in you when exploring the secretive grounds of this seminary. When Chelsea developer Clement Clarke Moore divided his estate, he deeded a block-size section to the Episcopal seminary, where he taught Hebrew and Greek (though it's easy to miss its great size behind the heavy exterior fencing). The campus is accessible through the unremarkable 1960s-era building on 9th Avenue, which houses administrative offices, a bookstore, and the 240,000-volume **St. Mark's Library**, among the nation's greatest ecclesiastical libraries, with a world-class collection of Latin and English Bibles. The 1836 **West Building** is a fine early example of Gothic revival architecture. For the most part, the rest was completed in 1883–1902, when the school hired architect Charles Coolidge Haight to design a campus to rival all other American colleges of the day using the English Collegiate Gothic style he pioneered. It worked. The hushed interior and the elm- and oak-graced lawns "sustain the pastoral illusion better than anything in New York besides Central Park," according to critic Paul Goldberger. ⊠ *175 9th Ave., at 20th St.,* ☎ *212/243–5150.* ☺ *Grounds weekdays noon–5, Sat. 11–3; call for information on using the library.*

③ **Hugh O'Neill Dry Goods Store.** Constructed in 1875, this cast-iron building, originally an emporium, features Corinthian columns and pilasters; its corner towers were once topped with huge bulbous domes. The name of the original tenant is proudly displayed on the pediment. ⊠ *655–671 6th Ave., between 20th and 21st Sts.*

⑦ **James N. Wells House.** This 1832 2½-story brick house was the home of Clement Clarke Moore's property manager, the man who planned

Chelsea. Wells was responsible for the strict housing codes that created the elegant residential neighborhood by prohibiting stables and manure piles and requiring tree planting. ⊠ *401 W. 21st St.*

NEED A BREAK? At **Le Gamin** (⊠ 183 9th Ave., at 21st St., ☎ 212/243–8864), a rustic French café where soup-bowl-size café au lait, crepes, and salads are de rigueur, you can sit for hours without being disturbed.

4 **Joyce Theater.** When the former Elgin movie house dating to 1942 was gutted, what emerged in 1982 was this sleek modern theater with art deco touches. Today it's one of the city's leading modern-dance venues. ⊠ *175 8th Ave., at 19th St.,* ☎ *212/242–0800.*

11 **London Terrace Apartments.** When this 20-story, block-long wall of red and black brick first opened in 1930, the doormen dressed as London bobbies. Today, the desirable real estate is home to the fashion glitterati who work just up 7th Avenue in the garment district. ⊠ *W. 23rd to W. 24th Sts., between 9th and 10th Aves.*

5 **St. Peter's Episcopal Church.** Built in 1836 to 1838 on a rising tide of enthusiasm for Gothic revival architecture, the modest fieldstone St. Peter's is one of New York's first examples of early Gothic revival, though retaining elements of Greek revival style. To the left of the church, the brick **parish hall** is now the home of the Atlantic Theater Company, founded by playwright David Mamet. ⊠ *344 W. 20th St., between 8th and 9th Aves.,* ☎ *212/929–2390.*

1 **Siegel-Cooper Dry Goods Store.** Built in 1896, much later than its neighbors, this impressive building adorned with glazed terra-cotta encompasses 15½ acres of space, and yet it was built in only five months. In its retail heyday, the store's main floor had an immense fountain—a circular marble terrace with an enormous white-marble-and-brass replica of *The Republic*, the statue Daniel Chester French displayed at the 1883 Chicago World's Fair—which became a favorite rendezvous point for New Yorkers. During World War I the site was a military hospital. The building's splendid exterior ornamentation contrasts with its otherwise unremarkable brick facade. Today its principal tenants are Bed, Bath & Beyond, Filene's Basement, and T. J. Maxx. ⊠ *620 6th Ave., between 18th and 19th Sts.*

NEED A BREAK? **La Petite Abeille** (⊠ 107 W. 18th St., ☎ 212/604–9350), just west of 6th Avenue, serves tasty café standards in addition to traditional Belgian waffles, chocolates, and cookies. Tintin, the Belgian comic book hero, brightens the walls.

42ND STREET

Few streets in America claim as many landmarks as midtown Manhattan's central axis, from Times Square, Bryant Park, and the main branch of the New York Public Library on its western half to Grand Central Terminal and the United Nations on its eastern flank. And few can claim as colorful a reputation. After World War II, 42nd Street took a nosedive, as once-grand theaters around Times Square switched from showing burlesque and legitimate theater to second-run and pornographic movies. With that decline came pickpockets, prostitutes, and the destitute, and the area became synonymous with tawdry blight.

But the street has changed again, its metamorphosis starting slowly in the late 1980s and then proceeding more rapidly in the 1990s. First Bryant Park and then the block between 7th and 8th Avenues were nurtured back to life. 42nd Street is now poised to reclaim its fame as the mythical Broadway, with a steady stream of real-estate deals and ground-breakings; traffic-stopping celebrity appearances outside the Virgin Megastore and ABC and MTV studios; and new stores, hotels, and restaurants, many with entertainment themes, each visually louder than the last. Of course, the construction of the Condé Nast and Reuters buildings on Broadway and 7th Avenue, respectively, promise to maintain a significant intellectual presence amid the general gaiety. In Times Square itself, however, the neon lights shine brighter than ever— a local ordinance requires that massive billboard-style ads are included in all new construction. Some critics decry the "Disney-fication" of this part of town, but, really, what New York neighborhood is more appropriate for this over-the-top treatment?

A Good Walk

Begin at the corner of 42nd Street and 10th Avenue (or for the intrepid, at the *Intrepid Sea-Air-Space Museum* ①, four blocks north at the Hudson River). The block of 42nd Street stretching toward 9th Avenue is home to a string of thriving off-Broadway playhouses, called Theatre Row. Across the street, at 330 West 42nd Street, stands the first McGraw-Hill Building, designed in 1931 by Raymond Hood, who later worked on Rockefeller Center, where there is a later McGraw-Hill building. The lobby is an art deco wonder of opaque glass and stainless steel.

The monolithic Port Authority Bus Terminal, at 8th Avenue and West 42nd Street, bustles with the millions of travelers arriving and departing the city by bus each year. On the northwest corner of Eighth Avenue and 43rd Street, a four-story bank building, empty for eight years, has been redesigned by Dutch architect Rem Koolhaas as the new Second Stage Theater. On the southeast corner, an 860-room Westin Hotel, scheduled to open in the spring of 2002, is being built. Of course, the big story is what's happening on 42nd Street between 8th and 7th Avenues. Nine theaters once lined the street here, and for decades X-rated bookstores and peep shows were their only tenants. Some of these theaters have been immaculately restored or rehabilitated, their facades now beaming with high-wattage signs, while others await their turn. The E Walk complex stretches across the northeast portion of the street, comprising movie theaters, restaurants, arcades, and nightclubs.

East of E Walk on West 42nd Street's north side is a 10-story building of studios and theater space that bears the original facade of the Selwyn Theater enhanced by a network of computer-controlled multicolor lights. The Times Square Theater (⊠ 215 W. 42nd St.) is next door, where for two decades after its 1920 opening, top hits such as *Gentlemen Prefer Blondes, The Front Page,* and *Strike Up the Band* were staged; Noël Coward's *Private Lives* opened here with Gertrude Lawrence, Laurence Olivier, and the author himself. Continuing east toward Times Square, you'll find the **Ford Center for the Performing Arts** ② (which presents only a slim entrance on 42nd Street—the main facade is on 43rd Street and worth a detour) and the **New Victory Theater** ③, a reclaimed treasure that mounts theatrical productions for children. Across from the New Victory is the **New Amsterdam Theater** ④, resuscitated by the Walt Disney Company. Just to the west is **Madame Tussaud's New York** ⑤, where you can see life-size wax figures of major celebrities.

Times Square ⑥ is one of New York's principal energy centers, not least because of its dazzling billboards. Before continuing east on West 42nd Street, head north through Times Square to **Duffy Square** ⑦, a triangle between West 46th and 47th streets, the home of the TKTS discount ticket booth. On the east side of Broadway, the **Times Square Visitors Center** ⑧ in the historic Embassy Theater is a helpful all-in-one resource.

Walk east on West 43rd Street toward 6th Avenue, where you'll pass **Town Hall** ⑨, one of the city's premier musical venues for much of the century. At 6th Avenue and West 43rd Street, visit the newly enlarged **International Center of Photography** ⑩.

Before returning to West 42nd Street, you may want to stroll by the hotels and clubs along West 44th Street. Walking east, you'll first see the comfortably understated **Algonquin Hotel** ⑪, an old celebrity haunt. Next door is the Iroquois Hotel (✉ 49 W. 44th St.), where struggling actor James Dean lived in the early 1950s. Across the street from them is the Royalton Hotel (✉ 44 W. 44th St.), a midtown hot spot that was stylishly redone by French designer Philippe Starck. Its neighbor, at 42 West 44th Street, the Association of the Bar of the City of New York, has one of the country's largest law libraries and an 1896 neo-classical facade resembling the courthouses. At 37 West 44th Street is the New York Yacht Club (1900), which until 1983 had displayed the America's Cup trophy for 150 years. The swelling beaux arts windows look just like the sterns of ships, complete with stone-carved water splashing over the sills. Farther east is the redbrick Harvard Club (✉ 27 W. 44th St.); the newer Penn Club (✉ 30 W. 44th St.), with its elegant blue awning, is on the other side of the street. And, yes, something on this block is open to the public: the General Society of Mechanics and Tradesmen Building has Colonial-era objects on display.

At the southwest corner of 5th Avenue and 44th Street, notice the 19-ft-tall 1907 sidewalk clock on a pedestal set in the 5th Avenue sidewalk, a relic of an era when only the wealthy could afford watches.

At West 42nd Street and 6th Avenue, steps rise into the shrubbery and trees of the handsomely renovated **Bryant Park** ⑫, a perfect place to relax for a few minutes. The park has been adopted as the backyard of all midtown workers. It's directly behind the magnificent beaux arts building that houses the **New York Public Library Humanities and Social Sciences Library** ⑬, the central research branch of the city's library system.

Continue east on 42nd Street to **Grand Central Terminal** ⑭. Park Avenue wraps around Grand Central and continues to the north. The once-problematic architectural space beneath the overpass, directly opposite Grand Central's main entrance, is now brightly occupied by the Pershing Square Café, a restaurant with a tavern feel at night. On the southwest corner of Park Avenue and East 42nd Street, the **Whitney Museum of American Art at Philip Morris** ⑮ takes up the large ground floor of the Philip Morris Building. Back across the overpass is the monumental space of the former Bowery Savings Bank, (✉ 110 E. 42nd St.), built in 1923. With a five-story Romanesque arch and 70-ft-high marble columns, this indeed must have seemed, as critic Paul Goldberger has noted, "like the safest place in the world to place your dollars." At the end of the block is the 1929 Chanin Building (✉ 122 E. 42nd St.), notable for its inventive lobby detailing and the floral art deco patterns adorning its facade.

Ask New Yorkers to name their favorite skyscraper, and most will choose the art deco **Chrysler Building** ⑯ at East 42nd Street and Lexington Avenue. Although the Chrysler Corporation itself moved out long ago, this graceful shaft culminating in a stainless-steel spire still captivates the eye and the imagination. On the south side of East 42nd Street and east one block, the ***Daily News* Building** ⑰, where the newspaper was produced until the spring of 1995, is another art deco tower with a lobby worth visiting. The modern **Ford Foundation Building** ⑱ on the next block encloses a 160-ft-high, ⅓-acre greenhouse.

Climb the steps along East 42nd Street between 1st and 2nd avenues to enter **Tudor City** ⑲, a self-contained complex of a dozen buildings with half-timbering and stained glass. From here you have a great view of the **United Nations Headquarters** ⑳. To end this walk on a quiet note, walk up 1st Avenue and turn left on East 47th Street, where you will find the **Japan Society** ㉑, a lovely oasis of fine and performing arts from Japan.

TIMING

This long walk covers vastly different types of sights, from frenzied Times Square to bucolic Bryant Park, and from the ornate Grand Central Terminal to the sleek United Nations complex. If you start at the *Intrepid,* you could easily eat up most of a day even before you reach 5th Avenue. If you can, time your sight-seeing so you visit Times Square at night, perhaps for a meal or a show, to take in the spectacle of bright lights.

Sights to See
Numbers in the text correspond to numbers in the margin and on the Midtown map.

⓫ **Algonquin Hotel.** Considering its history as a haunt of well-known writers and actors, this 1902 hotel is surprisingly unpretentious. Its most famous association is with the Algonquin Round Table, a witty group of literary Manhattanites who gathered in its lobby and dining rooms in the 1920s—a clique that included short-story writer and critic Dorothy Parker, humorist Robert Benchley, playwright George S. Kaufman, journalist and critic Alexander Woolcott, and actress Tallulah Bankhead. One reason they met here was the hotel's proximity to the former offices of *The New Yorker* magazine at 28 West 44th Street (the magazine now resides in the new Condé Nast tower on Times Square). Come here for a cozy drink at the bar, dinner and cabaret performances in the intimate Oak Room, or just a walk through the muraled lobby. ⊠ *59 W. 44th St., between 5th and 6th Aves.,* ☎ *212/840–6800.*

OFF THE
BEATEN PATH
BEEKMAN PLACE – This secluded and exclusive two-block-long East Side enclave has an aura of imperturbably elegant calm. Residents of its town houses have included the Rockefellers; Alfred Lunt and Lynn Fontanne; Ethel Barrymore; Irving Berlin; and, of course, Auntie Mame, a character in the well-known Patrick Dennis play (and later movie) of the same name. Steps at East 51st Street lead to an esplanade along the East River. ⊠ *East of 1st Ave. between 49th and 51st Sts.*

★ ⓬ **Bryant Park.** Midtown's only major green spac, has become one of the best-loved and most beautiful small parks in the city. Named for the poet and editor William Cullen Bryant (1794–1878), the 8-acre park was originally known as Reservoir Square (the adjacent main branch of the **New York Public Library** stands on the former site of the city reservoir). America's first World's Fair, the Crystal Palace Exhibition, was held here in 1853–54. Today London plane trees and formal flower beds line the perimeter of its grassy central square. In temperate months the park draws thousands of lunching office workers; in summer it hosts live jazz and comedy concerts and sponsors free outdoor film screenings on Monday at dusk. At the east side of the park, near a squatting bronze cast of Gertrude Stein, is the open-air Bryant Park Café, which is open April 15–October 15, and the stylish Bryant Park Grill, which has a rooftop garden. The New York Chess Society sets up public tables near the west end fountain in good weather (a sign set in the lawn reads "Sociable Games Arranged"). In February and early September giant white tents spring up here for the New York fashion shows. ⊠ *6th Ave. between 40th and 42nd Sts.*, ☎ *212/768-4242*, 🆆🅔🅑 *www.bryantpark.org.* ☉ *Sept.–May, daily 7–7; June–Aug., daily 7 AM–9 PM.*

★ ⑯ **Chrysler Building.** An art deco masterpiece designed by William Van Alen and built between 1928 and 1930, the Chrysler Building is one of New York's most iconic and beloved skyscrapers. It's at its best at dusk, when the setting sun makes the stainless-steel spire glow, and at night, when its illuminated geometric design looks like the backdrop to a Hollywood musical. The Chrysler Corporation moved out in the mid-1950s, but the building retains its name and many automotive details: gargoyles shaped like car-hood ornaments sprout from the building's upper stories—wings from the 31st floor, eagle heads from the 61st. At 1,048 ft, the building only briefly held the world's-tallest title—for 40 days before the Empire State Building snatched it away. The Chrysler Building has no observation deck, but the elegant lobby faced with African marble is worth a visit; the ceiling mural salutes transportation and human endeavor. ⊠ *405 Lexington Ave., at 42nd St.*

⑰ *Daily News* **Building.** This Raymond Hood–designed art deco tower (1930) has brown-brick spandrels and windows that make it seem loftier than its 37 stories. The newspaper moved to the west side in 1995, but the famous, illuminated, 12-ft-wide globe set into a sunken space beneath a black dome continues to impress adults and children alike. The floor is laid out like a gigantic compass, with bronze lines indicating mileage from New York to various international destinations. ⊠ *220 E. 42nd St., between 2nd and 3rd Aves.*

❼ **Duffy Square.** This triangle at the north end of is named after World War I hero Father Francis P. Duffy (1871–1932), known as "the fighting chaplain," who later was pastor of Holy Cross Church on West 42nd Street. There's also a statue of George M. Cohan (1878–1942), who wrote "Yankee Doodle Dandy." The square is one of the best places for a panoramic view of Times Square's riotous assemblage of signs. At its north end the **TKTS discount ticket booth** sells discounted tickets to Broadway and off-Broadway shows. ⊠ *In traffic island between W. 46th and 47th Sts.*

❷ **Ford Center for the Performing Arts.** On the site of two classic 42nd Street theaters, the Ford Center incorporates a landmark 43rd Street exterior wall from the Lyric (built in 1903) and architectural elements from the Apollo (1910), including its stage, proscenium, and dome (the other parts of the theaters, which had fallen into disrepair, were demolished). A 1,006-seat orchestra, two 350-seat balconies, and a huge stage make it likely the Ford will continue to be a leading venue for large-scale productions. Such a future is in keeping with the Lyric's and Apollo's history: in the early part of this century, the top talents they attracted to their stages included the Marx Brothers, Fred Astaire, Ethel Merman, and W. C. Fields. ⊠ *213 W. 42nd St., between 7th and 8th Aves.*, ☎ *212/307–4100 for tickets.*

⑱ **Ford Foundation Building.** Home to one of the largest philanthropic organizations in the world, the Ford Foundation Building, built by Kevin Roche, John Dinkeloo & Associates in 1967, is best known for its glass-wall, 12-story-high atrium, which doubles as a ⅓-acre greenhouse. Workers whose offices line the interior walls enjoy a placid view of its trees, terraced garden, and still-water pool. ⊠ *320 E. 43rd St., between 1st and 2nd Aves., with an entrance on 42nd St.* 🆓 *Free.* ☉ *Weekdays 9–5:30.*

OFF THE
BEATEN PATH

GARMENT DISTRICT – This district, which runs along 7th Avenue between West 31st and 41st streets (where it's known as Fashion Avenue), teems with warehouses, workshops, and showrooms that manufacture and finish mostly women's and children's clothing, and countless fabric, button, and notions shops. On weekdays the streets are crowded with trucks and the sidewalks swarm with daredevil deliverymen wheeling garment racks between factories and subcontractors. At the southern edge of the district you'll find New York's Amtrak terminal at **Pennsylvania Station** (⌧ W. 31st to 34th Sts., between 7th and 8th Aves.); major sporting, entertainment and other events at **Madison Square Garden** (⌧ W. 31st to 34th Sts., between 7th and 8th Aves.); and the **General Post Office** (⌧ 8th Ave. and 33rd St., ☎ 212/967–8585), which is open 24 hours a day, 365 days a year.

★ ⓮ **Grand Central Terminal.** Grand Central is not only the world's largest railway station (76 acres) and the nation's busiest (500,000 commuters and subway riders use it daily); it's also one of the world's greatest public spaces, "justly famous," as critic Tony Hiss has said, "as a crossroads, a noble building . . . and an ingenious piece of engineering." A massive four-year renovation completed in October 1998 restored the 1913 landmark to its original splendor—and then some.

The south side of East 42nd Street is the best vantage point from which to admire Grand Central's dramatic beaux arts facade, which is dominated by three 75-ft-high arched windows separated by pairs of fluted columns. At the top are a beautiful clock and a crowning sculpture, *Transportation,* which depicts Mercury flanked by Hercules and Minerva. The facade is particularly beautiful at night, when bathed in golden light. Doors on Vanderbilt Avenue and on East 42nd Street lead past gleaming gold- and nickel-plated chandeliers to the cavernous **main concourse.** This majestic space is 200 ft long, 120 ft wide, and 120 ft—roughly 12 stories—high. Overhead, you'll see a massive, robin's egg–blue ceiling covered with a celestial map that gloriously displays the constellations of the zodiac (the major stars actually glow with fiber-optic lights). A new marble staircase modeled after the Garnier stair at the Paris Opera has been belatedly, yet seamlessly, installed onto the concourse's east end. Up the west staircase to the left you'll find the Campbell Apartment, an extremely comfortable and stylish cocktail and cigar bar in what was once a rather secretive pied-à-terre. To the right is the mahogany-and-leather Michael Jordan's The Steak House, which overlooks the main concourse.

Dozens of other restaurants (including an outpost of the popular Brooklyn deli, Junior's, and the mammoth Oyster Bar) and shops, many in spaces long closed to the public, are making the downstairs **dining concourse** a destination in its own right. It has an entrance on Lexington Avenue and 43rd Street.

Despite all its grandeur, Grand Central still functions primarily as a railroad station. Underground, more than 60 ingeniously integrated railroad tracks lead trains upstate and to Connecticut via MetroNorth Commuter Rail. The best (and worst) time to visit is at rush hour, when the concourse whirs with the frenzy of commuters dashing every which way. ⌧ *Main entrance: E. 42nd St. at Park Ave.,* ☎ *212/935–3960 for tour information.* 🎫 *Tour free (donations to the Municipal Art Society accepted).* ☉ *Tours Wed. at 12:30 (meet in front of information booth inside terminal on main level).*

EVERYTHING YOU ALWAYS WANTED TO KNOW ABOUT THE SUBWAY

NEW YORK CITY has always had a reputation for innovation, so it's not surprising that the world's first elevated railcar ran on tracks between Prince and 14th streets. The fledgling journey took place in 1832, marking the advent of New York City public transit. Necessity was the mother of this invention—the city's population was growing rapidly, fostering the need for affordable and accessible rapid transit. But it would be seven decades before New York's transportation went underground.

By the end of the 19th century New York City was the largest commercial and industrial metropolis in the world. But while subways had already opened in many other cities worldwide, New York's "public" transportation consisted primarily of horse-drawn streetcars owned and operated by private companies. A few steam-powered elevated trains known as "els" ran above the congested city streets, offering the only alternative to the omnibuses. The omnibuses and els were clearly inadequate for New York, but the proposed subway system spent the last three decades of the 19th century on hold, a victim of bureaucratic corruption and incompetence.

The stranglehold finally broke in 1894 when New Yorkers voted overwhelmingly for public ownership of the subway. This decision, one of the first major public issues decided by the city's people, gave the city ownership of the yet-to-be built subway system's physical plant. At the groundbreaking ceremony on March 24, 1900, Mayor Robert A. Van Wyck used a silver spade from Tiffany's. Over the next four years, 12,000 mostly immigrant workers built the first subway routes. These laborers worked 10-hour days for 20¢ an hour. More than 50 men died and thousands were maimed while building what became the Interborough Rapid Transit (IRT) line. The 9.1 miles of track began at City Hall, continued north to Grand Central, crossed town, and then ran up Broadway to West 145th Street.

On October 27, 1904, the IRT finally opened. And while New York's subway was not the world's first, it was the first to use electric signals on all its tracks. On opening day, a nickel bought a ticket. Platform attendants watched the "ticket chopper," a collection box made of oak and glass. In the IRT's first year, passengers took more than a billion rides. Many changes were to come. Turnstiles appeared in 1928, but tickets remained, and it would be another 20 years before the fare rose to a dime. In 1953 tokens replaced tickets and the fare rose to 15¢.

Those original 9 mi of track have now grown to over 700 mi. The fare has grown too, of course, to $1.50, but the New York City subway is still one of this city's great bargains—and one of its most distinctive features. To learn more, visit **The New York Transit Museum** (✉ Boerum Pl. at Schermerhorn St., ☎ 718/243–3060) in downtown Brooklyn.

OFF THE
BEATEN PATH

HELL'S KITCHEN – In an area bordered by West 59th Street, the Hudson River, West 30th Street, and 8th Avenue, with such uninviting landmarks as the Port Authority Bus Terminal and the entrances to the Lincoln Tunnel, Hell's Kitchen has made a neighborhood of itself. As the name suggests, the first waves of immigrants who settled here did not find the living easy. The gritty appellation came either from a gang that ruled the area in the late 1860s, or a nickname local cops gave it in the 1870s. Today the area is home to dozens of restaurants and take-out eateries, and developers have taken to calling it Clinton.

From West 34th to 39th streets between 11th Avenue and the West Side Highway, the massive **Jacob Javits Convention Center** (✉ 655 W. 34th Street, ☎ 212/216–2000) brings thousands of visitors to the neighborhood each month for business and entertainment events. Along **9th Avenue,** sidewalks are lined with perhaps the world's largest assortment of ethnic cafés and groceries. In an area short on attractions, it's easy to entertain yourself for an afternoon in the many storefronts offering international delicacies. Each May, the **9th Avenue Food Festival** brings tens of thousands of visitors to Hell's Kitchen for exotic tasting treats.

NEED A
BREAK?

On 9th Avenue at West 42nd Street, the handsome **Chimichurri Grill** (✉ No. 606) serves Argentine steak. **Lakuwana** (✉ 358 W. 44th St., east of 9th Ave.) prepares the food of Sri Lanka. Across the avenue, the pastry masters at **Poseidon Bakery** (✉ No. 629) have been rolling out beautiful homemade phyllo dough and putting it to delectable use since 1923. **Bali Nusa Indah** (✉ No. 651) has a spicy and highly satisfying Indonesian menu. **Amy's Bread** (✉ No. 672) has quickly become a New York institution. Guess what you'll be eating at **Rice and Beans** (✉ No. 744) at West 50th Street, a tiny and excellent Brazilian restaurant?

❿ International Center of Photography (ICP). The city's leading photography-only venue recently consolidated a former uptown collection and underwent a large expansion, including an expanded bookstore facing 6th Avenue, a doubling of exhibition space, and the addition of a café. Founded in 1974 by photojournalist Cornell Capa (photographer Robert Capa's brother), ICP's exhibits from its permanent collection of 45,000 works often focus on one photographic genre (portraits, architecture, etc.) or the work of a single prominent photographer. The bookstore carries books, prints, and postcards. ✉ *1133 6th Ave., at 43rd St.,* ☎ *212/860–1777,* WEB *www.icp.org.* ✎ *$8; Fri. 5–8 pay what you wish.* ☉ *Tues.–Thurs. 10–5, Fri. 10–8, weekends 10–6.*

☝ ❶ Intrepid Sea-Air-Space Museum. Formerly the USS *Intrepid,* this 900-ft aircraft carrier is serving out its retirement as the centerpiece of Manhattan's only floating museum. An A-12 Blackbird spy plane, lunar landing modules, helicopters, seaplanes, and other aircraft are on deck. Docked alongside, and also part of the museum, are the *Growler,* a strategic-missile submarine; the *Edson,* a Vietnam-era destroyer; and several other battle-scarred naval veterans. Children will enjoy exploring the ships' skinny hallways and winding staircases, as well as manipulating countless knobs, buttons, and wheels. For an extra thrill (and an extra $5), they can try the Navy Flight Simulator and "land" an aircraft onboard. ✉ *Hudson River, Pier 86 (12th Ave. and 46th St.),* ☎ *212/245–0072,* WEB *www.intrepidmuseum.org.* ✎ *$12; free to active U.S. military personnel.* ☉ *May–Sept., weekdays 10–5, weekends 10–6; Oct.–Apr., Tues.–Sun. 10–5 (last admission 1 hr before closing).*

㉑ Japan Society. The stylish and serene lobby of the Society has interior bamboo gardens linked by a second-floor waterfall. Works by well-known Japanese artists are exhibited in the second-floor gallery—a recent exhibition showcased the first-ever retrospective of Yoko Ono's works. Cultural events, movies, lectures, language classes, concerts, and dramatic performances are also hosted. ⊠ *333 E. 47th St., between 1st and 2nd Aves.,* ☎ *212/832–1155,* WEB *www.japansociety.org.* ⊠ *$5.* ☉ *Tues.–Fri. 11–6, weekends 11–5.*

❺ Madame Tussaud's New York. Go ahead, get close to Oprah, stare down Don King, and heckle Regis Philbin. You'll encounter all three celebs at this display of nearly 200 astoundingly lifelike historical, cultural, and popular characters in wax. The original Madame Tussaud's, which she opened in London in 1835, is now England's top tourist draw; the opening of this branch on West 42nd Street confirms Times Square's status as New York's major entertainment destination. Inside, eerie Parisian tableaus, with a simulated guillotine and heads lying about cobblestone streets, make Halloween an excellent time to visit. But the realism of the American celebrities depicted in the "Opening Night Party" room is creepy all year: crowded with A-list celebs and a gawking swirl of tourists, the room induces a kind of vertigo, and you can't tell who's fake anymore—though Woody Allen, grinning alone in a corner, seems to get the last laugh. ⊠ *234 W. 42nd St., between 7th and 8th Aves.,* ☎ *212/512–9600,* WEB *www.madame-tussauds.com.* ⊠ *$19.95 (includes movie).* ☉ *Sun.–Thurs. 10–6, Fri.–Sat. 10–8.*

★ **❹ New Amsterdam Theater.** The street's most glorious theater, neglected for decades, triumphantly returned to life in 1997 following a breathtaking restoration. Built in 1903 by Herts & Tallant, the dazzling theater had an innovative cantilevered balcony and was the original home of the Ziegfeld Follies. Years of decay—the flooded orchestra pit was home to an 8-ft tree complete with birds' nests—had left the theater in structural and aesthetic ruins. With the backing of its new tenant, the Walt Disney Company, the 1,814-seat Art Nouveau theater was painstakingly restored by Hardy, Holzman, Pfeiffer, the New York firm that also rehabilitated the New Victory Theater, Radio City Music Hall, and Bryant Park. Today the theater is "a magical place," architecture critic Ada Louise Huxtable has said, "from the elaborate peacock proscenium arch to the nymphet heads illuminating columns with halos of incandescent lights." Outside, the 1940s-vintage art deco facade, installed when the theater became a movie house, was retained in the renovation. The stage version of Disney's *The Lion King,* which opened in 1997 to critical accolades and commercial success, is likely to run here for years to come. If you can't get tickets, tours reveal the now-gorgeous theater contrasted with large mounted photographs documenting its pre-renovation disrepair. The theater's old, ruined state is also captured in the movie *Uncle Vanya on 42nd Street.* ⊠ *214 W. 42nd St., between 7th and 8th Aves.,* ☎ *212/282–2900; 212/282–2907 for information on theater tours.* ☉ *Tours: Mon. 10–5 and Tues. 10–1, every hour on the hour.* ⊠ *Tour admission $10.*

★ ☺ **❸ New Victory Theater.** Since its superb restoration in 1995, the New Victory can make three unique claims: it was the first 42nd Street theater to be renovated as part of the revitalization of Times Square, it's the oldest New York theater still in operation, and it's the city's only theater devoted exclusively to productions for children and families. Special programs for teenagers, called VicTeens, include a night out with the cast. Oscar Hammerstein built the theater in 1900 (his more famous grandson, Oscar Hammerstein II, wrote the lyrics to such shows as *Oklahoma!* and *Carousel*). Acting legends Lionel Barrymore, Lillian Gish, Mary Pickford, and Tyrone Power strutted across its stage, and in the 1930s it was Broadway's first burlesque house. Today yellow-and-purple signs beckon from the elegant Venetian facade, and a gracious double staircase rises to a second-floor entry. Inside, garland-bearing *putti* (cupids) perch casually on the edge of the theater's dome above gilded deep-red walls. Unlike its neighboring theaters with long-running shows, the productions at the New Victory change every two weeks. ⊠ *209 W. 42nd St., between 7th and 8th Aves.,* ☎ *212/382–4000 for tickets,* WEB *www.newvictory.org.*

★ ⑬ **New York Public Library (NYPL) Humanities and Social Sciences Library.** This 1911 masterpiece of beaux arts design (Carrère and Hastings, architects) is one of the great research institutions in the world, with 6 million books, 12 million manuscripts, and 2.8 million pictures. But you don't have to crack a book to make it worth visiting: both inside and out, this stunning building, a National Historic Landmark, will take your breath away with its opulence.

Originally financed in large part by a bequest from former New York governor Samuel J. Tilden, the library combined the resources of two 19th-century libraries: the Lenox Library and the Astor Library. The latter, founded by John Jacob Astor, was housed in a building downtown that has since been turned into the Joseph Papp Public Theater. Today, the library anchors a network of close to 200 local branches throughout the city and encompasses a variety of unusual behind-the-scenes collections, ranging from sets of 19th- and early 20th-century menus to the personal library of magician Harry Houdini.

To make a grand entry, walk around to 5th Avenue just south of 42nd Street, where **two marble lions** guard the flagstone plaza in front. Mayor Fiorello La Guardia, who said he visited the facility to "read between the lions," dubbed them "Patience" and "Fortitude." Statues and inscriptions cover the white-marble neoclassical facade; in good weather the block-long grand marble staircase is a perfect spot to people-watch.

The library's bronze front doors open into the magnificent marble **Astor Hall,** flanked by a sweeping double staircase. Upstairs on the third floor, the magisterial **Rose Main Reading Room**—297 ft long (almost two full north–south city blocks), 78 ft wide, and just over 51 ft high—is one of the world's grandest library interiors. Completely renovated in 1998, it has original chandeliers, oak tables, and bronze reading lamps that gleam as if they were new. Gaze up at the ceiling and you'll see newly repainted murals of blue sky and puffy clouds, inspired by Tiepolo and Tintoretto. Exhibitions on photography, typography, literature, book-making, and maps are held regularly in the **Gottesman Exhibition Hall,** the **Edna B. Salomon Room,** the **Third Floor Galleries,** and the **Berg Exhibition Room** (exhibit information is available at 212/869–8089). Among the treasures you might see are Gilbert Stuart's portrait of George Washington, Charles Dickens's desk, and Charles Addams cartoons. Free one-hour tours leave Monday–Saturday at 11 and 2 from Astor Hall. ⊠ *5th Ave. between 40th and 42nd Sts.,* ☎ *212/930–0800.* ☉ *Mon. and Thurs.–Sat. 10–6, Tues.–Wed. 11–7:30 (exhibitions until 6).*

⑥ **Times Square.** Whirling in a chaos of dazzling light, Times Square is New York's white-hot energy center. Hordes of people, mostly tourists, crowd it day and night to walk and gawk. It would take hours of fixed concentration to really see what's going on here, in the confusion of lights, billboards, people, stores, and traffic. Like many New York City "squares," it's actually two triangles formed by the angle of Broadway slashing across 7th Avenue between West 42nd and 47th streets. Times Square (the name also applies to the general area, beyond the intersection of these streets) has been the city's main theater district since the turn of the century: from West 44th to 51st streets, the cross streets west of Broadway are lined with some 30 major theaters; film houses joined the fray beginning in the 1920s.

Before the turn of the 20th century, this was New York's horse-trading center, known as Long Acre Square. Substantial change came with the arrival of the subway and the *New York Times,* then a less prestigious paper, which moved here in exchange for having its name grace the square. On December 31, 1904, the *Times* celebrated the opening of its new headquarters, at Times Tower (⊠ W. 42nd St. between Broadway and 7th Ave.), with a fireworks show at midnight, thereby starting a New Year's Eve tradition. Now resheathed in marble and called **One Times Square Plaza,** the building is topped with the world's most famous rooftop pole, down which an illuminated 200-pound ball is lowered each December 31 to the wild enthusiasm of revelers below. (In the 1920s the *Times* moved to its present building, a green-copper-roof neo-Gothic behemoth, at 229 West 43rd Street.)

Times Square is hardly more sedate on the other 364 nights of the year, mesmerizing visitors with its usual high-wattage thunder: two-story-high cups of coffee that actually steam; a 42-ft-tall bottle of Coca-Cola; huge billboards of underwear models; a mammoth, superfast digital display offering world news and stock quotes; on-location network studios; and countless other technologically sophisticated allurements. Such madness often leads Times Square to be called the center of the world. For American teenagers, there can be no doubt. MTV moved its studios to the heart of the square recently, and throngs of teens gather each afternoon hoping to be chosen to be part of a show called Total Request Live. TRL, as it's popularly known, is filmed live from the second-floor glass windows at West 44th Street and Broadway. Since such well-known acts as the Backstreet Boys, Eminem, and Britney Spears make regular rounds here, Times Square has become a mecca for youth. The cleanup of Times Square will not turn out the lights, because current zoning *requires* that buildings be decked out with ads, as they have been for nearly a century. The traffic island in front of the Armed Forces Recruiting Office (it, too, has been re-done, in a larger, shinier metal box with neon American flags) provides the best angles on the whole of Times Square's helter-skelter welter. ⊠ *W. 42nd to 47th Sts. at Broadway and 7th Ave.*

❽ Times Square Visitors Center. When it opened in 1925, the Embassy Theater was an exclusive, high-society movie theater; a few years ago the lobby of this landmark theater was transformed into the city's first comprehensive visitor's center. Now anyone can get general Times Square information; buy sightseeing and theater tickets, MetroCards, and transit memorabilia; use ATMs; and get free Internet access. There is also a video camera that shoots and e-mails instant photos. Free walking tours are given Friday at noon. Perhaps most important, its rest rooms are the only facilities in the vicinity open to the non-paying public. ⊠ *1560 Broadway, between 46th and 47th Sts.,* ☏ *212/869–1890,* WEB *www.timessquarebid.com.* ✆ *Daily 8–8.*

❾ Town Hall. Founded by suffragists in 1921 seeking a venue from which to educate women on political issues (Margaret Sanger was arrested here on November 12, 1921, while speaking about birth control), Town Hall instead quickly became one of the city's premier musical venues when its acoustics were accidentally discovered in its inaugural year. The landmark McKim, Mead and White Federal revival building was designed with democracy in mind—there are no box seats and no obstructed views, giving rise to the phrase "not a bad seat in the house." Today a mix of musicians and entertainers, from Ravi Shankar to Garrison Keillor, performs here. ⊠ *123 W. 43rd St., between 6th and 7th Aves.,* ☎ *212/840–2824.* ⊙ *Box Office Mon.–Sat. noon–6.*

⑲ Tudor City. Built between 1925 and 1928 to attract middle-income residents, this private "city" on a bluff above East 42nd Street west of 1st Avenue occupies 12 buildings containing 3,000 apartments. Two of the buildings originally had no east-side windows, so the tenants wouldn't be forced to gaze at the slaughterhouses, breweries, and glue factories then crowding the shore of the East River. The terrace at the end of East 43rd Street now affords great views of the **United Nations headquarters** and stands at the head of **Sharansky Steps** (named for Natan [Anatoly] Sharansky, the Soviet dissident). The steps run along **Isaiah Wall** (inscribed THEY SHALL BEAT THEIR SWORDS INTO PLOW-SHARES); below are **Ralph J. Bunche Park,** named for the African-American former U.N. undersecretary, and **Raoul Wallenberg Walk,** named for the Swedish diplomat and World War II hero who saved many Hungarian Jews from the Nazis. ⊠ *1st and 2nd Aves. from 40th to 43rd Sts.*

★ ⑳ United Nations Headquarters. Officially an "international zone," not part of the United States, the U.N. Headquarters is a working symbol of global cooperation. The 18-acre riverside tract, now lushly landscaped, was bought and donated by oil magnate John D. Rockefeller Jr. in 1946. The headquarters were built in 1947–53 by an international team led by Wallace Harrison. The slim, 505-ft-tall green-glass **Secretariat Building;** the much smaller, domed **General Assembly Building;** and the **Dag Hammarskjöld Library** (1963) form the complex, before which fly the flags of member nations in alphabetical order, from Afghanistan to Zimbabwe, when the General Assembly is in session (mid-September to mid-December). Architecturally, the U.N. buildings are evocative of Le Corbusier, and their windswept park and plaza remain visionary: there is a beautiful riverside promenade, a rose garden with 1,400 rosebushes, and sculptures donated by member nations.

An hour-long guided tour (given in 20 languages) is the main visitor attraction; it includes the **General Assembly,** the **Security Council Chamber,** the **Trustee Council Chamber,** and the **Economic and Social Council Chamber,** though some rooms may be closed on any given day. Displays on war, nuclear energy, and refugees are also part of the tour; corridors overflow with imaginatively diverse artwork donated by member nations. Free tickets to assemblies are sometimes available on a first-come, first-served basis before sessions begin; pick them up in the General Assembly lobby. The **Delegates Dining Room** (☎ 212/963–7625) is open for a reasonably priced (up to $20) lunch weekdays (jackets required for men; reservations required at least one day in advance). The public concourse, one level down from the visitor entrance, has a coffee shop, gift shops, bookstore, and a post office where you can mail letters with U.N. stamps. ⊠ *Visitor entrance: 1st Ave. and 46th St.,* ☎ *212/963–7713.* ▣ *Tour $7.50.* ⊙ *Tours daily 9:15–4:45; hour-long tours in English leave General Assembly lobby every 15 mins. Children under 5 not admitted.*

⑮ Whitney Museum of American Art at Philip Morris. An enormous, 42-ft-high sculpture court with outstanding examples of 20th-century sculpture, many of which are simply too big for the Whitney's uptown base, is the centerpiece of the museum's midtown branch. In the adjacent gallery five shows a year cover all aspects of American art. An espresso bar and seating areas make this an agreeable place to rest. ⊠ *120 Park Ave., at 42nd St.,* ☎ *917/663–2453.* ▣ *Free.* ⊙ *Sculpture court Mon.–Sat. 7:30 AM–9:30 PM, Sun. 11–7; gallery Mon.–Wed. and Fri. 11–6, Thurs. 11–7:30.*

ROCKEFELLER CENTER
AND MIDTOWN SKYSCRAPERS

Athens has its Parthenon and Rome its Colosseum. New York's temples, which you see on this mile-long tour along six avenues and five streets, are its concrete-and-glass skyscrapers. Many of them, including the Lever House and the Seagram Building, have been pivotal in the history of modern architecture, and the 19 limestone-and-aluminum buildings of Rockefeller Center constitute one of the world's most famous pieces of real estate.

Conceived by John D. Rockefeller during the Great Depression of the 1930s, the Rockefeller center complex—"the greatest urban complex of the 20th century," according to the *AIA Guide to New York City*—occupies nearly 22 acres of prime real estate between 5th and 7th Avenues and West 47th and 52nd streets. Its central cluster of buildings consists of smooth shafts of warm-hued limestone, streamlined with glistening aluminum. Plazas, concourses, and shops create a sense of community for the nearly quarter of a million people who use it daily. Restaurants, shoe-repair shops, doctors' offices, barbershops, banks, a post office, bookstores, clothing shops, variety stores—all are accommodated within the center, and all parts of the complex are linked by underground passageways.

Rockefeller Center helped turn midtown into New York City's second "downtown" area. The neighborhood now rivals the Wall Street area in its number of prestigious tenants. The center itself is a capital of the communications industry, containing the headquarters of a TV network (NBC), several major publishing companies (Time-Warner, McGraw-Hill, Simon & Schuster), and the world's largest news-gathering organization, the Associated Press.

Numbers in the text correspond to numbers in the margin and on the Midtown map.

A Good Walk

An anchor of midtown Manhattan is **Rockefeller Center** (212/632–3975 for information), one of the greatest achievements in 20th-century urban planning. A fun way to navigate among its myriad buildings is to move from east to west, following a trail past three famous figures from Greek mythology. Atlas stands sentry outside the classically inspired **International Building** ㉒, on 5th Avenue between 50th and 51st streets directly across from St. Patrick's Cathedral. Head one block south on 5th Avenue and turn west to walk along the **Channel Gardens** ㉓, a promenade of rock pools and seasonal flower beds. At the far end is the sunken **Lower Plaza** ㉔ and its famous gold-leaf statue of Prometheus. The backdrop to this scene is the 70-story **GE Building** ㉕, originally known as the RCA Building, whose entrance is guarded by another striking statue of Prometheus. Straight across bustling West 50th Street is America's largest indoor theater, the titanic **Radio City Music Hall** ㉖.

On the west side of 6th Avenue, from West 47th to 51st streets, stand four towers that form the **Rockefeller Center Extension** ㉗, part of a mid-1960s expansion.

Continue north on 6th Avenue, leaving Rockefeller Center. On the east side of 6th Avenue between West 52nd and 53rd Streets, the monolithic black **CBS Building** ㉘ (also known as Black Rock) stands out from the crowd. From here it's a short stroll to three museums enshrining contemporary culture. Go east on West 52nd Street to the **Museum of**

Television and Radio ㉙, devoted to the two key mediums of the modern era. Right next door is the landmark **"21" Club** ㉚. A shortcut through the outdoor public space close to the CBS Building or through a shopping arcade farther east, at 666 5th Avenue, takes you to West 53rd Street's museums: on the south side, the **American Craft Museum** ㉛, and on the north side, the **Museum of Modern Art (MoMA)** ㉜. (Note that this location will be closed beginning summer 2002 for renovations. During construction, the museum will relocate to 45–20 33rd Street, Long Island City, Queens. For more information, call 212/708–9400.) A block east of MoMA, across 5th Avenue at 3 East 53rd Street, is **Paley Park** ㉝, a small vest-pocket park with a waterfall.

The true muse of midtown is not art, however, but business, as you'll see on a brisk walk east on 53rd Street across 5th Avenue, where you'll encounter four office towers named after their corporate owners. First head north on Madison Avenue to East 55th Street and the elegant rose-granite tower known as the **Sony Building** ㉞, immediately recognizable from afar by its Chippendale-style pediment. Farther east and a little south on Park Avenue stand two prime examples of the functionalist International Style: **Lever House** ㉟ and the **Seagram Building** ㊱, the only New York building designed by Ludwig Mies van der Rohe. Finally, go one block east to Lexington Avenue and the Turtle Bay district where, between East 53rd and 54th streets, the luminous silvery shaft of the **Citicorp Center** ㊲ houses thousands more New Yorkers engaged in the daily ritual that built the city—commerce. To end your walk on a less material note, return to Park Avenue and turn southeast to 51st Street and **St. Bartholomew's Church** ㊳.

TIMING

To see only the buildings, block out an hour and a half. Allow more time depending on your interest in the museums en route. At minimum you might spend 45 minutes in the American Craft Museum; the same in the Museum of Television and Radio; and 2½ hours in the Museum of Modern Art—even then you'll only dip briefly into the collections; it would be easy to pass an entire day there, ending with a movie in the museum's theater. Keep in mind that some parts of Rockefeller Center are open only during the week.

Start early in order to arrive at the Museum of Television and Radio when it opens, so you won't have to wait for a TV console on which to watch your shows; break up your MoMA visit with lunch in its café.

Sights to See

㉛ **American Craft Museum.** Distinctions between the terms *craft* and *high art* become irrelevant at this small museum, which showcases works in clay, glass, fabric, wood, metal, paper, and even chocolate by contemporary American and international artisans. ⊠ *40 W. 53rd St., between 5th and 6th Aves.,* ☏ *212/956–3535,* WEB *www.americancraftmuseum. org.* ⊑ *$5.* ☉ *Tues., Wed., and Fri.–Sun. 10–6; Thurs. 10–8.*

㉘ **CBS Building.** The only high-rise designed by Eero Saarinen, Black Rock, as this 38-story building is known, was built in 1965. Its dark-gray granite facade actually helps to hold the building up, imparting a sense of towering solidity. ⊠ *51 W. 52nd St., at 6th Ave.*

㉓ **Channel Gardens.** Separating the British Empire Building to the north from the Maison Française to the south (and thus the "Channel"), this busy promenade of six pools surrounded by seasonal gardens leads the eye from 5th Avenue to the **Lower Plaza.** The center's horticulturist conceived the gardens and presents around 10 often stunning shows a season. The French building contains, among other shops, the Metropolitan Museum of Art gift shop and the Librairie de France,

Midtown

Columbus Circle

W. 58th St.
W. 57th St.
W. 56th St.
W. 55th St.
W. 54th St.
W. 53rd St.
W. 52nd St.
W. 51st St.
W. 50th St.
W. 49th St.
W. 48th St.
W. 47th St.
W. 46th St.
W. 45th St.
W. 44th St.
W. 43rd St.
W. 42nd St.
W. 41st St.
W. 40th St.
W. 39th St.
W. 38th St.

Broadway
Ninth Ave.
Eighth Ave.
Seventh Ave.
Avenue of the Americas
[Sixth Ave.]
Fifth Ave.
Rockefeller Plaza

Russian Tea Room
Fifth Avenue Presbyterian Church
New York Hilton
Sheraton New York
Equitable Center
Paine Webber Art Gallery
Time & Life Building
Rockefeller Center
Dahesh Museum
TKTS Ticket Booth
Marriott Marquis
Times Square
Theatre Row
Port Authority Bus Terminal
Bryant Park

THEATER DISTRICT
HELL'S KITCHEN
DIAMOND DISTRICT
GARMENT DISTRICT

42nd Street
Algonquin Hotel **11**
Bryant Park **12**
Chrysler Building **16**
Daily News Building **17**
Duffy Square **7**
Ford Center for the Performing Arts **2**
Ford Foundation Building **18**

Grand Central Terminal **14**
International Center of Photography (ICP) . . .**10**
Intrepid Sea-Air-Space Museum **1**
Japan Society **21**
Madame Tussaud's New York **5**
New Amsterdam Theater **4**

New Victory Theater **3**
New York Public Library Humanities and Social Sciences Library **13**
Times Square **6**
Times Square Visitors Center **8**
Town Hall **9**
Tudor City **19**

United Nations Headquarters **20**
Whitney Museum of American Art at Philip Morris **15**

Rockefeller Center and Midtown Skyscrapers
American Craft Museum **31**
CBS Building **28**

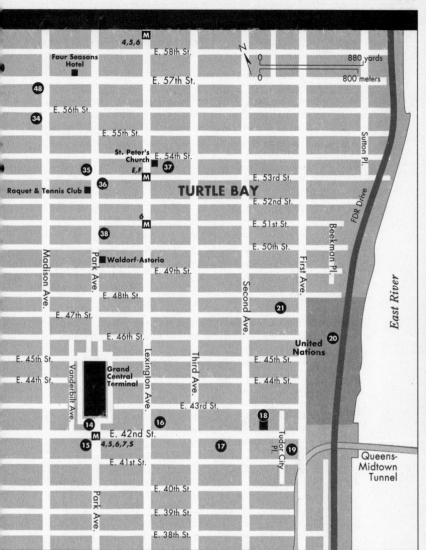

which sells French-language books, periodicals, tapes, and recordings. The building's surprisingly large basement contains a Spanish bookstore and a foreign-language dictionary store. ⊠ *5th Ave. between 49th and 50th Sts.*

㊲ **Citicorp Center.** The most striking feature of this 1977 design by Hugh Stubbins & Associates is the angled top. The immense solar-energy collector it was designed to carry was never installed, but the building's unique profile changed the New York City skyline. At the base of Citicorp Center is an atrium mall of restaurants and shops, where occasionally there's music at lunchtime. **St. Peter's Church** (☏ 212/935-2200), whose angled roof is tucked under the Citicorp shadow, is known for its Sunday-afternoon jazz vespers, at 5. ⊠ *Lexington Ave. between 53rd and 54th Sts.*

OFF THE
BEATEN PATH

CORPORATE-SPONSORED EXHIBITS – Although it's not Museum Mile, midtown does benefit from companies that use part of their space to present free public exhibits. The **Paine Webber Art Gallery** (⊠ 1285 6th Ave., between 51st and 52nd Sts., ☏ 212/713-2885), open weekdays 8–6, hosts four exhibits a year in the base of its building. The **Equitable Center** (⊠ 787 7th Ave., at 51st St., ☏ 212/554-4818) has an enormous Roy Lichtenstein work in its atrium and a gallery with changing exhibits; it's open weekdays 11–6, Saturday noon–5.

DIAMOND DISTRICT – The relatively unglitzy jewelry shops at street level on West 47th Street between 5th and 6th Avenues are just the tip of the iceberg; upstairs, millions of dollars' worth of gems are traded, and skilled craftsmen cut precious stones. Wheeling and dealing goes on at fever pitch amongst the host of Hasidic Jews in severe black dress, beards, and curled side locks. So thronged with people is this street during the day that it becomes one of the slowest to navigate on foot in Manhattan. Nearly lost in the shuffle is a sign hung over the northern sidewalk that reads "Wise Men Fish Here": a lure to the Gotham Book Mart, a New York literary landmark.

㉕ **GE Building.** The backdrop to the **Channel Gardens, Prometheus,** and the **Lower Plaza,** this 70-story (850-ft tall) building is the tallest tower in Rockefeller Center. It was known as the RCA Building until GE acquired its namesake company in 1986 (it is also known as 30 Rock): today it's also the headquarters of the NBC television network. The block-long street called Rockefeller Plaza, which runs north–south between the GE Building and the Lower Plaza, is each year the site of the Rockefeller Center Christmas tree. From 30 Rock emanated some of the first TV programs, including the *Today* show, now broadcast from ground-floor studios at the southwest corner of 49th Street and Rockefeller Plaza. Crowds of perky onlookers gather each morning between 7 and 9 hoping for a moment of national air time. The new, two-level, monitor-spiked NBC merchandise store, directly across West 49th Street from the *Today* studio, is the departure point for 70-minute tours of the **NBC Studios** (children under 6 are not permitted). Ticket information for other NBC shows is available here as well. ⊠ *30 Rockefeller Plaza,* ☏ *212/ 664-7174.* 🎟 *Tour $17.50.* ☉ *Tour departs from NBC store at street level of GE Bldg. every 15 mins Mon.–Sat. 8–7, Sun. 9–4:30. Thanksgiving–New Year's Day, Mon.–Sat. 7–10, Sun. 7–9.*

Poised above the GE Building's entrance doors on Rockefeller Plaza is a striking sculpture of Zeus by Lee Lawrie, the same artist who sculpted the big Atlas in front of the **International Building** on 5th Avenue. Inside, a dramatic mural entitled *Time,* by José María Sert, covers the ceiling of the foyer. Marble catacombs beneath Rockefeller Center house restaurants in all price ranges, from the formal Sea Grill to McDonald's; a post office and clean public rest rooms (scarce in midtown); and just about every kind of store. To find your way around the concourse, consult the strategically placed directories or obtain the free brochure "Walking Tour of Rockefeller Center" at the **GE Building information desk** (☎ 212/332–6868). When you've seen all there is to see, leave the GE Building from the 6th Avenue side to view the allegorical mosaics above that entrance. ✉ *Bounded by Rockefeller Plaza, 6th Ave., and 49th and 50th Sts.*

NEED A BREAK?   **Dean & DeLuca** (✉ 1 Rockefeller Plaza, at 49th St., ☎ 212/664–1363), at the foot of the *Today* show studio, serves coffee, pastries, and sandwiches. Restaurateur Pino Luongo's **Tuscan Square** (✉ 16 W. 51st St., at Rockefeller Center, ☎ 212/977–7777), a restaurant, wine cellar, espresso bar, and housewares and accessories market, delivers an old-world Tuscan feel.

㉒ International Building. A huge statue of Atlas supporting the world stands sentry before this heavily visited Rockefeller Center structure, which houses many foreign consulates, international airlines, and a U.S. passport office. The lobby is fitted with Grecian marble. ✉ *5th Ave. between 50th and 51st Sts.*

㉟ Lever House. According to the *AIA Guide to New York City*, this 1952 skyscraper built for the Lever Brothers soap company is "where the glass curtain wall began." Gordon Bunshaft, of Skidmore, Owings & Merrill, designed a sheer, slim glass box that rests on the end of a one-story-thick shelf balanced on square chrome columns. The whole building seems to float above the street. Because the tower occupies only half the air space above the lower floors, its side wall reflects a shimmering image of its neighbors. ✉ *390 Park Ave., between 53rd and 54th Sts.*

㉔ Lower Plaza. Sprawled on his ledge above this Rockefeller Center plaza, the great gold-leaf statue of the fire-stealing Greek hero **Prometheus** is one of the most famous sights in the complex, if not in all of New York. A quotation from Aeschylus—PROMETHEUS, TEACHER IN EVERY ART, BROUGHT THE FIRE THAT HATH PROVED TO MORTALS A MEANS TO MIGHTY ENDS—is carved into the red-granite wall behind. The plaza's trademark ice-skating rink is open from October through April; the rest of the year it becomes an open-air café. In December an enormous live Christmas tree towers above. Most days on the Esplanade above the plaza, flags of the United Nations' members alternate with flags of the American states. ✉ *Between 5th and 6th Aves. and 49th and 50th Sts.*, ☎ 212/332–7654 for the rink.

★ **㉜ Museum of Modern Art (MoMA).** MoMA is the city's—and the world's—foremost showcase of 20th-century art. Opened in 1929 on the heels of the stock market crash, the museum presented a revolutionary first exhibition—*Cézanne, Gauguin, Seurat, van Gogh*. Fortunately, Alfred Barr, the museum's first director, found an enthusiastic audience in New York City, and he continued to challenge museumgoers, not only with avant-garde painting and sculpture but also by including photography, architecture, industrial arts, decorative arts, drawings, prints, illustrated books, and film under the rubric of fine art. MoMA expanded several times before moving in 1939 into its present six-story building, designed by Edward Durell Stone and Philip Goodwin. The building has subsequently lost much of its original detailing, as well as its context—19th-century town houses and brownstones now sandwich it on either side, so it now "appears to be the back end of a back office," as Christopher Gray once noted in the *New York Times*.

But forget all that: A major overhaul, led by Japanese architect Yoshio Taniguchi, and begun in 1997, aims to radically change the look and feel of the museum. In summer 2002, the museum will move to a temporary home in Long Island City, Queens. The Manhattan renovations, expected to be completed by late 2004 or early 2005, will nearly double the museum's square footage, from 378,000 to 630,000. When the museum re-opens the Abby Aldrich Rockefeller Sculpture Garden, designed by Philip Johnson on the site of John D. Rockefeller's first New York home—and now closed until 2005—will be used more boldly; the space around the garden will open dramatically into the museum. The chronological arrangement of the galleries will also be reversed, with contemporary work now beginning on the larger, lower floors to provide an easier transition from the modern public spaces of the main lobby and new atrium.

Collection Highlights inaugurates the Long Island City location in summer 2002. The exhibition presents an installation of masterpieces from MoMAs weighty collection, including Vincent van Gogh's *The Starry Night* (1889), Pablo Picasso's *Les Demoiselles d'Avignon* (1907), and Andy Warhol's *Gold Marilyn Monroe* (1962).

MoMA's two movie theaters are among the city's finest venues for foreign, independent, and classic films, and they're free with admission. ⊠ *11 W. 53rd St.; 45-20 33rd St., at Queens Blvd.,* ☏ *212/708–9400; 212/708–9491 for jazz program,* WEB *www.moma.org.* ⌨ *$10; pay what you wish Fri. 4:30–8:15.* ☉ *Sat.–Tues. and Thurs. 10:30–5:45, Fri. 10:30–8:15.*

🖐 ㉙ **Museum of Television and Radio.** Three galleries of photographs and artifacts document the history of broadcasting in this 1989 limestone building by Philip Johnson and John Burgee. A computerized catalog of more than 100,000 television and radio shows and commercials is the main draw; you can then view or listen to your picks in private screening rooms. ⊠ *25 W. 52nd St.,* ☏ *212/621–6800 for general information and daily events; 212/621–6600 for other information,* WEB *www.mtr.org.* ⌨ *$6 (suggested donation).* ☉ *Tues.–Wed. and Fri.–Sun. noon–6, Thurs. noon–8.*

🖐 ㉝ **Paley Park.** This was the first of New York's vest-pocket parks—small open spaces squeezed between high-rise behemoths—which first sprouted in the '60s. A waterfall blocks out traffic noise, and feathery honey locust trees provide shade for relatively relaxing lunches. A snack bar opens when weather permits. ⊠ *3 E. 53rd St.*

★ ㉖ **Radio City Music Hall.** One of the jewels in the crown of Rockefeller Center, this 6,000-seat art deco masterpiece is America's largest indoor theater. Opened in 1932, it astonished the hall's Depression-era patrons with its 60-ft-high foyer, ceiling representing a sunset, and 2-ton chandeliers. The theater originally presented first-run movies in conjunction with live shows featuring the fabled Rockettes chorus line. In 1979 the theater was awarded landmark status. Its year-round schedule now includes major performers, awards presentations, and special events, along with its own Christmas and Easter extravaganzas. A very popular one-hour tour of the theater is offered most days. A $70-million renovation was completed in 1999 that gladdened critics and the public alike by, among other things, revealing the hall's originally intended, gleaming colors. ⊠ *1260 6th Ave., at 50th St.,* ☏ *212/247–4777; 212/632–4041 for tour information,* WEB *www.radiocity.com.* ⌨ *Tour $16.* ☉ *Tours usually leave from main lobby every 30 mins Mon.–Sat. 10–5, Sun. 11–5, call for current schedules.*

②⃝ Rockefeller Center Extension. Twelve corporate skyscrapers define Sixth Avenue's west side, including these four nearly identical ones from West 47th to 51st Streets built in the mid-1960s expansion of Rockefeller Center. Fountains and spacious street-level lobbies lessen the imposing solidity. The **1211 Building** at West 48th Street has a Fox News tickertape larger than the NBC model on Rockefeller Plaza; Fox broadcasts many of its cable shows from the ground-floor glass studios. The sunken plaza of the **McGraw-Hill Building** between West 48th and 49th Streets is notable for its 50-ft steel sun triangle that points to the seasonal positions of the sun at noon. The **Time & Life Building** stands between West 50th and 51st Streets. ⊠ *6th Ave., between 47th and 51st Sts.*

★ **㊳ St. Bartholomew's Church.** Like the Racquet & Tennis Club two blocks north, this handsome 1919 limestone-and-brick church represents a generation of midtown Park Avenue buildings long since replaced by such modernist landmarks as the **Seagram** and the **Lever** buildings. The incongruous juxtaposition plays up the church's finest features—a McKim, Mead & White Romanesque portal from an earlier (1904) church and the intricately tiled Byzantine dome. St. Bart's sponsors major music events throughout the year, including the summer's Festival of Sacred Music, which features full-length masses and other choral works; an annual Christmas concert; and an organ recital series that showcases the church's 12,422-pipe organ, the city's largest. ⊠ *109 E. 50th St., between Park and Lexington Aves.,* ☏ *212/378–0200; 212/ 378–0248 for music program information,* WEB *www.stbarts.org.* ☉ *Mon.–Sat. 8–6, Sun. 8–9.*

NEED A **Café St. Bart's** (⊠ Park Ave. and 50th St., ☏ 212/378–2664), a
BREAK? charming and tranquil outdoor spot for a relatively inexpensive meal or
a glass of wine or beer during the summer.

㊱ Seagram Building. Ludwig Mies van der Rohe, a leading interpreter of International Style architecture, built this simple, boxlike bronze-and-glass tower in 1958. The austere facade belies its wit: I-beams, used to hold buildings up, are here attached to the surface, representing the *idea* of support. The Seagram's innovative ground-level plaza, extending out to the sidewalk, has since become a common element in urban skyscraper design. It is a perfect place to contemplate the monumental brick-and-limestone neo-Renaissance **Racquet & Tennis Club** (1916) across the street, which exhibits a complementary restraint and classicism. Inside the Seagram Building is one of New York's most venerated restaurants, the **Four Seasons Grill and Pool Room.** ⊠ *375 Park Ave., between 52nd and 53rd Sts.,* ☏ *212/572–7404.* 🎟 *Free.* ☉ *Tours Tues. at 3.*

㉞ Sony Building. Commissioned by AT&T, which has since decamped to New Jersey, the Sony Building was designed by Philip Johnson in 1984. Sony's rose-granite columns, and its giant-size Chippendale-style pediment made the skyscraper an instant landmark. The first-floor arcade is home to Sony electronics stores; a restaurant; a café; and, to the delight of children, a conversant robot. The **Sony Wonder Technology Lab** on the fourth floor is a carnival of interactive exhibits, including a recording studio, and video-game and TV production studios. ⊠ *550 Madison Ave., between 55th and 56th Sts.,* ☏ *212/833–8830 for Sony Wonder Technology Lab.* 🎟 *Free.* ☉ *Technology Lab Tues.– Wed. and Fri.–Sat. 10–6, Thurs. 10–8, Sun. noon–6 (last entrance 30 mins before closing); Sony Plaza daily 7 AM–11 PM.*

㉚ "21" Club. A trademark row of jockey statuettes parades along the wrought-iron balcony of this landmark restaurant, which has a burnished men's-club atmosphere and a great downstairs bar. After a period of decline in the 1980s, when its menu aged along with its wealthy clientele, "21" reinvented itself in the 1990s. Today the power brokers are back, along with the luster of the past. ⊠ *21 W. 52nd St.,* ☎ *212/582–7200.*

5TH AVENUE AND 57TH STREET

This stretch of 5th Avenue, just north of Rockefeller Center, is still one of the world's great shopping districts, as evidenced by its many elegant shops and international fashion firms. The rents are even higher along East 57th Street, where there's a parade of exclusive boutiques and fine art galleries. But the area's character has changed as brand-name stores with slick marketing schemes have moved in. Hype aside, these stores can be fun even if you don't want to buy anything, and the many shoppers they attract to the neighborhood bring down the snootiness level in the pricier stores, too. Theme restaurants dominate 57th Street west of 5th Avenue, though that fad is on the wane.

Numbers in the text correspond to numbers in the margin and on the Midtown map.

A Good Walk

Start right across the street from Rockefeller Center's Channel Gardens, at the renowned **Saks Fifth Avenue** ㊴, the flagship of the national department store chain. Across 50th Street is the Gothic-style Roman Catholic **St. Patrick's Cathedral** ㊵. From outside, catch one of the city's most photographed views: the ornate white spires of St. Pat's against the black-glass curtain of Olympic Tower, a multiuse building of shops, offices, and luxury apartments at 51st Street and 5th Avenue.

Cartier displays its wares in a jewel-box turn-of-the-20th-century mansion on the southeast corner of 52nd Street and 5th Avenue; similar houses used to line this street, and many of their residents were parishioners of **St. Thomas Church** ㊶, at the northwest corner of 53rd Street and 5th Avenue. If you are in need of guidance of the earthly variety, take a detour west to 7th Avenue, between 52nd and 53rd Streets to **NYC & Company Visitor Information Center** ㊷. Continuing north on 5th Avenue, you'll see the imposing bulk of the **University Club** ㊸ at the northwest corner of 5th Avenue and 54th Street. It shares the block with the Peninsula, one of the city's finer hotels. Across the street is **Takashimaya New York** ㊹, a branch of the elegant Japanese department store chain.

Fifth Avenue Presbyterian Church, a grand brownstone church (1875), sits on the northwest corner of 5th Avenue and 55th Street. On the same block is **Henri Bendel** ㊺, a bustling women's fashion store. Next door is Harry Winston (⊠ 718 5th Ave.), with a spectacular selection of fine jewelry. Across the street, on the northeast corner of 5th Avenue and 55th Street, is the Disney Store (⊠ 711 5th Ave.), where you can buy everything Disney, from key chains to vacations.

Trump Tower ㊻, on the east side of 5th Avenue between 56th and 57th streets, is an apartment and office building named for its developer, Donald Trump. To the north, the intersection of 5th Avenue and 57th Street is ground zero for high-end shopping. And what more fitting resident for this spot than **Tiffany & Co.** ㊼, the renowned jewelers? Around the corner on 57th Street, NikeTown (⊠ 6 E. 57th St.) is a shrine to sports and sports marketing: TVs and scoreboards on the first floor let you keep track of how your team is doing. As you pass through the revolving doors of Tourneau TimeMachine (⊠ 12 E. 57th St.), an audible ticking welcomes you to its four floors of timepieces. Between these two stores you can relax amid clusters of bamboo in the public atrium of 590 Madison Avenue, a five-side, 20-story sheath of dark gray-green granite and glass by Edward Larrabee Barnes. An Alexander Calder mobile hangs in the lobby. Also in the building is **Newseum/NY** ④⑧, a media-monitoring institution with changing exhibits.

Cross 57th Street and head back toward 5th Avenue on the north side of the street, with its stellar lineup of boutiques: the French classics Chanel (⊠ 15 E. 57th St.), Hermès (⊠ 11 E. 57th St.), and **Christian Dior** (⊠ 21 E. 57th St.); the English Burberrys Ltd. (⊠ 9 E. 57th St.); and the German Escada (⊠ 7 E. 57th St.). The fragmented form of the white-glass Louis Vuitton Moet Hennesy headquarters (parent company and home of Dior) lends a light hearted elegance to the street. Farther west are the watch store Swatch Timeship (⊠ 5 E. 57th St.), the Original Levi's Store (⊠ 3 E. 57th St.), and Warner Brothers Studio Store (⊠ 1 E. 57th St.), an eight-story extravaganza filled with movie, television, and cartoon paraphernalia as well as interactive displays, movies, and a café. From outside you can watch a larger-than-life Superman pushing up the store's elevator. The two **Bergdorf Goodman** ④⑨ stores flank 5th Avenue: the extravagant women's boutiques are on the west side of the avenue between 57th and 58th Streets, and the men's store is on the east side at 58th Street. Van Cleef & Arpels jewelers is within Bergdorf's West 57th Street corner.

Cross 58th Street to **Grand Army Plaza** ⑤⓪, the open space along 5th Avenue between 58th and 60th Streets. Appropriately named **The Plaza** ⑤①, the famous hotel stands at the western edge of this square. Across the street, on the southeast corner of 58th Street and 5th Avenue, is the legendary **F.A.O. Schwarz** ⑤② toy store, ensconced in the General Motors Building.

Now return to 57th Street and head west, where the glamour eases off a bit. The large red NO. 9 on the sidewalk, in front of 9 West 57th Street, was designed by Ivan Chermayeff. (If you approach it from the other direction, it resembles an "e," thereby orienting passersby—you're facing east.) Continuing west, you'll pass the Rizzoli Bookstore (⊠ 31 W. 57th St.), with a neoclassical-inspired ceiling as elegant as the art books it carries. Across 6th Avenue (New Yorkers *never* call it Avenue of the Americas, despite the street signs), you'll know you're in classical-music territory when you peer through the showroom windows at Steinway and Sons (⊠ 109 W. 57th St.). Further west across the street, you'll spot the green and pink jungle-stripe awning of Planet Hollywood. The revamped Russian Tea Room (⊠ 150 W. 57th St.), however, teaches all nearby restaurants a lesson in ornamentation. Even if you're not hungry, take a peek at the four floors of shimmering, outré decor, including a revolving acrylic bear-shape aquarium. Presiding over the southeast corner of 7th Avenue and West 57th Street, **Carnegie Hall** ⑤③ has for decades reigned as a premier international concert hall.

TIMING

This walk isn't long and can be completed in about 1½ hours. Add at least an hour for basic browsing and several more hours for serious shopping. Make sure the stores are open before you set out. Bear in mind that 5th Avenue is jam-packed with holiday shoppers from Halloween until New Year's. Year-round, if you want to experience one of the theme restaurants, plan on waiting up to an hour for a table.

Sights to See

④⑨ **Bergdorf Goodman.** Good taste—at a price—defines this understated department store with dependable service. The seventh floor has room after exquisite room of wonderful linens, tabletop items, and gifts. ⊠ *Main store, 754 5th Ave., between 57th and 58th Sts.,* ☎ *212/753–7300; men's store, 745 5th Ave., at 58th St.*

★ ❺❸ **Carnegie Hall.** Musicians the world over have dreamed of playing Carnegie Hall ever since 1891, when none other than Tchaikovsky—direct from Russia—came to conduct his own work on opening night. Designed by William Barnet Tuthill, who was also an amateur cellist, this renowned concert hall was paid for almost entirely by Andrew Carnegie. Outside, the stout, square brown building has a few Moorish-style arches added, almost as an afterthought, to the facade. Inside, however, the simply decorated 2,804-seat white auditorium is one of the world's finest. The hall has attracted the world's leading orchestras and solo and group performers, from Arturo Toscanini and Leonard Bernstein (he made his triumphant debut here in 1943, standing in for New York Philharmonic conductor Bruno Walter) to Duke Ellington, Ella Fitzgerald, Judy Garland, Frank Sinatra, Bob Dylan, the Beatles (playing one of their first U.S. concerts)—and thousands of others.

Carnegie Hall was extensively restored in the 1980s; a subsequent mid-1990s renovation removed concrete from beneath the stage's wooden floor, vastly improving the acoustics. The work also increased the size of the lobby and added the small **Rose Museum** (⊠ 154 W. 57th St., ☎ 212/247–7800), which is free and open Thursday–Tuesday 11–4:30 and through intermission during concerts. Located just east of the main auditorium, it displays mementos from the hall's illustrious history, such as a Benny Goodman clarinet and Arturo Toscanini's baton. A sensational concert series run by the hall's education department introduces children to classical music through informal sessions with performers, with a low $5 ticket price. You can take a guided one-hour tour of Carnegie Hall, or even rent it if you've always dreamed of singing from its stage. ⊠ *W. 57th St. at 7th Ave.,* ☎ *212/247–7800,* WEB *www.carnegiehall.org.* ☑ *$6.* ☉ *Tours Mon.–Tues. and Thurs.–Fri. at 11:30, 2, and 3 (performance schedule permitting).*

OFF THE
BEATEN PATH   **DAHESH MUSEUM –** Donating his collection of approximately 3,000 works, a Lebanese doctor named Dahesh (1909–84) endowed this small, second-floor exhibition space dedicated to the European academic tradition. Among the well-known painters represented in changing exhibitions are Bonheur, Bouguereau, Gérôme, and Troyon—all painters who have since been upstaged by their contemporaries, the Impressionists, but who once claimed greater popularity. ⊠ *601 5th Ave., between 48th and 49th Sts.,* ☎ *212/759–0606.* ☑ *Free.* ☉ *Tues.–Sat. 11–6.*

❺❷ **F.A.O. Schwarz.** A wondrously fun selection of toys lies just beyond the fantastic mechanical clock standing inside the front doors of this famous toy-o-rama. Take a ride up a larger-than-life robot elevator for a view of the oversize decorations and role-playing employees. If the line to get in looks impossibly long, try walking around the block to the Madison Avenue entrance, where the wait may be shorter. ⊠ *767 5th Ave., at 58th St.,* ☎ *212/644–9400,* WEB *www.fao.com.*

❺⓪ **Grand Army Plaza.** At the southeast corner of Central Park is this open space along 5th Avenue between 58th and 60th Streets. The **Pulitzer Fountain,** donated by publisher Joseph Pulitzer, dominates the southern portion of the square. Appropriately enough in this prosperous neighborhood, the fountain is crowned by a female figure representing Abundance. To the north prances Augustus Saint-Gaudens's gilded equestrian statue of Civil War general William Tecumseh Sherman. Real horses pull carriages through a southern loop of the park and are available at fixed prices ($34 for the first half-hour, $10 each additional quarter-hour). Across 60th Street is **Doris C. Freedman Plaza,** with outdoor sculpture courtesy of the Public Art Fund, at the grand Scholars' Gate. Follow the path from this gate direct to the entrance of the **Central Park Zoo. The Plaza,** the internationally famous hotel, stands at the square's western edge.

45 Henri Bendel. Chic Henri Bendel sells whimsical, expensive women's clothing in a beautiful store, where inventive displays and sophisticated boutiques are hallmarks. You can have a meal in the second-floor café in front of the facade's René Lalique art-glass windows (1912) or view the windows from balconies ringing the four-story atrium. ⊠ *712 5th Ave., between 55th and 56th Sts.,* ☎ *212/247–1100.* ⊙ *Mon.–Wed. 10–7, Thurs. 10–8, Fri. and Sat. 10–7, Sun. noon–6.*

48 Newseum/NY. A sister to the larger Newseum in Arlington, Virginia, the New York Newseum is operated by The Freedom Forum. It offers changing exhibits as well as public roundtables and other programs related to journalism, free speech, and freedom of the press. Exhibits have included a selection of new photographs from 1968, and Pulitzer Prize winner Lucian Perkins's behind-the-scenes shots of runway models. ⊠ *580 Madison Ave., between 56th and 57th Sts.,* ☎ *212/317–7503.* 🎟 *Free.* ⊙ *Mon.–Sat. 10–5:30.*

42 NYC & Company Visitor Information Center. For tourist information, maps, tickets to attractions, souvenirs, and ATMs, stop by this bustling spot. ⊠ *810 7th Ave., between 52nd and 53rd Sts.,* ☎ *212/484–1222,* WEB *nycvisit.com.* ⊙ *Weekdays 8–6, weekends 9–5.*

51 The Plaza. With Grand Army Plaza, 5th Avenue, *and* Central Park at its doorstep, this world-famous hotel claims one of Manhattan's prize real estate corners. A registered historical landmark built in 1907, The Plaza was designed by Henry Hardenbergh, who also built the Dakota apartment building. Here he concocted a birthday-cake effect of highly ornamented white-glazed brick topped with a copper-and-slate mansard roof. The hotel is home to Eloise, the fictional star of Kay Thompson's children's books, and has been featured in many movies, from Alfred Hitchcock's *North by Northwest* to *Plaza Suite.* Past real-life guests include the Duke and Duchess of Windsor and the Beatles. ⊠ *5th Ave. at 59th St.,* ☎ *212/759–3000.*

★ **40 St. Patrick's Cathedral.** The Gothic, double-spired, Roman Catholic cathedral of New York is one of the city's largest (seating approximately 2,400) and most striking churches. It is dedicated to the patron saint of the Irish, then as now one of New York's principal ethnic groups. The 1859 white marble-and-stone structure by architect James Renwick was consecrated in 1879. Additions over the years include the archbishop's house and rectory, the two 330-ft spires, and the intimate Lady Chapel. The original, predominantly Irish, members of the congregation made a statement when they chose the 5th Avenue location for their church: during the week, most of them came to the neighborhood only as employees of the wealthy. But on Sunday, at least, they could claim a prestigious spot for themselves. Among the statues in the alcoves around the nave is a modern depiction of the first American-born saint, Mother Elizabeth Ann Seton. The steps outside are a convenient, scenic rendezvous spot. ⊠ *5th Ave. at 50th St.,* ☎ *212/753–2261 rectory.* ⊙ *Daily 8 AM–8:45 PM.*

41 St. Thomas Church. This Episcopal institution with a grand, darkly brooding French Gothic interior was consecrated on its present site in 1916. The impressive huge stone reredos behind the altar holds the statues of more than 50 apostles, saints, martyrs, missionaries, and other church figures, all designed by Lee Lawrie. The church is also known for its men's and boys' choir; Christmas Eve services here have become a seasonal highlight. ⊠ *5th Ave. at 53rd St.,* ☎ *212/757–7013.* ⏱ *Daily 7–6.*

㊴   **Saks Fifth Avenue.** On a breezy day, the 14 American flags fluttering from the block-long facade of Saks's flagship store make for the most patriotic shopping scene in town. In 1926, the department store's move from its original Broadway location solidified midtown 5th Avenue's new status as a prestigious retail mecca. Saks remains a civilized favorite among New York shoppers. The eighth-floor Café SFA serves delicious light fare, served with a view of Rockefeller Center, and the rooftop pools and gardens of the buildings flanking **Channel Gardens.** Saks's annual Christmas window displays, on view from late November through the first week of January, are among New York's most festive. ⊠ *611 5th Ave., between 49th and 50th Sts.,* ☎ *212/753–4000.* ⏱ *Mon.–Wed. 10–6:30, Thurs. 10–8, weekends 10–6:30.*

㊹   **Takashimaya New York.** A tearoom, a florist within a garden atrium, and gifts and accessories that combine Eastern and Western styles make this six-floor branch of Japan's largest department store chain supremely elegant. ⊠ *693 5th Ave., between 54th and 55th Sts.,* ☎ *212/350–0100.*

★ ㊼   **Tiffany & Co.** One of the most famous jewelers in the world and the quintessential New York store, Tiffany anchors the southeast corner of one of the city's great intersections. The fortresslike art deco entrance and dramatic miniature window displays have been a fixture here since 1940. Founded in 1837 at 237 Broadway, Tiffany slowly made its way uptown in six moves. The store's signature light blue bags and boxes are perennially in style, especially on gift-giving occasions. A New York icon, Tiffany is immortalized in the 1961 Hollywood classic *Breakfast at Tiffany's,* in which a Givenchy-clad Audrey Hepburn emerges from a yellow cab at dawn to window-shop, coffee and Danish in hand. ⊠ *727 5th St., at 57th St.,* ☎ *212/755–8000,* 🕸 *www. tiffany.com.*

NEED A BREAK?   **Mangia,** an Italian and American food shop, is a great place to stop for coffee and a snack, especially if good food is the only theme you want in a restaurant. Desserts are scrumptious, and the salad bar is exceptional. ⊠ *50 W. 57th St.,* ☎ *212/582–5882. Closed Sun.*

㊻   **Trump Tower.** As he has done with other projects, developer Donald Trump named this exclusive 68-story apartment and office building after himself. The grand 5th Avenue entrance leads into a glitzy six-story shopping atrium paneled in pinkish-orange marble and trimmed with lustrous brass. A fountain cascades against one wall, drowning out the clamor of the city, while trees and ivy climb the setbacks outside. ⊠ *5th Ave. between 56th and 57th Sts.*

㊸   **University Club.** New York's leading turn-of-the-20th-century architects, McKim, Mead & White, designed this 1899 granite palace for an exclusive midtown club of degree-holding men. (The crests of various prestigious universities hang above its windows.) The club's popularity declined as individual universities built their own clubs and as gentlemen's clubs became less important on the New York social scene, but the seven-story Renaissance revival building (the facade looks as though it's three stories) is as grand as ever. Architectural critics rate this among Charles McKim's best surviving works. ⊠ *1 W. 54th St., at 5th Ave.*

THE UPPER EAST SIDE

To many New Yorkers, the words *Upper East Side* connote old money, conservative values, and even snobbery. For others, this neighborhood is the epitome of the high-style, high-society way of life often associated with the Big Apple. Alongside Central Park, between 5th and Lexington Avenues, up to about East 96th Street or so, the trappings of wealth are everywhere apparent: well-kept buildings, children in private-school uniforms, nannies wheeling grand baby carriages, dog walkers, limousines, doormen in braided livery.

But like all other New York neighborhoods, this one is diverse, too, and plenty of local residents live modestly. The northeast section, which is known as Yorkville, is more affordable and ethnically mixed, a jumble of high and low buildings, old and young people. Until the 1830s, when the New York & Harlem Railroad and a stagecoach line began racing through, Yorkville was a quiet, remote hamlet with a large German population. Over the years it has also welcomed waves of immigrants from Austria, Hungary, and Czechoslovakia, and local shops and restaurants still bear reminders of this European heritage.

A Good Walk

A fitting place to begin your exploration of the moneyed Upper East Side is that infamous shrine to conspicuous consumption, **Bloomingdale's** ①, at 59th Street between Lexington and 3rd avenues. Leaving Bloomingdale's, head west on East 60th Street toward 5th Avenue. As you cross Park Avenue, notice the wide, neatly planted median strip. Railroad tracks once ran aboveground here; they were not completely covered with a roadway until after World War I, and the grand, sweeping street that resulted became a distinguished residential address. Look south toward midtown, and you'll see the Met Life Building; squished up against it, the Helmsley Building looks small and frilly by comparison. Then turn to look uptown, and you'll see a thoroughfare lined with massive buildings that are more like mansions stacked atop one another than apartment complexes. Colorful tulips and cherry blossoms in the spring and lighted pine trees in December make Park Avenue true to its name.

On the northwest corner of East 60th Street and Park Avenue is Christ Church United Methodist Church, built during the Depression but designed to look centuries old, with its random pattern of limestone blocks. Inside, the Byzantine-style sanctuary (open Sunday and holidays) glitters with golden mosaics. Continue west on 60th Street to pass a grouping of membership-only societies and clubs that have catered to the privileged since the 1800s. Although the clubs remain exclusive, their admirable architecture is there for all to see. The scholarly **Grolier Club** ②, with its fanciful grillwork curled over the doorway, is an exception in that it *is* open to the public. On the south side of the block just east of the park is the **Harmonie Club** ③, and across 60th Street is the even more lordly **Metropolitan Club** ④.

Take a right at 5th Avenue. At 60th Street you'll pass the Pierre, a hotel with a lovely mansard roof and tower that opened in 1930. As you cross East 62nd Street, look at the elegant brick-and-limestone mansion (1915) at 2 East 62nd Street, the home of the **Knickerbocker Club** ⑤, another private social club.

Across East 62nd Street is the Fifth Avenue Synagogue (⊠ 5 E. 62nd St.), a limestone temple built in 1959. Its pointed oval windows are filled with stained glass in striking abstract designs. You may want to detour down this elegant block of town houses; take special note of

No. 11, which has elaborate Corinthian pilasters and an impressive wrought-iron entryway. Farther up 5th Avenue, at East 64th Street, is the Central Park Zoo and the fortlike Arsenal. At East 65th Street is another notable house of worship: **Temple Emanu-El** ⑥, one of the world's largest synagogues.

From 5th Avenue, turn right on East 66th Street, past the site of the house (✉ 3 E. 66th St.) where Ulysses S. Grant spent his final years, before he was moved permanently up to Grant's Tomb. If presidential homes interest you, take a detour over to East 65th Street between Madison and Park avenues to Nos. 47 and 49, two town houses built in 1908 for Sara Delano Roosevelt and her son, Franklin, after his marriage to Eleanor. If you walk east another block on 65th Street, you'll reach the **China Institute** ⑦, whose museum exhibits Chinese art.

Back toward 5th Avenue, next door to Grant's house, at 5 East 66th Street, is the **Lotos Club** ⑧, a private arts and literature club. Continue east across Madison Avenue to Park Avenue. The large landmark apartment building (✉ 45 E. 66th St.) on the northeast corner of Madison Avenue and 66th Street was built from 1906 to 1908 with lovely Gothic-style detail. The red Victorian castle-fortress at East 66th Street and Park Avenue is the **Seventh Regiment Armory** ⑨, now often used as an exhibition space.

Although houses have generally been replaced by apartment buildings along Park Avenue, a few surviving mansions give you an idea of how the neighborhood once looked. The grandly simple silvery-limestone palace on the southwest corner of East 68th Street and Park Avenue, built in 1919, now houses the prestigious Council on Foreign Relations (✉ 58 E. 68th St.). The dark-redbrick town house on the northwest corner houses the **Americas Society** ⑩, which has a public art gallery. The three houses to the north—built during the following decade and designed by three architects—maintain the same neo-Georgian design to create a unified block; the modern-day uses of these former homes add to the international flavor of the area. The Spanish Institute (✉ 684 Park Ave.) offers film series, lectures, and language lessons. The Italian Cultural Institute (✉ 686 Park Ave.) sponsors readings, concerts, and performances. The Italian Consulate (✉ 690 Park Ave.) is home to the Italian diplomatic corps. Two blocks north, on the east side of Park Avenue, is the **Asia Society and Museum** ⑪, a museum and educational center dedicated to the art of South, Southeast, and East Asia.

At this point, shoppers may want to get down to business on Madison Avenue between East 59th and 79th streets. The area is packed with haute couture designer boutiques, patrician art galleries, and unique stores specializing in fine wares from hair combs to truffles. Larger brand-name stores such as Calvin Klein (at East 60th Street) and the Giorgio Armani Boutique (at East 65th Street) have also flocked to the prestigious neighborhood. Even if you're just window-shopping, it's fun to step inside the tony digs of **Polo/Ralph Lauren** ⑫, at Madison Avenue and East 72nd Street, which hardly seems like a store at all. Look for the venerable **Whitney Museum of American Art** ⑬ looming on the right at East 75th Street—its striking building has a base smaller than its upper floors. Take at least two hours to view the collection. At Madison Avenue and 76th Street is the **Carlyle Hotel** ⑭, one of the city's most elite and discreet properties.

The final leg of this tour is several blocks away. How you get through Yorkville is up to you, but we suggest walking four blocks east on 78th Street, then north on 2nd Avenue, and east again on 86th. The quiet blocks of 78th Street between Park and 2nd Avenues are home to rows of well-maintained Italianate town houses from the late 1800s. Many shops and restaurants line 2nd Avenue, some reflecting the area's Eastern European heritage. At East 81st Street the Hungarian Meat Market (✉ 1560 2nd Ave.) serves up delicious fresh-made sausages. At East 86th Street, the German store Schaller & Weber (✉ 1654 2nd Ave.) has enticing bratwurst, imported chocolates, and stollen. Secondhand stores in the area sell all sorts of odds and ends discarded by the well-to-do.

On East 86th Street and East End Avenue, the **Henderson Place Historic District** ⑮ includes 24 small-scale town houses built in the late 1880s. Across the street is **Carl Schurz Park** ⑯, overlooking the East River. **Gracie Mansion** ⑰, the mayor's house, sits at its north end. The park comes to a narrow stop at East 90th Street, but the foliage continues at **Asphalt Green** ⑱, a concrete parabolic structure.

TIMING

This tour covers a lot of ground, although many sights merely warrant looking, not stopping. Allow about three leisurely hours for the walk. The art institutions—the Americas Society, Asia Society, and the Whitney Museum—may take more of your time if you like, so check their hours.

Sights to See

Numbers in the text correspond to numbers in the margin and on the Upper East Side, Museum Mile map.

❿ **Americas Society.** This McKim, Mead & White–designed neo-Federal town house was among the first on this stretch of Park Avenue (built 1909–11). It was commissioned by Percy Rivington Pyne, the grandson of financier Moses Taylor and a notable financier himself. From 1948 to 1963 the mansion housed the Soviet Mission to the United Nations. In 1965 it was saved from developers by the Marquesa de Cuevas (a Rockefeller descendant), who acquired the property and presented it to the Center for Inter-American Relations, now called the Americas Society, whose mission is to educate U.S. citizens about the rest of the western hemisphere. The society has frequent literary events and its art gallery hosts changing exhibits. ✉ *680 Park Ave., at 68th St.,* ☎ *212/249–8950,* WEB *www.americas-society.org.* 🖭 *$3 (suggested gallery donation).* ☉ *Tues.–Sun. noon–6.*

⓫ **Asia Society and Museum.** The eight-story red-granite building that houses this museum and educational center complements Park Avenue's older, more traditional architecture. This nonprofit educational society, founded in 1956, offers a regular program of lectures, films, and performances, in addition to permanent and changing exhibitions. The Asian art collection of Mr. and Mrs. John D. Rockefeller III forms the museum's major holdings. A major renovation created a permanent space for exhibiting these works. The collection includes South Asian stone and bronze sculptures; art from India, Nepal, Pakistan, and Afghanistan; bronze vessels, ceramics, sculpture, and paintings from China; Korean ceramics; and paintings, wooden sculptures, and ceramics from Japan. A glassed-in atrium, sculpture garden, café, and visitor's center on the first floor make the Asia Society one of the Upper East Side's most inviting stops. ✉ *725 Park Ave., at 70th St.,* ☎ *212/288–6400,* WEB *www.asiasociety.org.* 🖭 *$4; free Thurs. 6–8.* ☉ *Tues., Wed., Fri., and Sat. 10–6, Thurs. 10–8, Sun. noon–5.*

🐾 ⓲ **Asphalt Green.** When this former asphalt plant was built by Kahn and Jacobs in 1941–44, it was the country's first reinforced concrete arch, and it will be here for the ages thanks to landmark status. The plant is now part of a fitness complex—there are often games on the bright green lawn out front, and the adjoining natatorium (AquaCenter) houses one of Manhattan's largest pools. A puppet and marionette playhouse has weekend shows for children. ⊠ *E. 90th St. between York Ave. and FDR Dr.,* ☏ *212/369–8890,* WEB *www.asphaltgreen.org.*

❶ **Bloomingdale's.** A New York institution, this noisy and crowded block-long behemoth sells everything from designer clothes to high-tech tea kettles in slick, sophisticated displays. Most selections are high quality, and sale prices on designer goods can be extremely satisfying. In addition to full his, hers, and home sections, Bloomingdale's has four restaurants, a chocolatier, and a coffee shop. ⊠ *E. 59th St. and Lexington Ave.,* ☏ *212/705–2000,* WEB *www.bloomingdales.com.* ☉ *Daily 10–8:30.*

⓰ **Carl Schurz Park.** During the American Revolution, a house on this promontory was used as a fortification by the Continental Army, then was taken over as a British outpost. In more peaceful times the land became known as East End Park. It was renamed in 1911 to honor Carl Schurz (1829–1906), a famous 19th-century German immigrant who eventually served the United States as a minister to Spain, a major general in the Union Army, and a senator from Missouri. During the Hayes administration, Schurz was secretary of the interior; he later moved back to Yorkville and worked as editor of the *New York Evening Post* and *Harper's Weekly.*

From the park's southern entrance at East 86th Street, a curved stone staircase leads up to the wrought-iron railings at the edge of John Finley Walk, which overlooks the churning East River—actually just an estuary connecting Long Island Sound with Upper New York Bay. You can see the Triborough, Hell Gate, and Queensboro bridges; Wards, Randall's, and Roosevelt islands; and on the other side of the river, Astoria, Queens. The view is so tranquil you'd never guess you're directly above the FDR Drive. Behind you along the walk are raised flower beds planted with interesting blooms, recreation areas, and a playground. Although it doesn't compare in size with the West Side's Riverside Park, Upper East Siders cherish it nonetheless.

Stroll to the north end of Carl Schurz Park to reach **Gracie Mansion**, where the city's mayor resides. The park tapers to an end at East 90th Street, where there is a dock from which ferry boats depart to lower Manhattan and up to Yankee Stadium. ⊠ *E. 84th to E. 90th St., between East End Ave. and East River.*

★ ⓮ **Carlyle Hotel.** The mood here is English manor house. The hotel has the elegant Café Carlyle, where top performers such as Bobby Short, Eartha Kitt, and Woody Allen (the latter on clarinet) appear regularly, and the more relaxed Bemelmans Bar, with murals by Ludwig Bemelmans, the famed illustrator of the Madeline children's books. Stargazers, take note: this hotel's roster of rich-and-famous guests has included Elizabeth Taylor, George C. Scott, Steve Martin, and Warren Beatty and Annette Bening. In the early 1960s President John F. Kennedy frequently stayed here; rumor has it he entertained Marilyn Monroe in his rooms. ⊠ *35 E. 76th St., at Madison Ave.,* ☏ *212/744–1600.*

❼ **China Institute.** A pair of fierce, fat stone lions guards the doorway of this pleasant redbrick town house, which houses a gallery and educational center. In addition to regular lectures, the institute hosts two annual exhibitions focusing on traditional Chinese art, including painting, calligraphy, folk art, architecture, and textiles. ⊠ *125 E. 65th St., between Lexington and Park Aves.,* ☏ *212/744–8181,* WEB *www. chinainstitute.org.* ▦ *$3; free Tues. and Thurs. 6–8.* ☉ *Mon., Wed.,*

Fri., and Sat. 10–5, Tues. and Thurs. 10–8, Sun. 1–5. Closed between exhibitions.

⑰ Gracie Mansion. Surrounded by a small lawn and flower beds, this Federal-style yellow-frame residence, the official home of the mayor of New York still feels like a country manor house, which it was when built in 1799 by wealthy merchant Archibald Gracie. The Gracie family entertained many notable guests here, including Louis-Philippe (later king of France), President John Quincy Adams, the Marquis de Lafayette, Alexander Hamilton, James Fenimore Cooper, Washington Irving, and John Jacob Astor. The city purchased Gracie Mansion in 1887, and after a period of use as the Museum of the City of New York, Mayor Fiorello H. La Guardia made it the official mayor's residence in 1942. Rudy Giuliani and his family were the most recent inhabitants, but the mansion will be home to new mayoral residents in 2002. ⊠ *Carl Schurz Park, East End Ave. opposite 88th St.,* ☎ *212/570–4751.* 🎫 *$4.* ☉ *Guided tours late Mar.–mid-Nov., Wed.; all tours by advance reservation only.*

② Grolier Club. Founded in 1884, this private club is named after the 16th-century French bibliophile Jean Grolier. Its members are devoted to the bookmaking crafts; one of them, Bertram G. Goodhue, designed this neatly proportioned Georgian-style redbrick building in 1917. The club presents public exhibitions on subjects related to books and has a reference library of more than 100,000 volumes (open by appointment only). ⊠ *47 E. 60th St., between Madison and Park Aves.,* ☎ *212/838–6690,* WEB *www.grolierclub.org.* 🎫 *Free.* ☉ *Gallery Sept.–July, Mon.–Sat. 10–5. Closed between exhibitions.*

❸ Harmonie Club. Originally a private club for German Jews, this was the city's first men's club to allow women at dinner. (Stephen Birmingham's *Our Crowd: The Great Jewish Families of New York* profiles the club's original generation.) The building is a pseudo-Renaissance palace built in 1906 by McKim, Mead & White. ⊠ *4 E. 60th St., between 5th and Madison Aves.*

⑮ Henderson Place Historic District. Originally consisting of 32 small-scale town houses in the Queen Anne style, Henderson Place still has 24 stone-and-brick buildings. They were built in the late 1880s for "people of moderate means" by Richard Norman Shaw. Designed to be comfortable yet romantic dwellings, they combine elements of the Elizabethan manor house with classic Flemish details. Note the lovely bay windows, the turrets marking the corner of each block, and the symmetrical roof gables, pediments, parapets, chimneys, and dormer windows. ⊠ *Henderson Pl. and East End Ave. between 86th and 87th Sts.*

NEED A
BREAK?
DTUT (⊠ 1626 2nd Ave., at 84th St., ☎ 212/327–1327) is a hip coffee parlor with comfy chairs, sandwiches, s'mores, and pastries. Or try the more traditional **Viand** (⊠ 300 E. 86th St., at 2nd Ave., ☎ 212/879–9425), a diner with superlative service and an extensive menu of treats to tide you over on this long walk.

❺ Knickerbocker Club. Built in 1915, this serene limestone mansion, the third home of the club—originally founded in 1874 by such wheeler-dealers as John Jacob Astor and August Belmont—was designed by Delano and Aldrich. ⊠ *2 E. 62nd St., between 5th and Madison Aves.*

❽ Lotos Club. Founded in 1870, this private club attracts devotees of the arts and literature. Its current home is a handsomely ornate beaux arts mansion originally built in 1900 by Richard Howland Hunt for a member of the Vanderbilt family. ⊠ *5 E. 66th St., between 5th and Madison Aves.*

④ Metropolitan Club. A lordly neoclassical edifice, this exclusive club was built in 1891–94 by the grandest producers of such structures—McKim, Mead & White. Ironically, it was established by J. P. Morgan when a friend of his was refused membership in the Union League Club; its members today include leaders of foreign countries and presidents of major corporations. ⊠ *1 E. 60th St., between 5th and Madison Aves.*

OFF THE
BEATEN PATH

MOUNT VERNON HOTEL MUSEUM AND GARDEN – On property once owned by Colonel William Stephens Smith, the husband of Abigail Adams, daughter of former president John Adams, this 18th-century carriage house is now owned by the Colonial Dames of America and largely restored to look as it did when it served as a bustling day hotel during the early 19th century (a time when the city's population was just beginning to boom). Eight rooms display furniture and artifacts of the Federal and Empire periods, and an adjoining garden is designed in 18th-century style. ⊠ *421 E. 61st St., between York and 1st Aves.,* ☎ *212/838–6878.* 🎟 *$4.* ☼ *Aug.–May, Tues.–Sun. 11–4; June and July, Tues. 11–9, Wed.–Sun. 11–4.*

⑫ Polo/Ralph Lauren. Ralph Lauren's flagship New York store, in the landmark, French Renaissance–style Rhinelander mansion (built 1898), has preserved the grand house's walnut fittings, Oriental rugs, and family portraits as an aristocratic setting in which to display Lauren's to-the-manor-born clothing and home furnishings. ⊠ *867 Madison Ave., at 72nd St.,* ☎ *212/606–2100.* ☼ *Mon.–Sat. 10–6.*

OFF THE
BEATEN PATH

ROOSEVELT ISLAND – This 2-mi-long East River island, which lies parallel to Manhattan from East 48th to 85th streets, became residential in the 1970s and now houses some 8,000 people. The island has a 19th-century lighthouse designed by James Renwick, Jr. (architect of St. Patrick's Cathedral) and Blackwell House (1794), the fifth oldest wooden house in Manhattan. Some fragments remain of the asylums, hospitals, and jails once clustered here, when it was known as Welfare Island and before that Blackwell's Island (Mae West and William "Boss" Tweed are among those who served time in Blackwell Penitentiary). Walkways along the island's edge provide fine river views, and it's surprisingly quiet, considering that the city is so close. The real treat, however, is the 3½-minute ride over on the aerial **Roosevelt Island Tramway** (☎ 212/832–4543, 🎟 $1.50); the entrance is at 2nd Avenue and 60th Street, a few blocks east of Bloomingdale's. For more about the island, visit 🕸 www.roosevelt-island.ny.us.

⑨ Seventh Regiment Armory. The term *National Guard* derives from the Seventh Regiment, which has traditionally consisted of select New York men who volunteered for service. (The Seventh Regiment first used the term in 1824 in honor of the Garde National de Paris.) This huge structure, designed by Seventh Regiment veteran Charles W. Clinton in the late 1870s, is still used as an armory, though not exclusively; a homeless shelter, the Seventh Regiment Mess and Bar, and numerous exhibitions also use its space. Two posh annual antiques shows take place in the expansive drill hall. Both Louis Comfort Tiffany and Stanford White designed rooms in its surprisingly residential interior; go up the front stairs into the wood-paneled lobby and take a look around. Over the years, neglect and water damage have taken their toll on the building's interiors, and in 2000 the armory was listed by the World Monument Fund as one of the "100 Most Endangered Sites" internationally. A statewide commission has since been formed to make plans for restoring this oft-overlooked architectural gem. ⊠ *643 Park Ave., between 66th and 67th Sts.,* ☎ *212/744–2968 curator's office.*

❻ **Temple Emanu-El.** The world's largest Reform Jewish synagogue seats 2,500 worshipers. Built in 1928–29 of limestone and designed in the Romanesque style with Byzantine influences, the building has Moorish and art deco ornamentation, and its sanctuary is covered with mosaics. A free museum displays artifacts detailing the congregation's history and Jewish life. ✉ *1 E. 65th St., at 5th Ave.,* ☎ *212/744–1400,* WEB *www.emanuelnyc.org.* ☉ *Sabbath services Fri. 5:15, Sat. 10:30; weekday services Sun.–Thurs. 5:30. Temple and museum open Mon.–Thurs. 10–4:30, Fri. 10–4, and Sat. 1–4:30.*

★ ⓭ **Whitney Museum of American Art.** This museum grew out of a gallery in the studio of the sculptor and collector Gertrude Vanderbilt Whitney, whose talent and taste were fortuitously accompanied by the wealth of two prominent families. In 1929 she offered her collection of 20th-century American art to the Met, but they turned it down, so she established an independent museum. The current building, opened in 1966, is a minimalist gray-granite vault separated from Madison Avenue by a dry moat; it was designed by Marcel Breuer, a member of the Bauhaus school (its manifesto called for architects and artists to work toward "the building of the future"). The monolithic exterior is much more forbidding than the interior, where exhibitions offer an intelligent survey of 20th-century American works. The fifth floor's eight sleek galleries house "Hopper to Mid-Century: Highlights from the Permanent Collection" featuring works by Reginald Marsh, George Bellows, Robert Henri, and Marsden Hartley. Notable pieces include Hopper's *Early Sunday Morning* (1930) and *A Woman in the Sun* (1961), several of Georgia O'Keeffe's dazzling flower paintings, and Alexander Calder's beloved sculpture *Circus* (1926–31). The second floor picks up chronologically where the fifth floor leaves off, with "Pollock to Today," more highlights from the permanent collection, including paintings and sculpture by such postwar and contemporary artists as Willem de Kooning, Jim Dine, Jasper Johns, Mark Rothko, Frank Stella, Chuck Close, Cindy Sherman, and Roy Lichtenstein. The famed Whitney Biennial, which showcases the most important developments in American art over the past two years, takes place in even-numbered years. The Whitney also has a branch across from Grand Central Terminal. ✉ *945 Madison Ave., at 75th St.,* ☎ *212/570–3676,* WEB *www.whitney.org.* ✉ *$10; pay what you wish Fri. 6–9.* ☉ *Tues.– Thurs. and weekends 11–6, Fri. 1–9.*

NEED A BREAK? | The soft lighting, tasteful decor, and delicious, if somewhat pricey, pastries, chocolates, and drinks of **Payard Pâtisserie & Bistro** (✉ 1032 Lexington Ave., between E. 73rd and 74th Sts., ☎ 212/717–5252) are a perfect complement to a day on the chic Upper East Side. A full restaurant is in back, but you can nibble on sandwiches and desserts at the small café tables up front.

MUSEUM MILE

Once known as Millionaires' Row, the stretch of 5th Avenue between East 79th and 104th streets has been fittingly renamed Museum Mile, for it now contains New York's most distinguished cluster of cultural institutions. The connection is more than coincidental: many museums are housed in what used to be the great mansions of merchant princes and wealthy industrialists. A large percentage of these buildings were constructed of limestone (it's cheaper than marble) and reflect the beaux arts style, which was very popular among the wealthy at the turn of the century.

Numbers in the text correspond to numbers in the margin and on the Museum Mile, Upper East Side, map.

A Good Walk

This tour is a simple, straight walk up 5th Avenue, from East 70th to 105th Street, and it covers nearly 2 mi. If you walk up the west side of the street (crossing over to visit museums, of course), you'll be under the canopy of Central Park and have a good view of the mansions and apartments across the street. Try to catch the annual "Museum Mile" celebration—held annually on the second or third Tuesday in June—when 5th Avenue is closed to traffic, music fills the air, and museums open their doors, free to all, from 6 to 9.

Begin at 5th Avenue and East 70th Street (a bit south of Museum Mile proper), with the **Frick Collection** ⑲, housed in an ornate, imposing beaux arts mansion. Walk several blocks north, past former mansions, some of them now converted into multiple-family dwellings, among them the Gothic revival facade of the Ukrainian Institute of America, on the southeast corner of 5th Avenue at 79th Street. One block north is the **American Irish Historical Society** ⑳, another fine example of the French-influenced beaux arts style that was so popular at the turn of the 20th century.

From here you can't miss the immense and impressive **Metropolitan Museum of Art** ㉑, one of the world's largest art museums, encroaching on Central Park's turf.

Across from the Met, between East 82nd and 83rd Streets, one beaux arts town house stands amid newer apartment blocks. It now belongs to the Federal Republic of Germany, which has installed a branch of the **Goethe Institut** ㉒ here. At the corner of East 85th Street is 1040 5th Avenue, the former home of Jacqueline Kennedy Onassis, from which she could view Central Park and the reservoir that now bears her name.

At East 88th Street, Frank Lloyd Wright's **Solomon R. Guggenheim Museum** ㉓, opened in 1959, is the architect's only major New York building. A block north stands the **National Academy** ㉔, an art museum and school (previously known as the National Academy of Design). At East 91st Street you'll find the former residence of industrialist Andrew Carnegie, now a museum devoted to contemporary and historic design—the **Cooper-Hewitt National Design Museum** ㉕. From the museum, cross 91st Street. A huge Italianate limestone mansion, constructed between 1914 and 1918 for financier Otto Kahn and his wife, Addie, noted patrons of the arts, is now home to the Convent of the Sacred Heart (1 E. 91st St.).

As you continue north, look for the **Jewish Museum** ㉖ at East 92nd Street; designed to look like a French Gothic-style château, it was originally built for financier Felix Warburg in 1908. The handsome, well-proportioned Georgian-style mansion on the corner of 5th Avenue and 94th Street was built in 1914 for another 5th Avenue magnate, Willard Straight, founder of *The New Republic* magazine. For some architectural variety, take a short walk east on 97th Street. The baroque-style St. Nicholas Russian Orthodox Cathedral (✉ 15 E. 97th St.), built in 1901–02 has striking onion-dome cupolas.

At East 103rd Street, the intimate **Museum of the City of New York** ㉗ has exhibits related to Big Apple history. One block north, **El Museo del Barrio** ㉘, highlights Latin American culture. After filling up on all this culture, you may want to head for nature: cross the street to Central Park's Conservatory Garden, a formal, enclosed tract in the ram-

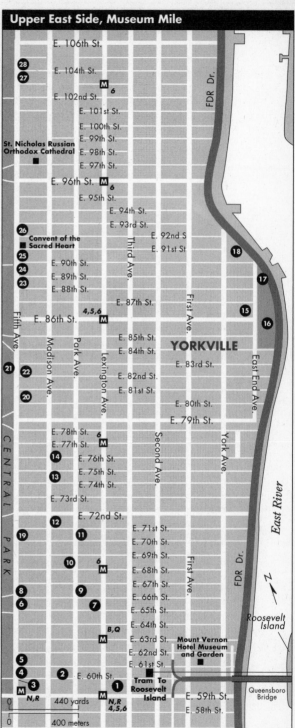

Upper East Side, Museum Mile

bling park, where you can sit on a bench and enjoy the scents of whatever's in bloom.

TIMING

It would be impossible to do justice to all these collections in one outing; the Metropolitan Museum alone contains too much to see in a week, much less a day. Consider selecting one or two museums or exhibits in which to linger and simply walk past the others, appreciating their exteriors (this in itself constitutes a minicourse in architecture). Save the rest for another day—or for your next trip.

Be sure to pick the right day for this tour: most museums are closed at least one day of the week, usually Monday, and a few have free admission during extended hours on specific days. Others have drinks, snacks, and/or music during late weekend hours. The Jewish Museum is closed Friday and Saturday; the Guggenheim is closed Thursday.

Sights to See

㉑ American Irish Historical Society (AIHS). U.S. Steel president William Ellis Corey, who scandalized his social class by marrying musical comedy star Mabelle Gilman, once owned this heavily ornamented, mansard-roof beaux arts town house; he died in 1934, and the building remained vacant until it was purchased and renovated by the AIHS (established 1897), which set up shop here in 1940. The society hosts frequent lectures, literary events, concerts, and exhibitions, and the library's holdings chronicle Irish and Irish-American history. Tours are usually available on request. ⊠ 991 5th Ave., at 80th St., ☎ 212/288–2263, WEB www.aihs.org. 🎫 Free. ⊙ Weekdays 10:30–5.

㉕ Cooper-Hewitt National Design Museum–Smithsonian Institution. Industrialist Andrew Carnegie sought comfort more than show when he built this 64-room house, designed by Babb, Cook & Williard, on what were the outskirts of town in 1901; he administered his extensive philanthropic projects from the first-floor study. (Note the low doorways—Carnegie was only 5 ft 2 inches tall.) The core of the museum's collection was assembled in 1897—not by Carnegie—but by the two Hewitt sisters, granddaughters of inventor and industrialist Peter Cooper. Major holdings focus on aspects of contemporary and historical design, including drawings, prints, textiles, furniture, metalwork, ceramics, glass, woodwork, and wall coverings. The Smithsonian Institution took over the museum in 1967, and in 1976 the collection was moved into the Carnegie mansion. Following a renovation completed in 1998, the museum's three buildings were linked and a Design Resource Center was opened. The changing exhibitions—which have covered such subjects as jewelry design and the construction of the Disney theme parks—are invariably enlightening and often amusing. In summer some exhibits make use of the lovely courtyard. ⊠ 2 E. 91st St., at 5th Ave., ☎ 212/849–8400, WEB www.si.edu/ndm/. 🎫 $8; free Tues. 5–9. ⊙ Tues. 10–9, Wed.–Sat. 10–5, Sun. noon–5.

㉘ El Museo del Barrio. *El barrio* is Spanish for "the neighborhood," and the museum, focusing on Latin American and Caribbean art, is fittingly located on the edge of East Harlem, where a largely Spanish-speaking, Puerto Rican community resides. Founded in 1969, the 8,000-object permanent collection includes numerous pre-Columbian artifacts, sculpture, film and video, and the museum's well-known *santos*, or saints—carved wooden folk-art figures from Puerto Rico. Shows also cull works from the Caribbean, Mexico, and Central and South America. A 599-seat theater with floor-to-ceiling murals by Willy Pogany opened in summer 2000. ⊠ 1230 5th Ave., between 104th and 105th Sts., ☎ 212/831–7272, WEB www.elmuseo.org. 🎫 $5 (suggested donation). ⊙ Wed.–Sun. 11–5; extended hrs in summer.

★ ⑲ **Frick Collection.** Coke-and-steel baron Henry Clay Frick amassed this superb art collection far from the soot and smoke of Pittsburgh, where he made his fortune. The mansion was designed by Thomas Hastings and built in 1913–14. It opened as a museum in 1935 and expanded in 1977, but still resembles a gracious private home, albeit one with bona fide masterpieces in almost every room. The number of famous paintings is astounding; you'll also see sculptures and decorative arts throughout the house. Many treasures bear special mention. Édouard Manet's *The Bullfight* (1864) hangs in the Garden Court. Two of the Frick's three Vermeers—*Officer and Laughing Girl* (circa 1658) and *Girl Interrupted at Her Music* (1660–61)—hang by the front staircase. Fra Filippo Lippi's *The Annunciation* (circa 1440) hangs in the Octagon Room. Gainsborough and Reynolds portraits are in the dining room; canvases by Gainsborough, Constable, Turner, and Gilbert Stuart are in the library; and several Titians (including *Portrait of a Man in a Red Cap,* circa 1516), Holbeins, a Giovanni Bellini (*St. Francis in the Desert,* circa 1480), and an El Greco (*St. Jerome,* circa 1590–1600) are in the "living hall." Nearly 50 additional paintings, as well as much sculpture, decorative arts, and furniture, are in the West and East galleries. Three Rembrandts, including *The Polish Rider* (circa 1655) and *Self-Portrait* (1658), as well as a third Vermeer, *Mistress and Maid* (circa 1667–68), hang in the former; paintings by Whistler, Goya, Van Dyck, Lorrain, David, and Corot in the latter. A free slide presentation introducing the collection runs every hour in the Music Room. Also recommended is the free "ArtPhone" audio tour, which guides you through the museum at your own pace and is available in several languages. When you're through, the tranquil indoor court with a fountain and glass ceiling is a lovely spot for a respite. ⊠ *1 E. 70th St., at 5th Ave.,* ☎ *212/288-0700,* WEB *www.frick.org.* ☞ *$10. Children under 10 not admitted.* ☼ *Tues.–Sat. 10–6, Sun. 1–6.*

㉒ **Goethe Institut.** In a 1907 beaux arts town house, this German cultural center hosts art exhibitions as well as lectures, films, and workshops; its extensive library includes current issues of German newspapers and periodicals. ⊠ *1014 5th Ave., at 82nd St.,* ☎ *212/439–8700,* WEB *www.goethe.de/newyork.* ☞ *Exhibitions free.* ☼ *Library hours, Tues. and Thurs. noon–7, Wed. and Fri. noon–5; Gallery hours, Mon., Wed., and Fri. 10–5; Tues. and Thurs. 10–7.*

㉖ **Jewish Museum.** One of the largest collections of Judaica in the world, the Jewish Museum explores the development and meaning of Jewish identity and culture over the course of 4,000 years. Housed in a graystone Gothic-style 1908 mansion, the exhibitions draw on the museum's collection of artwork and ceremonial objects, ranging from a 3rd-century Roman burial plaque to 20th-century sculpture by Elie Nadelman. The museum's two-floor permanent exhibition, "Culture and Continuity: The Jewish Journey" displays nearly 1,000 objects from the museum collection. Special exhibitions focusing on Jewish history and art can be very popular; the museum sometimes has a line to get in that extends down the block, so try to arrive early in the day. ⊠ *1109 5th Ave., at 92nd St.,* ☎ *212/423–3200,* WEB *www.jewishmuseum.org.* ☞ *$8; Tues. 5–8 pay what you wish.* ☼ *Sun., Mon., Wed., Thurs. 11–5:45, Tues. 11–8.*

★ ㉑ **Metropolitan Museum of Art.** The largest art museum in the western hemisphere (spanning four blocks, it encompasses 2 million square ft), the Met is one of the city's supreme cultural institutions. Its permanent collection of nearly 3 million works of art from all over the world includes objects from the Paleolithic era to modern times—an assemblage whose quality and range make this one of the world's greatest museums.

Founded in 1870, the Met first opened its doors 10 years later, on March 30, 1880, but the original Victorian Gothic redbrick building by Calvert Vaux has since been encased in other architecture, which in turn has been encased in other architecture. The majestic 5th Avenue facade, designed by Richard Morris Hunt, was built in 1902 of gray Indiana limestone; later additions eventually surrounded the original building on the sides and back. (You can glimpse part of the museum's original redbrick facade in a room to the left of the top of the main staircase and on a side wall of the ground-floor European Sculpture Court.)

The 5th Avenue entrance leads into the **Great Hall,** a soaring neoclassical chamber that has been designated a landmark. Past the admission booths, a wide marble staircase leads up to the **European paintings** galleries, whose 2,500 works include Botticelli's *The Last Communion of St. Jerome* (circa 1490), Pieter Brueghel's *The Harvesters* (1565), El Greco's *View of Toledo* (circa 1590), Johannes Vermeer's *Young Woman with a Water Jug* (circa 1660), Velázquez's *Juan de Pareja* (1648), and Rembrandt's *Aristotle with a Bust of Homer* (1653). The arcaded **European Sculpture Court** includes Auguste Rodin's massive bronze *The Burghers of Calais* (1884–95).

The **American Wing,** in the northwest corner, is best approached from the first floor, where you enter through a refreshingly light and airy garden court graced with Tiffany stained-glass windows, cast-iron staircases by Louis Sullivan, and a marble Federal-style facade taken from the Wall Street branch of the United States Bank. Take the elevator to the third floor and begin working your way down through the rooms decorated in period furniture—everything from a Shaker retiring room to a Federal-era ballroom to the living room of a Frank Lloyd Wright house—and the excellent galleries of American painting.

In the realm of 20th-century art, the Met was a latecomer, allowing the Museum of Modern Art and the Whitney to build their collections with little competition until the Metropolitan's contemporary art department was finally established in 1967. The Met has made up for lost time, however, and in 1987 it opened the three-story **Lila Acheson Wallace Wing,** in the southwest corner. Pablo Picasso's portrait of Gertrude Stein (1906) is the centerpiece of this collection. The **Iris and B. Gerald Cantor Roof Garden,** above this wing and open from May to late October, showcases 20th-century sculptures and provides a refreshing break with its unique view of Central Park and the Manhattan skyline.

Those with a taste for classical art should proceed to the left of the Great Hall on the first floor to see the **Greek galleries,** which were spectacularly renovated in 1999. Here, Grecian urns and mythological marble statuary are displayed beneath a skylit, barrel-vaulted stone ceiling that forms one of the grandest museum spaces in the city. Although still in progress, Roman galleries are slated to open behind the Greek galleries, with a court for Roman sculpture, and space for the museum's large collection of rare Roman wall paintings excavated from the lava of Mt. Vesuvius. The Met's awesome **Egyptian collection,** spanning some 4,000 years, is on the first floor, directly to the right of the Great Hall. Here you'll find papyrus pages from the Egyptian Book of the Dead, stone coffins engraved in hieroglyphics, and mummies. The collection's centerpiece is the **Temple of Dendur,** an entire Roman-period temple (circa 15 BC) donated by the Egyptian government in thanks for U.S. help in saving ancient monuments. Placed in a specially built gallery with views of Central Park, the temple faces east, as it did in its original location, and a pool of water has been installed at the same distance from it as the Nile once stood. Another spot suitable for contemplation is directly above the Egyptian treasures, in the **Asian galleries**: the Astor Court Chinese garden reproduces a Ming dynasty (1368–1644) scholar's courtyard, complete with water splashing over artfully positioned rocks.

Also on the first floor is a fine arms-and-armor exhibit (enter through the **Medieval galleries**, just behind the main staircase, and turn right). The Gothic sculptures, Byzantine enamels, and full-size Baroque choir screen built in 1668 are impressive and may whet your appetite for the thousands of medieval objects displayed at the **Cloisters**, the Met's annex in Washington Heights. From the Medieval galleries continue straight on until you enter the cool, skylit white space of the **Lehman Wing**, where the exquisite, mind-bogglingly large personal collection of the late donor, investment banker Robert Lehman, is displayed in rooms resembling those of his West 54th Street town house. The collection's strengths include old-master drawings; Renaissance paintings by Rembrandt, El Greco, Petrus Christus, and Hans Memling; French 18th-century furniture; and 19th-century canvases by Goya, Ingres, and Renoir. Even at peak periods, crowds tend to be sparse here (Lehman's insistence that his collection be exhibited in one place may be one of the reasons, for as great as the collection here is, it feels uncannily like an echo of the Met's main collections). The **Costume Institute**, one level below the main floor's Egyptian Art exhibit, has changing but always intriguing displays of clothing and fashion.

Although it exhibits roughly only a quarter of its vast holdings at any one time, the Met offers more than can reasonably be seen in one visit. The best advice for tackling the museum is to focus on two to four sections and know that, somewhere, there's an empty exhibit that just might be more rewarding than the one you can't see due to the crowds. Walking tours and lectures are free with your admission contribution. Tours covering various sections of the museum begin about every 15 minutes on weekdays, less frequently on weekends; they depart from the tour board in the Great Hall. Self-guided audio tours, which are recorded by Philippe de Montebello, the Met's longtime director, can be rented at a desk in the Great Hall and often at the entrance to major exhibitions. Lectures, often related to temporary exhibitions, are given frequently. ⊠ *5th Ave. at 82nd St.,* ☎ *212/535–7710,* WEB *www.met-museum.org.* ☞ *$10 (suggested donation); joint admission to the Cloisters, if viewed in the same day.* ⊙ *Tues.–Thurs. and Sun. 9:30–5:30, Fri. and Sat. 9:30–9.*

NEED A BREAK?   The first American branch of the very popular Belgian café chain, **Le Pain Quotidien** (⊠ 1131 Madison Ave., between 84th and 85th Sts., ☎ 212/327–4900) attracts Upper East Siders to its large, wide-plank pine communal table for croissants, tarts, brioche, and café au lait or simple meals of soup, open-face sandwiches, or salads. The quintessential Upper East Side café, **E.A.T.** (⊠ 1064 Madison Ave., between 80th and 81st Sts., ☎ 212/772–0022) serves everything from carrot soup and tabbouleh salad to roast lamb sandwiches and fish pâté. Silver-painted columns and a black-and-white check floor enliven the light and airy room, which bustles with diners from 7 AM to 10 PM daily.

★ ☺ ㉗ **Museum of the City of New York.** One of the best ways to start any visit to this daunting metropolis is with a visit to this museum, set in a massive Georgian mansion built in 1930. From the Dutch settlers of Nieuw Amsterdam to the present day, with period rooms, dioramas, slide shows, films, prints, paintings, sculpture, and clever displays of memorabilia, the museum's got it all. An exhibit on Broadway illuminates the history of American theater with costumes, set designs, and period photographs; the noteworthy toy gallery has several meticulously detailed dollhouses. Maps, nautical artifacts, Currier & Ives lithographs, and furniture collections constitute the rest of the museum's permanent displays, while special exhibitions showcase all aspects of the city's colorful history. Weekend programs are oriented especially to children. The museum will be leaving Museum Mile in 2003 and moving to a new space in the historic Tweed Courthouse in Lower Manhattan. ⊠ *1220 5th Ave., at 103rd St.,* ☎ *212/534–1672,* WEB *www.mcny.org.* ▣ *$7 (suggested donation).* ⊙ *Wed.–Sat. 10–5, Sun. noon–5.*

🔢 **National Academy.** Since its founding in 1825, the Academy has required each member elected to its Museum and School of Fine Arts (the oldest art school in New York) to donate a representative work of art. This criterion produced a strong collection of 19th- and 20th-century American art, as members have included Mary Cassatt, Samuel F. B. Morse, Winslow Homer, John Singer Sargent, Frank Lloyd Wright, Jacob Lawrence, I. M. Pei, Robert Rauschenberg, Jennifer Bartlett, Chuck Close, and Red Grooms. Changing art and architecture shows highlight both the permanent collection and loan exhibits. The collection's home is a stately 19th-century mansion donated in 1940 by sculptor and academy member Anna Hyatt Huntington and her husband Archer. Huntington's bronze, *Diana of the Chase* (1922), reigns triumphantly in the academy's foyer. ⊠ *1083 5th Ave., between 89th and 90th Sts.,* ☎ *212/369–4880,* WEB *www.nationalacademy.org.* ▣ *$8; free Fri. 5–6.* ⊙ *Wed.–Thurs. and weekends noon–5, Fri. 10–6.*

★ 🔢 **Solomon R. Guggenheim Museum.** Frank Lloyd Wright's landmark museum building is visited as much for its famous architecture as it is for its art. Opened in 1959, shortly after Wright died, the Guggenheim (which is shaped somewhat like an upside-down cone) is an icon of Modernist architecture and designed specifically to showcase—and complement—modern art. Outside, Wright's attention to detail is everywhere evident—in the circular pattern of the sidewalk outside the museum, the portholelike windows on its south side, and the smoothness of the hand-plastered concrete. Inside, under a 92-ft-high glass dome, a ¼-mi-long ramp spirals down past changing exhibitions. The museum has especially strong holdings in Vasily Kandinsky, Paul Klee, Pablo Picasso, and Robert Mapplethorpe. In 1992, the Guggenheim began what has become a global expansion, starting here with the opening of new galleries in its "little rotunda" (which displays the Thannhauser Collection comprised primarily of works by French Impressionists and neo-Impressionists including Toulouse-Lautrec and Cezanne) and its Tower galleries, a museum addition designed to accommodate the extraordinarily large art pieces that the Guggenheim owns but previously had no room to display. The museum also opened a SoHo branch, and now has branches around the world, including the renowned Frank O. Gehry-designed Guggenheim Bilbao (1997) in Spain and Guggenheim Las Vegas (2001). In 2004 or so, Manhattan will be getting its own *third* Guggenheim. After Gehry's success in Bilbao, he is designing a grand new building for the museum to be erected on piers above the East River, just below the South Street Seaport. ⊠ *1071 5th Ave., between 88th and 89th Sts.,* ☎ *212/423–3500,* WEB *www.guggenheim.org.* ▣ *$12, Fri. 6–8 pay what you wish.* ⊙ *Sun.–Wed. 9–6, Fri.–Sat. 9–8.*

CENTRAL PARK

For many residents, Central Park is the greatest—and most indispensable—part of New York City. Without the park's 843 acres of meandering paths, tranquil lakes, ponds, and open meadows, New Yorkers might be a lot less sane. Every day thousands of joggers, cyclists, in-line skaters, and walkers make their daily jaunts around the park's loop, the reservoir, and various other parts of the park. Come summertime the park serves as Manhattan's Riviera, with sun worshipers crowding every available patch of grass. Throughout the year pleasure seekers of all ages come to enjoy horseback riding, softball, ice-skating or roller-skating, rock climbing, croquet, tennis, bird-watching, boating, chess, checkers, theater, concerts, skateboarding, folk dancing, and more—or simply to escape from the rumble of traffic, walk through the trees, and feel, at least for a moment, far from the urban frenzy.

Although it appears to be nothing more than a swath of rolling countryside exempted from urban development, Central Park was in fact the first artificially landscaped park in the United States. The design for the park was conceived in 1857 by Frederick Law Olmsted and Calvert Vaux, the founders of the landscape architecture profession in the United States. Their design was one of 33 submitted in a contest arranged by the Central Park Commission—the first such contest in the country. The Greensward Plan, as it was called, combined pastoral, picturesque, and formal elements: open rolling meadows complement fanciful landscapes and grand, formal walkways. The southern portion of the park features many formal elements, while the north end is deliberately more rustic. Four transverse roads—at 66th, 79th, 86th, and 96th Streets—were designed to carry crosstown traffic beneath the park's hills and tunnels so that park goers would not be disturbed, and 40 bridges were conceived—each with its own unique design and name—to give strollers easy access to various areas.

The job of constructing the park was monumental. Hundreds of residents were displaced, swamps were drained, and great walls of Manhattan schist were blasted. Thousands of workers were employed to move some 5 million cubic yards of soil and plant thousands of trees and shrubs in a project that lasted 16 years and cost $14 million. Today, thanks to the efforts of the Central Park Conservancy, a private, not-for-profit organization that took over the reconstruction and maintenance of the park in 1980, Olmsted and Vaux's green oasis looks better than at any time in its history.

In the years following the park's opening in 1859, more than half its visitors arrived by carriage. Today, with a little imagination, you can still experience the park as they did, by hiring a horse-drawn carriage at Grand Army Plaza or any other major intersection of Central Park South at 59th Street between 5th Avenue and Columbus Circle. Rates, which are regulated, are $34 for the first half hour and $10 for each additional quarter hour for up to four people.

Numbers in the text correspond to numbers in the margin and on the Central Park map.

A Good Walk

To explore the park on foot, begin at the southeast corner, at Grand Army Plaza, at 59th Street. The first path off the main road (East Drive) leads to the **Pond** ①, where Gapstow Bridge provides a great vantage point for the oft-photographed midtown skyscrapers. Heading north on the road, you'll come to **Wollman Memorial Rink** ②, whose popularity is second only to that of the rink at Rockefeller Center. Turn your back to the rink, and you'll see the historic **Dairy** ③, which now serves as the park's main visitor center. As you walk up the hill to the Dairy, you'll pass the Chess and Checkers House to your left, where gamesters gather on weekends (playing pieces are available at the Dairy).

As you leave the Dairy, to your right (west) is the Playmates Arch, which leads to a large area of ball fields and playgrounds. Coming through

136

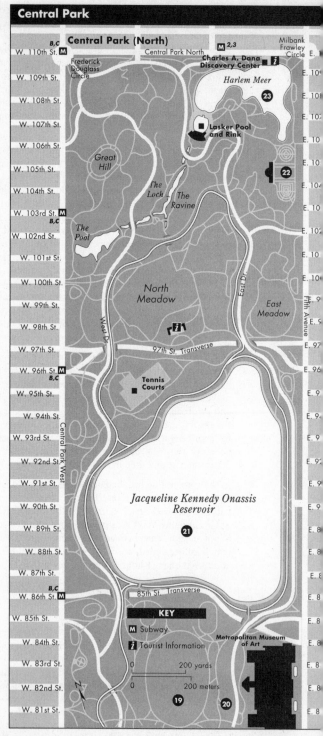

Central Park

Central Park (North)

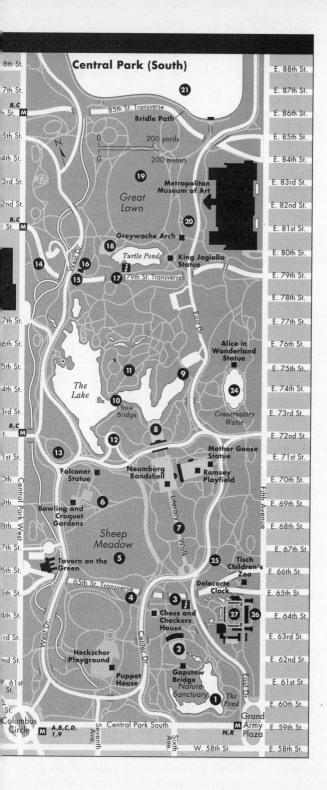

the arch, you'll hear the jaunty music of the antique **Friedsam Memorial Carousel** ④, the second oldest on the East Coast.

From the carousel, climb the slope to the left of the Playmates Arch and walk beside Center Drive, which veers to the right. Stop for a look at the **Sheep Meadow** ⑤, a 15-acre expanse, and the neighboring **Mineral Springs Pavilion** ⑥, one of the park's original refreshment stands. The grand, formal walkway east of the Sheep Meadow is **The Mall** ⑦, which is lined with statuary and magnificent American elms.

As you stroll up the Mall, note the buzzing road ahead, where joggers, rollerbladers, and cyclists speed by. This is the 72nd Street transverse, a crosstown street. Pass beneath it through a lovely tile arcade—elaborately carved birds and fruit trees adorn the upper parts of both staircases—to get to **Bethesda Fountain** ⑧, set on an elaborately patterned paved terrace on the edge of the lake.

For the **Loeb Boathouse** ⑨, take the path east from the terrace, where in season you can rent rowboats and bicycles. The path to the west of the terrace leads to **Bow Bridge** ⑩, a splendid cast-iron bridge arching over a neck of the lake. Across the bridge is **The Ramble** ⑪, a heavily wooded wild area. Then recross Bow Bridge and continue west along the lakeside path for a view of the lake from **Cherry Hill** ⑫.

Continue on the path back to the 72nd Street transverse; on the rocky outcrop across the road, you'll see a statue of a falconer gracefully lofting his bird. Turn to the right, and you'll see a more prosaic statue, the pompous bronze figure of Daniel Webster with his hand thrust into his coat. Cross West Drive behind Webster, being careful to watch for traffic coming around the corner. Tramp up the winding walk into **Strawberry Fields** ⑬, a memorial to John Lennon.

At the top of Strawberry Fields' hill, turn right through a rustic wood arbor thickly hung with wisteria vines and follow the path downhill. A view of the lake will open on your right. Start up the road that goes to 77th Street and take the path off the right to the southern end of the **Naturalists' Walk** ⑭. After you've explored the varied landscapes of the walk, head back toward the West Drive. Cross the street to the quaint wooden **Swedish Cottage** ⑮, scene of marionette shows.

Rising up behind the Swedish Cottage, the **Shakespeare Garden** ⑯ covers the hillside with flora that has figured in the Bard's work. From the top of the garden, turn east to the steps that lead up to the aptly named Vista Rock, which is dominated by the 1872 **Belvedere Castle** ⑰.

Look out from the castle terrace over Turtle Pond, populated by fish, ducks, and dragonflies, in addition to turtles, of course. To the left you'll see the back of the **Delacorte Theater** ⑱, where the Joseph Papp Public Theater's New York Shakespeare Festival performs each summer. And stretching out in front of you is the **Great Lawn** ⑲.

Walk out the south end of the terrace, turn left, and make your way downhill along the shaded path above the Turtle Pond. At the east end of the pond curve left past the statue of King Jagiello of Poland, where groups gather on weekends for folk dancing.

Continue around the pond and head uphill to **Cleopatra's Needle** ⑳, an Egyptian obelisk just across the East Drive from the Metropolitan Museum of Art. Vigorous walkers may want to continue north to the **Jacqueline Kennedy Onassis Reservoir** ㉑ for a glimpse of one of the city's most popular and scenic jogging paths, the spectacular **Conservatory Garden** ㉒, and onto the serene **Harlem Meer** ㉓. Others can return south from Cleopatra's Needle, following the path through

Greywacke Arch under the East Drive. Then angle right (south), around the back corner of the Metropolitan Museum, and take the first right.

After you pass the dog-walking mecca of Cedar Hill on the right, continue south to one of the park's most formal areas: the symmetrical stone basin of the **Conservatory Water** ㉔, which is usually crowded with remote-control model sailboats. Climb the hill at the far end of the water, cross the 72nd Street transverse, and follow the path south. When you see a rustic wooden shelter atop an outcrop of rock, take the path on the right to see **Balto** ㉕, a bronze statue of the real-life sled dog. The path circles back to the Tisch Children's Zoo, after which you'll pass under the Denesmouth Arch to the elaborately designed Delacorte Clock. A path to the left will take you around to the front entrance of the **Arsenal** ㉖, which houses various exhibits and some great WPA-era murals. Just past the clock is the **Central Park Wildlife Center** ㉗, formerly known as the zoo.

TIMING

Allow three to four hours for this route so that you can enjoy its pastoral pleasures in an appropriately leisurely mood. Bear in mind that the circular drive through the park is closed to auto traffic on weekdays 10–3 (except for the southeast portion of the road, up to 72nd Street) and 7–10, and on weekends and holidays. Nonautomotive traffic is often heavy and sometimes fast moving, so always be careful when you're crossing the road, and stay toward the inside when you're walking. Weekends are the liveliest time in the park—free entertainment is everywhere, and the entire social microcosm is on parade.

Despite its once bad reputation, Central Park has the lowest crime rate of any precinct in the city. Just use common sense and stay within sight of other park visitors. Weekend crowds make it safe to go into virtually any area of the park, although even on weekdays you should be safe anywhere along this tour. Take this walk only during the day, since the park is fairly empty after dark.

For a recorded schedule of weekend walks and talks led by Urban Park Rangers, call 888/697–2757. Or, visit the park's web site at www.centralparknyc.org. Information booths are scattered about the park.

Food for thought: Although there are cafés connected with several attractions, as well as food stands near many park entrances, food choices are limited; a picnic lunch is usually a good idea. For sit-down meals during the warmer months, however, **The Boathouse Café** (212/517–2233), overlooking the lake at the Loeb Boathouse, is a wonderfully pleasant spot.

Sights to See

㉖ **The Arsenal.** Constructed between 1847 and the early 1850s, the Arsenal, built as a storage facility for munitions, predates the park and is the oldest extant structure within its grounds. Between 1869 and 1877 it was the early home of the American Museum of Natural History, and it now serves as headquarters of the Parks and Recreation Department. The downstairs lobby has some great WPA-era murals, an upstairs gallery has changing exhibits relating to park and natural-environmental design, and a small public library offers information about New York City parks and other attractions. ✉ *830 5th Ave., at 64th St.,* ☎ *212/360–8111.* ☉ *Weekdays 9–5.*

㉕ **Balto.** This bronze statue commemorates Balto, a real-life sled dog who led a team of huskies that carried medicine for 60 mi across perilous ice to Nome, Alaska, during a 1925 diphtheria epidemic. The surface of the statue is shiny from being petted by thousands of children. *East of Center Dr. near Literary Walk.*

🔵 ⑰ **Belvedere Castle.** Standing regally atop Vista Rock, Belvedere Castle was built in 1872 of the same gray Manhattan schist that thrusts out of the soil in dramatic outcrops throughout the park (you can examine some of this schist, polished and striated by Ice Age glaciers, from the lip of the rock). From here you can also see the stage of **Delacorte Theater** and observe the picnickers and softball players on the Great Lawn. The castle, a typically 19th-century mishmash of styles—Gothic with Romanesque, Chinese, Moorish, and Egyptian motifs—was deliberately kept small so that when it was viewed from across the lake, the lake would seem bigger. (The Ramble's forest now obscures the lake's castle view.) Since 1919 it has been a U.S. Weather Bureau station; look for twirling meteorological instruments atop the tower. Inside, the Henry Luce Nature Observatory has nature exhibits, children's workshops, and educational programs. Free discovery kits containing binoculars, maps, and sketching materials are available for two pieces of identification. ☎ 212/772–0210. ✉ *Free.* ⊗ *Mid-Apr.–mid-Oct., Tues.–Sun. 9–5; mid-Oct.–mid-Apr., Tues.–Sun. 10–4.*

★ ⑧ **Bethesda Fountain.** Few New York views are more romantic than the one from the top of the magnificent stone staircase that leads down to the ornate, three-tier Bethesda Fountain. The fountain was dedicated in 1873 to commemorate the soldiers who died at sea during the Civil War. Named for the biblical pool in Jerusalem, which was supposedly given healing powers by an angel, it features the statue of an angel rising from the center. This statue is called *The Angel of the Waters,* and the four figures around the fountain's base symbolize Temperance, Purity, Health, and Peace. Beyond the terrace stretches the lake, filled with drifting swans and amateur rowboat captains. *Mid-park, at 72nd St.*

⑩ **Bow Bridge.** This splendid cast-iron bridge arches over a neck of the lake between Bethesda Fountain and The Ramble. Stand here to take in the picture-postcard view of the water reflecting a quintessentially New York image of vintage apartment buildings peeping above the treetops. *Mid-park, north of 72nd St.*

🔵 ㉗ **Central Park Wildlife Center (Zoo).** Even a leisurely visit to this small but delightful menagerie, home to about a hundred species, will take only about an hour. The biggest specimens here are the polar bears—go to the Bronx Zoo if you need tigers, giraffes, and elephants. Clustered around the central Sea Lion Pool are separate exhibits for each of the earth's major environments; the Polar Circle features a huge penguin tank and polar-bear floe; the open-air Temperate Territory is highlighted by a pit of chattering monkeys; and the Tropic Zone contains the flora and fauna of a miniature rain forest. The **Tisch Children's Zoo,** on the north side of the Denesmouth Arch, has interactive, hands-on exhibits where younglings and older wanna-be farmers can meet and touch such domestic animals as pigs, sheep, goats, and cows. There is also an enchanted forest area, designed to thrill the six and under set. Above a redbrick arcade near the Zoo is the **Delacorte Clock,** a delightful glockenspiel that was dedicated to the city by philanthropist George T. Delacorte. Its fanciful bronze face is decorated with a menagerie of mechanical animals, including a dancing bear, a kangaroo, a penguin, and monkeys that rotate and hammer their bells when the clock chimes its tune every half hour. ✉ *Entrance at 5th Ave. and 64th St.,* ☎ 212/439–6500, 🌐 *www.wcs.org/zoos/.* ✉ *$3.50. No children under 16 admitted without adult.* ⊗ *Apr.–Oct., weekdays 10–5, weekends 10:30–5:30; Nov.–Mar., daily 10–4:30.*

⑫ **Cherry Hill.** Originally a watering area for horses, this circular plaza with a small wrought-iron-and-gilt fountain is a great vantage point for the lake and the West Side skyline. *Mid-park, near W. 72nd St.*

⓴ Cleopatra's Needle. This exotic, hieroglyphic-covered obelisk began life in Heliopolis, Egypt, around 1600 BC, was eventually carted off to Alexandria by the Romans in 12 BC, and landed here on February 22, 1881, when the khedive of Egypt made it a gift to the city. It stands, appropriately, near the glass-enclosed wing of the Metropolitan Museum, which houses the Egyptian Temple of Dendur. Ironically, a century in New York has done more to ravage the Needle than millennia of globe-trotting, and the hieroglyphics have sadly worn away to a tabula rasa. The copper crabs supporting the huge stone at each corner almost seem squashed by its weight. *E. Park Dr., north of 79th St.*

★ **⓶ Conservatory Garden.** These magnificent formal gardens occupy 6 acres near Central Park's northeast corner, near **El Museo del Barrio**. The conservatory's entrance leads through elaborate wrought-iron gates that once graced the midtown 5th Avenue mansion of Cornelius Vanderbilt II. The **Central Garden,** in the classic Italian style, has a lawn bordered by yew hedges and cool crab-apple allées. Across the lawn is the large Conservatory Fountain, beyond which a semicircular wisteria-draped pergola rises into the hillside. The **North Garden,** in the French tradition, marshalls large numbers of bedding plants into elaborate floral patterns. The three spirited girls dancing in the Untermeyer Fountain are at the heart of a great circular bed where 20,000 tulips bloom in spring and 5,000 chrysanthemums herald autumn. Perrenials in the English–style **South Garden** surround a statue of characters from the classic children's book *The Secret Garden* by Frances Hodgson Burnett. ⊠ *Near Harlem Meer, 5th Ave. and 105th St.,* ☎ *212/360–2766.* ⌨ *Free.* ⊗ *Daily 8–dusk.*

🖐 **⓴ Conservatory Water.** The sophisticated model boats that sail this Renaissance revival–style stone basin are raced each Saturday morning at 10 from spring through fall. At the north end is one of the park's most beloved statues, José de Creeft's 1960 bronze sculpture of **Alice in Wonderland,** sitting on a giant mushroom with the Mad Hatter, White Rabbit, and leering Cheshire Cat in attendance; children are free to clamber all over it. On the west side of the pond, a bronze statue of **Hans Christian Andersen,** the Ugly Duckling at his feet, is the site of storytelling hours on summer weekends. A concession in the brick pavilion adjacent to Conservatory Water serves snacks and a fine hot chocolate for a cold day. *East side of park, near E. 74th St.*

❸ The Dairy. When it was built in the 19th century, the Dairy sat amid grazing cows and sold milk by the glass. Today the Dairy's painted, pointed eaves, steeple, and high-pitched slate roof harbor the **Central Park Visitor Center,** which has exhibits and interactive videos on the park's history, maps, and information about park events. *Mid-park, north of 65th St.,* ☎ *212/794–6564.* ⊗ *Apr.–Oct., Tues.–Sun. 10–5; Nov.–Mar., Tues.–Sun. 10–4.*

⓲ Delacorte Theater. Some of the best things in New York are, indeed, free— but have *long* lines—including summer performances by the Joseph Papp Public Theater New York Shakespeare Festival at this open-air theater. For free tickets (two per person), plan to arrive by mid-morning or earlier if there have been good reviews; the booth opens at 1 for that evening's performance. Same-day tickets are also given away at the Joseph Papp Public Theater, also at 1. *Mid-park, near W. 81st St.,* ☎ *212/539–8750 (seasonal).* ⊗ *Mid-June–Labor Day, Tues.–Sun. 8 PM.*

★ 🖐 **❹ Friedsam Memorial Carousel.** Remarkable for the size of its hand-carved steeds—all 57 are three-quarters the size of real horses—this carousel was built in 1908 and moved here from Coney Island in 1951. Today it's considered one of the finest examples of turn-of-the-

20th-century folk art. The organ plays a variety of tunes, new and old. *Mid-park, at 64th St., ☎ 212/879–0244. ☐ $1. ⊙ Apr.–Oct., daily 10–6; Nov.–Dec., daily 10–4; Jan.–Mar., weekends 10–4, weather permitting.*

⑲ Great Lawn. After millions of footsteps, thousands of ball games, hundreds of downpours, dozens of concerts, and one papal mass, the Great Lawn had had it. In 1997 the Great Dust Bowl, as it had come to be known, underwent high-tech reconstructive surgery. The central 14-acre oval is now the stuff of a suburbanite's dream—perfectly tended turf (a mix of rye and Kentucky bluegrass), state-of-the-art drainage systems, automatic sprinklers, and careful horticultural monitoring. The area hums with action on weekends and most summer evenings, when its softball fields and picnicking grounds provide a much-needed outlet for city dwellers of all ages. *Mid-park, between 81st and 85th Sts.*

㉓ Harlem Meer. Those who never venture beyond 96th Street miss out on two of the park's most unusual attractions: the Conservatory Garden and Harlem Meer, where as many as 100 people fish for stocked largemouth bass, catfish, golden shiners, and bluegills every day on a catch-and-release basis. At the meer's north end is the Victorian–style **Charles A. Dana Discovery Center,** where you can learn about geography, orienteering, ecology, and the history of the upper park. Within walking distance of the center are fortifications from the American Revolution and other historic sites, as well as woodlands, meadows, rocky bluffs, lakes, and streams. Fishing poles are available with identification from mid-April through October. *⊠ Between 5th and Lenox Aves., at 110th St., ☎ 212/860–1370. ⊙ Discovery Center: Apr.–Oct., Tues.–Sun. 10–5; Nov.–Mar., Tues.–Sun. 10–4.*

㉑ Jacqueline Kennedy Onassis Reservoir. Named for the former first lady, who frequently jogged in the area and lived nearby, this 106-acre body of water was built in 1862 to provide fresh water to Manhattan residents. Although it still contains 1 billion gallons, it's no longer used for drinking water—the city's main reservoirs are upstate. A 1.58-mi cinder track circling the lake is popular with runners year-round. If you come for some exercise, though, observe local traffic rules and run counterclockwise. Even if you're not training for the New York Marathon, it's worth visiting the reservoir for the stellar views of surrounding high-rises and the stirring sunsets; in spring and fall the hundreds of trees around it burst into color, and migrant waterfowl is plentiful. Just remember to look out for the athletes, as they have the right of way. *Mid-park, at 86th St.*

⑨ Loeb Boathouse. At the brick neo-Victorian boathouse, on the east side of the park's 18-acre lake, you can rent a dinghy (or the one authentic Venetian gondola) or pedal off on a rented bicycle. *East Park Dr., north of E. 72nd St., ☎ 212/517–2233 boat rental. ☐ Boat rental $10 per hr, $20 deposit ($30 per half hr for gondola); bicycle rental $10–$12 per hr, tandems $14 per hr, deposit required. ⊙ Mar.–Oct. daily 10–7, weather permitting.*

NEED A BREAK?   The **Boathouse Cafe** is a waterside, open-air restaurant and bar that serves lunch and dinner. An adjacent cafeteria dishes up a good cheap breakfast, including freshly made scones, and lunch. Both are open from March through October. Also note the decent public rest rooms on the southeast side of the building. *⊠ East Park Dr., north of E. 72nd St., ☎ 212/517–2233.*

★ **❼ The Mall.** Around the turn of the 20th century, fashionable ladies and gentlemen used to gather to see and be seen on this broad, formal walkway. Today the Mall looks as grand as ever. The south end of its main path, the **Literary Walk,** is covered by the majestic canopy of the largest collection of American elms in North America and lined by statues of famous and not-so-famous men—not all of whom are literary. For statues of the other sex, stretch your imagination and look toward **Alice in Wonderland** and **Mother Goose,** by East 72nd Street—but, sadly, the female bronze stops there. East of the Mall, behind the Naumburg Bandshell, is the site of **SummerStage,** a free summertime concert series. *Mid-park, between 66th and 70th Sts.*

❻ Mineral Springs Pavilion. The Moorish-style palace at the north end of the Sheep Meadow was designed by Calvert Vaux and J. Wrey Mould, who also designed Bethesda Terrace. Built as one of the park's four refreshment stands in the late 1860s, the pavilion still has a snack bar. Behind it are the croquet grounds and lawn-bowling greens. During the season (May–November) you can observe the players, dressed in their crisp whites. *Mid-park, near W. 68th St.*

⑭ Naturalists' Walk. Starting at the West 79th Street entrance to the park, across from the American Museum of Natural History, this landscaped nature walk (through which you can wind your way toward the **Swedish Cottage,** the **Shakespeare Garden,** and **Belvedere Castle**) has spectacular rock outcrops; a stream that attracts interesting birdlife; a woodland area with various native trees; stepping-stone trails; and, thankfully, benches. *Off Central Park W, between 77th and 81st Sts.*

❶ The Pond. Swans and ducks can sometimes be spotted on the calm waters of the Pond. For an unbeatable view of the city skyline, walk along the shore to **Gapstow Bridge.** From left to right you'll see the brown peak-roof Sherry-Netherland Hotel; the black-and-white former General Motors Building (now home to CBS); the rose-color Chippendale-style top of the Sony Building; the black-glass shaft of Trump Tower; and, in front, the green gables of the Plaza hotel. *Central Park S and 5th Ave.*

⑪ The Ramble. The Ramble is a heavily wooded, wild 37-acre area laced with twisting, climbing paths, designed to resemble upstate New York's Adirondack Mountain region. This is prime bird-watching territory; a rest stop along a major migratory route, it shelters many of the more than 260 species of birds that have been sighted in the park. The Urban Park Rangers lead **bird-watching tours** here; call ☎ 888/697–2757 for details. Because the Ramble is so dense and isolated, however, it is not a good place to wander alone or at night. *Mid-park, between E. 74th St. and 79th St. transverse.*

★ **⑯ Shakespeare Garden.** Inspired by the flora mentioned in the playwright's work, and nestled between Belvedere Castle and the Swedish Cottage, this somewhat hidden garden is a true find. Under the dedicated care of the gardener something is always blooming on the terraced hillside of lush beds. The fantastic spring bulb display beginning in March and June's peak bloom of antique roses are particularly stunning times to visit. The curving paths of the lower garden and the upper lawn leading to Belvedere Castle are furnished with handsome rustic benches that in this park-designated Quiet Zone make a superb spot for a good read or contemplative thought. *W. Park Dr. and 79th St. transverse.*

❺ Sheep Meadow. A sheep grazing area until 1934, this grassy 15-acre meadow is now a favorite of picnickers and sunbathers. It's an officially designated quiet zone; the most vigorous sports allowed are kite flying and Frisbee tossing. Just west of the meadow, the famous

Tavern on the Green, originally the sheepfold, was erected by Boss Tweed in 1870 and is now an overpriced Manhattan tourist destination. *West side of park, north of 65th St.*

★ ⓭ **Strawberry Fields.** This memorial to John Lennon, who penned the classic 1967 song "Strawberry Fields Forever," is sometimes called the "international garden of peace." Its curving paths, shrubs, trees, and flower beds donated by many countries create a deliberately informal pastoral landscape reminiscent of the English parks of Lennon's homeland. Every year on December 8, Beatles fans mark the anniversary of Lennon's death by gathering around the star-shape, black-and-white tile IMAGINE mosaic set into the sidewalk. Lennon's 1980 murder took place across the street at the Dakota, where he lived. *W. Park Dr. and 72nd St.*

⚞ ⓯ **Swedish Cottage.** This traditional Swedish schoolhouse was imported in 1876 for the Philadelphia Exhibition and brought to Central Park soon thereafter. Marionette theater is performed regularly to the delight of young park visitors. ⊠ *W. Park Dr., at 79th St.,* ☎ *212/ 988–9093.* ☞ *$5.* ⊙ *Shows Tues.–Fri. 10:30 and noon; Sat. 1; call for reservations.*

⚞ ❷ **Wollman Memorial Rink.** Its music blaring out into the tranquillity of the park can be a bit of an intrusion, but you can't deny that the lower park makes a great setting for a spin on the ice. Even if you don't want to join in, you can stand on the terrace here to watch ice-skaters throughout the winter and roller and in-line skaters and dancers in the summer. ⊠ *E. Park Dr., north of 59th St.,* ☎ *212/396–1010.* ☞ *$7 in winter, $4 in summer, skate rentals and lockers extra.* ⊙ *Mid-Oct.– Mar., Mon.–Tues. 10–3, Wed.–Thurs. 10–9:30, Fri.–Sat. 10 AM–11 PM, Sun. 10–9 for ice-skating; late Apr.–Sept., Thurs. and Fri. 11–6, Sat. 11–8, Sun. 11–6 for in-line skating. Call to confirm prices and hrs, as dates are subject to change due to weather.*

THE UPPER WEST SIDE

The Upper West Side—never as exclusive as the tony East Side—has always had an earthier appeal. Although real-estate prices keep going up (its restored brownstones and co-op apartments are among the city's most coveted residences), the Upper West Side is still a haven for families—albeit increasingly well-heeled ones—who give the area a pleasant, neighborhood feel. On weekends parents cram the sidewalks as they push babies around in their imported strollers, and shoppers jam the fantastic gourmet food stores and fashion emporiums that line Broadway, the Upper West Side's main drag. In the evenings, however, the action moves inside, where singles from the city and suburbs mingle in bars and restaurants. Columbus Avenue is one such boutique-and-restaurant strip; Amsterdam Avenue is quickly following suit, its shop fronts a mix of bodegas, new restaurants, and boutiques. These lively avenues, the Upper West Side's many quiet tree- and brownstone-lined side streets, its two flanking parks—Central on its east flank, Riverside on its west—as well as such leading cultural complexes as the American Museum of Natural History and Lincoln Center, are all perennial attractions and make for a great variety of things to do in one relatively compact area.

Numbers in the text correspond to numbers in the margin and on the Upper West Side, Morningside Heights map.

A Good Walk

The West Side story begins at **Columbus Circle** ①, the bustling intersection of Broadway, 8th Avenue, Central Park West, and Central

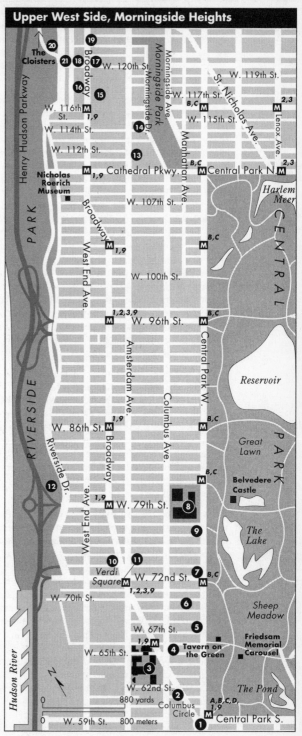

Upper West Side, Morningside Heights

Park South. Cars enter this enormous circle from any one of several directions (use caution and cross only at marked intersections). On the leafy southwest corner of Central Park, a line of horse-drawn carriages awaits fares. If you're in the mood for an ecclesiastical outing, stop in at the nearby **American Bible Society Gallery and Library** ②, home of the largest Bible collection in the United States.

With its parade of elegant, monumental apartment buildings on one side and Central Park on the other, Central Park West is one of the city's grandest avenues and the ideal place to begin a walk of the area. In the 1930s it was quite the rage to have your home address at the block-long Century (✉ 25 Central Park W, between 62nd and 63rd Sts.), which went up in 1931, taking with it one of the last large lots below 96th Street—only two buildings have gone up on this stretch since then. The solid brick-and-limestone New York Society for Ethical Culture buildings (✉ 33 Central Park W and 2 W. 64th St.), built in 1902–10, host Sunday services as well as periodic lectures and concerts. From this corner, the view up the avenue is particularly handsome. Turn west on 64th Street; on your left you may notice some unusual stonework on the back of one building. The West Side YMCA (✉ 10 W. 64th St., between Central Park W and Columbus Ave.) has a neo-Moorish portal that sports tiny carved figures representing the worlds of sport (golfers, tennis players) *and* religion (St. George slaying the dragon). As you approach Broadway, **Lincoln Center** ③, New York's premier performing arts venue, widens into view. On summer nights the brightly lit fountain in the central plaza with the Metropolitan Opera House behind is a lovely sight.

On the east side of Columbus Avenue just below 66th Street, stands a branch of the **Museum of American Folk Art** ④. Around the corner at 77 West 66th Street is the headquarters of the ABC television network; ABC owns several buildings along Columbus Avenue as well, including some studios where news shows and soap operas are filmed, so keep an eye out for your favorite daytime doctors, tycoons, and temptresses. Up Columbus Avenue one block, turn right onto West 67th Street and head toward Central Park West, where on the corner you'll encounter the Elizabethan front of the **Hotel des Artistes** ⑤. Across the street, just inside Central Park, is Tavern on the Green.

Walk north on the east (park) side of Central Park West for the best view of the stately apartment buildings that line the avenue. Mixed among them is the **Spanish & Portuguese Synagogue, Shearith Israel** ⑥ at West 70th Street, home of the country's oldest Jewish congregation. At 72nd Street cross back over Central Park West to get a close-up view of **The Dakota** ⑦, the châteaulike apartment building that presides over the block. Its neighbors to the north include several other famous apartment buildings and their famous residents: The Langham (✉ 135 Central Park W, at 73rd St.), is an Italian Renaissance–style highrise that was designed by leading apartment architect Emery Roth in 1929–30. The twin-tower San Remo (✉ 145–146 Central Park W, at 74th St.) was built in 1930 and, like its neighbor, The Langham, was designed by Emery Roth; over the years, it has been home to Rita Hayworth, Dustin Hoffman, Raquel Welch, Paul Simon, Barry Manilow, Tony Randall, and Diane Keaton. The Kenilworth (✉ 151 Central Park W, at 75th St.), built in 1908, with its immense pair of ornate front columns, was once the address of Basil Rathbone (Hollywood's quintessential Sherlock Holmes) and Michael Douglas. The final beauty is the cubic Beresford (✉ 211 Central Park W, at 81st St.), built in 1929 also by Emery Roth, whose lighted towers romantically haunt the night sky.

The row of massive buildings along Central Park West breaks between West 77th and 81st Streets to make room for the **American Museum of Natural History** ⑧. Also consider a stop at the **New-York Historical Society** ⑨ for a quick history lesson on the city itself.

At this point you've covered the major institutions in the neighborhood. If you've had enough sight-seeing, you could forsake the rest of this tour for a stroll through Central Park or for shopping along Columbus Avenue, which is directly behind the museum. If you're here on a Sunday, check out the flea market at the southwest corner of West 77th Street and Columbus Avenue. Food lovers should continue on to the four foodie shrines along the west side of Broadway: At Zabar's (⌖ 2245 Broadway, between 80th and 81st Sts.) shoppers battle it out for exquisite delicatessen items, prepared foods, gourmet groceries, coffee, and cheeses as well as cookware, dishes, and small appliances. H & H Bagels (⌖ 2239 Broadway, at 80th St.) sells—and ships around the world—a dozen varieties of chewy bagels hot from the oven. Citarella (⌖ 2135 Broadway, at 75th St.) always has an intricate arrangement of seafood on shaved ice in its front window. At the bountiful but unpretentious Fairway Market (⌖ 2127 Broadway, at 74th St.) snack food, cheeses, and produce practically overflow onto the street.

At West 73rd Street and Broadway are the white facade and fairy-castle turrets of the **Ansonia Hotel** ⑩, a turn-of-the-20th-century luxury building. At West 72nd Street, where Broadway cuts across Amsterdam Avenue, is triangular Verdi Square (named for Italian opera composer Giuseppe Verdi); here a marble statue of the composer is flanked by figures from Verdi's operas: *Aida, Otello,* and *Falstaff.* The triangle south of West 72nd Street is Sherman Square (named for Union Civil War general William Tecumseh Sherman); the **subway kiosk** ⑪ here is an official city landmark.

Blocks such as West 71st Street or West 74th Street between Broadway and Central Park West are perfect for casual strolling; Riverside Drive to West 116th Street and Columbia University in Morningside Heights makes another fine walk. The latter leads past **Riverside Park** ⑫, which many neighborhood residents consider their private backyard.

TIMING
Charming tree- and brownstone-lined park blocks comprise this tour, which will easily take two or three hours at a relaxed clip. The exhibits at the Museum of American Folk Art and the New-York Historical Society shouldn't take more than an hour or so to view, but the mammoth and often crowded American Museum of Natural History can eat up most of a day. In bad weather you might want to limit your itinerary to what's covered between Lincoln Center and the Museum of Natural History.

Sights to See

❷ **American Bible Society Gallery and Library.** With nearly 50,000 scriptural items in 2,000 languages, this is one of the largest Bible collections in the world outside the Vatican. The library, which can be toured by appointment, houses Helen Keller's massive 10-volume Braille Bible, leaves from a first edition Gutenberg Bible, and a Torah from China. The public gallery features changing exhibitions of sacred art, ranging from stained glass to sculpture. ⌖ *1865 Broadway, at 61st St.,* ☎ *212/408–1200,* WEB *www.americanbible.org.* ☉ *Bookstore and gallery, Mon.–Wed. and Fri. 10–6, Thurs. 10–7, Sat. 10–5; library, by appointment only.*

★ ☺ ❽   **American Museum of Natural History.** With 42 exhibition halls and more than 36 million artifacts and specimens, including its awe-inspiring collection of dinosaur skeletons, this is the world's largest and most important museum of natural history. Dinosaur-mania begins in the massive, barrel-vaulted **Theodore Roosevelt Rotunda,** where a 50-ft-tall skeleton of a barosaurus rears on its hind legs, protecting its fossilized baby from an enormous marauding allosaurus. Three spectacular dinosaur halls on the fourth floor—the **Hall of Saurischian Dinosaurs,** the **Hall of Ornithischian Dinosaurs,** and the **Hall of Vertebrate Origins**—use real fossils and interactive computer stations to present the most recent interpretations of how dinosaurs and pterodactyls might have behaved. The **Hall of Fossil Mammals** has interactive video monitors featuring museum curators explaining what caused the woolly mammoth to vanish from the earth and why mammals don't have to lay eggs to have babies. The **Hall of Biodiversity** focuses on Earth's wealth of plants and animals; its main attraction is the walk-through "Dzanga-Sangha Rainforest," a life-size diorama complete with the sounds of the African tropics—from bird calls to chain saws. The **Hall of Human Biology and Evolution**'s wondrously detailed dioramas trace human origins back to Lucy and feature a computerized archaeological dig and an electronic newspaper about human evolution. The **Hall of Ocean Life,** with its fiberglass replica of a 94-ft blue whale hanging from the ceiling, is the next area of the museum slated to undergo a high-tech make-over; plans for the hall, scheduled to re-open in 2003, call for a humongous fish-filled aquarium and a ceiling-wide video screen that will put the hall's whale into a virtual ocean habitat.

The spectacular **Hayden Planetarium** is contained in a 90-ft aluminum-clad sphere that appears to float inside an enormous glass cube, which in turn is home to the **Rose Center for Earth and Space.** Models of planets, stars, and galaxies dangle overhead, and an elevator whisks you to the top of the sphere and the new **Sky Theater,** which—using "all-dome video"—transports you from galaxy to galaxy as if you were traveling through space. The theater's inaugural show, "Passport to the Universe," narrated by Tom Hanks, is the most technologically advanced planetarium show in the world, incorporating up-to-the-minute scientific knowledge about the universe in computerized projections generated from a database of more than 2 billion stars. After the show, you descend a spiral walkway that tracks 13 billion years of the universe's evolution. The Rose Center also includes two major exhibits, the **Hall of the Universe,** in which black holes and colliding galaxies are explored through video and moving sculpture, and the **Hall of Planet Earth,** which explains the climate, geology, and evolution of our home planet with the help of over 100 giant rocks from the ocean floor, glaciers, and active volcanoes. On Friday evening, when the museum stays open late, the Rose Center turns into a cocktail lounge, with tapas-style dining and live jazz under the "stars."

Films on the museum's 40-ft-high, 66-ft-wide **IMAX Theater** (☎ 212/769–5034 for show times) screen are usually about nature (climbing Mt. Everest, a safari in the Serengeti, or an underwater journey to the wreck of the *Titanic*) and cost $15, including museum admission. ✉ *Central Park W at 79th St.,* ☎ *212/769–5200 for museum tickets and programs; 212/769–5100 for museum general information,* 🕸 *www. amnh.org.* 💲 *Museum $10 (suggested donation); museum and IMAX Theater combination tickets $15; museum and planetarium show combination tickets $19.* ☉ *Sun.–Thurs. 10–5:45; Fri.–Sat. 10–8:45.*

NEED A   For a diner-style cheeseburger or just a banana split, stop by **EJ's**
BREAK?   **Luncheonette** (✉ 447 Amsterdam Ave., between 81st and 82nd Sts.,

☎ 212/873–3444). Nearby **Big Nick's** pizza joint is a favorite with local youngsters (✉ 2175 Broadway, at 77th St., ☎ 212/724–2010).

⑩ Ansonia Hotel. This 1904 beaux arts masterpiece designed by Paul M. Duboy commands its corner of Broadway with as much architectural detail as good taste can stand. Inspiration for the Ansonia's turrets, mansard roof, and filigreed-iron balconies came from turn-of-the-20th-century Paris. Now a condominium apartment building, it was originally built as an apartment hotel, with suites without kitchens (and separate quarters for a staff that took care of the food). Designed to be fireproof, it has thick, soundproof walls that make it attractive to musicians; famous denizens of the past include Enrico Caruso, Igor Stravinsky, Arturo Toscanini, Florenz Ziegfeld, Theodore Dreiser, and Babe Ruth. ✉ *2109 Broadway, between 73rd and 74th Sts.*

❶ Columbus Circle. This confusing intersection—where Broadway, 8th Avenue, Central Park West, and Central Park South all meet—has never had the grandeur or the definition of Broadway's major intersections to the south, but it does have a 700-ton granite monument capped by a marble statue of Columbus himself in the middle of a tiny circular park. (The monument had to be elaborately supported when the land underneath was torn up during the construction of the Columbus Circle subway station in the early 1900s.) On the southwest quadrant of the circle, a multitower office, residential, and entertainment complex—scheduled for completion in fall 2003—is under construction on the former site of the New York Coliseum. In addition to being the new home for AOL Time-Warner with studios for CNN and the local all-news station New York 1, the complex will feature a new concert hall designed by architect Rafael Viñoly for Jazz at Lincoln Center.

Northeast of the circle, standing guard over the entrance to Central Park, is the **Maine Monument,** whose gleaming equestrian figures perch atop a formidable limestone pedestal. At the monument's foot, horse-drawn cabs await fares through Central Park, and a Victorian-style gazebo houses a 24-hour newsstand. The Trump International Hotel and Tower fills the wedge of land between Central Park West and Broadway; Donald Trump spent $250 million to gut this once marble-clad tower and rewrap it in a lamentable brown-glass curtain wall. Happily, it's also home to the self-named Jean Georges restaurant, where the celebrity chef works his culinary magic. You can sometimes see his white-clad assistants furiously stirring and chopping in the window as you walk past on Broadway.

★ ❼ The Dakota. The most famous of all the apartment buildings lining Central Park West, the Dakota set a high standard for the many that followed it. Designed by Henry Hardenbergh, who also built the Plaza, the Dakota was so far uptown when it was completed in 1884 that it was jokingly described as being "out in the Dakotas." Indeed, this buff-color château, with picturesque gables and copper turrets, housed some of the West Side's first residents. The Dakota is often depicted in scenes of old New York, and it was by looking out of a window here that Si Morley was able to travel back in time in Jack Finney's *Time and Again.* Its slightly spooky appearance was played up in the movie *Rosemary's Baby,* which was filmed here. The building's entrance is on West 72nd Street; the spacious, lovely courtyard is visible beyond the guard's station. At the Dakota's gate, in December 1980, a deranged fan shot John Lennon as he came home from a recording session. Other celebrity tenants have included Boris Karloff, Rudolf Nureyev, José Ferrer and Rosemary Clooney, Lauren Bacall, Rex Reed, Leonard Bernstein, and Gilda Radner. ✉ *1 W. 72nd St., at Central Park W.*

⑤ Hotel des Artistes. Built in 1918 with an elaborate, mock-Elizabethan lobby, this "studio building," like several others on West 67th Street, was designed with high ceilings and immense windows, making it ideal for artists. Its tenants have included Isadora Duncan, Rudolph Valentino, Norman Rockwell, Noël Coward, Fannie Hurst, and contemporary actors Joel Grey and Richard Thomas; another tenant, Howard Chandler Christy, designed the lush, soft-tone murals in the ground-floor restaurant, Café des Artistes. ⊠ *1 W. 67th St., at Central Park W.*

★ ❸ **Lincoln Center.** A unified complex of pale travertine, Lincoln Center (built 1962–68) is the largest performing arts center in the world—so large it can seat nearly 18,000 spectators at one time in its various halls. Here Kurt Masur conducts Schubert and Mahler, the American Ballet Theater performs *Swan Lake,* and Luciano Pavarotti sings arias and duets—and that's just an average day. The complex's three principal venues are grouped around the central Fountain Plaza: to the left, as you face west, is Philip Johnson's **New York State Theater,** home to the New York City Ballet and the New York City Opera. In the center, Wallace Harrison's **Metropolitan Opera House,** with its brilliantly colored Chagall murals visible through the arched lobby windows, is home to both the Metropolitan Opera and the American Ballet Theater. And to the right is Max Abramovitz's **Avery Fisher Hall,** host to the New York Philharmonic Orchestra. A great time to visit the complex is on summer evenings, when thousands of dancers trot and swing around the plaza during Midsummer Night Swing. One-hour guided "Introduction to Lincoln Center" tours, given daily, cover the center's history and wealth of artwork and usually visit these three theaters, performance schedules permitting.

Lincoln Center encompasses much more than its three core theaters. Its major outdoor venue is **Damrosch Park,** on the south flank of the Met, where summer open-air festivals are often accompanied by free concerts at the **Guggenheim Bandshell.** Accessible via the walk between the Metropolitan and Avery Fisher is the North Plaza—the best of Lincoln Center's spaces—with a massive Henry Moore sculpture reclining in a reflecting pool. The long lines and glass wall of Eero Saarinen's **Vivian Beaumont Theater** stand behind the pool. It is officially considered a Broadway house, despite its distance from the theater district. Below it is the smaller **Mitzi E. Newhouse Theater,** where many award-winning plays originate. To the rear is the **New York Public Library for the Performing Arts** (☎ 212/870–1600), a research and circulating library with an extensive collection of books, records, videos, and scores on music, theater, and dance. An overpass leads from this plaza across West 65th Street to the world-renowned **Juilliard School** (☎ 212/769–7406) for music and theater; actors Kevin Kline, Robin Williams, and Patti LuPone studied here. An elevator leads down to street level and **Alice Tully Hall,** home of the Chamber Music Society of Lincoln Center and the New York Film Festival. Or turn left from the overpass and follow the walkway west to Lincoln Center's **Walter Reade Theater,** one of the finest places in the city to watch films. ⊠ *W. 62nd to 66th St. between Broadway and Amsterdam Ave.,* ☎ *212/546–2656 for general information; 212/875–5350 for tour schedule and reservations,* ⊮ *www.lincolncenter.org.* 🎫 *Tour $9.50.*

NEED A BREAK? | Before or after a Lincoln Center performance, the pleasant **Café Mozart** (⊠ 154 W. 70th St., between Broadway and Columbus Ave., ☎ 212/595-9797) is the closest place to stop for conversation with a friend. The operatic atmosphere and espresso at **Café La Fortuna** (⊠ 69 W.

71st St., between Columbus Ave. and Central Park W, ☎ 212/724–5846) are just right.

④ Museum of American Folk Art. The collection of this intimate museum includes arts and decorative objects from the 18th century to the present day that are culled from all over the Americas. Folk paintings, quilts, sculpture, outsider art, dolls, trade signs, painted-wood carousel horses, and a giant Native American–chief copper weather vane are characteristic items on exhibition. The gift shop has intriguing craft items, books, and great cards. A brand-new, eight-floor building (at 45 W. 53rd St.) with quadruple the exhibition space opened in fall 2001. At press time there was talk of closing the Lincoln Square location; call in advance of your visit. Every other Sunday a workshop for children is held, usually based on the current exhibit. ⊠ *2 Lincoln Sq. (Columbus Ave. between 65th and 66th Sts.),* ☎ *212/595–9533,* WEB *www.folkartmuseum.org.* ◻ *Free.* ☉ *Tues.–Sun. 11:30–7:30.*

★ ④ New-York Historical Society. Founded in 1804, the New-York Historical Society is the city's oldest museum and one of its finest research libraries, with a collection of 6 million pieces of art, literature, and memorabilia. Exhibitions shed light on New York's—and America's—history, everyday life, art, and architecture. Highlights of the collection include George Washington's inaugural chair, 500,000 photographs from the 1850s to the present, original watercolors for John James Audubon's *Birds of America,* the architectural files of McKim, Mead & White, and the largest U.S. collection of Louis Comfort Tiffany's lamps. In 2000, 40,000 of the society's most treasured pieces went on long-awaited, permanent display in a new wing, the Henry Luce III Center for the Study of American Culture. Among them are the society's impressive collection of paintings by Hudson River School artists Thomas Cole, Asher Durant, and Frederic Church. There's also a permanent children's exhibit, "Kid City," which introduces young ones to New York's ever-evolving urban environment via the re-creation of an Upper West Side street corner—circa 1901. ⊠ *2 W. 77th St., at Central Park W,* ☎ *212/873–3400,* WEB *www.nychistory.org.* ◻ *Museum $5 (suggested donation).* ☉ *Museum: Tues.–Sun. 11–5; library: Tues.–Sat. 11–5.*

④ Riverside Park. Long and narrow, tree-lined Riverside Park—laid out by Central Park's designers Olmsted and Vaux between 1873 and 1888—runs along the Hudson from West 72nd to 159th streets. More manageable than Central Park—which can feel overwhelming—Riverside Park is best visited on weekends, when Upper West Side residents and their children throng its walkways. From the corner of West 72nd Street and Riverside Drive—where a **statue of Eleanor Roosevelt** stands at the park's entrance—head down the ramp (through an underpass beneath the West Side Highway) to the **79th Street Boat Basin,** a rare spot in Manhattan where you can walk right along the river's edge and watch a flotilla of houseboats bobbing in the water. These boats must sail at least once a year to prove their seaworthiness. Behind the boat basin, the **Rotunda** is home in summer to the Boat Basin Cafe, an open-air spot for a snack and river views. From the Rotunda, head up to the **Promenade,** a broad formal walkway, extending a few blocks north from West 80th Street, with a stone parapet overlooking the river.

At the end of the Promenade, a community garden explodes with flowers tended by nearby residents. To the right, cresting a hill along Riverside Drive at West 89th Street, stands the Civil War **Soldiers' and Sailors' Monument** (1902, designed by Paul M. Duboy), an imposing 96-ft-high circle of white-marble columns. From its base is a refreshing view of Riverside Park, the Hudson River, and the New Jersey waterfront. ✉ *W. 72nd to 159th Sts. between Riverside Dr. and the Hudson River.*

⑥ Spanish & Portuguese Synagogue, Shearith Israel. Built in 1897, this neoclassical edifice, with stained-glass windows by Louis Comfort Tiffany, is the fifth home of the oldest Jewish congregation in the United States, founded in 1654. A "Little Synagogue" inside is a replica of Shearith Israel's Georgian-style first synagogue (which was built on Mill Street in what is now the financial district) and filled with original, 350-year-old furnishings. ✉ *2 W. 70th St., at Central Park W,* ☏ *212/873–0300,* ⓦⒺⒷ *www.shearith-israel.org.* ⊙ *Morning services Sun.–Fri. 7:15, Sat. 8:15; evening services Sun.–Thurs. 6:30, Fri.–Sat. depending on time of sunset. Guided tours by appointment..*

⑪ Subway kiosk. This brick and terra-cotta building with rounded neo-Dutch molding is one of two remaining control houses from the original subway line (the other is at Bowling Green in lower Manhattan). Built 1904–05, it was the first express station north of 42nd Street. ✉ *W. 72nd St. and Broadway.*

MORNINGSIDE HEIGHTS

On the high ridge just north and west of Central Park, a cultural outpost grew up at the end of the 19th century, spearheaded by a triad of institutions: the relocated Columbia University, which developed the mind; St. Luke's Hospital, which cared for the body; and the Cathedral of St. John the Divine, which tended the soul. Idealistically conceived as an American Acropolis, the cluster of academic and religious institutions that developed here managed to keep these blocks stable during years when neighborhoods on all sides were collapsing. More recently, West Side gentrification has reclaimed the area to the south, while the areas north and east of here are beginning to bounce back as well. Within the gates of the Columbia or Barnard campuses or inside the hushed St. John the Divine or Riverside Church, New York City takes on a different character. This is an *uptown* student neighborhood—less hip than the Village, but friendly, fun, and intellectual.

Numbers in the text correspond to numbers in the margin and on the Upper West Side, Morningside Heights map.

A Good Walk

Broadway is the heartbeat of Morningside Heights, but many of the most remarkable sights will take you east and west of the main thoroughfare. Walk east from Broadway on West 112th Street and the massive **Cathedral Church of St. John the Divine** ⑬ will gradually loom up before you.

From here swing east on West 113th Street to secluded Morningside Drive. You'll pass the beaux arts–baroque 1896 core of St. Luke's Hospital, which has sprouted an awkward jumble of newer buildings. On Morningside Drive at West 114th Street, the **Church of Notre Dame** ⑭ nestles into its corner with as much personality but far less bulk than the other churches on this tour. At West 116th Street, catercorner from Columbia University's President's House (✉ 60 Morningside Dr.), pause at the overlook on the right to gaze out at the skyline and down into Morningside Park, tumbling precipitously into a wooded gorge. Designed by Olmsted and Vaux of Central Park fame, the park has a lovely landscape, but since it is bordered by some rough blocks, it's safest not to get any closer.

Turn back toward Amsterdam Avenue on West 116th Street, and walk past the Law School's streamlined Greene Hall to the eastern gates of

Columbia University ⑮. Across Broadway from Columbia proper is its sister institution, **Barnard College** ⑯. Institutes of higher learning abound as you follow Broadway on the east side of the street north to West 120th Street—on the right is **Teachers College** ⑰, a part of Columbia, and on the left, on the west side of the street, is the inter-denominational **Union Theological Seminary** ⑱. At the northeast corner of West 122nd Street and Broadway, behind a large blank-walled redbrick tower that fronts the intersection at an angle, is the **Jewish Theological Seminary** ⑲. Walk west on 122nd Street; between Claremont Avenue and Broadway the prestigious Manhattan School of Music (✉ 601 W. 122nd St.) is on your right, with musical instruments carved into the stone beneath its upper-story windows. Between Claremont and Riverside Drive is Sakura Park, a quiet formal garden, with cherry trees that achieve full, frothy bloom in spring.

Cross Riverside Drive at West 122nd Street into Riverside Park. The handsome white-marble **Grant's Tomb** ⑳ was once one of the city's most popular sights. Finish the walk at **Riverside Church** ㉑, at Riverside Drive and West 120th Street, then stroll back along Riverside Drive; you'll be able to admire Riverside Park and the Hudson to your right, and a long row of magnificent stone apartment buildings to your left.

TIMING

Allow yourself about two hours to leisurely walk the tour. To get the true flavor of the neighborhood, which is often student dominated, come during the week, when classes are in session. You'll be able to visit campus buildings, sample café life, and because the major churches on the tour are active weeklong, you won't miss seeing them in action. If you visit on a Sunday, you could attend church services.

Sights to See

⑯ **Barnard College.** Established in 1889 and one of the former Seven Sisters women's colleges, Barnard has steadfastly remained single-sex and independent from Columbia, although its students can take classes there (and vice versa). Note the bear (the college's mascot) on the shield above the main gates at West 117th Street. Through the gates is **Barnard Hall**, which houses classrooms, offices, a pool, and dance studios. Its brick-and-limestone design echoes the design of Columbia University's buildings. To the right of Barnard Hall, a path leads through the narrow but neatly landscaped campus. ✉ *Entrance at Broadway and 117th St.,* ☎ *212/854–2014,* WEB *www.barnard.edu.* ☼ *Student-led tours weekdays at 10:30 and 2:30 when classes are in session.*

★ ⑬ **Cathedral Church of St. John the Divine.** Everything about the cathedral is colossal, from its cavernous 601-ft-long nave, which can hold some 5,000 worshipers, to its 162-ft-tall dome crossing, which could comfortably contain the Statue of Liberty. Even though this divine behemoth is unfinished—the transepts and tower are the most noticeably uncompleted elements—it is already the largest Gothic cathedral in the world. To get the full effect of the building's mammoth size, approach it from Broadway on 112th Street. On the wide steps climbing to the Amsterdam Avenue entrance, five portals arch over the entrance doors. The central portal, known as the Portal of Paradise, depicts St. John witnessing the Transfiguration of Jesus, and 32 biblical characters, all intricately carved in stone. The three-ton bronze doors he presides over open only twice a year—on Easter and in October for the Feast of St. Francis, when animals as large as elephants and camels are brought in, along with cats and dogs, to be blessed. The doors have relief castings of scenes from the Old Testament on the left and the New Testament on the right.

The cathedral's first cornerstone was laid in 1892, and in 1911 a major change in architectural vision came at the hands of Ralph Adams Cram, a Gothic revival purist who insisted on a French Gothic style for the edifice. The granite of the original Romanesque-Byzantine design is visible inside at the crossing, where it has yet to be finished with the Gothic limestone facing. Note that the finished arches are pointed—Gothic—while the uncovered two are in the rounded Byzantine style. The **Great Rose Window** in the western facade, made from more than 10,000 pieces of colored glass, is the largest stained-glass window in the United States. Although work on the cathedral had continued for nearly 50 years, construction came to a screeching halt when the United States entered World War II. Work did not resume again until 1979, by which time stonecutting had become something of a lost art in this country; in order to continue building, stonecutters had to be imported from Europe to train local craftspeople. As it stands, the cathedral is now about two-thirds complete.

Inside, along the cathedral's side aisles, some chapels are dedicated to contemporary issues such as sports, poetry, and AIDS. The **Saint Saviour Chapel** contains a three-panel bronze altar in white gold leaf with religious scenes by artist Keith Haring (this was his last work before he died of AIDS in 1990). The more conventional **baptistry,** to the left of the altar, is an exquisite octagonal chapel with a 15-ft-high marble font and a polychrome sculpted frieze commemorating New York's Dutch heritage. The altar area expresses the cathedral's interfaith tradition and international mission—with menorahs, Shinto vases, and, in the **Chapels of the Seven Tongues** behind the altar, dedications to various ethnic groups.

A peaceful precinct of châteaulike Gothic-style buildings, known as the **Cathedral Close,** is behind the cathedral on the south side. In a corner by the Cathedral School is the **Biblical Garden.** Perennials, herbs, and an arbor are planted in and around the stone border of a Greek cross, bounded on the outside by the cathedral, a low stone wall, and a hedge. Around the bend from here, a rose garden will thrill your nose with floral scents. Back at Amsterdam Avenue, the **Peace Fountain** depicts the struggle of good and evil. The forces of good, embodied in the figure of the archangel Michael, triumph by decapitating Satan, whose head hangs from one side. The fountain is encircled by small, whimsical animal figures cast in bronze from pieces sculpted by children.

Along with Sunday services (8, 9, 9:30, 11, and 7), the cathedral runs a score of community outreach programs, has changing museum and art gallery displays, supports artists-in-residence and an early music consortium, and presents a full calendar of nonreligious (classical, folk, solstice) concerts. Christmastime programs are especially worth looking into. ⊠ *1047 Amsterdam Ave., at 112th St.,* ☎ *212/316–7540; 212/662–2133 box office; 212/932–7347 tours,* ᵂᴱᴮ *www.stjohndivine. org.* 🎫 *Tours $3, vertical tours $10.* 🕙 *Mon.–Sat. 8–6, Sun. 8–8; tours Tues.–Sat. at 11, Sun. at 1; vertical tours 1st and 3rd Sat. of month at noon and 2 (reservations required).*

NEED A BREAK? If St. John has filled your soul but your stomach is crying out for its share, head for the **Hungarian Pastry Shop** (⊠ 1030 Amsterdam Ave., at 111th St., ☎ 212/866–4230) for tasty desserts and coffee.

🄮 **Church of Notre Dame.** A French neoclassical landmark building (1911), this Roman Catholic church has a grand interior, including a replica of the French grotto of Lourdes behind its altar. It once served a predominantly French community of immigrants, but like the neighborhood, today's congregation is more ethnically diverse, with Irish, German, Italian, African-American, Hispanic, and Filipino members. The building is open 30 minutes before and after masses, which are held weekdays at 8 and 12:05; Saturday at 12:05 and 5:30; and Sunday at 8:30, 10 (in Spanish), 11:30, and 5:30. ⊠ *405 W. 114th St., at Morningside Dr.,* ☎ *212/866–1500.*

| OFF THE BEATEN PATH | **THE CLOISTERS** – Perched atop a wooded hill in Fort Tryon Park, near Manhattan's northernmost tip, the Cloisters houses the medieval collection of the Metropolitan Museum of Art in an appropriately medieval monasterylike setting. Colonnaded walks connect authentic French and Spanish monastic cloisters, a French Romanesque chapel, a 12th-century chapter house, and a Romanesque apse. An entire room is devoted to the richly woven and extraordinarily detailed 15th- and 16th-century Unicorn Tapestries—a must-see. Three enchanting gardens shelter more than 250 species of plants similar to those grown during the Middle Ages, including herbs and medicinals; the Unicorn Garden blooms with flowers and plants depicted in the tapestries. The Cloisters frequently hosts concerts of medieval music. The Cloisters is easily accessible by public transportation: the M4 Cloisters–Fort Tryon Park bus provides a lengthy but scenic ride; catch it along Madison Avenue below West 110th Street, or on Broadway above West 110th Street, or take the A train to West 190th Street. ⊠ *Fort Tryon Park,* ☎ *212/923–3700.* 🎫 *$10 (suggested donation).* ☾ *Mar.–Oct., Tues.–Sun. 9:30–5:15; Nov.–Feb., 9:30–4:45.* |
| | |

Also worthy of a detour uptown are two of the city's oldest houses: Washington Heights' **Morris–Jumel Mansion** is an elegant 1765 Palladian-style mansion with 12 period rooms. ⊠ *65 Jumel Terr., at 160th St.,* ☎ *212/923–8008.* 🎫 *$3.* ☾ *Wed.–Sun. 10–4.*

Inwood's homey **Dyckman Farmhouse Museum** is a Dutch colonial farmhouse from the 18th century with period furnishings. ⊠ *4881 Broadway, at 204th St.,* ☎ *212/304–9422.* 🎫 *Free.* ☾ *Tues.–Sun. 10–5.*

⓯ Columbia University. This wealthy, private, coed Ivy League school was New York's first college when it was founded in 1754. Back then, before American independence, it was called King's College—note the gilded crowns on the black wrought-iron gates at the Amsterdam Avenue entrance. The herringbone-pattern brick paths of College Walk lead into the refreshingly open main quadrangle, dominated by neoclassical **Butler Library** to the south and the rotunda-top **Low Memorial Library** to the north. Butler, built in 1934, holds the bulk of the university's 7 million books. Low was built in 1895–97 by McKim, Mead & White, which laid out the general campus plan when the college moved here in 1897. Modeled on the Roman Pantheon, Low is now mostly offices, but on weekdays you can go inside to see its domed, templelike former Reading Room. Low Library also houses the visitor center, where you can pick up a campus guide or arrange a tour. The steps of Low Library, presided over by Daniel Chester French's statue *Alma Mater,* have been a focal point for campus life, not least during the student riots of 1968. The southwest corner of the quad is the site of a new **student center,** with a six-story glass atrium and ultra-mod glass catwalks. ⊠ *Visitor Center, north of W. 116th St. between Amsterdam Ave. and Broadway,* ☎ *212/854–4900,* 🕸 *www.columbia.edu.* ☾ *Weekdays 9–5. Tours begin 11 and 2 weekdays from Room 213, Low Library.*

Before Columbia moved here, this land was occupied by the Bloomingdale Insane Asylum; the sole survivor of those days is **Buell Hall**

(1878), the gabled orange-red brick house, east of Low Library. North of Buell Hall is the interdenominational **St. Paul's Chapel** (1907), an exquisite little Byzantine-style dome church with fine tile vaulting inside. ☉ *Sept.–May, daily 10–10 (with multi-denomination services on Sun.). Greatly reduced hrs June–Aug. and during winter intercession; call 212/854–4900 for schedule.*

NEED A BREAK? The exterior of **Tom's Restaurant** (⊠ 2880 Broadway, at 112th St., ☎ 212/864–6137) made frequent appearances on the TV show *Seinfeld*. Whether or not you care about its claim to fame, this diner is still a good place for a New York bite.

⓴ Grant's Tomb. This commanding position along the Hudson River, within Riverside Park, is Civil War general and two-term president Ulysses S. Grant and wife Julia Dent Grant's final resting place. Opened in 1897, almost 12 years after Grant's death, it was a more popular sight than the Statue of Liberty until the end of World War I. The towering granite tomb, the largest mausoleum in North America, is engraved with the words LET US HAVE PEACE, recalling Grant's speech to the Republican convention upon his presidential nomination. Under a small white dome, the Grants' twin black-marble sarcophagi are sunk into a deep circular chamber visible from above; minigalleries to the sides display photographs and Grant memorabilia. ⊠ *Riverside Dr. and 122nd St.,* ☎ 212/666–1640, WEB *www.nps.gov/gegr.* ⌕ *Free.* ☉ *Daily 9–5, 20-min tours run on the hr.*

⓳ Jewish Theological Seminary. The seminary was founded in 1886 as a training ground for rabbis, cantors, and scholars of Conservative Judaism, but this complex wasn't built until 1930. You can visit the seminary's excellent library, which has frequent exhibits. ⊠ *3080 Broadway, at 122nd St.,* ☎ 212/678–8000, WEB *www.jtsa.edu.* ⌕ *Free.* ☉ *Call for library hours.*

OFF THE BEATEN PATH **NICHOLAS ROERICH MUSEUM –** An 1898 Upper West Side town house is the site of this small, eccentric museum dedicated to the work of Russian artist Nicholas Roerich, who immigrated to New York in the 1920s and quickly developed an ardent following. Some 200 of his paintings hang here—notably some vast canvases of the Himalayas. He also designed sets for ballets, such as *Rite of Spring,* photographs of which are also on view. Free chamber music concerts are usually held here on Sunday afternoon at 5. ⊠ *319 W. 107th St., between Broadway and Riverside Dr.,* ☎ 212/864–7752, WEB *www.roerich.org.* ⌕ *Free (donations accepted).* ☉ *Tues.–Sun. 2–5.*

★ ⓴ Riverside Church. In this modern (1930) Gothic-style edifice, the smooth, pale limestone walls seem the antithesis of the rougher hulk of the Cathedral of St. John the Divine. Most of the building is refined and restrained, but the main entrance, on Riverside Drive, explodes with elaborate stone carvings modeled on the French cathedral of Chartres (as are many other details here). Inside, look at the handsomely ornamented main sanctuary and take the elevator to the top of the 22-story, 356-ft tower, with its 74-bell carillon, the largest in the world. Although affiliated with the American Baptist church and the United Church of Christ, Riverside is interdenominational, interracial, international, and very politically and socially conscious. Its calendar includes political and community events, dance and theater programs, and concerts, along with regular Sunday services. ⊠ *Riverside Dr. and 120th St.,* ☎ 212/870–6700, WEB *www.theriversidechurchny.org.* ⌕ *Church free; tower $2.* ☉ *Church daily 9–6; service each Sun. 10:45; tower Tues.–Sat. 11–4, Sun. 12:15–4.*

Teachers College. Redbrick Victorian buildings house Columbia University's Teachers College, founded in 1887 and still the world's largest graduate school in the field of education. Names of famous teachers throughout history line the frieze along the Broadway facade. ✉ *525 W. 120th St.,* WEB *www.teacherscollege.edu.*

⑱ **Union Theological Seminary.** Founded in 1836, this progressive, all-denominational seminary moved here, to its rough, gray, collegiate Gothic quadrangle, in 1910; it has one of the world's finest theological libraries. Step inside the main entrance, on Broadway at West 121st Street, and ask to look around the serene central quadrangle. ✉ *W. 120th to 122nd Sts., between Broadway and Claremont Ave.,* ☎ *212/662–7100,* WEB *www.uts.columbia.edu.*

HARLEM

Harlem has been the mecca for African-American culture and life for nearly a century. Originally called Nieuw Haarlem and settled by Dutch farmers, Harlem became a well-to-do suburb by the 19th century; many Jews moved here from the Lower East Side in the late 1800s, and black New Yorkers began settling here in large numbers in about 1900, moving into a surplus of fine apartment buildings and town houses built by real estate developers for a middle-class white market that never materialized. By the 1920s Harlem had become the most famous black community in the United States.

In an astonishing confluence of talent known as the Harlem Renaissance, black novelists, playwrights, musicians, and artists—many of them seeking to escape discrimination and persecution in other parts of the country—gathered here. Black performers starred in chic Harlem jazz clubs—which, ironically, only whites could attend. Throughout the Roaring '20s, while whites flocked here for the infamous parties and nightlife, blacks settled in for the opportunity this self-sustaining community represented. But the Depression hit Harlem hard. By the late 1930s it was no longer a popular social spot for downtown New Yorkers, and many African-American families began moving out to houses in the suburbs of Queens and New Jersey.

By the 1960s Harlem's population had dropped dramatically, and many of those who remained were disillusioned enough with social injustices to join in civil rights riots. A vicious cycle of deteriorating housing, poverty, and crime turned the neighborhood into a simmering ghetto. Today, however, Harlem is restoring itself. Deserted buildings and yards of rubble still scar certain parts, but shining amid them are old jewels such as the refurbished Apollo Theatre, countless architecturally splendid churches, and cultural magnets such as the Studio Museum and Schomburg Center. Black (and, increasingly, white) professionals and young families are also restoring many of Harlem's classic brownstone and limestone buildings, bringing new life to the community.

Note that the city's north–south avenues acquire different names up here, commemorating heroes of black history: 6th Avenue becomes Lenox Avenue or Malcolm X Boulevard, 7th Avenue is Adam Clayton Powell Jr. Boulevard, and 8th Avenue is Frederick Douglass Boulevard; West 125th Street, the major east–west street, is Martin Luther King Jr. Boulevard. Many people still use the streets' former names, but the street signs use the new ones.

Numbers in the text correspond to numbers in the margin and on the Harlem map.

A Good Walk

Beginning on West 115th Street and Fredrick Douglass Boulevard, walk east to admire the facade of this branch of the **New York Public Library** ①. Continue east on West 115th Street, for two churches where, on Sunday, choirs fill the sanctuaries with soulful, moving, often joyous gospel music. Memorial Baptist Church (✉ 141 W. 115th St., ☎ 212/663–8830) welcomes visitors at its two-hour service, which begins promptly at 10:45 on Sunday. Gospel fans and visitors are also welcome at the 10:45 Sunday service at Canaan Baptist Church of Christ (✉ 132 W. 116th St., ☎ 212/866–0301); although the outside of this house of worship is unassuming, Martin Luther King, Jr., delivered his famous "A Knock at Midnight" sermon here one month before his assassination in 1968, and the current pastor, Rev. Wyatt Tee Walker, is known internationally as a crusader for civil rights.

On the southwest corner of West 116th Street and Malcolm X Boulevard, an aluminum onion dome tops the Malcolm Shabazz Masjid (✉ 102 W. 116th St.), a former casino that was converted in the mid-1960s to a black Muslim mosque, where El-Hajj Malik El-Shabazz (better known as Malcolm X) once preached. Across 116th Street, between Malcolm X Boulevard and Fifth Avenue, is the **Malcolm Shabazz Harlem Market** ②, a large indoor/outdoor bazaar. Continuing north along Malcolm X Boulevard and then east on West 120th Street brings you to **Marcus Garvey Park** ③, which interrupts 5th Avenue between 120th and 124th streets. At the north end of the park, walk east to 5th Avenue and then north one block to 125th Street.

Harlem's main thoroughfare is 125th Street (also known as Martin Luther King Jr. Boulevard), the chief artery of its cultural, retail, and economic life. A National Jazz Museum is being planned for the street in conjunction with the Smithsonian Institution. Above the street-level stores is the home of the National Black Theatre (✉ 2031-33 5th Ave., between 125th and 126th Sts., ☎ 212/722–3800), which produces new works by contemporary African-American writers. Walking west along 125th Street you'll pass a number of African-theme stores. On Malcolm X Boulevard, between West 124th and 125th streets, you'll find the art deco Lenox Lounge (✉ 288 Malcolm X Blvd., ☎ 212/427–0253), originally opened in the 1930s and currently host to jazz ensembles, blues acts, and jam sessions in its Zebra Room. Just a few steps north, between West 126th and 127th streets is **Sylvia's Soul Food Restaurant** ④.

Continuing along West 125th Street, you can't miss the striking **Theresa Towers** ⑤ office building at the southwest corner of Adam Clayton Powell Jr. Boulevard. Another community showplace is also on the block between Malcolm X Boulevard and Adam Clayton Powell Jr. Boulevard, the **Studio Museum in Harlem** ⑥, and on the next block across the street, the famous **Apollo Theatre** ⑦. One of the city's greatest cultural landmarks, the Apollo was fantastically restored in the 1980s.

Return to Adam Clayton Powell Jr. Boulevard and continue north, passing numerous large churches. Between West 131st and 132nd streets you'll pass what is today the Williams Institutional (Christian Methodist Episcopal) Church (✉ 2225 Adam Clayton Powell Jr. Blvd.). From 1912 to 1939 this was the Lafayette Theatre, which presented black revues in the 1920s and housed the WPA's Federal Negro Theater in the 1930s. Eubie Blake and Duke Ellington both got their big breaks here. A tree outside the theater was considered a lucky charm for black actors to touch, and it eventually became known as the Tree of Hope; though the original tree and then its live replacement were both cut down, it has been replaced by the colorful, abstract metal "tree" on

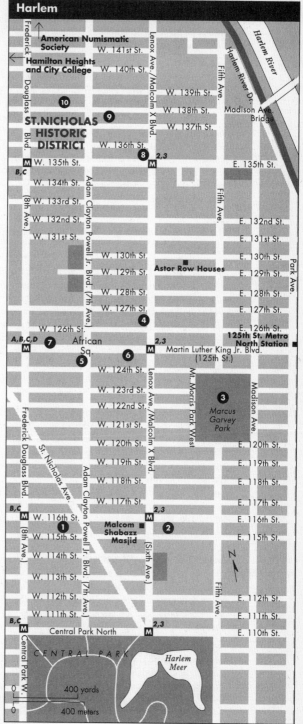

Harlem

the traffic island in the center of the street. A stump from the second tree is now a lucky charm for performers at the Apollo. To the west on 132nd Street is St. Aloysius Church (⊠ 209 W. 132nd St.), a stunningly detailed house of worship with intricately designed terra-cotta decoration.

At West 135th Street cross back east to Malcolm X Boulevard. Notice the branch of the YMCA (⊠ 180 W. 135th St.); writers Langston Hughes, Claude McKay, and Ralph Ellison all rented rooms here. At the corner of Malcolm X Boulevard you'll find the **Schomburg Center for Research in Black Culture** ⑧, a research branch of the New York Public Library that also functions as a cultural center. Three blocks north is another neighborhood landmark, the **Abyssinian Baptist Church** ⑨, one of the first black institutions to settle in Harlem. Across Adam Clayton Powell Jr. Boulevard from the church is St. Nicholas Historic District, a handsome set of town houses known as **Strivers' Row** ⑩.

TIMING
The walk takes about four hours, including stops at the Studio Museum and the Schomburg Center. Sunday is a good time to tour Harlem, especially if you'd like to stop by one of the many churches to listen to gospel music, and weekends in general are the liveliest time for walking around the neighborhood. If you do attend a church service, remember that most other people are there to worship and that they probably don't think of themselves or their church as tourist attractions. Show up on time for services, and be respectful of ushers, who may ask you to sit in a special section; don't take pictures or videos; dress in your Sunday best (not shorts and flip-flops); make a contribution when the collection comes around; and be prepared to stay for the full service, which may last as long as two hours.

Sights to See

⑨ **Abyssinian Baptist Church.** A famous family of ministers—Adam Clayton Powell Sr. and his son, Adam Clayton Powell Jr., the first black U.S. congressman—have presided over this Gothic-style church, which moved here in the 1920s. Stop in on Sunday to hear the gospel choir and the fiery sermon of its present activist minister, Reverend Calvin Butts. The Coptic Cross on the pulpit was a gift from Haile Selassie, then the king of Ethiopia. ⊠ *132 Odell Clark Pl. (W. 138th St.), between Adam Clayton Powell Jr. Blvd. and Malcolm X Blvd.,* ☎ *212/862–7474,* WEB *www.abyssinian.org.* ☉ *Sun. services 9 and 11. Groups of 10 or more call ahead, as seating is limited.*

OFF THE
BEATEN PATH
AMERICAN NUMISMATIC SOCIETY – The society, founded in 1858, displays its vast collection of coins and medals, including many that date from ancient civilizations, in two public galleries at the Audubon Terrace Museum complex. ⊠ *Audubon Terrace, Broadway at 155th St.,* ☎ *212/234–3130,* WEB *www.amnumsoc.org.* ☑ *Free (donations accepted).* ☉ *Tues.–Fri. 9:30–4:30.*

HISPANIC SOCIETY OF AMERICA – The Hispanic Society has the best collection of Spanish art outside the Prado, with paintings, sculptures, manuscripts, and decorative artworks from Spain, Portugal, Latin America, and the Philippines—including pieces by Goya, El Greco, and Velázquez. ⊠ *Audubon Terrace, Broadway between 155th and 156th Sts.,* ☎ *212/926–2234,* WEB *www.hispanicsociety.org.* ☑ *Free (donations accepted).* ☉ *Tues.–Sat. 10–4:30, Sun 1–4.*

★ ❼ **Apollo Theatre.** When it opened in 1913, it was a burlesque hall for white audiences only, but after 1934 music greats such as Billie Holiday, Ella Fitzgerald, Duke Ellington, Count Basie, Nat "King" Cole,

When you pack your MCI Calling Card, it's like packing your loved ones along too.

Your MCI Calling Card is the easy way to stay in touch when you travel. Use it to call to and from over 125 countries. Plus, every time you call, you can earn frequent flier miles. So wherever your travels take you, call home with your MCI Calling Card. It's even easy to get one. Just visit **www.mci.com/worldphone**.

EASY TO CALL WORLDWIDE

1. Just enter the WorldPhone® access number of the country you're calling from.

2. Enter or give the operator your MCI Calling Card number.

3. Enter or give the number you're calling.

Aruba ❖	800-888-8
Bahamas ❖	1-800-888-8000

Barbados ❖	1-800-888-8000
Bermuda ❖	1-800-888-8000
British Virgin Islands ❖	1-800-888-8000
Canada	1-800-888-8000
Mexico	01-800-021-8000
Puerto Rico	1-800-888-8000
United States	1-800-888-8000
U.S. Virgin Islands	1-800-888-8000

❖ Limited availability.

EARN FREQUENT FLIER MILES

SEE THE WORLD
IN FULL COLOR

Fodor's Exploring Guides bring all the great sights vividly to life with hundreds of photographs, fascinating historical background, and colorful anecdotes. Detailed maps and practical information keep you headed in the right direction.

Pair a **Fodor's** Exploring Guide with your trusted Gold Guide for a complete planning package.

Lionel Hampton, and Aretha Franklin performed at the Apollo. The theater fell on hard times and closed for a while in the early 1970s, but it has been renovated and in use again since 1983. The Apollo's current roster of stars isn't as consistent as it was in the past, but its regular Wednesday-night amateur performances at 7:30 are as wild and raucous as they were in the theater's heyday. Former winners of Amateur Night include Sarah Vaughn, James Brown, and The Jackson Five. The Wall of Fame, in the lobby, is a giant collage of Apollo entertainers. Included in an hour-long guided tour is a spirited, audience-participation-encouraged oral history of the theater, with many inside stories about past performers, as well as a chance to perform in a no-boos-allowed "Amateur Night" show. Tour goers also get to touch what's left of the Tree of Hope as they walk across the stage. A gift shop sells Apollo clothing, gift items, jewelry, and recordings. ⊠ *253 W. 125th St., between Adam Clayton Powell Jr. and Frederick Douglass Blvds.,* ☎ *212/749–5838 for performance schedules; 212/531–5337 for tours.* ☐ *Tours $8 weekdays, $10 weekends.*

NEED A BREAK? If you smell a sweet aroma, it's probably doughnuts frying at **Krispy Kreme** (⊠ 280 W. 125th St., at Frederick Douglass Blvd., ☎ 212/531–0111), New York's favorite chain of doughnut shops.

② Malcolm Shabazz Harlem Market. Sidewalk vendors used to line 125th Street with their wares, but in 1999—at the behest of the city—they relocated to this colorful indoor/outdoor bazaar. Specializing in imported African products, the market has 115 permanent stalls, displaying Mali mud-cloth coats, skirts, and scarves, as well as West African masks and figurines, herbal soaps, leather bags, and contemporary paintings. In summer, a food kiosk serves up tasty Caribbean and Southern-style dishes. ⊠ *52-60 W. 116th St., between Malcolm X Blvd. and 5th Ave.,* ☎ *212/987–8131,* WEB *www.malcolmshabazzmarket.com.* ☉ *daily 11–7.*

③ Marcus Garvey Park. Originally Mount Morris Square, this rocky plot of land was renamed in 1973 after Marcus Garvey (1887–1940), who preached from nearby street corners and led the back-to-Africa movement. From the street, you can see its three-tier, cast-iron **watchtower** (Julius Kroel, 1856), the only remaining part of a now defunct citywide network used to spot and report fires in the days before the telephone. The handsome neoclassical row houses of the **Mount Morris Park Historic District** front the west side of the park and line side streets. ⊠ *Interrupts 5th Ave. between 120th and 124th Sts., Madison Ave. to Mt. Morris Park W.*

① New York Public Library 115th Street Branch. This Italian Renaissance–style row house was designed by McKim, Mead & White in 1908. The money for the construction of this and more than 60 other branch libraries was donated by Andrew Carnegie in 1901, and almost all of these were narrow, midblock structures—because of Manhattan's expensive real estate. ⊠ *203 W. 115th St., between Adam Clayton Powell Jr. and Frederick Douglass Blvds.,* ☎ *212/666–9393.* ☉ *Mon. and Wed. 10–6, Tues. noon–8, Thurs.–Fri. noon–6, Sat. 1–5.*

★ ⑧ Schomburg Center for Research in Black Culture. The New York Public Library's Division of Negro Literature, History, and Prints first gained acclaim when it acquired in 1926 the vast collection of Arturo Alfonso Schomburg, a black scholar of Puerto Rican descent. Schomburg was curator from 1932–38, and, in 1940, when Schomburg died, what was then a collection of more than 10,000 books, documents, paintings, and photographs recording black history was renamed in his honor. Later designated a research library, the ever-growing collection moved in 1980 into this modern redbrick building from the handsome Victorian next door (designed by McKim, Mead & White), which is now a Schomburg exhibit hall. The collection today has more than 5 million items, including rare manuscripts, art and artifacts, motion pictures, records, and video-tapes. The Moving Image and Recorded Sound Division's music collection has early recordings of blues and jazz singers, as well as classic radio broadcasts, which can be heard in semi-private listening booths. The Schomburg complex also includes the **American Negro Theatre,** gallery space for changing exhibitions on African-American history, and the **Langston Hughes Auditorium,** where performing arts programs and lectures continue to contribute to Harlem culture. ⊠ *515 Malcolm X Blvd., at 135th St.,* ☎ *212/491-2200,* WEB *www.nypl.org/research/ sc/sc.html.* ⊡ *Free.* ☉ *Mon.–Wed. noon–8, Thurs.–Sat. 10–6; exhibits: Mon.–Wed. noon–8, Thurs.–Sat. 10–6, Sun. 1–5.*

NEED A BREAK?   A good place for coffee and maybe a bite to eat, whether it's grits, a delicious dessert, or fried chicken, is **Pan Pan Restaurant** (⊠ 500 Malcolm X Blvd., at 135th St., ☎ 212/926–4900), catercorner from the Schomburg Center.

★ ⑩ **Strivers' Row.** Since 1919, African-American doctors, lawyers, and other professionals have owned these elegant homes designed by such notable architects as Stanford White (his neo-Renaissance creations stand on the north side of West 139th Street). Behind each row are service alleys, a rare luxury in Manhattan. Musicians W. C. Handy ("The St. Louis Blues") and Eubie Blake ("I'm Just Wild About Harry") were among the residents here. The area, now officially known as the **St. Nicholas Historic District,** got its nickname because less affluent Harlemites felt that its residents were "striving" to become well-to-do. These quiet, tree-lined streets rank among the loveliest in Manhattan. ⊠ *W. 138th and 139th Sts., between Adam Clayton Powell Jr. and Frederick Douglass Blvds.*

NEED A BREAK?   If you're on Strivers' Row and you like fried chicken and sweet potato pie, stop by the **Sugar Shack** (⊠ 2611 Frederick Douglass Blvd., at 139th St., ☎ 212/491–4422). The Sunday brunch menu (waffles, biscuits, and gravy) is mouthwatering.

⑥ **Studio Museum in Harlem.** Focusing on African-American, Caribbean, and African art, this small museum houses a collection of paintings, sculpture (in a light-filled sculpture garden), and photographs (including historic photographs of Harlem by James Van Der Zee, popular in the 1930s, and works by Jacob Lawrence and Romare Bearden). The museum has changing exhibitions, special lectures and programs, and its gift shop is full of black American, Caribbean, and African-inspired books, posters, and jewelry. ⊠ *144 W. 125th St., between Malcolm X and Adam Clayton Powell Jr. Blvds.,* ☎ *212/864–4500,* WEB *www.studiomuseuminharlem.org.* ⊡ *$5 (suggested admission).* ☉ *Wed.–Thurs. noon–6, Fri. noon–8, weekends 10–6.*

④ **Sylvia's Soul Food Restaurant.** Although there have been rumors about her retiring, personable Sylvia Woods still stays late most nights chatting with her customers. Southern specialties and cordiality are the rule here. When the restaurant opened in 1962, it seated 35. Now it's taken over an entire city block and can seat 450. Sylvia's own line of foods—including BBQ sauce, corn-bread mix, and collard greens—is now available at the restaurant and in neighborhood supermarkets. ⊠ *328 Malcolm X Blvd., between 126th and 127th Sts.,* ☎ *212/996–0660.*

⑤ Theresa Towers. Its former incarnation as Harlem's poshest place to stay, the Hotel Theresa (1910), is still evident from the HT crests under some windows and a towering sign painted on its west side. It was once the only luxury hotel where blacks were welcome in New York City. Former guests include jazz greats Billie Holiday, Duke Ellington, Dizzy Gillespie, Lena Horne, and Cab Calloway. Fidel Castro left his midtown accommodations to stay here during his 1960 visit to the United Nations. Now an office building, Theresa Towers is home to several community organizations. ✉ *2090 Adam Clayton Powell Jr. Blvd., at 125th St.*

2 EXPLORING THE OUTER BOROUGHS

New York's four outer boroughs are often praised, if less frequently visited, for their stately parks, famous zoos, and world-class botanical gardens. They also harbor traces of their years as retreats for the wealthy— witness Brooklyn's elegant 19th-century "brownstone belt" and the jaw-dropping views of the Hudson from the Wave Hill estate in the Bronx. The outer boroughs now play the good-natured, bustling backstage to Manhattan's grand theater. Their closely knit ethnic enclaves range from a century-old Italian stronghold in the Bronx to a five-year-old Uzbekistani area in Queens. The public architecture here may not display Manhattan's hubris, but it reveals a subtler strain of New York ambition, the aspiration of millions of immigrants who moved in— and then moved up.

MANY VISITORS TO MANHATTAN notice the four outer boroughs—Brooklyn, Queens, the Bronx, and Staten Island—
only from an airplane window or the deck of a Circle Line
cruise. "Don't fall asleep on the subway," the wary tourist tells himself, "or you may end up in the Bronx!"

Updated by
Elise Harris

Manhattan, however, is less than half the New York story. Its population of about 1.53 million is smaller than that of either Brooklyn (2.3
million) or Queens (2 million) and only slightly larger than that of the
Bronx (1.2 million). Staten Island is less populous (399,000), but it's
2½ times the size of Manhattan. There's no doubt that the city center's spectacle and glamour are phenomenal, but they can't substitute
for the other boroughs' distinct, homegrown personalities.

Back in the 19th century, a prescient young newspaper editor at the
Brooklyn Eagle, Walt Whitman, noted that outside Manhattan, "men
of moderate means may find homes at a moderate rent," whereas in
Gotham itself "there is no median between a palatial mansion and a
dilapidated hovel." His vision of borough life was shared by many early
city officials and developers and is evident in pioneer public schools
as well as innovative garden apartments.

But now that many Manhattanites are being driven over the East River
by ever more astronomical rents, changes are afoot, and certain neighborhoods have become fashionable, highly desirable places to live. Some
parts of Brooklyn are as trendy as downtown Manhattan. Williamsburg is a catwalk of stylish young people, who have built a lively
nightlife scene. Over in working-class Italian Carroll Gardens, chefs
trained at elite Manhattan restaurants are opening bistros. The new
gentrification, however, sits uneasily with many longtime Brooklynites.

There are things to see and do in the outer boroughs that you simply
can't find in Manhattan, and most are just a subway ride from midtown. Some Manhattanites may act as if the world begins and ends in
their borough, but after a couple of beers they'll admit that they spent
last Friday night dancing at Frank's Lounge in Fort Greene, Brooklyn,
or they'll recall the quality of the Indian food in Jackson Heights. You
might even have to hear about the travail of planning a wedding at
beautiful Wave Hill—in the Bronx.

THE BRONX

The only one of New York's boroughs attached to the North American mainland, the Bronx has been an emblem of urban decay for the
past 30 years, but it's actually as rich in personality as the rest of the
city. The Bronx is home to a celebrated botanical garden, a world-
renowned zoo, the friendly Italian neighborhood of Belmont, and
stately Riverdale, with its riverside estates; and of course, Yankee Stadium, home of those perennial winners, the New York Yankees.

The New York Botanical Garden, the Bronx Zoo, and Belmont

Within the 5-mi vicinity covered in this tour, you can stroll among gardens of roses (250 kinds), peonies (58 varieties), and medicinal herbs;
watch red pandas swing from tree to tree; and sample biscotti at a third-
generation bakery where patrons greet each other by name.

*Numbers in the text correspond to numbers in the margin and on the
New York Botanical Garden and Bronx Zoo map.*

The Five Boroughs

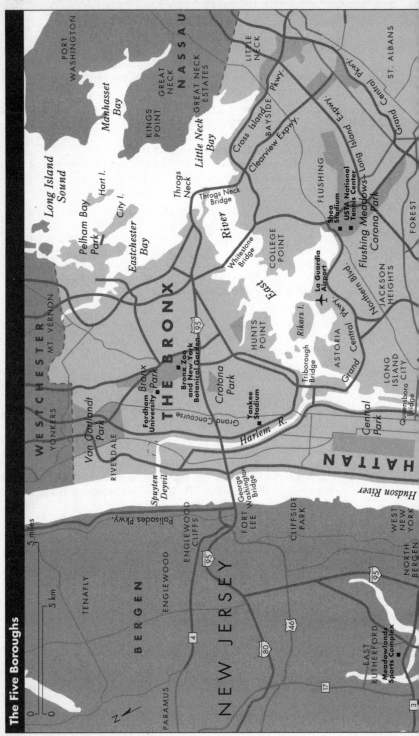

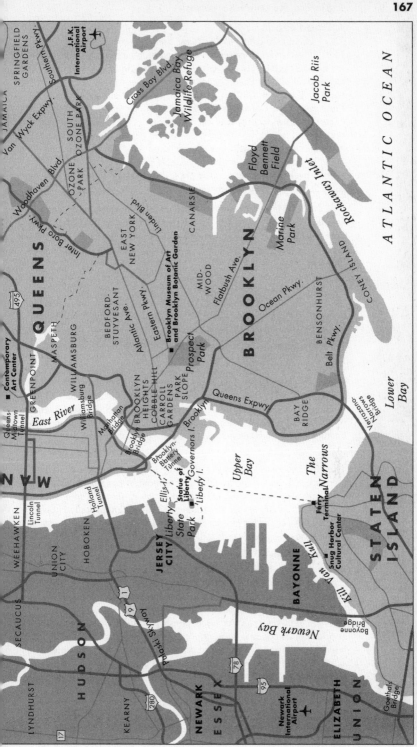

ATLANTIC OCEAN

Jacob Riis Park

J.F.K. International Airport

SPRINGFIELD GARDENS

Southern Pkwy.

JAMAICA

Van Wyck Expwy.

Cross Bay Blvd.

Jamaica Bay Wildlife Refuge

Floyd Bennett Field

Rockaway Inlet

Woodhaven Blvd.

SOUTH OZONE PARK

OZONE PARK

Inter Boro Pkwy.

Linden Blvd.

EAST NEW YORK

CANARSIE

Marine Park

CONEY ISLAND

QUEENS

MASPETH

BEDFORD-STUYVESANT

Atlantic Ave.

Eastern Pkwy.

Brooklyn Museum of Art and Brooklyn Botanic Garden

MID-WOOD

Flatbush Ave.

Ocean Pkwy.

BENSONHURST

Belt Pkwy.

BROOKLYN

495

WILLIAMSBURG

GREENPOINT

Contemporary Art Center

Queens-Midtown Tunnel

East River

Williamsburg Bridge

Manhattan Bridge

Brooklyn Bridge

BROOKLYN HEIGHTS

COBBLE HILL

CARROLL GARDENS

PARK SLOPE

Prospect Park

Brooklyn

Queens Expwy.

BAY RIDGE

Verrazano Narrows Bridge

The Narrows

Lower Bay

N E W

Brooklyn-Battery Tunnel

Governors I.

Ellis I.

Statue of Liberty

Liberty I.

Upper Bay

Ferry Terminal

Snug Harbor Cultural Center

STATEN ISLAND

Lincoln Tunnel

WEEHAWKEN

Holland Tunnel

HOBOKEN

Liberty State Park

UNION CITY

JERSEY CITY

SECAUCUS

HUDSON

LYNDHURST

KEARNY

Pulaski Skyway

1

9

BAYONNE

Kill Van Kull

Bayonne Bridge

Newark Bay

280

17

78

NEWARK

ESSEX

95

Newark International Airport

ELIZABETH

UNION

Goethals Bridge

A Good Walk

The most direct route to the **New York Botanical Garden** ① is via Metro North to the Botanical Garden stop, which is right across from the garden's pedestrian entrance (cross Kazimiroff Boulevard to the garden's Mosholu Gate). A cheaper alternative is to take the D train or the No. 4 to Bedford Park Boulevard. From the subway station continue east on Bedford Park Boulevard (a 10-minute walk) to the Kazimiroff Boulevard entrance of the garden. You may be tempted to spend most of the day here; when you do decide to leave the garden grounds, exit via the main gate. Turn left and walk along Southern Boulevard (10 minutes); turn left onto Fordham Road and continue (five minutes) to the Rainey Gate entrance of the **Bronx Zoo** ②—another must-see sight that could easily hold you for most of the day.

Exit the zoo via Southern Boulevard, turn right, and walk two blocks to East 187th Street; this will lead you straight into the heart of **Belmont** ③, an Italian neighborhood. You'll know you're in the right place when you see the imposing brick structure of **Our Lady of Mt. Carmel Roman Catholic Church** ④ (at Belmont Avenue and East 187th Street), the spiritual heart of the neighborhood—but for the true Belmont experience, a walk through the **Arthur Avenue Retail Market** ⑤ is essential. **Fordham University** ⑥ occupies a large plot of land north of Belmont. To get here, backtrack on Arthur Avenue to East Fordham Road (head toward the tall Gothic tower in the distance) and turn left. While the college prefers that you take the official tour, you can sneak a peek at the handsome inner campus on your own, too; turn right on Bathgate Avenue, which leads to a college gate manned by a security guard. To return to Manhattan, continue on East Fordham Road three blocks to chaotic Fordham Plaza, the "Times Square of the Bronx." From here, take Metro North at East Fordham Road and Webster Avenue, or continue on East Fordham Road about four blocks more up to the Fordham Road subway station (at Grand Concourse) for the D train.

TIMING

The Bronx Zoo and the New York Botanical Garden are each vast and interesting enough to merit half a day or more. If you plan to visit both, start early and plan on a late lunch or early dinner in Belmont. Saturday is the best day to see the Italian neighborhood at its liveliest; on Sunday most stores are closed. The zoo and the garden are less crowded on weekdays—except Wednesday, when admission to both is free.

Sights to See

⑤ **Arthur Avenue Retail Market.** An indoor shed sheltering more than a dozen stalls, the market is one of the last bastions of old-time New York. Here, amid piles of fresh produce, vendors still sell fresh beef hearts and occasionally burst into song. There's also fresh rabbit and tripe, 15 types of olives, gnocchi *freschi* (fresh), *bufula* (buffalo) mozzarella, and low-price ceramic ware imported from Italy. It's a delight to the senses, particularly to the sense of smell. Stop for a quick lunch—or at least a pizza square with toppings fresh from the market—at the Café al Mercato. ✉ 2344 Arthur Ave., at 187th St. ☉ Mon.–Sat. 7–6.

| NEED A BREAK? | At neighborhood favorite **Dominick's** (✉ 2335 Arthur Ave., at 187th St., ☎ 718/733–2807), there are no menus and no wine list. Instead, the question "What do you have?" is most often answered with "What do you want?" What you'll want is a heaping dish of spaghetti with meatballs—some of the best you'll find in New York City—along with crusty bread and wine poured from a jug. The same family has been cooking at Dominick's since the 1940s, serving loyal fans at congested communal tables covered with red-and-white check cloths. |

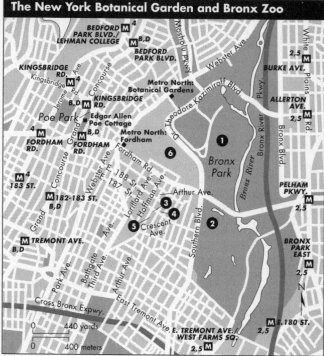

The New York Botanical Garden and Bronx Zoo

❸ Belmont. Often called the Little Italy of the Bronx, Belmont is where some 14,500 families socialize, shop, work, and eat, eat, eat. On Saturday afternoon, residents rush around buying freshly baked bread and homemade salami; don't be surprised to hear people speaking Italian in the neighborhood's tidy streets.

On Arthur Avenue, some of the gastronomic temptations come from the brick ovens at **Madonia Bros. Bakery** (✉ 2348 Arthur Ave.), which have been turning out golden-brown loaves since 1918. The staff will fill cannoli fresh on request. ✉ *Bordered by E. Fordham Rd., Southern Blvd., and Crescent and 3rd Aves.*

Around the corner at **Mount Carmel Wines & Spirits** (✉ 612 E. 187th St.), there's a tremendous selection of Italian wines and grappas in beautiful bottles. One block down, **Danny's Pork Store** (✉ 626 E. 187th St.) has homemade sausages. The **Catholic Goods Center** (✉ 630 E. 187th St.) sells multilingual Bibles and greeting cards as well as religious art, jewelry, and trinkets. Next to the Catholic Goods Center, **Borgatti's Ravioli & Egg Noodles** (✉ 632 E. 187th St.) is known for its homemade pastas.

NEED A BREAK? At **Egidio's Pastry Shop** (✉ 622 E. 187th St., ☎ 718/295–6077), a neighborhood favorite, you can sample handmade Italian pastries, washed down with a strong shot of espresso. The homemade gelati next door are top-notch. The **DeLillo Pastry Shop** (✉ 606 E. 187th St., ☎ 718/367–8198) serves not only the requisite espresso but also cappuccino–chocolate chip Italian ices in summer. Grab a fresh *sfogliatelle* (a flaky cheese-filled pastry) for the road.

★ ♻ ❷ **Bronx Zoo.** Opened in 1899, this 265-acre spread is the world's largest urban zoo. The zoo's nearly 6,500 animals, representing more than 600 species, mostly live in outdoor, parklike settings, often separated from you by no more than a moat. Among the best exhibitions are the **Congo Gorilla Forest,** a 6½-acre re-creation of an African rain forest with treetop lookouts, wooded pathways, lush greenery, and 400 animals—including two lowland gorilla troops, okapi, and red-river hogs; "Jungle World," an indoor Asian tropical rain forest filled with white-cheeked gibbons, tree kangaroos, Malayan tapirs, and other exotic critters; "Wild Asia" (open April to October only), where tigers and elephants roam free on nearly 40 acres of open meadows and dark forests; and "the World of Darkness," a windowless building that offers a rare glimpse into the nightlife of such nocturnal creatures as fruit-eating bats and naked mole rats. From late May to early October, a thousand butterflies and moths of 35 species dazzle visitors in the "Butterfly Zone." Three different rides, including a shuttle bus, a monorail, and an aerial tram, offer various perspectives of the grounds in summer. In winter, outdoor exhibitions are slightly modified, with fewer animals on view. The **Children's Zoo** (☐ $4), open from April to October, has many hands-on learning activities, as well as a large petting zoo. Youngsters can see the world from an animal's perspective by crawling through a prairie dog tunnel and trying on a turtle's shell for size. If you're visiting the city with children during the holidays, don't miss the zoo's spectacular **Holiday Lights** show. Every evening between Thanksgiving and New Year's, the zoo is ablaze with thousands of twinkling lights decorating 144 giant-size animal sculptures—from frogs to meercats (☐ $7; ☉ Sun.–Thurs. 5:30–9, Fri.–Sat. 5:30–9:30). To get to the zoo, take the No. 2 subway to Pelham Parkway and walk three blocks west to the zoo's Bronx Parkway entrance. You can also take the **Metro North** train (☎ 212/532–4900) from Grand Central Terminal or catch the **Liberty Line** (☎ 718/652–8400) Bronx M11 express bus from mid-Manhattan. ☒ *Bronx River Pkwy. and Fordham Rd.,* ☎ *718/367–1010,* WEB *www.wcs.org/zoos/bronxzoo.* ☐ *Apr.–Oct., Thurs.–Tues. $9; mid-Nov.–Dec., Thurs.–Tues. $7; Jan.–Mar., Thurs.–Tues. $5; free Wed. Extra charge for some exhibits. Parking $6.* ☉ *Apr.–Oct., weekdays 10–5, weekends 10–5:30; Nov.–Mar., daily 10–4:30; last ticket sold 1 hr before closing.*

OFF THE BEATEN PATH   **CITY ISLAND –** At the extreme northeast end of the Bronx is a bona fide island of 230 acres. (To reach City Island, take the No. 6 subway to Pelham Bay Parkway and then catch the No. 29 bus.) In 1761, a group of local residents planned a port to rival New York's, but when that scheme hit the shoals, they returned to perennial maritime pursuits such as fishing and boatbuilding. City Island–produced yachts have included a number of America's Cup contenders. Connected to Pelham Bay Park by bridge, City Island has a maritime atmosphere, fishing boat rentals, and hopping seafood restaurants. Worth visiting is the **North Wind Undersea Museum,** with its displays devoted to marine mammal rescue and deep-sea diving. ☒ *610 City Island Ave.,* ☎ *718/885–0701.* ☐ *$3.50* ☉ *Daily 10–5; hrs vary so call ahead.*

OFF THE BEATEN PATH   **EDGAR ALLAN POE COTTAGE –** If you finish your tour while it's still light out, venture up Fordham Road to East Kingsbridge Road, turn right, and walk the short block to Poe Park, where the Bronx County Historical Society maintains the Edgar Allan Poe Cottage, open weekends only. It was here that Poe and his sickly wife, Virginia, sought refuge from Manhattan and from the vicissitudes of the writerly life between 1846 and 1849. The family was so impoverished that Poe's mother sometimes picked dandelions by the roadside for dinner. Poe wandered the countryside on foot and listened to the sound of the church bells at nearby

St. John's College Church (now Fordham University); word has it
that these bells inspired one of his most famous poems, "The Bells."
⊠ *E. Kingsbridge Rd. and Grand Concourse,* ☎ *718/881–8900.*
☞ *$2.* ☉ *Mid-Jan.–mid-Dec., Sat. 10–4, Sun. 1–5.*

⑥ Fordham University. A small enclave of distinguished Collegiate Gothic
architecture in the midst of urban sprawl, this university opened in 1841
as a Jesuit college and was one of the country's preeminent schools.
Fordham now has an undergraduate enrollment of nearly 6,000 and
a second campus near Lincoln Center. With ID, you may be able to
(unofficially) enter the grounds via Bathgate Avenue, a few blocks
west of Arthur Avenue, to see **Old Rose Hill Manor Dig;** the **University Church,** whose stained glass was donated by King Louis Philippe
of France (1773–1850); **Edward's Parade** quadrangle in the center of
campus; and **Keating Hall,** sitting like a Gothic fortress in the center
of it all. Maps are posted around the campus and are available in the
security office on your left inside the gate. Call in advance for a free
campus tour. ⊠ *441 E. Fordham Rd.,* ☎ *718/817–1000.* ☉ *Daily 12:30
and 2 or by appointment.*

★ ① New York Botanical Garden. Considered one of the leading botany centers of the world, this 250-acre garden built around the dramatic gorge
of the Bronx River is one of the best reasons to make a trip to the Bronx.
The garden was founded by Dr. Nathaniel Lord Britton and his wife,
Elizabeth. After visiting England's Kew Gardens in 1889, they returned full of fervor to create a similar haven in New York. The
grounds encompass the historic **Lorillard Snuff Mill,** built by two
French Huguenot manufacturers in 1840 to power the grinding of tobacco for snuff. Nearby, the Lorillards grew roses to supply fragrance
for their blend. A path along the Bronx River from the mill leads to
the garden's 40-acre **Forest,** the only surviving remnant of the forest
that once covered New York City. Outdoor plant collections include
the **Peggy Rockefeller Rose Garden,** with 2,700 bushes of 230 varieties; the spectacular rock garden, which displays alpine flowers; and
the **Everett Children's Adventure Garden,** 8 acres of plant and science
exhibits for children, including a boulder maze, giant animal topiaries,
a wild wetland trail, and a plant discovery center.

In 1997 the historic **Enid A. Haupt Conservatory**—a Victorian-era glass
house with 17,000 individual panes—reopened after a four-year renovation. Inside are year-round re-creations of misty tropical rain forests
and arid African and North American deserts. The **Museum Building**
houses a gardening shop, a library, and a world-renowned herbarium
holding 6 million dried plant specimens.

To get to the Botanical Garden, take the **Metro North** train (☎ 212/532–
4900) from Grand Central Terminal to the Botanical Gardens stop; or
take the D or No. 4 train to the Bedford Park Boulevard stop and walk
eight blocks east to the entrance on Kazimiroff Boulevard. ⊠ *200th St.
and Kazimiroff Blvd.,* ☎ *718/817–8700,* 🕸 *www.nybg.org.* ☞ *$3; free
Sat. 10–noon and Wed.; Enid A. Haupt Conservatory $3.50; parking
$5.* ☉ *Nov.–Mar., Tues.–Sun. 10–4; Apr.–Oct., Tues.–Sun. 10–6.*

④ Our Lady of Mt. Carmel Roman Catholic Church. Rising like a beacon
of faith above the neighborhood, this is the spiritual center of Belmont.
In 1907, an Irish priest successfully petitioned the archdiocese for an
Italian church to serve the new Italian immigrant community. Many
residents of the neighborhood volunteered to help build the church in
order to keep the costs down. ⊠ *627 E. 187th St., between Hughes
and Belmont Aves.,* ☎ *718/295–3770.* ☉ *Weekdays 7–1 and 4–8, Sat.
7 AM–8 PM, Sun. 7–2 and 6–8:30.*

OFF THE
BEATEN PATH

WAVE HILL – In the mid- to late-19th century, Manhattan millionaires built summer homes in the Bronx suburb of Riverdale. Perched on a ridge above the Hudson River, the neighborhood commands stirring views of the New Jersey Palisades. Wave Hill, a 28-acre estate built in 1843, is the only one of these old estates open to the public. At various times Theodore Roosevelt, Mark Twain, and Arturo Toscanini all rented the property, which was donated to the city in 1960. Today the greenhouse and conservatory, plus 18 acres of exquisite herb, wildflower, and aquatic gardens, attract green thumbs from all over the world. Grand beech and oak trees adorn wide lawns, and elegant pergolas are hidden along curving pathways. Additional draws are gardening and crafts workshops; a summertime dance series; changing art exhibitions; Sunday concerts in Armor Hall from fall to spring; and a popular café overlooking the river and Palisades. From Manhattan you can drive up the Henry Hudson Parkway to Exit 21 and follow the signs to Wave Hill. Or you can take the Metro North Harlem line train to the Riverdale stop and walk up West 254th Street to Independence Avenue, turn right and proceed to the main gate. Or take the No. 1 or No. 9 train to 231st Street and then transfer to the Bx10 bus to 252nd street and Riverdale Avenue. Cross the overpass and follow the signs to Wave Hill. ✉ *W. 249th St. and Independence Ave.,* ☎ *718/549–2055,* WEB *www.wavehill.org.* ✍ *Mid-Mar.–mid-Nov. $4; Sat. am and Tues. free; mid-Nov.–mid-Mar. free.* ☉ *Mid-Apr.–mid-Oct., Tues. 9–5:30, Wed. 9–dusk, Thurs.–Sun. 9–5:30; mid-Oct.–mid-Apr., Tues.–Sun. 9–4:30; free garden tours Sun. 2:15. Call for program schedule.*

BROOKLYN

Brooklyn is New York City's most populous borough, and has always nurtured a sibling rivalry with Manhattan. More people visit Brooklyn than any of the other outer boroughs, and still more come here to live. Several Brooklyn neighborhoods, particularly Brooklyn Heights, Park Slope, Cobble Hill, Carroll Gardens, and Fort Greene, are favored more than ever by young families and professionals, who are drawn by the dignified brownstone- and tree-lined streets, handsome parks, cultural institutions such as the Brooklyn Academy of Music and the Brooklyn Museum of Art, and the less than frenetic pace of life.

Brooklyn Heights, Cobble Hill, and Carroll Gardens

"All the advantages of the country, with most of the conveniences of the city," ran the ads for a real-estate development that sprang up in the 1820s just across the East River from downtown Manhattan. Brooklyn Heights—named for its enviable hilltop position—was New York's first suburb, linked to the city originally by ferry and later by the Brooklyn Bridge. Feverish construction led by wealthy industrialists and shipping magnates quickly transformed the airy heights into a fashionable upper-middle-class community. It was characterized by radical politics, as in abolitionist Henry Ward Beecher, and a leisurely, aristocratic ambience. In the 1940s and '50s, the area became a bohemian haven, home to writers including Carson McCullers, W. H. Auden, Arthur Miller, Truman Capote, Richard Wright, Alfred Kazin, Norman Mailer, and Hart Crane.

Thanks to the vigorous efforts of preservationists in the 1960s, much of the Heights was designated New York's first historic district. Some 600 buildings more than 100 years old, representing a wide range of American building styles, are in excellent condition today. Cranberry and Pineapple are just two of the unusual street names in the Heights.

Brooklyn Heights, Cobble Hill, and Carroll Gardens

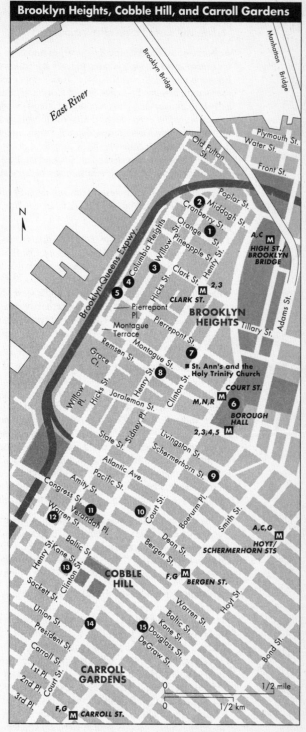

Rumor has it that these names were created by a certain Sarah Mid-dagh, who disliked the practice of naming streets for the town fathers and instead named them after various fruits.

A short hop across Atlantic Avenue from Brooklyn Heights, Cobble Hill is another quiet residential area of leafy streets lined with notable town houses built by 19th-century New York's upper middle class. A bit far-ther south, around President Street, Cobble Hill turns into the histori-cally Italian, working-class section of Carroll Gardens, a neighborhood distinguished by deep blocks that allow for unusually large front yards, at least by New York standards, and Smith Street's trendy boutiques and restaurants. It might be hard to believe you're in New York City, when, on nice days, residents can be found tending their front-yard gar-dens or stopping on the sidewalk to say hello to one another.

Numbers in the text correspond to numbers in the margin and on the Brooklyn Heights, Cobble Hill, and Carroll Gardens map.

A Good Walk

Take the No. 2 or 3 subway from Manhattan to Clark Street, or the No. 4 or 5 to Borough Hall and walk up Court Street to Clark Street. From Clark Street turn left on Henry Street toward Pineapple Street. From here you'll be able to see the blue towers of the Manhattan Bridge, which links Brooklyn to Manhattan, and a view of the Brooklyn Bridge will soon come into view. (As an alternative, walk across the Brook-lyn Bridge. At the bridge's Tillary Street terminus, turn right, walk two blocks to Cadman Plaza West, and swing right to Clark Street, where you'll see the No. 2 or 3 subway entrance.)

Turn left onto Orange Street. On the north side of the block (the right-hand side of the street) between Henry and Hicks streets is a formidable institution, the **Plymouth Church of the Pilgrims** ①, the center of abo-litionist sentiment in the years before the Civil War. Turn right on Hicks Street and follow it to Middagh Street (pronounced *mid*-awe). At its intersection with Willow Street is **24 Middagh Street** ②, the oldest home in the neighborhood. Venture a few steps west on Middagh Street to see the Manhattan Bridge reaching over the East River in the shadow of the dominating Watchtower building. The area is called DUMBO, a burgeoning artsy and residential neighborhood named for its indus-trial location—*D*own *U*nder the *M*anhattan *B*ridge *O*verpass.

Backtrack on **Willow Street** ③ and observe the masterful local archi-tecture between Clark and Pierrepont streets (Nos. 149, 155, 157, and 159 are especially notable). As you turn right on Pierrepont Street head-ing toward the river, glance down **Columbia Heights** ④ to your right, where the brownstones are particularly elegant and well-maintained.

Pierrepont Street ends at the **Brooklyn Heights Promenade** ⑤, one of the most famous vista points in all of New York City. This is a great place for a picnic, with take-out food from one of the many Montague Street restaurants or provisions from the exotic food stores on nearby Atlantic Avenue. (If the Promenade is under construction when you visit, access the open section that runs from Clark Street to Orange Street.) After you've soaked in the views from the Promenade, turn up Mon-tague Street. Look left to see Nos. 2 and 3 Pierrepont Place, two brick-and-brownstone palaces built in the 1850s. On your right lies Montague Terrace, where Thomas Wolfe lived when he was finishing *You Can't Go Home Again*. W. H. Auden lived on the top floor of the brown-stone at One Montague Terrace. Continue east along this commercial spine of the Heights, past a variety of restaurants, coffee shops, and retail clothing and gift stores. At the northwest corner of Montague and Clinton streets is St. Ann's and the Holy Trinity Church, known for its early-American stained-glass windows. The church is closed indefinitely.

Beyond Clinton on the north side of Montague Street, note an interesting and eclectic row of banks: Chase, a copy of the Palazzo della Gran Guardia in Verona, Italy. The Citibank looks like a latter-day Roman temple. Also remarkable is the art deco Municipal Credit Union. Farther down the street you'll find the historic **Brooklyn Borough Hall** ⑥, or you can detour a block north up Clinton Street to the elegant Romanesque redbrick **Brooklyn Historical Society** ⑦, slated to open from a long renovation in early 2002.

Return south along Clinton Street, and then turn right onto Remsen Street. At the corner of Remsen and Henry streets, stop to take in the Romanesque revival **Our Lady of Lebanon Maronite Church** ⑧. Continue west on Remsen Street and then turn left onto Hicks Street to visit the 1847 Gothic revival Grace Church at No. 254. Across Hicks Street is Grace Court Alley, a traditional mews with a score of beautifully restored redbrick carriage houses, which were once stables for the mansions on Remsen and Joralemon streets.

Just a few more steps down Hicks Street, turn right and stroll down cobblestone Joralemon Street, noting Nos. 29–75, a row of modest brick row houses that delicately sidestep their way down the hill toward the river. Follow Willow Place south along the peaceful block between Joralemon and State streets, where the quietly elegant former Willow Place Chapel, built in 1876, stands. Nos. 43–49, four redbrick houses, are linked by a majestic two-story colonnade that looks transplanted from an antebellum Southern mansion.

At the end of Willow Place, turn left on State Street and follow it past Hicks and Henry streets back to Clinton Street. You can make a left on Clinton and then the next right on Schermerhorn Street to visit the **New York City Transit Museum** ⑨. Otherwise turn right down Clinton to Atlantic Avenue, a busy thoroughfare with Middle Eastern food shops and restaurants. Farther east on Atlantic, between Hoyt and Bond streets, you can find more than a dozen antique furniture stores as well as two purveyors of modern housewares, Breukelen and Bark.

Atlantic Avenue is the dividing line between the neighborhoods of Brooklyn Heights and Cobble Hill. For a taste of the latter, go two blocks south down Clinton Street to Amity Street. You may want to turn left to **197 Amity Street** ⑩, where Jennie Jerome, the mother of Winston Churchill, was born in 1854. Return to Clinton and go one more block south, where on the west side of the street is **Cobble Hill Park** ⑪, bordered by Verandah Place, a graceful row of converted stable buildings. Proceed three blocks south down Clinton Street, which is lined with distinguished Romanesque revival, neoclassical, and Italianate brownstones. Take a right at Warren Street and walk past Henry Street. On the right you'll see Alfred P. Tredway's charming **Warren Place Workingmen's Cottages and Home and Tower "Model Tenements"** ⑫. The Workingmen's Cottages, 24 beautiful Romanesque revival residences, stand on a side street marked by a small, hanging wooden sign. Circle the gardens and exit back onto Warren Street. Starting at 136 Warren, you'll see the Home and Tower "Model Tenements," two of the 19th century's most important architectural structures. Go back to Clinton Street and turn right. Two blocks down, at 320 Clinton Street, stands the Episcopal **Christ Church** ⑬, designed by Richard Upjohn.

Another four blocks down Clinton Street, near President Street, Cobble Hill gives way to the largely Italian neighborhood of Carroll Gardens. If you stroll down President or Carroll street, or 1st and 2nd places, you'll see the lovingly tended gardens where the abundance of religious statuary attests to the neighborhood's Catholic influence. Or turn left (east) on DeGraw Street to **Court Street** ⑭, the neighborhood's main thoroughfare. Try to save some energy for exploring a new stretch of shops and restaurants on **Smith Street** ⑮, Carroll Gardens's burgeoning, slightly funky, neighborhood strip, one block west.

To continue on to the Park Slope tour, take the F train from the Carroll Street subway station (at the intersection of Carroll and Smith streets) three more stops toward Coney Island, to the 7th Avenue stop.

TIMING

Allow three to four hours for a leisurely tour of these three neighborhoods; more if you stop for lunch, dinner, or both. Ideally, you'll want to time your tour to include a picnic lunch along the Promenade and dinner on Smith Street. Try to come on a clear, sunny day, when the view from the Promenade is most spectacular.

Sights to See

★ ❻ **Brooklyn Borough Hall.** Built in 1848 and restored in the late 1980s, this Greek revival landmark is arguably Brooklyn's handsomest building. The hammered-brass top of the cast-iron cupola (a successor to the original wooden one, which burned in 1895) was restored by the same French craftsmen who restored the Statue of Liberty. The stately building is adorned with Tuckahoe marble both inside and out; other highlights are the square rotunda and the two-story beaux arts–style courtroom with plaster columns painted to look like wood. Today the hall serves as the office of Brooklyn's borough president. On Tuesday and Saturday a city greenmarket sets up on the flagstone plaza in front. ✉ *209 Joralemon St.,* ☎ *718/802–3900,* WEB *www.brooklyn-usa.org.* ✉ *Free.* ☉ *Tours Tues. 2.*

★ ☞ ❺ **Brooklyn Heights Promenade.** Stretching from Orange Street on the north to Remsen Street on the south, this ⅓-mi-long sliver of park hangs above Brooklyn's industrial waterfront like one of Babylon's fabled gardens. Cantilevered over two lanes of the Brooklyn–Queens Expressway, the esplanade offers enthralling views of the Manhattan skyline. Circling gulls squawk, tugboats honk, and the city seems like a magical place. This is a terrific vantage point from which to admire the Brooklyn Bridge, the transcendently impressive steel suspension bridge designed by John Augustus Roebling and completed in 1883. The small island to your left is Governors Island, a former military installation.

❼ **Brooklyn Historical Society.** Erected in 1878–80, this elegant redbrick museum and library was the first major structure in New York to feature terra-cotta ornamentation, such as capitals, friezes, and lifelike busts. After a major renovation, the building's exhibitions on Brooklyn history and its impressive library should be accessible in early 2002. Ongoing programs include Saturday neighborhood walking tours and off-site exhibitions; call for details. ✉ *128 Pierrepont St.,* ☎ *718/254–9830,* WEB *www.brooklynhistory.org.*

⓭ **Christ Church.** This sandstone Episcopal church, with its lean, tower-dominated facade, was designed by the prolific architect Richard Upjohn, who lived nearby at 296 Clinton Street. (He also designed Grace Church, at 254 Hicks Street, and **Our Lady of Lebanon Maronite Church.**) Inside, the pulpit, lectern, and altar are the work of Louis Comfort Tiffany; outside, the tranquil churchyard is enclosed by a wrought-iron fence. You can see the interior during services or by appointment. ✉ *320 Clinton St., at Kane St.,* ☎ *718/624–0083.* ☉ *Services Wed. 6:30 PM, Sun. 10:40, 11, 5:30, and 6.*

🖐 ⓫ **Cobble Hill Park.** One of the city's first vest-pocket parks, this green space has marble columns at its entrances, antique benches and tables, and a playground. Bordering the park's south side is **Verandah Place**, a charming row of converted stable buildings; Thomas Wolfe once resided in the basement of No. 40 (one of his many residences in the borough). ⊠ *Congress St. between Clinton and Henry Sts.*

NEED A BREAK? Between Court and Clinton streets on Atlantic Avenue are a half dozen Middle Eastern markets and eateries. The best of these is 45-year-old **Sahadi Importing** (⊠ 187–189 Atlantic Ave., ☎ 718/624–4550), where serious cooks stock up on cheap and delicious dried fruits, nuts, oils, olives, Turkish coffee, and spices. **Damascus Bread & Pastry** (⊠ 195 Atlantic Ave., ☎ 718/625–7070) purveys stellar baklava, spinach pie, and still-warm pita bread. **Peter's Ice Cream Parlor and Coffee House** (⊠ 185 Atlantic Ave., ☎ 718/852–3835) is another neighborhood institution.

❹ **Columbia Heights.** Among the majestic residences on this street, the brownstone grouping of **Nos. 210–220** is often cited as the most graceful in New York. Norman Mailer lives on this street, and from a rear window in **No. 111**, John Roebling's son Washington, who in 1869 succeeded his father as chief engineer for the Brooklyn Bridge, directed the completion of the bridge from his sickbed. ⊠ *Columbia Heights, between Pierrepont and Cranberry Sts.*

⓮ **Court Street.** Court Street's activity whirls around its cafés, restaurants, bookstores, and old-fashioned bakeries. In Cobble Hill, the **Attic** (⊠ 220 Court St., ☎ 718/643–9535) is a small antiques store worth seeking out. In Carroll Gardens, fresh pasta, mozzarella, sausages, olives, and prepared dishes are available at a number of shops, including **Pastosa Ravioli** (⊠ 347 Court St., ☎ 718/625–7952), where the gnocchi is particularly recommended, and **Caputo's Dairy** (⊠ 460 Court St., ☎ 718/855–8852), with a wide selection of homemade pastas and sauces. Italian sausages, *soppressata* (pork sausage), and homemade mozzarella can be had at **G. Esposito's & Sons** (⊠ 357 Court St., ☎ 718/875–6863), the neighborhood's best meat store.

NEED A BREAK? With its whirring ceiling fans, painted tin ceiling, and old wooden tables, the **Roberto Cappuccino** (⊠ 221 Court St., at Wycoff St., ☎ 718/858–7693) is a tiny, tasty spot for crêpes, sandwiches, and bowls of café au lait. At **Shakespeare's Sister** (⊠ 270 Court St., at Kane St., ☎ 718/694–0084), you can soothe yourself with any one of a great variety of teas and light snacks while viewing art exhibits—usually featuring work by women. Newcomer Sweet Melissa Patisserie (⊠ 276 Court St., ☎ 718/855–3410) sells sticky buns, madeleines, and finger sandwiches.

🖐 ❾ **New York City Transit Museum.** Inside a converted 1930s subway station, the Transit Museum displays 18 restored classic subway cars, working miniature subway trains, and has an operating signal tower. Its gift shop, like the one in Grand Central Terminal (☞ 42nd Street *in* Chapter 1), is a mother lode of subway-inspired memorabilia. ⊠ *Boerum Pl. at Schermerhorn St.,* ☎ 718/243–3060. ☑ *$3.* ☉ *Tues.–Fri. 10–4, weekends noon–5.*

❿ **197 Amity Street.** Jennie Jerome, the mother of Winston Churchill, was born in this modest house in 1854. A plaque at 426 Henry Street, southwest of here, incorrectly identifies *that* building as the famous woman's birthplace. The Henry Street address is actually where Jennie's parents lived before she was born.

❽ Our Lady of Lebanon Maronite Church. One of the oldest Romanesque revival buildings in the country, this Congregational church was designed by Richard Upjohn in 1844. Its doors, which depict Norman churches, were salvaged from the 1943 wreck of the ocean liner *Normandie*. ✉ *113 Remsen St., at Henry St.,* ☎ *718/624–7228.* ☾ *Services Sun. 9, 11 AM; tours by appointment.*

❶ Plymouth Church of the Pilgrims. Thanks to the stirring oratory of Brooklyn's most eminent theologian, Henry Ward Beecher (brother of Harriet Beecher Stowe, author of *Uncle Tom's Cabin*), this house of worship was the vortex of anti-slavery sentiment in the years before the Civil War. Because it provided refuge to American slaves, the church, which was built in 1850, is known as the Grand Central Terminal of the Underground Railroad in its latter years. Its windows, like those of many other neighborhood churches, were designed by Louis Comfort Tiffany. In the gated courtyard beside the church, a statue of Beecher depicts refugee slaves crouched in hiding behind the base. Nearby, at **22 Willow Street,** Beecher's house still stands—a prim Greek revival brownstone. ✉ *Orange St. between Henry and Hicks Sts.,* ☎ *718/624–4743.* ☾ *Service Sun. 11 AM; tours by appointment.*

❻ Smith Street. From humble beginnings, this otherwise low-key, semi-commercial Carroll Gardens street has become a fashionable neighborhood of boutiques, vintage clothing and furniture stores, and eclectic restaurants. Countering Brooklyn Heights's austerity and the prohibitive rents of Park Slope, this strip from Union to Sackett Street aspires to be Brooklyn's East Village: you'll often catch young, unpretentious designers selling their wares from their own shops. Restaurants here are some of the best Brooklyn has to offer, adorable bistros to refined New American.

❷ 24 Middagh Street. This 1824 Federal-style clapboard residence with a mansard roof is the oldest home in the neighborhood. Peer through a door in the wall on the Willow Street side for a glimpse of the cottage garden and carriage house in the rear.

❿ Warren Place Workingmen's Cottages and Home and Tower "Model Tenements." An early (1877) experiment in designing low-income multifamily housing, architect Alfred Tredway White's beautiful Home and Tower apartments prefigured the garden apartments built in the early 20th century in Forest Hills, Sunnyside, and Jackson Heights, Queens. White's structures stand in marked contrast to the enormous, block-like housing projects designed by later urban planners for low-income tenants. Now the Home and Tower apartments are the exclusive Cobble Hill Towers. the Workingmen's Cottages, which Tredway built for higher-income workers, is one of the most secret and charming enclaves in New York City. Each building is less than 12 ft wide. ✉ *The Tower: 136-142 Warren St. and 417-435 Hicks St. The Home: 439-445 Hicks St. and 129-135 Baltic St.*

❸ Willow Street. One of the prettiest and most architecturally varied blocks in Brooklyn Heights is Willow Street between Clark and Pierrepont streets. **Nos. 155–159** are three distinguished brick Federal row houses that were allegedly stops on the Underground Railroad.

OFF THE
BEATEN PATH   **WILLIAMSBURG –**Starting around the turn of the 20th century, immigrants—largely Jews, Poles, and Puerto Ricans—settled in this industrial section of Brooklyn along the East River, forming autonomous, prosperous communities side by side. Now the area is taking on a distinctly young, artsy face, as newcomers move into the few remaining converted lofts and affordable apartments here. The area's main drag is Bedford

Avenue, sometimes dubbed "Avenue E," as if it takes up where the East Village's Alphabet City (just across the East River) leaves off. The joke accurately describes the new Williamsburg, which is more Manhattan bohemia than Brooklyn enclave. The artists and other twenty- to thirtysomethings that have revived this otherwise barren neighborhood seem especially proficient at partying and shopping: Today independently owned bars, restaurants, stores, and art galleries line Bedford Avenue and its offshoots, revealing Williamsburg's future rather than its past.

From Manhattan, take the L train east one stop to **Bedford Avenue,** where everything is close at hand. The culturally inclined should seek out **Pierogi** (✉ 177 N. 9th St., between Bedford and Driggs Aves., ☎ 718/ 599–2144), a popular art gallery, or **Galapagos** (✉ 70 N. 6th St., between Wythe and Kent Aves., ☎ 718/782–5188), an all-in-one bar, art gallery, performance space, and movie house.

To experience what Williamsburg once was, attend the Italian Catholic **Giglio e Paradiso Feast and Bazaar** (718/384–0223), held for two weeks every summer starting the first Thursday in July. The remarkable processional that takes place on the festival's first Sunday leaves from Our Lady of Mt. Carmel church on Havermeyer Street between North 8 and North 9 streets.

Park Slope and Prospect Park

Park Slope grew up in the late 1800s and is today one of Brooklyn's most comfortable places to live. The largely residential neighborhood has row after row of immaculate brownstones dating from its turn-of-the-20th-century heyday, when Park Slope had the nation's highest per-capita income. The "Park" in Park Slope refers to Prospect Park, one of New York's most revered green spaces, encompassing 526 acres of meadow and woodland, man-made ponds and lakes, miles of drives and paths, a zoo, skating rink, concert bandshell, and much more. Nearby are the Grand Army Plaza, with its Soldiers' and Sailors' Memorial Arch; the stately Brooklyn Museum and Brooklyn Public Library; and the scenic Brooklyn Botanic Garden, a worthwhile destination virtually any time of year.

Numbers in the text correspond to numbers in the margin and on the Park Slope and Prospect Park map.

A Good Walk

Start your tour at the corner of Flatbush Avenue and **7th Avenue** ①, the neighborhood's commercial center, accessible by the D train (7th Ave. stop) and by the Nos. 2 and 3 (Grand Army Plaza stop). Walk up 7th Avenue and turn east onto Lincoln Place. At the top of Lincoln Place, at 8th Avenue, you'll see the **Montauk Club** ② whose sumptuous Venetian-palace style proclaims its standing as one of Brooklyn's most prestigious clubs. Make your way south along 8th Avenue, stopping to look at the brownstones on various streets along the way (President and Carroll streets are especially handsome), until you reach **Montgomery Place** ③, with its remarkable row of Romanesque revival brownstones.

From the top of Montgomery Place, take a left and walk one block north along Prospect Park West to **Grand Army Plaza** ④, whose center is dominated by the Soldiers' and Sailors' Memorial Arch, patterned on the Arc de Triomphe in Paris. Southeast of the plaza is the main entrance to the 526-acre Prospect Park, designed by Frederick Law Olmsted and Calvert Vaux. The designers liked it better than their other creation, Manhattan's Central Park, because no streets divide it and

180

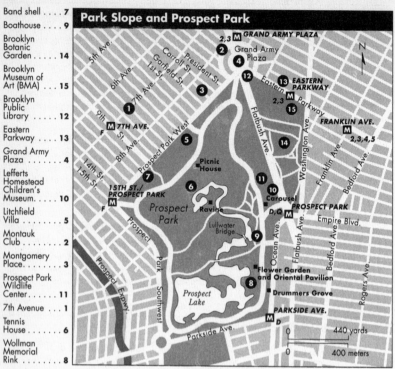

Park Slope and Prospect Park

no skyscrapers infringe on its borders. It is regarded by Olmsted aficionados as among his very best work, and a large number of restoration projects are now helping to revitalize the park.

Prospect Park's winding paths and drives, undulating hills, unexpected vistas, and open spaces serve up unanticipated pleasures at every turn. The best way to experience the park is to walk the entirety of its 3.3-mi circular drive and make detours off it as you wish. On summer evenings and weekends year-round, when the drive is closed to vehicular traffic, joggers, skaters, and bicyclists have it to themselves.

Immediately upon entering the park, veer right on the circular drive. Take a moment to admire the 90-acre Long Meadow, one of New York's greatest open spaces and a haven for picnickers, kite fliers, and dogs (on leashes). Remarkably, more than 130 years after the park's construction, the view down the Long Meadow from here still takes in no buildings—only grass, trees, and sky. A short distance down the drive, just beyond a circular playground on your right, a small access road leads you to **Litchfield Villa** ⑤, an elaborate Italianate mansion and home of the park's administrative offices. Continuing on the circular drive from the villa, you'll next come to two structures on your left—the Picnic House, frequently rented for weddings, and the **Tennis House** ⑥, home to the Brooklyn Center for Urban Education.

To the left, beyond the meadow, lies the Ravine, the wooded core of the park. The Ravine vividly conveys a sense of wilderness and demonstrates Olmsted's genius at juxtaposing vastly different landscapes. While an ongoing renewal project is underway, the majority of the Ravine is fenced off until the new plantings establish themselves. More paths open up each season and guided "Behind the Fences" tours, given on weekends from April to November, are a good way to see the otherwise inaccessible parts of the park (contact the Prospect Park hot line for details, ☎ 718/965–8999, www.prospectpark.org). Just off to the right is the **band shell** ⑦, site of the park's enormously popular free summer performing-arts series.

Continue along the circular drive, which curves to the left around the half-dozen baseball diamonds used by local leagues between Memorial Day and Labor Day; the diamonds mark the far southern end of Long Meadow. Down the hill on your left is the glorious 60-acre Prospect Lake, a refuge for waterfowl, including a few resident swans. Past the Ocean Parkway/Coney Island Avenue park entrance, as you arrive at the lake's outer reaches, you'll come upon Drummers Grove on the right. Designated an official Prospect Park site in 1996, this area has long been a popular informal weekend gathering spot for local African, Caribbean, and African-American musicians. Sunday afternoons when it's warm out, dozens of drummers, dancers, and other revelers get down, joined by an audience of sidetracked bicyclists, joggers, and skaters. Note that due to construction in this area of the park, the action sometimes moves to the Oriental Pavilion.

Just past the grove, on the left, is **Wollman Memorial Rink** ⑧. Moving on, you'll see the Flower Garden and Oriental Pavilion and reach the **Boathouse** ⑨. Unfortunately, construction of the Wollman Rink destroyed this area's original close connection with Prospect Lake. In the early days an orchestra would play on an island just offshore while spectators strolled along terraces and radial pathways. Busts of composers including Mozart and Beethoven added to the setting, and visitors sat in the beautiful pavilion, an open shelter supported by eight hand-painted wrought-iron columns and illuminated within by a central stained-glass skylight. Today the area is usually unwelcomingly deserted, and during the winter music blares from the rink.

Not far beyond the Boathouse, off on the eastern edge of the park (to your right) is the carousel, and beyond that the **Lefferts Homestead Children's Museum** ⑩ and the **Prospect Park Wildlife Center** ⑪, a small zoo. From here, you're just a short walk up the circular drive back to Grand Army Plaza, at which point you've come full circle around the park.

East (to your right) of the park's main entrance stands the main branch of the **Brooklyn Public Library** ⑫. A couple of hundred yards farther down the grand **Eastern Parkway** ⑬ lie the entrances to two of Brooklyn's most important cultural offerings: the beautifully tended **Brooklyn Botanic Garden** ⑭, which occupies 52 acres across Flatbush Avenue from Prospect Park, and the world-class **Brooklyn Museum of Art** ⑮. To return to Manhattan, you can take the No. 2 or 3 subway from the station in front of the museum. Or you could stay for dinner at Cucina or Rose Water, two happening spots on Park Slope's emerging restaurant row, a few blocks over on the southern end of 5th Avenue.

TIMING

You could easily spend a whole day at the Brooklyn Museum or the Brooklyn Botanic Garden—and another day exploring Prospect Park. If you must squeeze everything into one trip, break up your wanderings with a visit to 7th Avenue, where restaurants and cafés abound. Weekends are the best time to observe local life along 7th Avenue and to enjoy the park, when it's closed to vehicles. On weekends and holidays throughout the year, from noon to 5 PM, the red "Heart of Brooklyn" trolley circles Prospect Park, leaving Wollman Rink on the hour and hitting the zoo, the Botanic Garden, the Bandshell, and most other sights. Best of all it's free. Designed in collaboration with the Brooklyn Children's Museum, the "Heart of Brooklyn" connects with that museum's own trolley. Prospect Park has heaps of information for the Brooklyn visitor at their thorough Web site, www.prospectpark.org.

Sights to See

❼ Band shell. At the Park's 9th Street entrance (at Prospect Park West), the band shell is the home of the annual **Celebrate Brooklyn Festival,** which from mid-June through Labor Day sponsors free films and performances—with an emphasis on music—to please every taste, from African-Caribbean jazz to Kurt Weill, from the Brooklyn Philharmonic playing Duke Ellington to bluegrass and zydeco groups. A performance here on a glorious summer evening is *the* best way to enjoy the park and the Slope at their finest. ⊠ *Prospect Park W and 9th St.,* ☎ *718/965–8999 for park hot line; 718/855–7882 ext. 52 for Celebrate Brooklyn Festival,* ⓦⒺⒷ *www.brooklynx.org/celebrate.* ☞ *Free.* ☉ *Concerts late June–Labor Day; call for details.*

NEED A
BREAK?

A stone's throw from the park is **Dizzy's** (⊠ 511 9th St., at 8th Ave., ☎ 718/499–1966), which offers classic diner fare, although there may be a wait if you want to sit. Several Park Slope cafés feature great take-out, perfect for a Prospect Park picnic. Neighborhood favorite **Naidre's** (⊠ 384 7th Ave., at 12th St., ☎ 718/965–7585) makes great sandwiches from higher-end meats such as imported prosciutto. **Second Helpings** (⊠ 448 9th St, near 7th Ave., ☎ 718/965–1925) offers unbeatable gourmet wraps (try the seared tuna) and prepared foods. If you prefer coffee and something sweet, stop in at the neighborhood's best bakery, the **Two Little Red Hens** (⊠ 1112 8th Ave., at 12th St., ☎ 718/499–8108). The delicately adorned cakes with icing flowers cower before the sinful Brooklyn Blackout, a killer dark-chocolate cake. If you're closer to the Brooklyn Museum of Art or the botanical garden, dip into Prospect Heights for great diner fare and friendly service at **Tom's Restaurant** (⊠ 782 Washington St., at the corner of Sterling Pl., ☎ 718/636–9738).

❾ Boathouse. Styled after Sansovino's 16th-century Library at St. Mark's in Venice, this 1905 lakefront structure in Prospect Park, built about 40 years after the park was first created, sits opposite the **Lullwater Bridge,** setting a lovely scene, particularly on evenings when the light is just right and the lake reflects an exact image of the building. Just steps from the Boathouse (on the left as you face the Cleft Ridge Span) is the lovely **Camperdown Elm,** immortalized by the poet Marianne Moore, who in the 1960s was an early park preservationist.

★ ☾ **⓮ Brooklyn Botanic Garden.** A major attraction at this 52-acre botanic garden, one of the finest in the country, is the beguiling **Japanese Garden**—complete with a blazing red *torii* gate and a pond laid out in the shape of the Chinese character for "heart." The Japanese cherry arbor here turns into a breathtaking cloud of pink every spring. You can also wander through the **Cranford Rose Garden** (5,000 bushes, 1,200 varieties); the **Fragrance Garden,** designed especially for the blind; the **Shakespeare Garden,** featuring more than 80 plants immortalized by the Bard (including many kinds of roses); and **Celebrity Path,** Brooklyn's answer to Hollywood's Walk of Fame, with the names of New York stars—including Mel Brooks, Woody Allen, Mary Tyler Moore, Barbra Streisand, Mae West, and Maurice Sendak—inscribed on stepping-stones. The **Steinhardt Conservatory** (☉ Apr.–Sept., Tues.–Sun. 10–5:30; Oct.–Mar., Tues.–Sun. 10–4), a complex of handsome greenhouses, holds thriving desert, tropical, temperate, and aquatic vegetation, as well as a display charting the evolution of plants over the past 140 million years. The extraordinary C. V. Starr Bonsai Museum in the Conservatory exhibits about 80 miniature Japanese specimens.

Free tours are given weekends at 1 PM, except for holiday weekends. ⊠ *Eastern Parkway, west of the Brooklyn Museum; 1000 Washington Ave. at Empire Blvd.,* ☎ *718/623–7200,* WEB *www.bbg.org.* ✉ *$3; free Tues. and Sat. before noon.* ⊙ *Apr.–Sept., Tues.–Fri. 8–6, weekends 10–6; Oct.–Mar., Tues.–Fri. 8–4:30, weekends 10–4:30.*

★ ⑮ **Brooklyn Museum of Art (BMA).** Rudy Giuliani's aversion to elephant dung, and its use in a work of art, made the BMA and the mayor himself a subject of much controversy in 1999. The aptly named "Sensation" exhibition (Young British Artists from the Saatchi Collection), around which artists and art supporters rallied to protect freedom of speech and funding for the arts, was just one of the museum's recent efforts to bring more popular, cutting-edge works to the long-standing, venerable institution. With much less controversy but plenty of local attention, "First Saturdays" has also brought crowds to the museum, with late-night hours and special programs—such as live music, dancing, film screenings, and readings—on the first Saturday of every month.

A world-class museum, BMA was founded in 1823 as the Brooklyn Apprentices' Library Association (Walt Whitman was one of its first directors). Initial plans made this the largest art museum in the world, larger even than the Louvre. With approximately 1.5 million pieces in its permanent collection, it now ranks as the second-largest art museum in New York—only the Met is larger. As you approach the massive, regal building designed by McKim, Mead & White (1893), check out the allegorical figures of Brooklyn and Manhattan, originally carved by Daniel Chester French for the Manhattan Bridge.

Beyond the changing exhibitions, highlights include **Egyptian Art** (third floor), considered one of the best collections of its kind; and **African and Pre-Columbian Art** (first floor), another collection recognized worldwide. In the gallery of **American Painting and Sculpture** (fifth floor), *Brooklyn Bridge* by Georgia O'Keeffe hangs alongside nearly 200 first-rate works by Winslow Homer, John Singer Sargent, Thomas Eakins, George Bellows, and Milton Avery. The **Period Rooms** (fourth floor) include the complete interior of the Jan Martense Schenck House, built in the Brooklyn Flatlands section in 1675, as well as a Moorish-style room from the since-demolished 54th Street mansion of John D. Rockefeller (the MoMA sculpture garden now occupies the mansion's former site). **Asian Art** (second floor) includes galleries devoted to Chinese, Korean, Indian, and Islamic works. Outdoors, the **Frieda Schiff Warburg Memorial Sculpture Garden** showcases architectural fragments from demolished New York buildings, including Penn Station. ⊠ *200 Eastern Pkwy.,* ☎ *718/638–5000,* WEB *www.brooklynart. org.* ✉ *$4 (suggested donation).* ⊙ *Wed.–Fri. 10–5, weekends 11–6; first Sat. of every month, 11 AM–11 PM (call for program schedule).*

OFF THE BEATEN PATH **BROOKLYN CHILDREN'S MUSEUM** – This fully interactive museum for children has tunnels to crawl through and animals to pet. Exhibitions cover topics ranging from technology and oceanography to Caribbean music and international shoes. Free trolley service to the museum leaves Grand Army Plaza (corner of Union St. and Prospect Park W) at 15 minutes past the hour, and the Brooklyn Museum of Art at 25 minutes past the hour, from 10–5 on weekends. The trolley connects with the park's "Heart of Brooklyn" line. ⊠ *145 Brooklyn Ave., at St. Marks Ave.,* ☎ *718/735–4432,* WEB *www.bchildmus.org.* ✉ *$3 (suggested donation).* ⊙ *June–Aug., Mon. and Wed.–Sun. noon–5; Sept.–May, Wed.–Fri. 2–5, weekends 10–5.*

⓬ **Brooklyn Public Library.** Built in 1941, this grand neoclassical edifice was designed to resemble an open book, with a gilt-inscribed spine on Grand Army Plaza that opens out to Eastern Parkway and Flatbush Avenue. Bright limestone walls, perfect proportions, and ornate decorative details make this a rare 20th-century New York building. The 15 bronze figures over the entrance, representing characters in American literature, were sculpted by Thomas Hudson Jones, who also designed the Tomb of the Unknown Soldier in Arlington National Cemetery. ⊠ *Grand Army Plaza at intersection of Flatbush Ave. and Eastern Pkwy.,* ☎ *718/230–2100.* ⊙ *Mon.–Thurs. 9–8; Fri.–Sat. 9–6; Sun. 1–5.*

⓭ **Eastern Parkway.** The world's first six-lane parkway originates at Grand Army Plaza. When Olmsted and Vaux conceived the avenue's design in 1866, in tandem with their plans for Prospect Park, they wanted it to mimic the grand sweep of the boulevards of Paris and Vienna. Today it continues to play an important role in Brooklyn culture: every Labor Day weekend Eastern Parkway hosts the West Indian American Day Parade, the biggest and liveliest carnival outside the Caribbean.

❹ **Grand Army Plaza.** Prospect Park West, Eastern Parkway, and Flatbush and Vanderbilt avenues radiate out from this geographic star. Crossing the broad streets around here can be dangerous; be careful. At the center of the plaza stands the **Soldiers' and Sailors' Memorial Arch,** honoring Civil War veterans and patterned on the Arc de Triomphe in Paris. Three heroic sculptural groupings adorn the arch: atop, a four-horse chariot by Frederick MacMonnies, so dynamic it seems about to catapult off the arch; to either side, the victorious Union Army and Navy of the Civil War. Inside are bas-reliefs of presidents Abraham Lincoln and Ulysses S. Grant, sculpted by Thomas Eakins and William O'Donovan, respectively. On some spring and fall weekends the top of the arch is accessible; call ☎ 718/965–8999 for information.

To the northwest of the arch, Neptune and a passel of debauched Tritons leer over the edges of the **Bailey Fountain,** a popular spot for tulle-draped brides and grooms in Technicolor tuxes to pose after exchanging vows. On Saturday year-round, a large greenmarket sets up in the plaza; heaps of locally grown produce, flowers and plants, baked goods, and other foodstuffs attract throngs of neighborhood residents.

 ⓾ **Lefferts Homestead Children's Museum.** Built in 1783 and moved to Prospect Park in 1918, this gambrel-roof Dutch colonial farmhouse contains a historic house-museum for children. Adults will enjoy the two period rooms furnished with antiques, while children love playing in the two rooms with period reproduction furniture. Nearby is a restored 1912 **carousel** (⊡ 50¢ per ride on weekends, closed mid-Oct.–early Apr.). ⊠ *Flatbush Ave. north of junction with Park Loop,* ☎ *718/965–6505 museum.* ⊡ *Free.* ⊙ *Mid-Apr.–mid-Dec., Thurs.–Sun.; mid-Dec.–Mar. by appointment. Hours vary seasonally, so call ahead.*

❺ **Litchfield Villa.** The most important sight on the western border of Prospect Park, this Italianate mansion built in 1857 was designed by Alexander Jackson Davis, considered the foremost architect of his day, for a prominent railroad magnate. It has housed the park's headquarters since 1883, but visitors are welcome to step inside and view the domed octagonal rotunda. Not far from the Litchfield Villa on the park's circular drive is the **Picnic House,** one of the park's less architecturally distinguished buildings, used mostly for private functions. ⊠ *Prospect Park W and 3rd St.,* ☎ *718/965–8999 for park hot line.*

❷ **Montauk Club.** The home of a venerable club (and newly developed condominium apartments on its upper floors), this 1891 mansion designed by Francis H. Kimball is modeled on Venice's Ca' d'Oro and other Gothic Venetian palaces. It is Park Slope's most impressive building and easily rivals the showcase mansions on Manhattan's Upper East Side. You can view the building on three sides from the street; notice the friezes of Native American Montauks and the 19th-century private side entrance for members' wives. ⊠ *25 8th Ave.*

❸ Montgomery Place. This block-long street between 8th Avenue and Prospect Park West is considered to be one of Park Slope's finest thoroughfares; it's lined with stately town houses designed by the Romanesque revival genius C. P. H. Gilbert.

⑪ Prospect Park Wildlife Center. Small, friendly, and educational, this children's zoo off the main road of Prospect Park has just the right combination of indoor and outdoor exhibits along with a number of unusual and endangered species among its 390 inhabitants. The sea-lion pool is a hit with children, as are the indoor exhibits—"Animal Lifestyles," which explains habitats and adaptations, and "Animals in Our Lives," showcasing domesticated and farm animals. An outdoor discovery trail has a simulated prairie-dog burrow and a naturalistic pond. ⊠ *Flatbush Ave. at Empire Blvd.,* ☎ *718/399–7339.* ☞ *$2.50.* ☉ *Nov.–Mar., daily 10–4:30; Apr.–Oct., weekdays 10–5, weekends 10–5:30.*

OFF THE BEATEN PATH

PUPPETWORKS – With the mission of preserving puppet theater, the wooden marionettes at this 75-seat nonprofit theater perform classic children's stories drawn faithfully from original texts. Reservations are required for weekday shows for groups and for weekend showings at 12:30 and 2:30. ⊠ *338 6th Ave., at 4th St.,* ☎ *718/965-3391,* WEB *www.puppetworks.org.* ☞ *Adults $7, children $5.*

❶ 7th Avenue. Restaurants, groceries, bookstores, cafés, bakeries, churches, and more line Park Slope's commercial spine from Flatbush Avenue roughly to 15th Street. A few choice spots—beginning at the north (Flatbush) end and moving south—include the **New Prospect** (⊠ 52 7th Ave.), a place to pick up some ready-made food or bread; **Leaf & Bean** (⊠ 83 7th Ave.), a tea and coffee shop with lots of kitchen gadgets; **Leon Paley Ltd. Wines & Spirits** (⊠ 88 7th Ave.), a fine wine store; and **The Clay Pot** (⊠ 162 7th Ave.), known for original wares and ornaments for the home and for one-of-a-kind wedding bands made by local artisans. At the south end of Park Slope is **Lucky Bug** (⊠ 438 7th Ave.), a riotous mix of toys, kitsch, and folk art that will appeal to children and adults alike. A few doors down is **Bird** (⊠ 430 7th Ave.), a chic shop with well-designed women's clothing.

NEED A BREAK?

On the south end of the Slope, at 15th Street, the **Computer Caffé** is a good place to check your e-mail and have an espresso (⊠ 435 7th Ave.). Beloved local spot, **Max & Moritz** (⊠ 426A 7th Ave., at 14th St., ☎ 718/499–5557) attracts a crowd for weekend brunches. **2nd Street Café** (⊠ 189 7th Ave., at 2nd St., ☎ 718/768–4940) is a homey restaurant with lunch on weekdays, brunch on weekends, and counter service in late afternoons and evenings. Try the raisin-studded bread pudding or heartwarming soups such as curry pumpkin. There are two good local coffee joints among the many that line 7th Avenue. **Ozzie's Coffee & Tea** (⊠ 57 7th Ave., at Lincoln Pl., ☎ 718/398–6695), is a converted drugstore with its apothecary cases still intact. The **Community Bookstore and Café** (⊠ 143 7th Ave., at Garfield, ☎ 718/783–3075), offers pastries, quiche, and additional light offerings in the lovely, little garden out back or indoors among the bookcases.

6 Tennis House. The most prominent of several neoclassical structures in the park, this 1910 limestone and yellow-brick building postdates by 40 years the more rustic structures favored by Olmsted and Vaux, few of which survive. The Tennis House's most elegant features are the triple-bay Palladian arches on both its north and south facade, and its airy terra-cotta barrel-vaulted arcade on the south side. The building's large tiled central court has amazing acoustics—shout "hello" and listen to your voice bounce back at you. On the lower level, the **Brooklyn Center for the Urban Environment** has rotating exhibitions on urban issues. ☎ 718/788–8500. ⊠ *Free.* ⊙ *Weekdays 8:30–5 (Tennis House only) and weekends noon–5 (Tennis House and BCUE gallery, when an exhibition is up).*

8 Wollman Memorial Rink. A cousin to Wollman Rink in Central Park, this is one of Prospect Park's most popular destinations. Besides skating in the winter, pedal-boat rentals are available here weekends and holidays from April through the middle of October (☎ 718/282–7789 or 718/287–5538). The rink is directly across the circular drive from the **Drummers Grove** and adjacent to the **Flower Garden and Oriental Pavilion,** the most formally laid-out part of the park. Once a graceful setting where people strolled to the strains of an orchestra, the area is now rather desolate and ice-skaters are engulfed in loud music. ☎ 718/287–6431. ⊠ *$4; $3.50 skate rental.* ⊙ *Mid-Nov.–early Mar., Mon. 8:30–2, Tues. 8:30–5, Wed. 8:30–3, Thurs. 8:30–8, Fri. 8:30–9, Sat. 10–1, 2–6, and 7–10, Sun. 10–1 and 2–6.*

Coney Island

Named Konijn Eiland (Rabbit Island) by the Dutch for its wild rabbit population, Coney Island has a boardwalk, a 2½-mi-long beach, a legendary amusement park, the city's only aquarium, and easy proximity to Brighton Beach, a Russian enclave drenched in old-world atmosphere. Coney Island may have declined from its glory days in the early 1900s, when visitors lunched at a 34-room ocean-side hotel built in the shape of an elephant, glided across the nation's biggest dance floor at Dreamland, and toured a replica of old Baghdad called Luna Park. But it's still a great place to experience the sounds, smells, and sights of summer: hot dogs, suntan lotion, crowds, fried clams, and old men staring out to sea, not to mention the ponderous turning of the mighty Wonder Wheel and the heart-stopping plunging of the king of roller coasters—the Cyclone.

A Good Walk

Coney Island is the last stop on the B, D, F, and N trains in Brooklyn. The Coney Island boardwalk remains the hub of the action; amble along it to take in the local color. You'll find standard summer snacks here in the form of ice cream and saltwater taffy, but it is the chewy, deep-fried clams, hot dogs with spicy mustard, and ice-cold lemonade from **Nathan's Famous** ① that are truly synonymous with the Coney Island boardwalk experience.

Coney Island is a repository of times gone by, where fire-eaters and sword-swallowers carry on the traditions of what was once billed as the "World's Largest Playground" at **Sideshows by the Seashore and the Coney Island Museum** ②. The rickety 70-year old Cyclone roller-coaster at **Astroland** ③ and, farther down the boardwalk, the abandoned Space Needle–like structure, once the Parachute Jump, are testimony to this waning beachside culture. Be sure to take a ride on the Cyclone, which still packs a punch, or the Wonderwheel at **Deno's Wonderwheel Park** ④.

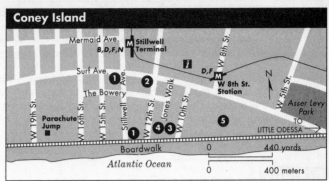

Today visitors are just as likely to come to Coney Island to see New York City's only aquarium, the **Aquarium for Wildlife Conservation** ⑤, where five beluga whales and some 10,000 other creatures of the sea make their home. From here, take a short walk east on Surf Avenue to Brighton Beach Avenue in "Little Odessa," where a community of some 90,000 Russian, Ukrainian, and Georgian emigrés operate fish markets, bakeries, and inexpensive restaurants. This is the place to find knishes with every filling imaginable, borscht, *blinis* (small crêpes or pancakes), and cups of dark-roast coffee, plus caviar at prices that can put Manhattan purveyors to shame.

TIMING

Coney Island is at its liveliest on weekends, when crowds come out to play, especially in summer. Brighton Beach is a vibrant neighborhood year-round. Allow most of a day for this trip, since the subway ride from Manhattan (one-way) takes at least an hour.

Sights to See

★ ☾ ⑤ **Aquarium for Wildlife Conservation.** Moved to Coney Island in 1957 from its former digs at Battery Park, New York City's only aquarium is worth a trip in itself. Here otters, walruses, penguins, and seals lounge on a replicated Pacific coast; a 180,000-gallon seawater complex hosts beluga whales; and dolphins and sea lions perform in the Aquatheater. ⊠ *W. 8th St. and Surf Ave.,* ☎ *718/265–3474,* WEB *www. wcs.org/zoos.* ☜ *$9.75.* ☼ *Daily, 10–4:30; last ticket sold 3:45.*

☾ ③ **Astroland.** The world-famous, wood-and-steel Cyclone is one of the oldest roller coasters still operating (it first rode in 1927); it was moved in 1975 to Astroland, which had recently opened as a "space-age" theme park. Today a visit is more like stepping into the past than the future, but the rides are still a thrill, as is the Skee-Ball. ⊠ *1000 Surf Ave.,* ☎ *718/372–0275.* ☼ *Call for seasonal hours.* ☜ *Free; $1–$4 per ride.*

☾ ④ **Deno's Wonderwheel Park.** You'll get a new perspective on the Island from the 80-year-old Wonder Wheel, which, though it appears tame, will still quicken your heart rate. ⊠ *1025 Boardwalk,* ☎ *718/449– 8836.* ☼ *Call for seasonal hours.* ☜ *Free; $2 per ride, 10 rides for $15.*

☾ ① **Nathan's Famous.** A Coney Island institution since 1916 for hot dogs (you can buy them by the pound), fries, and lemonade. Bring your antacid. ⊠ *On the Boardwalk,* ☼ *May–Sept.; 1310 Surf Ave. at 15th St.,* ☼ *year-round;* ☎ *718/946–2202 both locations.*

☾ ② **Sideshows by the Seashore and the Coney Island Museum.** A lively circus sideshow, complete with a fire-eater, sword-swallower, snake charmer, and contortionist, can be seen here. On the first Saturday after summer solstice, the cast of the sideshow, an amazing array of local legends, and a slew of (the more performative) New Yorkers take part in the **Mermaid Parade.** In a sometimes beautiful, sometimes absurd spectacle, imaginative floats and participants in wild costumes throng the Boardwalk and Surf Avenue to pay homage to the myth of the mermaid and the legend of the sea. For information call ☎ 718/372–5159. Upstairs from Sideshows, the **Coney Island Museum** (✉ 1208 Surf Ave., 🎫 99¢) has historic Coney Island memorabilia and a wealth of tourist information. It's open year-round but hours may vary so call ahead. ✉ *W. 12th St. and Surf Ave.,* ☎ *718/372–5159 for both.* 🎫 *$5.* ⊙ *Memorial Day–Labor Day, Fri.–Sun. 1–midnight; Labor Day–Memorial Day, weekends noon–5.*

QUEENS

Home of the La Guardia and John F. Kennedy international airports and many of Manhattan's bedroom communities, Queens is perhaps New York City's most underappreciated borough. It's certainly the most diverse, for the borough's countless ethnic neighborhoods continue to attract immigrants from all over the world. Its inhabitants represent maybe all nationalities and speak scores of languages, from Hindi to Hebrew. Queens communities such as Astoria (Greek and Italian), Jackson Heights (Colombian, Mexican, and Indian), Sunnyside (Turkish and Romanian), and Flushing (Korean and Chinese) are fascinating to explore, particularly if you're interested in experiencing some of the city's tastiest—and least expensive—cuisine. In addition, these areas often feature little-known historic sites, many of them just 10 minutes by subway from Grand Central Terminal. The Long Island City/Astoria area has emerged as the borough's destination of choice, largely because of its proximity to Manhattan, great museums, and superb ethnic dining.

Note: Queens streets, drives, and avenues—altogether different thoroughfares—sometimes have the same numerical name, for instance, 30th Drive is not the same as 30th Avenue.

Astoria and Long Island City

Astoria is like an archaeological site—each layer contains a trace of the area's successive denizens, from movie-makers to Greek immigrants to young artists and professionals. In the beginning, Astoria was the center of America's flashiest industry—namely, the movies. In the 1920s, Hollywood was still a dusty small town when such stars as Gloria Swanson, Rudolph Valentino, and the Marx Brothers came to this part of Queens to work at "the Big House," Paramount's movie-making center in the east. At that time the Kaufman-Astoria Studios were the largest and most important filmmaking studios in the country; today they remain the largest in the East, and they're still used for major films and television shows.

Originally German, then Italian, Astoria earned the nickname Little Athens in the late 1960s; by the early 1990s Greeks accounted for nearly half the population. Today there are also substantial numbers of Asians, Eastern Europeans, Irish, and Latino immigrants in Astoria, not to mention an ever-growing contingent of former Manhattan residents in search of cheaper rents and a friendlier atmosphere. Astoria is a place where people socialize on their front lawns at dusk and where mom-and-pop businesses thrive. Here you can buy Cypriot cured olives and feta cheese from store owners who will tell you where to go for the best spinach pie, or you can sit outside at one of the many *xaxaroplasteion* (pastry shops) drinking tall, frothy frappes and watching the subway's

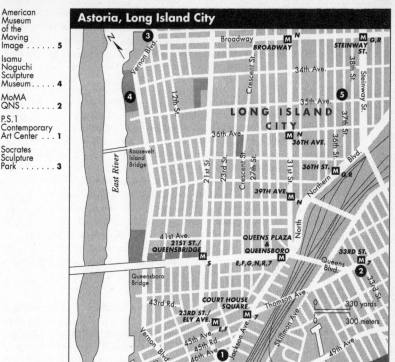

elevated trains roll by. Astoria's a perfect pit stop for food either before or after seeing the museums of Long Island City. The truly adventurous can also check out Astoria's vibrant ethnic nightlife and bars.

Numbers in the text correspond to numbers in the margin and on the Astoria, Long Island City map.

A Good Tour

By subway, take the E or F trains from Manhattan to the 23rd Street/Ely Avenue stop in Queens for the **P.S.1 Contemporary Art Center** ①, Or take the No. 7 train to the 33rd Street stop in Queens for the nearby **MoMA QNS** ②, the temporary space of the Museum of Modern Art, where some of the finest works of 20th-century modern art will be on display starting in the summer of 2002. Ask at either institution for walking directions between the two.

After you've done Long Island City, take the No. 7 train one stop (from 45th Road/Courthouse Square if you're coming from P.S.1; from 33rd Street if you're coming from MoMA QNS) to Queensboro Plaza. There, transfer to the N train to reach the Broadway stop in Astoria. You can eat lunch at one of the many restaurants and cafés up and down Broadway. Then walk (it's eight long blocks, about 20 minutes, from the Broadway subway station), hail a cab, or hop the Q104 bus toward the East River. At Vernon Boulevard and Broadway, the **Socrates Sculpture Park** ③ at first almost appears to be an urban hallucination, with its large, abstract artworks framed by the Manhattan skyline. Three blocks south on Vernon Boulevard, with its entrance on 33rd Road, the **Isamu Noguchi Sculpture Museum** ④ is the ultimate modernist experience. Hundreds of Noguchi's works are displayed in an indoor-outdoor setting that evokes the tranquillity of a Japanese garden.

Catch the Q104 bus along Broadway to 36th Street; when you get off turn right and walk two blocks to 35th Avenue. Here you'll find the

American Museum of the Moving Image ⑤, where cinema lovers can easily spend hours absorbed by the film production exhibits and the regularly scheduled film series and directors' talks. Next door, the imposing 13-acre Kaufman-Astoria Studios has been used for the filming of such movies as *The Cotton Club* and television series such as the *Cosby Show* and *Sesame Street*.

Head back to Broadway into the heart of the Greek community, between 31st and Steinway streets, where Greek pastry shops and coffee shops abound, and the elevated subway brings a constant stream of activity. Farther up, 30th Avenue has every kind of food store imaginable; between 35th and 36th streets alone you'll find a *salumeria* (Italian deli), a meat market, a bakery, a wholesale international-food store, and more. The largest Greek Orthodox congregation outside Greece worships at St. Demetrios Cathedral, just off 30th Avenue. You could end your day with a fine dinner at one of Astoria's Greek restaurants (on or near Broadway) or venture to the Middle Eastern restaurants farther out on Steinway Street. The truly adventurous can check out Astoria's vibrant ethnic nightlife and bars, which span the globe from Croatian to Brazilian. A particular jewel is the artsy Brick Cafe, on 33rd Street at 31st Avenue.

TIMING

To see Greek Astoria at its finest, visit on a Saturday, when sidewalk culture comes to life. To see all the art in Long Island City and Astoria would easily fill an entire day, so get an early start. Allow at least two hours for leisurely visits to P.S.1 and MoMA QNS; and two for the American Museum of the Moving Image and a tour of Greek Astoria. It's something of a schlepp to the Socrates Sculpture Park and the Isamu Noguchi Sculpture Museum (you may want to catch a cab); for these two sights, allow three hours altogether. (Note that the Noguchi museum is closed November–March.) Be aware that a visit to any one or two of these sights could fill up the better part of your day.

Sights to See

★ ⑤ **American Museum of the Moving Image.** Crossing the East River to Astoria for the nation's only museum devoted to the art, technology, and history of film, TV, and digital media is a worthwhile pilgrimage. Via artifacts, texts, live demonstrations, and video screenings, the core exhibition, "Behind the Screen," takes you step by step through the process of producing, marketing, and exhibiting moving images. Interactive computers allow you to make your own video flip book, edit sound effects, dub dialogue, and create animation. The museum's collection of movie memorabilia includes over 80,000 items, including costumes worn by Marlene Dietrich, Marilyn Monroe, and Robin Williams. Movie serials from the 1930s and '40s, such as Buck Rogers and Captain America, are shown daily in the 30-seat Tut's Fever Movie Palace. The museum also presents changing exhibits, lectures, and provocative film programs, including retrospectives, Hollywood classics, experimental videos, and TV documentaries. ⊠ *35th Ave. between 36th and 37th Sts., Astoria,* ☎ *718/784–0077,* WEB *www.ammi.org.* ☞ *$8.50.* ☺ *Tues.–Fri. noon–5, weekends 11–6.*

NEED A
BREAK?

Nearby is the hip, colorful **Café Bar** (⊠ 32-90 36th St., at 34th Ave., ☎ 718/204–5273), perfect for a snack, coffee, or an evening cocktail. **S'Agapo** (⊠ 43-21 34th Ave., at 35th St., ☎ 718/626–0303) is pricier than is average here, but it's been called the best food in Astoria. At **Omonia Café** (⊠ 32-20 Broadway, ☎ 718/274–6650) you can watch the constant activity on Broadway while nursing coffee and honey-sweet pastries. Across the street, **Uncle George's** (⊠ 33-19 Broadway,

☎ 718/626–0593) is a 24-hour Greek diner where rotisserie-roasted lamb and other Greek classics can be had for a song.

OFF THE
BEATEN PATH

FLUSHING MEADOWS–CORONA PARK – The site of both the 1939 and 1964 World's Fairs, Flushing Meadows–Corona Park is well worth the trek from Manhattan. A ride on the No. 7 subway from Times Square or Grand Central Station to the Willets Point–Shea Stadium stop puts you within walking distance of some of New York's most exciting cultural and recreational institutions. At the **Queens Museum of Art** check out the knock-your-socks-off New York City panorama, a 9,335-square-ft model of the five boroughs, made for the 1964 World's Fair. It faithfully replicates all the city's boroughs building by building, on a scale of 1 inch per 100 ft. The model's tiny brownstones and skyscrapers are updated periodically to look exactly like the real things. The museum has a "First Thursdays" program modeled after the Brooklyn Museum's successful "First Saturdays," with live music, film screenings, and access to current exhibitions. ✉ *Flushing Meadows–Corona Park,* ☎ *718/592–9700.* 🎫 *$4 (suggested donation); $7 "First Thursdays."* ⊙ *Wed.–Fri. 10–5, weekends noon–5; first Thurs. of every month 10–8.*

In front of the museum is one of the city's most stunning photo opportunities, the awe-inspiring **Unisphere.** Made entirely of stainless steel for the 1964 World's Fair, this massive sculpture of the Earth is 140 ft high and weighs 380 tons. If you're here with children, you'll also want to visit the **New York Hall of Science** (✉ 111th St. at 46th Ave., ☎ 718/699–0005), a top science museum with more than 160 hands-on experiments on subjects ranging from lasers to microbes. Outside, stations on the Science Playground coax youngsters into learning while they're horsing around—a seesaw, for example, becomes a lesson in balance and leverage. Children will also love the very manageable **Queens Wildlife Center** (✉ 53-51 111th St., at 53rd Ave., ☎ 718/271–7761), where American animals roam in settings loosely approximating their natural habitats. The residents include spectacled bears, mountain lions, sea lions, bobcats, coyotes, bison, and elk.

During baseball season, top the day off with a Mets game at **Shea Stadium** (☎ 718/507–8499 for a game schedule), just north of the park. If you're into tennis, catch such champs as Pete Sampras, Martina Hingis, and Venus Williams at the U.S. Open Tournament on and around Labor Day at the **USTA National Tennis Center** opposite the Unisphere. Or play a match yourself at one of the 29 courts open to the public (☎ 718/760–6200 for court reservations and fees).

★ ➍ **Isamu Noguchi Sculpture Museum.** In 1985, this space across the street from the studio of Japanese-American sculptor Isamu Noguchi (1904–88) became a museum devoted to his sculpture. A large, open-air garden and two floors of gallery space hold more than 250 of Noguchi's pieces in stone, bronze, wood, clay, and steel. Videos document his long career; there are also models, drawings, and even stage sets for Martha Graham's dance performances. Weekend bus service ($5) from Manhattan to the museum leaves every hour on the half hour, 11:30–3:30, from the northeast corner of Park Avenue and East 70th Street. ✉ *32-37 Vernon Blvd., at 33rd Rd., Long Island City,* ☎ *718/204–7088 or 718/721–1932,* ⬛WEB *www.noguchi.org.* 🎫 *$4 (suggested donation).* ⊙ *Apr.–Oct., Wed.–Fri. 10–5, weekends 11–6; closed Nov.–Mar.*

★ ➋ **MoMA QNS** Starting in the summer of 2002, while the Museum of Modern Art begins the $650 million reconstruction of its famous 53rd Street building, its peerless collection will be exhibited in a former Swingline factory in Long Island City near P.S.1. MoMA QNS opens with a special installation of masterworks, "Collection Highlights," to include Vincent Van Gogh's "Starry Night" (1889) and Picasso's "Les Demoiselles d'Avignon" (1907). A show of contemporary drawing will follow. *45-20 33rd St., at Queens Blvd., Long Island City,* ☎ *718/389–4729,* WEB *www.moma.org.* ☞ *$10.* ☉ *Sat.–Tues. and Thurs. 10:30–5:45, Fri. 10:30–8:15. No. 7 to 33rd St..*

★ ❶ **P.S.1 Contemporary Art Center.** A pioneer in the alternative-space movement, P.S.1 rose from the ruins of an abandoned school in 1971 as a sort of community arts center for the future. The focus is still on community involvement, with studio spaces for resident artists, educational programs, and outdoor summer concerts with DJs and cookouts. Its 1999 merge with Manhattan's Museum of Modern Art (moving temporarily to the neighborhood, *see above*) improved the quality of the curation and attracted new audiences. In summer, its Sunday afternoon outdoor dance parties with vogueish European DJs attract a glamorous crowd. P.S.1's exhibition space is enormous, and every available corner of the expansive building is used; four-odd floors, rooftop spaces, staircases and landings, bathrooms, the boiler room and basement, and outdoor galleries are all alive with works, making a thorough visit here an all-day affair (don't worry—there's a café). Exhibitions reflect the center's mission to present experimental and formally innovative contemporary art; you'll see things here you're not likely to encounter at other museums, from the progressive and interactive to the incomprehensible. Fortunately P.S.1's daring and spirited mission ensures that it's never dull. You can even exit the museum via a 45-ft corkscrew slide designed by Belgian artist Carsten Huller. ✉ *22-25 Jackson Ave., at 46th Ave., Long Island City,* ☎ *718/784–2084,* WEB *www.ps1.org.* ☞ *$4.* ☉ *Wed.–Sun. noon–6. E, F to 23d St.–Ely Ave.; No. 7 to 45 Rd.–Courthouse Sq.; G to Court Square.*

★ ☝ ❸ **Socrates Sculpture Park.** The ancient Greeks excelled in the art of sculpture, which was often displayed in outdoor temples. In 1985, local artist Mark DiSuvero and other residents rallied to transform what had been an illegal dump site into this 4⅕-acre park, devoted to the display of public art. Today a superb view of the river and the Manhattan skyline beyond frames huge works of art made of scrap metal, old tires, and other recycled products. You can climb on or walk through a number of the sculptures, making the park a good spot for children. ✉ *Vernon Blvd. at Broadway, Long Island City,* ☎ *718/956–1819.* ☉ *Daily 10–sunset.*

STATEN ISLAND

Even though Staten Island is officially a part of New York City, it is, for many New Yorkers, a forgotten borough. When it does come to mind, it's recollected for its expansive garbage dump and the island's perpetual agitation to secede from the city. Staten Island today still feels provincial and old-fashioned compared to the rest of the city. Residents use the ferry system that the other boroughs abandoned in the 1890s, and time stands still in the beautiful re-created villages of Richmondtown and Snug Harbor.

Staten Island keeps a low profile, but its privacy hides real attractions, such as the phenomenal views of lower Manhattan and the Statue of Liberty afforded by the the 20-minute ferry ride across New York Harbor. And the ride is free, an anomaly in New York. On weekend mornings until 11:30 AM, ferries leave the southern tip of Manhattan at Whitehall Terminal every hour on the half hour; from noon until 7:30 PM, they run every half-hour. On weekdays and weekend afternoons

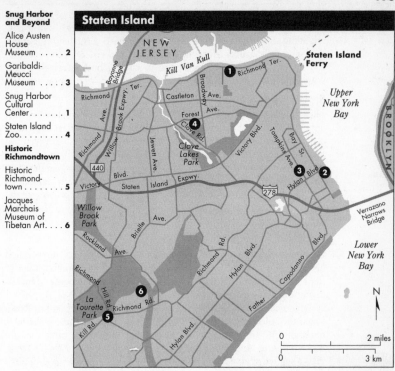

you can catch one at least every half-hour. To get to Whitehall Terminal, take a No. 4 or 5 train to Bowling Green, an N or R train to Whitehall, or a No. 1 or 9 train to South Ferry. You can also call the **Staten Island Ferry** (☎ 718/815–2628) for schedules and directions.

Snug Harbor and Beyond

Just 2 mi from the ferry terminal, the restored sailor's community of Snug Harbor is by far the most popular of Staten Island's attractions. For a highly enjoyable daytime outing, take the scenic ferry ride from Manhattan and visit Snug Harbor and two small but engaging nearby museums; then stop for a meal at Adobe Blues.

Numbers in the text correspond to numbers in the margin and on the Staten Island map.

A Good Tour

From the Staten Island Ferry terminal, a seven-minute (2-mi) ride on the S40 bus will take you to the **Snug Harbor Cultural Center** ①, an 83-acre complex with an art gallery, a botanical garden, a children's museum, and a colorful history. Signal the driver as soon as you glimpse the black iron fence along the edge of the property.

If the day is still young after you've toured Snug Harbor, return to the ferry terminal and catch the S51–Bay Street bus for the 15-minute ride to Hylan Boulevard to see the turn-of-the-20th-century photographs displayed in the ivy-covered **Alice Austen House Museum** ②. Italian history buffs should head to the **Garibaldi-Meucci Museum** ③, where General Giuseppe Garibaldi lived in exile with his friend Antonio Meucci—the true inventor of the telephone. You can also catch the S48 bus at the terminal to see farm animals and a faux African savannah at the **Staten Island Zoo** ④.

The Snug Harbor Cultural Center alone will take at least half a day, including the ferry commute; add to that the Alice Austen House and the Garibaldi-Meucci Museum, or the zoo, and you're in for a whole-day adventure. If you're interested in visiting both museums, plan your visit toward the end of the week, when they're both open.

Sights to See

② **Alice Austen House Museum.** Photographer Alice Austen (1866–1952) defied tradition when, as a girl of 10, she received her first camera as a gift from an uncle and promptly began taking pictures of everything around her. Austen went on to make photography her lifetime avocation, recording on film a vivid social history of Staten Island in the early part of the 20th century; one of the local ferries is actually named for her. The cozy, Dutch-style cottage known as Clear Comfort, where she lived almost all her life, has been restored, and many of her photographs are on display. ⊠ *2 Hylan Blvd.,* ☎ *718/816–4506.* ☞ *$2.* ☉ *Mar.–Dec., Thurs.–Sun. noon–5.*

❸ **Garibaldi-Meucci Museum.** The house Antonio Meucci once called home is now a small museum full of the letters and photographs of fiery Italian patriot Giuseppe Garibaldi. It also documents Meucci's invention of the telephone before Alexander Graham Bell. Appropriately, the museum is in the heart of the Italian neighborhood of Rosebank; the colorful **Our Lady of Mount Saint Carmel Society Shrine** is nearby, at 36 Amity Street. Ask the museum curator for directions. ⊠ *420 Tompkins Ave. (entrance on Chestnut Ave.),* ☎ *718/442–1608.* ☞ *$3 suggested donation.* ☉ *Tues.–Sun. 1–4:30 (but it's a good idea to call first).*

★ ☾ **❶** **Snug Harbor Cultural Center.** Once part of a sprawling farm, then a home for "aged, decrepit, and worn-out sailors," this 83-acre property is based around a row of five columned Greek revival temples, built between 1831 and 1880, and consists of 28 mostly restored historic buildings. The Main Hall—the oldest building on the property, dating from 1833—is home to the **Newhouse Center for Contemporary Art** (☎ 718/448–2500, ☞ $2 suggested donation, ☉ Wed.–Sun. noon–5 during exhibitions), which exhibits contemporary work, normally within a historical context. Thus, older works often sit beside multidisciplinary pieces—in costume, video, mixed-media, and performance, among others—in the expansive space. Next door is the **John A. Noble Collection** (☎ 718/447–6490, ☞ $2 suggested donation, ☉ Apr.–Oct., Wed. 10–5, Thurs. 1–9, Fri.–Sun. 1–5; Nov.–Mar., weekends only 10–4), where an old seaman's dormitory has been transformed into classrooms; a library and archive; a print-making studio; and galleries displaying maritime-inspired photography, lithographs, and artwork.

The cultural center grounds are graced by the **Staten Island Botanical Gardens,** which include a perennial garden, a greenhouse, a vineyard, 10 acres of natural marsh habitat, a rose garden, and a sensory garden with fragrant, touchable flowers and tinkling waterfalls intended for people with vision and hearing impairments. An authentic Chinese Scholars' Garden—hand-created by artisans from China and one of the only two in the United States—has reflecting ponds, waterfalls, pavilions, and a teahouse. The Carl Grillo Glass House keeps tropical, desert, and temperate plant environments, and the Connie Gretz Secret Garden is wonderfully child-friendly in design, with castles and moats among the flowers. Call for special programs, held throughout the year. ☎ *718/273–8200.* ☞ *Free; $5 for Chinese Garden and Secret Garden.* ☉ *Dawn–dusk; Chinese Garden, Tues.–Sun. 10–5.*

⊕ **Staten Island Children's Museum,** also on the grounds, has five galleries with hands-on exhibitions introducing such topics as nature's food chains, storytelling, and insects. Portia's Playhouse, an interactive children's theater, invites youngsters to step up to the stage and even try on costumes. ☎ *718/273–2060.* ⊠ *$4.* ⊙ *Tues.–Sun. noon–5.*

Snug Harbor's newly renovated **Music Hall,** the second-oldest hall in the city (after Carnegie, built in 1892), has frequent performances, including an annual music festival. The former chapel houses the 210-seat **Veterans Memorial Hall,** site of many indoor concerts and gatherings. The complex has a gift shop and a cafeteria. ⊠ *1000 Richmond Terr.,* ☎ *718/448–2500.* ⊠ *Cultural Center grounds free.* ⊙ *Dawn–dusk, tours weekends 2 PM (meet at the gift shop).*

NEED A BREAK?   Those with a powerful thirst should head straight to **Adobe Blues** (⊠ 63 Lafayette St., just off Richmond Terr., ☎ 718/720–2583), a Southwestern-style saloon and restaurant with more than 200 beers, 40 types of tequila, and a wicked chili con carne.

❹ **Staten Island Zoo.** At this small but high-quality zoo you'll find a "South American" tropical forest, a serpentarium (reptile house), an aquarium, an "African Savannah at Twilight," and a children's center. You can get here within half an hour from Snug Harbor by taking the S40 bus to Richmond Terrace, and there changing to the S53. ⊠ *Barrett Park, 614 Broadway, Staten Island,* ☎ *718/442–3100.* ⊠ *$3; pay as you wish Wed. 2–4:45.* ⊙ *Daily 10–4:45 (last admission 1 hr before closing).*

Historic Richmondtown

Hilly and full of green space, the scenic southern part of the island is far from the ferry terminal but worth the trip. Sprawling Historic Richmondtown takes you on a vivid journey into Staten Island's past, and the hilltop Jacques Marchais Museum of Tibetan Art transports you to the mountains of Asia.

A Good Tour

Take the S74–Richmond Road bus from the ferry terminal to **Historic Richmondtown** ⑤ (about 40 minutes), whose historic buildings date from the 17th, 18th, and 19th centuries. Afterward, grab lunch at the Parsonage restaurant, or walk about a half mi east on Richmond Road and up steep Lighthouse Avenue to the **Jacques Marchais Museum of Tibetan Art** ⑥, which has the largest collection of its kind outside Tibet.

TIMING
Set aside the better part of a day for a trip to Historic Richmondtown, which is on the opposite end of the island from the ferry terminal; add on a couple of hours for the Tibetan Museum. When you arrive, consult the schedule for the return bus, posted at the S74 stop across the street. The Tibetan Museum keeps irregular hours, so call ahead for an appointment. Historic Richmondtown hosts a variety of seasonal events, including an autumn crafts fair and a Christmas celebration.

Sights to See

★ ⊕ ❺ **Historic Richmondtown.** These 27 buildings, some of them constructed as early as 1685, are part of a 100-acre complex that was the site of Staten Island's original county seat. The buildings have been restored inside and out; some were built here, while others were relocated from other spots on the island. Many buildings, such as the Greek revival courthouse which serves as the **visitor center,** date from the 19th century; other architectural styles on site range from Dutch colonial to Victorian Gothic revival. During the warmer months costumed staff members demonstrate Early American crafts and trades such as printing, tinsmithing, and fireplace cooking.

The **Voorlezer's House,** built in 1695, is the oldest elementary schoolhouse still standing in the United States; it looks like the mold from which all little red schoolhouses were cast. The **Staten Island Historical Society Museum,** built in 1848 as the second county clerk's and surrogate's office, now houses American china, furniture, and tools, plus a collection of Staten Island photographs.

During a summer visit you might want to make reservations for the 19th-century dinner, cooked outdoors and served with utensils of the period. The Autumn Celebration shows off craftspeople demonstrating their skills; the annual Encampment in July is a reenactment of a Civil War battle; and December brings a monthlong Christmas celebration. Richmondtown regularly hosts other fairs, flea markets, and tours of the historic buildings. A tavern on the historic village grounds hosts a Saturday-night concert series showcasing ethnic and folk music; call the visitor center for details. ⊠ *441 Clarke Ave.,* ☎ *718/351–1611.* ☞ *$4.* ⊙ *Sept.–June, Wed.–Sun. 1–5; July–Aug., Wed.–Fri. 10–5, weekends 1–5.*

NEED A
BREAK?
For a taste of Richmondtown cuisine, head to the **Parsonage** (⊠ 74 Arthur Kill Rd., ☎ 718/351–7879), which serves rosemary-crusted pork tenderloin strudel and Black Angus steak au poivre in a fully restored 19th-century parish house.

---

❻ Jacques Marchais Museum of Tibetan Art. One of the largest private, nonprofit collections of Tibetan and Himalayan sculpture, scrolls, and paintings outside of Tibet is displayed in a museum resembling a Tibetan monastery. Try to visit on a day when the monks bless the monastery—and you. ⊠ *338 Lighthouse Ave.,* ☎ *718/987–3500.* ☞ *$3.* ⊙ *Call Wed.–Fri. for an appointment; closed weekends in winter, and on Mon. and Tues. year-round.*

3 THE ARTS

For lovers of the arts, New York is a kind of paradise. Theater fans can choose among Broadway crowd-pleasers and edgier works off-Broadway. Music devotees have the chance to see the world's top performers appear in incomparable showcases such as Carnegie Hall and the Metropolitan Opera House. For dance aficionados, there are two first-rate ballet troupes and an eclectic array of modern-dance companies. Film buffs can indulge in a full line of Hollywood releases, classics, foreign movies, and independent works. And fine-art enthusiasts can revel in the most extensive and varied selection of galleries and museums in the world.

Updated by
Lynda Hammes

NEW YORK CITY HAS A MAGNETIC PULL on artists and their audiences. From every corner of the earth, artists gather here to commune with their peers, study the masters, check out the competition, and—with luck and hard work—present their talents to the city's eager audiences. Whether performing the classics or more experimental fare, artists of all disciplines and styles can find a niche here. And discerning patrons strive to keep up with the latest—from flocking to a concert hall to hear a world-class soprano deliver a flawless performance to crowding in a cramped basement bookstore to support young writers nervously stumbling over their own prose.

New York has somewhere between 200 and 250 legitimate theaters, and many more ad hoc venues—parks, churches, universities, museums, lofts, galleries, streets, rooftops, and even parking lots. The city is, as well, a revolving door of festivals and special events: summer jazz, one-act-play marathons, international film series, and musical celebrations from the classical to the avant-garde, to name just a few.

FINDING OUT WHAT'S GOING ON

With so much to choose from, you might want to consult the critics— and in New York, there's one on every corner. From the journalists serving up their picks and pans at the newsstands to the opinionated cabbie who whisks you off to your next destination, there's plenty to go by. To find out who or what's playing where, check out the listings in the weekly publications. *Time Out New York* provides comprehensive information while the "Cue" section in the back of *New York* is more selective. The *New Yorker* has long been known for its "Goings On About Town" section that contains ruthlessly succinct reviews of theater, dance, art, music, film, and nightlife. The *Village Voice* and *New York Press* are free papers and offer extensive listings as well.

The New York Times comes in pretty handy, especially on Friday, with its two "Weekend" sections (Fine Arts and Leisure; Movies and Performing Arts). The Sunday "Arts and Leisure" section features longer articles on everything from opera to sitcoms, plus theater and movie ads and a full, detailed survey of cultural events for the coming week.

Paper magazine dishes the trendiest of the trendy scenes, and many of the above-mentioned publications plus *The New York Blade, LGNY, HX,* and *Next* illuminate the ever-changing gay and lesbian scene.

FILM AND TELEVISION

Film

On any given week New York City theaters screen all the major new releases, classics renowned and obscure, unusual foreign offerings, small independent flicks, and cutting-edge experimental works.

Getting Tickets

Alas, New York may be the global capital of cineasts, so sold-out shows are common. It's a good idea to purchase tickets in advance, if possible. If you do arrive around show time, you may have to endure a line that winds around the block, but even this can be entertaining—overheard conversations are often more interesting than the previews of coming attractions. Note that some queues are for people who have already bought their tickets; be sure to ask if the line is for ticket holders or ticket buyers.

For show times at theaters around the city, call **MovieFone** (☎ 212/777–3456). You can also use this service to order tickets in advance with a credit card. Not all movie theaters participate, however, and there's a $1.50 per ticket surcharge unless you purchase your ticket online, at WEB www.moviefone.com.

First-Run and Mainstream Movies
Wherever you are in the city, you usually don't have to walk far before coming across a movie theater showing new releases. Tickets to most of these theaters are about $9.50. There are no matinee discounts in Manhattan.

Two theaters preserve the flavor of grand old movie houses of times past. **Radio City Music Hall** (✉ 1260 6th Ave., at W. 50th St., ☎ 212/247–4777), with its art deco setting, 34-ft-high screen, and 4,500-watt projector, is occasionally used for movie screenings. **Clearview Ziegfeld** (✉ 141 W. 54th St., between 6th and 7th Aves., ☎ 212/765–7600) has a huge screen, brilliant red decor, and an awesome sound system.

Independent, Foreign, and Revival Films
New York is home to many cineasts who buck the Hollywood trends. The city has several cinemas that more or less specialize in foreign and innovative American films. The **Angelika Film Center** is a first stop for many indie- and foreign-film fans. In addition to premiering new releases, **Film Forum** hosts ongoing series of obscure films by directors such as William Castle or Samuel Fuller, never-before-seen cuts, and newly restored prints of classic works such as Orson Welles's *Touch of Evil* or the documentary on the Rolling Stones' 1969 tour called *Gimme Shelter*.

The **Quad Cinema** plays first-run art and foreign films on four relatively small screens. **The Paris,** next to the Plaza hotel, is an exquisite showcase for much-talked-about new American and foreign releases. **Cinema Village** has three screens that show mostly independent films, and the larger upstairs theater hosts somewhat more mainstream, although usually independent, films. **Anthology Film Archives** consists of two theaters housed in a renovated courthouse in the East Village. This "museum" is dedicated to preserving and exhibiting independent and avant-garde film.

Another great place to see films is the **Walter Reade Theater** at Lincoln Center. This comfortable, modern auditorium has wonderful sight lines. It presents series devoted to a particular theme, whether it's films by certain a director or from the same country. Movies for children are featured on weekends at 2 PM. Current mainstream movies are open-captioned for the deaf and shown once a month. Tickets can be purchased at the box office two weeks in advance.

You should keep in mind that many foreign and independent films are frequently screened at performing arts centers, cultural societies, and museums, such as the Asia Society, Goethe House, the Japan Society, Alliance Francaise, and the Whitney Museum of American Art. The four-screen complex at **Brooklyn Academy of Music: BAM Rose Cinemas** shows mostly first-run foreign-language and independent films and repertory programming. **Museum of Modern Art** includes rare classic films in its many excellent revival series. Tickets, free with the price of museum admission, are distributed at the main information desk in the lobby on the day of the screening (you can obtain tickets beginning at 10:30 AM for afternoon screenings and after 1 for evening films; they often go fast). New York's leading annual film event is the **New York Film Festival** (☎ 212/875–5610), sponsored by the Film Society of Lincoln Center every September and October. Its program includes exceptional movies, most never before seen in the United States; the festival's hits usually make their way into local movie houses over the next couple of months. Each March, the Film Society of Lincoln Center joins forces with the Museum of Modern Art to produce **New Directors/New Films** (☎ 212/708–9500), giving up-and-coming directors their moment to flicker. The series runs at MoMA's Roy and Niuta Titus Theaters.

During the summer you can bring a picnic and blankets to **HBO's Bryant Park Film Festival** (☎ 212/512–5700) on Monday just after sunset, when classics such as *On the Waterfront, Singing in the Rain,* and *King Kong* are screened for free. The lawn is always packed, so arrive early to secure a patch of green.

Catch a worthwhile flick at any of these theaters:

American Museum of the Moving Image. ⊠ *35th Ave. and 36th St., Astoria, Queens,* ☎ *718/784–0077.*
Angelika Film Center. ⊠ *W. Houston and Mercer Sts.,* ☎ *212/995–2000.*
Anthology Film Archives. ⊠ *32 2nd Ave., at E. 2nd St.,* ☎ *212/505–5181.*
Brooklyn Academy of Music: BAM Rose Cinemas. ⊠ *30 Lafayette Ave., off Flatbush Ave.,* ☎ *718/623–2770.*
Cinema Classics. ⊠ *332 E. 11th St., between 1st and 2nd Aves.,* ☎ *212/971–1015.*
Cinema Village. ⊠ *22 E. 12th St., between University Pl. and 5th Ave.,* ☎ *212/924–3363.*
Film Forum. ⊠ *209 W. Houston St., between 6th Ave. and Varick St.,* ☎ *212/727–8110.*
Lincoln Plaza Cinemas. ⊠ *1886 Broadway, at W. 62nd St.,* ☎ *212/757–2280.*
Millennium. ⊠ *66 E. 4th St., between Bowery and 2nd Ave.,* ☎ *212/673–0090.*
Museum of Modern Art. ⊠ *11 W. 53rd St., between 5th and 6th Aves.,* ☎ *212/708–9480.*
Paris. ⊠ *4 W. 58th St., between 5th and 6th Aves.,* ☎ *212/688–3800.*
Quad Cinema. ⊠ *34 W. 13th St., between 5th and 6th Aves.,* ☎ *212/255–8800.*
Screening Room. ⊠ *54 Varick St., at Canal St.,* ☎ *212/334–2100.*
Two Boots Pioneer Theater. ⊠ *155 E. 3rd St., between Aves. A and B,* ☎ *212/254–3300.*
Walter Reade Theater. ⊠ *Lincoln Center, 165 W. 65th St., between Broadway and Amsterdam Ave., plaza level,* ☎ *212/875–5600.*

Film for Children

Several museums sponsor special film programs aimed at families and children, including the Museum of Modern Art, the Museum of Television and Radio, and the American Museum of the Moving Image. Children marvel at the amazing nature and science films shown on the huge screen in the **IMAX Theater** (⊠ Central Park W and W. 79th St., ☎ 212/769–5034) at the American Museum of Natural History. At the **Sony IMAX Theater** (⊠ 1998 Broadway, at W. 68th St., ☎ 212/336–5000) audience members strap on high-tech headgear that makes specially created feature films appear in 3-D. The **Walter Reade Theater** shows feature films for children on weekend afternoons and sponsors children's film festivals. The innovative series **Reel to Real** (☎ 212/875–5370) take place on weekends from November to June. A typical program pairs a double billing of classic films—a collection of Betty Boop cartoons, for example—with a live dance or music performance.

Television

Tickets to tapings of television shows are free, but can be difficult to come by on short notice. Most shows require that you send a postcard with your name, address, and phone number for each pair of tickets requested, at least a month and up to 10 months in advance. Even then, that card may be thrown into a lottery hopper. But same-day standby tickets are available to people willing to wait in line for several hours, sometimes starting at 5 or 6 AM, depending on the level of celebrity involved at a particular taping.

The Daily Show with Jon Stewart. With a knowing smirk, the amiable Jon Stewart pokes fun at news headlines on this half-hour cable show. The program tapes Monday through Thursday and free tickets can be obtained by calling the Daily Show Studios. ⊠ *The Daily Show studios, 513 W. 54th St.,* ☎ *212/586–2477.*

Late Night with Conan O'Brien. This popular variety show hosted by O'Brien and his sidekick Andy Richter targets hip, savvy viewers and attracts consistently interesting guests. Standby tickets are available Tuesday through Friday after 9 AM at the 49th Street side of 30 Rockefeller Plaza. Call the ticket information line for reservations or you can write for tickets three or four months in advance. No one under 16 can attend a taping. ⊠ *NBC Tickets, Late Night with Conan O'Brien, 30 Rockefeller Plaza, between W. 49th and W. 50th Sts., 10112,* ☎ *212/664–4000.*

The Late Show with David Letterman. The tried-and-true variety-show format and Letterman's quirky, idiomatic manner continue to please devoted fans. Standby tickets can be obtained by calling 212/247–6497 at 11 AM on tape days, but it's better to write ahead. No one under 16 can attend. ⊠ *Late Show Tickets, c/o Ed Sullivan Theater, 1697 Broadway, 10019,* ☎ *212/975–1003.*

Live with Regis. This popular morning program books an eclectic and engaging roster of guests. Standby tickets become available weekdays at 7 AM at the **ABC studio** (⊠ 71 Lincoln Sq., between W. 67th St. and Columbus Ave.). Otherwise, write for tickets a full year in advance. Children under 10 cannot attend. ⊠ *Live Tickets, Ansonia Station, Box 777, 10023,* ☎ *212/456–3537.*

MTV Studios. If you're between the ages of 18 and 26 years old, you can be an audience member of **Total Request Live** with host Carson Daly. This hugely popular show is taped weekdays at 4 PM on the second-floor of the high-energy MTV studios in Times Square. Call the TRL hotline in advance for reservations. ⊠ *1515 Broadway, at 43rd St.,* ☎ *212/398–8549.*

The Rosie O'Donnell Show. With her incisive stand-up-comic timing and mom-next-door attitude, O'Donnell has shot to the top of the ratings. Not surprisingly, tapings of this show are one of the hottest tickets in town. Last-minute tickets are available by a lottery system at 7:30 AM Monday through Thursday at the West 49th Street entrance to Rockefeller Plaza. If you prefer to plan (way) ahead, you can mail in a request for two tickets for the following season. Children under five cannot attend. ⊠ *NBC Studios, Rosie O'Donnell Show, Ticket Request, 30 Rockefeller Plaza, 10112,* ☎ *212/506–3288.*

Saturday Night Live. Probably the most influential comedy variety show in the history of television, *SNL* continues to captivate audiences. This show tapes 20 times per season. Standby tickets are distributed on a first-come, first-serve basis at 9:15 AM on the day of the show at the West 49th Street entrance to 30 Rockefeller Plaza. You may receive either standby for a dress rehearsal (7 PM arrival time) or the live show (10 PM arrival time). Written requests for tickets must be submitted in August; your card is then entered in ticket lotteries held throughout the season. You will be notified one to two weeks in advance if you're selected. No one under 16 may attend. ✉ *NBC Tickets, Saturday Night Live, 30 Rockefeller Plaza, 10112,* ☎ *212/664–4000.*

Today is taped weekdays from 7 AM to 10 AM in the glass-enclosed, ground-level NBC studio at the southwest corner of West 49th Street and Rockefeller Plaza. If you're in the area and are so inclined, you can watch the action through the giant windows, and you may well be spotted on TV by friends back home, standing behind anchors Katie Couric and Matt Lauer. In the summer, live outdoor concerts featuring performers such as Ricky Martin and Mariah Carey are presented in the last half hour of the program.

PERFORMING ARTS

New York is indisputably the performing arts capital of America. In the course of a year, celebrated artists from around the world perform in the city's legendary concert halls and theaters. But the city's own artistic resources are what make the exciting performing arts scene here so terrific. Thousands of great actors, singers, musicians, and other artists populate the city, infusing New York's cultural scene with unparalleled levels of creative energy.

Getting Tickets

Major concerts and recitals, especially prime seats at venues such as the Metropolitan Opera, can cost twice as much as a Broadway play. For the most part, the top ticket prices for musicals are $80, although top prices for seats at a few productions have been known to hit $100. The best seats for nonmusicals can cost almost as much as $65. The League of American Theatres and Producers sponsors **The Broadway Line** (☎ 888/276–2392 toll-free; 212/302–4111 in the tri-state area), which gives information about show times, theater addresses, and ticket prices. Once you've heard the information you seek, the line can connect you directly to Tele-Charge or Ticketmaster to buy your tickets.

Scoring tickets to shows and concerts is fairly easy—unless, of course, you're dead set on attending the season's hottest events, which are often sold out months in advance. Generally, the box office is the best place to buy tickets, since in-house ticket sellers make it their business to know about their theaters and can point out (on a chart) where you'll be seated. It's always a good idea to purchase tickets in advance to avoid disappointment.

To purchase tickets in advance from the box office, send a certified check or money order, several alternate dates, and a self-addressed, stamped envelope. You can also use a credit card to reserve tickets for Broadway and off-Broadway shows. **Tele-charge** (☎ 212/239–6200, WEB www.telecharge.com) handles a great many Broadway shows. **Ticketmaster** (☎ 212/307–4100, WEB www.ticketmaster.com) handles New York State Theater, Town Hall, and Brooklyn Academy of Music tickets. Newspaper ads generally specify which service you should use for a given event. Both add a surcharge ($2.50–$5.75 per ticket) and Ticketmaster adds an additional handling charge ($1.25–$3.50). You can arrange to have your tickets mailed to you or to have them waiting for you at the theater's box office. Off- and off-off-Broadway theaters have their own joint box office called **Ticket Central** (✉ 416 W. 42nd St., between 9th and 10th Aves., ☎ 212/279–4200). It's open daily between 1 and 8. Although there are no discounts here, tickets to performances in these theaters are usually less expensive than Broadway tickets, and they cover events including theater, performance art, and dance.

You'll generally find that tickets are more readily available for evening performances from Tuesday through Thursday and matinees on Wednesday. Tickets for weekend matinees are tougher to secure. Most Broadway productions take Sunday and Monday nights off. If you're in town without tickets, try visiting the **Broadway Ticket Center** (1560 Broadway, between W. 46th and W. 47th Sts., ☎ no phone), at the Times Square Visitors Center, open daily 8–8. There are descriptions and videotaped excerpts from shows, theater location maps, and a box office that handles tickets for all Broadway shows (except *The Lion King*) and several off-Broadway shows. Tickets are usually full-price, with a $4.50 handling charge per ticket.

For those willing to pay top dollar to see that show or concert everyone's talking about but no one can get tickets for, try a ticket broker. You might have to pay $250 for tickets that would have cost $80 at the box office, but you can get last-minute seats for hot shows. **Continental Golden/Leblangs Theatre Ticket Services** (☎ 212/944–8910 or 800/299–8587) is one of the best-known brokers in Manhattan. Check the lobbies of major hotels for others.

You may be tempted to buy from ticket scalpers. But beware, as they have reportedly sold tickets for as much as $200 to shows that were available at the box office for much less. And lately there has been an upswing in the selling of counterfeit tickets and tickets for seats that don't exist. Ticket scalping is against the law in New York.

DISCOUNT TICKETS

TKTS (✉ Duffy Sq., W. 47th St. and Broadway; 2 World Trade Center, mezzanine, ☎ 212/221–0013) is New York's best-known discount-ticket source. Operated by the Theatre Development Fund, the two TKTS booths sell day-of-performance tickets for Broadway and off-Broadway plays at 25%–50% off the usual price (plus a $2.50 service fee). The names of shows for which tickets are available are posted on electronic boards. You can pay with cash or traveler's checks; credit cards are not accepted.

For evening performances Monday–Saturday, the Duffy Square booth is open from 3 to 8; for Wednesday and Saturday matinee performances, from 10 to 2; for Sunday matinee and evening performances, from 11 to 7:30. Lines at Duffy Square can be long, especially on weekends, but the wait is generally pleasant (if the weather cooperates), as the bright lights and babble of Times Square surround you.

The World Trade Center branch is open weekdays from 11 to 5:30 and Saturday from 11 to 3:30. For matinees (on Wednesday, Saturday, and Sunday), you have to purchase tickets the day before the performance (which means matinee tickets are available to downtown customers before customers in midtown). The lines at the World Trade Center booth are indoors and usually shorter than those at Duffy Square.

Discounts on well-known long-running shows (such as *Beauty and the Beast* and *Les Misérables*) are often available if you can lay your hands on a couple of "twofers"—discount ticket coupons found at the Broadway Ticket Center. The **NYC & Company Visitor Information Center** (✉ 810 7th Ave., between W. 52nd and W. 53rd Sts., ☎ 212/484–1222) is another good place to score half-price ticket vouchers.

Some theaters and performance spaces offer reduced rates for unsold tickets on the day of the performance, usually a half-hour before curtain time. Other shows have front-row orchestra seats available at a reduced price (about $20) the day of the performance. These discounts vary widely and are sometimes noted in the newspaper theater listings or ads. Occasionally, box offices offer same-day standing-room tickets ($10–$20) for sold-out shows (the Metropolitan Opera House sells standing-room tickets in advance); check with the particular theater for more information.

Some Broadway and off-Broadway shows sell reduced-price tickets for preview performances prior to the official opening night. Look at newspaper ads for discounted previews or consult the box office. Tickets for matinees may cost less, particularly on Wednesday.

Performing Arts Centers

New York's most renowned centers for the arts are tourist attractions in themselves.

Brooklyn Academy of Music (✉ 30 Lafayette Ave., Brooklyn, ☎ 718/636–4100), America's oldest performing arts center, opened in 1859, has a reputation for daring and innovative dance, music, opera, and theater productions. BAM's main performance spaces are the 2,000-seat Howard Gilman Opera House, a white-brick Renaissance Revival palace built in 1908, and the 900-seat Harvey Lichtenstein Theater, a spartanly restored 1904 theater around the corner on Fulton Street. Acclaimed international companies are often on the bill. You can grab a bite at the BAM Café, which is often the venue for weekend dances. The BAMbus provides round-trip transportation between Manhattan and BAM. The bus picks up passengers from the Whitney at Philip Morris (✉ 120 Park Ave., at E. 42nd St.) one hour prior to a performance. **Carnegie Hall** (✉ 881 7th Ave., at W. 57th St., ☎ 212/247–7800) is one of the world's most famous concert halls. Performances are given in the beautifully restored 2,804-seat Isaac Stern Auditorium and the far more intimate Weill Recital Hall, where many young talents make their New York debuts. Although the emphasis is on classical music, Carnegie Hall also hosts jazz, pop, cabaret, and folk music concerts. **City Center** (✉ 131 W. 55th St., between 6th and 7th Aves.; mailing address for ticket orders, CityTix, 130 W. 56th St., 4th floor, 10019; ☎ 212/581–1212) has a neo-Moorish look (it was built in 1923 by the Ancient and Accepted Order of the Mystic Shrine and saved from demolition in 1943 by Mayor Fiorello La Guardia) and presents major dance troupes such as Alvin Ailey and Paul Taylor, as well as concert versions of classic American musicals. The Manhattan Theatre Club, with its highly regarded and popular program of innovative contemporary drama, also resides here. **Lincoln Center** (✉ W. 62nd to W. 66th Sts., Broadway to Amsterdam Ave., ☎ 212/875–2656) is a 16-acre complex that houses the Metropolitan Opera, New York Philharmonic, New York City Ballet, New York City Opera, Juilliard School, Lincoln Center Theater, New York Public Library for the Performing Arts, Film Society of Lincoln Center, Chamber Music Society of Lincoln Center, Jazz at Lincoln Center, School of American Ballet, the Vivian Beaumont Theater, and Walter Reade Theater. **Tours of Lincoln Center** are available at $9.50 per person (☎ 212/875–5350).

The **Lincoln Center Festival** (☎ 212/875–5928) is a three-week summertime event. The programs include classical and contemporary music concerts, dance, film, and theater works. **Midsummer Night Swing** (☎ 212/875–5766) is a monthlong dance party outdoors on Lincoln Center's Josie Robertson Plaza. With an emphasis on live music, visitors can see and hear everything from swing, merengue, salsa, and tango to polka, rockabilly, and more. In August, **Mostly Mozart Festival** (☎ 212/875–5399) is Lincoln Center's longest running classical series featuring the music of Mozart and other classical favorites. Also during that month, **Lincoln Center Out-of-Doors** (☎ 212/875–5108) is an almost nightly festival of free performances featuring music, dance, and special family programs taking place throughout Lincoln Center's Plaza and adjacent Damrosch Park. **Jazz at Lincoln Center** (☎ 212/ 258–9822) includes Jazz for Young People, an annual concert series hosted by Wynton Marsalis for children.

Classical Music

"Gentlemen," conductor Serge Koussevitzky once told the assembled Boston Symphony Orchestra, "maybe it's good enough for Cleveland or Cincinnati, but it's not good enough for New York." In a nutshell he described New York's place at the center of the musical world.

New York possesses not only the country's oldest symphony orchestra (the New York Philharmonic) but also three renowned conservatories—the Juilliard School, the Manhattan School of Music, and Mannes College of Music. Since the turn of the 20th century, the world's great orchestras and soloists have made Manhattan a principal stopping point.

New York's early music scene has increased dramatically over the last few years. A half dozen performing groups and presenting organizations offer early music concerts throughout the year in many venues, including various churches.In an average week, between 50 and 150 events appear in newspaper and magazine listings, and weekly concert calendars are published in all the major newspapers. Record and music shops serve as information centers.

Most venues also host children's programs. The **Little Orchestra Society** (☎ 212/971–9500) organizes concerts that introduce classical music to children ages three–five at **Florence Gould Hall** (✉ 55 E. 59th St., between Park and Madison Aves., ☎ 212/971–9500) and ages 5– 12 at **Avery Fisher Hall at Lincoln Center.**

Concert Halls
The **Brooklyn Academy of Music** is the home of the Brooklyn Philharmonic, which under music director Robert Spano has the city's most adventurous symphonic programming. Both the Howard Gilman Opera House and the Harvey Lichtenstein Theater have extraordinary acoustics. They are homes for the Next Wave festival, which has featured some of the most important concerts, dance events, and theatrical and opera productions of the last 15 years, including the Welsh National Opera and productions of new works by Philip Glass and John (*Nixon in China*) Adams.

Carnegie Hall has been in operation for over a century. Virtually every important musician of the 20th century performed in this Italian Renaissance–style building, often at the peak of his or her creative powers. Tchaikovsky conducted the opening night concert on May 5, 1891; Leonard Bernstein had his famous debut here; Vladimir Horowitz made his historic return to the concert stage; and world-class orchestras sound their very best here in the lush, perhaps incomparable, acoustics of the 2,804-seat auditorium. The Opera Orchestra of New York, under the direction of Eve Queler, puts on concert versions of rarely performed operas here several times a year, usually with superstar soloists.

Lincoln Center is the city's musical nerve center, especially when it comes to the classics. The **New York Philharmonic** (☎ 212/875–5656), led by music director Kurt Masur, performs at Avery Fisher Hall from late September to early June. In addition to its concerts showcasing exceptional guest artists and the works of specific composers, the Philharmonic also schedules weeknight Rush Hour Concerts at 7:30 or 8 and Saturday Matinee Concerts at 2; these special events, offered throughout the season, last an hour and are priced lower than the regular subscription concerts. Rush Hour Concerts are followed by receptions with the conductor on the Grand Promenade, and Saturday Matinee Concerts feature discussions after the performances. A note for New York Philharmonic devotees: in season and when conductors and soloists are amenable, weekday orchestra rehearsals at 9:45 AM are open to the public on selected mornings for $12.

Intimate **Alice Tully Hall** (☎ 212/875–5050), Lincoln Center's "little white box," is considered to be as acoustically perfect as a concert hall can get. You can hear the Chamber Music Society of Lincoln Center, promising Juilliard students, Jazz at Lincoln Center, chamber music ensembles, music on period instruments, choral music, famous soloists, and concert groups.

Avery Fisher Hall (☎ 212/875–5030) follows the classic European rectangular pattern. To its stage come the world's great musicians; to its boxes, the black-tie-and-diamond-tiara set. Within the Library of the Performing Arts, **Bruno Walter Auditorium** (☎ 212/870–1630) often offers free concerts.

Other Venues

Aaron Davis Hall at City College (✉ W. 133rd St. at Convent Ave., ☎ 212/650–6900) is an uptown venue for world music events and a variety of classical music and dance programs. In Brooklyn, **Bargemusic** (✉ Fulton Ferry Landing at Old Fulton and Furman Sts., Brooklyn, ☎ 718/624–2083) keeps chamber music groups busy year-round on an old barge with a fabulous view of the Manhattan skyline. New York's Ensemble for Early Music performs about 20 medieval and Renaissance music concerts in the **Cathedral of St. John the Divine** (✉ 1047 Amsterdam Ave., at W. 112th St., ☎ 212/662–2133).

At the **Church of the Ascension** (✉ 5th Ave. at W. 10th St., ☎ 212/254–8553), Voices of Ascension, well known for its recordings, performs concerts of all periods. Choral and organ concerts take place at the **Church of St. Ignatius Loyola** (✉ 980 Park Ave., at E. 84th St., ☎ 212/288–2520) about twice a month from September to April with a special series at Christmastime. Single performances and seasonal series of sacred and secular music from the Middle Ages take place in the 12th-century chapel of the **Cloisters** (✉ Fort Tryon Park, ☎ 212/650–2290).

Kaufmann Concert Hall (✉ 92nd St. Y, 1395 Lexington Ave., at E. 92nd St., ☎ 212/996–1100) showcases well known recitalists and chamber music groups. **Merkin Concert Hall** (✉ Abraham Goodman House, 129 W. 67th St., between Columbus Ave. and Broadway, ☎ 212/501–3330) presents mostly chamber music ensembles.

The **Metropolitan Museum of Art** (✉ 1000 5th Ave., at E. 82nd St., ☎ 212/570–3949) holds three stages—the Temple of Dendur; the Grace Rainey Rogers Auditorium; and, at Christmas, the Medieval Sculpture Hall—with concerts by leading vocal, chamber, and jazz musicians. Other than Friday and Saturday evenings when the museum is open late, access is through the street-level entrance at East 83rd Street and 5th Avenue.

Miller Theatre (✉ Columbia University, Broadway at W. 116th St., ☎ 212/854–7740) features a varied program of jazz and classical performers, such as the New York Virtuosi Chamber Symphony. The **Sylvia and Danny Kaye Playhouse** (✉ Hunter College, E. 68th St. between Park and Lexington Aves., ☎ 212/772–4448) presents a varied program, including distinguished soloists, in a small concert hall.

Outdoor Music

All kinds of music waft through the air of the city's great outdoors. In the summertime both the Metropolitan Opera and the New York Philharmonic play free concerts in municipal parks, filling verdant spaces with the haunting strains of *La Bohème* or the thunder of the *1812 Overture* (for information call the **City Parks Special Events Hotline,** ☎ 212/360–3456 or 888/697–2757).

From the middle of June through Labor Day, Prospect Park comes alive with the sounds of its annual **Celebrate Brooklyn Performing Arts Festival** (✉ 9th St. Band Shell, enter from 9th St. and Prospect Park W, Brooklyn, ☎ 718/855–7882). The enormously popular **Central Park SummerStage** (✉ Rumsey Playfield, Fifth Ave. and 72nd St., ☎ 212/360–2777) presents free programs, ranging from alternative rock to spoken word, June through August. A **Jazzmobile** (☎ 212/866–4900) transports jazz and Latin music to parks throughout the five boroughs in July and August; Wednesday-evening concerts are held at Grant's Tomb. Pier 16 at **South Street Seaport** ☎ 212/732–7678) is the setting for a cornucopia of concerts Thursday through Saturday evenings from Memorial Day to Labor Day; it also sponsors holiday music programs from late November through January 1 on weekday evenings and weekend afternoons. The sculpture garden of **Museum of Modern Art** (✉ 11 W. 53rd St., between 5th and 6th Aves., ☎ 212/708–9480) is the site of free Friday- and Saturday-evening concerts of 20th-century music mid-June through August.

Dance

In a city that seems never to stop moving, dance is a thriving art form. On any given night, there's a wide variety of performances, be it of ballet, Japanese *butoh,* improvisation, or the increasingly popular dance-based Broadway show. Hardcore dance fans are often devoted to the virtuosity of ballet or the heady, experimental "downtown scene." Several New York–based companies blur the line, such as Merce Cunningham, the Mark Morris Dance Group, or Bill T. Jones/Arnie Zane Dance Company.

Ballet

Two powerhouse companies—the New York City Ballet and the American Ballet Theatre—continue to please and astonish huge audiences season after season. The intimate Joyce Theater hosts ballet companies focusing on contemporary works, including Eliot Feld's Ballet Tech, Ballet Hispanico, and Dance Theatre of Harlem.

The **American Ballet Theatre (ABT)** (☎ 212/477–3030) is renowned for its brilliant renditions of the great 19th-century classics (*Swan Lake, Giselle, The Sleeping Beauty,* and *La Bayardère*) as well as its eclectic contemporary repertoire (including works by all the 20th-century masters such as Balanchine, Tudor, Robbins, and de Mille). Since its inception in 1940, the company has included some of the great dancers, such as Mikhail Baryshnikov, Natalia Makarova, Rudolf Nureyev, Gelsey Kirkland, and Cynthia Gregory. The ballet has two New York seasons—eight weeks beginning in early May at its home in the Metropolitan Opera House and two weeks beginning in late October at City Center.

New York City Ballet (NYCB) (☎ 212/870–5570), founded in 1948, has two seasons. The winter season, which runs from mid-November through February, includes the beloved annual holiday production of

George Balanchine's *The Nutcracker.* Its spring season lasts from late April through June. The company continues to stress the works themselves rather than individual performers, although that hasn't stopped a number of principal dancers (such as Kyra Nichols, Darci Kistler, Damian Woetzel, and Jock Soto) from standing out. The company has more than 90 dancers and performs and maintains an active repertoire of 20th-century works unmatched in the world, including works by Balanchine, Jerome Robbins, Ballet Master-in-Chief Peter Martins, and others. NYCB performs in Lincoln Center's **New York State Theater,** where you can call for tickets and schedule information (✉ W. 62nd to W. 66th Sts., Broadway to Amsterdam Aves., ☎ 212/870–5570).

Modern Dance

The most innovative dance companies in the world perform in New York throughout the year, especially in the autumn and spring, showcasing the thrilling work of such legendary choreographers as Martha Graham, Merce Cunningham, Alvin Ailey, Mark Morris, Twyla Tharp, and Paul Taylor.

The **Brooklyn Academy of Music** features contemporary dance troupes as part of its Next Wave Festival every fall; this is where to catch the Mark Morris Dance Group or German choreographer Pina Bausch's troupe. At **City Center** the modern masters such as Ailey and Taylor hold sway. **Dance Theater Workshop** (✉ 219 W. 19th St., between 7th and 8th Aves., ☎ 212/924–0077) serves as one of New York's most successful laboratories for new dance. **Danspace Project** (✉ St. Mark's Church-in-the-Bowery, 131 E. 10th St., at 2nd Ave., ☎ 212/674–8194) sponsors a series of avant-garde choreography that runs from September through June.

In a former art deco movie house in Chelsea, the **Joyce Theater** (✉ 175 8th Ave., at w. 19th St., ☎ 212/242–0800) is one of the city's top venues for modern dance. Its eclectic program includes tap, ballet, jazz, ballroom, and ethnic dance. Up-and-coming choreographers are spotlighted in the Altogether Different series. It has another space downtown, the **Joyce SoHo** (✉ 155 Mercer St., between Houston and Prince Sts., ☎ 212/431–9233), which hosts performances by talented local dancers. At the 92nd St. Y, the **Harkness Dance Project** presents emerging dance troupes with discussions following performances. **P.S.122** (✉ 150 1st Ave., at E. 9th St., ☎ 212/477–5288) in the East Village is where dance often borders on performance art.

Opera

The greatest singers in the world all clamor to test their mettle at the Metropolitan Opera, where they can work alongside internationally admired directors and designers. The Met's lavish opera productions can be seen at prices significantly lower than what you'd pay in Europe, but tickets are far from cheap (unless you buy standing room). Another opera right next door—the New York City Opera—isn't as fancy, but often strays from the classics to perform less common works.

Major Companies

These are good times for opera lovers in New York, as the city's two major companies, the Metropolitan Opera and New York City Opera, are winning raves. The titan of American opera companies, **Metropolitan Opera** brings the world's leading singers to its massive stage at Lincoln Center's **Metropolitan Opera House** (W. 64th St. off Columbus Ave., ☎ 212/799–3100) from October to mid-April. Under the direction of James Levine, the Met's artistic director and principal conductor, and principal guest conductor Valery Gergiev, the opera orchestra performs with an intensity and quality that rival the world's finest symphonic orchestras. All performances, including operas sung in English, are unobtrusively subtitled on small screens (which can be turned off) on the back of the seat in front of you. For children, the Met offers its **Growing Up with Opera** program (☎ 212/769–7008).

Tickets, such as the sought-after center box seats, can cost more than $200. There are many price tiers below that: for example, mid-range seats in the Family Circle might run about $80, and about 700 seats sell for closer to $30. Standing-room tickets for the week's performances go on sale on Saturday at 10 AM for even less. Weekday prices are slightly lower than weekend prices. Saturday matinee performances from early December through the end of the season are broadcast live around the world on the Texaco-Metropolitan Opera International Radio Network.

Although not as widely known as the Met, the **New York City Opera** is just as vital to the city's operagoers as its more famous next-door neighbor. Under the leadership of artistic director Paul Kellogg, City Opera offers a diverse repertoire, including rarely seen baroque operas such as *Acis and Galatea* and *Rinaldo,* adventurous new works such as *Of Mice and Men* and *Central Park,* and beloved classic operas such as *La Bohème, Carmen,* and the like. Placido Domingo, Frederica von Stade, and Beverly Sills began their careers at City Opera, and if recent performances are any indication, the next generation of great voices is following in their footsteps. City Opera performs from September through November and in March and April at Lincoln Center's New York State Theater. All performances of foreign-language operas have supertitles—line-by-line English translations displayed above the stage.

Smaller Companies

The **Amato Opera Theatre** (✉ 319 Bowery, at E. 2nd St., ☎ 212/228–8200) is an intimate, well-established showcase for rising singers. The theater seats only 107, and the performances of Verdi, Mozart, and other composers of the standard opera repertory are often sold out. **Brooklyn Academy of Music** is an outstanding venue for opera, particularly less famous baroque masterpieces by such composers as Rameau, Gluck, and Handel. Opera aficionados should also keep track of the Carnegie Hall schedule for debuting singers and performances by the **Opera Orchestra of New York** (☎ 212/799–1982), which specializes in presenting concert versions of rarely performed operas, often with star soloists. A libretto of the opera is provided, and lights are kept up for those following along. **New York Gilbert and Sullivan Players** (✉ Symphony Space, 2537 Broadway, at W. 95th St., ☎ 212/769–1000; 212/864–5400 for box office) presents lively productions of Gilbert and Sullivan classics such as *Pirates of Penzance* and *The Mikado* performed with full orchestra. The **New York Grand Opera** (✉ 154 W. 57th St., near 7th Ave., Suite 125, ☎ 212/245–8837) mounts free summer performances of operas by Verdi and other composers—with a full orchestra and professional singers—at Central Park SummerStage.

Theater

Broadway—not the Statue of Liberty or even the Empire State Building—is the city's number-one tourist attraction. The renovation and restoration of some of the city's oldest and grandest theaters on and near 42nd Street has drawn New Yorkers' attention to the rebirth of Times Square. As in decades long past, everyone wants to be here, in the heart of the theater world.

The twice-monthly *Broadway Theatre Guide,* published by the League of American Theatres and Producers, and *Playbill* are available in hotels and theaters around town. The **Broadway Line** (☎ 212/302–4111 in CT, NJ, and NY; 888/411–2929 elsewhere) provides show times, plot summaries, theater addresses, and ticket prices. **NYC/ON STAGE** (☎ 212/768–1818), the Theatre Development Fund's 24-hour information service, covers performing arts events in all five boroughs.

Broadway

To most people, New York theater means Broadway, that region roughly bounded by West 41st and West 53rd streets, between 7th and 9th Avenues, where bright lights shine on newly restored theaters, gleaming entertainment complexes, theme stores, and restaurants. The names of the many theaters read like a roll call of American theater history: Edwin Booth, the Barrymores (Ethel, John, and Lionel), Eugene O'Neill, George Gershwin, Alfred Lunt and Lynn Fontanne, Helen Hayes, Richard Rodgers, and Neil Simon, among others.

Some old playhouses are as interesting for their history as for their current offerings. The **St. James** is where Lauren Bacall was an usherette in the '40s and where a little show called *Oklahoma!* ushered in the era of the musical play. The **Ford Center for the Performing Arts,** a lavish 1,839-seat theater constructed on the site of two classic houses, the Lyric and the Apollo, incorporates original architectural elements from both theaters, along with state-of-the-art facilities to accommodate grand-scale musicals. The Walt Disney Company has refurbished the art nouveau **New Amsterdam,** where Eddie Cantor, Will Rogers, Fanny Brice, and the Ziegfeld Follies once drew crowds. Today it is the den of *The Lion King*. The ongoing revamping of the Times Square district has most recently included the handsome renovation of the Selwyn, now known as the **American Airlines Theatre.** After various reincarnations as a Venetian-style theater, burlesque hall, and pornographic movie house, it's now the home of the Roundabout Theatre Company, which is acclaimed for its revivals of classic plays and musicals.

Check the arts listings in *The New York Times* to see which ticket vendor is handling the production you want to see.

Ambassador. ✉ *215 W. 49th St., between Broadway and 8th Ave.*
American Airlines Theatre. ✉ *227 W. 42nd St., between 7th and 8th Aves.*
Belasco. ✉ *111 W. 44th St., between Broadway and 6th Ave.*
Booth. ✉ *222 W. 45th St., between Broadway and 8th Ave.*
Broadhurst. ✉ *235 W. 44th St., between Broadway and 8th Ave.*
Broadway. ✉ *1681 Broadway, at W. 53rd St.*
Brooks Atkinson. ✉ *256 W. 47th St., between Broadway and 8th Ave.*
Cort. ✉ *138 W. 48th St., between 6th and 7th Aves.*
Ethel Barrymore. ✉ *243 W. 47th St., between Broadway and 8th Ave.*
Eugene O'Neill. ✉ *230 W. 49th St., between Broadway and 8th Ave.*
Ford Center for the Performing Arts. ✉ *213–215 W. 43rd St., between 7th and 8th Aves.*
Gershwin. ✉ *222 W. 51st St., between Broadway and 8th Ave.*
Harold Clurman. ✉ *412 W. 42nd St., between 9th and 10th Aves.*
Helen Hayes. ✉ *240 W. 44th St., between Broadway and 8th Ave.*
Imperial. ✉ *249 W. 45th St., between Broadway and 8th Ave.*
John Golden. ✉ *252 W. 45th St., at 8th Ave.*
Judith Anderson. ✉ *412 W. 42nd St., between 9th and 10th Aves.*
Kaufman. ✉ *534 W. 42nd St., between 10th and 11th Aves.*
Lunt-Fontanne. ✉ *205 W. 46th St., between Broadway and 8th Ave.*
Lyceum. ✉ *149 W. 45th St., between 6th and 7th Aves.*
Majestic. ✉ *247 W. 44th St., between Broadway and 8th Ave.*
Marquis. ✉ *1535 Broadway, at W. 45th St.*
Martin Beck. ✉ *302 W. 45th St., between 8th and 9th Aves.*
Minskoff. ✉ *200 W. 45th St., at Broadway.*

Music Box. ⊠ *239 W. 45th St., between Broadway and 8th Ave.*
Nat Horne. ⊠ *9th Ave. and W. 42nd St.*
Nederlander. ⊠ *208 W. 41st St., between 7th and 8th Aves.*
Neil Simon. ⊠ *250 W. 52nd St., between Broadway and 8th Ave.*
New Amsterdam. ⊠ *214 W. 42nd St., between 7th and 8th Aves.*
New Victory. ⊠ *209 W. 42nd St., between Broadway and 7th Ave.*
Palace. ⊠ *1564 Broadway, at W. 47th St.*
Plymouth. ⊠ *236 W. 45th St., between Broadway and 8th Ave.*
Richard Rodgers. ⊠ *226 W. 46th St., between Broadway and 8th Ave.*
Royale. ⊠ *242 W. 45th St., between Broadway and 8th Ave.*
St. James. ⊠ *246 W. 44th St., between Broadway and 8th Ave.*
Samuel Beckett. ⊠ *412 W. 42nd St., between 9th and 10th Aves.*
Shubert. ⊠ *225 W. 44th St., between Broadway and 8th Ave.*
Studio 54. ⊠ *254 W. 54th St., between Broadway and 8th Ave.*
Virginia. ⊠ *245 W. 52nd St., between Broadway and 8th Ave.*
Vivian Beaumont. ⊠ *Lincoln Center, 150 W. 65th St., at Broadway.*
Walter Kerr. ⊠ *219 W. 48th St., between Broadway and 8th Ave.*
Winter Garden. ⊠ *1634 Broadway, at W. 50th St.*

[handwritten annotations: Confirmation #A2214259? *(left margin);* 194 *; ticket charge* 212- 239- 6200 *(right margin);* Cabaret *(next to Studio 54)]*

Beyond Broadway

The best of New York theater is often found far away from 42nd Street. Off- and off-off-Broadway is where Eric Bogosian, Ann Magnuson, John Leguizamo, Danny Hoch, and Laurie Anderson often make their home. It's where you'll find crowd-pleasers such as the high-flying acrobatics of *De la Guarda* and the daffy dancing of *Stomp*. It's also still home to the romantic musical *The Fantasticks*, the longest-running play in American theater history.

In terms of quality and popularity, productions at many of the best-known off-Broadway theaters rival those seen in the larger houses on Broadway. In fact, some of Broadway's biggest hits had their start off-Broadway. **Manhattan Theatre Club,** with two stages in the basement of City Center, presents some of the most talked-about new plays and musicals in town. Always interesting and often controversial works by Terrence McNally, Athol Fugard, August Wilson, and A. R. Gurney have all had their work produced here. Call ahead, as most of the tickets go to subscribers. Lincoln Center's intimate 299-seat **Mitzi E. Newhouse** stages slightly edgier works than the Broadway-size Vivian Beaumont upstairs, but it's not unusual for popular shows such as Tony-winning *Contact* to move from the Newhouse to the Beaumont.

The **Joseph Papp Public Theater,** renamed in honor of its late founder and guiding light, continues to present new, innovative theater. This is the theater that first staged *Bring In 'Da Noise, Bring In 'Da Funk,* which went on to a successful Broadway run. In summer the Public heads to Central Park's **Delacorte Theater** (☎ 212/539–8750 [seasonal]) to mount free outdoor productions of plays by Shakepeare and others. Tickets for evening performances are distributed at around 1 PM on the day of the performance (to those who have been waiting several hours in line) downtown at the Public and uptown at the Delacorte.

The smaller off-Broadway and off-off-Broadway theaters are where you'll find more cutting-edge work. Here, in houses ranging in size from a few hundred to a few dozen seats, you often catch plays by the big names of tomorrow, or revivals of neglected works by the best known playwrights of the past. In the East Village the **Classic Stage Company** revives older works that still have relevance today. The **Ensemble Studio Theatre,** with its tried-and-true roster of players, develops new American plays. Each spring it presents a marathon of one-acts by prominent playwrights. With the help of its resident acting troupe, **Jean Cocteau Repertory** revives classics by playwrights such as Beckett and Brecht.

The **New York Theater Workshop** produces new work by playwrights such as Paul Rudnick, Tony Kushner, and Claudia Shear, whose play about Mae West, *Dirty Blonde,* premiered here before heading to Broadway. **Playwrights Horizons** produces promising new works, and it has the Pulitzers to prove it—for the plays *Driving Miss Daisy* and *The Heidi Chronicles* and the musical *Sunday in the Park with George.* The **Signature Theatre Company** devotes each season to a works by a single playwright, which in the past has included luminaries such as Edward Albee, Sam Shepard, and Maria Irene Fornes.

A four-theater cultural complex is home to the **Theater for the New City,** which devotes its experimental productions to new playwrights. The complex also sponsors a free street-theater program, arts festivals, and a Christmas spectacular. The **Vineyard Theater,** one of the best-regarded off-Broadway companies, knows how to pick a winner. Its productions of Paula Vogel's *How I Learned to Drive* and Edward Albee's *Three Tall Women* both won Pulitzers.

Also off-Broadway you'll find venues staging performance art—a curious mélange of artistic disciplines blending music and sound, dance, video and lights, words, and whatever else comes to the performance artist's mind. The product is sometimes fascinating, sometimes stupefying. Performance art is almost exclusively a downtown, small-scale endeavor, although it is also showcased in the outer boroughs, especially Brooklyn. The **Brooklyn Academy of Music** has built its considerable reputation on its annual **Next Wave Festival,** which takes place every November and December and features avant-garde works of the highest professional standards.

Here in SoHo started in 1993 as a collaboration between two small theater companies, and has grown into an arts center with café, art gallery, and three theaters. The company runs a free performance series sponsored by NBC that runs Monday through Thursday and is devoted to nurturing up-and-coming local performers. **The Kitchen** is *the* place for performance art, although video, dance, and music have their moments here, too. **P.S.122** occupies a former public school that was comedian George Burns's alma mater. This scruffy, vibrant East Village venue presents exhibitions and productions that come and go quickly, and they're never boring. Look especially for its annual marathon in February.

Ellen Stewart, also known—simply and elegantly—as La Mama, started the theater complex **La MaMa E.T.C.** in 1961. Over the past several decades, her East Village organization has branched out to import international innovators and has grown to include two theatres and a club. Productions include everything from African fables to new-wave opera to reinterpretations of the Greek classics. Past triumphs have included the original productions of *Godspell* and *Torch Song Trilogy.*

Hailed by *The New York Times* as "a first-class magician of the avant-garde," Richard Foreman oversees the **Ontological-Hysteric Theater,** whose unconventional productions illuminate the human condition, often exploring the realm of dreams and nightmares. During the summer the theater sponsors the Blueprint Series, which allows novice directors to test their skills in front of an audience.

Circus Amok (WEB www.circusamok.org) presents edgy performances oriented toward adult audiences in venues around town, including the Coney Island boardwalk. **De la Guarda** (✉ Union Sq. E, at 15th St., WEB www.dlgsite.com), a wet and wild spectacle that mixes theater and circus, performs above and amidst an audience that stands and moves about during the entire show (children under eight are not permitted);

purchase tickets through Tele-Charge. The magazines and newspapers with a downtown orientation, such as *New York Press, New York Blade, Paper, Time Out,* and the *Village Voice,* are an especially good source of information on what's going on off-off-Broadway and in performance art. Some off-Broadway venues sell tickets through the major agencies, but to obtain tickets to most off-off-Broadway and performance art events, contact the theater directly.

Actors' Playhouse. ⊠ *100 7th Ave. S, near Grove St.,* ☎ *212/239–6200.*

American Place Theatre. ⊠ *111 W. 46th St., between 6th and 7th Aves.,* ☎ *212/840–3074.*

Astor Place Theatre. ⊠ *434 Lafayette St., near Astor Pl.,* ☎ *212/254–4370.*

Atlantic Theater Company. ⊠ *336 W. 20th St., at 5th Ave.,* ☎ *212/239–6200.*

Chelsea Playhouse. ⊠ *125 W. 22nd St., between 6th and 7th Aves.,* ☎ *212/924–7415.*

Classic Stage Company. ⊠ *136 E. 13th St., between 3rd and 4th Aves.,* ☎ *212/239–6200.*

Culture Project. ⊠ *45 Bleecker St., between Broadway and Lafayette St.,* ☎ *212/253–7017.*

Daryl Roth Theater. ⊠ *20 Union Sq. E, at E. 15th St.,* ☎ *212/375–1110.*

Dixon Place. ⊠ *309 E. 26th St., between 1st and 2nd Aves.,* ☎ *212/532–1546.*

Douglas Fairbanks Theatre. ⊠ *432 W. 42nd St., between 9th and 10th Aves.,* ☎ *212/239–4321.*

Drama Department. ⊠ *27 Barrow St., at 7th Ave.,* ☎ *212/633–9108.*

Ensemble Studio Theatre. ⊠ *549 W. 52nd St., between 10th and 11th Aves.,* ☎ *212/247–3405.*

Flea Theatre. ⊠ *41 White St., between Broadway and Church St.,* ☎ *212/226–2407.*

47th Street Theatre. ⊠ *304 W. 47th St., at 8th Ave.,* ☎ *212/239–6200.*

Gramercy Theater. ⊠ *127 E. 23rd St., between Lexington and Park Aves.,* ☎ *212/777–4900.*

Irish Repertory Theatre. ⊠ *132 W. 22nd St., between 6th and 7th Aves.,* ☎ *212/727–2737.*

Jane Street Theater. ⊠ *113 Jane St., between the West Side Hwy. and Washington St.,* ☎ *212/239–6200.*

Jean Cocteau Repertory. ⊠ *Bowery Lane Theatre, 330 Bowery, at Bond St.,* ☎ *212/677–0060.*

Jewish Repertory Theatre. ⊠ *Playhouse 91, 316 E. 91st St., between 1st and 2nd Aves.,* ☎ *212/831–2000.*

John Houseman Theatre. ⊠ *450 W. 42nd St., at 10th Ave.,* ☎ *212/967–7079.*

Joseph Papp Public Theater. ⊠ *425 Lafayette St., south of Astor Pl.,* ☎ *212/260–2400.*

The Kitchen. ⊠ *512 W. 19th St., between 10th and 11th Aves.,* ☎ *212/255–5793.*

La MaMa E.T.C. ⊠ *74A E. 4th St., between Bowery and 2nd Ave.,* ☎ *212/475–7710.*

Lamb's Theatre. ⊠ *130 W. 44th St., between 6th and 7th Aves.,* ☎ *212/997–1780.*

Lucille Lortel Theatre. ⊠ *121 Christopher St., between Hudson and Bleecker Sts.,* ☎ *212/239–6200.*

Minetta Lane Theatre. ⊠ *18 Minetta La., between 6th Ave. and Mac-Dougal St.,* ☎ *212/420–8000.*

Mitzi E. Newhouse Theatre. ⊠ *Lincoln Center, 150 W. 65th St., at Broadway,* ☎ *212/239–6200.*

New York TheatreWorkshop. ⊠ 79 E. 4th St., between 2nd and 3rd Aves., ☎ 212/460–5475.

Ontological-Hysteric Theater. ⊠ St. Mark's Church-in-the-Bowery, 131 E. 10th St., at 2nd Ave., ☎ 212/533–4650.

Orpheum Theatre. ⊠ 126 2nd Ave., at E. 8th St., ☎ 212/477–2477.

Pan Asian Repertory Theatre. ⊠ West End Theatre in the church of St. Paul and St. Andrew, 263 W. 86th St., between Broadway and West End Ave., ☎ 212/505–5655.

Pearl Theatre Company. ⊠ 80 St. Marks Pl., between 2nd and 3rd Aves., ☎ 212/598–9802.

Performing Garage. ⊠ 33 Wooster St., between Broome and Grand Sts., ☎ 212/966–9796.

Players Theater. ⊠ 115 MacDougal St., between W. 3rd and Bleecker Sts., ☎ 212/254–5076.

Playwrights Horizons. ⊠ 416 W. 42nd St., between 9th and 10th Aves., ☎ 212/279–4200.

Primary Stages. ⊠ 354 W. 45th St., between 8th and 9th Aves., ☎ 212/333–4052.

Promenade Theatre. ⊠ 2162 Broadway, at W. 76th St., ☎ 212/580–1313.

P.S.122. ⊠ 150 1st Ave., at E. 9th St., ☎ 212/477–5288.

Repertorio Español. ⊠ Arts Theatre, 138 E. 27th St., between 3rd and Lexington Aves., ☎ 212/889–2850.

Second Stage. ⊠ Cazale Theatre, 2162 Broadway, at W. 76th St., ☎ 212/873–6103.

Signature Theatre Company. ⊠ 555 W. 42nd St., between 10th and 11th Aves., ☎ 212/244–7529.

SoHo Playhouse. ⊠ 15 Vandam St., between 6th and 7th Aves., ☎ 212/239–6200.

Sullivan Street Playhouse. ⊠ 181 Sullivan St., between Bleecker and Houston Sts., ☎ 212/674–3838.

Theater for the New City. ⊠ 155 1st Ave., between 9th and 10th Sts., ☎ 212/254–1109.

Theatre Four. ⊠ 424 W. 55th St., between 9th and 10th Aves., ☎ 212/757–3900.

Triad Theatre. ⊠ 158 W. 72nd St., between Columbus and Amsterdam Aves., ☎ 212/239–6200.

Union Square Theatre. ⊠ 100 E. 17th St., between Park Ave. S and Irving Pl., ☎ 212/505–0700.

Variety Arts Theatre. ⊠ 110 3rd Ave., at E. 13th St., ☎ 212/239–6200.

Vineyard Theater. ⊠ 108 E. 15th St., between Park Ave. S and Irving Pl., ☎ 212/353–3366.

Westside Theatre. ⊠ 407 W. 43rd St., between 9th and 10th Aves., ☎ 212/307–4100.

WPA Theatre. ⊠ 159 W. 25th St., between 6th and 7th Aves., ☎ 212/206–0523.

York Theatre Company. ⊠ Theatre at St. Peter's Church, 619 Lexington Ave., at E. 54th St., ☎ 212/935–5820.

Theater for Children

Miss Majesty's Lollipop Playhouse (⊠ Grove Street Playhouse, 39 Grove St., between W. 4th St. and 7th Ave. S, ☎ 212/741–6436) brings fairy tales and nursery rhymes to life on weekend afternoons. **New Victory Theater** (⊠ 209 W. 42nd St., between Broadway and 7th Ave., ☎ 212/239–6255) stages plays, musical performances, and even mini-circuses. The **Paper Bag Players** (⊠ Sylvia and Danny Kaye Playhouse, Hunter College, E. 68th St. between Park and Lexington Aves., ☎ 212/772–4448), the longest-running children's theater group in the nation, stages plays for children under 10. **Tada!** (⊠ 120 W. 28th St., between

6th and 7th Aves., ☎ 212/627–1732) is a popular children's group with a multiethnic perspective. **Theaterworks/USA** (✉ Promenade Theater, Broadway at W. 76th St., ☎ 212/647–1100) mounts original productions based on well-known children's books.

THE CIRCUS

In addition to the big traveling shows that visit the city throughout the year, New York has three circuses of its very own. The **Big Apple Circus** (✉ Lincoln Center Plaza, ☎ 800/922–3772) entertains kids and their families both in New York and in shows around the country. Sometimes the world-renowned **Cirque du Soleil** visits New York, and **Ringling Bros. and Barnum & Bailey Circus** pitches its tents in Madison Square Garden each spring. Look in the newspaper for dates, times, and ticket information.

PUPPET SHOWS

Marionette Theater (✉ Swedish Cottage, Central Park W at W. 81st St., ☎ 212/988–9093) entertains children Tuesday–Saturday. **Puppet Playhouse** (✉ Asphalt Green, 555 E. 90th St., between York and East End Aves., ☎ 212/369–8890) offers weekend shows of puppets and marionettes. The marionettes at **Puppetworks** (✉ 338 6th Ave., at 4th St., Park Slope, Brooklyn, ☎ 718/965–3391) perform classic children's stories.

READINGS AND LECTURES

New York is still the center of American publishing, and as a result many writers eventually find reason to settle here. It is easy to catch a glimpse of literary figures great and small in the dozens of New York readings—prose, drama, and poetry—held each week. Readings sponsored by distinguished groups such as the Academy of American Poets, Dia Center for the Arts, the Poetry Project, the Poetry Society of America, and Poets House bring out some of the top names in contemporary literature, including John Updike, Don DeLillo, Toni Morrison, Frank McCourt, Philip Roth, and Kazuo Ishiguro. Those in bookstores, libraries, bars, and theaters often are a chance to catch debuting talents.

Poetry Calendar (✉ *611 Broadway, Suite 905, 10012,* ☎ *212/260–7097*), published monthly from September through June, provides extensive listings of literary events all around the city. The calendar is available by subscription or for free at several Manhattan bookstores, libraries, and nightclubs. You can also check the listings of readings in *New York* magazine, *New York Press,* the *New Yorker, Time Out New York,* and the *Village Voice.*

Authors, poets, lyricists, and playwrights take the stage at the **92nd St. Y.** A number of readings are held at **Symphony Space** including the Selected Shorts series of stories read by prominent actors and broadcast on National Public Radio. **Makor** is a sleek new Jewish cultural arts center with a program of music, theater, seminars and excellent literary events geared toward a crowd in their twenties and thirties. In its City Center home **Manhattan Theatre Club** sponsors **Writers in Performance,** a provocative program of dramatic readings and roundtable discussions that showcase novelists, poets, and playwrights from the United States and abroad.

Downtown **Dixon Place** sponsors readings regularly, some of which border on performance art. The **Kitchen** also presents readings from the edges of the literary world. One of the most influential and avant-garde reading series around town is **Nightlight,** held one Wednesday a month at the **Drawing Center,** an art space in SoHo.

Informal poetry readings, sometimes with an open-mike policy that allows audience members to read their own work, crop up with frequency in New York City clubs and bars. These events are fairly popular, particularly with a younger crowd. There may be a low cover charge ($2–$5), and food and drink are usually available. Some reliable spots include **Biblio's, Cornelia Street Café, Ear Inn,** and the **Knitting Factory.** The **Nuyorican Poets Café** schedules daily readings by multicultural poets and hosts a Poetry Slam competition each Friday (you'll also find Latin jazz, comedy, and play readings here).

Many Manhattan bookstores organize evening readings by authors of recently published books. Best bets are **Barnes & Noble, Borders, Posman Books, Rizzoli, Shakespeare & Co.,** and **Three Lives & Co.** For readings by gay and lesbian authors, try the commodious **A Different Light.**

A major reading and talk series is held at the **New York Public Library for the Performing Arts,** at Lincoln Center, specializing in presentations by musicians, directors, singers, and actors. Several branches of the **New York Public Library** present lectures and reading events. A monthly calendar of free library readings is available at each branch.

Academy of American Poets. ⊠ *584 Broadway, between Prince and Houston Sts.,* ☎ *212/274–0343.*

Cornelia Street Café. ⊠ *29 Cornelia St., between W. 4th and Bleecker Sts.,* ☎ *212/989–9319.*

Dia Center for the Arts. ⊠ *548 W. 22nd St., between 10th and 11th Aves.,* ☎ *212/989–5566.*

Drawing Center. ⊠ *35 Wooster St., between Grand and Broome Sts.,* ☎ *212/219–2166.*

Ear Inn. ⊠ *326 Spring St., between Greenwich and Washington Sts.,* ☎ *212/226–9060.*

KGB. ⊠ *85 E. 4th St., between 2nd and 3rd Aves.,* ☎ *212/505–3360.*

Knitting Factory. ⊠ *74 Leonard St., between Broadway and Church St.,* ☎ *212/219–3055*

Makor. ⊠ *35 W. 67th St., between Central Park W and Columbus Ave.,* ☎ *212/601–1000.*

New York Library for the Performing Arts. ⊠ *150 W. 65th St., between Columbus and Amsterdam Aves.,* ☎ *212/870–1630.*

New York Public Library. ⊠ *Branches around town,* ☎ *212/930–0830.*

Nuyorican Poets Café. ⊠ *236 E. 3rd St., between Aves. B and C,* ☎ *212/505–8183.*

The Poetry Project. ⊠ *St. Mark's Church-in-the-Bowery, 131 E. 10th St., at 2nd Ave.,* ☎ *212/674–0910.*

Poetry Society of America. ⊠ *15 Gramercy Park S, between Park Ave. S and 3rd Ave.,* ☎ *212/254–9628.*

Poets House. ⊠ *72 Spring St., between Broadway and Lafayette St.,* ☎ *212/431–7920.*

Symphony Space. ⊠ *2537 Broadway, at W. 95th St.,* ☎ *212/864–5400.*

Writers in Performance. ⊠ *131 W. 55th St., between 6th and 7th Aves.,* ☎ *212/399–3000.*

VISUAL ARTS

New York City's contemporary art scene is experiencing an exciting shift. As the historic downtown art enclave of SoHo has been commercialized into a high-end shopping district, galleries have relocated to converted industrial spaces in Chelsea and the Meatpacking District in Manhattan's western reaches. What was a no-man's-land in the early 1990s has become a fashionable destination, with chic restaurants, bars, and the occasional shop, such as Commes des Garcons (its interior design and funky clothes are art works unto themselves) popping up everywhere.

Art Galleries

As America's art capital, New York has hundreds of galleries and thousands of artists. Exhibitions showcase artists ranging from established names, whose works can also be seen in major museum collections, to art school graduates making their debut in group shows. Both midtown (5th Avenue and 57th Street) and the Upper East Side (the East 60s and 70s) have clusters of established galleries showing anything from Old Masters to contemporary art. The most cutting-edge galleries, once concentrated in SoHo (south of Houston and west of Mulberry Street), are rapidly migrating to Chelsea (from West 14th Street through the 20s, between 10th and 11th Avenues). A burgeoning art scene is also making itself known in Brooklyn's Williamsburg, Greenpoint, and DUMBO sections. Most Manhattan galleries are open Tuesday through Saturday. Brooklyn galleries are mostly open on weekends. To find out what's on view, consult the listings in *Time Out New York* or the *Village Voice*. Another helpful resource is the *Art Now Gallery Guide,* available in most galleries.

Chelsea

Andrea Rosen. The gallery showcases young artists on the cutting edge, such as Andrea Zittel, John Currin, and Wolfgang Tillmans, who won Britain's prestigious Turner Prize in 2000 for his striking photography, which appears both staged and documentary. ⊠ *525 W. 24th St., between 10th and 11th Aves.,* ☎ *212/627–6000.*

Barbara Gladstone. Gladstone shows a range of interesting contemporary work, with paintings by Lari Pittman, photographs by Sharon Lockhart, and video by Gary Hill. ⊠ *515 W. 24th St., between 10th and 11th Aves.,* ☎ *212/206–9300.*

Bonakdar Jancou. This gallery presents such contemporary artists as Uta Barth, whose blurry photos challenge ideas about perception, and Ernesto Neto, a Brazilian artist who has made stunning room-size installations of large nylon sacks filled with spices. ⊠ *521 W. 21st St., between 10th and 11th Aves.,* ☎ *212/414–4144.*

Casey Kaplan. Kaplan has a keen eye for conceptual artists. Among them is Anna Gaskell, who has made photos of young girls dressed in costume and engaged in some menacing but inexplicable activity. ⊠ *416 W. 14th St., between 9th and 10th Aves.,* ☎ *212/645–7335.*

Cheim & Read. This prestigious gallery represents modern painters and photographers such as Louise Bourgeois and shows work by the late Jean-Michel Basquiat and Diane Arbus. ⊠ *521 W. 23rd St., between 10th and 11th Aves.,* ☎ *212/242–7727.*

Gagosian. This enterprising modern gallery has two branches in New York City, one in Los Angeles, and one in London. The warehouse-size Chelsea space opened with a star-studded opening for Damien Hirst's office scenes in vitrines filled with water and fish. ⊠ *555 W. 24th St., at 11th Ave.,* ☎ *212/741–1111; 980 Madison Ave., between E. 76th and E. 77th Sts.,* ☎ *212/744–2313.*

Gavin Brown's Enterprise. Smart and lively, this space has hosted the avant-garde performances of the duo of German artist-musicians Fischerspooner and a flea market for upstart artists to sell both their clutter and their art. You can ruminate about the art at Passersby, a bar that Brown opened next door. ⊠ *436 W. 15th St., between 9th and 10th Aves.,* ☎ *212/627–5258.*

Holly Solomon. Solomon's foresight is legendary—she was an early champion of photographer Robert Mapplethorpe—and now she shows works by artists such as William Wegman and Nick Waplington. ⊠

Galleries & Museums: Chelsea and SoHo

Room 425, Chelsea Hotel, 222 W. 23rd St., between 7th and 8th Aves., ☎ 212/941–5777.

Jack Shainman. Both emerging and established artists are shown here. You might find works by Phil Frost, whose imagery is derived from graffiti. The duo of Aziz + Cucher make digital photos of figures with erased features, suggesting body imaging gone awry. ✉ *513 W. 20th St., between 10th and 11th Aves., ☎ 212/645–1701.*

Jay Grimm. In the northernmost reaches of Chelsea, this gallery always surprises with contemporary artists ranging from the internationally established Dutch painter Karel Appel to the Japanese-American artist Masami Teraoka, who executes realist tableaux in his epic paintings. ✉ *505 W. 28th St., between 10th and 11th Aves., ☎ 212/564–7662.*

Luhring Augustine. Since 1985 owners Lawrence Luhring and Roland Augustine have been working with established and less well-known artists from Europe, Japan, and America. A 2000 show featured Gregory Crewdson's elaborately staged photographs of small town scenes tweaked with elements of fantasy or science fiction. ✉ *531 W. 24th St., between 10th and 11th Aves., ☎ 212/219–9100.*

Mary Boone. A hot SoHo gallery during the 1980s this venue moved first uptown, and has now opened a Chelsea space. Boone continues to show established artists such as Barbara Kruger and Eric Fischl, as well as newcomers Tom Sachs and Micha Klein. ✉ *541 W. 24th St., between 10th and 11th Aves., ☎ 212/752–2929; 745 5th Ave., between E. 57th and 58th Sts., ☎ 212/752–2929.*

Matthew Marks. At two Chelsea spaces Marks shows prominent modern artists such as the painters Ellsworth Kelly and Willem de Kooning, as well as up-to-the-minute luminaries such as photographers Andreas Gursky, Inez van Lamsweerde, and Sam Taylor-Wood. ✉ *522 W. 22nd St., between 10th and 11th Aves., ☎ 212/243–1650; 523 W. 24th St., between 10th and 11th Aves., ☎ 212/243–0200.*

Metro Pictures. Some of contemporary art's hottest talents are here including Cindy Sherman, whose provocative and often disturbing photographs have brought her international prominence. ✉ *519 W. 24th St., between 10th and 11th Aves., ☎ 212/206–7100.*

Paula Cooper. SoHo pioneer Paula Cooper moved to Chelsea in 1996 and enlisted architect Richard Gluckman to transform a warehouse into a dramatic space with tall ceilings and handsome skylights. Now she has two galleries on the same block that showcase the minimalist sculptures of Carl André, the dot paintings of Yayoi Kusama, and the provocative photos of Andres Serrano, among other works. ✉ *534 W. 21st St., between 10th and 11th Aves., ☎ 212/255–1105; 521 W. 21st St., between 10th and 11th Aves., ☎ 212/255–5247.*

Robert Miller. Miller represents the estates of some of the biggest names in modern painting and photography, such as Joan Mitchell, Robert Mapplethorpe, and Diane Arbus. ✉ *524 W. 26th St., between 10th and 11th Aves., ☎ 212/980–5454.*

Sean Kelly. Drop in here for top artists including Ann Hamilton, Cathy de Monchaux, and James Casebere. ✉ *524–532 W. 29th St., between 10th and 11th Aves., ☎ 212/343–2405.*

Sonnabend. This gallery, a pioneer of the SoHo art scene, has continued to show important modern artists in its Chelsea space, including Jeff Koons, Ashley Bickerton, and Californian conceptualist John Baldessari. ✉ *536 W. 22nd St., between 10th and 11th Aves., ☎ 212/627–1018.*

303. International artists including photographers Doug Aitken, painter Sue Williams, and installation artist Karen Kilimnik are displayed here. ✉ *525 W. 22nd St., between 10th and 11th Aves., ☎ 212/255–1121.*

Midtown/57th Street

David Findlay Jr. Fine Art. This gallery concentrates on American 19th- and 20th-century painters from John Singer Sargent to Arthur Dove to Andrew Wyeth. ⊠ *41 E. 57th St., between 5th and Madison Aves.,* ☎ *212/486–7660.*

Edwynn Houk. The gallery's impressive stable of 20th-century photographers includes Sally Mann, Lynn Davis, and Brassaï. It also shows prints by masters Edward Weston and Alfred Steiglitz. ⊠ *745 5th Ave., between E. 57th and 58th Sts.,* ☎ *212/750–7070.*

Galerie Lelong. Displayed here are works by Andy Goldsworthy, Cildo Meireles, and Petah Coyne, among others. ⊠ *20 W. 57th St., between 5th and 6th Aves.,* ☎ *212/315–0470.*

Joseph Helman. Contemporary masters such as Claes Oldenburg, Robert Moskowitz, Joe Andoe, and Tom Wesselman are shown here. ⊠ *20 W. 57th St., between 5th and 6th Aves.,* ☎ *212/245–2888.*

Lawrence Rubin Greenberg Van Doren Fine Art. This photography gallery continues to intrigue by hosting shows featuring the works of young photographers or glamorous party pictures from Studio 54 to Cannes. ⊠ *730 5th Ave., at E. 57th St.,* ☎ *212/445–0534.*

Marian Goodman. The excellent contemporary art here includes Jeff Wall's staged photographs presented on lightboxes, South African artist William Kentridge's video animations, and Rebecca Horn's mechanized sculptures. ⊠ *24 W. 57th St., between 5th and 6th Aves.,* ☎ *212/977–7160.*

Marlborough. With galleries in London, Monte Carlo, Madrid, Santiago, and Boca Raton, the Marlborough empire also operates one of the largest and most influential galleries in New York City. The gallery represents modern artists including Alex Katz, Magdalena Abakanowicz, and Paula Rego, and publishes prints by important 20th-century artists such as Matisse, Picasso, Hockney, Johns, and Rauschenberg. Check out its space in Chelsea, too. ⊠ *40 W. 57th St., between 5th and 6th Aves.,* ☎ *212/541–4900; 211 W. 19th St., between 7th and 8th Aves.,* ☎ *212/463–8634.*

Pace Wildenstein. The giant gallery focuses on such modern and contemporary painters as Piet Mondrian, Julian Schnabel, and New York School painter Ad Reinhardt. Upstairs is **Pace Prints** (☎ *212/421–3237*), where you can rifle through open racks of prints by artists such as Richard Diebenkorn, David Hockney, and Kiki Smith. The gallery also has a SoHo location that features 20th-century paintings and sculpture, and is scheduled to open a Chelsea location in fall 2002. ⊠ *32 E. 57th St., between Park and Madison Aves.,* ☎ *212/421–3292; 52 Greene St., at Prince St.,* ☎ *212/431–9224.*

Peter Findlay. Covering 19th- and 20th-century works by American and European artists, this gallery shows pieces by Mary Cassatt, Paul Klee, and Alberto Giacometti. ⊠ *41 E. 57th St., at Madison Ave.,* ☎ *212/644–4433.*

Spanierman. This venerable gallery deals in 19th- and early 20th-century American painting and sculpture. ⊠ *45 E. 58th St., between Park and Madison Aves.,* ☎ *212/832–0208.*

Tibor de Nagy. Founded in 1950 this reputable gallery shows work by 20th-century artists such as Arthur Dove, Georgia O'Keeffe, Allen Ginsberg, and Trevor Winkfield. ⊠ *724 5th Ave., between W. 56th and 57th Sts.,* ☎ *212/262–5050.*

SoHo

Ace. Just west of SoHo proper, Ace is a cavernous space where contemporary artists present large-scale works. Recent shows have included work by Sylvie Fleury, John Armleder, and fashion designer Issey Miyake. ⊠ *275 Hudson St., between Spring and Canal Sts.,* ☎ *212/255–5599.*

Art in General. This nonprofit organization, a few blocks below SoHo, often presents group exhibitions organized by guest curators. ⊠ 79 *Walker St., between Broadway and Lafayette St.,* ☎ 212/219–0473.

David Zwirner. Proving his finger is on the pulse of contemporary art, Zwirner shows works by Luc Tuymans, Franz West, Diana Thater, Yutaka Sone, and Katy Schimert. ⊠ *43 Greene St., between Broome and Grand Sts.,* ☎ 212/966–9074.

Deitch Projects. This energetic enterprise composed of two gallery spaces usually shows an emerging must-see plucked from the global art scene. Artists on view have included Cecily Brown, Teresita Fernandez, and Shazia Sikhander. ⊠ *76 Grand St., between Greene and Wooster Sts.,* ☎ 212/343–7300; 18 Wooster St., at Grand St., ☎ 212/343–7300.

Dia Center for the Arts: New York Earth Room. Conceptual artist Walter De Maria's installation, on view since 1977, consists of 250 cubic yards of dirt piled 22 inches deep. It's sublime. ⊠ *141 Wooster St., between Houston and Prince Sts.,* ☎ 212/473–8072.

Drawing Center. This nonprofit organization focuses on contemporary and historical sketches. Surprising works often push the envelope on what's considered drawing. ⊠ *35 Wooster St., between Broome and Grand Sts.,* ☎ 212/219–2166.

Tony Shafrazi. Shafrazi is the exclusive representative of the estate of the painter Francis Bacon. Among the other artists shown here are Keith Haring, Dennis Hopper, Michael Ray Charles, and David LaChapelle. ⊠ *119 Wooster St., between Prince and Spring Sts.,* ☎ 212/274–9300.

Upper East Side

David Findlay. Descend into a warren of rooms to view contemporary, color-soaked paintings. Represented artists include Pierre Lesieur, Roger Mühl, and (for a striking slice of New York streets) Tom Christopher. ⊠ *984 Madison Ave., between E. 76th and E. 77th Sts.,* ☎ 212/249–2909.

Hirschl & Adler. Although this gallery has a selection of European works, it is best known for its American paintings, prints, and decorative arts. Among the celebrated 19th- and 20th-century artists whose works are featured: Thomas Cole, Frederick Church, Childe Hassam, John Storrs, and William Merritt Chase. ⊠ *21 E. 70th St., between 5th and Madison Aves.,* ☎ 212/535–8810.

Jane Kahan. Besides ceramics by Picasso (this gallery's specialty), you'll see works by 19th- and 20th-century artists such as Fernand Léger, Joan Miró, and Marc Chagall. ⊠ *922 Madison Ave., between E. 73rd and E. 74th Sts.,* ☎ 212/744–1490.

Knoedler & Company. Knoedler helped many great American collectors, including industrialist Henry Clay Frick, start their collections. Now its represented artists include 20th-century painters Helen Frankenthaler, Robert Motherwell, and Frank Stella. ⊠ *19 E. 70th St., between 5th and Madison Aves.,* ☎ 212/794–0550.

Leo Castelli. Castelli, who passed away in 1999, was one of the most influential dealers of the 20th century. An early supporter of pop, minimalist, and conceptual art, he helped foster the careers of many important artists including one of his first discoveries, Jasper Johns. The gallery moved here from SoHo and continues to show works by Roy Lichtenstein, Ed Ruscha, and others. ⊠ *59 E. 79th St., between Madison and Park Aves.,* ☎ 212/249–4470.

Margo Feiden. Illustrations by theatrical caricaturist Al Hirschfeld, who has been delighting readers of the *New York Times* for more than 60 years, are the draw here. ⊠ *699 Madison Ave., between E. 62nd and E. 63rd Sts.,* ☎ 212/677–5330.

Michael Werner. This German art dealer mounts smart shows of such early-20th-century masters as Marcel Duchamp, Francis Picabia, and

222

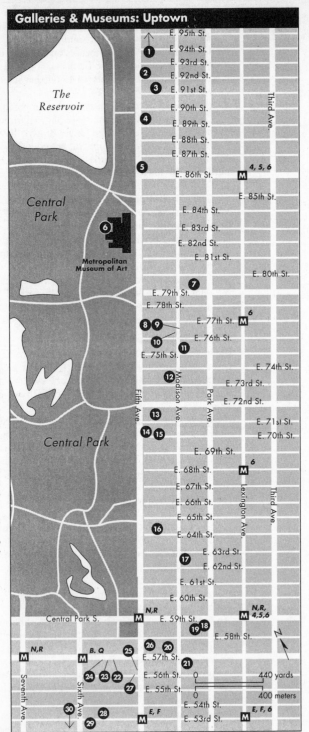

Galleries & Museums: Uptown

Henri Michaux in his refined, uptown locale. ⊠ *4 E. 77th St., between 5th and Madison Aves.,* ☎ *212/988–1623.*

Wildenstein & Co. This branch of the Wildenstein art empire was the first to take root in New York; its reputation for brilliant holdings was cemented by the acquisition of significant private collections. Look for impressionist exhibitions. ⊠ *19 E. 64th St., between 5th and Madison Aves.,* ☎ *212/879–0500.*

Brooklyn

Bellwether. Located in Greenpoint, this non-profit, artist-run gallery hosts shows by emerging and established local artists. It offers weekend shuttle bus service (call ahead of time to reserve) from the Bedford Ave. subway station on the L line. *150 Franklin St., near Kent St.,* ☎ *718/389–3213.*

GAle GAtes et. al. Located in DUMBO, this warehouse space presents changing exhibitions and performances. ⊠ *37 Main St.,* ☎ *718/522–4596.*

Momenta Art. This artist-run, not-for-profit space features changing exhibitions with a focus on emerging artists. ⊠ *72 Berry St., between N. 9th and N. 10th Sts.,* ☎ *718/218–8058.*

Pierogi 2000. Here you'll find mostly solo shows of Williamsburg artists. Check out its drawers containing drawings by some 500 artists. ⊠ *177 N. 9th St., between Bedford and Driggs Aves.,* ☎ *718/599–2144.*

Art Museums

For more information on art museums, *see* Chapters 1 and 2.

American Craft Museum. The intricate crafts on display here defy you to call them anything other than art. ⊠ *40 W. 53rd St., at 5th Ave.,* ☎ *212/956–3535.*

Asia Society. While its Park Avenue headquarters undergo renovation and expansion (until late 2001), the Asia Society temporarily sets up shop in midtown, presenting changing exhibitions of Asian art. ⊠ *725 Park Ave., at 70th St.,* ☎ *212/288–6400.*

Bronx Museum of the Arts. The Bronx Museum displays 20th-century works, with an emphasis on African-American, Latin American, and Asian American art. ⊠ *1040 Grand Concourse, at 165th St.,* ☎ *718/681–6000.*

Brooklyn Museum of Art. This is the second-largest museum in New York with over a million works in its collection. Its accumulation of Egyptian, African, and Pre-Columbian Art is recognized worldwide for its excellence. ⊠ *200 Eastern Pkwy., at Washington Ave.,* ☎ *718/638–5000.*

Children's Museum of the Arts. Youngsters get a hands-on experience of the visual and performing arts at this SoHo space. ⊠ *182 Lafayette St., between Broome and Grand Sts.,* ☎ *212/274–0986.*

The Cloisters. To house its medieval collection the Metropolitan Museum of Art built its northern branch from pieces of five medieval monasteries. Organized chronologically, the oldest pieces date from 1200 and the latest from about 1520. The famous 15th- and 16th-century Unicorn Tapestries are here. ⊠ *Ft. Tryon Park, Riverside Dr. and Broadway from W. 192nd to Dyckman Sts.,* ☎ *212/923–3700.*

Cooper-Hewitt National Design Museum. The Smithsonian's design and decorative arts collection is displayed in this 5th Avenue mansion. ⊠ *2 E. 91st St., between 5th and Madison Aves.,* ☎ *212/849–8300.*

Dahesh Museum. This museum is devoted to 19th- and early 20th-century European academic art. ⊠ *601 5th Ave., between E. 48th and 49th Sts.,* ☎ *212/759–0606.*

Dia Center for the Arts. This top-notch contemporary art space hosts long-term exhibitions, usually featuring a single artist. Recent shows have included Bridget Riley and Donald Judd. Be sure to check out Dan

Graham's glass pavilion on the rooftop and the funky new bookstore/reading room designed by artist Jorge Pardo. ✉ *548 W. 22nd St., between 10th and 11th Aves.,* ☎ *212/989–5566.*

El Museo del Barrio. Examples of Central and South American, Caribbean, and especially Puerto Rican art make up a permanent collection of more than 8,000 pieces. ✉ *1230 5th Ave., at E. 104th St.,* ☎ *212/831–7272.*

Forbes Magazine Galleries. The collection of the late Malcolm Forbes fills the ground floor of the Forbes Magazine Building, including such treasures as the exquisitely rendered Faberge eggs. ✉ *62 5th Ave., at W. 12th St.,* ☎ *212/206–5548.*

Frick Collection. The former mansion of steel magnate Henry Clay Frick houses this intimate but extensive and haunting collection of 14th-to 19th-century paintings and 18th-century furniture. ✉ *1 E. 70th St., at 5th Ave.,* ☎ *212/288–0700.*

Grey Art Gallery. New York University's fine arts museum presents high-caliber historical and contemporary shows. ✉ *100 Washington Sq. E,* ☎ *212/998–6780.*

Guggenheim Museum SoHo. This elegant downtown branch of the famed Solomon R. Guggenheim Museum specializes in multimedia installations and video art in addition to more traditional fare. ✉ *575 Broadway, at Prince St.,* ☎ *212/423–3500.*

International Center of Photography (ICP). This impressive center for photojournalism and fine art photography houses a notable permanent collection and hosts frequently changing exhibitions. ✉ *1133 Ave. of the Americas, at W. 43rd St.,* ☎ *212/768–4682.*

Jacques Marchais Museum of Tibetan Art. A building that resembles a Tibetan monastery houses one of the largest private collections of Tibetan and Himalayan art outside of Tibet. ✉ *338 Lighthouse Ave.,* ☎ *718/987–3500.*

Jewish Museum. This museum holds one of the largest collections of Judaica in America. Changing exhibitions explore Jewish history and culture of the past 4,000 years. ✉ *1109 5th Ave., at E. 92nd St.,* ☎ *212/423–3230.*

Madame Tussaud's Wax Museum. The world-renowned chain of wax museums opened its newest outpost in the heart of Times Square in 2000. See over 250 lifelike figures of celebrities from Michael Jackson to Jackie Onassis. ✉ *234 W. 42nd St., between 7th and 8th Aves.,* ☎ *212/512–9600.*

Metropolitan Museum of Art. Exhibits at the largest museum in the Western Hemisphere cover 5,000 years of artistic and cultural history, from Greek statuary to modern photography. ✉ *1000 5th Ave., at E. 82nd St.,* ☎ *212/535–7710.*

MoMA QNS. This former factory houses the collection of the Museum of Modern Art while that facility undergoes renovation and expansion. ✉ *45-20 33rd St., at Queens Blvd., Long Island City,* ☎ *718/389–4729.*

Morgan Library. The extensive collection includes drawings, prints, medieval and Renaissance manuscripts, and music manuscripts. The Morgan's covered courtyard café is the neighborhood's most pleasant place to lunch. ✉ *29 E. 36th St., at Madison Ave.,* ☎ *212/685–0610.*

Museum of American Folk Art. Quilts, weather vanes, and Shaker furniture are among some of the objects featured here in changing exhibitions. ✉ *2 Lincoln Sq., Columbus Ave. between W. 65th and W. 66th Sts.,* ☎ *212/977–7298.*

Museum of Modern Art (MoMA). MoMA holds one of the world's greatest collections of modern art. Until 2003, it is undergoing renovation and expansion, so highlights of the collection will be on display at the museum's annex in Long Island City, Queens. ✉ *11 W. 53rd St., between 5th and 6th Aves.,* ☎ *212/708–9400.*

Neue Galerie New York. Scheduled to open in autumn 2001, this museum includes works by modern German and Austrian artists, including masters Gustav Klimt and Egon Schiele. ⊠ *1048 5th Ave., at E. 86th St.,* ☎ *212/628–6200.*

New Museum of Contemporary Art. The SoHo veteran puts on provocative solo and group shows by artists from all over the world. Check out the bookstore on the lower level for cutting-edge publications and funky gifts. ⊠ *583 Broadway, between Houston and Prince Sts.,* ☎ *212/219–1222.*

P.S.1 Contemporary Art Center. Housed in a former school in Queens, P.S.1 presents a wide range of rigorous and energetic contemporary art exhibitions. ⊠ *22–25 Jackson Ave., at 46th Ave., Long Island City,* ☎ *718/784–2084.*

Solomon R. Guggenheim Museum. Within its spiraling gallery, Frank Lloyd Wright's famous building houses a permanent collection of important American and European 20th-century paintings and sculpture. In 2000, the Guggenheim won the financial backing of the city to build a gigantic new museum—to be designed by celebrity architect Frank Gehry—on the East River in lower Manhattan. ⊠ *1071 5th Ave., at E. 89th St.,* ☎ *212/423–3500.*

Studio Museum in Harlem. Changing exhibitions and a permanent collection of notable African-American paintings, sculpture and photographs fill this museum in the heart of Harlem. ⊠ *144 W. 125th St., between 6th and 7th Aves.,* ☎ *212/864–4500.*

Whitney Museum of American Art. A wide range of modern American works fill this fortresslike landmark. The Whitney Biennial, its provocative showcase of recent American art, is a major art-world event every other summer. The fifth floor has selections from the permanent collection, with choice works by 20th-century artists such as Edward Hopper, Georgia O'Keeffe, and Alexander Calder. ⊠ *945 Madison Ave., at 75th St.,* ☎ *212/570–3676.*

4 DINING

New York City may just be the greatest restaurant city in the world. Its cultural diversity produces an amazing breadth and depth of dining options, from temples of fine French cuisine to distinguished dim sum palaces. New Yorkers have a passion for good food. They will travel crosstown to buy their favorite bagels and into the outer boroughs to taste authentic Malaysian cuisine. This is a city where deciding where to eat is as important as deciding what to see and do. To experience the town like a native, make dining a priority.

By Mitchell
Davis and
Jane Miller

IN THE WAKE OF THE RESTAURANT BOOM OF THE LAST COUPLE OF **YEARS,** there is now almost a glut of dining options in New York City. At the same time menu prices, even at casual neighborhood eateries, have soared. With so many choices, and such high checks, making the right decision about where to eat has become even more of a challenge.

The most significant international culinary event of 2000 was the arrival of French chef Alain Ducasse in New York. More acclaimed than any French chef in history, Ducasse installed a gastronomic temple of Michelin three-star proportions at the Essex House hotel. New Yorkers, who are usually proud to outspend their dining neighbors, gasped at the exorbitant menu prices—a *New York Times* reviewer reportedly spent more than $2,000 on dinner for four. At first the dining elite found the neo-Victorian experience pretentious and the food sub-par. But as the kitchen hit its stride, the over-articulated service was toned down, and Ducasse actually stepped up to the stove to cook, the restaurant assumed a place at the top of the dining heap.

New restaurant rows (the original is in the theater district, on West 46th Street between 8th and 9th avenues) are sprouting up all around town, as restaurateurs transform city blocks into dining destinations. One-block-long Cornelia Street in the West Village was one of the first to appear. Now there's 1st Street between 1st and 2nd Avenues in the East Village and Elizabeth Street in NoLita, both of which attract a chic downtown crowd. Diners from all over town are trying to direct cab drivers to unlikely Clinton Street addresses on the Lower East Side. For 20 years Florent sat alone on Gansevoort Street in the Meatpacking District; now the tiny, cobblestone stretch that was once lined with meat lockers and warehouses boasts no fewer than five serious restaurants. Perhaps the most talked about new restaurant row is Smith Street in the Carroll Gardens neighborhood of Brooklyn, where expatriate Manhattan chefs and local residents have created a destination-dining enclave.

Once stigmatized as sub-standard, hotel dining continues to remake its image. Todd English opened an outpost of his Boston-based Olives empire in the W on Union Square. Celebutantes pile into Hudson Cafeteria in the Hudson hotel. The Iroquois is home to Triomphe. The Giraffe houses Chinoiserie (drink, but don't eat there). As we've already mentioned, Ducasse opened in the Essex House and District opened in the Muse. It isn't easy to get New Yorkers to eat in a hotel. Those who manage to do it have created quite a coup.

One last trend concerns the style of restaurants rather than the style of cooking. In New York, as in Paris, the neighborhood restaurant has undergone a serious change. Pedigreed chefs have opened small, casual restaurants that normally wouldn't attract city-wide attention, except that their food is superlative. 71 Clinton Fresh Food exemplifies the trend, but Annisa, The Tasting Room, Fleur de Sel, Wallsé, and Miss Williamsburg Diner also fall into this category. The food at these places isn't cheap, but neither is the overall experience.

A word of caution: some of the dishes recommended in the following reviews may not be on the menu you receive when you finally make it to the restaurant. Chefs often change their menus with the season and with the availability of ingredients in the market. Use our recommendations as guidelines and you won't be disappointed.

Children

Though it is unusual to see children in the dining rooms of Manhattan's most elite restaurants, dining with your youngsters in New York does not have to mean culinary exile. Many of the restaurants reviewed in this chapter are excellent choices for families. Upscale restaurants that offer some simple menu items and accommodating service, such as An American Place, Osteria del Circo, Tribeca Grill, or "21" Club, can satisfy the pickiest adults and children alike. More casual options include Café Habana, Kitchenette, Serendipity 3, or Shopsin's General Store. For an interactive experience, consider Korean barbecue (such as Kang Suh), where you grill your own meal, or Brazilian *churrascaria* (such as Churrascaria Plataforma or Green Fields Churrascaria), where waiters parade about with skewers of roasted meat. Most Chinese restaurants, such as Jing Fong, Great New York Noodletown, and Dim Sum Go Go, are very child-friendly. And all of the New York steak houses—Gallagher's, The Palm, Peter Luger, and Sparks, for example—offer good, old-fashioned satisfaction in the form of onion rings, crispy potatoes, and creamed spinach. Some restaurants are so much fun they feel like they're simply made for children; *see* the "For the Kids" feature box, *below,* for a list of these.

Dress

It was only a matter of time before restaurants followed Wall Street's lead and made casual attire acceptable most of the time. But casual in New York is not the same as casual elsewhere. In fact, the term most often used when you call and ask about the dress code is "casual chic," which loosely translates to "black and expensive" (whether a T-shirt or a little dress). For an example, Helmut Lang jeans are usually acceptable, while Levis are not. A few of the most formal placesstill require jackets and/or ties. As a rule, dress at restaurants in Midtown and around Wall Street is more conservative than in other, more residential neighborhoods, especially at lunch. SoHo and TriBeCa are trendier than the Upper East and Upper West sides. Shorts are appropriate only in the most casual spots. Don't be embarrassed to call and ask.

Hours

Timing is everything. Most New York restaurants keep long hours, so you should be able to make arrangements that suit your needs. Many stay open between lunch and dinner, some offer late-night seating, and still others serve around the clock. European and Latin American tourists are relieved that at least one American city allows them to dine as late as they do at home. But tourists from other parts of the United States marvel when sometime after 11 PM the entire dining room at Balthazar is re-seated, or a table of four orders the tasting menu at Daniel, or a group of friends fires up the coals for an authentic Korean barbecue. The city that never sleeps eats on the same schedule.

Prices

Although value is better than it has been in the past, prices continue to creep up in ways that aren't always obvious. Entrées have inched up and over the $30 mark, even in casual establishments, and appetizers run the full gamut of prices. Many restaurants have also begun charging $5–$10 for side dishes. Beware of the $10 bottle of water poured eagerly for unsuspecting diners. The increasingly ubiquitous $60-plus prix-fixe menu ensures that restaurateurs maintain a high check average, but bargains can still be had if you play your *cartes* right. One strategy is to order two or three appetizers and skip the entrée. Starters are usually more creative, and by ordering a selection you get a good idea of the chef's *oeuvre*.

A word of warning: if you are watching your budget, be sure to ask the price of daily specials recited by the waiter or captain. The charge for specials at some restaurants is noticeably out of line with the other prices on the menu. And of course, always review your bill. Even on computerized checks, mistakes do occur. No matter whose favor the mistake is in, it is a courtesy to bring it to your server's attention.

If you eat early or late you may be able to take advantage of a prix-fixe deal not offered at peak hours, and get more attentive service in the bargain. Most upscale restaurants offer fantastic lunch deals with special menus at cut-rate prices designed to give a true taste of the place, sometimes at half the cost of dinner. One dining bargain has become a New York institution. In 1992, the city's restaurants devised the idea of charging $19.92 for a prix-fixe lunch during the Democratic Convention in June. It was a huge success, and you can still find lunches (and some dinners) with prices tied to the year at restaurants throughout the city, not only during "Restaurant Week" in June, but all year round.

CATEGORY	COST*
$$$$	over $32
$$$	$25–$32
$$	$15–$24
$	under $15

per person for a main course at dinner

Some restaurants are marked with a price range ($$–$$$, for example). This indicates one of two things: either the average cost straddles two categories, or if you order strategically, you can get out for less than most diners spend.

Reservations

Most visitors to New York know you can eat better here than just about anywhere else in the country, but they may not realize that it takes some planning. If you want to eat in one of the top restaurants, you can't just call the same day and expect to get a table; tables are especially hard to come by if you want to dine between 7 and 9, or on Friday or Saturday night. At the hottest restaurants reservations need to be made weeks in advance, no matter how connected the concierge at your hotel is. For many of the more popular spots in town, the reservation books open at 9 AM exactly one month before the desired date and close (because all the tables are booked) by noon the same day.

Though it is by no means a guarantee, sometimes just showing up in person at a restaurant that has turned you away on the phone will get you a seat, if you are willing to wait for it. Last-minute cancellations and no-shows unexpectedly free up tables, and if you happen to be in the right place at the right time, one of those tables might be yours.

If you change your mind or your plans, cancel your reservation—it's only courteous, plus some of the busiest places have started to charge up to $25 a head for a no-show (they take a credit card number when you reserve). Many restaurants will ask you to call the day before or the morning of your scheduled meal to reconfirm: remember to do so or you could lose out. If your original time isn't ideal, ask when you confirm if a better one has become available. When you call, double-check that the information listed in these reviews hasn't changed. Credit card acceptance, hours of operation, chefs, and prices are subject to (and often do) change.

Smoking

New York has one of the country's strictest smoking laws: smoking is not allowed in restaurants with fewer than 30 seats, though you may

be able to smoke at the bar or at a table outdoors, if such seating is
available. Call ahead for details. Some restaurants that can't legally allow
smoking will ask if you mind if someone at a nearby table smokes. Don't
be afraid to say it does. There are also restaurants—often small establishments with a European staff and clientele—that ignore the law
altogether and are known as havens for smokers. Many restaurants
have added cigar rooms, and some establishments are devoted solely
to this pastime. Restaurant owners or patrons who break the smoking law are subject to a fine. Call the New York City Department of
Health at 212/442–9666 for information or with complaints.

Tipping

New Yorkers tip big, maybe because they can appreciate what it must
be like to serve people as demanding and impatient as they are all day
long. The rules are simple. Never tip the maître d' unless you're out
to impress your guests or if you expect to pay another visit soon. In
most restaurants, tip the waiter at least 15%–20%. (To figure the
amount quickly, just double the tax noted on the check—it's 8¼% of
your bill—and, if you like, add a little more.) Tip at least $2 per drink
at the bar, and $1 for each coat checked.

Wine

Gone for the most part are the hefty tomes filled with lists of historic
vintages of French Bourdeaux that used to be the norm at the city's
top restaurants. Sommeliers all over the city are focusing on small-pro-
duction, lesser-known wineries. Some are even keeping their wine lists
purposefully small, so that they can change them frequently to match
the season and the menu. Markups vary so much from bottle to bottle, restaurant to restaurant, that you should scan the entire list before
making a selection. Half-bottles are hard to find, but good wines by
the glass are everywhere. If you are intimidated by the selection or the
prices, don't hesitate to ask for recommendations. A well-trained waitstaff will know something about the wines they're serving, and many
restaurants with no sommelier on staff designate special people to
lend a hand.

MANHATTAN RESTAURANTS

Lower Manhattan

New York City grew from the southern tip of Manhattan up, and much
of what makes the city a world capital still transpires on or around
Wall Street. Yet history and commerce haven't produced many great
places to eat in Lower Manhattan. Then Roy Yamaguchi opened one
of his pan-Asian restaurants just off Wall Street and Eberhard Müller
took over the kitchen at Bayard's on Hanover Square. Not much has
changed in the rest of the neighborhood, though. If good, inexpensive
food is what you're looking for, you are better off in nearby Chinatown. And don't forget Tribeca, where an eclectic assortment of restaurants offers food at all price levels.

American

$$$–$$$$ ✕ **Wild Blue.** Decidedly more intimate, more casual, and less touristy
than its sky-high neighbor Windows on the World, this American
restaurant offers a steak house–style menu: simple fare such as grilled
meats, fish, and poultry; sides are à la carte. The view from the 107th
floor is awe-inspiring, as is the wine list, which was inherited from this
space's former incarnation as Cellar in the Sky. Desserts are fun, if a
bit hokey, and service is attentive. ⊠ *1 World Trade Center, 107th floor,
West St. between Liberty and Vesey Sts.,* ☎ *212/524–7107. Reserva-
tions essential. AE, DC, MC, V.*

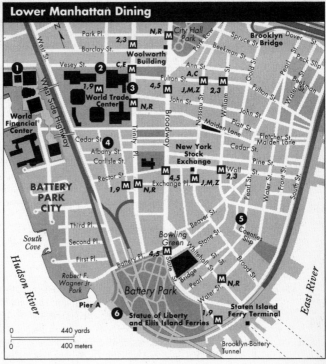

Lower Manhattan Dining

Contemporary

$$$–$$$$ ✕ **Hudson River Club.** Spacious wood-panel rooms with paisley banquettes, spectacular views of the Hudson River and the Statue of Liberty, and a spirited bar with piano music distinguish this World Financial Center restaurant. At lunch the light-filled room teems with expense accounts, at dinner the atmosphere is more romantic. The kitchen celebrates Hudson River Valley produce in seasonal dishes such as roasted wild pheasant with butternut squash puree and grilled salmon with fennel nage (broth). Desserts are strikingly presented. The wine list features regional American varietals. ⊠ *4 World Financial Center, 250 Vesey St., at West St.,* ☎ *212/786–1500. Reservations essential. AE, DC, MC, V. No lunch Sat.*

$$$–$$$$ ✕ **Windows on the World.** This monumental restaurant is part of a complex perched on the 107th floor of One World Trade Center. In the main dining room, panoramic views of Manhattan compete with artwork by Milton Glazer and an interior design that feels at once futuristic and retro. Executive chef Michael Lomonaco turns out updated American fare, such as oak-smoked salmon with buckwheat tortillas, grilled venison chops in cabernet sauce, and poached Maine lobster potpie to an out-of-town crowd more interested in the view than the food. The wine list is exceptional. ⊠ *1 World Trade Center, 107th floor, West St. between Liberty and Vesey Sts.,* ☎ *212/524–7011. Reservations essential. Jacket required. AE, DC, MC, V.*

$$–$$$ ✕ **American Park at the Battery.** Situated on the water with an incredible view of the Statue of Liberty and Ellis Island, this restaurant is part of the revamp of Battery Park. True to the spirit of New York, chef Rad Matmati's menu is more or less American, with flavors borrowed from many cuisines. An outdoor café opens right onto the water. Also outside is an ingenious table for groups of 10–12 that has a hollowed out pool in the middle, where your family-style dinner floats in wooden

dishes. Alas, the setting somehow surpasses the food, but the overall experience doesn't disappoint. ⊠ *Battery Park, opposite 175 State St.,* ☎ *212/809–5508. AE, DC, MC, V. No lunch weekends.*

French

$$$–$$$$ ✕ **Bayard's.** A historic change has happened in the kitchen of this elegant restaurant, located in the building that once housed the India House private merchant's club. Eberhard Müller, a darling of uptown dining (he once manned the stoves at Le Bernardin), suddenly left his post at Lutèce to migrate south. Müller's cooking is as sophisticated as the nautical-theme decor and much more contemporary. Some of the produce comes from his Long Island farm, and it finds itself incorporated into succulent dishes such as crisp snapper with a ragoût of artichoke, carrot, and celery; tender quail on a bed of Savoy cabbage; and rack of lamb with a mustard-honey glaze. The restaurant remains a private club at lunch. At dinner the energy of the room ranges from sedate to somnambulant. If you can't get a reservation for a fine meal anywhere on a Saturday night, remember you can probably get in here. ⊠ *1 Hanover Sq., between Pearl and Stone Sts.,* ☎ *212/514–9454. AE, D, DC, MC, V. Closed Sun. No lunch.*

Italian

$$–$$$ ✕ **Gemelli.** Tony May, who also owns San Domenico, brought authentic Italian cooking downtown at this bright and cheerful Wall Street trattoria. The name is Italian for "twins," but it also denotes the restaurant's signature shape of pasta, a double-rolled noodle served *alla gricia* with onion, pancetta, and pecorino cheese. The food is simple in an Italian way—cured beef with goat cheese, sea bass in clam broth, roasted lamb chops with grilled vegetables. The quality of service depends on how busy the room is. ⊠ *4 World Trade Center, between Church and Day Sts.,* ☎ *212/488–2100. AE, DC, MC, V. No lunch weekends.*

Pan-Asian

$$$ ✕ **Roy's New York.** The light fixtures at the cheery Roy's New York look like huge pineapple slices suspended from the ceiling, appropriate enough considering owner Roy Yamaguchi has almost single-handedly put Hawaiian–Pacific Rim cooking on the world map. This is Yamaguchi's 14th restaurant worldwide, joining other outposts in California, Guam, Tokyo, and—of course—Hawaii. The menu features such appetizers as skewered coconut shrimp with pineapple chili sauce, individual pizzas along the lines of a Chinese-style barbecued chicken pie with fresh avocado & spice sprout salad, and rich entrées such as tender slow-braised char-broiled honey-mustard short ribs of beef. Roy's provides a bit of welcome culinary contrast in its Wall Street neighborhood, where most of the menus tend toward meat and potatoes. ⊠ *130 Washington St., between Albany and Carlisle Sts.,* ☎ *212/266–6262. AE, D, DC, MC, V.*

Little Italy and Chinatown

As Chinatown encroaches from the south, Little Italy keeps getting littler, and from a restaurant standpoint nobody's grieving. Although many of the city's most authentic Asian restaurants are found in the Flushing section of Queens (a handful of entrepreneurs even run sister restaurants in both neighborhoods), Chinatown is still home to some exquisite Asian cooking. Shanghai has replaced Cantonese and Szechuan as the cuisine of choice, but good regional Chinese, Vietnamese, and Thai restaurants are also represented.

Cafés

$ ✕ **Caffe Roma.** Manhattan's most authentic Italian coffeehouse has worn walls, marble tables, and strong, bracing, foamy cappuccino. ⊠ *385 Broome St., at Mulberry St.,* ☎ *212/226–8413. No credit cards.*

$ ✕ **Dragon Land Bakery.** Modern industrial design meets traditional Chinese pastry in this fantastical, steel-lined bakery. Note the live fish and turtles in the bolted, curio-cabinet tables, the pastel-color bubble tea drinks in the refrigerated case, and the wall of delicious, heated buns ⊠ *125 Walker St., at Baxter St.,* ☎ *212/219–2012. Reservations not accepted. No credit cards..*

$ ✕ **Saint's Alp Tea House.** You needn't resist the urge to giggle when you are presented with a frothy, pastel-color drink in which beads of tapioca are teasingly suspended. Bubble tea, as this Hong Kong specialty is called, is goofy, and judging by the hip youth who crowd the cute cafés that serve it, wildly popular. There is even a branch in an NYU dorm in the East Village. Milky black tea with tapioca balls is refreshing and not too sweet, and the balls have the chewy texture of gummy bears. You can also order "pizza" (essentially cheese melted on a slab of white bread) or an assortment of dumplings or sweets to go with your drink. ⊠ *51 Mott St., between Canal and Bayard Sts.,* ☎ *212/766–9889; 39 3rd Ave., between 9th and 10th Sts,* ☎ *212/598–1890. No credit cards.*

Chinese

$$–$$$$ ✕ **Joe's Shanghai.** Joe's Shanghai first opened in Queens, but buoyed by the accolades accorded his steamed soup dumplings—magically filled with a rich, fragrant broth and a pork or pork-and-crabmeat mixture—Joe saw fit to open in Manhattan's Chinatown, and then midtown. At each location there is always a wait, but the line moves fast. Menu highlights include turnip shortcakes and dried bean curd salad to start, and succulent braised pork shoulder, ropey homemade Shanghai noodles, and traditional lion's head—rich pork meatballs braised in brown sauce and embellished with steamed baby bok choy—to follow. Other more familiar Chinese dishes are also excellent. ⊠ *9 Pell St., between Bowery and Mott St.* ☎ *212/233–8888; 24 W. 56th St., between 5th and 6th Aves.,* ☎ *212/333–3868; 136-21 37th St., between Main and Unions Sts., Astoria, Queens,* ☎ *718/539–3838; 82-74 Broadway, between 45th and Whitney Aves., Elmhurst, Queens,* ☎ *718/639–6888. No credit cards.*

$$–$$$ ✕ **Sweet 'n' Tart Restaurant.** When you sit down at a table in this mul-
★ tilevel restaurant, you will be handed four different menus. One lists an extensive selection of dim sum prepared to order; another offers special dishes organized according to principles of Chinese medicine; a third lists more familiar sounding dishes, such as hot-and-sour soup; and the final one lists curative "teas" (more like soups or fruit shakes, really). Don't miss the yam noodle soup with assorted dumplings, the fried rice with taro and Chinese sausage served in a bamboo container, or the panfried chow fun noodles with dried shrimp. The original café, with a more limited menu, is still located up the street (⊠ *76 Mott St., at Canal St.,* ☎ *212/334–8088*). ⊠ *20 Mott St., between Chatham Sq. and Pell St.,* ☎ *212/964–0380. No credit cards.*

$–$$ ✕ **Dim Sum Go Go.** Chinatown is known for cheap, authentic food in bare-bones surroundings. But a growing number of restaurants in the neighborhood are paying attention to design and offering menus that evidence some creativity. One of the most notable examples is this attractive red-and-white spot. Certain menu items are marked with a star, which in most Chinese restaurants means hot and spicy, but here it's an indication of chef Guy Liu's specialties. Nothing on the menu is run-of-the-mill. There are panfried halibut with garlic sauce, quail on baby

Little Italy, Chinatown, TriBeCa, SoHo, and NoLita Dining

SoHo and NoLita

Aquagrill	32	Meigas	30
Balthazar	46	The Mercer Kitchen	42
Blue Ribbon	38	Once Upon a Tart	35
Blue Ribbon Sushi	37	Palačinka	33
Café Habana	50	Pepe Rosso	34
Cendrillon	44	Peasant	51
Eight Mile Creek	52	Quilty's	36
Fanelli	43	Rialto	49
Le Gamin	31	Rice	53
Ghenet	48	Savoy	47
Honmura An	40	Soho Steak	39
Le Pain Quotidien	45	Woo Lae Oak	41

bok choy, and wonderful fresh soy beans served with pickled vegetables. Dim sum comes in several varieties, including pork and vegetable, shrimp with fresh ginger, and chicken in beet dough, all of which are expertly wrapped and steamed to perfection. ⊠ *5 E. Broadway, at Chatham Sq.,* ☏ *212/732–0797. AE, MC, V.*

$–$$ ✕ **Great New York Noodletown.** Lacquered ducks, roasted pork, crunchy baby pig, and soy sauce chicken hang in the window of this clean, no-frills restaurant. Each is superb, especially with the pungent garlic and ginger sauce served on the side. The soups and noodles are unbeatable—try the shrimp dumplings in broth or the panfried noodles with beef. Seasonal specialties such as duck with flowering chives and salt-baked soft-shell crabs are excellent. So is the *congee* (rice porridge), available with any number of garnishes. Solo diners may end up at a communal table, but everyone ends up happy. ⊠ *28½ Bowery, at Bayard St.,* ☏ *212/349–0923. Reservations not accepted. No credit cards.*

$–$$ ✕ **Ping's Seafood.** It was only a matter of time before the personable chef/owner Chuen Ping Hui branched out from his Elmhurst restaurant to open not one, but two Manhattan outposts. Although the original location in Queens still has the most elaborate menu with the most extensive selection of live seafood, the Manhattan locales are more accessible both geographically and gastronomically. Helpful menus have pictures of most of the specialties. Among them are Dungeness crab in black bean sauce, crisp fried tofu, silken braised *e-fu* noodles, and Peking duck. Pricier than some other Chinatown haunts, these restaurants are also a notch above in terms of setting and service. ⊠ *27 Mott St., at Chatham Sq.,* ☏ *212/602–9988; 20 E. Broadway, between Catherine and Market Sts.,* ☏ *212/965–0808; 83-02 Queens Blvd., at Goldsmith St., Elmhurst, Queens,* ☏ *718/396–1238. AE, MC, V.*

$ ✕ **Jing Fong.** Come to this authentic dim sum palace and pretend you're in Hong Kong. On weekend mornings hundreds of people crowd onto the escalator to the second-floor dining room. Chinese women call out in Cantonese while they push carts of dumplings, noodles, tofu, and a few things you might not want to order. The selection always includes *hargow* (steamed shrimp dumplings), *shu mai* (steamed pork dumplings), *chow fun* (wide rice noodles with dried shrimp or beef), sesame balls, and custard tarts. For the adventurous there are chicken feet, tripe, and snails. Depending on when you arrive—earlier is better, service starts at 10 AM—you may also see fresh, sweetened bean curd served from a barrel and deep-fried shrimp with their heads and shells intact. ⊠ *20 Elizabeth St., between Bayard and Canal Sts.,* ☏ *212/964–5256. AE, MC, V.*

Italian

$–$$ ✕ **Benito II.** As at most of the remaining Italian restaurants on this shrinking stretch of Mulberry Street, atmosphere and food are less than top-notch here. But unlike its neighbors (including the separately owned Benito I across the street), Benito II doesn't pretend to be anything but a decent, cheap place to eat. The tomato sauce tastes freshly made and the spaghetti is cooked al dente. What more could you want? For a filling meal try anything *alla Parmesan.* There is no shortage of garlic and the service is always friendly. ⊠ *163 Mulberry St., between Broome and Grand Sts.,* ☏ *212/226–9012. No credit cards.*

Pizza

$–$$ ✕ **Lombardi's.** Brick walls, red-and-white check tablecloths, and the
★   aroma of thin-crust pies emerging from the coal oven set the mood for some of the best pizza in Manhattan. Lombardi's has served pizza since 1905 (though not in the same location), and business has not died down a bit. The mozzarella is always fresh, resulting in an almost greaseless

slice, and the toppings, such as homemade meatballs, pancetta, or imported anchovies, are also top quality. ⊠ *32 Spring St., between Mott and Mulberry Sts.,* ☎ *212/941–7994. No credit cards.*

Thai

$–$$ ✕ **Thailand Restaurant.** It's hard to find a Thai restaurant in New York where everything is top-notch, but this large, popular Chinatown destination has a few terrific dishes. Among them are Penang duck in a fiery red curry sauce enriched with coconut milk and perfumed with opal basil, and shrimp simmered in your choice of red, green, or yellow curries. An order of steamed jasmine rice or sticky rice will help cool things off a little. ⊠ *106 Bayard St., between Baxter and Mulberry Sts.,* ☎ *212/349–3132. AE.*

Vietnamese

$–$$ ✕ **Nha Trang.** You can get a good meal at this inexpensive Vietnamese restaurant if you know how to order, so stick to the dishes you see others eating. Start with a steaming bowl of spicy sweet-and-sour seafood soup (the small order is enough for three or four people) and shrimp grilled on sugarcane. Follow that up with paper-thin pork chops grilled until crisp, and crunchy deep-fried squid served on a bed of shredded lettuce with a tangy dipping sauce. If the line is long, which it usually is, you may be asked to sit at a table with strangers. ⊠ *87 Baxter St., between Bayard and Canal Sts.,* ☎ *212/233–5948. No credit cards.*

$ ✕ **Viet-Nam.** It may be difficult to find the little elbow of a street where this basement dive is located—tell cab drivers to turn right onto Pell Street from Bowery and then left on Doyers—but after one bite of the tasty, cheap, and seductive Vietnamese food you'll remember how to get back. The sweet-and-sour dressing of the green papaya and beef jerky salad is positively addictive, as are the beef cubes with watercress, or anything served in the pungent black bean sauce. Genuinely proud of their food, the staff are extremely helpful, offering advice on what to order, help in how to eat some of the unusual dishes, and clues as to what exotic ingredients make the food so good. ⊠ *11–13 Doyers St., between Bowery and Pell St.,* ☎ *212/693–0725. AE.*

TriBeCa

This once industrial neighborhood now attracts affluent residents seeking spacious lofts. The same warehouselike spaces provide dramatic settings for neighborhood restaurants, many of them destinations for diners from all over the city. At night the streets seem deserted, but walk into any dining room and you'll find crowds of stylish people.

American

$$$–$$$$ ✕ **City Hall.** Chef/owner Henry Meer has created a tasteful New York–theme restaurant, complete with back-lit black-and-white photographs of old New York and an impressive raw seafood bar. The menu tempts with contemporary interpretations of classic urban fare, such as she-crab soup, Delmonico steak, broiled salmon, and grilled calves' liver. You can't help but laugh at the iceberg lettuce–wedge salad served with Russian dressing (which happens to be delicious). Even the warm onion-and-poppy seed rolls are transporting. An Apple Manhattan (bourbon with apple liqueur and chunks of fresh apple) will take the chill off a cold city night. ⊠ *131 Duane St., between Church St. and W. Broadway,* ☎ *212/227–7777. AE, MC, V. Closed Sun.*

American Casual

$–$$ ✕ **Bubby's.** Crowds clamoring for coffee and freshly squeezed juice line up for brunch at this TriBeCa mainstay. The dining room is homey and comfortable with attractive furnishings and plate-glass windows;

in summer, neighbors bring their dogs and sit outside. For breakfast you can order grits, homemade granola, or such entrées as sour cream pancakes and smoked trout with scrambled eggs. Eclectic comfort food—macaroni and cheese, fusilli with wild mushrooms, shepherd's pie—make up the lunch and dinner menus. Be sure to get a piece of homemade pie for dessert. ⊠ *120 Hudson St., at N. Moore St.,* ☎ *212/219–0666. AE, DC, MC, V.*

$–$$ ✕ **Kitchenette.** This small, comfy restaurant lives up to its name. The dining room feels like a neighbor's breakfast nook, and the food tastes like your mom made it—provided she's a great cook. There are no frills, just good, solid cooking, friendly service, and a long line at peak times. For brunch don't miss the pancakes, French toast, and thick-cut bacon. At dinner enjoy the meat loaf, chicken, grits, or mashed potatoes. The homemade pies and cakes are pretty good, too. If you need privacy, be warned that the tables are so close together you're likely to make new friends. ⊠ *80 W. Broadway, at Warren St.,* ☎ *212/267–6740. AE.*

Austrian

$$$$ ✕ **Danube.** This jewel box of a restaurant evokes turn-of-the-20th-century Vienna. The elegant bar is alight with shimmering mosaic swirls, and the diminutive dining room is lined with sparkling Klimt reproductions. To sample the breadth of David Bouley's nouveau Austrian cuisine, try the multicourse dégustation. A signature wine soup with smoked trout crêpes is delicious, as are the braised beef cheeks, which might be served with Zweigelt wine sauce, spaetzle, and ramps. The wine list is notable for hard-to-find Austrian and German labels. The food rises to the heights of the Austrian Alps, but the service still has some climbing to do before it reaches the summit. ⊠ *30 Hudson St., at Duane St.,* ☎ *212/791–3771. Reservations essential. Jacket and tie. AE, D, MC, V. Closed Sun.*

Contemporary

$$–$$$ ✕ **Tribeca Grill.** Anchored by the bar from the old Maxwell's Plum, this cavernous brick-wall restaurant displays art by Robert De Niro Sr., whose movie-actor son is one of restaurateur Drew Nieporent's partners. Chef Don Pintabona oversees the kitchen, but his contemporary American food doesn't seem as important to the nightly crowd of diners as does the prospect of sighting somebody famous. Still, you can eat well if you stick to the simplest dishes. Desserts are rich and satisfying. This is where the warm caramelized banana tart you find on menus around town began, and where, served with chocolate malt ice cream, it is still the best. ⊠ *375 Greenwich St., near Franklin St.,* ☎ *212/941–3900. Reservations essential. AE, DC, MC, V. No lunch Sat.*

French

$$$$ ✕ **Chanterelle.** Soft peach walls, luxuriously spaced tables, towering
★ floral arrangements, and stylish servers set the stage for what is certainly the most understated of New York's fancy French restaurants. Unassuming service complements chef David Waltuck's simple creations. Although the signature seafood sausage, charred on the outside and succulent within, and the Japanese-style raw seafood are both always available, the rest of the prix-fixe menu is dictated by the season. Roger Dagorn, the restaurant's exceptional sommelier, can help find value in the discriminating, beautifully chosen wine list. ⊠ *2 Harrison St., near Hudson St.,* ☎ *212/966–6960. Reservations essential. AE, DC, MC, V. Closed Sun.–Mon. No lunch.*

$$$–$$$$ ✕ **Bouley Bakery.** Under a vaulted red ceiling, fresh flower arrangements grace each table at David Bouley's bakery-cum-restaurant. Gone is the cumbersome table-side bread service, but the waiters' snooty attitude remains. Bouley's devotion to the freshest local produce is evident in the asparagus and peeky-toe crab salad. Unlikely combinations, such as roasted foie gras with green coffee-bean sauce and horseradish-pickled cherries, and salmon with organic vegetables and toasted hazelnut dressing, exemplify his innovative style. ✉ *120 W. Broadway, between Duane and Reade Sts.,* ☎ *212/964–2525. Reservations essential. AE, DC, MC, V.*

$$$–$$$$ ✕ **Montrachet.** Every chef Drew Nieporent selects for this, his first (and one suspects dearest) restaurant, excels. Currently Remi Lauvand offers seasonal three- and six-course menus. If you are lucky, you will be able to choose from the spicy crab salad with avocado and watermelon or the creamy oysters in champagne sauce to start, and follow them up with a truffle-crusted salmon or roasted veal chop with artichokes, mushrooms, and scallion mashed potatoes. Pastel walls, plush mauve banquettes, engaging works of art, and the occasional line cook traversing the dining room to the inconvenient walk-in refrigerator, set an unpretentious tone. The distinguished wine list emphasizes diminutive regional vineyards. ✉ *239 W. Broadway, between Walker and White Sts.,* ☎ *212/219–2777. Reservations essential. AE. Closed Sun. No lunch Mon.–Thurs. or Sat.*

$–$$$ ✕ **Odeon.** New York trendsetters change hangouts faster than they can press speed-dial on their cell phones, but this spot has managed to maintain its quality and style for 20 years and counting. Even with the buzz at Keith McNally's other hot spots, Balthazar and Pastis, the room is still packed nightly with chic revelers. Somehow, the neon lighting, the vinyl banquettes, and the Formica tables that comprise the neo–art deco setting don't seem dated. And the pleasant service, relatively low prices, and well-chosen wine list are always in style. The bistro menu highlights include meaty crab cakes, a hearty cassoulet, oversize goat cheese ravioli, and a generous serving of steak frites. ✉ *145 W. Broadway, at Thomas St.,* ☎ *212/233–0507. Reservations essential. AE, DC, MC, V.*

Japanese

$$$–$$$$ ✕ **Nobu.** A curved wall of river-worn black pebbles, a hand-painted
★ beech floor, bare wood tables, and birch trees set the stage for Nobu Matsuhisa's dramatic, contemporary Japanese-inspired food. The vast menu makes deciding what direction to take difficult (and unfortunately the impatient waitstaff don't seem to want to help). One road will take you to classic Japanese sushi and sashimi, among the best in town. Another leads you to contemporary dishes, such as the defyingly delicious seared black cod with sweet miso, or Peruvian-style sashimi. You are probably best off putting yourself in the hands of the chef by ordering the *omikase*—you specify how much you want to spend (the minimum is $80 per person) and the kitchen does the rest. Sake is the drink of choice, but there is also a serious wine list. To handle the overflow, restaurateur Drew Nieporent opened **Next Door Nobu** (☎ 212/334–4445), where diners can enjoy a slightly less-expensive menu on a first-come, first-served basis. ✉ *105 Hudson St., off Franklin St.,* ☎ *212/219–0500; 212/219–8095 for same-day reservations. Reservations essential. AE, DC, MC, V. Closed Sun. No lunch.*

Mediterranean

$$ ✕ **Spartina.** The bright, seasonal cooking of chef/owner Stephen Kalt evokes the sunny warmth of the Mediterranean. An emphasis on the food of Catalonia and the Basque country accounts for some of the more hearty and fragrant dishes, such as trout à la Basquaise, with a chunky sauce of celery, leeks, clams, and clam juice. Depending on the season, oversize pizzas may be topped with ricotta and white truffle oil or pumpkin and duck confit. For meat eaters the selections are equally satisfying. Spartina is one of the few TriBeCa restaurants that is both a serious dining destination and a friendly neighborhood hangout.

✉ *355 Greenwich St., at Harrison St.,* ☎ *212/274–9310. Reservations essential. AE, DC, MC, V. No lunch weekends.*

Steak

$$–$$$ ✕ **Dylan Prime.** The former home of City Wine & Cigar Co.—which was all dark wood and dim lighting—has been feminized to include plush booths, pale wood, and dainty floral arrangements. Dry-aged filet mignon is offered in 7- or 11-ounce portions, rib eye comes in 12- or 16-ounce slabs—the owners knew better than to dub them "his" and "hers." Sides, such as mascarpone pumpkin risotto and sautéed wild greens, are called "Accessories," and toppings for meat, such as Maytag blue cheese, are referred to as "Chapeaux." There are other options, such as salmon, veal, tuna, and lobster—also available with fashionable "hats." Adjacent to the restaurant is a bar/lounge that serves such sharable appetizers as Appenzeller and Gruyère fondue, scallop ceviche, and mini beef Wellingtons. ✉ *62 Laight St., at Greenwich St.,* ☎ *212/334–2274. AE, DC, MC, V. No lunch weekends.*

SoHo and NoLita

Many of the galleries and artists that made SoHo famous have been replaced by chain stores and tourists who swarm the sidewalks on weekends, but the eating is still good and the prices surprisingly reasonable. NoLita (North of Little Italy), the trendy next-door neighborhood of small shops and restaurants, is reminiscent of a bygone SoHo, with fresh new eateries popping up every month. Expect beautiful crowds dressed in black and service that is refreshingly unpretentious given the clientele.

American

$$ ✕ **Rialto.** The shabby-chic dining room with pressed-tin walls, plain wooden chairs, and burgundy banquettes provides a backdrop for the attractive crowd that makes this place pulsate with energy. The food is interesting without being fussy, well suited to the noisy space where people-watching can often distract you from your plate. But those who like to eat will have no trouble focusing on such dishes as marinated yellowfin tuna with Asian-spiced fries, roasted garlic soup, and a generous pork chop. The hamburger's pretty good, too. The lovely back garden is a great spot for summer dining. ✉ *26 Elizabeth St., between Houston and Prince Sts.,* ☎ *212/334–7900. AE, MC, V.*

American Casual

$ ✕ **Fanelli.** In a neighborhood that constantly morphs according to the whims of fashion and commercialism, Fanelli is refreshingly stable. Housed in a building erected in 1857, when the area was known more for upscale brothels than European designer boutiques, it is one of the most popular bar-restaurants in the city. The menu is unpretentious and serviceable, with burgers, sandwiches, omelettes, and pastas at reasonable prices. And the gorgeously time-worn original bar serves good draft beer to clamoring customers who can do without bizarre cocktails. ✉ *94 Prince St., at Mercer St.,* ☎ *212/226–9412. AE, MC, V.*

Cafés

$ ✕ **Le Gamin.** It's easy to confuse New York for Paris at these hip little havens, where the menu includes all the French café standards: croque monsieur, quiche Lorraine, salade Niçoise, crêpes (both sweet and savory), and big bowls of café au lait. Service can be desultory, but the upside is that you're free to lounge for hours. ✉ *50 MacDougal St., between Houston and Prince Sts.,* ☎ *212/254–4678; 536 E. 5th St., between Aves. A and B,* ☎ *212/254–8409; 183 9th Ave., at 21st St.,* ☎ *212/243–8864.*

$ ✕ **Once Upon a Tart.** Delicious baked goods unite this two-sided venture (one side "to stay," the other "to go"). The sandwich/salad/soup offerings satisfy, but you should definitely indulge in the unusual scones (cheddar-dill, apricot); cornmeal-almond biscotti; and, of course, the toothsome tarts. ⊠ *135 Sullivan St., between Houston and Prince Sts.,* ☎ *212/387–8869.*

Contemporary

$$–$$$ ✕ **Mercer Kitchen.** One of New York's premier chefs, Jean-Georges Vongerichten, runs this downtown outpost in the basement of the achingly hip Mercer Hotel. The sleek, modern, industrial space is warm and comfortable, and the room sizzles with the energy of the downtown elite. The menu of dishes (more casual than at Vongerichten's other eateries) is grouped according to which section of the kitchen prepares them. Dinner might include black sea bass carpaccio with lime juice, coriander, and mint (from the raw bar); Alsatian tarte flambé with fromage blanc, onions, and bacon (from the pizza oven); or roasted lobster with tagliatelle pasta and red wine sauce (from the rotisserie). ⊠ *The Mercer Hotel, 99 Prince St., at Mercer St.,* ☎ *212/966–5454. Reservations essential. AE, DC, MC, V. No dinner Sun.*

$$–$$$ ✕ **Quilty's.** One of the city's few star women chefs, Katy Sparks has built a reputation for her unique brand of American cooking that is at once intriguingly innovative and satisfyingly familiar. Squash soup with foie gras–stuffed seckel pears, and East Coast oysters in gewürztraminer cream, are representative starters. Pancetta-wrapped monkfish with braised cabbage and ginger fumet speaks to her flare with entrées. The restaurant has a comfortable, American atmosphere that feels more like New England than SoHo. Lunch offers better value and a quieter setting than dinner. ⊠ *177 Prince St., between Sullivan and Thompson Sts.,* ☎ *212/254–1260. Reservations essential. AE, DC, MC, V. No lunch Mon.*

$$–$$$ ✕ **Savoy.** Chef-owner Peter Hoffman serves an eclectic mix of dishes inspired by the Mediterranean in this cozy restaurant on a quiet cobblestone corner. A bronze wire-mesh ceiling, arched wood accents, and blazing fireplace lend the downstairs space a country feel, the perfect setting for such down-to-earth dishes as baby chicken with Moroccan sausage or penne with rabbit. Upstairs, the original tin ceiling, artwork, and open hearth are the backdrop for an expensive nightly prix-fixe menu, which includes a special grilled dish (cooked in the dining room hearth). The wine list emphasizes small producers. ⊠ *70 Prince St., at Crosby St.,* ☎ *212/219–8570. Reservations essential. AE.*

Eclectic

$$–$$$ ✕ **Blue Ribbon.** Open for dinner from 4 PM until 4 AM, Bruce and Eric
★ Bromberg's small American bistro is a popular hangout for off-duty chefs and other night crawlers, and it is common to have to wait for a table even at three in the morning. The staff has a knack of making everyone feel like a regular, and in fact most of the patrons are. There is a raw bar in front with terrifically fresh oysters and other seasonal delicacies from the sea. The something-for-everyone menu offers dishes from around the world—excellent sautéed sweetbreads, a towering pupu platter, a duck club sandwich, and matzoh ball soup. ⊠ *97 Sullivan St., between Prince and Spring Sts.,* ☎ *212/274–0404. Reservations essential. AE, MC, V. Closed Mon. No lunch.*

$ ✕ **Palačinka.** The delicate, buttery smell of warm crêpes wafts from the tiny open kitchen—really just a griddle top—at this quaint crêperie that's perfect for a leisurely breakfast, lunch, or afternoon snack. The decor is a pleasing hodgepodge of vintage objects: tin ceilings, small metal tables, and folding chairs. There are savory and sweet crêpes, as well as simple French sandwiches and salads. Savory fillings include roasted tarragon chicken with goat cheese and roasted peppers, or ham, Gruyère, and egg, and each comes with a pile of lightly dressed greens.

The sweet crêpes range from the classic butter and sugar to a rich concoction of chestnut cream and crème fraîche. Add a huge cup of frothy hot chocolate and you might never want to leave. ⊠ *28 Grand St., between 6th Ave. and Thompson St.,* ☎ *212/625–0362. No credit cards.*

$ ✕ **Rice.** All meals are built on a bowl of rice at this dark, cozy storefront where you can sit on chairs or bar stools while you dine at small tables. Choose from an array of rice varieties, such as basmati, brown, Thai black, or Bhutanese red, and create a meal by adding a savory topping such as Jamaican jerk chicken wings, warm lentil stew, or Indian chicken curry. The fresh, well-seasoned, budget-price menu affords a satisfying mix of multicultural cuisine and comfort food. ⊠ *227 Mott St., between Prince and Spring Sts.,* ☎ *212/226–5775. Reservations not accepted. No credit cards.*

Ethiopian

$ ✕ **Ghenet.** A rotating exhibit of local, African-inspired art hangs on
★ the walls of this welcoming Ethiopian restaurant where the food is authentic and delicious. By ordering one of the combination platters you can sample a variety of dishes, mounded on a platter lined with spongy *injera* flat bread. Use the bread to scoop the food to your mouth (no utensils are offered); servers will bring more while you eat. In addition to the tasty poultry and meat options, there's a good selection of vegetarian dishes such as rich and fragrant collard greens with Ethiopian spices, fiery potatoes and cabbage, and carrots in an onion sauce. The staff has even made an effort to match the food with wine and gives suggested pairings for each dish. ⊠ *284 Mulberry St., between Houston and Prince Sts.,* ☎ *212/343–1888. AE, MC, V. Closed Mon.*

French

$$–$$$ ✕ **Balthazar.** When he opened this celebrity-friendly spot, restaurant
★ impresario Keith McNally, of Odeon and Pastis fame, went to extraordinary lengths to re-create the look and feel of a Parisian brasserie. Balthazar is still going strong and it may be difficult to get a reservation at a normal dinnertime, but they will seat you until 1:30 AM. Nightly specials are based on classic French dishes; Tuesday it's *choucroute garni* (veal and garlic sausages, smoked meats, sauerkraut, and juniper simmered in white Alsatian wine). The roast chicken for two is hard to beat. Wonderful bread is baked in the restaurant's own bakery; you can buy some at the tiny shop next door. Prices are not exorbitant by today's standards, the wine list is fair, and average (read: not famous) diners are treated quite well. ⊠ *80 Spring St., between Broadway and Crosby St.,* ☎ *212/965–1414. Reservations essential. AE, DC, MC, V.*

$$ ✕ **Soho Steak.** The name suggests huge sides of beef in a manly room, but Soho Steak is really a French bistro offering a creative, mostly meat menu at reasonable prices. Throngs of fashionable French types crowd into the small dining room with tables that are so close together they might as well be communal. They come for the well-prepared food, such as a braised oxtail raviolo (a single ravioli), double-cut pork chops from the wood-burning oven, or filet mignon with potato Roquefort *galette,* spinach, and foie gras mousse. There are a couple of selections from the sea for non-carnivores, as well as a pleasant weekend brunch. ⊠ *90 Thompson St., between Prince and Spring Sts.,* ☎ *212/ 226–0602. No credit cards.*

Italian

$$ ✕ **Peasant.** Though the name suggests otherwise, the crowd at the rustic-yet-hip restaurant is stylishly urban. Most of Frank DeCarlo's menu is prepared in a bank of wood-burning ovens, from which the heady aroma of garlic perfumes the room. The ovens also serve as the focal

point of the dining room. Sizzling cuttlefish arrive at the table in the terra-cotta pots in which they were baked. Rotisserie lamb is redolent with the scent of fresh herbs. ✉ *194 Elizabeth St., between Spring and Prince Sts.,* ☎ *212/965–9511. Reservations essential. AE, MC, V.*

Japanese

$$–$$$$ ✕ **Blue Ribbon Sushi.** Though the sushi is pricier than at some of the popular Japanese restaurants in the neighborhood, they can't compete with this narrow, wood-lined restaurant for freshness, creativity, or atmosphere. Owned by the same people who own Blue Ribbon and Blue Ribbon Bakery, Blue Ribbon Sushi is also open late and has a fun, downtown vibe. A decent sake selection is served in traditional wooden boxes. ✉ *119 Sullivan St., between Prince and Spring Sts.,* ☎ *212/343–0404. AE, MC, V. Closed Mon. No lunch.*

$–$$ ✕ **Honmura An.** As you ascend the staircase into this serene, teak-lined space, you will find no sushi bar, no teppanyaki grill: only the noodle, soba. It is made in full view by a master who works in a glass-enclosed cube at the back of the dining room. Like the best restaurants in Tokyo, where the original Honmura An still operates, this one focuses on doing one thing well. The true test of quality is the cold soba, served on square trays with a dipping sauce and a ladle full of cooking water you are expected to slurp as you eat. But everything on the menu is exquisite, from the tiny dumplings and stuffed tofu appetizers to the steaming bowls of soba, udon, and other fresh noodles served in broth. Service is efficient and reserved. ✉ *170 Mercer St., between Houston and Prince Sts.,* ☎ *212/334–5253. AE, D, DC, MC, V.*

Korean

$$–$$$ ✕ **Woo Lae Oak.** Little Korea meets SoHo head-on at this chic eatery ★ where patrons order traditional Korean dishes and tabletop barbecue. The food is spicy and flavorful: kimchee burns the lips and prepares the palate for such dishes as *jang au gui* (broiled eel served sizzling on a hot stone), a wonderful Korean version of steak tartare, sweet black cod simmered in a rich soy broth, or the *bul go gi*—slices of beef grilled at the table. The food tastes like Seoul, but the ambiance is firmly grounded in SoHo. Tables are dark marble slabs, the lighting is romantically low, and attractive servers are dressed head to toe in black. ✉ *148 Mercer St., between Prince and Houston Sts.,* ☎ *212/925–8200. AE, DC, MC, V.*

Latin

$ ✕ **Café Habana.** When they opened this small Latin-theme restaurant the owners, who also operate Rialto down the block, wanted it to remain the neighborhood hangout the previous occupants had managed to create. The simple Cuban/Latin menu reflects the friendly, casual atmosphere: Cubano sandwiches, rice and beans, and *camarones al ajillo* (shrimp in garlic sauce), all at budget prices. True to their vision, the cheery space with blue booths and pale green Formica tables fills with locals eating breakfast in the afternoon, chatting with the waitresses, and humming along to Latin beats. ✉ *17 Prince Sts.,* ☎ *212/625–2001.*

Modern Australian

$$ ✕ **Eight Mile Creek.** The non-descript storefront entrance of this restaurant belies the fact that it is New York's first, and so far only, serious Australian restaurant. Didn't know Australian was a cuisine? Well grab a table in the narrow, dimly lit dining room and dig into yabbies (crawfish that are served with perfect lemony risotto), emu (appealingly gamy served as a carpaccio doused with truffle oil), or just a simple salad of kangaroo. Though Australia has been stereotyped as—how shall we put it—unsophisticated, Eight Mile Creek is doing all they can to change that image. The wine list—all Australian with a couple of ex-

cellent New Zealand whites thrown in for good measure—showcases
the best of what Australia has to offer, with a number of hard-to-find
boutique bottlings readily available. A less expensive bar menu is
served in the lounge downstairs. ✉ *240 Mulberry St., between Prince
and Spring Sts.,* ☎ *212/431–4635. AE, D, DC, MC, V. Closed Mon.
No lunch.*

Philippine

$$ ✕ **Cendrillon Asian Grill and Marienda Bar.** Cendrillon means Cinderella
in French, so the slipper-shape bar here is "fitting." Delicate inlay de-
signs ornament the redbrick dining room's wood tables. Don't miss
the spring rolls, Asian barbecue (duck, spareribs, and chicken), black
rice salad, or adobo—the national dish of the Philippines, prepared here
with quail and rabbit in the traditional vinegar and garlic sauce. ✉ *45
Mercer St., between Broome and Grand Sts.,* ☎ *212/343–9012. AE,
DC, MC, V. Closed Sun.*

Seafood

$$–$$$ ✕ **Aquagrill.** For an island at the edge of the Atlantic Ocean, Manhattan
has surprisingly few good seafood restaurants, especially downtown.
But Aquagrill has a friendly staff, comfortable decor, and an extensive
menu that places it among the best. Chef/owner Jeremy Marshall mans
the stove, while his wife, Jennifer, works the host stand. Specialties in-
clude tiny pillows of garlic-drenched escargot baked in homemade puff
pastry and falafel-crusted salmon served on hummus with tomato and
cucumber. Then there's a vast selection of oysters on the half shell and
many types of grilled fresh fish. Of the desserts, don't miss the skillet
cake or the pink grapefruit gratin. ✉ *210 Spring St., at 6th Ave.,* ☎
212/274–0505. Reservations essential. AE, DC, MC. Closed Mon.

Spanish

$$–$$$ ✕ **Meigas.** It's been said that Luis Bollo, chef of this nuevo Spanish
restaurant, will do for Spanish cooking in America what chefs like Daniel
Boulud and Jean-Georges Vongerichten have done for French. It's a
pity he has to do it in such an uninspired setting. Bollo's food is highly
conceptualized but grounded in Spanish tradition: A better squid in
black ink sauce would be difficult to find. Suckling pig is superb.
Braised oxtail croquettes are heady and satisfying. A chilled octopus
terrine forms a beautiful mosaic on the plate. But some dishes, par-
ticularly desserts, fall flat on their abstract face. (Beware of the herb
foam.) And don't expect a lively scene–a kitsch mural of a sorcerer
(*meigas* in Spanish) painted without any irony and an energy-zapping
atmosphere give the restaurant an inexplicably sedate feeling, even when
it's packed. ✉ *250 Hudson St., at King St.,* ☎ *212/627–5800. Reser-
vations essential. AE, MC, V. Closed Sun. No lunch.*

Greenwich Village

One of the most difficult Manhattan neighborhoods to navigate, Green-
wich Village has enchanted many a tourist (and frustrated many a cab
driver). Only in recent years has the local food risen to match the charm
of the environment. Cornelia Street has become a mini Restaurant Row,
and tiny alcoves around the neighborhood are being transformed into
serious eateries. To the far west, the Meatpacking District—where you
can still see people carting around sides of beef—has blossomed into
one of the most chic restaurant destinations in town.

American

$$ ✕ **Home.** In this sliver of a storefront restaurant, owners David Page
and Barbara Shinn encourage you to make yourself at home. Page cooks

FOR THE KIDS

WHEN MANY PEOPLE think New York dining they think white tablecloths and high prices or slick minimalism and, well . . . high prices. Classic or trendy, many Manhattan restaurants are not exactly child-friendly, or friendly to your wallet if you are feeding a crew. But there are plenty of dining options to keep the younger set happily full.

Lower Manhattan: The South Street Seaport has a variety of family dining options, from fresh fish to food court, in its Pier 17 (South St. at Fulton St., ☎ 212/732–7678).

Chinatown: Any of the restaurants in Chinatown are good for children. If they (or you) are clamoring for a snack, stop by the Chinatown Ice Cream Factory (✉ 65 Bayard St., between Mott and Elizabeth Sts., ☎ 212/608–4170), which has such exotic flavors as lychee and ginger.

SoHo and NoLita: Introduce the kids to French food in Le Jardin Bistro's (25 Cleveland Pl., between Kenmare and Spring Sts., ☎ 212/343–9599) casual NoLita garden.

Greenwich Village: For a quick sugar fix, Cones (✉ 272 Bleecker St., between 6th and 7th Aves., ☎ 212/414–1795) offers European–style gelato in traditional flavors. Cowgirl Hall of Fame (✉ 519 Hudson St., at 10th St., ☎ 212/633–1133) serves corn dogs and Frito pie (a slit-open bag of corn chips drowned with spicy chili) in a kitschy dining room that feels like a garage sale in Texas circa 1948. Peanut Butter & Co. (✉ 240 Sullivan St., between Bleecker and W. 3rd Sts., ☎ 212/677–3995) has gussied up school lunch with more than 10 varieties of peanut butter sandwiches, all served with carrot sticks and potato chips.

East Village and Lower East Side: If the kids want a snack, head to Pommes Frites (✉ 123 2nd Ave., between 7th St. and St. Marks Pl., ☎ 212/674–1234), a tiny kiosk spawned by the Belgian boom; the fabulous fries come with a choice of wild toppings.

Murray Hill, Flatiron District, and Gramercy: The roadhouselike Chat 'n Chew (✉ 10 E. 16th St., between 5th Ave. and Union Sq. W, ☎ 212/243–1616) serves huge portions of such American comfort food as macaroni and cheese, meat loaf, and overstuffed BLT's.

Chelsea: If you've managed to introduce your kids to art in Chelsea's galleries, reward them with a juicy burger at the old-fashioned, stainless steel Empire Diner (210 10th Ave., at 22nd St., ☎ 212/243–2736.

Midtown West: Sports fans and their little sluggers deserve a trip to ESPN Zone (✉ 1472 Broadway, at 42nd St., ☎ 212/921–3776) a jock's paradise with huge TVs, sports paraphernalia, and stadiumlike food. Jekyll & Hyde (✉ 1409 6th Ave., between 57th and 58th Sts., ☎ 212/541–9505), a macabre multilevel fantasy world of trick doors, animated skeletons, and so-so food will appeal to the budding Stephen Kings in your brood (and you'll appreciate the extensive beer list). At Mars 2112 (✉ 1633 Broadway, at 51st St., ☎ 212/582–2112), take the kids on a five-minute spaceship ride to Mars (be warned the ride is a bit bumpy) and tuck into decent food served up by Martian waitstaff.

Midtown East: For a sweet snack take the little ones to Buttercup Bake Shop (✉ 973 2nd Ave., between 51st and 52nd Sts., ☎ 212/350–4144) for luscious, colorful cupcakes with thick, yummy frosting. The dining concourse at Grand Central Terminal (✉ 42nd St. at Lexington Ave.), which includes the Oyster Bar and Two Boots (☎ 212/557–7992), will please hungry children who won't sit still for the neighborhood's more formal dining.

Upper East Side: If you've got the kids in tow, take a break for grilled cheese at Barking Dog Luncheonette (✉ 1678 3rd Ave., at 94th St., ☎ 212/831–1800). Children will also love E.J.'s Luncheonette (✉ 1271 3rd Ave., at 73rd St., ☎ 212/472–0600) for salads, sandwiches, chicken, and other goodies.

Upper West Side and Harlem: Jackson Hole (✉ 517 Columbus Ave., at 85th St., ☎ 212/362–5177) is known for huge, juicy hamburgers with a multitude of topping choices. For a big, chewy chocolate cookie, head to Levain (✉ 167 W. 74th St., between Amsterdam and Columbus Aves., ☎ 212/874–6080).

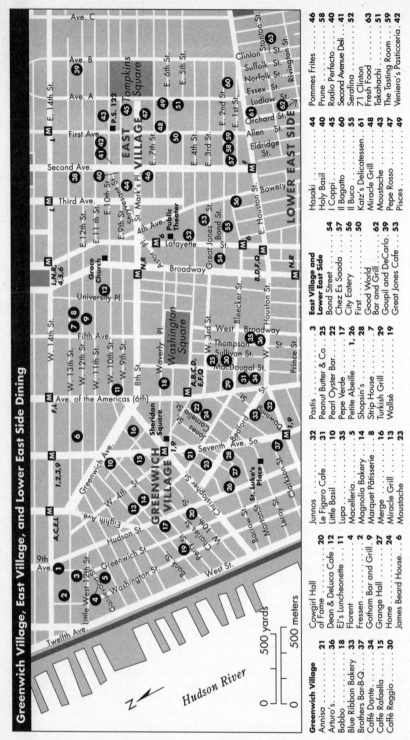

Greenwich Village, East Village, and Lower East Side Dining

Greenwich Village

Annisa	21
Arturo's	36
Babbo	18
Blue Ribbon Bakery	33
Brothers Bar-B-Q.	37
Caffé Dante	34
Caffé Rafaella	15
Caffé Reggio	30
Cowgirl Hall of Fame	20
Dean & Deluca Cafe	12
EJ's Luncheonette	11
Florent	4
Fressen	2
Gotham Bar and Grill	9
Grange Hall	15
Home	24
James Beard House	30
Junno's	32
Le Figaro Cafe	31
Little Basil	10
Lupa	35
Macelleria	5
Magnolia Bakery	14
Marquet Pâtisserie	8
Merge	16
Miracle Grill	24
Moustache	23
Pastis	3
Peanut Butter & Co.	25
Pearl Oyster Bar.	22
Pepe Verde	17
Petite Abeille	1, 26
Shopsin's	28
Strip House	7
Turkish Grill	29
Wallsé	19

East Village and Lower East Side

Bond Street	54
Chez Es Saada	57
City Eatery	56
First	50
Good World Bar and Grill	62
Goupil and DeCarlo.	39
Great Jones Cafe	53
Hasaki	44
Holy Basil	40
I Coppi	45
Il Bagatto	60
Il Buco	55
Katz's Delicatessen	61
Miracle Grill	48
Moustache	43
Pepe Rosso	47
Pisces	49
Pommes Frites	46
Prune	58
Radio Perfecto	40
Second Avenue Deli	41
Serafina	52
71 Clinton Fresh Food	63
Takahachi	51
The Tasting Room	59
Veniero's Pasticceria	42

with authority and honesty, utilizing recipes from his Midwestern background. Check out the blue cheese fondue with caramelized shallots and rosemary toast, the oyster stew studded with pieces of bacon, the moist roast chicken, and the juicy pork chop stuffed with apple and thyme and served with braised red cabbage and mashed sweet potato. The creamy chocolate pudding and homemade cookies won't disappoint. Home also offers an interesting wine list, highlighting American varietals, and serves brunch on weekends. ⊠ *20 Cornelia St., between Bleecker and W. 4th Sts.,* ☎ *212/243–9579. Reservations essential. AE. Closed Mon.*

$$ ✗ **Merge.** Chef/owner Sam DeMarco, of First and District, has created an amusing menu of the modern American comfort food he's become known for. Everything from fiery chicken wings to sophisticated salmon to camp-style s'mores are served with elegance and humor in generous portions. The flavors are bold and the service is friendly. Sunday night the format changes, and the restaurant serves an old-fashioned, family-style, prix-fixe Italian American menu in honor of the hit HBO series *The Sopranos.*⊠ *142 W. 10th St., between Greenwich Ave. and Waverly Pl.,* ☎ *212/691–7757. AE. No lunch weekdays.*

$–$$ ✗ **Grange Hall.** Updated all-American cuisine, affordable prices, a friendly bar, and a room that alludes to the W.P.A. style of architecture attract a lively local bar crowd nightly to this former speakeasy on one of Greenwich Village's most charming, tucked-away streets. Order one of the small plates, such as potato pancakes with chive-spiked sour cream, for starters or make an entire meal by ordering several of the sides. Entrées—including the center-cut cranberry-glazed pork chops and grilled salmon—may be ordered by themselves or with a choice of soup or salad for a couple of dollars more. Excellent iced devil's food cake is a dessert staple. ⊠ *50 Commerce St., at Barrow St.,* ☎ *212/924–5246. Reservations essential. AE.*

Austrian

$$$ ✗ **Wallsé.** For many, Kurt Gutenbrunner's modern Austrian menu at this comfortable, neighborhoody restaurant is everything David Bouley's at Danube is not: rich, soulful, and satisfying, with a strong emphasis on Austrian tradition and an urban New York attitude. It's hard to argue with such dishes as smoked trout and eel salad, herbed spaetzle with braised rabbit, weiner schnitzel, and *rostbraten*—roasted beef in a delicate brown sauce—with kohlrabi gratin, each prepared with a light hand and beautifully presented. Forget the veal goulash, but order at least one portion of the quark dumplings–steaming hot puffs of an ethereal dough served with buttered bread crumbs and fruit compote. And don't be embarrassed to order a second; you wouldn't be the first to do so. The Austrian-heavy wine selections complement the menu. ⊠ *344 W. 11th St., at Washington St.,* ☎ *212/352–2300. Reservations essential. AE, MC, V. No lunch.*

Barbecue

$–$$ ✗ **Brothers Bar-B-Q.** This barnlike space has a lounge decorated in the style of the American South circa 1949, with hair dryers; tacky period plastic furniture; signs from Texaco, Esso, and Shell; even a garage door. Sample the puffy hush puppies with hot sauce, smoked sausage over black-eyed peas, fried wings and smoked rib tips in bourbon sauce, shrimp po' boy sandwiches, and terrific chicken and ribs. Several combination plates allow you to try a variety of barbecued meats. There's a wide selection of tequila shots, plus 11 bottled beers and seven beers on tap. ⊠ *225 Varick St., at Clarkston St.,* ☎ *212/727–2775. AE.*

Belgian

$-$$ ✕ **Petite Abeille.** There are only seven small tables in the original
★   closet-size Hudson Street storefront, which remains the most inviting
outpost of an expanding chain of Belgian bistros. The menu tempts
with salads, frites, sandwiches, omelettes, poached salmon, and other
light fare for early in the day, and sausages, *stoemp* (mashed sweet potatoes and veggies), steak, stew, and mussels later on. Two styles of waffles are always available, *de Bruxelles* (made fresh to order and topped
with ice cream, whipped cream, and fresh fruit) and *de Liège* (imported
from Belgium and reheated until the subtle caramelized sugar coating
crunches and melts in your mouth). ✉ *466 Hudson St., at Barrow St.,*
☎ *212/741–6479; 400 W. 14th St., at 9th Ave.,* ☎ *212/727–1505; 107
W. 18th St., between 6th and 7th Aves.,* ☎ *212/604–9350; 134 W. Broadway, between Duane and Reade Sts.,* ☎ *212/791–1360. AE, MC, V.*

Cafés

$ ✕ **Caffè Dante.** A longtime Village haunt, this convivial spot has su-
perlative espresso and knockout tiramisu. The regulars here have been
coming for years. ✉ *79–81 MacDougal St., between Houston and
Bleecker Sts.,* ☎ *212/982–5275.*

$ ✕ **Caffe Rafaella.** Parchment-paper lamp shades adorned with fluttering
red fringe, variously hued marble-top tables, and an antiques-store assortment of chairs make this one of the homiest Old World cafés anywhere in the city. ✉ *134 7th Ave. S, between 10th and Charles Sts.,*
☎ *212/929–7247.*

$ ✕ **Caffè Reggio.** In the neighborhood's oldest coffeehouse, where a huge
antique espresso machine gleams in the gloom, the tiny tables are
really close together, perfect for eavesdropping. One of the paintings
is an original from the school of Caravaggio. ✉ *119 MacDougal St.,
between 3rd and Bleecker Sts.,* ☎ *212/475–9557.*

$ ✕ **Dean & DeLuca.** Known for gourmet goodies, this small local chain
is a spin-off of the SoHo gourmet market. Think fast as the line snakes
past the gingerbread, cakes, cookies, sandwiches, and salads. ✉ *75 University Pl., at 11th St.,* ☎ *212/473–1908; 1 Rockefeller Plaza, at 49th
St.,* ☎ *212/664–1363; 235 W. 46th St., between Broadway and 8th
Ave., in the Paramount Hotel,* ☎ *212/869–6890.*

$ ✕ **Le Figaro Cafe.** A major beat hangout long ago, Le Figaro today at-
tracts herds of tourists and students, but during off-hours it can be quiet
enough to read Kerouac. Sadly, the live jazz has been usurped by twice-
a-week karaoke nights. ✉ *184 Bleecker St., at MacDougal St.,* ☎ *212/
677–1100.*

$ ✕ **Magnolia Bakery.** Sky-high homestyle cakes, cupcakes, puddings,
★   and pies keep this adorable bakery packed into the wee hours. They
will even serve you a glass of milk to wash it all down. A second location, called the **Buttercup Bake Shop** (✉ *973 2nd Ave., between 51st
and 52nd Sts.,* ☎ *212/350–4144), is in Midtown. ✉ *401 Bleecker St.,
at 11th St.,* ☎ *212/462–2572.*

$ ✕ **Marquet Pâtisserie.** At this friendly café you can savor a crisp
palmier cookie and a café au lait served in a bowl; the menu also includes inventive salads, thick sandwiches, and soups. ✉ *15 E. 12th St.,
between 5th Ave. and University Pl.,* ☎ *212/229–9313.*

Contemporary

$$$–$$$$ ✕ **Gotham Bar & Grill.** Celebrated chef Alfred Portale virtually invented
an art form with his towering architectural presentations. The secret
to their success is that they are built on a foundation of simple, clean
flavors. Chilled seafood salad is a light and refreshing way to start; the
rack of lamb is always reliable. The Gotham chocolate cake, served
with toasted-almond ice cream, should not be overlooked. Gotham's
loftlike space was *the* prototype for New York restaurants in the go-

go 1980s, and lo these many years later you can't help but enjoy the retro, power-dining feel. Solo diners at the bar are treated to a special place setting that makes it a pleasure to dine alone. Also, a prix-fixe lunch special is almost too good to be true. ⊠ *12 E. 12th St., between 5th Ave. and University Pl., ☎ 212/620–4020. Reservations essential. AE, DC, MC, V. No lunch weekends.*

$$–$$$ ✕ **Annisa.** Anita Lo and her partner Jennifer Schism have transformed this once dreary space into a bright, elegant restaurant. They built a platform to elevate the dining room and back-lit a wall of white sheer curtains to create a soft airiness. Lo's food is similarly light and creative. The menu is modern French, though Asian influences poke through. Soft-shell crab on a corn and sea urchin salad and falafel-stuffed squash blossoms are tempting openers. Pan-roasted chicken stuffed with pig's feet and truffles is an earthy entrée delight. The wine list, created by Roger Dagorn of Chanterelle features the work of women winemakers and winery owners. From the creative hors d'oeuvres to the delicate petit-fours, Annisa raises the bar (and the price tag) on neighborhood dining. ⊠ *13 Barrow St., between Bleecker and W. 4th Sts., ☎ 212/741–6699. Reservations essential. AE, MC, V. Closed Sun. No lunch.*

$$–$$$ ✕ **Fressen.** At the end of a dark street lined with meatpacking warehouses and strolled by the occasional prostitute, this trendy restaurant is hard to locate. But once inside, you will know you have found the right place, if only because of the loud music, the throngs of beautiful people, and the pulsating energy. Described as a "postmodern garage," the cement-floor dining room is about as chic as anyone could stand it to be. And the short menu, which changes every day and emphasizes organically grown ingredients, has something to please just about everyone. Whole steamed fish, roasted chicken, sautéed vegetables, and a variety of potato preparations are always available. Though some question the high prices, others believe the place is such a New York experience that it's worth every penny. Don your best all-black outfit and judge for yourself. ⊠ *421 W. 13th St., between 9th Ave. and Washington St., ☎ 212/645–7775. AE, MC, V. Closed Sun. No lunch.*

Eclectic

$$$$ ✕ **James Beard House.** Though not a restaurant per se, this landmark town house presents an extravagant dinner to the public almost every night. The James Beard Foundation, a nonprofit culinary organization, invites chefs from around the world to cook in what was once the home of the famous American cookbook author and television personality. Reservations must be made well in advance for the prepaid, prix-fixe dinners. One night you might be able to sample the food of a great chef from France, the next you might have a dinner prepared by a team of chefs from California. All dinners begin at 7 PM with a cocktail reception, during which you can stand in the kitchen and watch the chefs in action. Call in advance to find out what's on the calendar and on the menu, and have an insider's gastronomic experience. ⊠ *167 W. 12th St., between 6th and 7th Aves., ☎ 212/675–4984. Reservations essential. Jacket required. AE, DC, MC, V.*

$ ✕ **Shopsin's General Store.** It's hard to recommend Shopsin's, but it's even harder to leave it out. The temperament of chef/owner Kenny Shopsin, who sometimes falls asleep on the window banquette of his tiny storefront restaurant, makes dining a risk. If he doesn't like your attitude he won't hesitate to throw you out—a shame considering you'd be missing a selection of more than 200 soups and hundreds of entrées (each prepared à la minute). One of the best meals is breakfast. Offerings include homemade pumpkin pancakes, corn and cornmeal waffles, and an open-face chorizo omelette that will keep you feeling full for the entire day. The coffee is good, but you have to get it yourself (the milk is in the fridge). If you don't like it, you know what you can do. ⊠ *63 Bedford St., at Morton St.,* ☎ *212/924–5160. DC, MC, V. Closed weekdays 7* PM *and weekends.*

French

$$–$$$$ ✕ **Pastis.** A spinoff of Balthazar, Pastis offers similar faux-French ambiance and a no-reservations policy that assures you'll get a seat, though you'll have to wait for it. The menu includes simple French dishes such as steak frites, frisée aux lardons, leeks vinaigrette, salmon in a herbal sauce, and excellent crusty bread (imported from Balthazar). The restaurant also serves a full breakfast menu. The bar area in the front is a haven for smokers (and New York's no-smoking law is not strictly adhered to in the main dining room) and the back room is a festive combination of bathhouse-meets-brasserie, with gilt-edged mirrors and white ceramic tile. The casual atmosphere, with everything from French accordion music to the Rolling Stones emanating from the booming sound system, makes Pastis suitable for any occasion. ⊠ *9 9th Ave., at Little W. 12th St.,* ☎ *212/929–4844. Reservations not accepted. AE, DC, MC, V.*

$$–$$$ ✕ **Blue Ribbon Bakery.** When the owners of Blue Ribbon and Blue Ribbon Sushi renovated this space they uncovered a 100-year-old coal-burning oven made from Italian tile. They were so happy with their discovery, they let the oven dictate the destiny of their restaurant. They built a bakery–restaurant with an eclectic menu featuring substantial sandwiches on homemade bread (from the oven, of course) and entrées that include trout and Cornish game hen. A whole section of the menu presents small plates of charcuterie, pâté, aged cheeses, and tapas-style dishes. The basement dining room (which has more atmosphere) is dark and intimate; upstairs is a Parisian-style café, perfect for lingering over a glass of good wine from the well-chosen list. ⊠ *33 Downing St., at Bedford St.,* ☎ *212/337–0404. AE, DC, MC, V. Closed Mon.*

$–$$ ✕ **Florent.** When it's 4 AM and pierogis in the East Village or a slice on Bleecker Street just won't cut it, head to Florent, the true pioneer of dining in the Meatpacking District. Open each night until 5 AM (on Saturday they stay open 24 hours) this brushed steel and Formica diner is always a blast—expect loud music, drag queens, and members of every walk of city life. The simple French menu features decent versions of everything you crave: onion soup, mussels steamed in white wine, blood sausage, pâté; and in the early morning hours you can also order from a full breakfast menu. Wash it all down with some cheap red wine, or coffee if you're trying to kill your hangover before heading out for the day. ⊠ *69 Gansevoort St., between Greenwich and Washington Sts.,* ☎ *212/989–5779. No credit cards.*

Italian

$$$ ✕ **Babbo.** After your first bite of the kitchen's ethereal homemade pasta
★ or the tender suckling pig, you won't wonder why this place was an instant sensation when it opened, and why reservations are still so hard to get. A five-course pasta tasting menu is the best way to get your fill of fresh noodles, such as the luscious lamb and fresh mint "love letters," or the rich beef-cheek ravioli. Adventuresome eaters will rejoice in the delicious lamb's tongue salad or the custardy brain ravioli, but more timid diners gravitate toward such simple dishes as succulent whole fish baked in salt. The only challenge is getting a reservation. Once you're finally seated, the service is friendly. ⊠ *110 Waverly Pl., between MacDougal St. and 6th Ave.,* ☎ *212/777–0303. Reservations essential. AE, MC, V. No lunch.*

$$–$$$ ✕ **Macelleria.** Italian for "butcher shop," the name of this new restaurant in the red-hot Meatpacking District presages the menu, which features Italian-style preparations of meat. The double-cut porterhouse

for two is a deliciously aged piece of beef that comes with fresh-cut fries. Salads, pastas, side dishes, and other simple fare are skillfully prepared. The minimalist decor manages to feel simultaneously homey and chic with a stylish combination of brick, cement, and pine. As at many of the restaurants in this new destination neighborhood, the service can be sporadic. ⊠ *48 Gansevoort St., between Greenwich and Washington Sts.,* ☎ *212/741–2555. AE, MC, V.*

$$ ✕ **Lupa.** Mario Batali and Joseph Bastianich, the team behind the ever-packed Italian sensation Babbo, also run this more casual, more moderately priced offspring just a couple of blocks away. Like the setting, the food is more casual than at Babbo, but antipasti such as the board of *salumeria* (cold cuts), fresh pasta dishes like pappardelle with rabbit ragù, and hearty entrées such as braised oxtail are every bit as satisfying, despite small-ish portions. The front room of the restaurant is seated on a first-come, first-served basis, while reservations are taken for the back. ⊠ *170 Thompson St., between Bleecker and Houston Sts.,* ☎ *212/982–5089. AE, DC, MC, V. Closed Sun.*

Korean

$–$$ ✕ **Junno's.** A fun-loving crowd of regulars congregates at the blue-top bar of this diminutive Korean-esque restaurant, known for its creative cocktails and spicy food. Grilled calamari is served with a thick, tasty miso sauce; seaweed salad is flavored generously with sesame oil; and such entrées as fishy mackerel and savory short ribs are satisfying. Be forewarned: on a slow evening, if the owners are in the mood, they pull out the karaoke machine and everyone is encouraged to participate. ⊠ *64 Downing St., between Bedford and Varick Sts.,* ☎ *212/ 627–7995. AE, MC, V. Closed Sun. No lunch.*

Middle Eastern

$ ✕ **Moustache.** There's always a crowd waiting outside for one of the ★ copper-top tables at this appealing Middle Eastern restaurant. The focal point is the pita, steam-filled pillows of dough rolled before your eyes and baked in a searingly hot oven. They are the perfect vehicle for the tasty salads—lemony chick-pea and spinach and hearty lentil and bulghur among them. For entrées, try the leg of lamb or merguez sausage sandwiches or, if you are feeling particularly hungry, tackle the *ouzi,* a large phyllo package stuffed with chicken and fragrant rice. Except for the bland falafel, nothing on the menu will disappoint. Although the service can be slow, it is always friendly. ⊠ *90 Bedford St., between Barrow and Grove Sts.,* ☎ *212/229–2220; 265 E. 10th St., between Ave. A and 1st Ave.,* ☎ *212/228–2022. No credit cards.*

Pizza

$–$$$ ✕ **Arturo's.** Few guidebooks list this brick-walled Village landmark, but the jam-packed room and the smell of well-done pies augur a good meal to come. The pizza is terrific, cooked in a coal-fired oven. Basic pastas as well as seafood, veal, and chicken concoctions with mozzarella and lots of tomato sauce come at giveaway prices. Let everyone else stand in line at John's Pizzeria on Bleecker Street. ⊠ *106 W. Houston St., off Thompson St.,* ☎ *212/677–3820. AE, MC, V.*

Seafood

$–$$ ✕ **Pearl Oyster Bar.** Although the big rents and small scale of the ★ buildings in Greenwich Village make it a neighborhood of compact restaurants, none is tinier (or more charming) than this friendly New England–style oyster bar run by Rebecca Charles. There is only one table (two if they split it in half) and a handful of stools at the bar. But that doesn't mean you can't enjoy an excellent meal of the freshest seafood—only that at times you may have to wait for it. Menu highlights include a selection of chilled seafood, cocktails, chowders, whole fish, lobster, and bouillabaisse, but the specifics depend on the market. At lunch it may be easier to find a seat in which to enjoy the Maine-style lobster roll, fried oyster po' boy, and garlicky Caesar salad. ⊠ *18 Cornelia St., between Bleecker and W. 4th Sts.,* ☎ *212/691–8211. MC, V. Closed Sun.*

Steak

$$$ ✗ **Strip House.** From the pin-up girl logo, to the bordello-red walls, to the signature New York strip steak, to the cutesy name, Strip House attempts to be a serious steak house that doesn't take itself too seriously. Though chef David Walzog has been perfecting his beef cookery at Michael Jordan's Steak House in Grand Central Station, the menu at Strip House shows off his more sophisticated culinary leanings. In addition to a variety of steaks, Walzog serves appetizers, such as foie gras torchon and carpaccio; non-beef entrées, such as Dover sole and roast duck breast; and sides, such as melted heirloom tomatoes, and potatoes cooked in goose fat, that inspire instant adulation. ⊠ *13 E. 12th St., between 5th Ave. and University Pl.,* ☎ *212/328–0000. AE, DC, MC, V. Closed Mon. No lunch weekends.*

East Village and Lower East Side

Once Manhattan's bohemian enclave, the East Village is fast becoming just another high-rent neighborhood. Luckily, some of the commercial spaces still have low-rent leases that enable restaurateurs to open creative, inexpensive restaurants. The Lower East Side has not yet attracted luxury real-estate developers, but a number of ambitious young chefs have opened destination restaurants that are helping to transform the neighborhood.

American

$$–$$$ ✗ **First.** This quintessentially downtown restaurant—stylish waiters, loud music, risqué artwork, and dark, horseshoe-shape banquettes—was one of the first in the area to offer serious food. Chef/owner Sam DeMarco of Merge and District commands an open kitchen that makes everything from the bread to the mayonnaise. You will usually find seafood tacos, pork chops, hanger steak, and salmon prepared in some yummy and filling way. Several fine vintages from the carefully chosen wine list are available by the glass. Late hours prevail, and on Sunday there's a fun brunch and some family-style Italian-American specials for dinner. ⊠ *87 1st Ave., between 5th and 6th Sts.,* ☎ *212/ 674–3823. Reservations essential. AE, MC, V. No lunch.*

$–$$ ✗ **Prune.** This adorable restaurant serves a quirky brand of eclectic American food that matches perfectly with the offbeat, homey decor. Roasted capon is served over garlicky toasted bread, fried oysters are coated in a thick layer of batter, and a bacon-wrapped pork chop is grilled to perfection. The home-style touches are evident in an appetizer of housemade bologna and a dessert of buttered bread with sugar. There is usually a wait, and the quarters are cramped, so don't expect to linger at your table. ⊠ *54 E. 1st St., between 1st and 2nd Aves.,* ☎ *212/677– 6221. AE, MC, V. Closed Mon. No lunch.*

American Casual

$ ✗ **Radio Perfecto.** The music is loud, the wine comes in water glasses, and the owner really seems to care about his guests. Radio Perfecto is a part of the Avenue B restaurant revolution and it is a perfect neighborhood spot, lively but completely casual, with such decent, inexpensive food as hamburgers, pasta, french fries, and an exemplary roast chicken served with a choice of sauces each night. The waitstaff, all dressed according to the prevailing neighborhood aesthetic, are friendly and personable, if occasionally forgetful. ✉ *190 Ave. B, between 11th and 12th Sts.,* ☎ *212/477–3366. No credit cards. No lunch.*

Cafés

$ ✕ **Goupil and DeCarlo.** The almond croissants at this small bakery/café rival any baked in France. There is a complete selection of French baked goods and a special dish of the day (think beef bourguignon). ✉ *244 E. 13th St., between 2nd and 3rd Aves.,* ☎ *212/473–3320. MC, V.*

$ ✕ **Veniero's Pasticceria.** More than a century old, this bustling bakery-café sells every kind of Italian *dolci* (sweet), from cherry-topped cookies to creamy cannoli. ✉ *342 E. 11th St., near 1st Ave.,* ☎ *212/674–7264.*

Cajun/Creole

$ ✕ **Great Jones Cafe.** When you pass through the bright orange door into this small, crowded Cajun joint you'll feel like you're in a honky-tonk. The menu, posted on the brightly colored walls, always features cornmeal-fried or blackened catfish, gumbo, jambalaya, popcorn shrimp, and rice. Brunch is also festive, and if the strong coffee isn't enough to wake you up, the spicy food definitely will be. ✉ *54 Great Jones St., between Bowery and Lafayette St.,* ☎ *212/674–9304. No credit cards.*

Contemporary

$$–$$$ ✕ **Tasting Room.** Although you may think there's something wrong with the math, this tiny spot on East First Street's restaurant row really does have only eight tables and more than 300 different bottles on its American-only wine list. There's an ever-changing list of about 10 wines by the glass, and the menu depends on the season. Owners Collin and Renee Alevras want to give diners the option of trying a lot of different dishes with a glass or a bottle from the fine list, so the menu items come in small ("tastes") and large ("shares") portions. They might include beautifully presented contemporary creations such as an heirloom tomato salad, earthy lamb tartare, tender roasted duck leg with yam sauce, sweet Maine lobster in parsley sauce, and a selection of cheeses. ✉ *72 E. 1st St., between 1st and 2nd Aves.,* ☎ *212/358–7831. AE, D, MC, V. Closed Sun. No lunch.*

$$ ✕ **71 Clinton Fresh Food.** The name does little to indicate the sophis-
★ ticated experience that awaits at this off-the-beaten-path restaurant. Food really is the focus here—though the decor of the small, intimate room is certainly pleasant enough. A striking appetizer features smoked salmon wrapped around avocado and served with pickled horseradish; black sea bass is encrusted with rye and soy and roasted until crisp; and short ribs are braised in beer and served with hanger steak and chervil spaetzle. The goat cheese tart with crisped potato and apple-wood-smoked bacon is simple but right on target. The success of this place proves that New Yorkers really will travel anywhere for a good meal. Follow their lead. ✉ *71 Clinton St., between Stanton and Rivington Sts.,* ☎ *212/614–6960. AE, DC, MC, V. No lunch.*

Delicatessens

$$ ✕ **Second Avenue Deli.** Memorabilia inside and Hollywood-style stars
★ embedded in the sidewalk outside commemorate the luminaries of the Yiddish theaters that once reigned along this stretch of 2nd Avenue. A face-lift may have removed the wrinkles of time, but the strictly kosher food is as good as ever. The deli's bevy of Jewish classics includes chicken in the pot, matzo-ball soup, chopped liver, Romanian tenderloin, and *cholent* (a Sabbath dish of meat, beans, and grain). A better pastrami sandwich you can't find (don't ask for it lean). A welcome bowl of pickles, sour green tomatoes, and coleslaw satisfies from the start, but at

the finish forego dessert—it's non-dairy to comply with the rules of kashruth. ⊠ *156 2nd Ave., at 10th St.,* ☎ *212/677–0606. AE.*

$ ✕ **Katz's Delicatessen.** Everything and nothing has changed at Katz's since it first opened in 1888, when the neighborhood was dominated by Jewish immigrants. The rows of Formica tables, the long self-service counter, and such signs as "send a salami to your boy in the army" are all completely authentic. What's different are the area's demographics, but the new locals still flock here for succulent hand-carved corned beef and pastrami sandwiches, soul-warming soups, juicy hot dogs, crisp half-sour pickles, and a little old-school attitude thrown in for good measure. ⊠ *205 E. Houston St., at Ludlow St.,* ☎ *212/254–2246. AE, MC, V.*

Italian

$$–$$$ ✕ **Il Buco.** The unabashed clutter of rusty kitchen gadgets, vintage tableware, and old pine cabinets harkens back to Il Buco's past as an antiques store. The tables, some of which are communal, are each unique and provide varying levels of comfort. They are rather close together and tend to wobble when the staff, who are often harried, whiz past across creaking floorboards. The effect is a festive, almost romantic country-house atmosphere. A long menu of Mediterranean tapaslike appetizers lets you try many different dishes and specials that change daily. Consider the salt-cured codfish croquettes with aiöli, grilled quail with pomegranate, or homemade egg pasta with wild mushrooms. ⊠ *47 Bond St., between Bowery and Lafayette St.,* ☎ *212/533–1932. AE. No lunch Sun.–Mon.*

$$ ✕ **City Eatery.** Though the somewhat cold brasserie decor, complete with red banquettes, remains intact from this restaurant's previous incarnation, the menu has been transformed from run-of-the-mill French to inventive Italian by chef Scott Conant, who formerly plied his trade at San Domenico. Conant cooks Italian staples with confidence, evidenced by the impossibly small and tender gnocchi that are served with nothing more than a sweet tomato sauce and a grating of Parmigiano-Reggiano. Polenta, heady with the scent of truffle oil, is a rich, satisfying dish. Conant gets creative with entrées such as olive oil–poached tuna and a selection of ever-changing homemade pastas. ⊠ *316 Bowery, at Bleecker St.,* ☎ *212/253–8644. MC, V. No lunch.*

$$ ✕ **I Coppi.** Named for the terra-cotta urns used to store olive oil in Tuscany, this rustic East Village eatery has been embraced by a neighborhood crowd that's outgrown falafel and cheap bar grub. Good choices include the assorted crostini with toppings such as chicken liver or sautéed black kale, or a hearty soup of red beans and pasta. Entrées are equally appealing: slow-roasted pork loin is delicately perfumed with fennel seed, thin slices of eggplant are cooked with cheese and tomato sauce until they are delectably tender, and thin pizzas are whisked from the wood-burning oven while still crisp. There is an excellent assortment of Italian wines to choose from and the back garden may be one of the prettiest in all of the city. ⊠ *432 E. 9th St., between Ave. A and 1st Ave.,* ☎ *212/254–2263. AE, MC, V. Closed Mon.*

$–$$ ✕ **Il Bagatto.** You have to be a magician (*il bagatto* in Italian) to get a table before 11:30 PM at this hip, inexpensive restaurant, but as the reservationist says in her Italian-accented drawl "you go home, take a shower, relax, everyone else will be tired and drunk, you will come to dinner refreshed and happy." How true, and Il Bagatto is just the kind of restaurant where you want to arrive refreshed—so as to enjoy its electric ambience, rich Italian food (order the lasagna special), and fun, rustic decor. It's like being at a party every night, only the food is better. ⊠ *192 E. 2nd St., between Aves. A and B,* ☎ *212/228–0977. No credit cards. Closed Mon. No lunch.*

Japanese

$$–$$$ ✕ **Bond Street.** The hipper-than-thou setting—sheer curtains, sleek black tables, and taupe screens—matches the look of the ultra-chic people who dine on the contemporary Japanese fare at Bond Street. The sushi is well prepared, with offerings you will not find in many other restaurants, such as four types of yellowtail and tuna or a selection of unusual caviars. The kitchen does an admirable job of preparing interesting alternatives to raw fish, such as broiled Chilean sea bass marinated in saikyo miso, rack of lamb with Asian pear and shiso sauce, and hot buckwheat soba soup with duck and scallion. But be warned: as is the case in many restaurants where the waitstaff is better dressed than the clientele, the service can be maddening. ⊠ *6 Bond St., between Broadway and Lafayette St.,* ☎ *212/777–2500. AE, MC, V.*

$$–$$$ ✕ **Hasaki.** Otherwise impatient New Yorkers are usually willing to wait for good food. And wait they do at Hasaki, a simple Japanese restaurant that serves excellent sushi. If the sushi chef is in the mood, you can ask him to surprise you with a beautiful platter of delicacies from the sushi bar. Toro, yellowtail, and eel are among the fresh-as-the-sea selections. Nor can you go wrong ordering off the menu. The staples are always fresh and nicely presented, and the service is always gracious. ⊠ *210 E. 9th St., between 2nd and 3rd Aves.,* ☎ *212/473–3327. AE, MC, V.*

$–$$ ✕ **Takahachi.** One of Manhattan's least expensive but best small Japanese restaurants, Takahachi serves very fresh sushi standards that attract a loyal following of East Village residents, plus the occasional celebrity. The food is not exactly distinctive, but the freshness and the price make the restaurant better than many around town. ⊠ *85 Ave. A, between 5th and 6th Sts.,* ☎ *212/505–6524. Reservations not accepted. AE, MC, V. No lunch.*

Moroccan

$$–$$$ ✕ **Chez Es Saada.** Come with us to the Casbah, past the street-level bar, down the tile staircase sprinkled with fresh rose petals, into this brick-lined, underground den of a modern Moroccan restaurant, where beautiful men and women recline on large cushions. Although all the food isn't as tantalizing as the setting, you can still manage to eat a pretty good *tagine* (stew) of lamb with ginger and dates, or a buttery *bisteeya* (chicken wrapped in phyllo and served with a saffron and lemon butter sauce). Simpler is better. Don't focus on your plate; instead sit back in an alcove and watch the room come alive. ⊠ *42 E. 1st St., between 1st and 2nd Aves.,* ☎ *212/777–5617. Reservations essential. AE, DC, MC, V. No lunch.*

Scandinavian

$–$$ ✕ **Good World Bar and Grill.** This quirky Scandinavian bar/restaurant is located on the fringes of Chinatown in a storefront marked by an old sign for the Good World Barber Shop, the original tenant. Despite the groovy crowd of non-blonds smoking cigarettes in the shabby, bohemian space, the menu is traditional Swedish. There are, of course, Swedish meatballs, as well as fish soup and a tasting plate of herring; lingonberries are used liberally. ⊠ *3 Orchard St., at Division St.,* ☎ *212/925–9975. AE, D, DC, MC, V. No lunch weekdays.*

Seafood

$–$$ ✕ **Pisces.** As the name suggests, the thrust here is fish, and the kitchen handles its charge well. Sweet sea scallops, Chilean sea bass, and other creatures from the depths are skillfully prepared. A couple of entrées nod to more carnivorous cravings. The sophisticated menu, reasonable prices, and, weather permitting, outdoor café seating make this a worthwhile destination. A ventilated cigar room on the second floor is also a draw. Brunch is served on weekends. ⊠ *95 Ave. A, at 6th St.,* ☎ *212/260–6660. AE, DC, MC, V. No lunch weekdays.*

Southwestern

$–$$ ✕ **Miracle Grill.** In fair weather, your long wait for an outdoor table at this Southwestern restaurant will be rewarded by a seat in a large and pretty garden. The food is reasonably priced, tasty, and the perfect complement to one of the bar's fabulous margaritas. Appetizers of grilled steak carnitas with soft corn tortillas, warm tomato picadillo, and chipotle cream are out of this world, as are the catfish tacos. And vegetarians will appreciate the grilled Portobello mushroom fajita. A second location in the West Village serves equally delicious fare in a casual bistro setting. ⊠ *112 1st Ave., between 6th and 7th Sts.,* ☎ *212/ 254–2353; 415 Bleecker St., between Bank and 11th Sts.,* ☎ *212/924– 9709. AE, MC, V. No lunch weekdays.*

Thai

$–$$ ✕ **Holy Basil.** Holy Basil counters New York City's dearth of good Thai restaurants by offering better-than-average Thai food at a reasonable price in an elegant setting. The second-floor dining room is decorated like the living quarters of an aristocrat, with dark paneling, huge gilt-framed mirrors, and old-fashioned paintings. The vibrant food—enlivened by chilies, opal basil, and kaffir lime—comes carefully composed. A spicy *som tum* (green papaya salad) and rich *tom kah gai* (chicken and coconut milk soup), not to mention anything in *kaw praw* (a traditional curried preparation), excite your taste buds. A large and informative wine list is an added bonus. A Greenwich Village outpost called **Little Basil** (⊠ 39 Greenwich Ave., at Charles St., ☎ 212/645– 8965), doesn't offer as much atmosphere or spice. ⊠ *149 2nd Ave., between 9th and 10th Sts.,* ☎ *212/460–5557. AE, MC, V.*

Murray Hill, Flatiron District, and Gramercy

Murray Hill, a quiet residential neighborhood, is home to some of the city's most charming boutique hotels and has begun to experience a restaurant boom. A giant movie theater and shopping complex called Kips Bay brings people from all over town, as do the Indian restaurants along Lexington Avenue, which surpass most in the city for reasonably priced, authentic, regional food. South of Murray Hill, Gramercy saw little restaurant action until the mid-1990s, when a healthy crop of fashionable eateries sprouted in the neighborhood's stately buildings, especially on lower Madison Avenue. The neighboring Flatiron district, which radiates south from its architectural centerpiece, the Flatiron Building, is home to some of the most characteristic architecture in the city and many of the city's best dining establishments.

American

$$$$ ✕ **Gramercy Tavern.** Danny Meyer's ever-popular restaurant has ex-
★ posed beams, heavy drapes, antique wooden furniture, and a friendly, knowledgable staff. The space is divided into two areas—the first-come, first-served tavern in the front offers a light menu prepared in the wood-burning oven (on display), plus a menu of small dishes and desserts between lunch and dinner service. The more formal (but unintimidating) dining room in the back features a prix-fixe American table d'hôte menu carefully conceived by executive chef Tom Colicchio. For $65 (plus an occasional supplement), choose from seasonal dishes such as wild Scottish partridge in consommé, fondue of sea urchin and Maine crabmeat, and roasted sirloin with braised beef cheeks and leeks. Pastry chef Claudia Fleming has devised a dessert menu that rivals any in the city. An excellent cheese selection and a fine wine list complete the

Murray Hill, Flatiron District, Gramercy, and Chelsea Dining

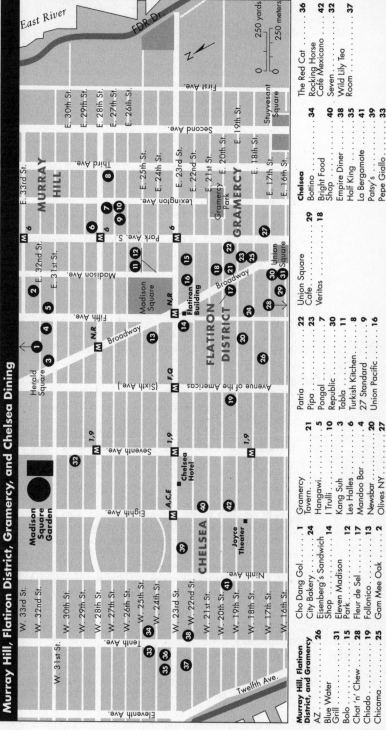

East River

FDR Dr.

0 — 250 yards
0 — 250 meters

MURRAY HILL

GRAMERCY

FLATIRON DISTRICT

CHELSEA

Madison Square Garden

Madison Square

Herald Square

Chelsea Hotel

Joyce Theater

Flatiron Building

Gramercy Park

Stuyvesant Square

Union Square

experience. ⊠ *42 E. 20th St., between Broadway and Park Ave. S,* ☎ *212/477–0777. Reservations essential. AE, DC, MC, V.*

$$–$$$ ✕ **Union Square Cafe.** New Yorkers consistently rate Union Square as one of their favorite restaurants—thanks in large measure to executive-chef Michael Romano's crowd-pleasing menu and to the restaurant's consistently unpretentious disposition and excellent, low-key service. Mahogany moldings outline white walls hung with bright modern paintings; in addition to the three main dining areas, there's a long bar perfect for solo diners. The cuisine is more-or-less American with a thick Italian accent: for example the signature filet mignon of tuna with Asian slaw can land on the same table as homemade gnocchi in a creamy mushroom sauce. ⊠ *21 E. 16th St., between 5th Ave. and Union Sq. W,* ☎ *212/243–4020. Reservations essential. AE, DC, MC, V. No lunch Sun.*

American Casual

$ ✕ **Eisenberg's Sandwich Shop.** Since the 1930s this narrow coffee shop with its time-worn counter and cramped tables has been providing the city with some of the best tuna, chicken, and egg salad sandwiches. During the lunch rush the colorful countermen shout orders at one another down the line as they make sandwiches, ladle soups, and slice dill pickles. They still use the cryptic language of soda jerks and diner cooks, in which "whisky down" means rye toast and "Adam and Eve on a raft" means two eggs on toast. Considering the usual feeling of mayhem in the place, it's always a pleasant surprise when you actually get your sandwich, quickly and precisely as ordered. Stick to sandwiches; the soups come from a can. ⊠ *174 5th Ave., between 22nd and 23rd Sts.,* ☎ *212/675–5096. AE. Closed Sun.*

Cafés

$ ✕ **City Bakery.** This self-service bakery/restaurant has the urban aesthetic to match its name. Owner Maury Rubin has a strong sense of humor and design, and both show in his creative window displays and his elegant tarts. The baked goods—giant cookies, chocolate croissants, tender scones–are rich with creamy butter. But one of the major draws here is the salad bar, a large selection of impeccably fresh food—including whole sides of baked salmon, sautéed vegetables, pasta salads, and several Asian-flavored dishes—that puts most others to shame. Much of the produce comes from the nearby farmers' market, and the quality shows in the clean flavors and high prices. In winter, the bakery hosts a hot chocolate festival; in summer it's lemonade time. At dinner there is table service and expanded counter service; small dishes are available upstairs at the bar. ⊠ *3 W. 18th St., between 5th and 6th Aves.,* ☎ *212/366–1414. Closed Sun. No dinner.*

$ ✕ **Newsbar.** This ultracasual resting place with four other Manhattan locations has good coffee and tea, a generous offering of magazines, and CNN on the tube. ⊠ *2 W. 19th St., between 5th and 6th Aves.,* ☎ *212/255–3996. No credit cards.*

Contemporary

$$$$ ✕ **AZ.** To get to the roof-top dining room of this sizzling Flatiron restaurant you must suffer an impatient crowd trying to squeeze into the first-floor lounge, an attitude-throwing hostess, and a claustrophobic ride in a glass elevator. Thankfully, once you leave the elevator, you can breathe a little easier because of the numerous plants, the spacious table arrangement, and the atrium ceiling that opens in warm weather. Once you tuck into Patricia Yeo's pan-world prix-fixe menu of tempura soft-shell crabs, duck schnitzel, tea-smoked chicken, and the like, you'll probably leave all the commotion behind—that is, if you don't let the under-zealous and over-attitudinal service get to you. ⊠ *21 W. 17th*

St., between 5th and 6th Aves., ☎ *212/691–8888. Reservations essential. No open-toe shoes for men. AE, DC, MC, V.*

$$$$ ✕ **Union Pacific.** In a neighborhood of serious restaurants, chef Rocco
★ DiSpirito's elegant dining room stands out as a favorite among serious foodies. Every meal is an education in exotic ingredients, unusual
flavor combinations, elegant presentations, and precise technique.
Consider raw bay scallops with fresh sea urchin and mustard oil,
which combines the taste of the ocean with the temperature of a hot
summer's day. Your education continues through the entrées: sea bass
with fig and sunflower seeds and lamb with hearts of palm, raisins,
and *kokum* (dried Indian black plums). Rarely does anything on his
seasonal prix-fixe ($65) menus disappoint. An unusual wine list, heavy
on German labels, has something to teach you, too. ✉ *111 E. 22nd
St., between Broadway and Park Ave. S,* ☎ *212/995–8500. Reservations essential. AE, MC, V. Closed Sun. No lunch Sat.*

$$$$ ✕ **Veritas.** What do you do when you own more wine than you can
★ drink? The partners who own this Flatiron newcomer decided to open
a restaurant. The wine list culled from their private collections originally boasted more than 1,300 producers, and although much of the
initial inventory has been drunk, the list remains exemplary. Chef
Scott Bryan's prix-fixe contemporary menu runs from such rich, earthy
dishes as braised veal cheeks with truffled celery root purée to the Asian-
inspired salmon with greens and curry emulsion. The dining room is
distinguished by clean, natural lines, with one wall made of Italian tile
and another displaying a collection of pretty hand-blown vases. ✉ *43
E. 20th St., between Broadway and Park Ave. S,* ☎ *212/353–3700.
AE, DC, MC, V. No lunch Sun.*

$$$ ✕ **27 Standard.** Jazz is the theme at this spacious, bi-level restaurant
on a small strip in Murray Hill that has undergone some recent restau-
rant revitalization. Downstairs is a serious jazz club, where headlin-
ing musicians and vocalists are the major draw. Upstairs is a serious
restaurant, where the contemporary cooking of chef Matthew Lake
brings people in. Select from a variety of salads (mushroom is a favorite),
beer-battered oysters, cashew chicken, pan-fried cod, and other satis-
fying choices. ✉ *116 E. 27th St., between Lexington Ave. and Park
Ave. S,* ☎ *212/447–7733. AE, DC, MC, V. Closed Sun.*

$$–$$$ ✕ **Eleven Madison Park.** Danny Meyer has created a contemporary
★ restaurant in the lobby of the landmark Metropolitan Life Building.
The design incorporates the original art deco fixtures, but the place
feels very modern. Meyer has entrusted the kitchen to Kerry Heffer-
nan, whose menu includes satisfying starters such as a leek and Ap-
penzeller cheese tart, a terrine of beef shanks, foie gras and pig's feet,
and a salad of Maine lobster with fennel and black trumpet mushrooms.
Of the main courses, the skate *grenobloise* (with brown butter), the
braised pork shoulder, and the aged prime rib of beef for two display
the chef's hearty style. A beautiful bar and views of Madison Square
Park complete the environment. ✉ *11 Madison Ave., at 24th St.,* ☎
212/889–0905. Reservations essential. AE, DC, MC, V. No lunch.

Eclectic

$$$$ ✕ **Tabla.** In concert with restaurant guru Danny Meyer, chef Floyd Car-
doz creates exciting cuisine based on the tastes and traditions of his
native India, filtered through his formal European training. Give your-
self up to appetizers such as lamb and turmeric raviolo with tomato
kasundi (sauce) and mint oil, or seared quail with quail samosa, fen-
nel salad, and grape–pine nut chutney. Don't think too hard about the
main courses, such as skate crusted with *rawa* (a blend of spices), sweet
spice-braised oxtail, and black-spice roasted poussin with *kokum* (a
dried black plum) jus. This is a restaurant where the chef knows more

than you do, so trust in the prix-fixe menu and you will be rewarded. If you feel compelled to know, your server will explain ingredients in a friendly, unintimidating way. At the more casual bread bar downstairs, you can get in and out faster and for less money while watching the tandoor ovens in operation. ⊠ *11 Madison Ave., at 25th St.,* ☎ *212/889–0667. Reservations essential. AE, MC, V.*

French

$$$$ ✕ **Fleur de Sel.** Could this charming, cozy French restaurant be the same space that just moments ago was an unconvincing Italian trattoria? It is, and the neighborhood is better served for it. Chef/owner Cyril Renaud, who's danced behind the stoves at such high-falutin' restaurants as La Caravelle and the now-closed Bouley, has settled down in the shadow of the Flatiron Building. He's brought his watercolors (which adorn the walls and the menus), his love of French food, his thirst for creativity, and his beloved salt from Brittany, which gives the restaurant its name. The prix-fix menu is limited but perfectly tuned to the season and the scale of the dining room. A cream-free parsnip purée comes with chestnut-truffle ravioli, venison medallions are served in an earth beet-licorice sauce, dessert crêpes are plump with sautéed apples and Devonshire cream. The professionalism of the service is commendable. ⊠ *5 E. 20th St., between 5th Ave. and Broadway,* ☎ *212/ 460–9100. Reservations essential.. AE, MC, V. Closed Sun. No lunch.*

$$–$$$ ✕ **Les Halles.** Chef Anthony Bourdain has become famous not for his cooking, but for his best-selling exposé of kitchen life entitled *Kitchen Confidential.* But his restaurant remains strikingly unpretentious, a French bistro–cum–butcher shop that is a great place to eat steak. French posters, a tin ceiling, and a windowed kitchen contribute to the atmosphere. This may be the only place in town where covering the tables with butcher paper actually makes sense. A good bet is the *côte de boeuf* with béarnaise sauce, a massive rib steak for two served on a wooden board. Other prime choices include crispy duck-leg confit and frisée salad, warm sausages with lentils, and heaping plates of garlicky cold cuts. ⊠ *411 Park Ave. S, between 28th and 29th Sts.,* ☎ *212/679- 4111. AE, DC, MC, V.*

Indian

$ ✕ **Pongal.** Some people will direct you to 6th Street in the East Village for Indian food. Don't go. Instead, follow the off-duty cabs to the real locus of authentic regional Indian cooking, which radiates from the intersection of 28th Street and Lexington Avenue. There you will find Pongal, an attractive, narrow restaurant with a cow in the window. Fragrant (and kosher) vegetarian southern Indian food issues forth from the kitchen. Start with one of the combination platters (*thalis*) on the back of the overwhelming menu. The Gujarati thali comes with a selection of southern specialties, including a vegetable stew with eggplant and lotus root, seasoned yogurt, fragrant basmati rice, steamed lentil cake, and other treats. ⊠ *110 Lexington Ave., between 27th and 28th Sts.,* ☎ *212/696–9458. No credit cards.*

Italian

$$–$$$ ✕ **Follonico.** The wood trim, earth tones, open kitchen, wood-burning oven, and chef-owner Alan Tardi's personal interpretation of Tuscan cuisine will transport you to Italy. Wood-roasted calamari or other soulful appetizers are so good you'll want to overindulge, but save room for one of the unusual pastas, such as *fazzoletti*, a handkerchief pasta imprinted with fresh herbs. For a third course try the whole red snapper baked in a rock-salt crust. Fresh fruit granita is refreshing, but it would be a shame to leave without dunking a biscotti into dessert wine and drinking some bracing espresso. ⊠ *6 W. 24th St., between 5th and*

6th Aves., ☎ 212/691–6359. *Reservations essential. AE, DC, MC, V. Closed Sun. No lunch Sat.*

$$–$$$ ✕ **I Trulli.** Rough-hewn gold walls, a fireplace, a garden for summer dining, and a whitewashed open grill with the traditional beehive shape of early Pugliese houses distinguish this Italian winner from its competitors. An out-of-the-ordinary glass of wine from a little-known producer and one of the enticing appetizers—baked oysters with pancetta, Tallegio cheese, and bread crumbs—are a great way to start. Almost all the pasta is made by hand by the owner's mother, and the departure of chef Mauro Mafrici hasn't seemed to affect the quality of the rest of the menu. Entrées of game, meat, and fish are cooked in the wood-fired oven. **Enoteca** (⊠ 124 E. 27th St., between Lexington and Park Aves., ☎ 212/481–7372), a lovely casual wine bar next door, offers a simple menu of the same exquisite food and an impressive selection of wines, available by the glass or in tasting flights. ⊠ *122 E. 27th St., between Lexington Ave. and Park Ave. S, ☎ 212/481–7372. Reservations essential. AE, DC, MC, V. Closed Sun. No lunch Sat.*

$$–$$$ ✕ **Olives NY.** Ten years ago, if you had said that New Yorkers would one day be excited about a chef from Boston opening a restaurant in a hotel, you would have been locked up in Bellevue Hospital. But in December 2000 that's exactly what happened. Todd English opened a branch of Olives in the lobby of the just-opened W Hotel on Union Square, and from the difficulty of getting a reservation, to the bouncer at the door, to the crush of attractive young people at the bar, you'd think New York had been starving for a decent Italian restaurant. In direct contrast to the heart-healthy fare served at Heartbeat in the midtown W, English's menu is filled with butter, cream, foie gras, duck fat, and meat. He raises a chicken wing to new levels by filling it with a mousse of chicken, foie gras, and truffles, and simmering it in duck fat until crisp. The delicate, over-stuffed pastas are made by hand, and most come dripping in butter. The hearty entrées all have a creative twist, such as the rack of venison that comes wrapped in pear. Unfortunately, the design of the room is so drab it almost detracts from the food. And it seems the designer forgot to place a rest room within walking distance of the dining room. ⊠ *201 Park Ave. S, at 17th St., ☎ 212/353–8345. Reservations essential. AE, D, DC, MC, V.*

Korean

$–$$ ✕ **Cho Dang Gol.** A few blocks away from the main drag of Little Korea, this restaurant specializes in tofu (*doo-boo* in Korean). Myriad varieties of bean curd are made on the premises and then incorporated into a vast array of traditional Korean dishes of varying heat and spice. Anyone who thinks of tofu as a bland, jiggling substance should try *doo-boo dong-ka-rang-deng,* puffy rounds of tofu filled with shredded vegetables and beef, or *cho-dan-gol jung-sik,* a three-part dish of tofu dregs, pork stew, and rice. The only drawback is that the staff, who are lovely and eager to please, don't speak enough English to be of much help. ⊠ *55 W. 35th St., between 5th and 6th Aves., ☎ 212/695–8222. AE, DC, MC, V.*

$–$$ ✕ **Gam Mee Ok.** It's hard to say whether it's the deconstructed industrial design, the inexpensive menu of Korean comfort foods, or the late-night hours that attracts such a young and stylish crowd to this restaurant in the heart of Little Korea, but they come in droves. As soon as you sit down, an aloof waitress will approach your table and snip whole turnip and cabbage kimchee into bite-size pieces. Every item on the very limited menu has a photo to help you order. But all you need to remember is oxtail and bone marrow soup—a subtle, satisfying milky-white bowl of soup with rice noodles and beef that you season at your table with Korean sea salt and chopped scallions—and mung bean pancakes, made fresh from mung bean flour and scallions, and fried until crisp and chewy. ⊠ *43 W. 32nd St., between 5th and 6th Aves.,* ☎ *212/695–4113. Reservations not accepted. No credit cards.*

$–$$ ✕ **Kang Suh.** "Seoul" food at its best is served at this lively second-floor restaurant on one end of the strip of West 32nd Street known as Little Korea. Cook thin slices of ginger-marinated beef ribs (*bul go gui*) or other meats over red-hot coals; top them with hot chilies, bean paste, and pickled cabbage; and wrap them all up with lettuce for a satisfying meal. Dinner starts with 10 or more delicious types of kimchee, spicy pickles and condiments that are almost a meal in themselves. A crisp oyster-and-scallion pancake, sautéed yam noodles, and other traditional dishes are all expertly prepared. The waitstaff speaks little English but the menu has lots of pictures, so you can just point and smile. ⊠ *32 W. 32nd St., between 5th and 6th Aves.,* ☎ *212/947–8482. AE, MC, V.*

$ ✕ **Mandoo Bar.** This appealing little dumpling shop is a welcome addition to Little Korea's main drag, which is filled mostly with huge eateries lit up with neon and fluorescent lighting. You can watch the ladies making dumplings in the window on your way to one of the blond-wood cafeterialike tables in the back. There are plenty of dumplings, or *mandoo,* to choose from, such as broiled shrimp and sea cucumber, Korean kimchee, beef, pork, or leek. There are also traditional noodle and rice dishes and a couple of specialties like *tangsuyook*—fried pork with sweet and sour sauce. ⊠ *2 W. 32nd St.,* ☎ *212/279–3075. AE, MC, V.*

Latin

$$$ ✕ **Chicama.** Douglas Rodriguez has created a hit with Chicama, an utterly festive Latin spot in the home furnishings store ABC Carpet & Home. Much of the restaurant's wood-panel interior was imported from a restaurant in Brazil and the effect is that of a rustic hacienda. Rodriguez is the undisputed master of interpretive Latin cooking, and the menu here delivers. There's a ceviche bar, from which a wide array of excellent fish "cocktails" are served. Tender grilled octopus is skewered and served on a bed of nutty quinoa. Adobo-rubbed steak served with huge slabs of tomato and nuggets of cabrales cheese packs a deceptively subtle spiciness. Tapioca pudding, dramatically served in a coconut, is the favorite dessert. Rodriguez lists the name of every staff member, down to the dishwashers, on the menu, and the servers seem to take their role seriously; for such a trendy spot, service is surprisingly caring. ⊠ *35 E. 18th St., between Broadway and Park Ave.,* ☎ *212/505–2233. Reservations essential. AE, D, DC, MC, V.*

$$–$$$ ✕ **Patria.** Caribbean colors and festive mosaics provide the setting for what has been described as electric cooking. After the 1999 departure of opening chef Douglas Rodriguez (now at Chicama), longtime sous-chef Andrew DiCataldo took the helm and changed the focus of the menu to reflect all of Latin America's cuisines. Contemporary variations on traditional appetizers, such as meat, vegetable, or seafood empanadas, soups, and an impressive selection of ceviches, are an exciting way to begin. Entrées build to a Peruvian stew of guinea hen and or an Argentinian beef tenderloin with *chimimchurri* seasoning. The wine list focuses on offerings from Spain, Argentina, and California. The service isn't as good as it once was, but the overall experience is pleasant. ⊠ *250 Park Ave. S, at 20th St.,* ☎ *212/777–6211. Reservations essential. AE, MC, V.*

Pan-Asian

$ ✕ **Republic.** Epicureans on the run flock to this innovative Asian noodle emporium that looks like a cross between a downtown art gallery and a Japanese school cafeteria. Dressed in black T-shirts and pants and holding remote-control ordering devices, the attractive young waitstaff could have walked out of a Calvin Klein ad. At the long, blue-stone bar, you can simultaneously dine and enjoy the spectacle of chefs scurrying amid clouds of steam in the open kitchen. Otherwise you can eat at the picnic-style tables. Appetizers include a smoky grilled eggplant with sesame and spicy fried wantons. Entrées are based on noodles or rice. The curried coconut milk, lemongrass, Asian basil, and lime leaf broth and the Vietnamese-style barbecued pork are particularly delicious. ⊠ *37A Union Sq. W, between 16th and 17th Sts.,* ☎ *212/627–7172. AE, DC, MC, V.*

Seafood

$$–$$$$ ✕ **Blue Water Grill.** A copper-and-tile raw bar anchors one end of this warm, sweeping room of indigo, siena, and yellow. The original 1904 molded ceiling and marble everywhere recall the space's former life as a bank. Strong on fresh seafood served neat (chilled whole lobster, shrimp in the rough), the menu also has international flair—Moroccan-spiced red snapper, Maryland crab cakes, warm shrimp cocktail in bamboo steamers with Japanese and Shanghai sauces—and simple preparations that issue forth from a wood-burning oven. For dessert, try the brownie ice cream sundae. A lounge and dining room in the basement vault features live jazz. ⊠ *31 Union Sq. W, at 16th St.,* ☎ *212/675–9500. Reservations essential. AE, DC, MC, V.*

Spanish

$$$ ✕ **Bolo.** With its tile-edge brick oven, primary color scheme, open kitchen, and polished wood bar, Bolo's design fuses Manhattan and some fictional version of Barcelona. Bobby Flay's loosely Spanish-inspired food takes aim at New York palates, but it doesn't always hit: green onion gazpacho is refreshing and spicy, but squid ink risotto is gummy and overcooked. If you're not in the mood for sangria, select from the well-priced wine list. ⊠ *23 E. 22nd St., between Broadway and Park Ave. S,* ☎ *212/228–2200. Reservations essential. AE, MC, V. No lunch weekends.*

$$–$$$ ✕ **Pipa.** The father of Nuevo Latino cuisine, Douglas Rodriguez, turns his attention to Spain at this festive tapas bar in home furnishings store ABC Carpet & Home, next door to his restaurant Chicama. The menu has over 50 items, such as *cocas,* flavorful pizzalike flatbreads covered with savory toppings such as delicious garlicky clams, tender sautéed porcini mushrooms, and white beans and serrano ham. More traditional tapas on the order of garlic shrimp and grilled chorizo come in traditional clay dishes, and are perfect for nibbling with one of the many sherries on the wine list. ABC made all of Pipa's design decisions, and the resulting look is that of a Victorian interior decorator gone mad. Chandeliers hang on top of one another and one concrete wall is oozing with shells. There's a fountain that gurgles to one side and an abundant array of colorful pillows in each booth. ⊠ *38 E. 19th St., between Broadway and Park Ave. S,* ☎ *212/677–2233. Reservations not accepted. AE, D, DC, MC, V.*

Turkish

$–$$ ✕ **Turkish Kitchen.** Manhattan's best Turkish restaurant is housed in a striking multilevel room with lipstick-red walls, chairs with skirted slipcovers, framed prints, and colorful kilims. The young staff dressed in long white chefs' aprons serve authentic food. For appetizers choose from such delectable offerings as velvety char-grilled eggplant salad, deep-fried cubes of calves' liver tossed with lemon and parsley, and fried calamari. The stuffed cabbage and the bulghur-wheat patties filled with ground lamb, pine nuts, and currants, are both highly recommended. The newer, smaller **Turkish Grill** (⊠ *193 Bleecker St., at MacDougal*

St., ☎ 212/674–8833) is less expensive but has only a few tables. ✉ *386 3rd Ave., between 27th and 28th Sts., ☎ 212/679–1810. AE, DC, MC, V. No lunch weekends.*

Vegetarian

$$–$$$ ✕ **Hangawi.** In a city of limited vegetarian offerings, Hangawi holds a special place. The food is billed as "vegetarian mountain Korean cooking," and it and the strongly Japanese-influenced environment are transporting. For the full experience choose the emperor's menu, a parade of more than 10 courses designed as a complete introduction to this unusual style of eating. Offerings include delicate soups, one a miso broth, the other a savory pumpkin purée; stuffed tofu; marinated wild mountain herbs; and a main-course spread of more than 15 bowls of assorted kimchee—some taste like earth, some are brazenly spiced. To accompany the meal, a selection of exotic teas, including one made from a purée of dates, and an unfiltered milky white Korean sake served from a wooden bowl are recommended. ✉ *12 E. 32nd St., between 5th and Madison Aves., ☎ 212/213–0077. AE, DC, MC, V.*

Chelsea

Chelsea has become a neighborhood of "immigrants"—art galleries from SoHo have settled in the west and gay men have migrated north from the Village. The result is a vibrant neighborhood of trendy shops, serious art, buff men, and lively restaurants. A few downtown restaurants have opened outposts here to capture the audience of northward-moving trendsetters.

American

$$–$$$ ✕ **Red Cat.** Chef/owner Jimmy Bradley has created a comfortable neighborhood restaurant with a contemporary American menu to match. Seasonal appetizers include sautéed zucchini with almonds and pecorino, clam and octopus stew, and a signature chicken-and-apple sausage served with braised cabbage. Satisfying entrées include sautéed skate with capers and brown butter, steak and golden potatoes with fennel and cabernet sauce, and whole trout in beurre blanc. The service is friendly and welcoming and the wine list is reasonably priced. The inexpensive lunch menu is a delicious way to refuel during a day of gallery hopping. ✉ *227 10th Ave., between 23rd and 24th Sts., ☎ 212/242–1122. AE, D, DC, MC, V.*

$$–$$$ ✕ **Seven.** In the culinary wasteland around Penn Station, there actually is a serious restaurant. The contemporary American menu runs the gamut from over-stuffed sandwiches (at lunch), to seasonal soups, to homemade pastas, to creative entrées such as roasted cod with aioli-crushed potatoes in saffron broth. The decor, like the menu, plays it safe but sophisticated. In all honesty, in another neighborhood this restaurant might not warrant mention, but as an oasis in a desert of fast-food outlets and diners it deserves special mention. ✉ *350 7th Ave., between 29th and 30th Sts., ☎ 212/967–1919. AE, MC, V. Closed Sun..*

Cafes

$ ✕ **La Bergamote.** Exemplary French pastries are served in this simple café. Try the buttery pain au chocolate and chewy meringues. ✉ *169 9th Ave., at 20th St., ☎ 212/627–9091.*

Eclectic

$$ ✕ **Bright Food Shop.** Asia and the American Southwest meet at this converted coffee shop, one of the first restaurants to find its way to 8th Avenue before Chelsea's gentrification in the 1990s. The atmosphere is early 20th-century lunch counter, but the food is from some futuristic place. Don't be scared by bizarre-sounding concoctions such as

"salmon wonton tostadas" and "moo shu mex vegetable handrolls with chipotle peanut sauce": somehow the kitchen manages to make this mega-fusion cooking taste good. The flavors are bold and the portions are filling. An equally eclectic menu is available for breakfast, brunch, and lunch, and a simpler takeout menu is available next door at Kitchen Market. ⊠ *216 8th Ave., between 21st and 22nd Sts.,* ☎ *212/ 243–4433. No credit cards.*

$ ✕ **Wild Lily Tea Room.** A true gem worthy of its setting among the Chelsea galleries, this tearoom offers a serene break from the bustle of the art world. Colorful fish swim in a stone pond set into the floor. Food is served on china made in the shape of lily pads, and teas are described with such eloquence that you might mistake the list for a book of poetry. Treat yourself to a contemporary afternoon tea, complete with dainty finger sandwiches, desserts, and delectable scones with jam and clotted cream, or choose from an assortment of tasty Asian treats, such as *shu mai* dumplings with shrimp, crab, or vegetables; spicy Thai sausage in puff pastry; or an ingenious ginger chicken "hamburger." ⊠ *511A W. 22nd St., between 10th and 11th Aves.,* ☎ *212/691–2258. Reservations essential. AE, MC, V. Closed Mon.*

Irish

$–$$ ✕ **Half King.** The owner wanted to create an authentic, low-key Irish pub where he (and anyone who wanted to) could hang out, meet friends, talk to the bartender, drink pints, and eat hearty Irish food. Inasmuch as such a place can exist amid the art galleries and gay gathering places of Manhattan's trendy Chelsea neighborhood, he has actually succeeded. The casual pub has large booths, friendly service, plenty of beer on tap, and inexpensive Irish food served in generous portions. As might be expected, potatoes and cabbage are given a prominent role on the menu; there's also lamb steak and fish and chips. ⊠ *505 W. 23rd St., between 10th and 11th Aves.,* ☎ *212/462–4300. AE, DC, MC, V.*

Italian

$$–$$$ ✕ **Bottino.** Despite some convincing evidence to the contrary, chic people dressed in black like good food too. They get it *alla italiana* at this smartly designed west Chelsea restaurant, where a table is almost as hard to get as at Balthazar or Daniel. The menu is straightforward— fresh mozzarella with tomato and basil or ripe Anjou pears with Tuscan pecorino to start; homemade leek tortelloni, grilled salmon, roast chicken, lamb, or steak to follow. In the summer, a garagelike glass door opens to a secluded garden. Service is slow but friendly. The take-out shop of the same name, next door (⊠ *248 8th Ave., between 24th and 25th Sts.,* ☎ *212/206–6766*), has a nice selection of Italian lunch items. ⊠ *246 10th Ave., between 24th and 25th Sts.,* ☎ *212/206–6766. AE, DC, MC, V. No lunch Sun.–Mon.*

$ ✕ **Pepe Giallo.** The crown of a growing chain of tiny Italian eateries, this Chelsea outpost is the most spacious and charming of the lot. A long list of specials changes daily, but the menu always includes a variety of pastas (prepared fresh in the open kitchen and served in generous portions) antipasti, salads, entrées and sandwiches. The gnocchi are surprisingly light, the pesto sauce is fragrant with basil and garlic, and the veal is tender and flavorful. Inexpensive wine is available in carafes or by the bottle. Considering dinner can cost less than $15, these restaurants may be the best Italian value in the city. Other locations include **Pepe Rosso** (⊠ *149 Sullivan St.,* ☎ *212/677–4555*) in SoHo, **Pepe Verde** (⊠ *559 Hudson St.,* ☎ *212/255–2221*) in the West Village, and **Pepe Viola** (⊠ *200 Smith St.,* ☎ *718/222–8279*) in Brooklyn. ⊠ *253 10th Ave., at 25th St.,* ☎ *212/242–6055. No credit cards.*

Mexican

$$ ✗ **Rocking Horse Cafe Mexicano.** Fresh tortillas and funky corn husk light fixtures help place this bright, colorful restaurant a cut above the others on the 8th Avenue strip. Chef Joseph Cacace's nouveau Mexican menu features creative culinary riffs such as duck confit in blue corn/*epazote* (a wild Mexican herb) crepas and chipotle-chile glazed tuna. Take in the buff Chelsea crowd while enjoying a potent margarita and some homemade tortilla chips served in a metal bucket at the bar. ✉ *182 8th Ave., between 19th and 20th Sts.,* ☎ *212/463–9511. AE, MC, V.*

Midtown West

Big hotels and big businesses dominate the western half of midtown. With a few exceptions, restaurants cater to tourists, culture seekers, and people looking for a more casual, less restrained atmosphere than the dining rooms of Midtown East afford. Now that Times Square and the theater district resemble theme parks and Hell's Kitchen has been gentrified (you'll hear it called Clinton), the seedy edge of the area is all but gone. The exorcism of the tawdry element has not done much to improve the overall variety or quality of Midtown West restaurants, though Hell's Kitchen is rich with an array of inexpensive ethnic eateries. But amid the dizzying wattage are some real culinary finds; you can even eat well on Restaurant Row.

American

$$$$ ✗ **"21" Club.** It's exciting to hobnob with celebrities and tycoons at this four-story brownstone landmark, a former speakeasy that opened on December 31, 1929. With its large banquettes, red-and-white check tablecloths, and a ceiling hung with toys, the Grill Room is the place to be. In the past the restaurant was mostly noted for the costly signature dish, the "21" burger, but executive chef Erik Blauberg now turns the menu toward inventive New American food with subtle Asian accents. Asian-style seared tuna and seasonal game preparations such as succulent antelope are delicious examples of his style. Dramatic desserts and specialty coffee flambés bring flair to meal's end, and the service is seamless. ✉ *21 W. 52nd St., between 5th and 6th Aves.,* ☎ *212/582–7200. Reservations essential. Jacket and tie. AE, DC, MC, V. Closed Sun. No lunch Sat.*

$$$–$$$$ ✗ **Beacon.** Chef Waldy Malouf has established himself in this multilevel restaurant just around the corner from the Rainbow Room, his former home. Meat, fish, and even vegetables roast in his wood-fired oven, with delicious results. The crusty bread, baked on the premises, is also notable, as are the rich, satisfying, and desserts by pastry chef Martin Howard, another Rainbow alum. Although the atmosphere is midtown business, the simple, almost rustic food pleases people from all walks of life. ✉ *25 W. 56th St., between 5th and 6th Aves.,* ☎ *212/332–0500. AE, D, MC, V. Closed Sun. No lunch Sat.*

$$$–$$$$ ✗ **District.** This contemporary American restaurant in the Muse Hotel is named for the theater district in which it is located. The dining room, with its metal curtains and plush, neutral-color furniture, is certainly comfortable enough, but it may not inspire you. Sam DeMarco's cooking is another story. The chef of the popular late-night haunt First is following his muse in creating grown-up food with an irrepressible, almost childlike, sense of humor. The menu has a section called the "luxury box," where foie gras is available in three sizes—Huey, Dewey, and Louis—and an entire truffle can be yours for the asking. While many of the main dishes, such as juniper-crusted venison au poivre or roasted diver scallops with truffled potatoes, may not warrant a chuckle, the seafood tacos have made a happy journey here from First. ✉ *130 W. 46th St., between 5th and 6th Aves.,* ☎ *212/485–2999. AE, D, MC, V.*

Midtown West Dining

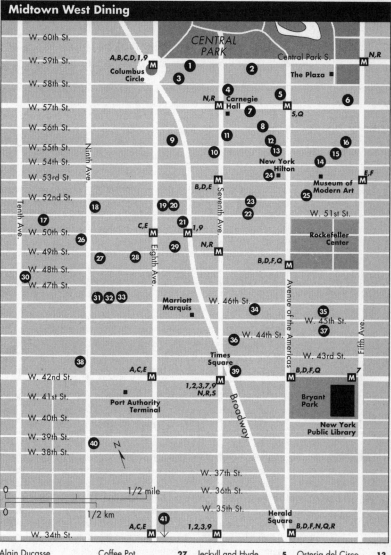

Alain Ducasse New York 3	Coffee Pot 27
Atlas 2	Cupcake Café 40
Aquavit 14	District 35
Baldoria 29	Esca 38
Barbetta 33	ESPN Zone 39
Beacon 8	Estatorio Milos . . . 12
Becco 32	Firebird 31
Brasserie 8½ 6	Gallagher's Steak House 20
Carnegie Deli 10	Hallo Berlin 17
Churrascaria Plataforma 28	Island Burgers and Shakes 18

Jeckyll and Hyde 5	Osteria del Circo . . . 13
JUdson Grill 23	Petrossian 4
La Caravelle 16	Remi 24
La Côte Basque . . . 15	Russian Tea Room . . 7
La Locanda 26	San Domenico 1
Le Bernardin 22	Sugiyama 9
Le Marais 34	Triomphe 37
Mars 2112 21	Victor's Café 19
Meskerem 30	Virgil's Real BBQ . . . 36
Molyvos 11	"21" Club 25
Nick and Stef's Steakhouse 41	

$$$–$$$$ ✕ **JUdson Grill.** Owner Jerome Kretchmer conceived JUdson Grill on
★ the same grand scale as his flagship venture, Gotham Bar & Grill. The
bi-level space has a freestanding bar that hosts a lively after-work
crowd. The main dining room and balcony have red velour banquettes,
mirrored walls, lofty ceilings, engaging John Parks murals, and immense
gold vases. In the open kitchen, chef Bill Telepan produces such sump-
tuous dishes as New York State foie gras terrine with Sauternes-onion
marmalade, inventive fish entrées like wild striped bass with a Meyer
lemon crust, and well-executed, down-to-earth seasonal preparations.
The wine list is beautifully organized and has many hard-to-find bot-
tles. ✉ *152 W. 52nd St., between 6th and 7th Aves.,* ☎ *212/582–5252.*
AE, DC, MC, V. Closed Sun. No lunch Sat.

American Casual

$ ✕ **Island Burgers and Shakes.** Burgers rule at this bright and cheery
café with multicolored round tables and funky chairs. The menu of-
fers belly-busting hamburgers with a wide variety of toppings to please
every taste. Every sandwich can be ordered with grilled chicken instead
of the usual beef patty, but true believers stick to the real thing. And
if you're in the mood for even more calories, the tempting selection of
milk shakes is extremely hard to pass up. The only drawback is that
there are no French fries—you'll have to settle for potato chips. ✉ *766*
9th Ave., between 51st and 52nd Sts., ☎ *212/307–7934. No credit cards.*

Barbecue

$–$$ ✕ **Virgil's Real BBQ.** Neon, wood, and Formica set the scene at this
massive roadhouse in the theater district. Start with stuffed jalapeños
or buttermilk onion rings with blue-cheese dip. Then go for the "pig
out"—a rack of pork ribs, Texas hot links, pulled pork, rack of lamb,
chicken, and more. If you prefer seafood, the New Orleans-style barbecued shrimp are giant and tasty. There's also a good list of top beers
from around the world. ✉ *152 W. 44th St., between 6th Ave. and*
Broadway, ☎ *212/921–9494. Reservations essential. AE, MC, V.*

Brazilian

$$$–$$$$ ✕ **Churrascaria Plataforma.** This sprawling, boisterous shrine to meat,
★ with it's generous all-you-can-eat prix-fixe menu, is best experienced
with a group of hungry friends. Order a full pitcher of *caipirinhas* (a
cocktail of sugarcane liquor and lime), and head for the center of the
room, where a vast salad bar beckons with vegetables (including fresh
hearts of palm), meats, and cheeses, plus hot tureens of *fejoida* (the
Brazilian national dish of beans, pork, greens, and manioc). But exer-
cise restraint—the real show begins with the parade of lamb, beef,
chicken, ham, sausage, and innards, brought to the table on skewers.
The only relief is to turn over your chip, marked green on one side
(MORE!), red on the other (STOP!). Side dishes include plantains, french
fries, rice, mashed potatoes, manioc, and a tangy vinegar sauce. The
heavy, gooey desserts, such as the coconut flan, are perfect with the
strong Brazilian coffee. ✉ *316 W. 49th St., between 8th and 9th Aves.,*
☎ *212/245–0505. AE, DC, MC, V.*

Cafés

$ ✕ **Coffee Pot.** Overstuffed sofas and chairs, mirrors, brass chandeliers,
good deals on the coffee of the day, and pleasant service make this one
of the theater district's most pleasant options. ✉ *350 W. 49th St., at*
9th Ave., ☎ *212/265–3566.*

$ ✕ **Cupcake Café.** Intensely buttery, magnificently decorated cakes and
cupcakes, as well as doughnuts, coffee cake, and hearty soup are worth
the trek to this funky spot on the western flank of the Port Authority
Bus Terminal (a somewhat sketchy area). ✉ *522 9th Ave., at 39th St.,*
☎ *212/465–1530.*

Contemporary

$$$$ ✕ **Atlas.** Located on a swank strip of New York real estate, and serving only from a prix-fixe menu, Atlas feels like a very cosmopolitan restaurant. The space is tasteful and sophisticated with a marble floor, a sculptural globe that spins from time to time, and a small bar in front. The tables are well appointed and widely spaced, with attractive seasonal flower arrangements. Service is solicitous and professional. One might expect a very safe menu in such a coddling setting, but the cocky young chef, Paul Leibrandt, delivers anything but. Guaranteed, Leibrandt is the only chef in town cooking croquet of pigs' trotter, an earthy dish enhanced by a cucumber-anchovy chutney. Poached chicken *jus gras* (in a rich broth) sounds simple, but it comes with an unusual risotto heavily scented with herbs. Eel paired with watermelon and crystallized violets misses the mark, but Leibrandt's culinary daring should be applauded anyway. ✉ *40 Central Park S, between 5th and 6th Aves.,* ☎ *212/759–9191. Reservations essential. AE, D, MC, V. Close Sun. No lunch.*

Continental

$$$ ✕ **Petrossian.** A pristine glass of iced Russian vodka, a dollop of fresh, briny Beluga resting on a warm blini—that's what this restaurant, an outpost of the Parisian caviar purveyor, is about. The recently expanded dining room is enhanced by art deco accents, a granite bar, a profusion of marble, and *objets* by Erté and Lalique. The only way to begin a meal at Petrossian is with caviar—beluga, osetra, or sevruga—presented in a Christofle server, or with a selection of smoked salmon, eel, and other delicacies. The rest of the menu, overseen by Parisian-based consulting chef Philippe Contacini and executive chef David Cunningham, features a mélange of contemporary dishes, solidly prepared and satisfying. Service can be exceptional. A new café next door sells fine pastries and a selection of creative treats—plus caviar, of course. ✉ *182 W. 58th St., at 7th Ave.,* ☎ *212/245–2214. Reservations essential. AE, DC, MC, V.*

Cuban

$–$$$ ✕ **Victor's Café.** You can smell the authentic Cuban cooking as you enter this Technicolor restaurant, a neighborhood fixture since 1963. The high-back booths, tile floor, rattan chairs, and skylight evoke golden-age movies set in Old Havana. Better than average, the food is a contemporary transcription of Cuban, Puerto Rican, and Latin dishes, such as hearty adobo, black bean soup, and fried plantains. The staff couldn't be friendlier. ✉ *236 W. 52nd St., between Broadway and 8th Ave.,* ☎ *212/586–7714. AE, DC, MC, V.*

Delicatessens

$$ ✕ **Carnegie Deli.** Although not what it once was, this no-nonsense deli is still a favorite of out-of-towners. The portions are so huge you feel like a child in a surreal culinary fairy tale. Two giant matzoh balls come in a bowl of soup, the knishes hang off the edge of the plates, and some combination sandwiches are so tall they are held together with bamboo skewers, not toothpicks. Don't miss the cheesecake, to our palates the best (and, of course, biggest) in the city. Don't be fooled: you pay for that excessive amount of food, but you can take home what you don't eat. To drink? Try cream soda or Cel-Ray tonic. ✉ *854 7th Ave., between 54th and 55th Sts.,* ☎ *212/757–2245. No credit cards.*

Ethiopian

$ ✕ **Meskerem.** Ethiopian art adorns the yellow walls in this no-nonsense Hell's Kitchen storefront. The tasty delicacies include *kitfo,* (spiced ground steak), which can be ordered raw, rare, or well done, and *yebeg alecha,* tender pieces of lamb marinated in Ethiopian butter flavored with curry, rosemary, and an herb called *kosart,* and then sautéed with fresh ginger and a bit more curry. The vegetarian combination, an array of five vegetable and grain preparations served on *injera* (a yeasty flat bread) is a terrific deal. ⊠ *468 W. 47th St., at 10th Ave.,* ☎ *212/664–0520. AE, DC, MC, V.*

French

$$$$ ✕ **Alain Ducasse New York.** The arrival in New York of France's most decorated chef created quite a stir in 2000. Could he get away with charging more than anyone else in this already overpriced city? The short answer is yes: Alain Ducasse New York has evolved into one of the most drop-dead fabulous dining experiences the city has ever seen. Much has been made of opulent flourishes such as the stools on which to place your purse and the opportunity to select your own steak knife, but the pomp has been pared down (the selection of pens with which to sign the check has disappeared, probably into the pockets of diners with sticker shock), and the menu is now a prix-fixe format. For that you get on-the-ball service that manages to be friendly and unintimidating; food that sings with the freshness of seasonal ingredients, like the royale (a flan or custard) with morels and the line-caught sea bass with lemon rock salt and citrus fondue; a parade of sweets that includes all manner of eye-popping delights—petits fours, madeleines, fresh cherry tarts, lollipops, and more—that you are encouraged to take home; and a fresh-baked brioche bagged and waiting for you at the door as you leave. It's worth maxing out your credit card. ⊠ *Essex House, 155 W. 58th St., between 6th and 7th Aves.,* ☎ *212/265–7300. Reservations essential. Jacket and tie. AE, D, DC, MC, V. Closed Sat., Sun. No lunch Mon., Tues., or Fri.*

$$$$ ✕ **La Caravelle.** In what was once one of New York's most opulent dining rooms, owners Rita and André Jammet have been celebrating the good life Parisian style for 40 years. Although the decor may be worse for the wear, it is enlivened by Jean Pagés murals, their colors spilling over to the pink-peach banquettes. Mirrors, flowers, and the Caravelle coat of arms add to the richness, as does Kitty Carlyle, who's often sitting at the table by the door. The cuisine is classic and refined, with seasonal selections that change often, served to you in a prix-fixe format. Enjoy truffled pike quenelles in lobster sauce, the perfectly roasted chicken in a delicate bath of champagne and cream, and one of the cloudlike soufflés (which must be requested at the beginning of the meal). ⊠ *33 W. 55th St., between 5th and 6th Aves.,* ☎ *212/586–4252. Reservations essential. Jacket and tie. AE, DC, MC, V. Closed Sun. No lunch Sat.*

$$$$ ✕ **La Côte Basque.** Though not in its original location, Jean-Jacques Rachou's landmark French restaurant preserves many elements of its design: dark wooden crossbeams, murals by Bernard Lamotte, faux windows, and even the revolving door. The cuisine is classic French—begin with the trio of pâtés or one of the gossamer soufflés. The roast duckling with honey, Grand Marnier, and black-cherry sauce is prepared for two and carved table-side. A hearty cassoulet will leave you happily sated. The prix-fixe-only menu offers reasonable value given the quality of the food and the service. ⊠ *60 W. 55th St., between 5th and 6th Aves.,* ☎ *212/688–6525. Reservations essential. Jacket and tie. AE, DC, MC, V. No lunch Sun.*

$$$$ ✕ **Le Bernardin.** Owner Maguy LeCoze presides over the power scene
  ★ in the dining room at this trend-setting French seafood restaurant. Chef Eric Ripert works magic with anything that swims—preferring at times not to cook it at all. Spanish mackerel tartare with osetra caviar, red snapper in sherry vinaigrette, thyme and pepper crusted rare yellowfin tuna on a truffled herb salad, and some of the finest desserts in town,

such as chocolate millefeuille and a honeyed-pear-and-almond-cream tart, are highlights of the menu. The teak-panel dining room is plush, expansive, and hushed; late-19th-century French oil paintings adorn the walls. The wine list is strong on white Burgundies, which perfectly accompany the exceptional food. ⊠ *155 W. 51st St., between 6th and 7th Aves.,* ☎ *212/489–1515. Reservations essential. Jacket required. AE, DC, MC, V. Closed Sun. No lunch Sat.*

$$$ ✕ **Triomphe.** You must be confident to name your restaurant Triomphe, and indeed the team behind this petite spot in the Iroquois Hotel have created a winner. Once past the busy but tasteful bar, you enter a dining room that manages to please without dazzle. The simple decor features a recessed ceiling set off by crown moldings, and a single flower on every table. Chef Steve Zobel's menu is ambitious yet understated, with a range of well-prepared dishes that will appeal to a variety of tastes. There's an appetizer of chicken liver with three onions that is earthy and elegant at the same time, and seared scallops with a light dressing of truffle oil that are slightly more refined. Zobel's rabbit coq au vin is a winning entrée. Desserts are simple but impeccable, especially the tarte Tatin, which is caramelized to perfection. ⊠ *49 W. 44th St., between 5th and 6th Aves.,* ☎ *212/453–4233. Reservations essential. AE, D, MC, V.*

$$–$$$ ✕ **Brasserie 8 1/2.** The less attractive sister to Brasserie, this subterranean restaurant nevertheless has some visual and culinary charms of its own. The dramatic staircase releases you into a spacious cocktail lounge with black leather sofas, where drinks made with unusual-flavor vodkas are offered. The dining room is lined with serious modern art, and the menu is flush with the creative cooking of Julian Alonzo. Nothing Fellini-esque, just solid contemporary French cooking. The frites alone are worth a trip to Midtown. ⊠ *9 W. 57th St., between 5th and 6th Aves.,* ☎ *212/829–0812. AE, D, MC, V.*

German

$ ✕ **Hallo Berlin.** When nothing but bratwurst will do, head to Hell's Kitchen for a meal at Hallo Berlin. In addition to "brat" there are over 10 other varieties of wurst to choose from, accompanied by traditional German dishes such as sauerkraut, spaetzle, or addictive pan-fried potatoes. The atmosphere is low-budget Berlin beer garden, but the low, low prices match the lack of pretension. There are other authentic dishes on the menu, but none can compete with a sausage paired with a cold pint of German beer. ⊠ *402 W. 51st St., between 9th and 10th Aves.,* ☎ *212/541–6248. No credit cards. No lunch Sun.*

Greek

$$–$$$$ ✕ **Estiatorio Milos.** Like a stylized version of the Plaka in Athens, this dramatic restaurant comes alive with whitewashed walls, large-scale decorations in the classical style, table umbrellas, and beautiful European diners. The snipping of fresh herbs into bowls full of olive oil starts the evening off. Classic salads—of lentil, chick-pea, or smoked carp roe—and a signature pile of paper-thin fried vegetables are delicious appetizers. You can pick a fish from the display of fresh seafood flown in everyday, and have it grilled whole. The only drawback is that you have to be a shipping tycoon to afford a meal here. ⊠ *125 W. 55th St., between 6th and 7th Aves.,* ☎ *212/245–7400. Reservations essential. AE, D, MC, V.*

$$–$$$ ✕ **Molyvos.** Fresh ingredients, bold flavors, fine olive oil, and fragrant herbs inform the kitchen of this upscale taverna. Meals start with a selection of salads, or *meze.* They include gigantes beans stewed with tomatoes, *taramasalata* (a creamy spread made with smoked carp roe), garlicky *skordalia* (potato puree), *saganaki* (fried *kefalotiri* cheese), and a real Greek salad with vegetables, olives, and feta—but no lettuce. Entrées include traditional Greek dishes, such as *pastitsio* (baked pasta casserole), moussaka (a custard-topped casserole of eggplant and ground lamb), and whole grilled snapper drizzled with olive oil and sprinkled with fresh herbs. ⊠ *871 7th Ave., between 55th and 56th Sts.,* ☎ *212/582–7500. AE, DC, MC, V.*

Italian

$$$–$$$$ ✕ **Barbetta.** Operated by the same family since it opened in 1906, Barbetta offers a uniquely authentic Piemontese experience. The ornately luxurious throwback of a dining room evokes the Old-World atmosphere of royal Turin, seat of the Savoy kingdom. The food on the seasonally changing menu is classic for the area: *fonduta* (made of melted Fontina cheese, eggs, and truffles), *agnolotti del plin* (similar to ravioli), *bue al barolo* (beef braised in red wine), and fresh-baked cakes and tortes for dessert. The more creative dishes aren't always successful, but the mature, professional staff dotes. When white truffles are in season (October through December) there is no better place to enjoy them; they are imported from the owner's estate in Italy, where she keeps her own truffle hounds. A beautiful garden is a lovely summertime setting. ⊠ *321 W. 46th St., between 8th and 9th Aves.,* ☎ *212/246–9171. AE, D, DC, MC, V. Closed Sun.–Mon. in winter.*

$$–$$$$ ✕ **Becco.** In general, Restaurant Row caters (poorly) to a clientele that wants to eat quickly before or after the theater. Becco is one of the only restaurants specifically to plan its menu to accommodate the demands of this audience. The restaurant offers two pricing scenarios: one includes an all-you-can-eat selection of three or four pastas served hot out of pans carried around the dining room by waiters; the other starts with the pastas and concludes with a generous entrée. Either way you'll be in and out quickly, and you won't leave hungry. The selection changes daily but often includes gnocchi, fresh ravioli, and something in a cream sauce. The entrées include braised lamb shank, veal, and an assortment of fish. If you have room, which is unlikely, order the bread pudding for dessert. ⊠ *355 W. 46th St., between 8th and 9th Aves.,* ☎ *212/397–7597. Reservations essential. AE, DC, MC, V.*

$$–$$$$ ✕ **San Domenico.** The self-appointed ambassador of authentic Italian cuisine in New York, owner Tony May presides over the dining room of this temple to *alta cucina.* Dark wood, terra-cotta floors, leather chairs, and earthy hues set an understated, elegant tone. Unfortunately, the enthusiasm of the kitchen and the dining room staff has waned. Executive chef Odette Fada creates what some consider overly refined versions of Italian dishes, such as risotto flecked with prosciutto and flavored with balsamic vinegar, or rabbit with fennel and black olives, scented with lemon. A showcase of Italy's great vintages, the huge wine list is impressive. ⊠ *240 Central Park S, between Broadway and 7th Ave.,* ☎ *212/265–5959. Reservations essential. Jacket and tie AE, DC, MC, V. No lunch weekends.*

$$$ ✕ **Remi.** A Venetian sensibility pervades this stylish restaurant designed by Adam Tihany. A skylighted atrium, blue-and-white stripe banquettes, Venetian glass chandeliers, and a soaring room-length mural of the city of canals make this the perfect spot for a power lunch or a satisfying meal before a night on the town. Chef Francesco Antonucci's contemporary Venetian cuisine is highly favored among Italians living in New York. Fresh sardines make a lovely beginning, with their contrasting sweet-and-sour onion garnish, and you can't go wrong with the sumptuous pastas, expertly prepared rack of lamb, or any of the wonderful desserts. ⊠ *145 W. 53rd St., between 6th and 7th Aves.,* ☎ *212/581–4242. Reservations essential. AE, DC, MC, V. No lunch weekends.*

$$–$$$ ✕ **Baldoria.** Frank Pellegrino's beloved Rao's, an Italian dining institution in Harlem, is so impossible to get into we took it out of the guide years ago. But lucky for everyone, last year Frank Pellegrino Jr. set up shop downtown in the theater district. The bi-level restaurant is almost 10 times the size of the original, but the atmosphere is almost as homey and personal. Many of the signature dishes that made the original restaurant famous are served, perhaps the best among them an inexplicably wonderful fusilli with sausage and cabbage in red sauce. Other exemplary dishes include a large veal chop smothered with wild mushrooms and an excellent grilled octopus. ⊠ *249 W. 49th St., between Broadway and 8th Ave.,* ☎ *212/582–0460. Reservations essential. AE, D, MC, V. Closed Sun. No lunch.*

$$–$$$ ✕ **Osteria del Circo.** Opened by the sons of celebrity restaurateur Sirio Maccioni (Le Cirque 2000), this less formal place celebrates the Tuscan cooking of their mother Egi. Mechanical monkeys do tricks around the dining room's center pillar, and large statues of circus animals dance over the open kitchen. The contemporary menu offers a wide selection (the lobster salad is always available) and includes some traditional Tuscan specialties, such as Egi's ricotta-and-spinach filled ravioli, tossed in butter and sage and gratinéed with imported Parmesan. The *pizza pazza* (crazy pizza) has a delicate layer of mascarpone cheese and tomato topped with thin slices of prosciutto di Parma. Don't miss the fanciful Circo desserts, amusingly presented and thoroughly decadent. ⊠ *120 W. 55th St., between 6th and 7th Aves.,* ☎ *212/265–3636. Reservations essential. AE, DC, MC, V. No lunch Sun.*

$$ ✕ **La Locanda.** In a neighborhood of popular but unsatisfying restaurants, La Locanda stands out as an authentic re-creation of an Italian trattoria. The owners, a restaurant family from Italy, have stuck with the familiar in New York: all the staff is Italian, Italian pop music plays on the radio, and their bakery next door supplies the authentic Italian bread (for better or worse). The antipasti portions are generous and the pastas, finished in the kitchen with sauce, butter, and cheese as they ought to be, are excellent. Grilled meats are also tempting. ⊠ *737 9th Ave., at 50th St.,* ☎ *212/258–2900. AE, MC, V.*

Japanese

$$$$ ✕ **Sugiyama.** If you are not familiar with the Japanese style of eating known as *kaiseki,* (a meal of small tasting portions that are presented in a ritualized order) then you should make a reservation at this charming prix-fixe-only restaurant, where Nao Sugiyama will give you a delicious crash course. First timers should order the *omikase,* or chef's tasting, so you can appreciate the true breadth of the genre, which unfolds in front of you like a kabuki performance. It may start with a wild mountain plum floating in a glasslike cube of gelatin and served with a selection of other intriguing cold starters. It could proceed to a gurgling pot of blowfish or to sweet lobster or delicate squid that you cook on a hot stone. There will probably be sashimi and sushi and miso-marinated cod. The experience is exhilarating and delicious. ⊠ *251 W. 55th St., between Broadway and 8th Ave.,* ☎ *212/956–0670. AE, D, MC, V. Closed Sun.–Mon. No lunch.*

Kosher

$$–$$$ ✕ **Le Marais.** The appetizing display of meats and terrines at the entrance, the bare wood floors, tables covered with butcher paper, the French wall posters, and maroon banquettes may remind you of a Parisian bistro. Yet the clientele (mostly male) is strictly kosher, and they don't speak French. A cold *terrine de boeuf en gelée façon pot au feu* (marinated short ribs) starts the meal on the right note, and rib steak for two is cooked until it is tender and juicy. The accompanying fries are perfect. ⊠ *150 W. 46th St., between 6th and 7th Aves.,* ☎ *212/ 869–0900. AE, MC, V. No dinner Fri., no lunch Sat.*

Russian

$$$-$$$$ ✕ **Russian Tea Room.** The late Warner Le Roy (famous for Tavern on the Green) created this posh Winter Palace of a restaurant. The first-floor power scene is decorated with deep, red booths, year-round Christmas ornaments, and glistening ice sculptures. A clear, hollow acrylic bear in the second-floor dining room serves as an aquarium for the fish du jour. Fur coats flock to the bar to throw back frozen vodka and toast successful shopping sprees. There is so much glitz and glam that you almost forget about the food, a good thing considering much of it tastes like standard Bolshevik issue. The hearty borscht and tender short ribs are among your best bets. The oversize chicken kiev shoots butter across the room. ⊠ *150 W. 57th St., between 6th and 7th Aves.,* ☎ *212/974–2111. Reservations essential. AE, D, DC, MC, V.*

$$-$$$$ ✕ **Firebird.** Housed in two brownstones renovated to resemble a pre-
★ Revolutionary St. Petersburg mansion, Firebird boasts eight dining rooms full of objets d'art and period antiques. Staples of the regional cuisine here range from caviar and *zakuska* (assorted Russian hors d'oeuvres) to tea with cherry preserves, and great desserts (an assortment of terrific Russian cookies steal the show). Don't fail to sample the extraordinary vodka selection. And the elegant caviar presentation—steaming hot blini drenched in butter, slathered with sour cream and filled with beluga, sevruga, or osetra by waiters in white gloves—is a giddy indulgence. **Firebird Cafe** (⊠ 363 W. 46th St., between 9th and 10th Aves.,, ☎ 212/586–0244), next door, has become a fashionable cabaret nightspot and serves desserts as well as vodkas. ⊠ *365 W. 46th St., between 8th and 9th Aves.,* ☎ *212/586–0244. Reservations essential. AE, DC, MC, V. No lunch Sun.*

Scandinavian

$$$$ ✕ **Aquavit.** Cool as a dip in the Baltic Sea, this airy atrium that was
★ once Nelson Rockefeller's town house is decorated with contemporary art, Roger Smith kites, and an inspiring waterfall. The nouveau Swedish fare of wunderkind chef Marcus Sammuelsson is dressed in chic contemporary garb, and offered only through a prix-fixe menu in the main dining room. Forget herring, smoked eel, lingonberries, and pea soup (although they're better here than anywhere else): think miso-glazed lobster in carrot-ginger broth and halibut in marrow crust. Desserts are equally creative and delicious. An upstairs dining room is less formal and less expensive. Appropriately, New York's largest selection of aquavits keeps company with the well-chosen wine list. Sunday brunch is literally a smorgasbord. ⊠ *13 W. 54th St., between 5th and 6th Aves.,* ☎ *212/307–7311. Reservations essential.. AE, DC, MC, V.*

Seafood

$$$ ✕ **Esca.** Mario Batali's latest venture takes its inspiration from the sea. Esca, Italian for "bait," lures diners in with delectable raw preparations called *cruda*—which might include scallops with tangerine oil or fluke with a douse of olive oil and sprinkle of crunchy sea salt—and hooks them with such entrées as a whole, salt-crusted *branzino* (striped sea bass), or *bucatini* pasta with baby octopus. The dining room, done up in hues of tan, aqua, and terra-cotta, conjures images of sea and sand, though the high-powered media crowd could exist nowhere but Manhattan. Batali's partner, Joe Bastianich, is in charge of the wine cellar, so expect an adventurous list of esoteric Italian bottles. ⊠ *402 W. 43rd St., at 9th Ave.,* ☎ *212/564–7272. Reservations essential. AE, D, MC, V. Closed Sun.*

SPECIAL EXPERIENCES

CRAVING KOREAN AT 2 AM?
Wanna catch some rays along
with a dish of homemade pasta?
As you might expect, New York
City can fulfill your every dining desire,
whether for a really good brunch or a
side of celebrities. All of these special spots
are reviewed in this chapter.

Al fresco: Although New York is an asphalt jungle, there are still a few restaurants where you can dine in the open air,
off the sidewalk. Old World charm flows
from the fountain in the middle of **Bar-
betta**'s handsome garden on Restaurant
Row in the theater district. For a romantic al fresco dinner over a dish of handmade Pugliese pasta try the garden at **I
Trulli** in Murray Hill. You would never guess
a ramshackle East Village block could hide
a garden as beautiful as the one behind
I Coppi, where a ban on large parties
keeps it quiet and serene. On the other
hand, if margarita-induced mayhem is more
your East Village speed, the lovely garden at **Miracle Grill** beckons. If you'd like
the company of Lady Liberty while you
dine, head to Lower Manhattan and
American Park at the Battery.

Brunch: Brunch with a few friends and
the Sunday paper is a weekly tradition.
Upper West Side institutions such as **Bar-
ney Greengrass** and **Sarabeth's** offer
good food at good prices (and often a
good long wait for a table), while **Avenue** serves French pastries along with
fine brunch fare. On the Upper East Side,
Le Pain Quotidien serves up Belgian
treats. In TriBeCa, **Bubby's** always has
a line on weekend mornings, but these
days the overflow is handled by **Kitchenette.** Long before the Meatpacking
District became trendy, **Florent** had a loyal
brunch following. Farther East, **Home**
and **Petit Abeille** offer cozy environments and good food. For nontraditional
brunch fare, try the Spanish tapas at

Pipa or the Swedish smorgasbord at
Aquavit.

Celebrity spotting: True New Yorkers
will never admit to choosing a dining destination based on the chance of seeing
a celebrity, but if star-studded glam is the
evening's aim, some excellent restaurants usually come through. Everyone
from Jerry Seinfeld to Martha Stewart have
been caught with their hand in the bread
basket at SoHo's **Balthazar.** Giorgio Armani, Sandra Bernhardt, and Isaac
Mizrahi have been seen getting take-out
from **Second Avenue Deli** in the East
Village. For the billionaire celebrity set,
like Ron Perlman, Donald Trump, and
Larry Tish, nothing but Midtown's **Le
Cirque 2000** will do, but for media
moguls, such as Edgar Bronfman, Tina
Brown, and Barbara Walters, the Grill
Room at **Four Seasons** is the place to lunch.
If none of these restaurants is what you're
looking for, there's bound to be someone
famous at **Jean Georges, Daniel,** or
Nobu any night of the week.

Late-night: If you'd rather eat at 3 AM
than wake up early to stand on line for
Sunday brunch, there are a wealth of late-
night dining options to choose from. In
TriBeCa you can wind down to the wee
hours at **Le Zinc.** In SoHo, you can eat
your way around the world at **Blue Ribbon** until 4 AM. In the Meatpacking District **Pastis** serves French bistro fare
almost as late. If wine's your thing, head
to the East Village's **Tasting Room** (open
until 2 AM) for an excellent selection of
American labels and contemporary cooking, but if it's martinis and creative American fare you desire, your first priority should
be **First** (until 3 AM). If you want a more
ethnic experience, try the 24-hour **Kang
Suh** Korean barbecue place in Midtown,
or Chinese noodles at **Great New York
Noodletown,** where you can get *mei fun*
until 4 AM.

Steak

$$$–$$$$ ✕ **Nick & Stef's Steakhouse.** The menu here, at the first New York venture of L.A. chef Joachim Splichal, can be a daunting proposition. It's a stately steakhouse, but with a mix-and-match philosophy and a French sensibility. Diners must choose among a lengthy list of meats and seafood, sauces, potatoes, and vegetables—12 of each, in fact, though we're not sure what the significance of that number is. This means that in addition to the steakhouse staples of New York strip, lobster, mashed potatoes, creamed spinach, and Worcestershire sauce, there's also a venison chop, pommes Maxim's—thin slices of potato arranged like scales and cooked in clarified butter, grilled Portobello mushrooms with red wine-shallot jus, and bordelaise sauce with bone marrow. The setting is appropriately large and corporate for the Penn Station locale. ✉ 9 *Penn Plaza, W. 33rd St., between 7th and 8th Aves.,* ☎ *212/563–4444. AE, D, DC, MC, V. No lunch Sun.*

$$–$$$$ ✕ **Gallagher's Steak House.** The most casual of the great New York
★   steak houses, with red-and-white check tablecloths, photos of sports greats on the walls, and a large, friendly bar, Gallagher's has almost no pretensions and nothing to hide—through the window from the street you can even peer into the dry-aging room where slabs of meat ripen to perfection. You won't be disappointed with the famous aged sirloin steaks, oversize lobsters, or any of the fabulous potato dishes (try the potatoes O'Brien with sweet pepper and onion). Don't miss the creamy rice pudding. ✉ *228 W. 52nd St., between Broadway and 8th Ave.,* ☎ *212/245–5336. Reservations essential. AE, DC, MC, V.*

Midtown East

Power brokers like to seal their deals over lunch on the East Side, so that means lots of suits and ties at the restaurants during the day. At night the streets are deserted, but the restaurants are filled with people celebrating success over some of the finest, most expensive, and most formal food in town.

American

$$$$ ✕ **Four Seasons.** Mies van der Rohe's landmark Seagram Building houses one of New York's most famous restaurants, designed by architect Philip Johnson in a timeless Modern style. The starkly masculine Grill Room, a longtime bastion of the power lunch, has inviting leather banquettes, rosewood walls, a floating sculpture, and one of the best bars in New York. Illuminated trees, a gurgling pool of Carrara marble, and undulating chain curtains distinguish the more romantic Pool Room. As the name implies, the eclectic international menu changes seasonally; the pre-theater prix-fixe dinner is a relatively inexpensive way to experience it. Otherwise, the menu is one of the priciest in town. You can't go wrong with the Dover sole, the steak tartare, or the duck. Old-fashioned service and an aristocratic wine list keep the Four Seasons at the top of its class. ✉ *99 E. 52nd St., between Park and Lexington Aves.,* ☎ *212/754–9494. Reservations essential. Jacket required. AE, DC, MC, V. Closed Sun. No lunch Sat.*

$$$ ✕ **Larry Forgione's An American Place.** Executive chef Forgione, one of the original practitioners of New American cooking, captures the hearts of New York diners by preparing what has become classic American restaurant food. The menu ranges from fresh Maine deviled-crab spring rolls to cedar-planked salmon with seasonal vegetables. In the Benjamin Hotel, the room has a high ceiling, art deco brasserie-style light fixtures, colorful china, and generously spaced tables that impart a sense of luxury. Kindly service adds polish to this solid experience. If you have to

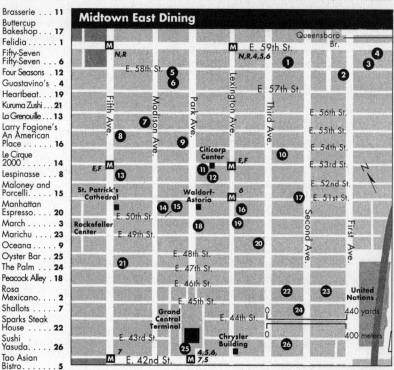

Midtown East Dining

spend Thanksgiving away from home, this is where you should do it. ✉ *565 Lexington Ave., at 50th St.,* ☎ *212/888–5650. Reservations essential. AE, DC, MC, V. No lunch weekends.*

Cafés

$ ✕ **Manhattan Espresso.** Foreign languages are heard as often as English at this favorite with international businesspeople, who hone in on the Illy espresso and treats from Bouley Bakery. ✉ *146 E. 49th St., between 3rd and Lexington Aves.,* ☎ *212/832–3010. Closed weekends.*

Contemporary

$$$$ ✕ **March.** With its travertine floor, working fireplace, and burled teak-and-elm wainscoting, this romantic restaurant tucked into a small town house is elegantly understated. Co-owner Joseph Scalice supervises the polished service and the expert wine list that complement the inspired cuisine of chef Wayne Nish. Demonstrating a mastery of classical French technique coupled with a strong Asian influence, the all-table d'hôte prix-fixe menu is organized into categories designed for tasting. You can select any number of courses, and then choose from a long list of seasonal offerings to customize your menu. The menu includes a range of dishes, many with a Japanese flair, such as sashimi of Japanese yellowfin tuna with olive oil and soy sauce, and such luxury offerings as the "Beggar's Purses," filled with caviar and crème fraîche or lobster and truffles. ✉ *405 E. 58th St., between 1st Ave. and Sutton Pl.,* ☎ *212/754–6272. Reservations essential. AE, DC, MC, V. No lunch.*

$$$–$$$$ ✕ **Heartbeat.** The omnipresent Drew Nieporent is behind this unfortunately named restaurant in the W New York hotel. The room, designed by David Rockwell, feels a little bit like sitting in a Mondrian painting. Executive chef Michel Nischan has devised a menu of modern-day spa food that emphasizes healthful preparations full of flavor, not fat. Starters include a sashimi of fluke and sweet shrimp and a de-

fyingly rich heirloom squash soup. The entrées are creative and appealing despite having no added fat. Highlights might include a sautéed trout with lump crab cake and succotash and a spiced seared venison chop. Don't worry, desserts are full of fat. Finish with a selection from the impressive tea menu. ⊠ *149 E. 49th St., at Lexington Ave.,* ☎ *212/ 407–2900. AE, DC, MC, V. No lunch weekends.*

$$$–$$$$ ✕ **Maloney & Porcelli.** Pictures of eagles and a large fish suspended from the ceiling brighten up this lively bi-level space, decorated in a green-and-beige color scheme with wood accents. A large, square bar marks the center of the room. The definitive dish is a huge, juicy crackling pork shank served on a bed of poppy-seed sauerkraut with a Mason jar of tangy, homemade "Firecracker" jalapeño-spiced apple sauce. Drunken doughnuts, served with three small pots of liqueur-flavored jam, are one of the fun desserts. The inventive wine list includes 40 wines priced under $40. ⊠ *37 E. 50th St., between Madison and Park Aves.,* ☎ *212/750–2233. AE, DC, MC, V.*

$$$–$$$$ ✕ **Fifty Seven Fifty Seven.** Designed by I. M. Pei, the Four Seasons Hotel, which houses this room and a sophisticated adjacent bar, is strikingly sleek. With 22-ft coffered ceilings, inlaid maple floors, onyx-studded bronze chandeliers, and a contemporary American menu, the restaurant even attracts locals. Creative interpretations of familiar dishes such as lobster Caesar salad are very well prepared, and it's hard to choose between the pepper-crusted tuna niçoise or the perfectly cooked herb-roasted veal chop with artichokes and oven-roasted tomatoes. For breakfast, don't miss the lemon ricotta pancakes. ⊠ *57 E. 57th St., between Madison and Park Aves.,* ☎ *212/758–5757. Reservations essential. AE, DC, MC, V.*

Eclectic

$$–$$$$ ✕ **Guastavino's.** Under the 59th Street Bridge, in an incredible space that shows the pristine tile work of Rapphael Guastavino, is something of a marvel to New Yorkers, who remember when this was nothing but a deserted tunnel you would not want to walk through on a lonely night. Of course it took Terrance Conran, a Brit with a penchant for huge, out-of-the-way spaces in his native London, to summon the guts to turn it into a restaurant. The restaurant has two dining rooms; the bustling downstairs is where you can order fish and chips, raw shellfish, roast baby chicken, or a catfish club sandwich. Upstairs, in Club Guastavino, the atmosphere and the food is more refined, if not outstanding, and the menu is prix fixe. There, you can sample the fancier dishes of French-trained chef Daniel Orr, such as frog's legs with parsley and garlic or John Dory with cockles. ⊠ *409 E. 59th St., between 1st and Sutton Pl.,* ☎ *212/980–2455. AE, DC, MC, V.*

French

$$$$ ✕ **La Grenouille.** Flowers and fur: that's how some people describe the scene at La Grenouille (French for "frog"). It is the quintessential Manhattan French restaurant, so much so that it almost feels like a retro theme restaurant. The menu, written only in French, presents a $90 prix fixe (with several tempting supplements that can add to your bill) of three courses, which may consist of salmon tartare with caviar vinaigrette, lobster and scallop ravioli, or frogs' legs and escargot to start, followed by duck breast with chestnuts, baby chicken with lavender, or a flambé of kidneys with mustard sauce. Expect to add anywhere from $3.50 to $85 for lobster, sole, foie gras, steak, or beluga. La Grenouille isn't so much about having a wonderful meal as it is about having a wonderful experience, complete with a thick French accent. ⊠ *3 E. 52nd St., between 5th and Madison Aves.,* ☎ *212/752–1495. Reservations essential. AE, DC, MC, V. Closed Sun.–Mon.*

$$$$ ✕ **Le Cirque 2000.** Sirio Maccioni has fed the world's elite for more than 25 years, first at Le Cirque, now at Le Cirque 2000 in the landmark Villard House at the New York Palace Hotel. Whimsical, futuristic circus decor contrasts with the original gilded interior in two ornate dining rooms—you either love it or you hate it. French native Pierre Schaedlin has injected the classic French menu with contemporary overtones and has included a few homages to Sirio's Italian roots (although the lobster salad is still served at lunch). Each weeknight also brings a different special. Though the dessert presentations are still over the top, without former pastry chef Jacques Torres many have become more show than substance. The large wine list spans the spectrum of the world's varietals. ⊠ *455 Madison Ave., between 50th and 51st Sts.,* ☎ *212/303–7788. Reservations essential. Jacket and tie. AE, DC, MC, V. No lunch Sun.*

$$$$ ✕ **Lespinasse.** Christian Delouvrier's extravagant French cooking fits
★ the opulent, stuffy, Louis XV dining room of the luxurious St. Regis hotel like a dainty hand in a kid glove. The gilded trim, extravagant floral arrangements, and commodious seating provide a perfect setting for his seasonal menu, which includes a wide selection of game (*civet* of hare, roasted pheasant, grilled venison), seafood (pan-roasted lobster, jumbo scallops with tomato confit, grilled halibut), and vegetarian (a complete dégustation menu is available) dishes. Everything is exquisitely prepared and presented with enough pomp to justify the extravagant prices. The service is exceptional. A thoughtful wine list offers few bargains, but that's not why you're here. ⊠ *2 E. 55th St., between 5th and Madison Aves.,* ☎ *212/339–6719. Reservations essential. Jacket required. AE, DC, MC, V. Closed Sun.*

$$$–$$$$ ✕ **Peacock Alley.** As New Yorkers learn to love eating in hotel dining
★ rooms, grande dames such as the Waldorf-Astoria pose a challenge. But foodies are flocking to the distinguished Peacock Alley to sample Laurent Gras's cooking. He's a product of Alain Ducasse's Louis XV kitchen in Monaco, and his style reflects the elegant restraint and indulgent simplicity of his mentor. Gras performs miracles with every course on the prix-fixe menu: a savory soup—pumpkin consommé with sweet-and-sour chicken wings, cockscombs, and San Danielle ham—is a triumph, as is a dessert soup, garnished with passion-fruit sorbet and tropical fruits. Tranquil lighting, banquette seating, roomy tables, fine china, professional service, and a comprehensive wine cellar add up to an exquisite experience. ⊠ *301 Park Ave., between 49th and 50th Sts.,* ☎ *212/872–4895. AE, DC, MC, V. Closed Sun. No lunch Sat.*

$$–$$$ ✕ **Brasserie.** If ever there was a midtown restaurant with a downtown vibe, this ultra-modern rathskeller brasserie fits the bill. The award-winning design by architects Diller & Scofidio uses molded pearwood, lime green resin, pastry-bag sculptures, and digital flat-screen technology to create an otherworldly eating environment. As an added bonus, the contemporary brasserie fare—served from morning to late night—is excellent. The baguettes are superb and the daily specials speak French without an accent. Don't leave without sampling dessert or taking a trip to the cool bathroom. ⊠ *100 E. 53rd St., between Lexington and Park Aves.,* ☎ *212/751–4840. AE, D, DC, MC, V.*

Italian

$$–$$$$ ✕ **Felidia.** Manhattanites frequent this *ristorante* as much for the winning enthusiasm of owner Lidia Bastianich as for the food. The emphasis here is on the authentic regional cuisines of Italy, with a bow to dishes from Ms. Bastianich's homeland, Istria, on the Adriatic. Sit in an attractive front room with a wooden bar (great for a solo dish of pasta and a glass of excellent wine), a rustic room beyond (you might forget you're in New York City), or an elegant second floor (good for

quiet conversation while you eat). Regional and seasonal menu items include dishes featuring white truffles and exceptional game preparations (in fall). Order risotto (no matter the flavor), fresh homemade pasta, or roasted whole fish, and choose from a wine list representing Italy's finest vineyards. They offer an interesting menu of olive oils to pair with the food. ⊠ *243 E. 58th St., between 2nd and 3rd Aves.,* ☎ *212/758–1479. Reservations essential. Jacket and tie. AE, DC, MC, V. Closed Sun. No lunch Sat.*

Japanese

$$–$$$$ ✕ **Kuruma Zushi.** Only a small sign in Japanese indicates the location
★ of this extraordinary restaurant that serves only one thing, sushi (well, two—they also have sashimi). Don't let the stark decor fool you into believing this is like any other sushi restaurant. Regulars know that the best way to enjoy the exotic delicacies available here is to bypass the tables, sit at the sushi bar, and put yourself in the hands of Toshihiro Uezu, the owner and fantastically talented chef. Uezu imports hard-to-find fish from Japan, and on a typical night he will offer several different types of tuna, the prices of which vary according to the degree of fattiness and the size of the fish from which they are cut. The sea scallops are so fresh they literally move on the plate. Exotic pickled vegetables, freshly grated wasabi, and the most quietly attentive service staff in the city complete the wildly expensive but worth it experience. ⊠ *7 E. 47th St., 2nd floor, between 5th and Madison Aves.,* ☎ *212/317–2802. AE, MC, V. Closed Sun.*

$$–$$$ ✕ **Sushi Yasuda.** The chic bamboo-lined space in which chef Maomichi Yasuda works his marine magic is as clean and elegant as his food. It couldn't be more out of place, surrounded by car rental companies on a nondescript block near Grand Central Station. But whether he's using hard-to-pronounce fish flown in daily from Japan, or the creamiest sea urchin with a subtle taste of the sea, Yasuda makes sushi so fresh and delicate it is transporting. A number of special appetizers change daily, and a fine selection of sake and beer complement the food. In typical Japanese fashion, the service is doting but unobtrusive. Certainly this adds up to one of the best Japanese restaurants in town. ⊠ *204 E. 43rd St., between 2nd and 3rd Aves.,* ☎ *212/972–1001. AE, D, MC, V. Closed Sun., no lunch Sat.*

Kosher

$$$–$$$$ ✕ **Shallots.** The owners here hope no one notices that their restaurant is Kosher, and feel certain that even the non-observant will like it so much they'll want to eat here anyway. Kosher or not, Shallots is certainly an ambitious restaurant. The decor is tasteful and romantic (though walking through the deserted Sony Atrium at night kind of ruins it) with backlit glass panels, low lighting, and impressive floral arrangements. The food comes on oversize, colored, frosted-glass plates, and leans toward such dishes as porcini-dusted sweetbreads and parsnip and garlic soup rather than to knishes and corned beef sandwiches. Everything is attractively presented and priced for the big leagues. The only moment that you'll really notice you're not in a secular restaurant is when you first look at the wine list, which is—you guessed it—all kosher. ⊠ *The Sony Atrium, 550 Madison Ave., between 55th and 56th Sts.,* ☎ *212/833–7800. AE, D, MC, V. Closed Fri. and Sat. No lunch.*

Mexican

$$–$$$ ✕ **Rosa Mexicano.** Owner Josefina Howard is serious about Mexican
★ cooking, and the vibrant cuisine at her lively restaurant makes you believe whatever she has to say. When the staff slips open the parchment package that contains a lamb shank braised in a three-chili sauce, the

room fills with the fragrance of Oaxaca. Duck enchiladas and chicken steamed in beer stand out among the interesting regional dishes. A better guacamole, prepared table-side and served with warm corn tortillas, cannot be found—not even in Mexico. The assortment of chilled seafood served as an appetizer is terrific, and the chocolate-chili mousse cake has real kick. The jam-packed bar room in the front makes you feel as though you've happened upon a Mexican fiesta (or a frat party). Howard has opened a second **Rosa Mexicano** (⊠ 51 Columbus Ave., ☎ 212/977–7700) across from Lincoln Center, with fancifully modern decor and a similar menu. ⊠ *1063 1st Ave., at 58th St.,* ☎ *212/ 753–7407. Reservations essential. AE, DC, MC, V. No lunch.*

Pan-Asian

$$–$$$$ ✕ **Tao Asian Bistro.** The scene here offers little of the serenity suggested by its name. This is a see-and-be-seen, people-watching fest, with every guest trying to look hipper and better dressed then the next. Housed in a former movie theater, the huge restaurant has plenty of room for all the beautiful people and wanna-bes. With its Asian screens, red lighting, and soaring brick walls, the restaurant seems to go on forever in every direction. The menu explores the cuisines of Asia, throwing in a liberal dose of creative license. There are several sushi-style appetizers that are satisfying for the non-purist, and dishes such as dragon tail spare ribs in a sweet and sour sauce, Chilean sea bass in soy, and pad thai. Dominating the dining room is a 40-ft high gilt Chinese Buddha, who sits in a fountain strewn with black stones. He seems thoroughly amused by the spectacle. ⊠ *42 E. 58th St., between Park and Madison Aves.,* ☎ *212/888–2288. AE, D, MC, V.*

$$–$$$$ ✕ **Vong.** A stint at Bangkok's Oriental Hotel inspired Jean-Georges Vongerichten to create this radiant restaurant of potted palms, gold-leaf ceilings, and patchwork murals. Presentation is vital here: the food is showcased on dazzling dishes of varying size, color, and shape. The menu changes with the seasons, but reliable standbys include quail rubbed with Thai spices and grilled beef and noodles in a ginger broth. As is often the case these days, the appetizers are more interesting than the entrées. Order two or three and you won't be disappointed. The desserts are also terrific. It's not an authentic Thai experience—more like French-Thai fusion—but the food is flavorful, fun, and delicious. ⊠ *200 E. 54th St.,* ☎ *212/486–9592. Reservations essential. AE, DC, MC, V. No lunch weekends.*

Seafood

$$$$ ✕ **Oceana.** The long, narrow first-floor dining room of this contemporary seafood prix-fixe restaurant feels so much like the inside of a ship you almost have the sensation of floating. Rich wood, subdued lighting, bright murals, and posters of luxury ocean liners enhance the feeling. Chef Rick Moonen has a deft hand with seafood; everything on the menu is well prepared. Crab cakes, lobster ravioli, bouillabaisse, and salmon tartare wrapped in smoked salmon all score high marks as starters. More than 100 whites are offered on the first-rate wine list; the Bordeaux selection is especially choice. ⊠ *55 E. 54th St., between Madison and Park Aves.,* ☎ *212/759–5941. Reservations essential. Jacket required. AE, DC, MC, V. Closed Sun. No lunch Sat.*

$–$$$ ✕ **Oyster Bar.** Deep in the heart of Grand Central Station, the Oyster Bar has been a worthy seafood destination for almost nine decades. In separate areas, the cavernous tile space combines Old New York splendor with the camp of a 1970s airport-style lounge, the noir style of a serpentine lunch counter, and the appealing tackiness of a smoke-filled commuter tavern. Sit at the counter and slurp an assortment of bracingly fresh oysters, washed down with an ice-cold brew or a steaming hot bowl of clam chowder. Or enter the grand main dining room and

experience the forgotten pleasure of fresh, unadorned seafood such as
lobster with drawn butter, lightly grilled fish, or matjes herring in season. Avoid anything that sounds new-fangled. ✉ *Grand Central Station, dining concourse, 42nd St. and Vanderbilt Ave.,* ☎ *212/490–6650.
AE, D, MC, V.*

Spanish

$$ ✕ **Marichu.** Natural brick, old beams, and a lovely garden grace New
York's only Basque restaurant, an overlooked find just steps from the
United Nations. A fascinating list of Spanish wines nicely comple-
ments the refined and elegant cuisine, which is particularly strong on
seafood. There's no better way to start than with Rioja peppers stuffed
with a puree of salt cod. Other preparations, such as Florida snapper
in garlic vinaigrette and baby squid in black ink sauce, are fresh and
boldly seasoned. The small, bright dining room with white walls and
wooden tables doesn't feel like Manhattan. ✉ *342 E. 46th St., between
1st and 2nd Aves.,* ☎ *212/370–1866. AE, DC, MC, V. No lunch
weekends.*

Steak

$$$–$$$$ ✕ **Sparks Steak House.** Magnums and jeroboams of wines that cost
more than most people earn in a week decorate the large dining rooms
of this classic New York steak house. The tone is set by the black-tie
waiters at the door, who seem so sincerely pleased to see you it's
startling to realize there are about 600 other people in the place. Al-
though seafood is given fair play on the menu, Sparks is about steak
(lobster and fish just don't match well with all of that aged Bordeaux).
The menu includes dry-aged steaks from every section of the cow—
sirloin, filet, and rib among them. The lamb chops and veal chops are
also noteworthy. Classic sides of home fries, spinach, mushrooms,
onions, and broccoli are all you need to complete the experience. Oh,
and a bottle of fine red wine. ✉ *210 E. 46th St., between 2nd and 3rd
Aves.,* ☎ *212/687–4855. Reservations essential. AE, DC, MC, V. No
lunch weekends.*

$$–$$$$ ✕ **The Palm.** They may have added tablecloths in recent years, but a
piece of white cotton does little to hide the true nature of this legendary
steak house, where sawdust on the floor, brusque waiters, and caricatures of legendary New Yorkers drawn right on the wall set the tone.
You will either eat steak—the sirloin and filet are always impeccable—
or lobster so big there may not be room at the table for such classic
side dishes as rich creamed spinach. Those in the know order the "half
and half," an addictive combination of cottage-fried potatoes and
fried onions. Overflow from the restaurant caused the owners to open
Palm Too (✉ 840 2nd Ave., between 44th and 45th Sts., ☎ 212/697–
5198), a slightly less raffish version of the original, across the street.
In the Theater District, **Palm West** (✉ 250 W. 50th St., between Broadway and 8th Ave.) offers roomier quarters. ✉ *837 2nd Ave., between
44th and 45th Sts.,* ☎ *212/687–2953. Reservations essential. AE, DC,
MC, V. No lunch weekends.*

Upper East Side

Enclave of the privileged, where lunching ladies air-kiss over pricey bowls
of pasta and bankers sip single malts at the end of the day, the Upper
East Side nevertheless harbors some exciting eateries. They range from
temples of haute cuisine to neighborhood coffee shops, offering something appropriate whether you are visiting a museum or shopping
along Madison Avenue.

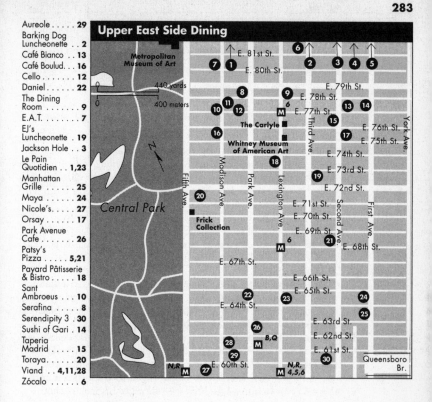

Upper East Side Dining

American

$$–$$$ ✕ **Dining Room.** Mark Spangenthal's restaurant, a welcome presence on the Upper East Side, feels like a plush neighborhood restaurant for people with money. As the name suggests, the place has no ulterior motives, and Spanganthal is happy to let his contemporary American food shine. His zingy fried artichokes are a favorite, alongside a copious raw bar with several types of oyster and a selection of ceviche; seasonal entrées include pan-roasted wild snapper with summer vegetables. ⊠ *154 E. 79th St., at Lexington Ave.,* ☎ *212/327–2500. AE, D, MC, V. No lunch Sat.*

American Casual

✕ **E.A.T.** Located a block from the Metropolitan Museum of Art, E.A.T. was Eli Zabar's first foray to the east side of town. The pleasant no-frills atmosphere (think butcher paper over metal tables) has long been a favorite haunt of the ladies-who-lunch set. Maybe they like it because the food is simple, fresh, and very good, or maybe they like it because everything is so overpriced. Try any of the wonderful soups and be sure to get a basket of the bread for which Zabar is famous. On the way out, buy a first-class brownie from the retail counter. Just be sure to rob a bank before you get here. ⊠ *1064 Madison Ave., between 80th and 81st Sts.,* ☎ *212/772–0022. AE.*

$–$$ ✕ **Serendipity 3.** This fun ice-cream parlor café has been producing excellent burgers, foot-long hot dogs (with or without chili), French toast, omelets, salads, and other satisfying plates since 1954. The shepherd's pie isn't bad either. But most people come for the fantasy sundaes—huge, naughty, and decadent—and Serendipity's most famous dessert, frozen hot chocolate (now available in a mix you can prepare at home). ⊠ *225 E. 60th St., between 2nd and 3rd Aves.,* ☎ *212/838–3531. AE, DC, MC, V. BYOB.*

$ ✕ **Viand.** Okay, this is only a diner—well, the one on Madison Avenue is really only a lunch counter. But in the land of expensive restaurants and stuffy waitstaff, there is something appealing, almost oasislike, about the old-fashioned, friendly attitude of the talkative line-cooks. Turkeys are roasted fresh all day long. And the rice pudding is the best of its kind in the city. ⊠ *673 Madison Ave., between 61st and 62nd Sts.,* ☎ *212/751–6622; 1011 Madison Ave., at 78th St.,* ☎ *212/249–8250; 300 E. 86th St., at 2nd Ave.,* ☎ *212/879–9425. AE, MC, V.*

Cafés

$–$$$$ ✕ **Sant Ambroeus.** You'll swear you're in Milan at this very Italian café with red leather banquettes and Murano chandeliers, where you can enjoy magnificent coffee and desserts, including intense gelato. For a quick jolt, visit the tuxedoed man at the espresso bar. ⊠ *1000 Madison Ave., between 77th and 78th Sts.,* ☎ *212/570–2211.*

$–$$ ✕ **Toraya.** This traditional Japanese tea room is tucked into a row of town houses just off Fifth Avenue. Along with green tea, you can try some of the seasonal *wagashi*, a sweet treat that's often shaped like flowers or leaves. ⊠ *17 E. 71st St., between 5th and Madison Aves.,* ☎ *212/861–1700.*

$ ✕ **Café Bianco.** Settle in here for excellent coffee, sinful desserts (such as the chocolate-covered *tartufo*), and light meals; in warm weather, try the back garden with its pint-size pond. ⊠ *1486 2nd Ave., between 77th and 78th Sts.,* ☎ *212/988–2655.*

$ ✕ **Le Pain Quotidien.** This international Belgian chain is proud of its
★   heritage—they use Belgian jams, Belgian flour for the crusty breads, even Belgian chocolate for their café mochas and hot chocolates. For a more substantial meal, take a seat at the long, wooden communal table. ⊠ *1131 Madison Ave., between 84th and 85th Sts.,* ☎ *212/327–4900; 833 Lexington Ave., between 63rd and 64th Sts.,* ☎ *212/744–5810; 100 Grand St.,* ☎ *212/625–9009.*

Contemporary

$$$$ ✕ **Aureole.** Charlie Palmer's once fashionable prix-fixe-only restaurant, with its alluring bas-reliefs, striking floral displays, and swank townhouse location, is a long-standing favorite, although these days the clientele is usually from out of town. Presentations are striking architectural constructions that on occasion leave you wishing more attention were paid to the taste than the look. Steer clear of the sea scallops, which are sandwiched between two potato latkes and fried until overcooked. Instead order the fricassee of lobster with Provençale artichokes or the pepper-seared tuna on green-onion risotto. Meat and game dishes are served in large, satisfying portions. Desserts are stunning visual masterpieces—the bittersweet chocolate and praline "opera" with caramelized hazelnut nougats is a high-rise wonder that requires some dexterity to dissect without destroying it. The small pristine garden is open in the summer. ⊠ *34 E. 61st St., between Madison and Park Aves.,* ☎ *212/319–1660. Reservations essential. AE, DC, MC, V. Closed Sun. No lunch Sat.*

$$$–$$$$ ✕ **Park Avenue Cafe.** American folk art, antique toys, and sheaves of dried wheat decorate this quintessentially New York restaurant that was an innovator of New American cooking (and plating) when it opened in 1992. David Burke's presentations are imaginative and often whimsical: salmon is cured like pastrami and arrives on a marble slab with warm corn blini, while the swordfish chop sports a numbered tag that automatically enters the bearer into a raffle to win a travel package. A selection of oysters on the half shell with a variety of garnishes is served on an ice sculpture so large it requires two people to carry it. The pastry chef's visual masterpieces, presented with equal flair, include a milk-chocolate crème brûlée. Of late, service has been sporadic and

some of the visual creativity of the dishes has come at the expense of flavor. ☒ *100 E. 63rd St., between Park and Lexington Aves.,* ☎ *212/644–1900. Reservations essential. AE, DC, MC, V. No lunch Sat.*

$$$ ✗ **Nicole's.** After a morning of shopping for the casually elegant designs of London's hot fashion talent, Nicole Farhi, why not take the elevator to the basement for an equally stylish lunch in her restaurant? The food is simple: crisp salads, fresh fish, light desserts; its calculated minimalism fits the soothing decor. At lunch the crowd is a mix of fashionistas, publishing-world players, and ladies who lunch. At dinner, it's hardly a crowd at all. ☒ *Nicole Farhi, 10 E. 60th St., between 5th and Madison Aves.,* ☎ *212/223–2288. AE, D, MC, V.*

French

$$$$ ✗ **Daniel.** In this grand space, historic elements of the old Mayfair Hotel
★ ballroom mix with modern accents to create a bi-level dining room and lounge area with a rich, timeless feel. The prix-fixe menu is contemporary French to the nth degree—nobody else prepares such contemporary dishes as Jerusalem artichoke soup with crispy bacon or chestnut-crusted venison with caramelized pear, and nobody else creates such modern classics as sea bass in a potato crust or scallops in black tie (dressed with truffles), with more confidence. The service and wine list are on par with the food. For a more casual evening you can reserve a table in the lounge. ☒ *60 E. 65th St., between Madison and Park Aves.,* ☎ *212/288–0033. Reservations essential. Jacket required. AE, DC, MC, V.*

$$$–$$$$ ✗ **Café Boulud.** At Daniel Boulud's "casual bistro" in the Surrey Hotel,
★ only the atmosphere is relaxed; the food and service are as serious and as disciplined as ever. Though overseen by Boulud, the cafe's kitchen is now in the hands of Andrew Carmellini, late of Le Cirque 2000, Lespinasse, and San Domenico. The collaboration results in a four-part menu: under *La Tradition* you'll find such classic French dishes as baked fresh pork belly with lentils; *Le Potager* is flush with tempting vegetarian offerings such as oven-roasted vegetable casserole; *La Saison* reflects the bounty of the market, which if you are lucky will include white truffles or fresh fava beans; and *Le Voyage* is where the kitchen interprets the myriad cuisines of the world. One month you might find yourself in Italy, eating a dish of freshly made *macheroni alla chitarra*—slightly thicker than usual pasta cut on a wire "guitar" and resembling square-cut spaghetti—and the next you could be in Vietnam enjoying fish steamed with ginger, soy, and garlic. ☒ *20 E. 76th St., at Madison Ave.,* ☎ *212/772–2600. Reservations essential. AE, DC, MC, V. No lunch Sun.–Mon.*

$$–$$$$ ✗ **Orsay.** It's hard to believe that this elegant, neo–art nouveau brasserie was once the socialite hangout Mortimers. Gone are the party favors, the mini-hamburgers, and most of the face-lift crowd. Of particular note on the extensive menu are unique sections, such as a long list of tartares and an array of house-smoked items. Both the traditional brasserie fare and the creative options are skillfully executed. A reasonably priced wine list and good service complete the dining experience. ☒ *1057–59 Lexington Ave., at 75th St.,* ☎ *212/517–6400. AE, D, MC, V.*

$$$ ✗ **Payard Pâtisserie & Bistro.** Pastry chef François Payard created this knockout combination bistro and pastry shop. The decor of the room feels time-honored and traditional until you look at the details: croissant motifs in the mosaic tile floor and sculpted moldings, futuristic bulbous sconces on the wall. The effect is at once familiar and innovative. Appetizers on the bistro menu include an adventurous salad of pig's-feet fritters and haricots verts, and a fresh terrine of homemade foie gras. Among the entrées are melt-in-your-mouth lamb shank with

baby artichokes and eggplant, and delicious caramelized sweetbreads with orange, rosemary, carrot, and turnip confit. Payard's desserts— tarts, soufflés, and cakes—are extraordinary. ⊠ *1032 Lexington Ave., between 73rd and 74th Sts.,* ☎ *212/717–5252. Reservations essential. AE, MC, V. Closed Sun.*

Japanese

$$–$$$ ✕ **Sushi of Gari.** The chef's creative, personal style with sushi trans-
★   lates into an exciting food experience. You can order the chef's choice at a number of prices, and you can even ask that he give you only creations that aren't on the menu. These might include an ethereally fresh tuna sushi with a creamy tofu sauce or an unusual salmon sushi with tomato and onion on rice (it tastes like it could use a bagel). Other more traditional sushi are excellent, and the Japanese noodles (udon and soba) and meat dishes (such as teriyaki) are all well prepared. The service is friendly, but because the restaurant is always packed you might have to wait for your order. ⊠ *402 E. 78th St., at 1st Ave.,* ☎ *212/517–5340. Reservations essential. AE, D, MC, V. No lunch.*

Mexican

$$–$$$ ✕ **Zócalo.** Peruse the unusual menu while enjoying a first-class margarita and one of the beguiling dips—warm tomatillo (green tomato), tomato chipotle, *pico de gallo* (raw onion-tomato salsa), and chunky guacamole, beautifully presented in the traditional *molcajete* (lava-rock mortar). Among the inventive dishes are grilled clams in a banana-leaf wrapping with peanut-tomato sauce, and chocolate sorbet laced with jalapeño peppers. Burnt-orange and blue walls add zest to the attractive long main dining room. *174 82nd St., between Lexington and 3rd Aves.,* ☎ *212/717–7772. AE, DC, MC, V.*

$$ ✕ **Maya.** The upscale hacienda decor is an appropriate setting for some
★   of the best Mexican food in the city. Begin with a delicious mango margarita or a shot of tequila from the premium list. Richard Sandoval, the chef and owner, prepares an array of dishes. Exciting starters include the *sopa de elote,* a creamy roasted corn soup served with a dumpling made from *cuitlacoche* (corn fungus), and *tamal Oaxaqueno,* steamed cornmeal and chicken wrapped in a banana leaf and served with molé sauce. The entrées include *quetzal,* a pan-roasted sea bass served with cactus salad and grilled cilantro shrimp, and *pato poblano,* grilled duck breast with butternut squash puree and prune molé. The boldly flavored food here will revive even the most jaded palate. ⊠ *1191 1st Ave., between 64th and 65th Sts.,* ☎ *212/585–1818. Reservations essential. AE, DC, MC, V. No lunch.*

Pizza

$–$$ ✕ **Patsy's Pizza.** One of the few remaining signs that this neighborhood was once largely Italian, this pizzeria, which opened in 1933, still serves some of the best slices in the city. In recent years a mini-chain of Patsy's has opened around Manhattan, but none makes a pie as thin, crisp, or flavorful as the original on upper 1st Avenue. A newly built dining room with a congenial bar offers minimal atmosphere. ⊠ *2287–91 1st Ave., between 117th and 118th Sts.,* ☎ *212/534–9783;* ⊠ *67 University Pl., between 10th and 11th. Sts.,* ☎ *212/533–3500;* ⊠ *318 W. 23rd St., between 8th and 9th. Aves.,* ☎ *646/486–7400;* ⊠ *509 3rd Ave., between 34th and 35th Sts.,* ☎ *212/689–7500;* ⊠ *1312 2nd Ave., at 69th St.,* ☎ *212/639–1000;* ⊠ *61 W. 74th St., between Columbus Ave. and Central Park W,* ☎ *212/579–3000. No credit cards.*

$–$$ ✕ **Serafina Fabulous Pizza.** Mediterranean-hued friezes, an inviting upstairs terrace, and hordes of models and celebrities grace this very Italian café adorned with wine racks and paper wall sconces. Scene aside, the draw is some of Manhattan's most authentic Neopolitan pizza and variations on focaccia (the menu claims the water used in the dough is filtered to resemble the water of Naples). The mozzarella used on the thin-crust pizza is made daily with fresh milk. For a singular treat, try the mashed potatoes slathered with homemade tomato sauce and Parmesan cheese and then baked in the oven. The downtown location is packed until the wee hours. ✉ *1022 Madison Ave., near 79th St.,* ☎ *212/734–2676; 393 Lafayette St., at E. 4th St.,* ☎ *212/995–9595. AE, DC, MC, V.*

Seafood

$$$$ ✕ **Cello.** Cello may be the only restaurant in town that could give Le Bernardin a run for its seafood money. The clubby spot has an elegant clientele and even more elegant tableware. The prix-fixe menu could best be described as *haute poisson,* for chef Laurent Tourondel coddles the fruits of the sea with impeccable French technique and fine, fresh ingredients. Highlights include a multicourse lobster tasting menu, baby mussels, and the sweetest diver sea scallops. Don't miss dessert, which you will probably have time to enjoy, for the service has a tendency to come on strong and then peter out toward the end. ✉ *53 E. 77th St., between Madison and Park Aves.,* ☎ *212/517–1200. Reservations essential. Jacket required. AE, D, MC, V. Closed Sun. No lunch Sat.*

Spanish

$$ ✕ **Taperia Madrid.** A ceramic tile façade and communal tables within set the stage for a well-conceived culinary journey to Spain. The red sangria, enhanced by plenty of fruit, is quite delicious. The plates of tapas consist of such safe bets as sausages, Spanish cheese, olives, and grilled octopus. The whole experience works, making this an ultra-fun place to come with a date or a group of friends. ✉ *1471 2nd Ave., between 76th and 77th Sts.,* ☎ *212/794–2923. AE, MC, V. No lunch.*

Steak

$$–$$$ ✕ **Manhattan Grille.** A bronze doorway that once graced the old Biltmore hotel is the appropriately grand portal of this steak house, which even a non-carnivore can love. Cut flowers, Victorian chandeliers, Persian carpets, mahogany moldings, deep hunter-green upholstery, and a gracious greeting from the host create a sophisticated alternative to the burly atmosphere of the typical New York steak house. The first-class double sirloin or Porterhouse rival any in town: huge, dry-aged, well-marbled, juicy, and perfectly grilled. The prime rib is also luscious, and there are seafood offerings such as baby lobster cocktail or stone crab claws (in season) as well. The wine list is easy to negotiate and offers several good choices under $30. ✉ *1161 1st Ave., between 63rd and 64th Sts.,* ☎ *212/888–6556. AE, DC, MC, V. No lunch Sat.*

Upper West Side and Harlem

Considering that Lincoln Center's theaters can accommodate more than 18,000 spectators at one time, you'd think the area would be chock-ablock with restaurants catering to all tastes and budgets. Alas, perhaps because this captive audience has to eat in a hurry, the pickings are slim. The streets of the upper West Side are lined with restaurants, but finding something good to eat can be a challenge—unless you buy a picnic at some of the city's best retail food outlets. In Harlem, a soul-food renaissance is underway. Brunch is the busiest time, but you might have to wait no matter when you want to eat.

American

$–$$ ✕ **Henry's.** Located on a forlorn strip between the Upper West Side proper and Columbia University, Henry's is like an oasis in a culinary desert. The red-checked tablecloths and rich wood arts-and-crafts ac-

288

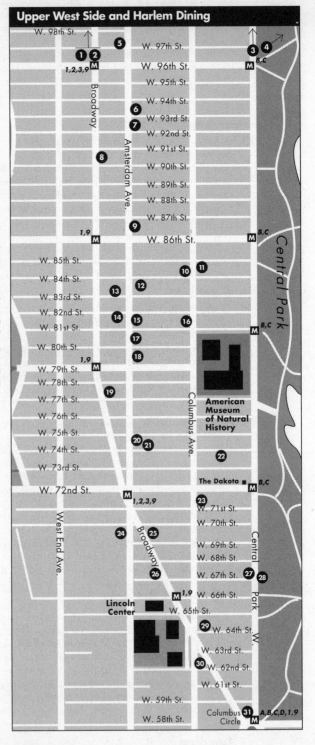

cents create a homey feel, and the menu offers something for all. There's everything from a fine meaty hamburger to a rich San Francisco-style cioppino, with stops in between such as fried calamari and Southern pork chops. ⌧ *2745 Broadway, at 105th St.,* ☎ *212/866–0600. AE, MC, V.*

American Casual

$–$$ ✕ **Barney Greengrass.** The self-proclaimed sturgeon king, Barney Greengrass hasn't changed its formula since this Jewish "appetizing" take-out shop and restaurant opened in 1908: good food, friendly, in-your-face service, Formica, and plenty of salt. Four generations later, the wait can sometimes reach two hours during prime weekend brunch time. Order anything with smoked salmon or sturgeon—scrambled eggs with onions; bagels or bialys with cream cheese, tomato, and red onion; or the austere platters of fish. A full range of Jewish food is available, including glasses of chilled borscht with sour cream, potato knishes that are split in half and toasted, and chopped liver that some consider the embodiment of fine Jewish cuisine. Finish with an individual chocolate babka "muffin." ⌧ *541 Amsterdam Ave., between 86th and 87th Sts.,* ☎ *212/724–4707. MC, V. No credit cards on weekends. Closed Mon.*

$–$$ ✕ **Sarabeth's Kitchen.** Lining up for brunch at Sarabeth's is as much an Upper West Side tradition as strolling in Riverside Park. Filled with bric-a-brac and imbued with a homespun charm, this is a favorite for its eclectic American menu with such entrées as chicken potpie; a delicious shrimp sandwich; and outstanding baked goods like muffins, scones, and a cranberry-pear bread pudding. The affordable wine list includes some unexpected bottles from small producers. The restaurant has a couple of offshoots on the Upper East Side, as well. ⌧ *423 Amsterdam Ave., between 80th and 81st Sts.,* ☎ *212/496–6280; 1295 Madison Ave., between 92nd and 93rd Sts.,* ☎ *212/410–7335; 945 Madison Ave., at 75th St. (in Whitney Museum),* ☎ *212/570–3670. AE, DC, MC, V.*

Argentine

$–$$ ✕ **Pampa.** Now that imported Argentine beef is legal in the United States a crop of restaurants serving the delicacy have sprouted up in the city. Although Pampa offers a variety of dishes to cater to all tastes, the main reason to go is for the beef, served *asado* style, cooked on the *parilla,* or "grill." The room is not particularly South American in feel, but the speckled yellow walls are pleasant and evoke a sun-drenched atmosphere. ⌧ *768 Amsterdam Ave., between 97th and 98th Sts.,* ☎ *212/865–2929. No credit cards. No lunch Mon.–Thurs.*

Cafés

$ ✕ **Café La Fortuna.** Weary Columbus Avenue strollers have long flocked to this comforting refuge that offers Italian pastries, serious coffee, and opera music. In summer enjoy an iced cappuccino with a chocolate Italian ice in the garden out back. ⌧ *69 W. 71st St., between Columbus Ave. and Central Park W,* ☎ *212/724–5846.*

$ ✕ **Cafe Lalo.** Linger over cappuccino, liqueurs, and crossword puzzles at this flashy, Toulouse Lautrec–theme spot off Amsterdam Avenue. Some cakes fall short of their menu descriptions. ⌧ *201 W. 83rd St., between Broadway and Amsterdam Ave.,* ☎ *212/496–6031.*

$–$$ ✕ **Cafe Mozart.** Images of Mozart cover the walls at this spot that's perfect after a night at Lincoln Center. Creamy desserts are the specialty. A pianist or classical duo often performs. On Friday and Saturday nights it's open until 3 AM, on other nights until 1. ⌧ *154 W. 70th St., between Broadway and Columbus Ave.,* ☎ *212/595–9797.*

$ ✕ Drip. Blind-date notebooks containing the personal ads of other patrons have earned this café a notoriety that, alone, its vintage 1970s couches wouldn't garner. The retro atmosphere will make you crave one of their Rice Krispy treats. ⊠ *489 Amsterdam Ave., between 83rd and 84th Sts.,* ☎ *212/875–1032.*

Chinese

$ ✕ Ollie's. This no-frills Chinese restaurant, one in a growing mini chain, is a blessing for Lincoln Center–goers in search of a quick budget meal. The best dishes are the noodle soups (available in a number of variations) and the dumplings that are prepared by superfast chefs whom you can watch while you wait for a table. The other standards are all well executed, and portions are generous. Don't expect any culinary revelations; do expect fast, efficient service and low prices. ⊠ *1991 Broadway, at 67th St.,* ☎ *212/595–8181. AE, MC, V.*

Contemporary

$$$–$$$$ ✕ Tavern on the Green. The late Warner LeRoy's lavishly tacky restaurant in Central Park is a visual fantasy, a maze of dining rooms each with a different theme. There's jazz and cabaret in the Chestnut Room, and a view of the trademark Christmas-lighted trees and ornate chandeliers in the Crystal Room. Weather permitting, you may opt for alfresco dining in the garden. A meal here is not about the food (and service can be slow): it's about eating in Central Park with people from out of town. Nevertheless, careful selection from the menu can provide a passable meal. The simplest dishes are the best bet: filet mignon, salmon, and fettuccine with shrimp and bay scallops, and any of the above-average desserts, such as fruit cobbler or a decadent ice-cream sundae. The wine list is well chosen, if expensive. ⊠ *Central Park at W. 67th St.,* ☎ *212/873–3200. Reservations essential. AE, DC, MC, V.*

Continental

$$$ ✕ Café des Artistes. Howard Chandler Christy murals of nymphs at play grace the walls of this sensual belle epoque dining room owned by Hungarian restaurant impresario and writer George Lang. The food, very disappointing on a culinary level but somehow satisfying on a nostalgic one, complements the setting. Four-way salmon is served smoked, poached, dill-marinated, and raw, and pot-au-feu, the French boiled dinner, is presented with bone marrow and traditional accompaniments. Desserts are classic and appealing; the mocha *dacquoise* layers hazelnut meringue with French butter cream. For wines, go with the George Lang selections, especially Gundel wines from Hungary. Brunch is particularly festive. ⊠ *1 W. 67th St., at Central Park W,* ☎ *212/877–3500. Reservations essential. Jacket required. AE, DC, MC, V.*

French

$$$–$$$$ ✕ Jean Georges. Jean-Georges Vongerichten's eponymous prix-fixe
★ restaurant in the Trump International Hotel and Towers is a true dining destination. The main dining room, with picture windows overlooking the park, embodies a less-is-more, Asian-inspired aesthetic, and all the furnishings, in neutral colors, are luxurious but understated. The same might be said of Vongerichten's cooking—restrained, with unusual combinations that intrigue the palate without overwhelming it. Sea scallops in caper-raisin emulsion with caramelized cauliflower, or spring garlic soup perfumed with thyme and dotted with nuggets of boned, sautéed frogs' legs are standout examples. For dessert try the breathtakingly simple strawberry "water" or a thin rhubarb tart with brown sugar and rhubarb crème *glacée.* Personalized service and a beautifully selected wine list contribute to the dining experience. In sum-

mer the terrace restaurant, **Le Mistral,** offers a less expensive menu and a more casual setting. Year-round, the elegant **Nougatine** serves a more moderate à la carte menu in the bar area, with a view of the open kitchen. ⊠ *1 Central Park W, at 59th St.,* ☎ *212/299–3900. Reservations essential. Jacket and tie. AE, DC, MC, V. Closed Sun.*

$$$–$$$$ ✕ **Picholine.** Named for a small green Mediterranean olive (a bowl of
★ which is brought to your table at the start of your meal), this mellow restaurant is patterned on a Provençal farmhouse, with soft colors, wood floors, and dried flowers. Chef-proprietor Terrance Brennan's French food with Mediterranean accents is among the finest in Manhattan. Top dishes include the grilled octopus with fennel, potato, and lemon-pepper dressing; Moroccan-spiced loin of lamb with vegetable couscous and mint-yogurt sauce; and tournedos of salmon with horseradish crust, cucumbers, and salmon caviar. The wine list is extensive, offering many hard-to-find bottles, as well as wonderful wines by the glass. Be sure to save some wine to enjoy with the superlative cheese course, a selection of some 30 varieties that are sought out and ripened by the knowledgable *fromagier.* There's a small wine room that seats up to eight for special tasting menus. ⊠ *35 W. 64th St., off Broadway,* ☎ *212/724–8585. Reservations essential. AE, DC, MC, V. Closed Sun. No lunch Mon.*

$$–$$$ ✕ **Café Luxembourg.** This lively, sophisticated bistro with arched windows and a zinc-top bar, operated by the same crew responsible for TriBeCa's ever-trendy Odeon, has a definite downtown vibe, rare among the restaurants in this uptown neighborhood. The café is a terrific spot for a post–Lincoln Center meal. The menu offers classic bistro dishes such as cassoulet, steak frites, and roast duck, as well as a decent selection of wines. ⊠ *200 W. 70th St., between Amsterdam and West End Aves.,* ☎ *212/873–7411. Reservations essential. AE, DC, MC, V. No lunch Mon.*

$$ ✕ **Avenue.** Scott Campbell's French bistro in the gastronomic no-man's-land of Upper Columbus Avenue has proven a success. The accent is French, and the food, at its best, is satisfying and delicious. At lunch and weekend brunch you place your order at the counter; at dinner there is table service, albeit sometimes indifferent and slow. During the day you can choose from an array of freshly baked French pâtisserie, eggs, pancakes, sandwiches, and salads. The seasonal bill of evening fare usually includes a selection of salads, soups, pâtés, and individual tartlets to start. Intermediate plates include tuna tartare on sesame spinach, succulent crab cakes, and goat cheese ravioli. Large plates tend toward serious main courses of smoked loin of pork, steak frites, and roasted duckling. ⊠ *520 Columbus Ave., at 85th St.,* ☎ *212/ 579–3194. AE, MC, V.*

Italian

$$–$$$$ ✕ **Carmine's.** Savvy West Siders and theater-goers line up at these huge, busy eateries adorned with dark woodwork and old-fashioned black-and-white tiles. Those who wait are rewarded with huge portions of home-style Italian cooking, served family style. The portions are enough for three to four people (really), so this a perfect place for groups and folks who like to share. Kick off a meal with fried calamari or stuffed artichoke, then move on to the pastas, classic chicken and veal dishes, or lobster fra diavolo. You will inevitably order too much, but don't worry, it all tastes great left over. ⊠ *2450 Broadway, between 90th and 91st Sts.,* ☎ *212/362–2200; 200 W. 44th St., between Broadway and 8th Ave.,* ☎ *212/221–3800. AE. No lunch.*

$–$$ ✕ **Gennaro.** Though it's difficult to believe when you first arrive, the food here is worth the interminable wait and uncomfortably crowded tables. When you finally sit down in the tiny storefront trattoria, you can sample some of the city's best and most fairly priced Italian food. The restaurant is dark, simply designed, cramped, and noisy, but the food is soulful, earthy, and richly satisfying. Share the huge antipasto platter or a selection of homemade pastas. For entrées choose from seasonal preparations of lamb, veal, fish, chicken, and beef. No one leaves hungry. ⊠ *665 Amsterdam Ave., between 92nd and 93rd Sts.,* ☎ *212/ 665–5348. No credit cards.*

$–$$ ✕ **La Grolla.** In a neighborhood bursting at the seams with mediocre Italian restaurants serving budget pastas, La Grolla provides a much needed contrast. The decor is a slight cut above most others in the area, offering a bit more sophistication and less chaos. The cuisine of the Val d'Aosta, a tiny region in the North of Italy, is the focal point of the menu and specialties of the region are indicated on the menu. *Fonduta,* an Italian fondue, is a hearty dish, perfect for sharing at the start of a meal. There are other substantial Northern Italian specialties such as rabbit stew and carbonado, and a selection of pastas, all homemade, that make good use of meat and game. To cater to the neighborhood, the owners opened a more casual, and cheaper version, **Café La Grolla** (411A Amsterdam Ave., between 79th and 80th Sts., ☎ 212/579–9200), right next door. ⊠ *413 Amsterdam Ave., between 79th and 80th Sts.,* ☎ *212/496–0890. AE, DC, MC, V.*

Latin

$$ ✕ **Calle Ocho.** Taking its name from the main drag of Miami's Little Havana neighborhood, Calle Ocho cultivates a festive vibe, with bright colors, a wall mural of Cuban imagery, and a terra-cotta fireplace. Chef Alex Garcia serves a Pan-Latin menu that incorporates dishes from various countries, especially his native Cuba. You can dine on Cuban-style steak frites with yuca fries, *arepas with bacalao* (corn fritters stuffed with salt cod), or crispy snapper with *malanga* (a South American tuber) mash. All of the dishes are best washed down with one of the restaurant's snappy specialty drinks, such as a refreshing *mojito* (rum with soda, mint, and sugar syrup) or an interesting *mamey* (a sweet Mexican fruit) daiquiri. ⊠ *446 Columbus Ave., between 81st and 82nd Sts.,* ☎ *212/873–5025. AE, DC, MC, V. No lunch.*

Mexican

$–$$ ✕ **Gabriela's.** These modest cantinas reward all who love authentic Mexican cuisine at rock-bottom prices (almost in line with those in Mexico itself). The menu has tasty tacos stuffed with beef tongue, and *chicharrones* (deep-fried pork skins) in a memorable bath of tomatillo and serrano sauce. The house specialty is a whole rotisserie chicken, Yucatán style, with rice, beans, and plantains. The *posole,* a hominy-based soup with a variety of garnishes, is a meal in itself. Overseen by ceramic parrots hanging from the ceiling, the atmosphere is noisy and festive. ⊠ *685 Amsterdam Ave., at 93rd St.,* ☎ *212/961–0574; 311 Amsterdam Ave., at 75th St.,* ☎ *212/875–8532. AE, DC, MC, V.*

Pan-Asian

$–$$ ✕ **Rain.** Located in a dramatic space just off Columbus Avenue, Rain offers first-rate Thai- and Vietnamese-inspired food. The menu includes all the favorites of Southeast Asian cooking, such as *bahn cuon* (steamed ravioli with lump crab, bean sprouts, and chili sauce), crispy whole fish in three-flavor sauce, and tantalizing charred-beef salad. Although some of the spices and flavorings are toned down, the food satisfies a certain craving. The spacious dining room is adorned with modern Asian touches, and the pretty bar area has rattan-and-chintz chairs and wooden floors covered with Oriental runners. ⊠ *100 W. 82nd St., between Amsterdam and Columbus Aves.,* ☎ *212/501–0776. Reservations essential. AE, DC, MC, V. No lunch.*

$–$$ ✕ **Ruby Foo's.** Upper West Siders flock to this over-the-top Asian fantasy lounge with a dramatic staircase ascending from the middle of the room. The menu incorporates favorites from most Asian cuisines with many dishes intended for sharing. Some dishes are not authentic—dim sum is filled with creative ingredients and sushi explores new combinations—but the chef, who is from Thailand, serves up some excellent traditional dishes from Southeast Asia. Among the best are pungent lemongrass hot-and-sour soup, green curries, and crispy whole fish. If some of the food doesn't measure up to the setting, it's safe to say the place is so lively and fun no one seems to mind a bit. ✉ *2182 Broadway, at 77th St., ☎ 212/724–6700; 1626 Broadway, between 49th and 50th Sts., ☎ 212/489–5600. Reservations essential. AE, MC, V.*

Southern

$–$$ ✕ **Emily's.** The best chopped-barbecue sandwiches, deep-fried chicken livers (dunk them into the zesty house sauce), corn-bread stuffing spiked with hot peppers and spices, and homemade potato salad this side of the Mason-Dixon line are the reasons to seek out this Harlem haunt. Bare Formica tables and paper napkins are the extent of the decor, but that's what makes the delicious soul food such a bargain. It's also a good place for breakfast and brunch. ✉ *1325 5th Ave., at 111th St., ☎ 212/996–1212. AE, DC, MC, V.*

$ ✕ **Charles's Southern-Style Kitchen.** Charles Gabriel serves some of the best soul food in Harlem. Fried chicken is the specialty, and if you stand by the takeout counter you can watch Charlie dip pieces of chicken into his peppery batter and fry it to a crispy golden brown in a giant cast-iron skillet. The value-packed all-you-can-eat buffet ($6.99 at lunch, $9.99 at dinner) includes all of soul food's greatest hits: barbecued ribs, oxtail, black-eyed peas, okra, macaroni and cheese, collard greens, and candied yams. And on occasion there are special treats, such as salmon cakes. ✉ *2839 8th Ave., between 151st and 152nd Sts., ☎ 212/926–4313. AE, MC, V.*

Turkish

$–$$ ✕ **Turkuaz.** As the upper reaches of the Upper West Side are increasingly gentrified, the restaurant scene is slowly evolving to keep pace. Enter Turkuaz, a surreal restaurant with fabric-draped ceilings and waiters in traditional costume, where the food is flavorful and authentic. The salads will look familiar to anyone who likes Middle Eastern food, but the entrées are somewhat of a departure. Yogurt and lamb factor heavily, and the kebabs are highly seasoned, if a little dry. Service is sporadic but personable. And in the area, that's a lot more than many diners expect. ✉ *2637 Broadway, at 100th St., ☎ 212/665–9541. AE, D, MC, V.*

OUTER-BOROUGH RESTAURANTS

Manhattan is where most of New York's dining excitement takes place, but you can find plenty of good food in the city's other four boroughs. Brooklyn, in particular, has become a hotbed for great neighborhood restaurants. As always, ethnic food excels outside Manhattan.

The Bronx

When it comes to food, just about the only area of the Bronx that's worth exploring is Arthur Avenue, a strip of bakeries, food stores, and butcher shops that suggest what Little Italy once was.

American

$–$$$$ ✕ **Jimmy's Bronx Cafe.** A sports bar, nightclub, and restaurant all in one, this is one of only a handful of destinations that attract New Yorkers from all boroughs to the Bronx (the others are a garden, a zoo, and the winningest team in baseball). The club features a lineup of Latino performers and other events. The restaurant serves a selection of American food with a Caribbean twist, which essentially means you can get rice and beans and plantains with any dish. In Harlem, an outpost of **Jimmy's** (2207 Adam Clayton Powell Blvd., between 130th and 131st Sts., ☎ 212/491–4000) attracts an eclectic crowd. ⊠ *281 W. Fordham Rd., between Cedar Ave., and Major Deegan Expressway,* ☎ *718/329–2000. AE, DC, MC, V.*

Italian

$–$$$ ✕ **Dominick's.** One of the best and most popular restaurants on the Avenue, Dominick's has tough waiters who preside over communal tables in a room that is more or less devoid of ambience. Garlic is the predominant flavor of everything that comes out of the kitchen (you can even smell it in the street). A bottle of Chianti is all you need for an authentic Italian-American meal. ⊠ *2335 Arthur Ave., at 187th St., Belmont,* ☎ *718/733–2807. No credit cards.*

Brooklyn

New York's most populous borough inspires fierce loyalty in the hearts of its residents, who will maintain that everything, including the restaurants, is as good here as it is in Manhattan. In light of the ongoing, white-hot restaurant boom in some neighborhoods, this heresy may in fact not be too far from the truth.

American

$–$$ ✕ **Diner.** Don't let the name fool you. Located in an old, beat-up diner, this trendy bistro has become ground zero for the bohemian renaissance underway in Williamsburg. In fact, the entire place was recently re-created as an art installation in Sweden, complete with the staff and some of the regular customers. The unusual thing is that the restaurant is actually a lovely place to pass an evening—the food is good, the crowd is beautiful, the service is friendly, and the price is right. ⊠ *85 Broadway, at Berry St, Williamsburg.,* ☎ *718/486–3077. Reservations not accepted. AE, D, MC, V.*

American Casual

$$–$$$ ✕ **Junior's.** The neighborhood has changed over the years, but Junior's remains a worthy reminder of another era. The huge menu has the Jewish specialties that made the restaurant famous: corned beef, pastrami, chopped liver, and other sandwiches served on freshly baked club rye. More substantial food is also available, such as complete dinners of roast chicken, ribs, meat loaf, and the like, with your choice of sides and fixin's. The cheesecake is still counted among the best in the city. The rugelach aren't bad either. ⊠ *386 Flatbush Ave. Ext., at DeKalb Ave., Downtown Brooklyn,* ☎ *718/852–5257. AE, DC, MC, V.*

Contemporary

$$–$$$ ✕ **Saul.** Smith Street in Brooklyn has become a dining destination for residents of all of New York City's boroughs, and this is one of the best additions to the strip. Opened by Saul Bolton, a chef who has worked in such venerable Manhattan establishments as Le Bernardin and the late, great Bouley, the inviting neighborhood restaurant has an approachable yet ambitious menu. Everything is well prepared, from simple bistro dishes such as a bacon-and-onion tart to more involved dishes such as a butternut squash soup that is poured over a lush squash custard. Manhattan's loss is definitely Brooklyn's gain. ⊠ *140 Smith St., between Dean and Pacific Sts., Boerum Hill,* ☎ *718/935–9844. MC, V. No lunch.*

French

$$ ✕ **Mignon.** A favorite in Carroll Gardens' thriving restaurant scene, this little place is as adorable as the name suggests (*mignon* means cute in French). The menu basks on the sunny shores of Provence, reflecting the experience of the chef, Pablo Trobo. You'll find an array of appealing choices; among the best are an intensely flavored chilled seafood bisque, merguez sausage *en brochette* served with dried fruit and an array of savory vegetables, and an enticing grilled red snapper. ⊠ *394 Court St., at Carroll St., Carroll Gardens,* ☎ *718/222–8383. No credit cards. Closed Mon. No lunch.*

$$ ✕ **Patois.** This small, cheery bistro with cartoony wallpaper and patterned Formica tables has a homespun feel, probably because chef/owner Alan Harding and his partners did most of the decorating themselves. The food, however, is more refined. A small tart adorned with Roquefort, potatoes, leeks, and egg is a good starter. Rich, earthy main courses like a lamb and white bean casserole or steak frites will make you think you're on Paris' Left Bank, not the East River's right bank. For dessert, nothing but the deeply caramelized tarte Tatin will do. ⊠ *255 Smith St., between Douglass and DeGraw Sts., Cobble Hill,* ☎ *718/855–1535. AE, D, DC, MC, V. Closed Mon. No lunch.*

$-$$ ✕ **La Bouillabaisse.** Like a small bistro you'd find in one of Paris's outer arrondissements, this spot serves simple but delicious food to a local clientele. The menu is presented on a blackboard brought to your table for inspection. It always includes the signature fish soup, a meal and a half of seafood bathed in a rich, aromatic broth. If you like sweetbreads, here's where to have them. A huge portion is crisply fried in butter and served with mashed potatoes and braised red cabbage. Other offerings change with the season. The staff is always friendly, if sometimes so busy it's hard to get their attention. ⊠ *145 Atlantic Ave., between Clinton and Henry Sts., Cobble Hill,* ☎ *718/522–8275. No credit cards. No lunch weekends.*

Italian

$-$$$ ✕ **Cucina.** One of the most serious restaurants in Park Slope is run by chef-owner Michael Ayoub. The style is Italian, and most meals commence with a selection of antipasti from the giant buffet at the back of the main dining room. Pastas are available in appetizer- and entrée-size portions. Depending on the season you might find lobster and pumpkin ravioli or pappardelle with duck and wild mushrooms among the selections. Of the entrées, you should consider the simple breaded veal cutlet *alla milanese,* the generous osso buco, or the grilled fillet mignon of pork, served with crisp mushroom risotto and a dried fruit and porcini sauce. Service can be slow at times and the room can be noisy, but both add to the neighborhood feel of the restaurant. ⊠ *256 5th Ave., between Carroll St. and Garfield Pl., Park Slope,* ☎ *718/230–0711. Reservations essential. AE, DC, MC, V. No lunch.*

$-$$ ✕ **al di la Trattoria.** You know you are approaching al di la when you see small clusters of people on the sidewalk waiting patiently for a table. Inside, the decor is comfortably rustic, with pretty curtains, plain wood tables, and vintage decorations. The menu, though, is the real draw—simple Italian food prepared without too much flourish, but with plenty of care. Homemade pastas such as *malfatti,* a vegetable gnocchi with ricotta and Parmesan, are generously flavored, and entrées like charred hanger steak *tagliata* with arugula truly hit the spot. ⊠ *248 5th Ave., at Carroll St., Park Slope,* ☎ *718/783–4565. MC, V. No lunch.*

$-$$ ✕ **Miss Williamsburg Diner.** This diminutive restaurant is one of the most successful examples of the refurbished diner trend that seems to have overtaken Williamsburg. It's casual, it's loud, the hospitable vibe

makes you feel like you're part of a loving dysfunctional family, and—
surprise, surprise—it's Italian. Chef Massimiliano Bartoli prepares his
simple salads, creative pastas and lasagnas, and wholesome entrées such
as herb-crusted pork chops in the area that once housed the diner's
griddle and deep-fat fryer. Running the dining room is Pilar Rigon, who
used to own the wildly popular East Village trattoria Il Bagatto, and
her Italian drawl will charm you into loving her new restaurant as much
as she does. ⊠ *206 Kent Ave., between Metropolitan Ave. and N. 3rd
St., Williamsburg, Brooklyn,* ☎ *718/963–0802. No credit cards. Closed
Mon. No lunch.*

$–$$ ✕ **Noodle Pudding.** Although the name conjures images of *lokshen kugel*
(Jewish noodle pudding), it is actually a loose translation of the owner's
last name, Migliaccio, which is also the name of a Neopolitan dessert.
The food here is Italian, and if you're going to eat one meal in Brooklyn Heights, this is where you should do it. Oddly, pasta is not the
kitchen's strong point (save for the lasagna, which changes daily). Instead, the chef excels at fish, usually generously portioned, lightly
grilled, and served with a dressing of extra-virgin olive oil and a bed
of fresh, steamed vegetables. Appetizers, such as beef carpaccio, fried
calamari, and mussels in spicy tomato sauce, are all good ways to start.
Braised osso buco, roasted chicken, and baked rabbit are fine alternatives to the fish. ⊠ *38 Henry St., between Cranberry and Middagh
Sts., Brooklyn Heights,* ☎ *718/625–3737. No credit cards. Closed Mon.
No lunch.*

Pizza

$ ✕ **Grimaldi's.** When you think of a New York–style pizza parlor,
Grimaldi's (formerly known as Patsy Grimaldi's or simply Patsy's; a
lawsuit forced the owners to change the name) is exactly what comes
to mind. The tables are covered in red-and-white check cloths, the walls
are covered with autographed black-and-white photos, and Frank
Sinatra croons from the jukebox. Owner Patsy Grimaldi usually sits
at the table in the far right corner, making sure everyone is happy with
the pies that come out of the coal-fired oven. Any combination of toppings is available, but be careful because the price adds up quickly. You
can get salads and pasta dishes with red sauce, but you should really
come here for the pizza. ⊠ *19 Old Fulton St., between Front and Water
Sts., Brooklyn Heights,* ☎ *718/858–4300. No credit cards.*

Russian

$$$$ ✕ **Rasputin.** Etched glass, hand-painted murals, crystal chandeliers, and
carved doors decorate this restaurant-cum-nightclub extravaganza in
Brighton Beach, Brooklyn's predominantly Russian neighborhood. A
multilevel stage, state-of-the-art sound system, and laser light show set
the mood for the lavish Rasputin Follies revue, in which nine dancers,
seven singers, and an eight-piece orchestra put on a floor show to rival
Vegas. The show starts at 10 PM Friday, Saturday, and Sunday. The mostly
Russian clientele arrives dressed to the nines and stays until the wee
hours, drinking vodka, dancing, and consuming a copious traditional
Russian banquet. The prix-fixe meal begins with *zakuska,* hot and cold
Russian appetizers ranging from smoked salmon to blini and caviar.
Entrées, which include a passable chicken Kiev, follow. A full bottle of
vodka (for four people) is included in the price. Alone, none of the el-
ements is very good, but together the experience is amazing. ⊠ *2670
Coney Island Ave. at Ave. X, Brighton Beach,* ☎ *718/332–8111.
Reservations essential. AE, DC, MC, V. No lunch.*

Southern

$ ✕ **Sweet Mamas.** The sweet mama in the name refers to Tennessee native Terrie Mangrum, the chef-owner of this small soul food restaurant that has Park Slopers clamoring for fried chicken, mac and cheese, grits, and homemade pies. The mismatched chairs and Southern kitsch set the scene, the friendly service and neighborhood crowd make you feel right at home. ⊠ *168 7th Ave., between 1st St. and Garfield Pl., Park Slope,* ☎ *718/768–8766. No credit cards.*

Steak

$$–$$$ ✕ **Peter Luger Steak House.** You cannot find a better porterhouse
★ steak anywhere. Period. Sure, you can find better lighting, a more sophisticated atmosphere, a more comfortable chair. You would have no trouble locating a steak house with a bigger wine list, a broader menu, a certain flair. But if prime aged beef is what you want, if you don't care if it only comes in the shape of a porterhouse, and if you don't want to dress up, then Peter Luger's is where you should be. It has been serving the same quality beef since 1873, when the place opened as a German beer hall. The atmosphere hasn't changed. You probably won't see a menu, but don't worry, here's all you need to know: onion rolls; shrimp cocktail; beefsteak tomato and onion salad; steak sauce (for the salad and the rolls, not the steak); steak for two, three, four, five, or however many people are in your party; home fries; french fries; creamed spinach; pecan pie; cheesecake and *schlagg* (whipped cream). Bring a lot of cash, because the restaurant doesn't take credit cards. If you ask, its own car service will carry you back to Manhattan (for a reasonable fee). ⊠ *178 Broadway, at Driggs Ave., Williamsburg,* ☎ *718/387–7400. Reservations essential. No credit cards.*

Thai

$ ✕ **Amarin Cafe.** A little community of Thai restaurants has developed in Williamsburg and Greenpoint, including this small, nondescript Thai café with food that keeps people coming back. The green papaya salad (practically Thailand's national dish), is tangy and delicious. The noodle dishes are fresh and fragrant with kaffir lime, tamarind, and opal basil. And the braised curries are fire-engine hot. ⊠ *716 Manhattan Ave., between Driggs and Nassau Sts., Williamsburg,* ☎ *718/349–2788. Reservations not accepted. No credit cards.*

Queens

The biggest borough geographically speaking, Queens is also the most ethnically diverse. A trip on the No. 7 train, from the Vernon Boulevard/Jackson Avenue station in Long Island City to the Main Street station in Flushing, is a veritable world tour. You'll hear less and less English spoken with each passing station. Because many immigrant communities have only recently settled here, Queens has restaurants serving a wide range of authentic national cuisines. Some have sister restaurants in Manhattan, but the Queens siblings are usually more reasonably priced.

Brazilian

$$ ✕ **Green Field Churrascaria.** This sprawling Corona restaurant, which looks like a parking garage, features a prix-fixe, all-you-can-eat *rodizio,* the Brazilian orgy of grilled meats. Waiters arrive at your table in a seemingly endless parade, carrying skewers of grilled sirloin, chicken hearts, turkey nuggets, skirt steak, shoulder steak, chicken, duck, sausage, and roasted pork that they slice directly onto your plate. Let them know when to stop by using the chip on your table (green means continue, red means stop). You can begin with a trip to the copious salad bar and hot buffet, or you can just save room for the succulent

meat. ✉ *108–01 Northern Blvd., at 108th St., Corona,* ☎ *718/672–5202. AE.*

Chinese

$–$$ ✗ **Joe's Shanghai.** This is the original location of the famous dumpling house. *See* Chinatown *in* Manhattan, *above.* ✉ *136-21 37th St., between Main and Unions Sts., Astoria,* ☎ *718/539–3838; 82-74 Broadway, between 45th and Whitney Aves., Elmhurst,* ☎ *718/639–6888.*

$–$$ ✗ **K. B. Garden.** There are so many superb Chinese restaurants in Flushing that it's difficult to decide where to eat. K. B. Garden stands out for its regular menu and for the weekend dim sum, when women push carts around the large dining rooms while calling out names of dishes (you just point to order). Of particular note are the soft and slightly soupy braised noodles served with a variety of garnishes, such as wild mushrooms. ✉ *136–28 39th Ave., between Main and Union Sts., Flushing,* ☎ *718/961–9088. AE, MC, V.*

Greek

$$ ✗ **Karyatis.** One of the oldest and most elegant of Astoria's Greek restaurants, airy multilevel Karyatis is perfect for a festive evening of live music and professional service. Whole grilled fish of the day, wonderful vegetables, and skillfully executed sauces (especially the traditional avgolemono) lead the list. Greek wines are the appropriate accompaniment; also try a glass of ouzo, followed by buttery baklava and a cup of thick Greek coffee. ✉ *35–03 Broadway, between 35th and 36th Sts., Astoria,* ☎ *718/204–0666. AE, DC, MC, V.*

$–$$ ✗ **Elias Corner.** There's always a line and never a menu in this casual Greek fish restaurant. Start with the crisp fried smelts or the tender grilled octopus and follow with whole red snapper, St. Peter's fish, shrimp, or whatever fish is fresh from the market that morning. Order a side of potatoes mashed with garlic or fried with cheese. Avoid the traditional Greek appetizers, which are uniformly uninteresting. Wines are limited to Greek selections; try the clean, grassy Kouras from the island of Patras. Weather permitting, head for the charming garden. ✉ *24–02 31st St. at 24th Ave., Astoria,* ☎ *718/932–1510. Reservations not accepted. No credit cards. No lunch.*

$–$$ ✗ **Zenon.** Astoria is filled with Greek restaurants, but only a handful actually offer regional Greek specialties. This is one of them, and the region highlighted is Cyprus. Among the Cypriot dishes on the extensive menu is *sheftalia,* a tasty cross between meatballs and sausage, and *glykadakia,* nuggets of veal sweetbreads sautéed with onions and mushrooms. For about $15 per person, you can order a feast of eight hot and eight cold appetizers. The setting is much as you would find in a restaurant in Athens, and the friendly staff help walk you through some of the more unusual menu items. ✉ *34-10 31st St. Ave., between 34th and 35th Sts.,* ☎ *718/956–0133. No credit cards.*

Indian

$ ✗ **Jackson Diner.** This popular Indian restaurant occupies a modern space with spice-colored, earth-toned accents. Neighborhood folk and Manhattanites alike flock here for cheap, spicy, authentic Indian fare served in generous portions. ✉ *37–47 74th St., between Roosevelt and 37th Aves., Jackson Heights,* ☎ *718/672–1232. No credit cards.*

Italian

$–$$ ✗ **Manducatis.** This classic red-sauce Italian restaurant, located on a deserted street in Long Island City, serves up hearty dishes that put it a cut above many of its family-style counterparts. On weekends the large bar area and two main dining rooms jump with a loyal clientele, who greet the friendly owners and accommodating hometown waitresses by name. Homemade pastas, served family style if you like, are always a good choice, and the menu is complemented by a large, well-chosen wine list with very reasonable prices. ✉ *13–27 Jackson Ave., at 47th Ave., Long Island City,* ☎ *718/729–4602. AE, MC, V.*

Malaysian

$–$$ ✕ **Penang.** This was the first in the chain that has since proliferated Manhattan-wide, and it is the only one that still serves superb, authentic Malaysian food. While you look over the menu, order the freshly made roti with curried chicken dipping sauce; you'll want to order another by the time you have decided on your entrée. Every meal ought to include the coconut fried shrimp and something based on the restaurant's homemade noodles. If you can't figure out what to order, the considerate staff will be happy to help. ✉ *38–04 Prince St., at Main St., Flushing,* ☎ *718/321–2078. AE, MC, V.*

Middle Eastern

$–$$ ✕ **Mombar.** Three blocks is a long way in Astoria, and that's how far Mombar is from any train station. But the hike is worth it. Egyptian artist Moustafa Rahman has opened this restaurant-cum-art-installation in a strip of other Egyptian businesses. There is no sign, but you can't mistake the neo-hieroglyph façade. Inside and out the tiny restaurant is a work of art. Rahman presides behind the small stove near the door, and he also likes to serve the food and come sit down at your table. His cooking is Egyptian through an artist's eye. The signature *mombar,* a lamb sausage, is light and delicious. The familiar Middle Eastern spreads and salads come garnished with fruit and other unusual pairings. The entrées are less exciting, but they include braised rabbit, lamb, and a vegetarian special that changes daily. ✉ *25-22 Steinway St., at 25th Ave., Astoria,* ☎ *718/726–2356. No credit cards.*

Thai

$ ✕ **Sripraphai.** According to Asiaphiles, this is the most authentic Thai
★ restaurant in the five boroughs. The setting is a tiny, clean storefront in Woodside, and the menu, which comes with a helpful photo album, includes a wide selection of rarely seen dishes. Among the best are the green papaya salad, barbecued pork, an unusual fried and shredded catfish salad, pungent seafood soups, duck in red curry, and a Chinese sausage dish with fried rice. The secret to fine Thai food is the delicate balance between sweet, salty, sour, and spicy, and here it is all zestily combined. The authentic desserts, which are salty and sweet, are challenging to Western tastes. ✉ *64-13 39th Ave., at 64th St., Woodside,* ☎ *718/429–9257. No credit cards. Closed Wed.*

Staten Island

The least urban of New York's five boroughs, Staten Island is a residential area where most diners prefer quantity without surprises.

Contemporary

$–$$ ✕ **Aesop's Tables.** Though Manhattan dwellers don't often venture to Staten Island, this New American restaurant located near the ferry is a good choice for a first excursion. Its pretty garden overlooks the Manhattan skyline, and the contemporary American food is reasonably priced and well prepared. The menu changes daily. Look for dishes such as bacon-wrapped monkfish medallions and pan-seared duck breast with winter squash and pancetta risotto. ✉ *1233 Bay St., at Maryland Ave., Rosebank,* ☎ *718/720–2005. AE, MC, V.*

5 LODGING

The economic boom of the late 1990s set the stage for unprecedented hotel development in Manhattan. Visitors to the city are now, more than ever, faced with an incredible range of choices when booking a room. Hoteliers have engaged in fierce competition to create hotels that are as striking as they are functional and luxurious, hiring top-name designers to create over-the-top lobbies and post-modern guest rooms. Although Midtown still boasts the highest concentration of hotels, visitors to New York can now choose a room in the celebrity-studded neighborhood of Tribeca, on the outskirts of Hell's Kitchen, or overlooking the unofficial gateway to downtown, Union Square Park. Room rates remain extremely high, with many hotels charging upwards of $500 a night.

Updated by
Jane Miller and
Eliot Rennert

NEW YORK IS STILL the fastest-growing and largest hotel market in the United States, and the overwhelming demand for lodging has allowed hoteliers to charge considerably more than their counterparts in other cities. The average price of a room at the hotels listed in these pages tops $300. In 2000 New York broke its own record for occupancy rates, coming in just below 84%, and there was a slew of openings of posh properties catering to affluent young professionals.

In an effort to attract this lucrative market, hoteliers have gone to great lengths to open lodging options that are hyper-designed, trendsetting, and high-tech. Top designers such as David Rockwell, Philippe Starck, and Larry Bogdanow have created some jaw-dropping interiors, and hotel bars and lobbies—once bastions of civility—can feel like nightclubs at many of the chic new hotels. Hoteliers have also hired big-name chefs to run their dining rooms, aiming to cook up instant buzz and to attract a hip local clientele. Some new hotels have become such popular meeting places that guests may be required to show a room key just to get into the lobby. If you are not into this sort of scene, you still have plenty to choose from at the many plush, old-guard, uptown establishments that are known for quietly pampering their guests.

Although few and far between, there are lodging bargains to be had in New York. With a little research you may be able to uncover special weekend or promotional rates. When calling the hotels directly be sure to ask about special corporate, AAA, or AARP discounts. The rates in this guide are based on the published rack rate, but you can usually book for much less depending on the time of year you travel. If you're willing to put up with tiny quarters and few amenities there are rooms available at decent budget properties in the $100 range. When considering a hotel browse their website, as it will usually include pictures of the rooms and lists of amenities down to the last detail. Many hotels even let you reserve online.

In general, Manhattan hotels don't measure up to those in other U.S. cities in terms of facilities such as parking and pools. Likewise, you may be shocked by the size of your room, especially if you are paying $300 a night: Like the typical city apartment, many New York hotel rooms can most kindly be described as compact and cozy. And unless you're paying extra for it, forget about a panoramic view. Still, the majority of local hotels more than compensate for these quirks—indeed, they often far outshine lodgings elsewhere in the country—with fastidious service, beautifully maintained properties, delightful amenities, and restaurants that more than hold their own in a city of knowledgeable diners.

CATEGORY	COST*
$$$$	over $400
$$$	$275–$400
$$	$150–$275
$	under $150

*All prices are for a standard double room, excluding 13¼% city and state taxes.

Reservations
Hotel reservations are an absolute necessity when planning your trip to New York—hotels fill up quickly, so book your room as far in advance as possible. Fierce competition means properties undergo frequent improvements, so while booking inquire about any ongoing renovations lest you get a room within earshot of noisy construction.

In this ever-changing city, travelers can find themselves temporarily, and most inconveniently, without commonplace amenities such as room service or spa access if their hotel is upgrading.

Once you decide on a hotel, use a major credit card to guarantee the reservation, another essential in an extremely tight market where overbooking can be a problem and "lost" reservations are not unheard-of. When signing in, take a pleasant but firm attitude; if there is a mix-up, chances are the outcome will be an upgrade or a free night.

Services

Unless otherwise noted in the individual descriptions, all the hotels listed have private baths, central heating, air-conditioning, private phones, no-smoking rooms or floors, and cable TV with pay-per-view films. Almost all hotels now have data ports and phones with voice mail, as well as valet service. Most large hotels have video or high-speed checkout capability, and many can arrange baby-sitting.

Pools are a rarity, but most properties have gyms or health clubs, and sometimes full-scale spas; hotels without facilities usually have arrangements for guests at nearby gyms, sometimes for a fee. Among those hotels with pools (all listed in this chapter) are Le Parker Meridien, The Peninsula, the Regal U.N. Plaza, and Trump International; on the other end of the price spectrum is the Vanderbilt YMCA.

Bringing a car to Manhattan can be the source of any number of headaches and can significantly add to your lodging expenses. Many properties in all price ranges do have parking facilities, but they are often at independent garages that charge as much as $20 or more per day, and valet parking can cost up to $40 a day. The few hotels that once offered free parking have abandoned the policy that, when combined with the city's exorbitant 18¾% parking tax, makes leaving your lemon out of the Big Apple a smart idea.

New York has gone to great lengths to attract family vacationers, and hotels have followed the family-friendly trend. One result is that properties that once drew mostly business travelers are finding themselves suddenly full of families—and are scrambling to add child-friendly amenities. Some properties offer diversions such as Web TV and in-room video games, while others have suites with kitchenettes and fold-out sofa beds. Most full-service Manhattan hotels provide roll-away beds, baby-sitting, and stroller rental, but be sure to make arrangements when booking the room, not when you arrive. Ask the reservations agent specific questions, since the list of services and amenities is constantly expanding.

HOTELS

Lower Manhattan

$$$$ 🏨 **Regent Wall Street.** The 1842 structure, originally a U.S. Customs
★   House (novelist Herman Melville worked here), still has basement cells once used to detain criminals, but today's Wall Street moguls gladly pay to stay. And pay they do. When rooms start at $545 it's easy to impress, but when the little things stand out—elevators that seem to defy gravity, sumptuous Bulgari toiletries, personalized service—the price approaches justification. The centerpiece is a 12,000-square-ft grand ballroom (once the NYSE trading floor) with a unique Wedgewood dome, whose spaceshiplike exterior anchors an upper-level courtyard. The accommodations are both stately and luxurious, and the immense, marble-clad bathrooms have what seem like the deepest tubs in town.

KID-FRIENDLY HOTELS

HERE ARE some especially good choices for those travelling with children.

The reasonably priced **Iroquois** offers family-size suites, in-room Nintendo, afternoon board games in the parlor, and child-size bathrobes at no extra charge.

The group of properties operated by **Manhattan East Suite Hotels** (☎ 212/465–3690) tends to have fully equipped suites at very reasonable rates.

Downtown, the **Millenium Hilton** is close to beautiful Rockefeller Park, whose designated children-only activities and play areas make it a summertime favorite.

The Paramount has a small playroom with children's videos and furniture made of Tweety Bird and Pink Panther stuffed animals. The guest rooms are fun but small, so book two.

Even your most finicky eaters will like the room service at the **Roger Smith**—it's a collection of delivery menus from half a dozen local restaurants (you can charge deliveries to your room), ranging from pizza to burgers; there's a free video library, too.

The rooms and suites at **Trump International Hotel and Towers** resemble mini-apartments: all have fully equipped kitchens, entertainment centers with stereos and VCRs, and mini-telescopes overlooking Central Park. There is also an indoor pool.

Courtyard rooms are most impressive, with plenty of light and an elongated design that makes standard rooms feel like suites. ✉ *55 Wall St., at Williams St., 10005,* ☎ *212/845–8600 or 800/545–4000,* ℻ *212/845–8601,* 🕸 *www.regenthotels.com. 138 rooms, 6 suites. Restaurant, bar, in-room data ports, in-room fax, in-room safes, in-room VCRs, minibars, room service, gym, dry cleaning, laundry service, concierge, business services, meeting room, parking (fee). AE, D, DC, MC, V.*

$$$–$$$$ 🏨 **Millenium Hilton.** The class act of downtown, this sleek black monolith is across the street from the World Trade Center. The modern, beige-and-wood rooms have a streamlined look, with contoured built-in desks and night tables; almost all have expansive views of landmark buildings and both the Hudson and the East rivers. The health club has an Olympic-size pool with windows that look out on St. Paul's Church. Live piano music adds sparkle to the smart lobby lounge. ✉ *55 Church St., between Cortland and Dey Sts., 10007,* ☎ *212/693–2001 or 800/445–8667,* ℻ *212/571–2317,* 🕸 *www.hilton.com. 481 rooms, 80 suites. 2 restaurants, 3 bars, in-room data ports, in-room safes, minibars, room service, indoor pool, massage, health club, piano, baby-sitting, dry cleaning, laundry service, concierge, business services, meeting room, parking (fee). AE, D, DC, MC, V.*

$$–$$$$ 🏨 **Embassy Suites Hotel New York.** Located in the heart of the financial district directly across from the World Trade Center is Manhattan's first Embassy Suites Hotel. As the name suggests, every room is at least a one-bedroom suite, with a living area that includes a pull-out sofa, microwave oven, and other amenities that make them ideal for families or business travelers who need to conduct meetings. ✉ *102*

304

Downtown Lodging

North End Ave., at Vesey St., 10281, ☎ *212/945–0100 or 800/362–
2779,* FAX *212/945–3012,* WEB *www.embassy-suites.com. 465 suites.
Restaurant, bar, in-room data ports, in-room fax, in-room safes, refrigerators, room service, concierge business services, meeting rooms,
parking (fee). AE, D, DC, MC, V.*

$$$ 🏨 **New York Marriott World Trade Center.** This downtown giant is nes-
tled between the World Trade Center's twin towers. The fabulous
skylit lobby has a contemporary green granite-and-marble entrance, a
grand curved staircase, and a fountain. The green and burgundy art
deco–style rooms are sleek and spacious by Manhattan standards.
The 22nd-floor health club has phenomenal views of Lower Manhat-
tan. ⊠ *3 World Trade Center, at Liberty and West Sts., 10048,* ☎ *212/
938–9100 or 800/550–2344,* FAX *212/444–3444,* WEB *www.marriott.com.
788 rooms, 29 suites. Restaurant, bar, in-room data ports, in-room safes,
minibars, room service, indoor pool, health club, dry cleaning, laun-
dry service, concierge, business services, meeting room, travel services,
car rental, parking (fee). AE, D, DC, MC, V.*

$$–$$$ 🏨 **Holiday Inn Wall Street.** You know the future has arrived when a
★ Holiday Inn offers T-1 Internet access in every room (a New York first),
express check-in lobby computers that dispense key-cards, and both
Web TV and Nintendo on 27-inch televisions. The comfortable rooms
are surprisingly spacious—many have 14-ft ceilings—a fact that's es-
pecially impressive when you consider that this 17-story redbrick struc-
ture was built in 1999. Thoughtful touches include ergonomically
designed workspaces with L-shape desks, full-length mirrors that open
to reveal ironing boards, and oversize shower heads that simulate
falling rain. ⊠ *15 Gold St., at Platt St., 10038,* ☎ *212/232–7700 or
800/465–4329,* FAX *212/425–0330,* WEB *www.holidayinnwsd.com. 124
rooms, 14 suites. Restaurant, bar, in-room data ports, in-room safes,
minibars, room service, gym, dry cleaning, laundry service, business
services, meeting room, parking (fee). AE, D, DC, MC, V.*

$$ 🏨 **Best Western Seaport Inn.** This thoroughly pleasant, restored 19th-
century building is one block from the waterfront, close to South Street
Seaport. Its cozy, librarylike lobby has the feel of a colonial sea captain's house, though the reasonably priced rooms are clearly those of
a chain hotel. For $25–$35 extra, you can have a room with a whirlpool tub and/or an outdoor terrace with a view of the Brooklyn Bridge.
⊠ *33 Peck Slip, between Front and Water Sts., 10038,* ☎ *212/766–
6600 or 800/468–3569,* FAX *212/766–6615. 72 rooms. In-room data ports,
in-room safes, in-room VCRs, refrigerators. AE, D, DC, MC, V.*

Chinatown, TriBeCa, and SoHo

$$$$ 🏨 **Tribeca Grand.** The first major hotel to open in this stylish neighborhood, the Tribeca Grand occupies a triangular lot and is itself triangular. Some might call the fresh, funky, yet formal hotel industrial-chic,
while others may refer to it as a dimly lit cell block. The hotel centers
around an eight-story atrium entered via a curving, 30-ft cleft-stone
ramp. The popular, fashionable Church Lounge occupies the atrium
and serves as bar, café, and dining room throughout the day and well
into the night (a separate restaurant, The Chambers, offers a more extensive menu). Eighty feet up, a frosted glass skylight encloses the
space. Hallways on the guest floors overlook the atrium and a steel
cage houses twin glass elevators in one corner of the triangle. The well-
appointed, sleek and modern rooms have a subdued color scheme of
blue and cream throughout, with floor-to-ceiling windows that make
average-size accommodations feel larger. High-tech amenities include
Web TV, cordless phones and high-speed internet access in all the
rooms. Like its sister hotel, the SoHo Grand, the Tribeca Grand wel-

comes pets. The service, meant to impress, is sometimes compromised by the hotel's nightclub atmosphere. ⊠ *2 Ave. of the Americas, between Walker and White Sts., 10013,* ☎ *212/519–6600,* FAX *212/519–6700,* WEB *www.tribecagrand.com. 195 rooms, 8 suites. Bar, café, in-room data ports, in-room fax, in-room VCR, room service, exercise room, dry cleaning, laundry service, concierge, business services, meeting rooms, parking (fee). AE, D, DC, MC, V.*

$$$–$$$$ 🏨 **SoHo Grand.** This is the hotel that started the downtown boutique boom, and it's still a central player in the see-and-be-seen hotel scene. The oversize cast-iron and bottle-glass staircase that leads up to the second-floor lobby evokes the neighborhood's 19th-century industrial past; the lobby bar's warehouse-size windows and stone pillars continue the theme. Guest rooms have custom-designed furnishings, including drafting table-style desks, nightstands that mimic sculptors' stands, and minibars made of old chests. The hotel's popularity has taken its toll on the furnishings, but a partial renovation of many of the guest rooms has helped to bring the rooms back to their original state. All rooms have stereos with CD players, and suites come equipped with Web TV. This is one of the few animal-friendly spots in town, with such options as pet room service and complimentary goldfish to keep lone travelers company, and if you get really attached you can even take your fishy home with you. Canal House serves the best macaroni-and-cheese east of Sheboygan, and the pricey store-front Caviarteria features live jazz. The concierge staff is top-notch. ⊠ *310 W. Broadway, at Grand St., 10013,* ☎ *212/965–3000 or 800/965–3000,* FAX *212/965–3244,* WEB *www.sohogrand.com. 365 rooms, 4 suites. Restaurant, bar, in-room data ports, in-room safes, minibars, room service, beauty salon, massage, gym, baby-sitting, dry cleaning, laundry service, concierge, business services, meeting room, parking (fee). AE, D, DC, MC, V.*

$$$ 🏨 **Mercer Hotel.** Owner Andre Balazs, known for his Château Marmont
★   in Hollywood, has a knack for adapting the aesthetic to the neighborhood. Here, it's SoHo loft all the way. So minimalist is the sprawling, hushed lobby with library and adjoining bar, that you may not even realize this is a hotel until you notice the unmarked reception desk along the back wall. Service is friendly and casual but professional, and guest rooms are generous to enormous, with long entryways, high ceilings, and walk-in closets. No fussy chintz or cheesy framed Monet prints here—instead, dark African woods and custom-designed furniture upholstered in muted solids lend serenity to the rooms. The bathrooms steal the show with their unusually designed shower stalls and decadent two-person, ultra-modern marble tubs—some of them surrounded by mirrors—but beware not all rooms come with a tub, so ask before booking a reservation. Downstairs is the Mercer Kitchen, a Jean-Georges Vongerichten venture. ⊠ *147 Mercer St., at Prince St., 10012,* ☎ *212/966–6060 or 888/918–6060,* FAX *212/965–3838. 67 rooms, 8 suites. Restaurant, 2 bars, in-room data ports, in-room safes, in-room VCRs, minibars, room service, concierge, business services. AE, DC, MC, V.*

$$ 🏨 **Holiday Inn Downtown.** Housed in a historic building in the heart of Chinatown and just a few steps from Little Italy and SoHo, this is one of the few hotels in the area. Although the Asian decor in the lobby and the excellent dim sum at Pacifica Restaurant attract plenty of Asian business travelers, many Europeans and young budget travelers are attracted to the reasonable rates and proximity to the downtown scene. The rooms are standard issue, but are clean and well maintained. The staff is well trained and works hard to please the hotel's guests. ⊠ *138 Lafayette St., near Canal St., 10013,* ☎ *212/966–8898 or 800/ 465–4329,* FAX *212/966–3933,* WEB *www.holi-inn.com. 215 rooms, 12 suites. Restaurant, bar, in-room data ports, room service, dry cleaning, laundry service, concierge, parking (fee). AE, D, DC, MC, V.*

Greenwich Village

$ ⊞ **Larchmont Hotel.** You might miss the entrance to this beaux arts
★ brownstone, whose geranium boxes and lanterns blend right in with
the Old New York feel of West 11th Street. If you don't mind shared
bathrooms and no room service or TV, the residential-style accommodations are all anyone could ask for, for the price. The small rooms
have a tasteful safari theme, with rattan furniture and ceiling fans; your
own private sink and stocked bookshelf will make you feel right at home.
Guests have use of a communal kitchen, a real bonus since Balducci's,
New York's premier gourmet grocery, is just around the corner on 6th
Avenue. ⊠ *27 W. 11th St., between 5th and 6th Aves., 10011,* ☎ *212/
989–9333,* FAX *212/989–9496,* WEB *www.larchmonthotel.citysearch.com.
55 rooms, none with bath. AE, D, DC, MC, V.*

$ ⊞ **Washington Square Hotel.** Situated at the northwest corner of Wash-
ington Square Park, this cozy hotel has a European feel and style, from
the wrought iron and gleaming brass in the small, elegant lobby to the
personal attention given by the staff. Rooms are simple but pleasant
and well maintained; some rooms have no window, so request one that
does. There's also a good, reasonably priced restaurant, C3, and a low-
key lounge of the same name; the Blue Note jazz club is just down the
street. ⊠ *103 Waverly Pl., at MacDougal St., 10011,* ☎ *212/777–9515
or 800/222–0418,* FAX *212/979–8373,* WEB *www.wshotel.com. 165
rooms. Restaurant, bar, in-room data ports, gym. AE, MC, V.*

Murray Hill, Flatiron District, and Gramercy

$$$–$$$$ ⊞ **Doral Park Avenue.** The lobby rotunda of this stately Park Avenue
hotel is neoclassical with a twist: a giant painting of an ancient Greek
city is offset by palm trees and art deco details. Styled headboards and
throw pillows in muted colors grace the warm, inviting guest rooms.
The swanky lounge off the lobby has big windows facing Park Avenue,
and the restaurant, Saturnia, has garden-theme murals that give the il-
lusion of dining in a greenhouse conservatory. ⊠ *70 Park Ave., at E.
38th St., 10016,* ☎ *212/687–7050 or 800/223–6725,* FAX *212/973–2497,*
WEB *www.doralparkavenue.com. 181 rooms, 7 suites. Restaurant, bar,
in-room data ports, in-room fax, in-room safes, minibars, room ser-
vice, massage, baby-sitting, dry cleaning, laundry service, concierge,
business services, meeting rooms, parking (fee). AE, D, DC, MC, V.*

$$$–$$$$ ⊞ **The Inn at Irving Place.** New York City's most charming small inn
★ occupies two grand 1830s town houses a few steps from Gramercy Park.
Its cozy tea salon (complete with a working fireplace and antique tea
pots), antiques-filled living room, and details such as an original 1834
curving stair banister vividly evoke a more genteel era. Each guest room
has an ornamental fireplace, a four-poster bed with embroidered linens,
wood shutters, and glossy cherrywood floors; Madame Olenska's
room has a bay window with a sitting nook. In the morning, steam-
ing pots of tea and coffee are served in the tea salon, along with home-
made pastries and breads. ⊠ *56 Irving Pl., between 17th and 18th Sts.,
10003,* ☎ *212/533–4600 or 800/685–1447,* FAX *212/533–4611,* WEB
*www.innatirving.com. 6 rooms, 6 suites. Bar, in-room data ports,
minibars, room service, massage, dry cleaning, laundry service, park-
ing (fee). AE, D, DC, MC, V.*

$$$–$$$$ ⊞ **The Kitano.** The Kitano brings austere grandeur to an otherwise low-
key stretch of Park Avenue South. A large Botero bronze of a stylized
dog presides over the chic mahogany and marble lobby. Handsome cherry
and mahogany furnishings, luxurious beds with duvet comforters,
Japanese tea makers, and watercolor still lifes impart an air of seren-
ity to the rooms and suites; soundproof windows make them among
Manhattan's quietest. The Nadaman restaurant is known for its high-

priced but authentic Japanese cuisine; and the swank, second-floor lounge has a Japanese jazz band on weekend nights. For business meetings, the Kitano is hard to beat: Two of the top-floor banquet rooms have floor-to-ceiling glass doors leading to expansive balconies with dazzling city views. ⊠ *66 Park Ave., at E. 38th St., 10016,* ☎ *212/885–7000 or 800/548–2666,* ℻ *212/885–7100,* WEB *www.kitano.com. 141 rooms, 8 suites. 2 restaurants, bar, in-room data ports, in-room fax, in-room safes, minibars, room service, spa, baby-sitting, dry cleaning, laundry service, concierge, business services, meeting rooms, parking (fee). AE, D, DC, MC, V.*

$$$–$$$$ 🏨 **W Union Square.** Starwood's W Hotel brand has conquered the landmark Guardian Life building at the northeast corner of Union Square Park. The exterior of the 1911 beaux-arts style building has been restored, revealing many of its original granite and limestone details. Inside, the W's trademark sleek botanical design elements prevail: Green grass and gerber daisys cling to the walls of the lobby (officially referred to as the "living room") and the front desk is a grass lawn with granite stepping stones. Style permeates each room, from the shiny sharkskin bed covering to the overstuffed velvet armchairs, and the amenities (high-speed Internet access, dual-line cordless phones) are up-to-the-minute. The room categories—"Wonderful," "Spectacular," "Mega," and "Urban"—vary in square footage and price. Generally, the service staff looks as though they just stepped out of a photo shoot, and at times it feels like that's where they'd rather be. Celebrity chef Todd English's first New York restaurant, Olives NY, and the hyperchic lobby bar draw huge crowds. ⊠ *201 Park Ave. S, at E. 17th St., 10003,* ☎ *212/253–9119 or 877/946–8357,* ℻ *212/779–0148,* WEB *www.whotels.com. 270 rooms, 16 suites. Restaurant, 2 bars, in-room data ports, in-room VCRs, mini-bars, room service, health club, dry cleaning, laundry service, concierge, business services, meeting rooms, parking (fee). AE, D, DC, MC, V.*

$$$ 🏨 **The Giraffe.** Inspired by the colors and textures of the art moderne period, this boutique property aspires to the indulgent comfort and sophisticated luxury of the 1920s and 1930s. Guest rooms with 10-ft ceilings are adorned with exotic features such as antique-rose velveteen armchairs, ivory diamond-quilted satin bedcovers, and pearlized platinum wall covers. Deluxe rooms have French doors opening onto private balconies that resemble the small balconies seen all over Paris. If you're ready to splurge, reserve one of the most beautiful penthouse suites in the city. The rooftop garden is accessible only to guests. ⊠ *365 Park Ave. S, at E. 26th St., 10016,* ☎ *212/685–7700 or 877/296–0009,* ℻ *212/685–7771,* WEB *www.hotelgiraffe.com. 73 rooms, 21 suites. Restaurant, 2 bars, in-room data ports, in-room VCRs, in-room safes, room service, dry cleaning, laundry service, business services, concierge. AE, D, DC, MC, V.*

$$$ 🏨 **Morgans.** Owner Ian Schrager started New York's boutique hotel craze when he opened this hipster way back in 1984, but Morgans is still up-to-the-minute as it ever was. Your first clue is that there's no sign outside. Inside, the stunning rooms have a minimalist, high-tech look, with low-lying, futonlike beds and 27-inch TVs on wheels; the tiny bathrooms have crystal shower doors, steel surgical sinks, and poured-granite floors. The chic Asia de Cuba, an enduring favorite, is a rarity among New York eateries—it actually lives up to all the hype. The same spirit prevails at the cavelike, candlelit Morgans Bar downstairs. ⊠ *237 Madison Ave., between E. 37th and E. 38th Sts., 10016,* ☎ *212/686–0300 or 800/334–3408,* ℻ *212/779–8352. 87 rooms, 26 suites. Restaurant, 2 bars, in-room data ports, in-room safes, minibars, room service, baby-sitting, dry cleaning, laundry service, concierge, business services, meeting rooms, parking (fee). AE, D, DC, MC, V.*

$$$ ⊞ **Roger Williams Hotel.** A masterpiece of industrial chic, this prop-
★ erty uses sleek maple walls and fluted zinc pillars to accentuate its cav-
ernous lobby. What they lack in space, bedrooms make up for in
high-style, custom-made blond-birch furnishings—including sliding
shoji screens behind the beds—and dramatic downlighting; each is
equipped with a 27-inch TV, VCR, and CD player. Some baths have
a cedarwood-floor shower stall. There's complimentary fresh fruit in
the evenings, as well as 24-hour cappuccino. ⊠ *131 Madison Ave., at
E. 31st St., 10016,* ☎ *212/448–7000,* FAX *212/448–7007,* WEB *www.
boutiquehg.com. 183 rooms, 1 suite. In-room data ports, in-room
VCRs, exercise room, concierge, parking (fee). AE, D, MC, V.*

$$$ ⊞ **W Court and W Tuscany.** Big black "W"s transform the guest room
headboards into billboards at these self-consciously stylish sister prop-
erties. The studied, design-for-design's-sake lobbies might strike some
as cold, but a friendly concierge and staff go a long way toward warm-
ing things up. Spacious rooms have vaguely Oriental black-and-blond
wood furnishings and ottomans with chenille throws (which, along with
most everything else, can be purchased through the in-room W catalog). The Tuscany is quieter with larger rooms, but the Court is hipper and louder thanks to the popular Wet Bar—expect well-dressed
crowds on weekends—and the starkly elegant, steamship-deco Icon
restaurant. ⊠ *Court: 130 E. 39th St., between Lexington and Park Aves.,
10016,* ☎ *212/685–1100 or 877/946–8357,* FAX *212/889–0287. Tuscany: 120 E. 39th St., near Lexington Ave., 10016,* ☎ *212/779–7822;
800/223–6725 reservations,* FAX *212/696–2095. Court: 150 rooms, 48
suites; Tuscany: 110 rooms, 12 suites. 2 restaurants, 2 bars, in-room
data ports, in-room safes, minibars, room service, gym, baby-sitting,
dry cleaning, laundry service, concierge, business services, meeting
rooms, parking (fee). AE, D, DC, MC, V.*

$$–$$$ ⊞ **Jolly Madison Towers.** The Italian Jolly Hotels chain brings a Eu-
ropean flair to this friendly hotel on a residential Murray Hill corner.
The tasteful and traditional rooms have dark-wood furnishings. Suites
are downright luxurious; huge bathrooms have glass shower stalls, bidets,
and make-up mirrors. Cinque Terre serves Northern Italian cuisine, and
the cozy Whaler Bar has a fireplace and a wood-beam ceiling. A separate concession on the premises offers shiatsu massage and Japanese
sauna. ⊠ *22 E. 38th St., between Madison and Park Aves., 10016,*
☎ *212/802–0600 or 800/225–4340,* FAX *212/447–0747,* WEB *www.
jollyhotels.it. 245 rooms, 6 suites. Restaurant, bar, in-room data ports,
in-room safes, minibars, massage, sauna, dry cleaning, laundry service,
concierge, parking (fee). AE, DC, MC, V.*

$$ ⊞ **Gramercy Park Hotel.** This 1920s curio has the air of a proud re-
tiree living on a fixed income. Accommodations in the north building
are bigger, and the kitchens in the suites are large enough to swing-
dance in. Although clean, the rooms are a bit tatty and not particu-
larly stylish, and the forgotten lobby bar is so completely B-movie noir
you'll swear you're seeing in black and white. Room service offers gi-
gantic burgers with fries for $7.95 (an incredible bargain for NYC),
and guests are granted access to the only private park in the city. It's
probably not for children (girlie mags are sold in the gift shop), but
the combination of low cost, large rooms, and quiet surroundings
makes the whole of this strange lady greater than the sum of her parts.
⊠ *2 Lexington Ave., at Gramercy Park, 10010,* ☎ *212/475–4320 or
800/221–4083,* FAX *212/205–0535. 360 rooms, 149 suites. Restau-
rant, bar, room service, parking (fee). AE, D, DC, MC, V.*

$ ⊞ **Carlton Arms.** Every wall, ceiling, and other surface here is covered
with murals, commissioned over the years by the free-spirited managers.
Each room has a theme; for instance, the Versailles Room (5A) is an
outré symphony of trompe l'oeil trellises and classical urns. All rooms

have double-glazed windows but are TV-less, almost free of furniture, and sometimes bathless. There are no room phones, either, and the front desk phone can go unanswered for periods of time, but most guests aren't in town on business, anyway. ✉ *160 E. 25th St., at 3rd Ave., 10010,* ☎ *212/684–8337; 212/679–0680 for reservations,* WEB *www. carltonarms.com. 54 rooms, 20 with bath. MC, V.*

$ ★ 🏨 **The Gershwin.** Young, foreign travelers flock to this budget hotel-cum-hostel, housed in a converted 13-story Greek Revival building. A giant primary-color cartoony sculpture, one of many works by house artist Brad Howe, visually assaults in the lobby. (A gallery next door show-cases other avant-garde creations.) Rooms are all painted in custard yellow and kelly green and are somewhat crumbly in places, with no air-conditioning. Dormitories have four or eight beds and a remarkable $22 rate. You won't be spending much time in your room, however, be-cause of all the activities here: concerts, stand-up comedy, film series, and occasional summer rooftop barbecues (which can draw the unwanted attention of New York's Finest, who sometimes choose to shut down the festivities). ✉ *7 E. 27th St., between 5th and Madison Aves., 10016,* ☎ *212/545–8000,* FAX *212/684–5546,* WEB *www.gershwinhotel.com. 110 rooms, 20 dorm rooms, 2 suites. Bar. AE, MC, V.*

Chelsea

$$ 🏨 **Chelsea Savoy Hotel.** Affordable rates and a friendly though often harried young staff make this a sensible choice. Jade-green carpets, but-terscotch-color wood furniture, and perhaps a framed van Gogh print enliven the small, basic rooms. Off the bland lobby, a huge, salmon-pink sitting room with mismatched chairs and sofas is a convenient place to meet and greet. ✉ *204 W. 23rd St., at 7th Ave., 10011,* ☎ *212/929–9353,* FAX *212/741–6309. 90 rooms. In-room data ports. AE, MC, V.*

$$ 🏨 **Inn on 23rd.** When you think Manhattan hotel, a cozy B&B is the last image to come to mind, but this inn would like to change that. It is the inspired creation of Annette and Barry Fisherman, who restored a 19th-century commercial building in the heart of Chelsea. All 11 guest rooms are spacious and unique, from the exotic and elegant bamboo room to the art-moderne style of the 1940s room. There is also a suite with an incomparable view of the quintessential New York landmark, the Empire State Building. Although it's small and homey, the inn pro-vides private baths and satellite TV in all rooms, an elevator, and, of course, breakfast. ✉ *131 W. 23rd St., between 6th and 7th Aves., 10011,* ☎ *212/463–0330,* FAX *212/463–0302. 11 rooms. In-room data ports. AE, MC, V.*

$ 🏨 **Chelsea Inn.** The eclectic, country ambience here is a refreshing change from the characterless hotels that dominate this price category. Housed in an old brownstone, it's a favorite of young budget travelers, who appreciate the in-room cooking facilities (some rooms have full kitch-enettes; others have just a refrigerator and sink). Rooms, with shared or private bath, are a cozy hodgepodge of country quilts and thrift-shop antiques. A few rooms in back overlook a little courtyard with an ivy-draped fence, and quiet prevails even though next door sits one of the largest, most popular gay bars in town. ✉ *46 W. 17th St., be-tween 5th and 6th Aves., 10011,* ☎ *212/645–8989 or 800/640–6469,* FAX *212/645–1903,* WEB *www.chelseainn.com. 27 rooms, 3 with bath. Kitchenettes (some), refrigerators. AE, D, MC, V.*

Midtown West

$$$$ 🏨 **Essex House, a Westin Hotel.** The lobby of this stately Central Park South property is an art deco masterpiece, with inlaid marble floors and bas-relief elevator doors. Reproductions of British Chippendale

or French Louis XIV antiques decorate the guest rooms, all of which have marble baths—some with walk-in showers. Many rooms have breathtaking views of the park, and in-room extras include ironing facilities and personal fax/copier/printers. In a major coup, the hotel managed to convince the celebrated French chef, Alain Ducasse, to open his first stateside venture in the space that once held Les Célébrites. The result is the city's most expensive restaurant, with service that will impress even the most jaded diner. Cafe Botanica still pleases with its greenhouselike setting overlooking the park. ⊠ *160 Central Park S, between 6th and 7th Aves., 10019,* ☎ *212/247–0300 or 800/645–5687,* FAX *212/315–1839,* WEB *www.westin.com. 516 rooms, 81 suites. Restaurant, bar, in-room data ports, in-room fax, in-room safes, in-room VCRs, minibars, room service, spa, health club, baby-sitting, dry cleaning, laundry service, concierge, business services, meeting rooms, parking (fee). AE, D, DC, MC, V.*

$$$$ ⊞ **Marriott Marquis.** This giant in the heart of the theater district is a place New Yorkers love to hate. It's obvious, brash, and bright, with its own little city of restaurants, shops, meeting rooms, ballrooms— there's even a large Broadway theater—within its vast confines. As at other Marriotts, all of the nearly 2,000 rooms here look alike, but all are clean, pleasant, and functional. Some rooms have dramatic urban views. The View, the aptly-named revolving bar/restaurant on the 49th floor, offers one of the most spectacular—and dizzying—panoramas in New York, but you may have to wait on line to get in. ⊠ *1535 Broadway, at W. 45th St., 10036,* ☎ *212/398–1900 or 800/843–4898,* FAX *212/704–8966,* WEB *www.marriott.com. 1,888 rooms, 56 suites. 4 restaurants, 3 bars, café, coffee shop, in-room data ports, in-room safes, room service, beauty salon, massage, health club, theater, baby-sitting, dry cleaning, laundry service, concierge, business services, meeting rooms, parking (fee). AE, D, DC, MC, V.*

$$$$ ⊞ **The Plaza.** Towering like a giant birthday cake on 5th Avenue opposite Central Park and F.A.O. Schwarz, this is one of New York's highest-profile hotels. The fictional Eloise ran riot in it, countless films have featured it, and the Oak Bar and Palm Court are city institutions. Owned and managed by Fairmont Hotels and Resorts, the hotel carefully maintains its high-traffic public areas and 9,000-square-ft health club. Suites are magnificent, but even the smallest guest rooms have crystal chandeliers and 14-ft ceilings. The hotel is as stately as a faded queen, if somewhat past its prime, and at times the service could be better. ⊠ *5th Ave. at 59th St., 10019,* ☎ *212/759–3000 or 800/759–3000,* FAX *212/546–5324. 692 rooms, 112 suites. 3 restaurants, 2 bars, in-room data ports, in-room safes, minibars, room service, health club, baby-sitting, dry cleaning, laundry service, concierge, business services, meeting rooms, parking (fee). AE, D, DC, MC, V.*

$$$$ ⊞ **Rihga Royal.** This discreet establishment has a loyal following among celebrities and business travelers. Each of its luxurious, contemporary-style suites—many of them quite spacious—has a living room, a bedroom, and a large marble bath with glass-enclosed shower and separate tub. Some suites feature French doors and bay windows, and the pricier Pinnacle Suites have CD players, cellular phones, and printer-copiers. The hotel's spectacular "Marketplace in the Sky" Sunday brunch, offered in the top-floor banquet rooms, has become a local favorite. ⊠ *151 W. 54th St., between 6th and 7th Aves., 10019,* ☎ *212/307–5000 or 800/937–5454,* FAX *212/765–6530,* WEB *www.rihga.com. 500 suites. Restaurant, bar, in-room data ports, in-room fax, in-room safes, in-room VCRs, minibars, room service, massage, gym, baby-sitting, dry cleaning, laundry service, concierge, business services, meeting rooms, parking (fee). AE, D, DC, MC, V.*

312

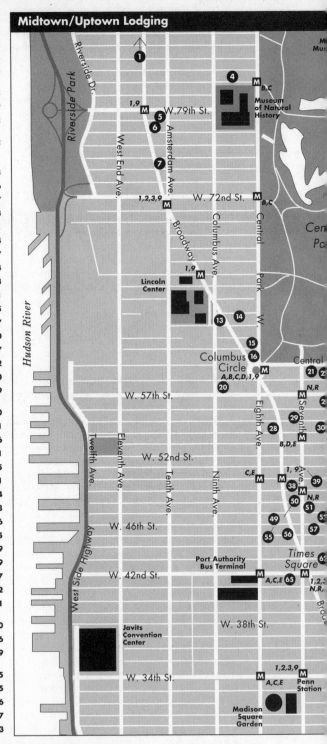

Midtown/Uptown Lodging

$$$–$$$$ 🏨 **Le Parker Meridien.** This dramatic, modern French hotel has one of the city's more striking entryways: A long atrium with an elaborate painted-mosaic ceiling and massive Doric columns leads into a cavernous lobby, where a sheer cliff of blond wood backs the registration desk. Equally impressive are the hotel's rooftop swimming pool and 15,000-square-ft Club La Raquette fitness facility. Upstairs, the well-kept rooms with in-room CD players and Biedermeier-style reproductions have a sleek, modern art deco feel; most rooms face toward Central Park, two blocks away. The hotel frequently offers unadvertised specials and package deals, so ask when you call. ⊠ *118 W. 57th St., between 6th and 7th Aves., 10019,* ☎ *212/245–5000 or 800/543–4300,* 𝖥𝖠𝖷 *212/708–7477,* 𝖶𝖤𝖡 *www.parkermeridien.com. 449 rooms, 249 suites. 2 restaurants, 2 bars, breakfast room, in-room data ports, in-room fax, in-room safes, in-room VCRs, minibars, room service, indoor pool, spa, health club, racquetball, baby-sitting, dry cleaning, laundry service, concierge, business services, meeting rooms. AE, D, DC, MC, V.*

$$$–$$$$ 🏨 **The Michelangelo.** Italophiles will feel right at home at this deluxe
★   hotel, whose very long, wide lobby lounge is full of multihued marble and Veronese-style oil paintings. Upstairs, the relatively spacious rooms (averaging 475 square ft) have varying decorative motifs, from neoclassical (cherrywood furnishings with black accents) to Asian—but all have marble foyers and marble bathrooms equipped with bidets, TVs, phones, and oversize 55-gallon tubs. The larger rooms have sitting areas and king beds. Complimentary cappuccino, pastries, and other Italian treats are served each morning in the baroque lobby lounge. ⊠ *152 W. 51st St., at 7th Ave., 10019,* ☎ *212/765–1900 or 800/237–0990,* 𝖥𝖠𝖷 *212/581–7618,* 𝖶𝖤𝖡 *www.michelangelohotel.com. 128 rooms, 50 suites. Restaurant, bar, in-room fax, in-room data ports, in-room safes, minibars, room service, gym, baby-sitting, dry cleaning, laundry service, concierge, business services, meeting rooms, parking (fee). AE, D, DC, MC, V.*

$$$–$$$$ 🏨 **Renaissance.** This link in the chain is a business hotel, but vacationers often take advantage of its low off-season rates and its proximity to Broadway. Elevators lead from street level to the third-floor art deco–style reception area. On the second floor are two bars and Foley's Fish House, a restaurant with up-close views of Times Square. Rooms are warm and inviting, and the marble bathrooms have deep soaking tubs. ⊠ *714 7th Ave., between W. 47th and W. 48th Sts., 10036,* ☎ *212/765–7676 or 800/628–5222,* 𝖥𝖠𝖷 *212/765–1962,* 𝖶𝖤𝖡 *www.renaissancehotels.com. 295 rooms, 10 suites. Restaurant, bar, in-room data ports, in-room safes, in-room VCRs, room service, minibars, massage, gym, baby-sitting, dry cleaning, laundry service, concierge, business services, meeting rooms, parking (fee). AE, D, DC, MC, V.*

$$$–$$$$ 🏨 **The Royalton.** This is a second home to media, music, and fashion-biz folk, who often meet for martinis in the spacious lobby lounge or the inconspicuous Vodka Bar. Each minimalist, Philippe Starck–designed guest room has a low-lying, custom-made bed, tasteful lighting, and fresh flowers. Some of the rooms have working fireplaces, and all have VCRs and CD players. Slate bathrooms with stainless steel and glass fixtures may also feature round, two-person tubs. The staff here does a good job of catering to people who feel it's their lot in life to be waited on. ⊠ *44 W. 44th St., between 5th and 6th Aves., 10036,* ☎ *212/869–4400 or 800/635–9013,* 𝖥𝖠𝖷 *212/575–0012. 145 rooms, 23 suites. Restaurant, bar, in-room data ports, in-room safes, minibars, room service, massage, gym, baby-sitting, dry cleaning, laundry service, concierge, business services, meeting rooms, parking (fee). AE, DC, MC, V.*

$$$-$$$$ ▥ **The Shoreham.** This is a miniature, low-attitude version of the Royalton—and it's comfortable to boot. Almost everything is metal or of metal color, from perforated steel headboards (lit from behind) to the steel sink in the shiny, tiny bathrooms to the silver-gray carpets. Pleasant touches include CD players and cedar-lined closets. Guests enjoy a complimentary Continental breakfast, and the Shoreham Bar and Grille offers an eclectic, light menu of sandwiches and salads. ⊠ *33 W. 55th St., between 5th and 6th Aves., 10019,* ☎ *212/247–6700 or 877/847–4444,* ℻ *212/765–9741,* ⓌⒺⒷ *www.boutiquehg.com. 47 rooms, 37 suites. Restaurant, bar, in-room data ports, in-room safes, in-room VCRs, massage, baby-sitting, dry cleaning, laundry service, concierge, business services, parking (fee). AE, DC, MC, V. CP.*

$$-$$$$ ▥ **The Gorham.** An inviting lobby with maple-paneled walls, marble floors, Persian rugs, and potted plants sets the cosmopolitan mood for this midtown gem, which prides itself on its cozy breakfast room and sunny, immaculate gym. Fully equipped kitchenettes and work desks make the spacious rooms a bargain, whether or not you like the Euromodern decor of red-lacquer furniture and marbleized countertops. Bathrooms have their own phones and nifty digital water-temperature settings. The quietest rooms are in the front of the hotel, on West 55th Street. ⊠ *136 W. 55th St., between 6th and 7th Aves., 10019,* ☎ *212/245–1800 or 800/735–0710,* ℻ *212/582–8332,* ⓌⒺⒷ *www. gorhamhotel.com. 70 rooms, 45 suites. Breakfast room, in-room safes, kitchenettes, gym. AE, DC, MC, V.*

$$-$$$$ ▥ **The Hudson.** Yet another hotel designed by Philippe Starck, the Hudson often puts up velvet ropes to manage the glitzy crowd of New York trendsters who have colonized its bar. More than 1,000 rooms are squeezed into 23 floors; some are as small as 150 square ft, and there are no king beds. Some rooms have see-through shower walls—a must for the modern voyeur—and all the bathrooms have a supply of candles for a relaxing atmosphere. The guest rooms have richly colored, dark walls that contrast with the comfortable, modern bright white furniture. Tight quarters in the small rooms are balanced by low (by Manhattan standards) rates. The Hudson Cafeteria has become the see-and-be-seen dining room of the moment, though it's not because the food is anything to swoon over. ⊠ *356 W. 58th St., between 8th and 9th Aves., 10019,* ☎ *212/554–6000,* ℻ *212/554–6001,* ⓌⒺⒷ *www. hudsonhotel.com. 1,000 rooms. Restaurant, bar, in-room data ports, in-room safes, room service, massage, health club, laundry service, concierge, business services, meeting rooms, parking (fee). AE, D, DC, MC, V.*

$$-$$$$ ▥ **The Mansfield.** Built in 1904 as lodging for distinguished bachelors, this small, clubby hotel has a Victorian mood. Turn-of-the-20th-century details abound, from the lobby's coffered ceiling, warm ivory walls, and yellow limestone floor to the black-marble bathrooms, darkwood venetian blinds, and sleigh beds in the guest rooms. A machine dispenses free cappuccino 24 hours a day in the breakfast nook, and the hotel's swank M Bar serves cocktails, caviar, and desserts until 2 AM—which you might need since room service is only available weekdays until 8 PM. ⊠ *12 W. 44th St., between 5th and 6th Aves., 10036,* ☎ *212/944–6050 or 877/847–4444,* ℻ *212/764–4477. 124 rooms, 24 suites. In-room data ports, in-room safes, in-room VCRs, room service, library, concierge, business services, meeting rooms, parking (fee). AE, DC, MC, V.*

$$-$$$$ ▥ **New York Hilton.** New York City's largest hotel and the epicenter of the city's hotel-based conventions, the Hilton has myriad business facilities, eating establishments, and shops, all designed for convenience. Considering the size of this property, guest rooms are surprisingly well maintained, and all have coffeemakers, hair dryers, and ironing boards. A variety of local ethnic cuisines is offered at the New York Marketplace, a mall-style food court in the hotel lobby. ⊠ *1335 6th Ave., between W. 53rd and W. 54th Sts., 10019,* ☏ *212/586–7000 or 800/445–8667,* FAX *212/315–1374,* WEB *www.hilton.com. 2,041 rooms, 20 suites. 2 restaurants, 2 bars, in-room data ports, in-room safes, minibars, room service, barbershop, hair salon, massage, sauna, health club, baby-sitting, dry cleaning, laundry service, concierge, concierge floors, business services, parking (fee). AE, D, DC, MC, V.*

$$–$$$$ ⊞ **Sofitel New York.** The European hotel group's first New York property is a dramatic, contemporary 30-story curved tower overlooking Fifth Avenue. The place feels professional, with a spacious, quiet lobby, an elegant French Brasserie (Gaby, named for a Parisian model who made a name for herself in the Big Apple in the 1920s), and courteous staff who are always on hand. Upstairs, the rooms are what you expect to find in a big corporate hotel—lots of earthtones and mahogany—but what they lack in aesthetics they more than make up for in amenities such as high-speed Internet access and plush bedding. ⊠ *45 W. 44th St., between 5th and 6th Aves., 10036,* ☏ *212/354–8844,* FAX *212/782–3002,* WEB *www.sofitel.com. 398 rooms, 52 suites. Restaurant, piano bar, in-room data ports, minibars, room service, gym, dry cleaning, laundry service, concierge, business services, meeting rooms, parking (fee). AE, D, DC, MC, V.*

$$$ ⊞ **The Algonquin.** The hallways of this New York landmark and publishing-world darling are papered with 100 years worth of *New Yorker* cartoons, and indeed, it's the mystique of the place that attracts guests. Small and boxy—even compared to those of less-expensive hotels—the rooms have a somewhat grandmotherly feel that you might find less than cheerful. Even Matilda, the resident cat who holds court in the parlorlike lobby, knows that the draw here is the litany of famously literate visitors, whose signed works can be checked out of the library and whose witticisms grace the doors of each guest room. The renowned Oak Room is one of the city's premier cabaret performance venues, and the publike Blue Bar has visitors from around the world feeling at home. ⊠ *59 W. 44th St., between 5th and 6th Aves., 10036,* ☏ *212/840–6800 or 800/555–8000,* FAX *212/944–1419,* WEB *www.camberleyhotels.com. 142 rooms, 23 suites. 2 restaurants, bar, in-room data ports, in-room safes, room service, gym, cabaret, library, dry cleaning, laundry service, concierge, business services, meeting rooms, parking (fee). AE, D, DC, MC, V.*

$$$ ⊞ **Casablanca.** Morocco meets the Mediterranean in this fanciful hotel: Moorish mosaic tiles, framed antique Berber scarves and rugs, and a mural of a North African cityscape conjure up the exotic desert oasis of Casablanca itself. In the spacious lounge with a fireplace, a piano, a 41-inch movie screen, and bookshelves stocked with Bogart-abilia, look for complimentary breakfast and wine and cheese on weeknights, in addition to complimentary 24-hour cappuccino and cookies. Rattan furniture, ceiling fans, and Moroccan-style wood shutters dress up the smallish rooms, which have elaborately tiled bathrooms. ⊠ *147 W. 43rd St., between 6th and 7th Aves., 10036,* ☏ *212/869–1212,* FAX *212/391–7585,* WEB *www.casablancahotel.com. 43 rooms, 5 suites. Bar, breakfast room, in-room data ports, in-room safes, in-room VCRs, refrigerators, piano, business services, meeting room, complimentary Continental breakfast, parking (fee). AE, DC, MC, V.*

$$$ ⊞ **Central Park Intercontinental.** A Central Park South classic, this property has not only a swank address but very polished service and fine art on virtually every wall. Everything about the hotel is first-class. Guest rooms are graced with rich brocades, polished woods, and marble bathrooms; some have breathtaking Central Park views. ⊠ *112 Central Park S, between 6th and 7th Aves., 10019,* ☏ *212/757–1900 or 800/937–*

8461, FAX 212/757–9620. *193 rooms, 15 suites. Restaurant, bar, in-room data ports, in-room safes, minibars, room service, steam room, health club, baby-sitting, dry cleaning, laundry service, concierge, business services, meeting room, parking (fee). AE, D, DC, MC, V.*

$$$ **The Time.** This spot half a block from the din of Times Square tempers trendiness with a touch of humor. A ridiculously futuristic glass elevator—eggshells line the bottom of the shaft—transports guests to the second-floor lobby. In the adjoining bar, nature videos lighten up the low-flung, serious gray-scale furnishings. The smallish guest rooms, each themed on one of the primary colors, have mood lighting and even specific aromas that create a unique, if contrived, hotel experience. Pino Luongo operates the popular Coco Pazzo Teatro restaurant on the first floor. ✉ *224 W. 49th St., between Broadway and 8th Ave., 10019,* ☎ *212/320–2900 or 877/846–3692,* FAX *212/245–2305,* WEB *www.thetimeny.com. 164 rooms, 29 suites. Restaurant, bar, in-room safes, minibars, room service, dry cleaning, laundry service, concierge, business services, parking (fee). AE, D, DC, MC, V.*

$$$ **Warwick.** Built by William Randolph Hearst in 1927 as a private res-
★   idence, the Warwick remains a midtown favorite, and is well placed for the Theater District and points west. The elegant, marble-floor lobby buzzes with activity; the Warwick Bar is on one side and Ciao Europa, an Italian restaurant, on the other. Handsome, Regency-style rooms have soft pastel color schemes, mahogany armoires, and marble bathrooms, and some have fax machines. The Cary Grant suite was the actor's New York residence. ✉ *65 W. 54th St., at 6th Ave., 10019,* ☎ *212/247–2700 or 800/223–4099,* FAX *212/489–3926,* WEB *www.warwickhotels.com. 357 rooms, 70 suites. Restaurant, bar, in-room data ports, in-room safes, minibars, room service, gym, dry cleaning, laundry service, business services, meeting rooms, parking (fee). AE, DC, MC, V.*

$$–$$$ **Ameritania Hotel.** Guests at this busy crash pad just off Broadway are divided pretty evenly: Half come for business, half for pleasure. Dimly lit hallways create a feeling of perpetual nighttime—an impression that lingers in the bedrooms, where black metal furniture dominates. The hotel's Bar 54 plays Top-40 music until 2 AM. Rates may drop by as much as $100 a night in off-season, depending on occupancy. ✉ *230 W. 54th St., at Broadway, 10019,* ☎ *212/247–5000 or 888/664–6835,* FAX *212/247–3316,* WEB *www.nycityhotels.com. 195 rooms, 12 suites. Restaurant, bar, in-room data ports, in-room safes, room service, dry cleaning, laundry service, concierge, business services, parking (fee). AE, D, DC, MC, V.*

$$–$$$ **Hilton Times Square.** The Hilton Times Square sits atop a 335,000-square-ft retail and entertainment complex that includes a 25-theater movie megaplex and Madame Tussaud's Wax Museum. The building has a handsome Mondrian-inspired façade, but room décor runs more to chain-hotel blandness. Nonetheless, the rooms are quite comfortable, with amenities that range from in-room coffee makers to bathrobes to premium cable TV. The hotel is efficiently run and the staff is pleasant. Because there are no guest rooms below the 22nd floor, many rooms afford excellent views of Times Square and midtown. Chef Larry Forgione's Restaurant Above is off the "sky lobby" on the 21st floor. ✉ *234 W. 42nd St., between 7th and 8th Aves., 10036,* ☎ *212/642–2500,* FAX *212/840–5516,* WEB *www.hilton.com. 444 rooms, 15 suites. Restaurant, bar, in-room data ports, in-room safes, minibars, room service, gym, laundry service, concierge, business services, meeting rooms, parking (fee). AE, D, DC, MC, V.*

$$–$$$ **The Iroquois.** Built during the Depression, this once prosaic hotel is now among the city's better boutique properties. Service is top-notch, and as the hotel is privately run it has more personality than many of the bigger chains. Amenities are abundant—children enjoy in-room Nin-

tendo systems and their very own Frette bathrobes. Cozy standard rooms have either a queen or two full beds, and the elegant marble-and-brass bathrooms have phones and pedestal sinks. The street-side James Dean suite was the actor's residence in the early 1950s. Triomphe, the hotel's French/Italian restaurant, has enjoyed such success that it has doubled in size since its opening. ✉ *49 W. 44th St., between 5th and 6th Aves., 10036,* ☎ *212/840–3080 or 800/332–7220,* FAX *212/398–1754,* WEB *www.iroqouisny.com. 114 rooms, 9 suites. Restaurant, bar, in-room data ports, in-room safes, room service, massage, gym, dry cleaning, laundry service, concierge, business services, parking (fee). AE, D, DC, MC, V.*

$$–$$$ 🏨 **The Muse.** In the heart of the Theater District, the Muse takes the theater as its inspiration. Although the lobby is oddly nondescript, the rooms are oversize and crammed with state-of-the-art amenities such as multiline cordless phones and high-speed Internet access. The beds are dressed in fine linens with feather duvets, and some rooms have a DVD player, wide-screen TV, exercise equipment, and desktop computer. There is also a "midnight pantry," where guests can enjoy a complimentary post-theater buffet. In keeping with the theatrical theme, chef Sam DeMarco prepares globally influenced American cuisine in a stagelike setting in the hotel's happening restaurant, District. ✉ *130 W. 46th St., between 6th and 7th Aves., 10018,* ☎ *212/485–2400,* FAX *212/485–2900,* WEB *www.themusehotel.com. 200 rooms, 10 suites. Restaurant, bar, in-room data ports, in-room safes, minibars, room service, gym, dry cleaning, laundry service, concierge, business services, meeting rooms, parking (fee). AE, D, DC, MC, V.*

$$–$$$ 🏨 **The Paramount.** The fashionable Paramount caters to a somewhat bohemian, fashionable, yet cost-conscious clientele. The very small rooms have black-and-gray check carpet, white furnishings and walls, and distinctive touches such as gilt-framed headboards and conical steel bathrooms sinks. In the lobby, a sheer platinum wall and a glamorous sweep of staircase lead to the Mezzanine Restaurant, where you can enjoy cocktails or dinner while gazing down upon the action below. The attached Whiskey Bar, once fiercely trendy, draws a somewhat diluted crowd now that other Whiskeys have opened in all of the W Hotels around town. Hotel drawbacks include limited room amenities and a sometimes harried staff. ✉ *235 W. 46th St., between Broadway and 8th Aves., 10036,* ☎ *212/764–5500 or 800/225–7474,* FAX *212/354–5737. 590 rooms, 10 suites. 2 restaurants, 2 bars, café, in-room data ports, in-room safes, in-room VCRs, room service, gym, nursery, dry cleaning, laundry service, concierge, business services, meeting rooms. AE, D, DC, MC, V.*

$$ 🏨 **Quality Hotel and Suites.** This small prewar hotel is near many theaters, Rockefeller Center, and some of the city's best-known Brazilian restaurants. The peculiar lobby has a narrow corridor that snakes off around a corner and is decorated with some rather handsome art deco Bakelite lights. The rooms are very plain, but most are well maintained and clean. This block is one of midtown's most deserted at night, so travelers should use caution coming and going. ✉ *59 W. 46th St., between 5th and 6th Aves., 10036,* ☎ *212/719–2300 or 212/790–2710 or 800/567–7720,* FAX *212/290–2760,* WEB *www.applecorehotels.com. 193 rooms, 21 suites. Cafeteria, in-room data ports, barbershop, beauty salon, business services. AE, D, DC, MC, V.*

$$ 🏨 **Wellington Hotel.** This large, old-fashioned property's main advantages are reasonable prices and its proximity to Central Park and Carnegie Hall. The lobby has an aura of faded glamor, from the lit-up red awning outside to the chandeliers and ornate artwork inside. The hotel appeals to families and to those traveling on a budget. Rooms are small but clean; baths are serviceable, and the staff is helpful.

✉ *871 7th Ave., at W. 55th St., 10019,* ☎ *212/247–3900 or 800/652–1212,* ℻ *212/581–1719,* ⓦⓔⓑ *www.wellingtonhotel.com. 487 rooms, 130 suites. Restaurant, bar, coffee shop, in-room data ports, beauty salon, parking (fee). AE, DC, MC, V.*

$–$$ ⊞ **Broadway Inn Bed & Breakfast.** In the heart of the theater district,
★ this friendly, comfortable, reasonably priced B&B has spartan but cheerful rooms, with black-lacquer beds and folding chairs. Breakfast is served in the Victorian-style lobby, whose brick walls, stocked bookshelves, and framed photos of Old New York encourage lingering. An extra $70 or $80 gets you a suite with an additional fold-out sofabed, and a kitchenette hidden by closet doors. Single travelers can get their own room for as little as $125, which very well might be one of the best deals in town. ✉ *264 W. 46th St., between Broadway and 8th Ave., 10036,* ☎ *212/997–9200 or 800/826–6300,* ℻ *212/768–2807. 22 rooms, 11 suites. In-room data ports, kitchenettes (some). AE, D, DC, MC, V.*

$–$$ ⊞ **Hotel Edison.** This offbeat old hotel is a popular budget stop for tour groups from the United States and abroad. The simple, serviceable guest rooms are clean and fresh, but the bathrooms tend to show their age. The loan-shark murder scene in *The Godfather* was shot in what is now Sophia's restaurant, and the pink-and-blue plaster Edison Café, known half-jokingly as the Polish Tea Room, is a theater-crowd landmark consistently recognized as NYC's best coffee shop. ✉ *228 W. 47th St., between Broadway and 8th Ave., 10036,* ☎ *212/840–5000 or 800/637–7070,* ℻ *212/596–6850. 800 rooms. Restaurant, bar, coffee shop, beauty salon, airport shuttle. AE, D, DC, MC, V.*

$ ⊞ **Herald Square Hotel.** Sculpted cherubs on the facade and vintage magazine covers adorning the common areas hint at this building's previous incarnation as *Life* magazine's 1886 headquarters. Rooms are basic and clean; all have TVs and phones with voice mail. There's no concierge and no room service, but nearby restaurants will deliver. A no-frills option, to be sure, but where else in the city can you find a clean, single room for the downright suburban sum of $60 (doubles start at $115). ✉ *19 W. 31st St., between 5th Ave. and Broadway, 10001,* ☎ *212/279–4017 or 800/727–1888,* ℻ *212/643–9208,* ⓦⓔⓑ *www.heraldsquarehotel.com. 120 rooms. In-room safes. AE, D, MC, V.*

$ ⊞ **Portland Square Hotel.** You can't beat this theater district old-timer for value, given its clean, simple rooms that invite with flower print bedspreads and curtains. James Cagney once lived in the building, and—as the story goes—a few of his Radio City Rockette acquaintances lived upstairs. There is certainly a feeling of history to the place—*Life* magazine used to have its offices here, and everything from the gilt-edged entryway to the original detailing evoke old New York. Rooms on the east wing have oversize bathrooms. ✉ *132 W. 47th St., between 6th and 7th Aves., 10036,* ☎ *212/382–0600 or 800/388–8988,* ℻ *212/382–0684,* ⓦⓔⓑ *www.portlandsquarehotel.com. 142 rooms, 112 with bath. In-room safes, gym, coin laundry, business services. AE, MC, V.*

Midtown East

$$$$ ⊞ **The Drake.** Just off Park Avenue in the heart of corporate Manhattan, this Swissôtel property caters to business travelers with modern, comfortable rooms that are a cut above the average corporate variety. The deco-style accomodations are a welcome alternative to the traditional decor of many hotels in this price category. The once-stuffy bar has been replaced by a sleek, contemporary restaurant, Quantum 56, and a branch of Fauchon, Paris' gourmet food emporium, has a shop and a lovely tea room off the lobby. ✉ *440 Park Ave., at E. 56th St., 10022,* ☎ *212/421–0900 or 800/372–5369,* ℻ *212/371–4190,* ⓦⓔⓑ *www.swissotel.com. 385 rooms, 100 suites. Restaurant, bar, in-room data*

Close-Up

COMING ATTRACTIONS

SOMETIMES IT SEEMS like a new hotel opens every month in the red-hot New York market. Among the latest as of press time were:

The Chambers. A swank, modern new hotel overlooking Bryant Park, with a well-known chef ensconced in the kitchen.

Red Roof Inn. The economy chain makes its New York debut with a convenient West 32nd Street location and a rooftop garden/bar. Planned: 172 rooms priced $89–$199.

Ritz-Carlton Battery Park City. Millennium Partners brings the world-renowned luxury brand back to New York with this new construction aimed at business travelers and weekenders. Planned: 300 rooms, plus condo-style residential suites.

Ritz-Carlton Central Park. After a complete overhaul of the old St. Moritz on Central Park South, Millennium Partners will open this showpiece.

60 Thompson. SoHo welcomes its third major lodging, a 100-room luxury boutique hotel with amenities such as in-room DVD players, laptop computers, and personal cell phones. There will also be a restaurant that is sure to attract attention.

---

ports, in-room fax, in-room safes, refrigerators, room service, spa, gym, baby-sitting, dry cleaning, laundry service, concierge, business services, meeting rooms, parking (fee). AE, D, DC, MC, V.

$$$$ Four Seasons. ★ Architect I. M. Pei designed this limestone-clad stepped spire amid the prime shops of 57th Street. Everything here comes in epic proportions—from the prices (rooms *start* at $585); to the guest rooms, which average 600 square ft; to the sky-high Grand Foyer, with French limestone pillars, marble, onyx, and acre upon acre of blond wood. The soundproof guest rooms have 10-ft-high ceilings, bedside controls for opening and closing window shades, enormous English sycamore walk-in closets, and blond-marble bathrooms with tubs that fill in 60 seconds. Service is impeccable. ⊠ *57 E. 57th St., between Park and Madison Aves., 10022,* ☎ *212/758–5700 or 800/487–3769,* FAX *212/758–5711,* WEB *www.fourseasons.com. 310 rooms, 62 suites. Restaurant, bar, in-room data ports, in-room safes, minibars, room service, spa, health club, piano, baby-sitting, dry cleaning, laundry service, concierge, business services, meeting room, car rental, parking (fee). AE, DC, MC, V.*

$$$$ New York Palace. ★ Among its many luxurious facilities, the Palace boasts the five-star restaurant Le Cirque 2000, inside the landmark 1882 Villard Houses. Other offerings include a snazzy lobby lounge, a Spanish restaurant (Istaña) with an olive bar and Mediterranean-style tapas tea service, and a tier of glamorous deco-style guest rooms on various floors of the plush Tower level—a modern alternative to the hotel's traditional Empire-style rooms. The 7,000-square-ft health club has TVs with videos and headphones at every treadmill, and terrific views of St. Patrick's Cathedral. This is among New York's very best (check out the decadent bathrooms!). ⊠ *455 Madison Ave., at E. 50th St., 10022,*

☎ 212/888–7000 or 800/697–2522, FAX 212/303–6000, WEB *www.newyorkpalace.com. 797 rooms, 100 suites. 2 restaurants, 2 bars, in-room data ports, in-room safes, minibars, room service, spa, health club, baby-sitting, dry cleaning, laundry service, concierge, concierge floors, business services, meeting room, parking (fee). AE, D, DC, MC, V.*

$$$$ ▥ **Omni Berkshire Place.** Omni Berkshire's flagship hotel brings sophistication to the Omni name. Although the cavernous reception area is less than inviting, there's a dramatic, two-story atrium lounge with a fireplace, an elaborately stained dark-wood floor, and bowls of Siamese fighting fish on every table. The spacious guest rooms (all of them 375 square ft) have a contemporary, Asian-influenced simplicity and plenty of modern amenities such as plush bedding, tasteful furnishings, and spacious bathrooms. Families will want to take advantage of the hotel's extensive kid's program. ⊠ *21 E. 52nd St., between 5th and Madison Aves., 10022,* ☎ *212/753–5800 or 800/843–6664,* FAX *212/754–5020,* WEB *www.omnihotels.com. 396 rooms, 47 suites. Restaurant, bar, in-room data ports, in-room fax, in-room safes, minibars, room service, massage, health club, dry cleaning, laundry service, concierge, business services, meeting rooms, parking (fee). AE, D, DC, MC, V.*

$$$$ ▥ **The Peninsula.** Step past the beaux arts facade of this 1905 gem and into a lobby that retains its original art nouveau accents and you'll find yourself comfortably ensconced in the lap of luxury. Guest rooms, many with sweeping views down 5th Avenue, have a modern sensibility. King-size beds have formal covers that are ingeniously tucked away in built-in drawers at turn-down; simple, attractive artwork adorns the walls. The high-tech amenities are excellent, from a bedside console that controls the lighting, sound, and thermostat for the room to a TV mounted over the tub for bathtime viewing. Sumptuous marble bathrooms have separate shower stalls. The rooftop health club, pool, and seasonal open-air bar—which has become something of a local hot spot—all have dazzling views of midtown. ⊠ *700 5th Ave., at 55th St., 10019,* ☎ *212/247–2200 or 800/262–9467,* FAX *212/903–3943,* WEB *www.peninsula.com. 200 rooms, 42 suites. 2 restaurants, 2 bars, in-room data ports, in-room fax, in-room safes, minibars, room service, pool, spa, health club, dry cleaning, laundry service, concierge, business services, meeting rooms, parking (fee). AE, D, DC, MC, V.*

$$$$ ▥ **Regal U.N. Plaza.** It's easy to miss the entrance to this favorite among the business and diplomatic set—it's on a quiet side street near (naturally) the United Nations. Rooms, which begin on the 28th floor, have particularly spacious bathrooms, plus breathtaking views and framed tapestries donated by various missions. The views also dazzle from the elegant 27th-floor pool and health club, and the rooftop tennis court attracts name players. Service throughout the hotel is first-rate, and the business center is open until 11 PM. If you plan to use the fitness facilities, ask to stay in the east tower, where they are located. ⊠ *1 United Nations Plaza, at E. 44th St. and 1st Ave., 10017,* ☎ *212/758–1234 or 800/222–8888,* FAX *212/702–5051,* WEB *www.unplaza.com. 393 rooms, 33 suites. Restaurant, bar, in-room data ports, in-room fax, in-room safes, minibars, room service, pool, massage, tennis court, health club, baby-sitting, dry cleaning, laundry service, concierge, business services, meeting rooms, parking (fee). AE, D, DC, MC, V.*

$$$$ ▥ **The Regency.** Rough-hewn travertine lines an understated lobby punctuated by modern Regency-style furnishings, potted palms, and burnished gold sconces. Guest rooms have taupe-color silk wallpaper, velvet throw pillows, and polished Honduran mahogany, but the smallish bathrooms with their marble countertops are unspectacular. Goose-down duvets and ergonomic leather desk chairs reinforce the pleasingly modern feel. Feinstein's at the Regency hosts some of the hottest (and

priciest) cabaret acts in town, and 540 Park has become a destination in its own right among restaurant-savvy locals. ⊠ *540 Park Ave., at 61st St., 10021,* ☎ *212/759–4100 or 800/235–6397,* FAX *212/826–5674,* WEB *www.loews.com. 260 rooms, 100 suites. Restaurant, lobby lounge, in-room data ports, in-room fax, in-room safes, minibars, room service, beauty salon, massage, gym, cabaret, baby-sitting, dry cleaning, laundry service, concierge, business services, meeting rooms, parking (fee). AE, D, DC, MC, V.*

$$$$ 🏨 **The St. Regis.** Long a one-of-a-kind New York classic, this 5th Av-
★ enue beaux arts landmark became the first link in a luxury hotel chain when Sheraton acquired it early in the 1990s. Public spaces are ultra-luxe, from the celebrated restaurant Lespinasse; to the Astor Court tea lounge with harpist and trompe l'oeil cloud ceiling; to the King Cole Bar, an institution in itself with its famous Maxfield Parrish mural (which somehow retains its lustre amid an ever-present cloud of Cohiba exhaust). Even the elevators have crystal chandeliers. Guest rooms, all serviced by extremely accommodating butlers, are straight out of a period film, with high ceilings, crystal chandeliers, silk wall coverings, Louis XV antiques, and world-class amenities such as Tiffany silver services. Marble bathrooms, with tubs, stall showers, and double sinks, are outstanding. ⊠ *2 E. 55th St., at 5th Ave., 10022,* ☎ *212/753–4500 or 800/759–7550,* FAX *212/787–3447,* WEB *www.ittsheraton.com. 221 rooms, 92 suites. Restaurant, bar, in-room data ports, in-room fax, in-room safes, minibars, room service, beauty salon, massage, sauna, health club, baby-sitting, dry cleaning, laundry service, concierge, business services, meeting rooms, parking (fee). AE, D, DC, MC, V.*

$$$$ 🏨 **W New York.** The first of the New York Ws brings nature's calming powers to midtown. Vast floor-to-ceiling windows pour sunlight into the airy lobby (a.k.a. "the living room"), where a fireplace and bar flank a sunken sitting area. Although tiny, the rooms display custom craftsmanship in natural materials, and soothe with signature linens, feather beds, CD players, and miniature window boxes. In the slate-floor baths, not a sliver of the all-too-familiar polished marble is to be found. Downstairs, Heartbeat Restaurant serves heart-healthy foods and a mezzanine dining area makes breakfast a quick buffet affair. In the attached Whiskey Blue bar—*if* you get in—you'll find a young, hip, and moneyed crowd. ⊠ *541 Lexington Ave., between E. 49th and E. 50th Sts., 10022,* ☎ *212/755–1200 or 877/946–8357,* FAX *212/ 319–8344,* WEB *www.whotels.com. 684 rooms, 36 suites. Restaurant, bar, breakfast room, lobby lounge, snack bar, in-room data ports, in-room safes, minibars, room service, massage, spa, health club, dry cleaning, laundry service, concierge, business services, meeting rooms. AE, D, DC, MC, V.*

$$$$ 🏨 **Waldorf-Astoria.** This landmark 1931 art deco masterpiece (the Empire State Building stands on the hotel's original 1893 site) is a hub of city life. The lobby, full of murals, mosaics, and elaborate plaster ornamentation, features a grand piano once owned by Cole Porter and still played daily. Guest rooms, each individually decorated, are all traditional and elegant; Astoria-level rooms have the added advantages of great views, fax machines, and access to the Astoria lounge, where a lovely, free afternoon tea is served. The curious Bull and Bear Bar, on the hotel's Lexington Avenue side, is a 1940s throwback complete with cigar smoke, miniature soda bottles, and no-nonsense barkeeps. Well known to U.S. presidents and other luminaries, the ultra-exclusive Waldorf Towers has a separate entrance, reception desk, and concierge. ⊠ *301 Park Ave., between E. 49th and E. 50th Sts., 10022,* ☎ *212/355– 3000 or 800/925–3673,* FAX *212/872–7272,* WEB *www.waldorf.com. 1,176 rooms, 276 suites. 4 restaurants, 2 bars, in-room data ports, in-room safes, minibars, room service, massage, health club, baby-sitting,*

dry cleaning, laundry service, concierge, concierge floors, business services, meeting rooms, parking (fee). AE, D, DC, MC, V.

$$$–$$$$ 🔲 **The Benjamin.** From the elegant marble-and-silver lobby with 30-ft ceilings and sweeping staircase, to the Frette bed linens and custom mattresses, to the hi-tech argon gas–filled windows that reduce street noises to near whispers, this place pleases in ways seen and unseen. Rooms are done in warm beiges and golds, and the extensive in-room offices come with personalized business cards. Bathrooms are disappointingly small, but you might be too busy choosing from the "pillow menu" or being pampered at the on-site Woodstock Spa to notice. ⊠ *125 E. 50th St., at Lexington Ave., 10022,* ☎ *212/715–2500 or 888/423–6526,* 𝔽𝔸𝕏 *212/764–4477,* 𝕎𝔼𝔹 *www.thebenjamin.com. 112 rooms, 97 suites. Restaurants, bar, in-room data ports, in-room safes, minibars, room service, massage, spa, health club, baby-sitting, dry cleaning, laundry service, concierge, concierge floors, business services, meeting rooms, parking (fee). AE, D, DC, MC, V.*

$$$–$$$$ 🔲 **The Dylan.** The 1903 beaux arts–style building occupied by this boutique hotel used to house the Chemists Club. Inside and out the structure has been completely revitalized, from the façade's ornate decorative plasterwork to the stunning marble grand staircase that spirals up three floors. Located near Grand Central Station in the heart of midtown, the Dylan is one of the more attractive and comfortable properties to hit the neighborhood in some time. The 11-ft ceilings, standard in all guest rooms, make the modern accommodations feel more spacious than many others in New York, but the carrara cut-marble bathrooms show the hotel's opulent intentions. The Alchemy Suite, which was built to replicate a medieval laboratory, has gothic columns and vaulted ceilings. ⊠ *52 E. 41st St., between Park and Madison Aves., 10017,* ☎ *212/338–0500,* 𝔽𝔸𝕏 *212/338–0569,* 𝕎𝔼𝔹 *www.dylanhotel.com. 108 rooms, 2 suites. Restaurant, bar, in-room data ports, in-room safes, minibars, health club, concierge, business services, meeting rooms. AE, D, DC, MC, V.*

$$$–$$$$ 🔲 **Sherry-Netherland.** This 5th Avenue grande dame is a cooperative apartment hotel with a three-to-one ratio of permanent residents to hotel guests. As a result, in-room amenities are somewhat hit-or-miss, depending on the whims of the individual owners. Still, the marble-lined lobby wows with fine, hand-loomed carpets, crystal chandeliers, and wall friezes from the Vanderbilt mansion, and it's hard not to be impressed by uniformed elevator operators. The enormous, utterly luxurious suites—some with unsurpassed midtown views—have separate living and dining areas, serving pantries, decorative fireplaces, fine antiques, and glorious marble baths. The incredibly cramped and stupendously expensive Harry Cipriani's provides room service (a liter of water costs about $20). ⊠ *781 5th Ave., at 59th St., 10022,* ☎ *212/355–2800,* 𝔽𝔸𝕏 *212/319–4306,* 𝕎𝔼𝔹 *www.sherrynetherland.com. 40 rooms, 35 suites. Restaurant, bar, in-room safes, in-room VCRs, refrigerators, room service, barbershop, beauty salon, gym, dry cleaning, laundry service, concierge, business services, meeting rooms, parking (fee). AE, D, DC, MC, V.*

$$–$$$$ 🔲 **Plaza Fifty.** This hotel has a distinctly businesslike mood—witness the granite-wall lobby outfitted with mirrors, stainless steel, and leather furniture—but it's also supremely comfortable. The spacious rooms and suites have a clean, modern design with abstract art and oversize chairs and couches. There is no restaurant in the hotel, but a restaurant next door provides room service 7 AM–11 PM. Plus, rooms have kitchenettes and suites have full-size kitchens. ⊠ *155 E. 50th St., at 3rd Ave., 10022,* ☎ *212/751–5710,* 𝔽𝔸𝕏 *212/753–1468,* 𝕎𝔼𝔹 *www.mesuite.com. 74 rooms, 138 suites. In-room data ports, in-room fax, in-room safes, kitchenettes, room service, gym, coin laundry, concierge, business services, meeting rooms, parking (fee). AE, D, DC, MC, V.*

$$$ ⊞ **Beekman Tower.** Situated just steps from the United Nations, this jazzy hotel has been designated an art deco architectural landmark by the NYC Landmarks Commission. Its swanky Top of the Towers lounge, a rooftop bar with live piano, is a superb place to take in the view of the East River and beyond; downstairs, the Zephyr Grill looks out on First Avenue. Suites, which range from studios to one-bedrooms, are all very spacious, and all have kitchens. Rooms are attractively decorated with chintz and dark-wood furniture, and all have separate sitting areas. The one-bedroom suites have dining tables as well. ⊠ *3 Mitchell Pl., at 1st Ave. and E. 49th St., 10017,* ☎ *212/320–8018 or 800/637–8483,* FAX *212/465–3697,* WEB *www.mesuite.com. 174 suites. Restaurant, 2 bars, in-room data ports, in-room safes, kitchenettes, room service, gym, dry cleaning, laundry service, concierge, business services, meeting rooms, parking (fee). AE, D, DC, MC, V.*

$$$ ⊞ **The Fitzpatrick.** This cozy hotel just south of Bloomingdale's brings Irish charm to the New York hotel scene, which might explain why Gregory Peck, Liam Neeson, various Kennedys, Sinead O'Connor, and the Chieftains have all been guests. More than half of the units are suites, and all have emerald carpets and traditional dark-wood furniture. Fitzer's, the publike bar at the heart of the hotel, is as welcoming as any in Dublin. ⊠ *687 Lexington Ave., at E. 57th St., 10022,* ☎ *212/ 355–0100 or 800/367–7701,* FAX *212/355–1371,* WEB *www. fitzpatrickhotels.com. 42 rooms, 50 suites. Restaurant, bar, in-room data ports, in-room safes, minibars, room service, massage, health club, dry cleaning, laundry service, concierge, business services, meeting rooms, parking (fee). AE, D, DC, MC, V.*

$$$ ⊞ **Hotel Elysée.** Best known as the site of the Monkey Bar, which remains a very popular watering hole, this hotel has relatively affordable rates, given its location. The feeling here is intimate and unpretentious, more like sleeping over at your great aunt's apartment than staying in a Manhattan hotel. All guests have access to the Club Room, which feels like a living room and offers complimentary coffee, tea, and snacks all day long. You can grab a breakfast pastry there in the morning and free wine and hors d'oeuvres on weeknights; and it's a good thing, too, since room service is limited and there are no minibars in the guestrooms. A few of the rather dowdy guest rooms have terraces at no extra charge; request one far in advance. ⊠ *60 E. 54th St., between Madison and Park Aves., 10022,* ☎ *212/753–1066 or 800/535–9733,* FAX *212/980–9278. 87 rooms, 12 suites. Restaurant, bar, in-room data ports, in-room safes, in-room VCRs, refrigerators, room service, massage, piano, dry cleaning, laundry service, concierge, business services, meeting room, parking (fee). AE, DC, MC, V.*

$$$ ⊞ **Library Hotel.** In a beautifully restored landmark buiding dating from 1900, this brick and terra-cotta boutique hotel feels like a mansion. Although the structure never housed a library, each of the hotel's 10 floors is dedicated to one of the 10 major categories of the Dewey Decimal System, its rooms decorated with art and books relevant to a topic within that category. Guests can choose rooms based on their interests—for example, those with a green thumb might opt for room 500.004, The Botany Room, on the Math and Science floor. Although the Library's theme is quirky, the full-service property delivers tremendous comfort with luxurious appointments and amenities. In addition to flower arrangements and books and art that complement each room's theme, there are padded headboards, marble sinks, and bathrobes for lounging as you catch up on your favorite subject. ⊠ *299 Madison Ave., at E. 41st St., 10017,* ☎ *212/983–4500 or 877/793–7323,* FAX *212/499– 9099,* WEB *www.libraryhotel.com. 60 rooms. Bar, in-room data ports, in-room safes, in-room VCRs, minibars, room service, dry cleaning, laundry service, business services, parking (fee). AE, DC, MC, V.*

$$–$$$ ▣ **Crowne Plaza at the United Nations.** This 20-story building built in 1931 is in historic Tudor City, a stone's throw from the United Nations and Grand Central Terminal. Interior spaces are classic and unassuming, with marble floors, handmade carpets, and hardwood reproduction furniture upholstered in brocades and velvets. The traditional, well-kept rooms all come with irons, ironing boards, and coffeemakers. For $30 extra per night, guests have access to the Crowne Club Lounge, where complimentary breakfast and evening cocktails are served. ✉ *304 E. 42nd St., between 1st and 2nd Aves., 10017,* ☎ *212/986–8800 or 800/879–8836,* FAX *212/986–1758,* WEB *www.crowneplaza.com. 278 rooms, 18 suites. Restaurant, bar, in-room data ports, in-room safes, minibars, room service, sauna, gym, concierge, business services, meeting rooms, parking (fee). AE, D, DC, MC, V.*

$$ ▣ **Barbizon.** Grace Kelly, Joan Crawford, and Liza Minnelli all lived here at various times, back when the hotel was an exclusive women's residence (from 1927 to 1981). The chic lobby has a marble-and-limestone floor and gilt chairs with mohair upholstery. Guest rooms glow with blond wood that complements fabrics in soft tones of shell-pink or celadon; zig-zag wrought-iron floor lamps and bedsteads recall the hotel's deco days. The three-floor spa facility, operated by the Equinox gym chain, includes a 55-ft lap pool. ✉ *140 E. 63rd St., at Lexington Ave., 10021,* ☎ *212/838–5700 or 800/223–1020,* FAX *212/888–4271,* WEB *www.barbizon.com. 306 rooms, 13 suites. Bar, breakfast room, in-room data ports, in-room safes, minibars, room service, indoor lap pool, spa, health club, baby-sitting, dry cleaning, laundry service, business services, parking (fee). AE, D, DC, MC, V.*

$$ ▣ **Roger Smith.** The elusive Roger Smith (see if *you* can find out who
★ he is) lends his name to this colorful boutique hotel and adjacent gallery. Riotous murals cover the walls in Lily's, the café, and the circular lobby is almost as zany. The art-filled rooms are homey and comfortable, and some have stocked bookshelves and fireplaces. An eclectic mix of room service is offered by five local restaurants. Guests have access to the nearby New York Sports Club ($10 fee). Rates can drop by as much as $75 per night in winter and summer, so ask when booking. ✉ *501 Lexington Ave., between E. 47th and E. 48th Sts., 10017,* ☎ *212/755–1400 or 800/445–0277,* FAX *212/758–4061,* WEB *www.rogersmith.com. 98 rooms, 32 suites. Restaurant, bar, in-room data ports, in-room safes, refrigerators, room service, complimentary Continental breakfast, laundry service, meeting room, parking (fee). AE, D, DC, MC, V. CP.*

$$ ▣ **San Carlos.** Comfortable and plain, this small residential-style property has friendly service and a safe, convenient location. The rooms are spacious, and all have a kitchenette, a walk-in closet, and two phones. Guests have access to the nearby YWCA, an impressive facility with two swimming pools, for only $5 a day. A major renovation to upgrade the humble hotel to luxury status is planned to start in 2002, so rates are subject to change. ✉ *150 E. 50th St., between Lexington and 3rd Aves., 10022,* ☎ *212/755–1800 or 800/722–2012,* FAX *212/688–9778,* WEB *www.sancarloshotel.com. 70 rooms, 80 suites. Breakfast room, in-room data ports, in-room safes, kitchenettes, room service. AE, DC, MC, V.*

$ ▣ **Pickwick Arms Hotel.** This no-frills but convenient East Side establishment is regularly booked solid by bargain hunters. Privations you endure to save a buck start and end with the Lilliputian size of some rooms, all of which have cheap-looking furnishings. However, some rooms look over the Manhattan skyline, and all are renovated on a regular basis. ✉ *230 E. 51st St., between 2nd and 3rd Aves., 10022,* ☎ *212/355–0300 or 800/742–5945,* FAX *212/755–5029. 370 rooms, 175 with bath. Café, refrigerators (some), airport shuttle. AE, DC, MC, V.*

$ 🏨 **Vanderbilt YMCA.** Of the various Manhattan Ys that offer overnight accommodations, this one has the best facilities, including a full-scale fitness center. Rooms are little more than dormitory-style cells, each with a bed (bunks in doubles), dresser drawer, and TV; singles have desks. Only five rooms have private baths (these cost extra), but communal showers and toilets are clean. The Turtle Bay neighborhood is safe and convenient; Grand Central Terminal and the United Nations are both a few blocks away. ⊠ *224 E. 47th St., between 2nd and 3rd Aves., 10017,* ☎ *212/756–9600,* 🅵🅰🆇 *212/752–0210. 370 rooms, 5 with bath. Restaurant, 2 indoor pools, sauna, steam room, basketball, health club, volleyball, coin laundry, meeting rooms, airport shuttle. MC, V.*

Upper East Side

$$$$ 🏨 **The Carlyle.** European tradition and Manhattan swank come together
★ at New York's most lovable grand hotel. Everything about this Madison Avenue landmark suggests refinement, from the Mark Hampton–designed rooms, with their fine antique furniture and artfully framed Audubons and botanicals, to the first-rate service. Cabaret luminaries Barbara Cook and Bobby Short take turns holding court at the clubby Café Carlyle, but the canny Peter Mintun steals the show at Bemelmans Bar, named after the illustrator responsible for the bar's wall murals and the beloved children's book character, Madeline. ⊠ *35 E. 76th St., at Madison Ave., 10021,* ☎ *212/744–1600 or 800/227–5737,* 🅵🅰🆇 *212/717–4682,* 🆆🅴🅱 *www.dir-dd.com. 145 rooms, 45 suites. Restaurant, bar, café, in-room data ports, in-room safes, kitchenettes, minibars, room service, spa, health club, dry cleaning, laundry service, concierge, business services, meeting rooms, parking (fee). AE, DC, MC, V.*

$$$$ 🏨 **The Mark.** A block north of the Carlyle and steps from Central Park,
★ the Mark is a haven of tranquillity. The feeling of calm that pervades the cool, Biedermeier-furnished marble lobby follows you into the clubby bar, where even lone women travelers feel comfortable. The serenity continues at Mark's Restaurant, where afternoon tea is served. Bedrooms are understated and elegant, with museum-quality prints, plump armchairs, a potted palm or two, and Frette bed linens. ⊠ *25 E. 77th St., between 5th and Madison Aves., 10021,* ☎ *212/744–4300 or 800/ 843–6275,* 🅵🅰🆇 *212/744–2749,* 🆆🅴🅱 *www.themark.com. 120 rooms, 60 suites. Restaurant, bar, in-room data ports, in-room fax, in-room safes, in-room VCRs, kitchenettes (some), minibars, room service, massage, health club, baby-sitting, dry cleaning, laundry service, concierge, business services, meeting rooms, parking (fee). AE, D, DC, MC, V.*

$$$$ 🏨 **The Pierre.** As ornate as the Four Seasons hotel on 57th Street is minimalist, the Pierre remains a grand presence among the Four Seasons hotel group's properties, all of which, including the Pierre, are known for their exceptional service. The landmark building owes a lot to the Palace of Versailles, with chandeliers, murals depicting putti, and Corinthian columns in the Rotunda lounge, where afternoon tea is an institution. Chintz and dark wood adorn the grand and traditional guest rooms, whose gleaming black-and-white art deco bathrooms are spacious for New York. ⊠ *2 E. 61st St., between 5th and Madison Aves., 10021,* ☎ *212/838–8000 or 800/332–3442,* 🅵🅰🆇 *212/758–1615,* 🆆🅴🅱 *www.fshr.com. 149 rooms, 54 suites. Restaurant, bar, in-room data ports, in-room safes, minibars, room service, beauty salon, massage, health club, concierge, business services, meeting rooms, parking (fee). AE, D, DC, MC, V.*

$$$$ 🏨 **Plaza Athénée.** When its penthouses aren't humming with photo shoots, the Plaza Athénée is just another luxurious hotel on the edge of the tony Madison Avenue shopping district. At this elegant French property in a building of a certain age, no two rooms share the same floor plan and all have ample space, making up for a staff that has more hauteur than warmth. Even the most modest rooms have sitting areas with inviting sofas, and generous closet space. Twelve of the handsomely furnished suites have enviable balconies, although tubs and showers in some rooms fall below the comfort level otherwise evident. Rooms above the 12th floor have over-the-rooftops views. The lounge-bar is a great spot for tea or drinks, and Sunday brunch at the hotel's La Régence restaurant ($46 per person) is a sumptuous local favorite. ⊠ 37 E. 64th St., 10021, ☎ 212/734–9100 or 800/447–8800, ℻ 212/772–0958. *124 rooms, 26 suites, 2 penthouses. Restaurant, bar, in-room data ports, in-room safes, minibars, room service, massage, gym, baby-sitting, dry cleaning, laundry service, concierge, business services, meeting rooms, parking (fee). AE, D, DC, MC, V.*

$$$–$$$$ ★ 🏨 **The Lowell.** Like Noël Coward, you may be tempted to check in long-term at this pied-à-terre–style landmark on a tree-lined street between Madison and Park avenues. Guest rooms, most of which are suites, have all the comforts of home—kitchenettes (or minibars), stocked bookshelves, and even umbrellas. Thirty-three of the suites have working fireplaces, and 10 have private terraces. A gym suite has its own fitness center and a garden suite has two beautifully planted terraces. The Pembroke Room serves a fine afternoon tea, and the Post House is renowned for its steaks. ⊠ 28 E. 63rd St., between Madison and Park Aves., 10021, ☎ 212/838–1400 or 800/221–4444, ℻ 212/319–4230, 🌐 www.preferredhotels.com. *21 rooms, 47 suites. Restaurant, breakfast room, in-room data ports, in-room fax, in-room safes, in-room VCRs, kitchenettes (some), minibars, room service, massage, health club, baby-sitting, dry cleaning, laundry service, concierge, parking (fee). AE, D, DC, MC, V.*

$$ 🏨 **The Franklin.** This stylish little property is a ravishing uptown version of the trendy downtown hotels. The tiny lobby—constructed of black granite, brushed steel, and cherrywood—looks like an art installation. Most rooms are also tiny (some measure 100 square ft), but what they lack in size they make up for in style: all have funky, custom-built steel furniture, gauzy white canopies over the beds, cedar closets, and CD players. Added bonuses are the daily breakfast buffet, fresh fruit in the evenings, and 24-hour cappuccino. ⊠ 164 E. 87th St., between Lexington and 3rd Aves., 10128, ☎ 212/369–1000 or 800/428–5252, ℻ 212/369–8000, 🌐 www.franklinhotel.com. *47 rooms. In-room data ports, in-room safes, in-room VCRs, complimentary Continental breakfast, library, parking (fee). AE, DC, MC, V.*

$$ 🏨 **Hotel Wales.** Every effort has been made to retain the turn-of-the-20th-century mood of this 1901 Carnegie Hill landmark—from the cavernous lobby to the Pied Piper parlor, where vintage children's illustrations cover the walls. Fireplaces, fine oak woodwork, fresh flowers, and in-room CD players make up for minuscule bathrooms. A generous European-style breakfast is served in the parlor, along with 24-hour cappuccino. ⊠ 1295 Madison Ave., between E. 91st and E. 92nd Sts., 10128, ☎ 212/876–6000 or 800/528–5252, ℻ 212/860–7000. *46 rooms, 41 suites. Restaurant, bar, in-room safes, in-room VCRs, room service, dry cleaning, laundry service, parking (fee). AE, DC, MC, V.*

Upper West Side

$$$–$$$$ 🏨 **Trump International Hotel and Towers.** A large unisphere gleams outside this expensive, showy hotel, which occupies the first 17 floors of a well-situated, black-glass tower. Rooms and suites resemble mini-apartments: all have fully equipped kitchens with black-granite countertops,

entertainment centers with stereos and CD players, and mini-telescopes, which you can use to gaze through the floor-to-ceiling windows. Creamy-beige marble bathrooms are stocked with bath salts and loofahs. Complimentary cellular phones and personalized stationery and business cards are also offered. The hotel's restaurant, Jean Georges, is one of the city's finest; if you want to dine in, a Jean Georges chef is on hand to prepare meals in your suite. ⊠ *1 Central Park W, between W. 59th and W. 60th Sts., 10023,* ☎ *212/299–1000 or 888/448–7867,* FAX *212/299–1150,* WEB *www.trumpintl.com. 38 rooms, 129 suites. Restaurant, bar, café, in-room data ports, in-room fax, in-room safes, in-room VCRs, kitchenettes, minibars, indoor pool, spa, health club, baby-sitting, dry cleaning, laundry service, concierge, business services, meeting room, parking (fee). AE, D, DC, MC, V.*

$$–$$$ ⊞ **Mayflower.** This spot across the street from Central Park has a long, low, wood-paneled lobby, with gilt-framed oils of tall ships. Although not high-style, the rooms are large and comfortable (spend the extra few bucks for a park view). All have dark-wood colonial-style furniture and walk-in closets; most also have walk-in pantries with a refrigerator and sink. Service has been shaky at times, but most of the staff is friendly and helpful, and complimentary coffee and cookies are offered in the evenings. ⊠ *15 Central Park W, between W. 61st and W. 62nd Sts., 10023,* ☎ *212/265–0060 or 800/223–4164,* FAX *212/265–2026,* WEB *www.mayflowerhotel.com. 117 rooms, 160 suites. Restaurant, bar, in-room data ports, in-room safes, refrigerators, room service, gym, meeting rooms, parking (fee). AE, DC, MC, V.*

$$ ⊞ **Empire Hotel.** One of the city's better buys, this property has an unbeatable location across from Lincoln Center. Crimson carpet and hanging tapestries adorn its warm, inviting English country–style lobby. Rooms and suites are small but appealing; all have textured teal carpets, dark-wood furnishings, and entertainment centers with CD players. A nearby New York Sports Club is accessible for a small fee. Downstairs is the 63rd Street Steakhouse as well as the subterranean Iridium club, one of Manhattan's premier jazz venues. ⊠ *44 W. 63rd St., between Broadway and Columbus Ave., 10023,* ☎ *212/265–7400 or 800/333–3333,* FAX *212/244–3382. 355 rooms, 20 suites. Restaurant, bar, in-room data ports, in-room safes, in-room VCRs, minibars, room service, meeting rooms, parking (fee). AE, D, DC, MC, V.*

$$ ⊞ **Excelsior.** Directly across the street from the American Museum of Natural History, this well-kept spot rubs shoulders with fine pre-war doorman apartment buildings. The attractive rooms have in-room PCs, and all have T-1 Internet access and satellite TV. The library lounge, with leather sofas, cozy fireplace, and tables with built-in game boards, is an unexpected plus. ⊠ *45 W. 81st St., between Central Park W and Columbus Ave., 10024,* ☎ *212/362–9200 or 800/368–4575,* FAX *212/721–2994,* WEB *www.excelsiorhotelny.com. 116 rooms, 80 suites. Restaurant, breakfast room, in-room data ports, in-room fax, in-room safes, gym, library, parking (fee). AE, D, DC, MC, V.*

$$ ⊞ **Hotel Beacon.** The Upper West Side's best budget buy is three blocks
★ from both Central Park and Lincoln Center, and just footsteps from Zabar's gourmet bazaar. All rooms and suites have kitchenettes with coffeemakers, full-size refrigerators, stoves, microwaves, and ironing facilities. Closets are huge, and some of the bathrooms have Hollywood dressing room–style mirrors. Although technically not part of the hotel, the American Restaurant downstairs is open 24 hours and will deliver to your room. ⊠ *2130 Broadway, between W. 74th and W. 75th Sts., 10023,* ☎ *212/787–1100 or 800/572–4969,* FAX *212/724–0839,* WEB *www.beaconhotel.com. 110 rooms, 100 suites. In-room safes, kitchenettes, refrigerators, business services, meeting room, parking (fee). AE, D, DC, MC, V.*

$$ 🏨 **The Lucerne.** In a handsome brownstone building, this reasonably priced option enjoys a constant buzz of activity, thanks to the publike Wilson's Bar & Grill next door. The multihue-marble lobby has more pizzazz than the predictable guest rooms, with their requisite dark-wood reproduction furniture and chintz bedspreads. Health-conscious adults might like the gym on the top floor, with its dramatic city views, but children will be glued to the TV, playing the in-room Nintendo games. ✉ *201 W. 79th St., at Amsterdam Ave., 10024,* ☎ *212/875–1000 or 800/492–8122,* 𝔽𝔸𝕏 *212/721–1179,* 𝕎𝔼𝔹 *www.newyorkhotel.com. 200 rooms, 50 suites. Restaurant, bar, in-room data ports, room service, gym, dry cleaning, meeting rooms, concierge. AE, D, DC, MC, V.*

$$ 🏨 **On the Ave.** A slice of sophistication and service on the Upper West Side, this reasonably priced boutique hotel appeals to families, to business travelers who will do anything to avoid midtown, and to the budget conscious. There is no restaurant or room service, but the amenities in the basic rooms, like high-speed internet access, hairdryers, and terrycloth robes, are more than adequate and penthouse floors afford views of Central Park and/or the Hudson River. On the Ave. combines modern style—unlike most of the other moderately priced Upper West Side hotels—with comfort and gives guests a little taste of what it's like to live in New York. ✉ *2177 Broadway, at W. 77th St., 10024,* ☎ *212/362–1100 or 800/509–7598,* 𝔽𝔸𝕏 *212/787–9521. 251 rooms, 4 suites. In-room data ports, in-room safes, business services. AE, D, DC, MC, V.*

$ 🏨 **Malibu Studios Hotel.** This youth-oriented budget crash pad could almost pass for a college dorm, especially given its proximity to Columbia University. Although it's farther north than you may care to venture, it's in a lively, safe neighborhood. Double-occupancy rooms offer private or shared baths; every room has a TV and a desk with a writing lamp. ✉ *2688 Broadway, at W. 103rd St., 10025,* ☎ *212/222–2954 or 800/647–2227,* 𝔽𝔸𝕏 *212/678–6842,* 𝕎𝔼𝔹 *www.malibuhotelnyc.com. 150 rooms, 110 with bath. No credit cards.*

$ 🏨 **YMCA West Side.** Although the fitness center here is not quite as polished as the one at the Vanderbilt YMCA, you can't beat this Y for value, location, and atmosphere: two blocks from Lincoln Center and a short jaunt from Central Park, it's housed in a building that looks like a Spanish cloister, with gargoyles adorning its arched neo-Byzantine entrance. Rooms are as tiny as jail cells, but red carpeting and spreads make them a little more cheerful. Those with private bath cost extra. ✉ *5 W. 63rd St., at Central Park W, 10023,* ☎ *212/875–4100 or 800/ 348–9622,* 𝔽𝔸𝕏 *212/875–1334. 488 rooms, 30 with bath. Cafeteria, 2 indoor pools, sauna, health club, racquetball, coin laundry, meeting room, airport shuttle. AE, MC, V.*

Brooklyn

$$ 🏨 **New York Marriott Brooklyn.** Guests here won't miss Manhattan, with amenities that include an Olympic-length lap pool, a 1,100-car valet parking garage, an 18,000-square-ft Grand Ball Room (one of New York's biggest), and even a dedicated Kosher kitchen. The large rooms are enhanced by niceties such as 11-ft ceilings, massaging showerheads, and rolling desks, but the lobby displays of Brooklyn-abilia— including seats salvaged from historic Ebbett's Field—are more likely to impress. Beautiful trompe l'oeil ceilings transform the multilevel foyer into a virtual open-air atrium, where a mural of the Brooklyn Bridge backs the long reception desk. Major subway lines only a block away make for a mere 10-minute commute into Manhattan. ✉ *333 Adams St., between Johnson and Willoughby Sts., Brooklyn, 11201,* ☎ *718/ 246–7000 or 800/843–4898,* 𝔽𝔸𝕏 *718/246–0563,* 𝕎𝔼𝔹 *www.marriott.com.*

355 rooms, 21 suites. Restaurant, bar, in-room data ports, in-room fax, in-room safes, minibars, room service, pool, health club, dry cleaning, laundry service, concierge, business services, meeting rooms, airport shuttle, parking (fee). AE, D, DC, MC, V.

BED-AND-BREAKFASTS

For value-conscious travelers who prefer a lived-in, low-key style and are willing to bypass such luxuries as room service and personal voice mail, hundreds of bed-and-breakfasts can be found in residential neighborhoods of Manhattan and the other boroughs—especially Brooklyn. These are not the gingerbread-house B&Bs of smaller towns and cities: in Manhattan, the term simply refers to a private apartment you may rent for a few nights' stay. Although amenities, service, and privacy may fall short of what you get in hotels (often you don't even get breakfast, despite the B&B name) you may pay as little as $100 for this type of accommodation; and depending on the apartment you choose, it may even be more comfortable than a hotel. Be sure to ask your booking service for details on decor, location, and amenities: predictably, you'll pay more for a central location, a doorman building, and special features such as balconies and gardens.

B&Bs booked through a service may either be hosted (you are the guest in someone's occupied apartment) or unhosted (you have full use of someone's vacant apartment, including kitchen privileges—though you may not get maid service). Most B&B services represent both kinds. Make reservations as far in advance as possible; in general, refunds (minus a $25 service charge) are given up to 10 days before arrival. A minimum three-night stay is the norm.

Abode Bed and Breakfasts Ltd. (⊠ Box 20022, 10021, ☎ 212/472–2000 or 800/835–8880, WEB www.abodenyc.com). **A Hospitality Co.** (⊠ 580 Broadway, Suite 1009, 10012, ☎ 212/965–1102 or 800/987–1235, FAX 212/965–1149, WEB www.hospitalitycompany.com). **Bed & Breakfast (& Books)** (⊠ 35 W. 92nd St., 10025, ☎ 212/865–8740). **Bed and Breakfast Network of New York** (⊠ 134 W. 32nd St., Suite 602, 10001, ☎ 212/645–8134 or 800/900–8134). **City Lights Bed and Breakfast** (⊠ Box 20355, Cherokee Station, 10021, ☎ 212/737–7049, FAX 212/535–2755). **Manhattan Home Stays** (⊠ Box 20684, Cherokee Station, 10021, ☎ 212/737–3868, FAX 212/452–1604, WEB www.manhattanstays.com). **New World Bed and Breakfast** (⊠ 150 5th Ave., Suite 711, 10011, ☎ 212/675–5600; 800/443–3800 in the U.S., FAX 212/675–6366). **New York Habitat** (⊠ 307 7th Ave., Suite 306, 10001, ☎ 212/647–9365, FAX 212/627–1416, WEB www.nyhabitat.com). **Urban Ventures** (⊠ Box 426, 10024; 38 W. 32nd St., 10001, ☎ 212/594–5650 for both locations, FAX 212/947–9320).

6 NIGHTLIFE

The city that never sleeps has enough diversions to keep even the most inveterate night owls occupied for weeks. In the same evening you can head for a classic West Village jazz haunt, a sleek TriBeCa lounge, a sophisticated uptown cabaret, a grungy East Village bar, or a raucous comedy club. Whether you're in the mood for loud rock, Broadway ballads, a Brazilian beat, blues, or bluegrass, you're sure to find it in Manhattan.

Updated by
John J.
Donohue

NEW YORK NIGHTLIFE REALLY STARTED TO SWING in 1914, when ballroom dancers Florence and Maurice Walton took over management of the Parisian Room, in what is today's theater district. At Chez Maurice, as their club was called, the city's café society learned a sensual dance at Tango Teas. Then came the Harlem Renaissance of the 1920s and '30s, and the New York jazz scene shifted north of 110th Street. In the 1950s, nightclubs mushroomed in Greenwich Village and the East 50s. Along 52nd Street in those years, recalls journalist Pete Hamill, "you could walk down a single block and hear Art Tatum, Billie Holiday, and Charlie Parker. And you could go to the Latin Quarter and see girls running around with bananas on their heads."

Well, fruit as headgear is out, but night-owling while wearing the look of the moment never will be. The scene is now downtown—in drab-by-day East Village dives, classic jazz joints in the West Village, and TriBeCa see-and-be-seen boîtes. Preppy hangouts are also still alive and well on the Upper East and Upper West sides. And all over town, you can find lounges. You'll know you're in one if you see lots of crushed velvet and zinc-top bars.

There are enough committed club-crawlers in Manhattan to support venues for almost every idiosyncratic taste. But keep in mind that *when* you go is just as important as *where* you go. These days night prowlers are more loyal to floating parties, DJs, even party promoters, than they are to addresses. A spot is only hot when it's hopping, and you may find the same party or bar that raged last night completely empty tonight. The other thing to remember is to dress properly, something that is easily accomplished by wearing black and leaving your sneakers at home.

For the totally hip, **Paper** magazine's "P.M. 'Til Dawn" and bar sections have as good a listing as exists of the roving parties and the best of the fashionable crowd's hangouts. **Time Out New York** offers a comprehensive weekly listing of amusements by category. The more staid Friday **New York Times** "Weekend/Movies and Performing Arts" section runs "Pop and Jazz" and "Cabaret" columns that can clue you in to what's in the air, as can the **Village Voice,** a weekly newspaper that probably has more nightclub ads than any other rag in the world. The *Voice* is free and disappears from its red kiosks on street corners all over the city often by the afternoon it arrives in them (Wednesday). Some newsstands and bookstores also stock it. Look also for that weekly's competitor, **New York Press,** which has pages and pages of nightlife listings. Flyers about and passes to coming events are stacked in the entry at **Tower Records** (⊠ Broadway and 4th St., ☎ 212/505–1500; Broadway and 66th St., ☎ 212/799–2500). You may also get good tips from a suitably au courant hotel concierge. Keep in mind that events change almost weekly, and venues have the life span of the tsetse fly, so phone ahead to make sure your target hasn't closed or turned into a polka hall. Most charge a cover, which can range from $2 to $25 or more depending on the club and the night. And take cash, because many places don't accept plastic.

CLUBS AND ENTERTAINMENT

Quintessential New York

These are the crème de la crème of New York's nightlife venues—distinguished by locale, age (you'd think even the newest of these has been there for years), style (elegance prevails), or a peerless combination of the three. Reservations are essential.

The Carlyle. Bobby Short plays the hotel's discreetly sophisticated Café Carlyle when he's in town, and Barbara Cook and Eartha Kitt also often purr by the piano here. Stop by on a Monday night and take in Woody Allen, who swings on the clarinet with his New Orleans Jazz Band. Bemelmans Bar, with murals by the author of the Madeline books, regularly stars pianist-singers Barbara Carroll and Peter Mintun. ⊠ *35 E. 76th St., between Madison and Park Aves.,* ☎ *212/744–1600.*

Four Seasons. Miró tapestries in the lobby greet you as you enter this power bar in the Grill Room. New York City (and American) history is made here. Watch for politicos and media moguls. ⊠ *99 E. 52nd St., between Park and Lexington Aves.,* ☎ *212/754–9494.*

Greatest Bar on Earth. Although it doesn't live up to its name (what bar could?), this glittering, oversize bar—actually three bars—at Windows on the World does afford one of the greatest views on earth. A multi-ethnic bar menu, dancing after 10 PM, and the adjacent Skybox— an oasis for cigar smokers—are additional draws. ⊠ *1 World Trade Center, 107th fl.,* ☎ *212/524–7000, ext. 6.*

Oak Room. This fabled room in one of New York's most famous hotels presents a string of top-notch performers. The wood-paneled corner still offers yesteryear's charms, now with a bit of polish. You might find the hopelessly romantic singer Andrea Marcovicci crooning here. ⊠ *Algonquin Hotel, 59 W. 44th St., near 6th Ave.,* ☎ *212/840–6800.*

Palio. Colorful swirling murals of the horse race in Siena for which this hall of sophistication is named dominate the walls here, making this room one of the nicest in the city. The drinks and the service are top-notch, too, and Palio is perfect for business or a romantic cocktail. ⊠ *151 W. 51st St., between 6th and 7th Aves.,* ☎ *212/245–4850.*

Rainbow Room. Heavenly views top the bill of fare at this romantic, 65th-floor institution, where the revolving dance floor and 12-piece orchestra ensure high spirits, even on a cloudy night. ⊠ *30 Rockefeller Plaza, between 5th and 6th Aves.,* ☎ *212/632–5000.*

River Café. If you're looking for an eminently romantic locale, head out to this restaurant hidden at the foot of the Brooklyn Bridge. The bar offers smashing views of the downtown Manhattan skyline across the East River, and after cocktails you can enjoy a splendid meal. ⊠ *1 Water St., near Old Fulton St., Brooklyn,* ☎ *718/522–5200.*

Supper Club. The last four digits of the telephone number give it all away: this huge prix-fixe dinner-and-dancing club specializes in cheek-to-cheek big-band sounds with a full orchestra on Friday and Saturday nights followed by swing dancing from midnight until early morning. It also occasionally turns into a concert venue featuring touring alternative and rock-and-roll acts. ⊠ *240 W. 47th St.,* ☎ *212/921–1940.*

"21" Club. Famous for its clubby atmosphere even before it became a setting in *All About Eve,* "21" still has a conservative air that evokes a sense of connections, power, and prestige. A New York City classic. ⊠ *21 W. 52nd St., between 5th and 6th Aves.,* ☎ *212/582–7200.*

Dance Clubs

The city's busiest clubs are as much places to shake your booty as to see and be seen. Revelers come to socialize, to find romance, to scream business deals over the music, to show off their glad rags, or to be photographed rubbing shoulders with stars. Some clubs are cavernous spaces filled with throbbing music and a churning sea of bodies. Others are like parties thrown by a mutual friend for people who don't know one another; comers are drawn by a common interest, a likeness of spirit,

DANCE WITH ME!

DANCE CLUBS IN NEW YORK that cater to every flavor, from swinging hep-cats to smoldering salseros, offering live music and sometimes lessons for toe tappers of all levels.

Ballroom: In summer there's dancing under the stars at the popular **Midsummer Night Swing** (☎ 212/875–5766) at Lincoln Center's Fountain Plaza. The bloom may be off the rose at the legendary **Roseland Ballroom** (✉ 239 W. 52nd St., between Broadway and 8th Ave., ☎ 212/247–0200), but it's still Manhattan's most spacious place to waltz, fox-trot, and rumba with a crowd that remembers when. An increasingly popular option for serious hoofers is dance socials held at ballroom studios, such as **Dance New York** (✉ 237 W. 54th St., ☎ 212/246–5797), citywide. What they tend to lack in atmosphere (canned music, folding chairs, no booze), studios such as **Dance-Sport** (✉ 1845 Broadway, ☎ 212/307–1111) make up for it by providing an enthusiastic learning-oriented environment. The skill level is mixed but generally high at the more established schools, such as **Dance Manhattan** (✉ 39 W. 19th St., ☎ 212/807–0802). You can trip the light fantastic at **Pierre Dulaine Dance Club** (✉ 25 W. 31st St., ☎ 212/244–8400), or show off your moves at **Stepping Out** (✉ 1780 Broadway, ☎ 212/245–5200).

Salsa/Mambo/Merengue: "On 2" salseros shouldn't ignore **Bistro Latino** (✉ 1711 Broadway, ☎ 212/956–1000). You can mambo downtown at **Cafe Remy** (✉ 104 Greenwich St., near Rector St., ☎ 212/267–4646), or try the swank **Copacabana**—the later the better, especially on weekends. For pop-salsa music and a younger crowd, try the **Latin Quarter** (✉ 2551 Broadway, at 96th St., ☎ 212/864–7600). At **SOB's** couples sway to the Latin rhythms of hot new salsa bands.

Swing: The Flipped Fedoras swing out at **Chicago Blues** (✉ 73 8th Ave., between 13th and 14th Sts., ☎ 212/924–9755).

Tasty food and a sizeable dance floor are seductive at the **Cotton Club** (✉ 656 W. 125th St., between Broadway and Riverside Dr., ☎ 212/663–7980). At **Greatest Bar on Earth,** you can shimmy before spectacular 107th-floor views. The Roy Gerson Orchestra fills the dance floor on Savoy Sundays, organized by the New York Swing Dance Society (☎ 212/696–9737), at **Irving Plaza.** Neo-swing bands play the retro **Supper Club** in the theater district. You can also hop, swing, and jump to George Gee's orchestra at **Swing 46** (✉ 349 W. 46th St., between 8th and 9th Aves., ☎ 212/262–9554). For a roundup of swing-dancing events, call the **Lo-Fi Hotline** (☎ 212/462–3250).

Tango: Tango between courses at **Il Campanello** (✉ 136 W. 31st St., ☎ 212/695–6111). Practice your *ochos* at the comfortable **Lafayette Grill** (✉ 54 Franklin St., ☎ 212/732–5600). Just watching the pros from the balcony could send you head over heels at romantic **La Belle Epoque** (✉ 827 Broadway, between 12th and 13th Sts., ☎ 212/254–6436). At unpretentious **La Nacional** (✉ 239 W. 14th St., ☎ 212/243–9308) the *milonga* fires up late. Brush up with a lesson, then dance all night at **Moscow Restaurant** (✉ 137 E. 55th St., ☎ 212/579–9278).

Know Before You Go: Expect a cover charge ($5–$25) and, at some places, a drink minimum. Latin clubs are usually cheaper for women and more expensive after 10 PM. Heels and skirts for women and suits for men are required at upscale and Latin places. Swing parties attract couples in retro costume; ballroom dancing is done in everything from gowns to jeans. Going solo is common; both men and women can expect to find willing partners in most clubs and studios. Many clubs offer lessons for a small additional fee. Schedules change often, so call to confirm, check the listings in *Time Out* or the *New York Press,* or hit www.nycdc.com.

— Karen Deaver

which can be created almost any place. The venues mentioned below are dance clubs, but parties—dance and otherwise—with DJs and themes ranging from '60s bossa nova nights to soul-and-drag galas have been known to crop up at such places as Irving Plaza. So read some rags of the paper variety and make some calls.

Centro-Fly. This eye-popping lounge and dance hall is a geometric wonderland—black and white circles and other geometric patterns cover its interior. You'll find house music on the weekends, an enthusiastic crowd, and a refreshingly cheap ($10) cover. ✉ *51 W. 21st St., between 5th and 6th Aves.,* ☎ *212/627–7770.*

Cheetah. One of *the* hot places (the 20th-anniversary party for Studio 54 was held here), Cheetah pays homage to the '70s with disco in a faux-leopard setting. ✉ *12 W. 21st St., between 5th and 6th Aves.,* ☎ *212/206–7770.*

China Club. Further proof that the '80s are back with a vengeance, this symbol of high-living excess has relocated from its original Upper West Side location to an 8,000-square-ft bi-level space in Hell's Kitchen. The exclusionary velvet ropes are again in place, but there's also a mass-market gift shop. ✉ *268 W. 47th St., between Broadway and 8th Ave.,* ☎ *212/398–3800.*

Cream. Five rooms, two dance floors, and wildly eclectic decor (everything from Persian rugs to fake snow) induce a crowd of young professionals to cut the rug. In this neighborhood, Cream can't be beat for dancing. ✉ *246 Columbus Ave., between 71st and 72nd Sts.,* ☎ *212/712–1666.*

Culture Club. From the Pac Man illustration on the outside awning to the interior murals of Adam Ant and the cast from "The Breakfast Club," if you're desperately seeking a dose of '80s nostalgia, this is your place. ✉ *179 Varick St., between Charlton and King Sts.,* ☎ *212/398–3800.*

Float. Skinny trust-fund girls and the bankers who chase them crowd into this three-level dance hall that feels like a funhouse: A maze of VIP rooms and small lounges lead off the main dance floor. ✉ *240 W. 52nd St., between Broadway and 8th Ave.,* ☎ *212/581–0055.*

Le Bar Bat. This bamboo-encrusted, multi-tier monster fits right in with the Planet Hollywood–type places on 57th Street's theme-restaurant row, but you can have a flashy good time here among the Euro and prepster poseurs. ✉ *311 W. 57th St., between 8th and 9th Aves.,* ☎ *212/307–7228.*

Limelight. Located in a deconsecrated church, this classic of 1990s New York nightlife reinvented itself after a hiatus in 1998. Now, 10-ft waterfalls, video installations, and an art gallery have replaced the dancers who once shimmied in cages above the crowd. ✉ *47 W. 20th St., at 6th Ave.,* ☎ *212/807–7059.*

Nell's. Here, in the 1990s, Nell Campbell (of *Rocky Horror* fame) reintroduced sophistication to nightlife. The tone in the upstairs live-music jazz salon is Victorian; downstairs you can dance to a DJ. The boîte opens at 10 PM and closes at 4 AM nightly. ✉ *246 W. 14th St., near 8th Ave.,* ☎ *212/675–1567.*

Roxy. Most nights this huge hall is a standard bridge-and-tunnel magnet, mostly attracting those who live in other New York boroughs and in New Jersey and occasionally drawing a mixed rave crowd. Wednesday is roller-disco night. Call ahead for special events. ✉ *515 W. 18th St., between 10th and 11th Aves.,* ☎ *212/645–5156.*

Saci. Don't let the midtown address fool you. This airy dance hall draws an ultra-fashion-conscious crowd. They appreciate the minimalistic elevated bars and pulsing walls of light, which look just as good as their fellow patrons. ✉ *135 W. 41st St., between 6th Ave. and Broadway,* ☎ *212/278–0988.*

Sapphire. The party at this small Lower East Side contender gets started late, but the DJ keeps the lively, diverse crowd going with every kind of music from ska to disco. Ultrafriendly patrons might drag you onto the floor to strut your stuff. ✉ *249 Eldridge St., between Houston and Stanton Sts.,* ☎ *212/777–5153.*

Sound Factory. A cavernous, super-high-energy dance mecca, this club is only open on Friday and Saturday nights, though the action does continue through noon on Sunday. ✉ *618 W. 46th St., between 11th and 12th Aves.,* ☎ *212/489–0001.*

Spa. Massage your psyche in the entrance lounge, where a waterfall cascades down behind the bar, before working out to the R&B and hip-hop beats on the dance floor. The super-fit and attractive set can be found in the exclusive alabaster banquettes of the White Room. ✉ *76 E. 13th St., between Broadway and 4th Ave.,* ☎ *212/388–1060.*

Tunnel. Like the Roxy this is another mega-club standard bearer; it attracts a similar crowd, though unlike the Roxy, there's never any roller skating. ✉ *220 12th Ave., at 27th St.,* ☎ *212/695–4682.*

Twilo. Friday brings DJs from around the globe to this massive dance warehouse with an ear-rattling sound system. On Saturday, New York City legend Junior Vasquez takes over the "wheels of steel." ✉ *530 W. 27th St., between 10th and 11th Aves.,* ☎ *212/268–1600.*

Vinyl. Perhaps the no-alcohol policy here draws a more determined gang, but whatever the reason, the crowd is friendly, the vibe is good, and the dancing is among the city's hottest at this legendary Tribeca institution. Expect house music and a great time. ✉ *6 Hubert St., at Hudson St.,* ☎ *212/343–1379.*

Webster Hall. Five kinds of music are played on the four floors of this fave among NYU students and similar species. ✉ *125 E. 11th St., between 3rd and 4th Aves.,* ☎ *212/353–1600.*

Jazz Clubs

Greenwich Village is still New York's jazz mecca, with more than a dozen jazz nightclubs, although many others are strewn around town.

Arthur's Tavern. Unless there's a festival in town, you won't find any big names jamming here. But you will find live jazz nightly, without a cover charge, amidst the smoke-filled, dark-wood ambience of the Greenwich Village of old. ✉ *57 Grove St., between 7th Ave. S and Bleecker St.,* ☎ *212/675–6879.*

Birdland. At the place that gets its name from saxophone great Charlie Parker, you'll find serious, up-and-coming groups. The dining room serves moderately priced Southern cuisine. ✉ *315 W. 44th St., between 8th and 9th Aves.,* ☎ *212/581–3080.*

Blue Note. Considered by many to be the jazz capital of the world, the Blue Note could see on an average week Spyro Gyra, Ron Carter, and Jon Hendricks. Expect a steep music charge, except on Monday, when record labels promote their artists' new releases for an average ticket price of $15. ✉ *131 W. 3rd St., near 6th Ave.,* ☎ *212/475–8592.*

Garage Restaurant and Cafe. There's no cover at this bi-level Village hot spot; a fireplace sets the mood upstairs. ✉ *98 7th Ave. S, near Grove St.,* ☎ *212/645–0600.*

Iridium. This intimate subterranean space often hosts some of the biggest names in jazz. On Monday, electric-guitar innovator Les Paul runs the show. ✉ *48 W. 63rd St., at Columbus Ave.,* ☎ *212/582–2121.*

Jazz Standard. This sizable underground room is a reliable spot to hear the top names in the business. ✉ *116 E. 27th St., between Park and Lexington Aves.,* ☎ *212/576–2232.*

Downtown Nightlife

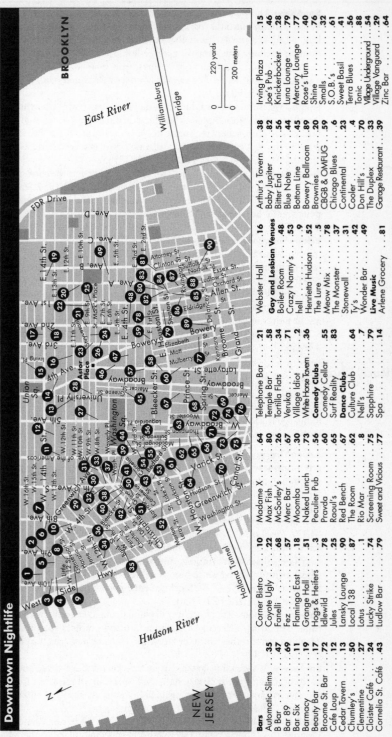

Bars
Automatic Slims **35**
B Bar **47**
Bar 89 . . . . **69**
Bar Six **11**
Barmacy **19**
Beauty Bar **17**
Broome St. Bar **72**
Cafe Loup **12**
Cedar Tavern **13**
Chumley's **50**
Clementine **27**
Cloister Café **24**
Cornelia St. Café **43**

Corner Bistro **10**
Coyote Ugly **22**
Fanelli **68**
Fez **57**
Flamingo East **18**
Grange Hall **51**
Hogs & Heifers **3**
Idlewild **78**
Jules **25**
Lansky Lounge **90**
Local 138 . . . . **87**
Lotus **1**
Lucky Strike **74**
Ludlow Bar **79**

Madame X **64**
Max Fish **80**
McSorley's **26**
Merc Bar **57**
Moomba **30**
Naked Lunch **73**
Peculier Pub **56**
Pravda **60**
Raoul's **65**
Red Bench **67**
The Room **62**
Rio Mar **8**
Screening Room **75**
Sweet and Vicious **77**

Telephone Bar **21**
Temple Bar **58**
Tortilla Flats **34**
Veruka **71**
Village Idiot **2**
White Horse Tavern **36**

Comedy Clubs
Comedy Cellar **55**
Surf Reality **83**

Dance Clubs
Culture Club **64**
Nell's **7**
Sapphire **79**
Spa **14**

Webster Hall **16**

Gay and Lesbian Venues
Boiler Room **48**
Crazy Nanny's **53**
hell **9**
Henrietta Hudson **52**
The Lure **5**
Meow Mix **78**
The Monster **37**
Stonewall **31**
Ty's **42**
Wonder Bar **49**

Live Music
Arlene Grocery **81**

Arthur's Tavern **38**
Baby Jupiter **82**
Bitter End **56**
Blue Note **44**
Bottom Line **45**
Bowery Ballroom **89**
Brownies **20**
CBGB & OMFUG **59**
Chicago Blues **6**
Continental **23**
Cooler **4**
Don Hill's **70**
The Duplex **33**
Garage Restaurant **39**

Irving Plaza **15**
Joe's Pub **46**
Knickerbocker **28**
Luna Lounge **79**
Mercury Lounge **77**
Rose's Turn **40**
Shine **76**
Smalls **32**
S.O.B.'s **61**
Sweet Basil **41**
Terra Blues **56**
Tonic **88**
Village Underground **54**
Village Vanguard **29**
Zinc Bar **64**

Knickerbocker. Piano and bass duets are the fare at this reliable steak-house with an old New York feel. Think red meat, smoke, and good jazz. ⊠ *33 University Pl., at 9th St.,* ☎ *212/228–8490.*

Knitting Factory. This sprawling, three-level space in TriBeCa features avant-garde jazz in a variety of settings, from a small homey room to a sizable theater. ⊠ *74 Leonard St., between Broadway and Church St.,* ☎ *212/219–3055.*

Smalls. Where can you find jazz till dawn and beyond? After the Village Vanguard closes, poke your head around the corner into this pocket-size club, where the music keeps coming until 8 AM. But if you want to tipple, bring your own bottle; no booze is served here. ⊠ *183 W. 10th St., near 7th Ave. S,* ☎ *212/929–7565.*

Sweet Basil. One of the top places for jazz, this joint gets the trios, quar-tets, quintets, and orchestras to keep a true jazz maven happy. Sunday brunch (from 2 to 6) with pianist Chuck Folds is truly a religious ex-perience. ⊠ *88 7th Ave. S, between Bleecker and Grove Sts.,* ☎ *212/242–1785.*

Village Vanguard. This former Thelonious Monk haunt, the prototypical old-world jazz club, lives on in a smoky cellar, where you might hear jams from the likes of Wynton Marsalis and James Carter, among others. ⊠ *178 7th Ave. S, between 11th and Perry Sts.,* ☎ *212/255–4037.*

Zinc Bar. This tiny underground spot features Brazilian jazz on Satur-day and Sunday. During the week the live music ranges from straight-ahead guitar work to Cuban tunes. It's a sure bet for a great night. ⊠ *90 W. Houston St., between Thompson St. and LaGuardia Pl.,* ☎ *212/477–8337.*

Rock Clubs

Crowds at the Big Apple's rocketerias are young, enthusiastic, and hun-gry; the noise is often deafening, but you can catch many a rising star in this lively scene. In summer, New York's parks and plazas come alive with performances of everything from acid jazz to zydeco.

Arlene Grocery. This rock club on the Lower East Side is known for recruiting new bands with promising futures. No cover charge and a welcoming atmosphere set it apart. ⊠ *95 Stanton St., between Lud-low and Orchard Sts.,* ☎ *212/358–1633.*

Baby Jupiter. Part cheap (and tasty) restaurant, part club, this Lower East Side spot can be counted on for decent live rock by local bands. ⊠ *170 Orchard St., at Stanton St.,* ☎ *212/982–2229.*

Bitter End. This old Village standby still serves up its share of talent; Lisa Loeb, Joan Armatrading, and Warren Zevon have played here. Check before arriving, since blues, country, rock, and jazz all make ap-pearances here. ⊠ *147 Bleecker St., between Thompson St. and La-Guardia Pl.,* ☎ *212/673–7030.*

Bowery Ballroom. This tastefully clean, balconied space is run by the folks behind the Mercury Lounge and often presents major stars. There's a comfortable bar in the basement. ⊠ *6 Delancey St., near Bow-ery,* ☎ *212/533–2111.*

Brownie's. It's catch-as-catch-can at this East Village dive, but the hard thrashing sounds occasionally pull people in off the street to join the pierced and tattooed throngs. ⊠ *169 Ave. A, between 10th and 11th Sts.,* ☎ *212/420–8392.*

CBGB & OMFUG. American punk rock and New Wave (the Ramones, Blondie, the Talking Heads) were born in this long, black tunnel of a club. Today expect Shirley Temple of Doom, Trick Babies, Xanax 25, and other inventively named bands. **CB's 313 Gallery,** next door at 313 Bowery, attracts a quieter (and older) crowd with mostly acoustic music. ⊠ *315 Bowery, at Bleecker St.,* ☎ *212/982–4052.*

Continental. A favorite haunt of New York University students, this East Village dive is loud, cheap, and lots of fun, in a delightfully sophomoric way. ⊠ *25 3rd Ave., at St. Marks Pl.,* ☎ *212/529–6924.*

The Cooler. A hip bar, live-music dive, and DJ dance party are all in one at this former meat cooler in the raw yet up-and-coming Meatpacking District. Come here for a mix of rap, reggae, techno, and jazz. ⊠ *416 W. 14th St., between 9th and 10th Aves.,* ☎ *212/229–0785.*

Don Hill's. At this TriBeCa favorite, you'll find bands both popular and not yet signed. Most of the time the crowd is authentically rock-and-roll; Friday night is Squeeze Box, a riotous party usually hosted by drag impresarios. ⊠ *511 Greenwich St., at Spring St.,* ☎ *212/334–1390.*

Irving Plaza. Looking for Joan Osborne, Weezer, or Wilco? You'll find them in this perfect-size place for general-admission live music. There's a small balcony with a bar and a tiny lounge area. ⊠ *17 Irving Pl., at 15th St.,* ☎ *212/777–6800; 212/777–1224 for concert hot line.*

Luna Lounge. Downtown hipsters pack the back room of this Ludlow Street staple to catch between two and four local rock acts a night, except on Monday when stand up comedy is on the bill. ⊠ *171 Ludlow St., between Houston and Stanton Sts.,* ☎ *212/260–2323.*

Maxwells. It's actually in New Jersey, but if you're looking for a small room to see some big names in indie rock, it's well worth the short PATH train ride. ⊠ *1039 Washington St., at 11th St., Hoboken, NJ,* ☎ *201/798–0406.*

Mercury Lounge. With one of the best sound systems in the city, this East Village club holds a quiet cachet with bands and industry insiders. ⊠ *217 E. Houston St., at Ave. A,* ☎ *212/260–4700.*

Tonic. This former kosher winery on the happening Lower East Side presents some of the most innovative rock and jazz in town. ⊠ *107 Norfolk St., between Delancey and Rivington Sts.,* ☎ *212/358–7501.*

Wetlands. If you can ignore the hokey broken-down VW bus–cum–gift shop, this hard-to-find club rules, mostly because it draws great, often danceable, often psychedelic bands. Dave Matthews, Soul Coughing, and Hootie and the Blowfish "developed" here. ⊠ *161 Hudson St., at Laight St.,* ☎ *212/966–4225.*

World Music Venues

A former mayor once called New York a "gorgeous mosaic" for the rich ethnic mix of its inhabitants, and the music in some of its clubs reflects that. Brazilian, Celtic, and of course Latin—salsa, samba, merengue—integrate with the ever-present energy of the streets.

Connolly's. This Irish pub with a "Cheers"-like atmosphere plays host to the Irish rock-and-roots hybrid Black 47 (named for the year of the great famine) on Saturday night. ⊠ *14 E. 47th St., between 5th and Madison Aves.,* ☎ *212/867–3767.*

Copacabana. Music and passion were always in fashion at this legendary nightclub, but now it's in the form of Latin music by such performers as the three Titos: Ruiz, Riojas, and Nieves. ⊠ *617 W. 57th St., between 11th and 12th Aves.,* ☎ *212/582–2672.*

Knitting Factory. This cross-genre music café regularly features performers from far and wide. ⊠ *74 Leonard St., between Broadway and Church St.,* ☎ *212/219–3055.*

Latin Quarter. Sharp-dressed patrons pack this second-story club that often features internationally known salsa performers. ⊠ *2551 Broadway, at 96th St.,* ☎ *212/864–7600.*

SOB's. The initials stand for Sounds of Brazil at *the* place for reggae, Trinidadian carnival, zydeco, African, and especially Latin tunes and salsa rhythms. The decor is à la Tropicana; the favored drink, a *caipir-*

inha, a mixture of Brazilian sugarcane liquor and lime. ✉ *204 Varick St., at Houston St.,* ☎ *212/243–4940.*

Blues, Acoustic, and R&B Venues

B. B. King Blues Club & Grill. It ain't no Mississippi juke joint. This lavish Times Square club, which opened at the end of 2000, is vast and shiny and host to a wide range of musicians, from Bo Diddley to Peter Frampton. Every so often the relentlessly touring owner stops by as well. ✉ *243 W. 42nd St., between 8th Ave. and Broadway,* ☎ *212/997–4144.*

Bottom Line. Clubs come and go, but this granddaddy prevails. Its reputation is for showcasing talents on their way up, as it did for both Stevie Wonder and Bruce Springsteen. Recent visitors include Buster Poindexter and Jane Siberry. When a name pulls in a crowd, patrons are packed like sardines at mostly long, thin tables. ✉ *15 W. 4th St., at Mercer St.,* ☎ *212/228–6300.*

Chicago Blues. Big Time Sarah, Jimmy Dawkins, the Holmes Brothers, and others have cozied into this nothing-fancy, just-plain-folksy West Village blues club. ✉ *73 8th Ave., between 13th and 14th Sts.,* ☎ *212/924–9755.*

Hogs & Heifers Uptown. The sibling of the West Village bar of the same name draws a slightly preppier, but equally inebriated, crowd. Plus it has free live music, in the country, blues, and rockabilly veins, nightly. ✉ *1843 1st Ave., between 95th and 96th Sts.,* ☎ *212/722–8635.*

Rodeo Bar. There's never a cover at this Texas-style roadhouse, complete with barn-wood siding, a barbecue and Tex-Mex menu, and "music with American roots"—country, rock, rockabilly, swing, bluegrass, and blues. ✉ *375 3rd Ave., at 27th St.,* ☎ *212/683–6500.*

Shine. This Tribeca club is home to Giant Step disk jockey parties (bringing the top names in the business to town weekly) as well as to one-night stands by up-and-coming rock bands. ✉ *285 W. Broadway, at Canal St.,* ☎ *212/941–0900.*

Terra Blues. A second-story haven for blues lovers, this cozy Village club is surprisingly short on New York University students and rowdy folk. It must be the candlelit tables and the great national and local acts that grace the stage. ✉ *149 Bleecker St., between Thompson and LaGuardia Sts.,* ☎ *212/777–7776.*

Tribeca Blues. Henry Butler, Michael Hill, and Papa Chubby are among the performers who stop by here when they're in this neck of the woods. ✉ *16 Warren St., between Trimble Pl. and Broadway,* ☎ *212/766–1070.*

Village Underground. This intimate subterranean club opened at the end of 2000 and immediately started booking such quality acts as John Cale, Graham Parker, and Dan Hicks. One bonus: the club is non-smoking. ✉ *130 W. 3rd St., near 6th Ave.,* ☎ *212/777–7745.*

Comedy Clubs

Neurotic New York comedy is known the world over, and a few minutes watching these hilarious Woody Allen types might just make your own problems seem laughable. Comedy isn't pretty here, nor is it especially cheap. Expect to pay around $15 per person on a weekend, sometimes on top of a drink minimum, and reservations are usually necessary. One warning: only those skilled in the art of repartee should sit in the front. The rest are advised to hide in a corner or risk being relentlessly heckled. The *Village Voice* and *Time Out New York* cover the comedy scene well.

Caroline's Comedy Club. This high-gloss club features established names as well as comedians on the edge of stardom. Joy Behar, Sandra Bernhard, and Gilbert Gottfried have appeared. ⊠ *1626 Broadway, between 49th and 50th Sts.,* ☎ *212/757–4100.*

Chicago City Limits. This troupe's been doing improvisational comedy for a long time, and it seldom fails to whip its audiences into a laughing frenzy. Chicago City Limits performs in a renovated movie theater and is very strong on audience participation. ⊠ *1105 1st Ave., at 61st St.,* ☎ *212/888–5233.*

Comedy Cellar. Laughter fills this space beneath the Olive Tree Café, with a bill that's a good barometer of who's hot. ⊠ *117 MacDougal St., between 3rd and Bleecker Sts.,* ☎ *212/254–3480.*

Comic Strip Live. The atmosphere here is strictly corner bar ("More comfortable than a nice pair of corduroys," says daytime manager J. R.). The stage is brilliantly lighted but minuscule; the bill is unpredictable but worth checking out. ⊠ *1568 2nd Ave., between 81st and 82nd Sts.,* ☎ *212/861–9386.*

Dangerfield's. Since 1969 this has been an important showcase for prime comic talent. It's owned by comedian Rodney Dangerfield. ⊠ *1118 1st Ave., between 61st and 62nd Sts.,* ☎ *212/593–1650.*

Freestyle Repertory Theater. On "Spontaneous Broadway" nights, an audience member shouts out a song title and the troupe improvises a show tune and then a whole musical. On other evenings teams compete in head-to-head "theater sports" matches. ⊠ *Various theaters,* ☎ *212/642–8202 for locations.*

Gotham Comedy Club. Housed in a landmark building in the Flatiron district, this club—complete with a turn-of-the-20th-century chandelier and copper bars—showcases popular headliners such as Chris Rock and David Brenner. Once a month there's a Latino comedy show. ⊠ *34 W. 22nd St., between 5th and 6th Aves.,* ☎ *212/367–9000.*

Luna Lounge. On Monday night, the back room at this Lower East Side watering hole hosts no-name stand ups as well as big name stars such as Janeane Garofalo. ⊠ *171 Ludlow St., between Houston and Stanton Sts.,* ☎ *212/260–2323.*

Surf Reality. At this downtown loft space—a showcase for what's known as alternative comedy—you won't find anyone telling jokes on a stage backed by an exposed brick wall. Instead, expect wacky sketch comedy and oddball skits. ⊠ *172 Allen St., between Stanton and Rivington Sts.,* ☎ *212/673–4182.*

Cabaret and Performance Spaces

Cabaret takes many forms in New York, from a lone crooner at the piano to a full-fledged song-and-dance revue. Some nightspots have stages; almost all have a cover and a minimum food–and/or–drink charge.

Arci's Place. Karen Mason, Marilyn Volpe, Wesla Whitfield are a few of the singers who have taken the stage at one of the city's newer cabaret rooms. ⊠ *450 Park Ave. S, between 30th and 31st Sts.,* ☎ *212/532–4370.*

Danny's Skylight Room. Housed in Danny's Grand Sea Palace, this fixture on Restaurant Row offers a little bit of everything: jazz performers, crooners, and ivory ticklers. ⊠ *346 W. 46th St., between 8th and 9th Aves.,* ☎ *212/265–8133.*

Don't Tell Mama. Composer-lyricist hopefuls and established talents show their stuff until 4 AM at this convivial theater district cabaret. Extroverts will be tempted by the piano bar's open-mike policy. In the two rooms you might find singers, comedians, or female impersonators. ⊠ *343 W. 46th St., between 8th and 9th Aves.,* ☎ *212/757–0788.*

Downstairs at the West Bank Café. Below an attractive bistro-type restaurant across from Theater Row, moonlighting musical-comedy triple threats (actor-singer-dancers) show off; on occasion, new plays are read. ☒ *407 W. 42nd St., between 8th and 9th Aves.,* ☎ *212/695–6909.*

The Duplex. Since 1951 this music-scene veteran on Greenwich Village's busy Sheridan Square has hosted young singers on the rise, drop-ins fresh from Broadway at the open mike, and comediennes polishing their acts. Plays and rock bands round out the scope of entertainment offerings. ☒ *61 Christopher St., at 7th Ave. S,* ☎ *212/255–5438.*

Feinstein's at the Regency. Located in the 540 Park Restaurant, this is the stomping ground of pianist Michael Feinstein, when it's not presenting some of the top names in the business. ☒ *540 Park Ave., at 61st St.,* ☎ *212/339–4095.*

Firebird Cafe. This swank spot, on Restaurant Row beside the restaurant of the same name, is the place to hear leading crooners while sampling a vast selection of rare vodkas. ☒ *363 W. 46th St., between 9th and 10th Aves.,* ☎ *212/586–0244.*

Joe's Pub. This cabaret is the work of the Public Theater, in which it's housed, and nightlife impresario Serge Becker, the man behind such legendary clubs as Area and M. K. Look for top-notch performers, as well as A-list celebrities. ☒ *425 Lafayette St., between 4th St. and Astor Pl.,* ☎ *212/539–8770.*

Judy's Restaurant and Cabaret. Both cabaret and piano bar, Judy's is known for singing pianists in the Michael Feinstein mold. ☒ *169 8th Ave., between 18th and 19th Sts.,* ☎ *212/929–5410.*

Rose's Turn. This landmark cabaret presents singers, sketch comedy groups, and various other performers; a recent show had a Judy Garland impersonator sparring with an Ann Miller impersonator. Downstairs is a popular piano bar. ☒ *55 Grove St., near Bleecker and 7th Ave. S,* ☎ *212/366–5438.*

BARS

Although working out is a way of life in New York, there's little danger that Manhattanites will abandon their bars, and drinking establishments continue to thrive and multiply. Exploring neighborhood by neighborhood, you'll find a glut of mahogany-encrusted historic taverns in the West Village; chichi wine bars in SoHo and TriBeCa; yuppie and collegiate minifrats on the Upper West and Upper East sides; and hipster bars all over downtown, especially in the East Village's Alphabet City and on the Lower East Side. No matter where you are in town, the city's liquor law allows bars to stay open until 4 AM, so it's easy to add on a watering stop at the end of an evening's merriment.

Lower Manhattan, SoHo, and TriBeCa

Bar 89. This bi-level lounge has the most entertaining bathrooms in town; the high-tech doors of unoccupied stalls are transparent, and (ideally) turn opaque as you lock the door. ☒ *89 Mercer St., between Spring and Broome Sts.,* ☎ *212/274–0989.*

Bridge Café. Just a hop away from South Street Seaport, this busy little restaurant flanking the Brooklyn Bridge is a world apart from that touristy district. The bar is one of the oldest in Manhattan, and though it's small, its inventory is huge: you can choose from a list of 80 domestic wines and about 50 single-malt scotches. ☒ *279 Water St., at Dover St.,* ☎ *212/227–3344.*

Broome Street Bar. A classic hangout, this SoHo standard attracts artsy types from Manhattan on weekdays and from the other boroughs on weekends. ☒ *363 W. Broadway, at Broome St.,* ☎ *212/925–2086.*

El Teddy's. You can't miss the gigantic Lady Liberty crown out front, and the "Judy Jetson goes to art camp" decor at this former mob haunt. The margaritas (straight up, *por favor*) at this enduring TriBeCa bar are phenomenal. ⊠ *219 W. Broadway, between White and Franklin Sts.,* ☎ *212/941–7070.*

Fanelli. On Sunday, many carry the fat *New York Times* under their arms when they come to this casual SoHo neighborhood bar. The food's good, too. ⊠ *94 Prince St., at Mercer St.,* ☎ *212/226–9412.*

Lucky Strike. Now that the supermodels party elsewhere, this ultra-cool SoHo bistro has quieted down. Young Euro types pose at the cozy back tables; DJs play funky tunes at crowded weekend parties. ⊠ *59 Grand St., between Broadway and Wooster St.,* ☎ *212/941–0479.*

Lush. One of TriBeCa's hottest lounges, this modern-looking space has a cool banquette running the length of its loftlike room, as well a couple of round chambers in the rear where the celebrities retire. ⊠ *110 Duane St., between Church St. and Broadway,* ☎ *212/766–1295.*

MercBar. A chic European crowd and New Yorkers in the know come to this dark, rather nondescript bar for the wonderful martinis. Its street number is barely visible—look for the French doors, which stay open in summer. ⊠ *151 Mercer St., between Prince and Houston Sts.,* ☎ *212/966–2727.*

Naked Lunch. Dazzlingly popular, this William Burroughs–inspired, earth-tone SoHo haunt is frequented by celebrities and other beautiful people. ⊠ *17 Thompson St., at Grand St.,* ☎ *212/343–0828.*

North Star Pub. This snug London-style pub is one of the only places at the South Street Seaport not completely overrun by tourists. Have an Imperial (20-ounce) pint of Guinness, but skip the greasy, expensive bar food. ⊠ *93 South St., at Fulton St.,* ☎ *212/509–6757.*

Pravda. Martinis are the rule at this stylish, Russian-theme bar and lounge, where there are more than 70 brands of vodka and nearly as many types of martinis. ⊠ *281 Lafayette St., between Prince and Houston Sts.,* ☎ *212/226–4696.*

Raoul's. One of the first trendy spots in SoHo, this smoky French restaurant has yet to lose its touch. Expect a chic bar scene filled with model-pretty men and women. ⊠ *180 Prince St., between Sullivan and Thompson Sts.,* ☎ *212/966–3518.*

Red Bench. A small, dark lounge popular with the attractive locals who want some time off from the usual SoHo scene. ⊠ *107 Sullivan St., between Prince and Spring Sts.,* ☎ *212/274–9120.*

The Room. It can get rather cozy in this minimilist but comfortable spot where the great selection of wine and beer draws a friendly international crowd. ⊠ *144 Sullivan St., between Houston and Prince Sts.,* ☎ *212/477–2102.*

Screening Room. People often have dinner or drinks on a night out at the movies, so it makes sense to hold that audience captive, as is often done in Britain. The movie theater here is small but inviting and the food is quite good, making it a favorite with the TriBeCa crowd. ⊠ *54 Varick St., at Canal St.,* ☎ *212/334–2100.*

Sweet and Vicious. A relaxing and completely unpretentious place for a drink. The crowd here is friendly and between 25 and 45 years old. If you visit during the summer you can enjoy its outside garden. ⊠ *5 Spring St., between the Bowery and Elizabeth Sts.,* ☎ *212/334–7915.*

Veruka. Getting past the velvet rope at this ultra-hot lounge is as difficult as driving a ground ball past New York Yankee shortstop Derek Jeter, who frequents this spot along with his friend David Cone, and other such celebrities as Serena Altschul. ⊠ *525 Broome St., between Thompson and Sullivan Sts.,* ☎ *212/625–1717.*

Walker's. First-precinct NYPD detectives, TriBeCa artists, Wall Street suits, and the odd celeb kick back at this cozy restaurant-bar. ⊠ *16 N. Moore St., at Varick St.,* ☎ *212/941–0142.*

Chelsea and the Village

Automatic Slim's, a cramped bar that gets patrons dancing on the counter to loud music, has amazingly good food. ⊠ *733 Washington St., at Bank St.,* ☎ *212/645–8660.*

Bar Six. This elegant bar and restaurant with French doors opening onto the street is an idyllic stop on a soft summer night. ⊠ *502 6th Ave., between 12th and 13th Sts.,* ☎ *212/691–1363.*

Café Loup. This French restaurant is something of a neighborhood institution, and its cozy bar serves some of the best margaritas in the city. They use only fresh fruit juices here. ⊠ *105 W. 13th St., between 5th and 6th Aves.,* ☎ *212/255–4746.*

Cedar Tavern. This old-fashioned Village tavern is located a block away from the site of the original, which was a popular haunt of the abstract expressionist crowd during the 1950s. ⊠ *82 University Pl., at 12th St.,* ☎ *212/741–9754.*

Chelsea Commons. Construction workers mingle with Chelsea dandies at this longtime neighborhood fave. It's got a lamplit brick courtyard straight out of olde London, and a welcome (on a cold February night) fireplace. ⊠ *242 10th Ave., at 24th St.,* ☎ *212/929–9424.*

Chumley's. There's no sign to help you find this place—they took it down during Chumley's speakeasy days—but when you reach the corner of Bedford and Barrow streets, you're very close. A fireplace warms the relaxed dining room, where the burgers are hearty and the clientele collegiate. ⊠ *86 Bedford St., at Barrow St.,* ☎ *212/675–4449.*

Ciel Rouge. Sip titillating cocktails such as Lady Love Fizz and Bitches Brew in a wicked all-red room straight out of the Left Bank. Don't miss cool happenings like live jazz and piano music on Monday and Tuesday nights. ⊠ *176 7th Ave., between 20th and 21st Sts.,* ☎ *212/929–5542.*

Clementine. The only stop on a barless stretch of 5th Avenue, this elegant restaurant with a long, burnished bar and soft lighting is the perfect place for a romantic pre- or postdinner drink. ⊠ *1 5th Ave., at 8th St.,* ☎ *212/253–0003.*

Cornelia Street Café. Share a bottle of merlot at a street-side table on a quaint West Village lane. Downstairs you can groove to live jazz from Wednesday through Saturday. ⊠ *29 Cornelia St., between 4th and Bleecker Sts.,* ☎ *212/989–9319.*

Corner Bistro. Founded in 1966, this pub-and-grub style bar serves the best hamburgers in town. The cozy place is so inviting and the young, professional crowd so friendly, you might think you're in a small town. ⊠ *331 W. 4th St., at 8th Ave.,* ☎ *212/242–9502.*

Grange Hall. Decorated in art deco style with WPA-ish murals, this West Village restaurant is an American classic, just like its all-domestic wine list. ⊠ *50 Commerce St., at Barrow St.,* ☎ *212/924–5246.*

Hogs & Heifers. This place seems to be Gotham's homage to the movie *Deliverance,* but it still manages to attract star power such as Drew Barrymore, Julia Roberts, and Harrison Ford. ⊠ *859 Washington St., at 13th St.,* ☎ *212/929–0655.*

Lot 61. This cavernous restaurant with sliding doors, rubber sofas, and contemporary art is as good looking, and coolly distant, as its model and movie-star patrons. ⊠ *550 W. 21st St., between 10th and 11th Aves.,* ☎ *212/243–6555.*

Lotus. Use your nose to help find this unmarked west side hot spot: incense burns in the entry to its blonde-wood panelled quarters, where unexpectedly mature patrons try not to get caught admiring the celebrities (Dennis Leary, Mick Jagger) in their midst. ⊠ *409 W. 14th St., between 9th and 10th Aves.,* ☎ *212/243–4420.*

Madame X. The bordello atmosphere here is accented by blood red walls and a sexy crowd. It's just across Houston Street from Soho, which means it's got just as attractive a crowd, but less attitude. There's also live jazz and, in the warmer months, a garden. ⊠ *94 W. Houston St., between La Guardia Pl. and Thompson St.,* ☎ *212/539–0808.*

Moomba. As soon as it opened, this restaurant-lounge was so popular with actor Leonardo DiCaprio, rap impresario Russell Simmons, and other celebrities that you couldn't get in the door. Now, if you do slip under the velvet rope, don't expect to see any famous faces. ⊠ *133 7th Ave. S, between Charles and 10th Sts.,* ☎ *212/989–1414.*

Peculier Pub. From Abbaye de Brooklyn to Zywiec—the nearly 500 beers, representing 43 countries, including Peru, Vietnam, and Zimbabwe, are the draw at this heart-of-the-Village pub. ⊠ *145 Bleecker St., at LaGuardia Pl.,* ☎ *212/353–1327.*

Rio-Mar. This throwback to Spain serves tapas until about 6 PM (there's also an adjoining dining room). ⊠ *7 9th Ave., at Little 12th St.,* ☎ *212/243–9015.*

Serena. This remarkably stylish subterranean lounge is the creation of top New York City caterer Serena Bass. Her chic friends are its most reliable patrons. ⊠ *Chelsea Hotel, 222 W. 23rd St., between 7th and 8th Aves.,* ☎ *212/255–4646.*

Tortilla Flats. The backroom "Vegas Lounge" here is a tribute to the stars of Vegas, from Lewis and Martin to Siegfried and Roy. ⊠ *767 Washington St., at 12th St.,* ☎ *212/243–1053.*

Village Idiot. George Thorogood plays on the jukebox, the drinks are nearly as cheap as a subway ride, and the crowd of young college students just loves it. ⊠ *355 W. 14th St., at 9th Ave.,* ☎ *212/989–7334.*

White Horse Tavern. According to (dubious) New York legend, Dylan Thomas drank himself to death in 1953 at this historic tavern founded in 1889. From April through October there's sidewalk seating. ⊠ *567 Hudson St., at 11th St.,* ☎ *212/989–3956.*

Lower East Side and East Village through East 20s

B Bar. Long lines peer through venetian blinds at the fabulous crowd within this trendy spot formerly known as the Bowery Bar. If the bouncer says there's a private party going on, more likely than not, it's his way of turning you away nicely. ⊠ *358 Bowery, at 4th St.,* ☎ *212/475–2220.*

Barmacy. Appealing to club kids and collegiate types, this East Village bar looks like a small-town old-fashioned pharmacy. But don't expect to have your prescription filled—unless it's in the form of a martini. ⊠ *538 E. 14th St., between Aves. A and B,* ☎ *212/228–2240.*

Beauty Bar. If you've ever wanted to try out the beauty parlor in *Steel Magnolias*, this is your chance. Come during happy hour to get your nails done. ⊠ *231 E. 14th St., between 2nd and 3rd Aves.,* ☎ *212/ 539–1389.*

Cloister Café. With one of Manhattan's largest and leafiest outdoor gardens, the Cloister is a perfect perch for lingering and elbow bending. ⊠ *238 E. 9th St., between 2nd and 3rd Aves.,* ☎ *212/777–9128.*

Coyote Ugly. The name is appropriate for this grimy dive, where the raucous regulars can be heard across the 'hood singing along with the Skynyrd wailing from the jukebox. ⊠ *153 1st Ave., between 9th and 10th Sts.,* ☎ *212/477–4431.*

Fez. Tucked away in the popular Time Café, this Moroccan-theme Casbah offers nightly events, including drag and comedy shows, readings, and jazz and pop music (make reservations in advance for big-name bands). ⊠ *380 Lafayette St., between 4th and Great Jones Sts.,* ☎ *212/ 533–2680.*

Flamingo East. Kidney-shape sofas, style-mad patrons, and moody lighting make this haute downtown restaurant and bar a cool good time. Upstairs starts late and is only sporadically open to the public, but the balcony overlooking 2nd Avenue is a treat, and the food is delicious. ⊠ *219 2nd Ave., between 13th and 14th Sts.,* ☎ *212/533–2860.*

Fun. True to its name, this bi-level club features amusing projections of computer animation and other video art on 10-ft screens, while all around a playful twentysomething crowd revels in the high-tech surroundings. ⊠ *130 Madison St., near Pike St.,* ☎ *212/964–0303.*

Idlewild. Tucked away on the edge of the East Village, this terminally kitschy bar paying homage to jet travel—it takes its name from the airstrip that became John F. Kennedy International Airport—succeeds as a cool drinking destination. The booths were created from real coach seats, the modular bathrooms remain intact, and waitresses are decked out in stewardess uniforms. ⊠ *145 E. Houston St., between 1st and 2nd Aves.,* ☎ *212/477–5005.*

Jules. This *très français, très romantique* bistro with wine bar is fronted by a perfect people-watching patio. ⊠ *65 St. Marks Pl., between 1st and 2nd Aves.,* ☎ *212/477–5560.*

Lansky Lounge and Grill. In the back room of a New York City institution, Ratner's Restaurant, Lansky occupies the site of a former speakeasy. You enter via a long, dark alley; once inside the tastefully decorated two-tier space you'll find young hipsters sipping potent cocktails. ⊠ *104 Norfolk St., between Delancey and Rivington Sts.,* ☎ *212/677–9489.*

Local 138. If you're looking for a neighborly spot to catch World Cup action, head to this new cozy, low-lit outpost. It's run by Irish lads who love football, er, soccer. ⊠ *138 Ludlow St., between Stanton and Rivington Sts.,* ☎ *212/477–0280.*

Ludlow Bar. This low-key bar is one of the main draws on the oh-so-happening main drag of the Lower East Side. ⊠ *165 Ludlow St., between Houston and Stanton Sts.,* ☎ *212/353–0536.*

Max Fish. This crowded, kitschy palace on a gentrified Lower East Side strip boasts a twisted image of a grimacing Julio Iglesias over the bar, a pool table in back, and a young, dot-com crowd. ⊠ *178 Ludlow St., between Houston and Stanton Sts.,* ☎ *212/529–3959.*

McSorley's Old Ale House. One of New York's oldest saloons (they claim to have opened in 1854), immortalized by *New Yorker* writer Joseph Mitchell, this is a must-see for beer-loving first-timers to Gotham. ⊠ *15 E. 7th St., between 2nd and 3rd Aves.,* ☎ *212/473–9148.*

Old Town Bar and Restaurant. Proudly unpretentious and stubbornly smoke-friendly, this watering hole is heavy on the mahogany and redolent of Old New York—it's been around since 1892. ⊠ *45 E. 18th St., between Broadway and Park Ave. S,* ☎ *212/529–6732.*

Pete's Tavern. This saloon is famous as the place where O. Henry is alleged to have written "The Gift of the Magi" (at the second booth to the right as you come in). These days it's still crowded with noisy, friendly souls. ⊠ *129 E. 18th St., at Irving Pl.,* ☎ *212/473–7676.*

Telephone Bar. Imported English telephone booths and a polite, handsome crowd mark this pub, which has great tap brews and killer mashed potatoes. ⊠ *149 2nd Ave., between 9th and 10th Sts.,* ☎ *212/529–5000.*

Temple Bar. Romantic and upscale, this unmarked haunt is famous for its martinis and is a treat at any price. ⊠ *332 Lafayette St., between Bleecker and Houston Sts.,* ☎ *212/925–4242.*

Midtown and the Theater District

Algonquin Hotel Lounge. This venerable hotel bar plays up its heritage as the site of the fabled literary Algonquin Roundtable. ⊠ *59 W. 44th St., between 5th and 6th Aves.,* ☎ *212/840–6800.*

Barrymore's. The requisite show posters hang on the wall at this pleasantly downscale theater-district bar. ⊠ *267 W. 45th St., between Broadway and 8th Ave.,* ☎ *212/391–8400.*

Campbell Apartment. One of Manhattan's more beautiful rooms, this restored space inside Grand Central Terminal dates back to the 1930s, when it was the private office of an executive named John W. Campbell. He knew how to live, and you can enjoy his good taste, too. ⊠ *15 Vanderbilt Ave., at 41st St.,* ☎ *212/953–0409.*

Café Un Deux Trois. In a charmingly converted old hotel lobby, this small bar is chicly peopled; it hops before and after the theater. ⊠ *123 W. 44th St., between Broadway and 6th Ave.,* ☎ *212/354–4148.*

Divine Bar. You may think you're in SoHo when you see this bar's zebra-stripe bar chairs, cigar area, and cozy velvet couches upstairs. There's a selection of tapas, wines, and beers, but no hard liquor is served. ⊠ *244 E. 51st St., between 2nd and 3rd Aves.,* ☎ *212/319–9463.*

Fantino. In the Central Park Inter-Continental, this restaurant bar is dressy and traditional—a very double-martini place. ⊠ *112 Central Park S, between 6th and 7th Aves.,* ☎ *212/757–1900.*

Joe Allen. At this old reliable on Restaurant Row, celebrated in the musical version of *All About Eve,* everybody's en route to or from a show. The posters that adorn the "flop wall" are from Broadway musicals that bombed. ⊠ *326 W. 46th St., between 8th and 9th Aves.,* ☎ *212/581–6464.*

Keens Steakhouse. Just around the corner from Madison Square Garden, this old New York City restaurant is stocked with more than 140 different single-malt scotches, and filled with cigar smoke. The ceilings here are lined with clay pipes that once belonged to patrons. ⊠ *72 W. 36th St., between 5th and 6th Aves.,* ☎ *212/947–3636.*

King Cole Bar. The famed Maxfield Parrish mural is a welcome sight at this classic and gorgeous midtown meeting place. ⊠ *St. Regis Hotel, 2 E. 55th St., near 5th Ave.,* ☎ *212/753–4500.*

Landmark Tavern. This aged redbrick pub (it opened in 1868) is warmed by the glow of potbellied stoves on each of its three floors. The original mahogany bar and hand-pressed tin ceilings and walls give the tavern a 19th-century feel. The waiters insist it's haunted. ⊠ *626 11th Ave., at 46th St.,* ☎ *212/757–8595.*

Monkey Bar. A big, hairless ape greets patrons at the door of this '90s creation, though neither it nor the jungle murals bring out much barbarism in the mannered banker-types who shoot back scotch here. ⊠ *60 E. 54th St., between Park and Madison Aves.,* ☎ *212/838–2600.*

Morgans Bar. Supermodels and their kin tuck themselves into this little bar, all gilt mirrors and candles, housed in the basement of the Morgans hotel. ⊠ *237 Madison Ave., at 37th St.,* ☎ *212/686–0300.*

Morrell Wine Bar and Café. Run by the wine purveyors of the same name (their store is next door), this cozy bar offers one of the city's best selections of wine by the glass. In summer you can sip your Viognier under the watchful gaze of Prometheus, at outdoor tables in the heart of Rockefeller Center. ⊠ *1 Rockefeller Center, 49th St., between 5th and 6th Aves.,* ☎ *212/262–7700.*

Oak Bar. Bedecked with plush leather chairs and oak walls, this old favorite continues to age well. Its great location draws sophisticates, shoppers, businesspeople, tourists in the know, and stars. ⊠ *Plaza Hotel, 5th Ave. and 59th St.,* ☎ *212/759–3000.*

Pen Top Bar and Lounge. Take a break from 5th Avenue shopping at this glass-lined penthouse hotel bar on the 22nd floor. Drinks are pricey, but the views are impressive, and it's well worth a visit during the hotter months for its open-air rooftop seating area. ⊠ *Peninsula Hotel, 700 5th Ave., at 55th St.,* ☎ *212/247–2200.*

P. J. Clarke's. Mirrors and polished wood adorn New York's most famous Irish bar, where scenes from the 1954 movie *Lost Weekend* were shot. Lots of after-work types unwind here. ⊠ *915 3rd Ave., at 55th St.,* ☎ *212/759–1650.*

Royalton. Philippe Starck's modernistic midtown hotel has two places to drink—the large lobby bar furnished with armchairs and chaise longues and the banquette-lined Round Bar in a separate, circular room to your right as you enter. ⊠ *44 W. 44th St., between 5th and 6th Aves.,* ☎ *212/869–4400.*

Sardi's. "The theater is certainly not what it was," crooned a cat in the long-running *Cats*—and he could be referring to this Broadway institution as well. Still, if you care for the theater, make time for a drink in one of the red-leather booths, which are surrounded by caricatures of stars past and present. ⊠ *234 W. 44th St., between Broadway and 8th Ave.,* ☎ *212/221–8440.*

Top of the Tower. There are higher hotel-top lounges, but this one on the 26th floor still feels halfway to heaven. The atmosphere is elegant and subdued. ⊠ *Beekman Tower, 3 Mitchell Pl., near 1st Ave. at 49th St.,* ☎ *212/355–7300.*

Water Club. Right on the East River, with a pleasing outside deck (you're not on a boat, but you'll somehow feel you are), this is a special-occasion kind of place—especially for those who've already been to all the special landlocked watering holes in town. ⊠ *500 E. 30th St., at FDR Dr.,* ☎ *212/683–3333.*

Whiskey Park. This urbane candlelit outpost across the street from Central Park quickly established itself as a place to see and be seen. ⊠ *100 Central Park S, at 6th Ave.,* ☎ *212/307–9222.*

Upper East Side

American Trash. The name refers to the decor, not necessarily to the clientele: old pipes, bike wheels, and golf clubs line the walls and ceilings. ⊠ *1471 1st Ave., between 76th and 77th Sts.,* ☎ *212/988–9008.*

Auction House. There's a modest dress code (no baseball hats, no sneakers) at this Upper East Side lounge with high ceilings and candlelight, so the neighborhood crowd is a little better in appearance, and behavior, than usual. ⊠ *300 E. 89th St., between 1st and 2nd Aves.,* ☎ *212/427–4458.*

Dakota Southwestern Bar & Grill. A mix of yuppies fresh out of college and neighborhood lifers congregate around the 52-ft, 4-inch bar, one of the longest in Manhattan. ⊠ *1576 3rd Ave., between 88th and 89th Sts.,* ☎ *212/427–8889.*

Elaine's. The food's nothing special, and you will be relegated to an inferior table, but go to gawk; try going late at night, when the stars rise in Elaine's firmament. Woody Allen's favorite table is by the cappuccino machine. ⊠ *1703 2nd Ave., at 88th St.,* ☎ *212/534–8103.*

Luvbuzz. This lounge has a refreshingly (for the neighborhood) cool look. It also offers an in-house computerized dating service. ⊠ *1438 3rd Ave., between 81st and 82nd Sts.,* ☎ *212/717–0100.*

Metropolitan Museum of Art. On Friday and Saturday evening, until 9, unwind to the sounds of a string quartet at the Great Hall Balcony Bar. During the summer, be sure to visit the bar on the Iris and B. Gerald Cantor Roof Garden for a view of Central Park and the skyline that's as stunning as anything in the museum's vast collections. ⊠ *1000 5th Ave., at 82nd St.,* ☎ *212/879–5500.*

Upper West Side

Café des Artistes. George Lang's restaurant, as well known for its glorious Art Nouveau murals as for its food, has a small, warm bar where interesting strangers tell their life stories and the house drink is pear champagne. It is one of the city's special hideaways. ⊠ *1 W. 67th St., near Central Park W,* ☎ *212/877–3500.*

Gabriel's. This highly regarded Northern Italian restaurant has a cool, modern interior, a 35-ft curved mahogany bar, and a stupendous selection of grappas. Smoking is not permitted. ⊠ *11 W. 60th St., between Broadway and Columbus Ave.,* ☎ *212/956–4600.*

Hi-Life. Big with the neighborhood's bon vivants, this is a good stop for cocktails. ⊠ *477 Amsterdam Ave., at 83rd St.,* ☎ *212/787–7199.*

O'Neal's. Mike O'Neal, the owner of the beloved but now defunct Ginger Man, has created a series of rooms (one with a fireplace) serving good pub food. ⊠ *49 W. 64th St., between Central Park W and Broadway,* ☎ *212/787–4663.*

Peter's. A staple of the Upper West Side singles scene since the early 1980s, this vast, noisy bar and restaurant features copies of the wall paintings at Pompeii and an ambitious crowd in its late twenties and early thirties. ⊠ *182 Columbus Ave., between 68th and 69th Sts.,* ☎ *212/877–4747.*

Potion Lounge. More of a downtown spot than you'd expect in this neighborhood, this attractive lounge serves eye-catching, multicolor drinks, or "potions," to a slightly more mature crowd. ⊠ *370 Columbus Ave., between 77th and 78th Sts.,* ☎ *212/721–4386.*

Raccoon Lodge. Baseball caps and shirts with collars is the dress code for the mostly male, mostly fresh out of college crowd here. ⊠ *480 Amsterdam Ave., at 83rd St.,* ☎ *212/874–9984.*

Shark Bar. A classy, loungy kind of place, this bar fills with eye candy every night. ⊠ *307 Amsterdam Ave., between 75th and 76th Sts.,* ☎ *212/874–8500.*

Gay and Lesbian Bars

Any night of the week, gay men and lesbians can find plentiful entertainment of every description in New York City. The thriving community enjoys gay-specific theater, concerts, comedy, readings, dining, parties, dance clubs, bars, and just about every other way to spend free time. For advice on gay and lesbian life and organizations in New York, call the **Gay and Lesbian National Hotline** (☎ 212/989–0999) or stop by the **Lesbian and Gay Community Services Center** (temporarily located at ⊠ 1 Little W. 12th St., near 9th Ave., ☎ 212/620–7310, while its permanent home is being renovated). For listings of gay events and places, check out *Homo Xtra (HX)*, *Next*, *New York Blade*, *Time Out New York*, *MetroSource*, the *Village Voice*, and *Paper*.

Dance Clubs and Parties

Big Apple Ranch. You won't find house or disco beats at this mixed Saturday-night party. Instead you'll get country-western music, two-stepping, and, if you're there at 8, lessons. ⊠ *Dance Manhattan, 39 W. 19th St., between 5th and 6th Aves.,* ☎ *212/358–5752.*

Click and Drag. A periodic cyber-fetish party brought to you by some of the hippest party promoters in town, this phenomenon attracts a mixed gay and straight crowd. ⊠ *Fun, 130 Madison St., near Pike St.,* ☎ *212/929–6060.*

Clit Club. Fab chicks bump and grind along with gyrating go-go girls every Friday night at this steamy glamorama. Call first, because the party roves. ⊠ *Flamingo East, 219 2nd Ave., between 13th and 14th Sts.,* ☎ *212/529–3300.*

1984. On Friday at this long, narrow space, energetic guys relive the '80s in all its new-wave, syntho-trash glory. ⊠ *Pyramid, 101 Ave. A, between 6th and 7th Sts.,* ☎ *212/462–9077.*

Trannie Chaser. Three times a week, from Thursday to Saturday, Glorya Wholesome plays hostess for her transvestite girlfriends. ⊠ *Now Bar, 22 7th Ave. S, at Leroy St.,* ☎ *212/802–9502.*

Twilo. Saturday is the gay boys' night at this super-modern club. ⊠ *530 W. 27th St., between 10th and 11th Aves.,* ☎ *212/268–1600.*

Men's Bars

Barracuda. The comfy couches in back are the big draw at this Chelsea hangout, where the pool table also helps draw a crowd. ⊠ *275 W. 22nd St., between 7th and 8th Aves.,* ☎ *212/645–8613.*

Boiler Room A neighborhood hangout with a pool table, a jukebox, and cheap drinks, this East Village bar gets packed with twenty- and thirtysomething locals late weeknights and on the weekends. ⊠ *86 E. 4th St., between 1st and 2nd Aves.,* ☎ *212/254–7536.*

Cleo's 9th Avenue Saloon. Near the theater district, this small, narrow neighborhood bar draws a convivial, laid-back older crowd. ⊠ *656 9th Ave., at 46th St.,* ☎ *212/307–1503.*

g. A huge circular bar and two airy, relaxed rooms lined with leather settees bring an upscale, mostly male crowd to this Chelsea favorite. ⊠ *223 W. 19th St., between 7th and 8th Aves.,* ☎ *212/929–1085.*

The Lure. Here, at the ultimate parade of black leather, chains, and Levi's, the bark is always bigger than the bite. ⊠ *409 W. 13th St., between 9th Ave. and Washington St.,* ☎ *212/741–3919.*

The Monster. A long-standing West Village contender, the Monster has a piano bar upstairs and a pitch-black disco downstairs that continue to draw a busy blend of ages, races, and genders. ⊠ *80 Grove St., between 4th St. and 7th Ave. S,* ☎ *212/924–3558.*

Splash Bar. Most nights go-go dancers writhe in translucent shower cubicles at this large, perennially crowded Chelsea hangout. ⊠ *50 W. 17th St., between 5th and 6th Aves.,* ☎ *212/691–0073.*

Stonewall. With its odd assortment of down-to-earth locals and tourists chasing gay history (though the famed riots actually started at the original Stonewall, which used to be next door), the scene here is definitely democratic. ⊠ *53 Christopher St., near 7th Ave. S,* ☎ *212/463–0950.*

The Townhouse. On some nights it's like stepping into a Brooks Brothers catalog—cashmere sweaters, Rolex watches, distinguished-looking gentlemen—and it's surprisingly festive. ⊠ *236 E. 58th St., between 2nd and 3rd Aves.,* ☎ *212/754–4649.*

Ty's. Although its clientele is close-knit and fiercely loyal, this small, jeans-and-flannel neighborhood saloon never turns away friendly strangers. ⊠ *114 Christopher St., near Bleecker St.,* ☎ *212/741–9641.*

The Works. The crowd is usually J. Crew–style or disco hangover at this Upper West Side institution. ⊠ *428 Columbus Ave., between 80th and 81st Sts.,* ☎ *212/799–7365.*

Mixed Bars

hell. Tucked away on a quiet street in the groovy Meatpacking District, this swanky lounge—with crystal chandeliers and red drapes—attracts a hip, mixed crowd of Chelsea-ites and downtowners. ⊠ *59 Gansevoort St., between Washington and Greenwich Sts.,* ☎ *212/727–1666.*

Wonder Bar. A youngish, happening crowd fills this friendly, popular lounge that has low sofas, an elevated disk jockey booth, and hypnotic music on the speakers. ⊠ *505 E. 6th St., between Avenues A and B,* ☎ *212/777–9105.*

Women's Bars

Crazy Nanny's. The hairstyles here range from mullet to shaved head, and you'll find more of a racial mix than at most of Manhattan's lesbian bars. Different nights of the week have different themes and events. ⊠ *21 7th Ave. S, at Leroy St.,* ☎ *212/366–6312.*

Henrietta Hudson. A little more laid back than Crazy Nanny's, the home of the original Cubby Hole attracts young professionals, out-of-towners, and longtime regulars with its two rooms, a pool table, and party nights. ⊠ *438 Hudson St., at Morton St.,* ☎ *212/924–3347.*

Julie's. Geographically and psychically removed from its downtown sisters, this brownstone basement draws more of a midtown bridge-and-tunnel crowd. Thursday is networking night (good for newcomers), and there's dancing most every night, especially Sunday and Wednesday. ✉ *204 E. 58th St., between 2nd and 3rd Aves.,* ☎ *212/688–1294.*

Meow Mix. The East Village's only lesbian bar offers live music, literary readings, cheap drinks, and the cutest girls in town. The young, sometimes outrageous, crowd pushes the fashion envelope way out there. ✉ *269 E. Houston St., at Suffolk St.,* ☎ *212/254–0688.*

7 OUTDOOR ACTIVITIES AND SPORTS

The Yankees and Knicks frequently rank in the top of their leagues, bolstering the pride and bravado of New York's die-hard sports fans. Look at any newspaper in the hands of a subway rider, and most likely it's turned to the sports section. But this isn't just a city of fans. From billiards to rock climbing, no matter what the sport, there's a place to pursue it. Head to Central Park and join cyclists zooming by on thousand-dollar bikes, blissed-out runners circling the Reservoir, bird-watchers admiring the latest avian arrivals, and in-line skaters literally dancing in the streets.

Y OU'LL FIND OASES OF GREENERY all over New York—13% of the city, or approximately 27,000 acres, is parkland. And if you strike up a conversation while waiting to rent a boat or a bike at the Loeb Boathouse, while stretching before a jog around the reservoir in Central Park, or before sliding your kayak into the Hudson River, you'll discover a friendly, relaxed side of the city. Just one word before you set out: weekends are very busy. If you need to rent equipment or secure space—for instance, a tennis court—go very early, or be prepared to wait.

Updated by
Jennifer L.
Kasoff

BEACHES

Good weather brings sun-worshiping New Yorkers out in force. Early in the season the nearest park or even a rooftop (affectionately known as Tar Beach) is just fine for catching rays, but later on everyone heads for beaches in the city or on Long Island. Before you go, call to check on swimming conditions.

City Beaches

Brighton Beach, in a largely Russian community sometimes called "Odessa by the Sea," this Brooklyn strand is easily reached via the D or Q train. The tame waves of **Coney Island** (☎ 718/946–1350) are the closest many New Yorkers get to the surf all year. Across the street from the last Brooklyn stop on the B, D, F, and N lines, the beach here has the boardwalk and the famous amusement-park skyline of the Cyclone and the Wonderwheel as its backdrop and is busy every day the sun shines. To see surfers riding the waves in wet suits, venture out on the A train to the beaches in the **Rockaways** (☎ 718/318–4000) section of Queens— at 9th Street, 23rd Street, or between 80th and 118th streets.

Long Island

The Long Island Railroad provides easy access to all Long Island beaches. New Yorkers' favorite strand may be **Jones Beach** (☎ 516/785–1600), one of the world's great man-made beaches, built in the late 1920s under the reign of former parks commissioner Robert Moses. The train station nearest to Jones Beach is in Freeport, where you can catch a shuttle to the water. The LIRR will take you directly to suburban **Long Beach,** which has a wide boardwalk along an even wider beach. On the west end of Fire Island, a narrow barrier island that runs along the southern coast of Long Island, there's a good beach at **Robert Moses State Park** (☎ 631/669–0449), also reachable via the LIRR and a bus.

PARKS AND PLAYGROUNDS

The outdoor amusements never end in New York—except maybe during thunderstorms or snowstorms. But when the skies are clear, which is very often, New Yorkers of all ages seek out fun in the city's parks and playgrounds.

The biggest park of them all, of course, is **Central Park.** Central Park's 21 playgrounds are full of slides, bridges, bars, swings, towers, and tunnels; they're carpeted with sand or soft rubber matting and often cooled in summer by sprinklers or fountains. Good playgrounds can be found along 5th Avenue at 67th Street near the zoo, at 71st and 77th streets, at 85th Street near the Metropolitan Museum, and at 96th Street. Along Central Park West, the best ones are at 68th, 82nd, 85th,

93rd, and 96th streets. The **Hecksher Playground,** in Central Park at 62nd Street, is the park's largest.

The **Asser Levy Playground** (⊠ E. 23rd St., 1 block from East River) is the first in Manhattan to cater fully to children with disabilities, with giant, multicolor mazelike structures; helter-skelter slides with wheel-chair stations; and textured pavement for children who are blind. Top-rated by Manhattan kids is the playground at **Hudson River Park** (⊠ West St. south of Vesey St.), where whimsical, child-size bronze sculptures of people and animals are integrated into the parkscape. In **Riverside Park,** west of Riverside Drive, the best playgrounds are at 77th and 91st streets; the one at 77th Street has a circle of spouting elephant fountains. **Washington Square Park** (⊠ South end of 5th Ave., between Waverly Pl. and W. 4th St.) has a popular and shady playground, as well as jugglers, magicians, and musicians in summertime.

Coney Island in Brooklyn is well known for its amusement parks: **Astroland** (⊠ 1000 Surf Ave., ☏ 718/372–0275) and **Deno's Wonderwheel Park** (⊠ 1025 Boardwalk, ☏ 718/449–8836) offer a colorful and slightly seedy slice of Brooklyn. Admission to both is free; fares are $2–$4 per ride at Astroland (certain hours you can buy a $13.99 "Pay One Price" ticket to the rides) and $1.75 per ride or 10 rides for $15 at Deno's. Call in advance for information about the parks' hours, which vary seasonally.

PARTICIPANT SPORTS

For information about athletic facilities in Manhattan as well as a calendar of sporting events, pick up a copy of *MetroSports* at sporting goods stores or health clubs. The magazine also has a good Web site, www.metrosportsny.com. *Time Out New York,* sold at most newsstands, is a great resource: Its "Sports" section lists upcoming events, times, dates, and ticket information.

Bicycling

Even in tiny Manhattan apartments, many locals keep a bicycle for transportation—the brave ones swear it's the best (and fastest) way to get around—and for rides on glorious days. A sleek pack of dedicated racers zooms around Central Park at dawn and at dusk daily, and on weekends the parks swarm with recreational cyclists. **Central Park** has a 6-mi circular drive with a couple of decent climbs. It is closed to automobile traffic from 10 AM to 3 PM (except the southeast portion between 6th Avenue and East 72nd Street) and 7 PM to 10 PM on weekdays, and from 7 PM Friday to 6 AM Monday. On holidays it's closed to automobile traffic from 7 PM the night before until 6 AM the day after. The bike lane along the **Hudson River Park's esplanade,** which forms the beginning of Bike Route 9 (a route that runs north through the state), parallels the waterfront from 14th Street down to Battery Park. From there it's a quick ride to the Wall Street area, which is deserted on weekends, and over to South Street and a bike lane along the East River. The 3½-mi circular drive in Brooklyn's beautiful **Prospect Park** is closed to cars on weekends year-round and from 9 AM to 5 PM and 7 PM to 10 PM on weekdays from April to November. In **Riverside Park** the promenade between West 72nd and West 110th streets, with its Hudson River view, gets an easygoing crowd of slow-pedaling cyclists.

Bike Rentals

Expect to leave a deposit or a credit card when renting a bike. **Bicycle Rentals at Loeb Boathouse** (⊠ Loeb Boathouse, midpark near E. 74th

St., ☎ 212/517–2233) provides sturdy cycles for the whole family. **Larry's & Jeff's Bicycles Plus** (✉ 1690 2nd Ave., at 87th St., ☎ 212/722–2201) rents mountain bikes and hybrids. **Pedal Pusher** (✉ 1306 2nd Ave., between 68th and 69th Sts., ☎ 212/288–5592) has everything from three-speeds to racing bikes to hybrids in its rental fleet. **Toga Bike Shop** (✉ 110 West End Ave., at 64th St., ☎ 212/799–9625) offers all kinds of bikes.

Group Trips

For organized rides with other cyclists, call or write before you come to New York. The **Five Borough Bicycle Club** (✉ 891 Amsterdam Ave., at 103rd St., ☎ 212/932–2300 ext. 115, WEB www.5bbc.org) organizes day and weekend rides. **Bike New York** (✉ 891 Amsterdam Ave., at 103rd St., ☎ 212/932–2300 ext. 111) runs the five-borough bike ride in May. The **New York Cycle Club** (✉ Box 20541, Columbus Circle Station, 10023, ☎ 212/828–5711, WEB www.nycc.org) sponsors weekend rides for every level of ability. **Time's Up!** (☎ 212/802–8222, WEB www.times-up.org), a non-profit environmental group, leads free recreational rides at least twice a month for cyclists as well as skaters; the Central Park Moonlight Ride, departing from Columbus Circle at 10 PM the first Friday of every month, is a favorite. **Transportation Alternatives** (✉ 115 W. 30th St., between 6th and 7th Aves., Suite 1207, 10001-4010, ☎ 212/629–8080, WEB www.transalt.org) lists group rides throughout the metropolitan area in its bimonthly newsletter, which is distributed in many local bike stores.

Billiards

Pool halls used to be dusty, grimy, sticky places—and there are still a few of those around. But in New York they're outnumbered by a group of spots with deluxe decor, high prices, and even classical music or jazz in the background. Most halls are open late.

Amsterdam Billiard Club (✉ 344 Amsterdam Ave., between 76th and 77th Sts., ☎ 212/496–8180) can satisfy your hustling desires until 3 AM weekdays and 4 AM weekends—365 days a year. The club has 32 pool tables and a full bar. **Amsterdam Billiard Club East** (✉ 210 E. 86th St., between 2nd and 3rd Aves., ☎ 212/570–4545) has 29 pool tables, three Ping-Pong tables, a café, and a full bar. **Billiard Club** (✉ 220 W. 19th St., between 7th and 8th Aves., ☎ 212/206–7665), in Chelsea, has a classy look and loud rock music. **Chelsea Billiards** (✉ 54 W. 21st St., between 5th and 6th Aves., ☎ 212/989–0096) has 30 pool tables and three for snooker on two floors. **Corner Billiards** (✉ 85 4th Ave., at 11th St., ☎ 212/995–1314) draws a college crowd to its 28 tables. **East Side Amusements** (✉ 163 E. 86th St., between 3rd and Lexington Aves., ☎ 212/831–7665) has 11 tables, plus a video game arcade. **Soho Billiards** (✉ 56 E. Houston St., between Mott and Mulberry Sts., ☎ 212/925–3753) has a great location to attract weary bar hoppers.

Bird-Watching

Manhattan's green parks and woodlands provide habitats for thousands of birds, everything from fork-tailed flycatchers to common nighthawks. Because the city is on the Atlantic flyway, a major migratory route, you can see birds that nest as far north as the high Arctic. April and May are the best months. The songbirds are in their freshest colors then, and so many sing at once that you can hardly distinguish their songs. Fall is also an excellent season for birding in New York. To find out what's been seen where, call the very helpful and thorough **Rare Bird Alert** (☎ 212/979–3070)—fascinating to call once even if you don't give a hoot about birds. For information on the best bird-watching spots in city parks, call the **Urban Park Rangers** (☎ 212/360–2774, WEB www.nycparks.org), a uniformed division of the Parks Department.

The Ramble in Manhattan's **Central Park** is full of warblers in spring-time and may attract as many birders as it does birds. In Brooklyn, **Green-Wood Cemetery** (☎ 718/768–7300 for permission to enter grounds) features Victorian-era headstones, as well as a nice woodland that attracts hawks and songbirds. In Queens try **Jamaica Bay Wildlife Refuge,** where birds are drawn to the 9,155 acres of salt marshes, fresh and brackish ponds, open water, and upland fields and woods; stop by the **visitor center** (⊠ Crossbay Blvd., Broad Channel, Queens, ☎ 718/318–4340) to get a free permit. Birders will like 1,146-acre **Van Cortlandt Park** (☎ 718/430–1890), in the Bronx, with its varied habi-tats, including freshwater marshes and upland woods. In Staten Island head for the mostly undeveloped 312-acre **Wolfe's Pond Park** (☎ 718/984–8266), where the pond and the nearby shore can be dense with geese and ducks during the annual migrations.

Guided Walks

The **New York City Audubon Society** (⊠ 71 W. 23rd St., between 5th and 6th Aves., ☎ 212/691–7483) has frequent bird-watching outings; call weekdays 10–4 for information. Also check with the Urban Park Rangers at the number listed above.

Boating and Kayaking

Central Park has rowboats (plus one Venetian gondola for nighttime glides in the moonlight) on the 18-acre Central Park Lake. Rent your boat at **Loeb Boathouse** (☎ 212/517–2233), near East 74th Street, from spring through fall. **Floating the Apple** (⊠ W. 44th St. and the Hud-son River, ☎ 212/564–5412) has free rows and sails in community group–made boats from Pier 84. In **Prospect Park,** pedal boats can be rented at **Kate's Corner** (☎ 718/282–7789) at the Wollman Memorial Rink weekends and holidays from April through the end of October; 60-acre Prospect Lake is one of the city's largest bodies of water.

Try kayaking at the **Downtown Boathouse** (⊠ Pier 26, N. Moore St. and the Hudson River, ☎ 212/385–8169, WEB www.downtown-boathouse.org), where you can take a kayak out for a paddle free on summer weekends. **Manhattan Kayak Company** (⊠ Chelsea Piers, Pier 60, W. 23rd St. and the Hudson River, ☎ 212/336–6068) runs trips and gives lessons for all levels.

Bowling

AMF Chelsea Piers Bowling Center (⊠ Between Piers 59 and 60, W. 18th St. and the Hudson River, ☎ 212/835–2695) has 40 lanes and all the latest bowling trends—glow-in-the-dark and "extreme" bowl-ing—and fine finger foods. The funky **Bowlmor Lanes** (⊠ 110 University Pl., between 12th and 13th Sts., ☎ 212/255–8188) is a 42-lane bi-level operation (with bar) frequented by a colorful Village crowd; many stay until closing time, as late as 4 AM a few nights a week. After 6 PM it's strictly 21-plus. The **Leisure Time Bowling & Recreation Center** (⊠ Port Authority Bus Terminal, south bldg., 2nd level, W. 42nd St. and 8th Ave., ☎ 212/268–6909) offers 30 lanes and New York's most tradi-tional bowling-alley atmosphere.

Boxing

Chelsea Piers Sports Center (⊠ W. 23rd St. and the Hudson River, ☎ 212/336–6000) has a boxing ring and equipment circuit. **Crunch Fit-ness** (⊠ 404 Lafayette St., at 4th St., ☎ 212/614–0120) gives classes in its boxing ring. Brooklyn's venerable **Gleason's** (⊠ 75 Front St., between Washington and Main Sts., ☎ 718/797–2872), home of more than 100 world champs, including Muhammad Ali, instructs visitors and allows spectators for a small fee. Don't miss the monthly White Collar Fight Night; it's exactly what it sounds like.

Chess and Checkers

In **Central Park,** the Chess & Checkers House perches atop a massive stone outcrop. Twenty-four outdoor tables are available during daylight hours. Bring your own or pick up playing pieces at the **Dairy** (⊠ Midpark at 64th St., ☎ 212/794–6564) Tuesday–Sunday 11–5; there is no charge, but a photo ID is required. The **Manhattan Chess Club** (⊠ The New Yorker Hotel, 481 8th Ave., Room 1521, between 34th and 35th Sts., ☎ 212/333–5888) sponsors tournaments and exhibitions. Visitors are welcome here for casual play. Downtown, the **Village Chess Shop** (⊠ 230 Thompson St., between Bleecker and 3rd Sts., ☎ 212/475–9580) has 30 boards that it rents by the hour for play in the store, along with timers for speed chess. Outdoor players congregate at the tables in the southwest corner of **Washington Square Park** (⊠ W. 4th and MacDougal Sts.) where, for a small donation to the regulars, you can borrow pieces and a timer. You can even play against the people in charge—who are very skilled chess players.

Dance and Cardio

Chelsea Piers Sports Center (⊠ W. 23rd St. and the Hudson River, ☎ 212/336–6000) sells a day pass for $40 that includes access to all the impressive facilities and classes this sports behemoth has to offer. **Crunch Fitness** (⊠ 404 Lafayette St., at 4th St., ☎ 212/614–0120; 54 E. 13th St., between Broadway and University Pl., ☎ 212/475–2018; 162 W. 83rd St., between Columbus and Amsterdam Aves., ☎ 212/875–1902; 1109 2nd Ave., at 59th St., ☎ 212/758–3434, and other locations) offers everything from straight-up cardio to kickboxing, yoga, pilates, and body sculpting. **New York Sports Clubs** (⊠ 30 Wall St., ☎ 212/482–4800; 1601 Broadway, at 49th St., ☎ 212/977–8880; 200 Madison Ave., at 36th St., ☎ 212/686–1144; 125 7th Ave. S, at 10th St., ☎ 212/206–1500; and other locations) are well equipped and offer conditioning and strength-training classes at times and locations likely to suit any travel schedule. The **Vanderbilt YMCA** (⊠ 224 E. 47th St., between 2nd and 3rd Aves., ☎ 212/756–9600) schedules more than 100 drop-in exercise classes every week. Day passes are available at all of these clubs.

Golf

Bethpage State Park (☎ 516/249–0700; 516/249–0707 for reservations), on the outskirts of the Long Island town of Farmingdale, about 1¼ hours from Manhattan, is home to five well-groomed golf courses, including its 7,295-yard, par-71 Black Course, generally ranked among the nation's top 25 public courses. All five courses are busy seven days a week; reservations can be made up to two days in advance. Greens fees for the five courses range from $24 to $39; electric carts are available on four of the courses for $27. There is also a driving range.

Queens has a 6,300-yard, par-70 course at **Forest Park** (⊠ 101 Forest Park Dr., ☎ 718/296–0999), in Woodhaven. The greens fee at Forest Park runs $19–$21.50; a cart costs $25–$26. Staten Island has the 6,050-yard, par-69 **Silver Lake Golf Course** (⊠ 915 Victory Blvd., 1 block south of Forest Ave., ☎ 718/447–5686). The greens fee is $19; a cart costs $12.50. Of the 14 city courses, the 6,281-yard, par-72 **Split Rock** (⊠ 870 Shore Rd., ☎ 718/885–1258) in Pelham Bay Park in the Bronx is the most challenging. Slightly easier is its sister course, the 6,405-yard, par-70 Pelham, which has fewer trees. Both courses cost $19–$27 plus $25 for a cart. Van Cortlandt Park, in the Bronx, has the nation's first public golf course, established in 1895, the hilly 6,102-yard, par-70 **Van Cortlandt** (⊠ Bailey Ave., ☏ 718/543–4595). The greens fee runs $19–$27, and a cart costs $25.

Driving Ranges

Jutting out into the Hudson, the **Golf Club at Chelsea Piers** (⊠ Pier 59, W. 23rd St. and the Hudson River, ☏ 212/336–6400) has a 200-yard artificial-turf fairway, a computerized tee-up system, and heated hitting stalls—so you can keep driving balls even in winter. **Bethpage State Park** has a driving range in addition to its five golf courses. **Family Golf Center at Randall's Island** has a 325-yard driving range with 80 heated stalls.

Miniature Golf

The 18-hole outdoor course at **Pier 25** (⊠ Hudson River at Reade St., ☏ 212/732–7467), open seasonally, has a great riverside location and fabulous fresh lemonade. **Family Golf Center at Randall's Island** (⊠ Randall's Island, ☏ 212/427–5689) has two 18-hole courses and a driving range; a shuttle bus from 3rd Ave. between 86th and 87th streets will get you there.

Horseback Riding

A trot on the bridle path around Central Park's reservoir provides a pleasant look at New York. The **Claremont Riding Academy** (⊠ 175 W. 89th St., between Columbus and Amsterdam Aves., ☏ 212/724–5100) is the city's oldest riding academy (established in 1892). Experienced English riders can rent horses for an unescorted walk, trot, or canter in nearby Central Park; call ahead to reserve, preferably a week in advance. The **Chelsea Equestrian Center** (⊠ Pier 63, Westside Hwy. at W. 23rd St., ☏ 212/367–9090) rents to the general public (English and Western saddles available) for rides on indoor and outdoor rings.

Ice-Skating

Each of the city's rinks has its own character, and all have scheduled skating sessions. Central Park's **Lasker Rink** (⊠ Midpark near 106th St., ☏ 212/534–7639), at the north end of the park, is smaller and usually less crowded than Wollman Memorial Rink. The outdoor rink in **Rockefeller Center** (⊠ 50th St. at 5th Ave., lower plaza, ☏ 212/332–7654) is fairly small yet utterly romantic, especially when the enormous Christmas tree towers above it. If you're a self-conscious skater, note that there are huge crowds watching. Chelsea Piers' **Sky Rink** (⊠ Pier 61, W. 23rd St. and the Hudson River, ☏ 212/336–6100) has two year-round indoor rinks overlooking the Hudson; one is almost always open for general skating, and the other hosts leagues, lessons, and special events. The beautifully situated **Wollman Memorial Rink** (⊠ 6th Ave. at 59th St., north of park entrance, ☏ 212/396–1010), in Central Park, offers skating beneath the lights of the city. Be prepared for crowds on weekends. Prospect Park has its own **Kate Wollman Memorial Rink** (⊠ Ocean Ave. and Parkside Ave., ☏ 718/287–6431) surrounded by trees.

In-Line Skating

The in-line skating craze has died down a bit in New York as scooters take over the streets. But you'll still find plenty of places to go for a whirl—and plenty of company. **Blades** has several Manhattan stores, including East (⊠ 160 E. 86th St., between 3rd and Lexington Aves., ☏ 212/996–1644), West (⊠ 120 W. 72nd St., between Broadway and

REALLY BIG SHOWS

NEW YORK CITY hosts dozens of major annual sporting events throughout the year. If your visit coincides with one of them, it's worth checking out the spectacle.

Winter

Manhattan is an island, after all, so it shouldn't come as too much of a surprise that the **New York National Boat Show** (☎ 212/216–2000) in January at the Javits Center draws fans from across the country. Stop by to fulfill your Coast Guard-inspired fantasies, or simply to dream about yachting around the world.

Did the movie *Best of Show* pique your interest? Simply missing Fido while you're vacationing in the Big Apple? You'll be barking for a walk to Madison Square Garden for February's **Westminster Kennel Club Dog Show** (☎ 212/465–6741).

Ladies and gentlemen, start your engines . . . and head straight to the **New York International Motorcycle Show** (☎ 212/216–2000), held at the Javits Center in February. Hulking bikes of all varieties will be on display.

Spring

Bring in the clowns! Spring (usually March/April) means the **Ringling Bros. and Barnum & Bailey Circus** (☎ 212/465–6741) is coming to town. Head to Madison Square Garden for a peak at the high-wire fun.

Duck inside on a rainy April day to see the **New York International Auto Show** (☎ 212/216–2000) at the Javits Center. Hundreds of the latest, hottest cars, along with auto oddities, are celebrated each year.

Summer

If you're visiting in late August/early September and the F train seems unusually crowded, here's why: the **U.S. Open Tennis Tournament** (☎ 718/760–6200) is rocking Flushing Meadows-Corona Park in Queens. The crowd's love for this end-of-the-summer tournament translates into one of the most exciting tennis events of the year.

Fall

Even if your idea of an intense workout is battling the biddies in Bloomingdale's, don't miss the **New York City Marathon** (☎ 212/860–4455) if you're in town at the right time (usually the first Sunday of November). Vantage points around the city fill up fast, so get there early and be ready with small treats for the runners (orange sections and bite-size banana pieces will be greatly appreciated).

After you've trotted through Central Park, follow the bridle path to November's **National Horse Show** (☎ 212/465–6741) at Madison Square Garden. All things equine have gathered in the city for this show for more than 115 years.

–Jennifer L. Kasoff

Columbus Ave., ☎ 212/787–3911), and TriBeCa (✉ 128 Chambers St., between West Broadway and Church Sts., ☎ 212/964–1944). They sell and rent skates along with all the protective gear. **Empire Skate Club** (☎ 212/774–1774) runs skate trips for members and fields skating questions. **Peck & Goodie** (✉ 917 8th Ave., at 54th St., ☎ 212/246–6123) sells and rents skates. Skaters are welcome on all **Time's Up!** (☎ 212/802–8222) bike rides.

Central Park is headquarters for city skaters. Most skaters seem to prefer circling the park, though not everyone is strong enough to make it up the hill at the park's northwest corner; to skip it, take the cutoff near 103rd Street. On weekends, between the Mall and Bethesda Fountain, dancing skaters whirl and twirl to disco music emanating from the huge speakers they set up. On weekends from April through October the **Central Park Skate Patrol** (☎ 212/439–1234) holds $20 clinics for skaters of all levels. Call for times and registration information. The **Hudson River Park Esplanade,** from West 14th Street down to Battery Park, is packed with skaters on warm days.

The two outdoor roller rinks at the **Chelsea Piers** complex (✉ Pier 62, W. 23rd St. and the Hudson River, ☎ 212/336–6200) have free skates, classes, Rollaerobics, and hip-hop dance parties. There's also a skate park, with ramps, half-pipes, rails, and other in-line challenges; it's open to skateboarders as well. The **Roxy** (✉ 515 W. 18th St., between 10th and 11th Aves., ☎ 212/645–5156), a downtown dance club, goes roller-disco on Tuesday and Wednesday nights. You must be 21 or older to enter.

Jogging and Racewalking

Jogging

All kinds of New Yorkers jog, some with dogs or babies in tow. Publicity notwithstanding, crime is not a problem as long as you jog when and where everybody else does. On Manhattan streets, figure 20 north–south blocks per mile.

In Manhattan, **Central Park** is the busiest spot, specifically along the 1⅗-mi track circling the **Jacqueline Kennedy Onassis Reservoir.** A runners' lane has been designated along the park roads. A good 1¾-mi route starts at Tavern on the Green along the West Drive, heads south around the bottom of the park to the East Drive, and circles back west on the 72nd Street park road to your starting point; the entire loop road is a hilly 6 mi. **Riverside Park,** along the Hudson River bank in Manhattan, is glorious at sunset. You can cover 4½ mi by running from 72nd to 116th Street and back.

Other favorite Manhattan circuits are the **Battery Park City Esplanade** (about 1⅕ mi), the **East River Esplanade** (just over 3 mi from 59th to 125th Street), and along the **Hudson River Park Esplanade** (about 1½ mi). Tiny, but pleasant loops are around **Gramercy Park** (⅕ mi) and **Washington Square Park** (½ mi). In Brooklyn try the **Brooklyn Heights Promenade** (⅓ mi), which faces the Manhattan skyline, or the loop in **Prospect Park** (3⅓ mi).

The **New York Road Runners Club** (✉ 9 E. 89th St., between Madison and 5th Aves., ☎ 212/860–4455) organizes a year-round schedule of races and group runs. The latter begin at 6:30 AM and 6:30 PM on weekdays and at 10 AM on weekends, at the club kiosk along the bridal path near the Central Park entrance at East 90th Street and 5th Avenue. The runs are open to runners—members or not—of all levels. At the 4-mi Midnight Run, held on New Year's Eve in Central Park, runners show up wearing costumes, and the night culminates with fireworks. The New York City Marathon is the club's best-known event.

The **Hash House Harriers** organize runs with a purpose: they always end up at a bar. There's usually more than one run in New York City each week. Call ☎ 212/427–4692 for times, fees, and locations.

Racewalking

Racewalkers can move as fast as some joggers, the great difference being that their heels are planted firmly with every stride. A number of competitive racewalking events are held regularly. For information contact the **Park Race Walkers' Club** (✉ mailing address: 320 E. 83rd St., 10028, ☎ 212/628–1317).

Rock Climbing

For rock jocks and beginners alike, New York's indoor climbing walls offer hand-cramping challenges of the vertical sort. Lessons and equipment rentals (harness and climbing shoes) are available at the walls listed below, and experienced climbers should expect to take a belay test before they're free to belay their partners. You can usually find a partner if you're solo. **Chelsea Piers** (✉ W. 23rd St. and the Hudson River, ☎ 212/336–6000) has two climbing areas: a 30-ft wall in the field house designed for children (but adults are welcome, too), and a 46-footer plus separate bouldering wall in the Sports Center. Both allow nonmembers, though the day rate is higher in the Sports Center. The **Extra Vertical Climbing Center** (✉ 61 W. 62 St., at Broadway, ☎ 212/586–5718) has an indoor-outdoor (covered) wall ranging from 30 to 50 ft high. Taking a climb above Broadway's jumble of honking taxis and gawking pedestrians is an only-in-NYC experience worth seeking out. It's a great place to watch, and they have a $9 "challenge" package for beginners that includes instruction, equipment, and two climbs.

Swimming

Asphalt Green (✉ York Ave. between 90th and 92nd Sts., ☎ 212/369–8890) has a breathtaking 50-meter pool (known as AquaCenter), which is usually sectioned off into 25-yard and 20-yard lap areas, and a full fitness center; the daily drop-in fee is $20 for either the pool or the fitness center. The **Carmine Recreation Center** (✉ 7th Ave. S and Clarkson St., ☎ 212/242–5228) has a 23-yard indoor pool and a 105-yard outdoor pool (only one is open at a time). For the $25 annual membership fee, you can use the pool and take advantage of fitness facilities and classes. Bring your own padlock, towel, and shower shoes; it's a no-frills kind of place. **Chelsea Piers Sports Center** (✉ Pier 60, W. 23rd St. and the Hudson River, ☎ 212/336–6000) has a six-lane, 25-yard lap pool surrounded by windows overlooking the Hudson, with an adjacent whirlpool and sundeck. Day passes for the exercise club, including the pool, are $40. The Vanderbilt **YMCA** (✉ 224 E. 47th St., between 2nd and 3rd Aves., ☎ 212/756–9600) has two clean, brightly lighted lap pools open to nonmembers for a $25 day fee. The **YWCA** (✉ 610 Lexington Ave., at 53rd St., ☎ 212/755–4500) has a sparkling 25-yard lap pool available at $15.

Tennis

The New York City Parks Department maintains scores of tennis courts. Some of the most scenic are the 26 clay courts and four hard courts in **Central Park** (✉ Midpark near 96th St., ☎ 212/280–0206), set in a thicket of trees with the skyline beyond. Admission is available without reservations or seasonal permits, for $5 per hour April through November.

The **USTA National Tennis Center** (✉ Flushing Meadows–Corona Park, Queens, ☎ 718/760–6200), site of the U.S. Open Tournament, has 42 courts (33 outdoor and 9 indoor, all Deco Turf II) open to the public all year except August and September. Reservations are accepted up to two days in advance, and prices are $15–$44 hourly, depending on which courts you reserve and when you play.

Several local clubs will book courts to nonmembers: **Crosstown Tennis** (⊠ 14 W. 31st St., between 5th and 6th Aves., ☎ 212/947–5780) has four indoor hard courts; fees range from $39 to $60. **HRC Tennis** (⊠ Piers 13 and 14, East River at Wall St., ☎ 212/422–9300) has eight Har-Tru courts under two bubbles. Off-peak play goes for $50 per hour, but peak times cost as much as $120 per hour. HRC Tennis also owns **Village Tennis Courts** (⊠ 110 University Pl., between 12th and 13th Sts., ☎ 212/989–2300), with two hard rubber courts. Hourly fees can be up to $110. **Manhattan Plaza Racquet Club** (⊠ 450 W. 43rd St., between 9th and 10th Aves., ☎ 212/594–0554) has five hard-surface courts and some famous regulars. The hourly fee for same-day reservations is $45 or $75, but the hours nonmembers can play are limited. At **Midtown Tennis Club** (⊠ 341 8th Ave., between 26th and 27th Sts., ☎ 212/989–8572) it's best to make reservations for one of their eight courts (some outdoor in summer, bubbled in winter) a couple of days in advance. Hourly rates are $40–$75.

Yoga

Has the pace of New York City gotten you wound up? Are you yearning to stretch your limbs and get in touch with your body? Yoga centers across the city offer classes with reasonable drop-in rates. The **Integral Yoga Institute** (⊠ 227 W. 13th St., between 7th and 8th Aves., ☎ 212/929–0586) offers drop-in classes every day of the week at all levels for varying prices. **Jivamukti Yoga Center** (⊠ 404 Lafayette St., between Astor Pl. and E. 4th St., ☎ 212/353–0214) lends a downtown vibe to your yoga. Be sure to take in one of this center's open, basic, or Astanga classes that last 1 hour and 35 minutes. Evening sessions fill up fast; arrive early to secure your $17 spot. Yoga classes may include meditation and chanting. The soothingly decorated **Soho Sanctuary** (⊠ 119 Mercer St., between Prince and Spring Sts., ☎ 212/334–5550), for women only, is truly rejuvenating. Yoga classes are offered every day but Monday. You must make a reservation for the class you want. The one-class rate of $20 includes use of the steam bath. **Yoga Zone** (⊠ 160 E. 56th St., between Lexington and 3rd Aves., ☎ 212/935–9642; 138 5th Ave., at 19th St., ☎ 212/647–9642) has a full schedule of group classes at both locations. A single class costs $20.

SPECTATOR SPORTS

No doubt about it, New York is a city of sports fans. Basketball, baseball, football, hockey—you name it, NYC fields at least one team in every major pro sport. And they're some of the winningest teams around, as local fans will constantly remind you.

Arenas

Many sporting events—ranging from boxing to figure skating—take place at **Madison Square Garden** (⊠ 7th Ave. between 31st and 33rd Sts.); tickets can be purchased in person at the **box office** (☎ 212/465–6741) or by phone through **Ticketmaster** (☎ 212/307–7171). Several New York pro teams, including its two football teams, a basketball team, and a hockey team, play across the Hudson River at the **Meadowlands Sports Complex** (⊠ Rte. 3 and New Jersey Tpke. Exit 16W, East Rutherford, NJ, ☎ 201/935–3900 for box office and information), which includes the **Continental Airlines Arena** and **Giants Stadium**. Whenever there's a game, buses run directly from the Port Authority Bus Terminal in Manhattan. When events are sold out, on the day of the game you can sometimes pick up a ticket outside any of these venues from a fellow sports fan. Ticket agencies, listed in the Manhattan Yellow Pages and the sports pages of the *Daily News,* can be helpful— for a price.

Baseball

Fans still talk about the Subway Series of 2000. With two champions, New Yorkers are rightfully proud of their baseball teams. The **New York Mets** play at **Shea Stadium** (⊠ Roosevelt Ave. off Grand Central Pkwy., ☎ 718/507–8499), at the penultimate stop on the No. 7 train, in Flushing, Queens. Start spreading the news: the **New York Yankees** reigned supreme in the 1996, 1998, 1999, and 2000 World Series. See them play at **Yankee Stadium** (⊠ 161st St. and River Ave., ☎ 718/293–6000), accessible by the No. 4 or D train to the 161st Street station in the Bronx. *Yankee Clipper* and *Mets Express* ferries (New York Waterways) also cruise from Manhattan's east side to the respective stadiums on game nights. The regular baseball season runs from April through September.

Basketball

The **New York Knicks** arouse intense hometown passions, which means tickets for home games at Madison Square Garden are *extremely* hard to come by. For up-to-date game roundups, phone the New York Knicks Fan Line (☎ 212/465–5867). The **New Jersey Nets,** the New York area's other NBA team, play at the Meadowlands in the Continental Airlines Arena. For tickets—which are remarkably easy to obtain—call the **Meadowlands box office** (☎ 201/935–3900) or **Ticketmaster** (☎ 201/507–8900). The men's basketball season goes from late October through April.

The **Liberty** (☎ 212/465–6741 for tickets; 212/564–9622 fan hotline), New York's Women's National Basketball Association team captured the 1999 and 2000 Eastern Conference Championships. Some of the team's more high-profile players are already legendary. In the stands you'll see many more women and girls than usually attend pro sports games, and there are followers who believe the women play a more skilled game than the guys. The season, from mid-June through August, fills a traditionally slow time for Madison Square Garden.

Boxing

Major and minor boxing bouts are staged in Madison Square Garden. **Church Street Boxing Gym** (⊠ 25 Park Pl., between Church St. and Broadway, ☎ 212/962–5046) has amateur boxing and kickboxing fights on some Friday nights.

Football

The enormously popular **New York Giants** (☎ 201/935–8111 for tickets) play at Giants Stadium in the Meadowlands Sports Complex. Most seats for Giants games are sold on a season-ticket basis—and there's a very long waiting list for those. However, single tickets are occasionally available at the stadium box office. The **New York Jets** (☎ 516/560–8200 tickets; 516/560–8288 fan club) play at Giants Stadium. Although they're not as scarce as Giants tickets, most Jets tickets are snapped up by fans before the season opener. The football season runs from September through December.

Hockey

The **New Jersey Devils** fight for the puck at the Continental Airlines Arena at the Meadowlands. The **New York Islanders** (☎ 631/888–9000 for tickets) skate at Nassau Veterans Memorial Coliseum in Uniondale, Long Island. The **New York Rangers** (☎ 212/308–6977 for Rangers hot line) play at Madison Square Garden. Tickets for the Islanders and Devils are usually available at game time; Rangers tickets are more difficult to find. The hockey season runs from October through April.

Horse Racing

Modern **Aqueduct Racetrack** (✉ 110th St. and Rockaway Blvd., Ozone Park, Queens, ☎ 718/641–4700), with its abundant lawns and gardens, holds Thoroughbred races from late October to early May, Wednesday–Sunday. In May the action moves from Aqueduct Racetrack to **Belmont Park** (✉ Hempstead Tpke., Elmont, Long Island, ☎ 718/641–4700), home of the third jewel in horse racing's triple crown, the Belmont Stakes. The horses run here May–June and late August through October, Wednesday–Sunday. The **Meadowlands** (☎ 201/935–8500 for race information) has Thoroughbred racing from September to mid-December and harness racing the rest of the year (from late December to mid-August). **Yonkers Raceway** (✉ Yonkers and Central Aves., Yonkers, ☎ 718/562–9500) features harness racing every evening except Sunday year-round.

Running

Since 1970 the **New York City Marathon** has rocked the city each year, on a Sunday in early November. It's grown to involve some 2 million spectators cheering on the pack of more than 30,000 international participants (some 96% of whom finish). World-class marathoners, racewalkers, senior citizens, competitors with disabilities, runners in costume, and thousands of volunteers help to make this an incredibly spirited event. Spectators line rooftops and sidewalks, promenades, and terraces along the route, which covers ground in all five boroughs. Just don't go near the finish line in Central Park around 2 PM unless you relish mob scenes. Contact the **New York Road Runners Club** (✉ 9 E. 89th St., between Madison and 5th Aves., ☎ 212/860–4455).

Soccer

Since 1996 the tristate area has had a national major-league soccer team, the **MetroStars.** Games take place at Giants Stadium from April to September. Tickets are easy to get, ☎ 201/583-7000.

Tennis

The annual **U.S. Open Tournament,** held from late August through early September at the **USTA National Tennis Center** (✉ Flushing Meadows–Corona Park, Queens, ☎ 718/760–6200), is one of the high points of the tennis buff's year, and tickets to watch the late rounds are some of the hottest in town. Early round matches are entertaining, too, and with a stadium-court ticket you can also view matches in outlying courts. The championships are played at the 23,000-seat Arthur Ashe Stadium. Tickets go on sale in May through **Tele-charge** (☎ 888/673–6849).

The tennis year winds up with the **WTA Tournament Championships** (☎ 212/465–6521), a major women's pro event held at Madison Square Garden in mid-November. Tickets go on sale in September.

8 SHOPPING

True to its nature, New York shops on a grand scale, at the world's finest department stores, glossy couture houses along Madison Avenue, renowned antiques dealers all over town, and fashion-forward SoHo boutiques. The East Village and the Lower East Side are getting busier by the minute. NoLita practically steams with chic, its streets full of upstart clothing lines and exotic home-design stores, and hip retailers continue to waft into Chelsea. No matter which threshold you cross, shopping in New York is, more than ever, an event.

Updated by
Amanda
Freeman

THERE'S SOMETHING FOR EVERYONE in every price range in New York. Do you have a sudden yearning for Japanese stress-reduction chewing gum? Head to Daily 235. Looking for vintage Pucci? Resurrection can set you up nicely. How about a handsome set of English darts? Darts Shoppe Ltd. is your destination.

One of Manhattan's biggest shopping lures is the bargain—a temptation fueled by the opening of Loehmann's, H&M, and other discount divas. Hawkers of not-so-real Rolex watches and Kate Spade bags are stationed at street corners (even on Madison Avenue), and Canal Street is lined with counterfeit Gucci logos and Burberry plaid. There are uptown thrift shops where well-known socialites send their castoffs, and downtown spots where the fashion crowd turns in last week's supertrendy must-haves to free up more closet space. In any given week (particularly mid-winter or early summer), designers' showroom sales and sample sales allow you to buy cheap at the source; auctions promise good prices as well.

Sales

Sales take place late June and July (for summer merchandise) and late December and January (for winter wares); these sales are announced in the papers. Be sure to check out *New York* magazine's "Sales and Bargains" column, which often lists sales in manufacturers' showrooms that are not otherwise promoted publicly, and *Time Out New York*'s "Shoptalk" page, which includes sales. The *Village Voice* is also a good source for tip-off sale ads.

Shopping Neighborhoods

New York City does not have a mall culture (the closest thing you'll find are the underground promenades below Rockefeller Center, the World Financial Center, and Grand Central Terminal)—although some New Yorkers complain that some chain-store-packed neighborhoods are beginning to resemble malls, without the food courts or free parking. So save the chain stores for home, and seek out the shops that are unique to New York, or at least unique to the world's shopping capitals. Stores tend to cluster in a few main neighborhoods, which makes shopping a good way to get to know the area. And, if you head off in search of an outlying store, you may end up discovering something else—new boutiques are constantly springing up, even on previously deserted streets. Below are the shopping highlights in each neighborhood from south to north. Addresses for shops, if not included in these rundowns, can be found in the store listings later in the chapter.

South Street Seaport

The past few years at the Seaport have been choppy. The Fulton Market Building, once a linchpin, is closed, as developers plan for the future. For now most shops are located along the cobbled, pedestrians-only extension to Fulton Street and on the three levels of Pier 17. Stores here tend toward the comfortably familiar. There is a sizeable **Abercrombie & Fitch** (⊠ 199 Water St., ☎ 212/889–9000) for plaid shirts and jeans. A branch of **Coach** leather goods is in the Seaport, and **J. Crew** is in one of the Seaport's former waterfront hotels. Pier 17 has few surprises, but there are some few-of-a-kind shops, including **Mariposa** (☎ 212/233–3221), for rare butterflies mounted under Lucite.

World Financial Center

The World Financial Center, due west across the West Side Highway from the World Trade Center (cross directly from one to the other via the pedestrian walkway above the highway), may yet emerge as a shopping and cultural destination in its own right. Beyond the elevator banks of such financial giants as Merrill Lynch and clustered around the huge marble-cloaked Winter Garden, which is the architectural centerpiece here, are suitably chichi stores such as a small **Barneys New York,** for clothing. There is a **Rizzoli** for books and magazines.

Lower East Side and the East Village

Once home to millions of Jewish immigrants from Russia and Eastern Europe, the Lower East Side has traditionally been New Yorkers' bargain beat. The center of it all is Orchard Street. The spirit of "Have I got a bargain for you!" still fills the narrow street crammed with tiny, no-nonsense clothing and lingerie stores and open stalls. A lot of the merchandise here is of dubious quality, but there are some finds to be made. The gentrification of the Lower East Side has introduced groovy boutiques—now you can check out everything for the modern lifestyle at **Zao** and high-tech fashion at **DDC Lab.** Among the Orchard Street veterans, essential stops include **Fine & Klein,** for handbags; **Forman's,** for women's clothing; **Marcoart** (⌧ 186 Orchard St., ☎ 212/253–1070), for colorful, cartooned tees and tanks; and the lovely **Klein's of Monticello,** for deals on dressy clothes. Off Orchard Street, Grand Street (south of Delancey Street) is chockablock with linens, towels, and other items for the home; the Bowery between Grand and Delancey streets, with lamps and lighting fixtures. Many shops on or near Orchard sell candy, nuts, dried fruit, and Israeli sweets. Ludlow Street, one block east of Orchard, is buzzing with little storefronts selling hipster gear such as electric guitars, vintage '60s and '70s furniture, and clothing and accessories from local designers. To the north, the East Village offers diverse, offbeat specialty stops, plenty of collectible kitsch, and some great vintage-clothing boutiques, especially along East 7th and East 9th Streets. Note: most shops along Orchard Street are closed on Saturday.

NoLita

This Nabokovian nickname, shorthand for "*North of Little Italy,*" describes a neighborhood that has taken over where SoHo left off—both were once edgy neighborhoods that have gone from deserted, locals-only areas to crowded weekend shopping destinations. NoLita's parallel north-south spines are Elizabeth, Mott, and Mulberry streets, between Houston and Kenmare streets. Tiny boutiques (as well as similarly diminutive but generally good eateries) continue to sprout like mushrooms after rain. Among the small, funky housewares and design shops is **Shi.** The clothing stores are equally stylish. A cache of shops—**Jade, Calypso,** and **Tracy Feith**—is rife with exotic glamour. There are oh-so trendy handbags at **Jamin Peuch** and **Blue Bag,** swank shoes at **Sigerson Morrison,** and perfectly tailored shirts at **Seize sur Vingt.**

SoHo

Once abandoned, then lined with artists' studios and galleries, the mad, commerce-filled streets of SoHo are now packed with high-rent fashion boutiques. A flock of makeup stores has swept in, including **Helena Rubenstein, Shiseido Studio,** and French import **Sephora.** Big fashion guns such as **Vivienne Westwood, Louis Vuitton, Bottega Veneta,** and **Prada Sport** also established themselves, raising local retail a notch above the secondary-line couture places, such as **D&G** and **Miu Miu.** Much to the distress of many locals, the mall element (**Victoria's Secret, Old Navy, J. Crew, French Connection,** and many more) has a firm foothold; however, there are still many unique shops, especially for housewares and fashion. For double take–worthy clothes, recent additions **Kirna Zabette** and **R by 45 rpm** hone two very different creative edges.

Some well-known stops include **Dean & DeLuca,** a gourmet food emporium; **Zona** and **Moss,** full of well-designed home furnishings and gifts; and the hallucinatory **Enchanted Forest** toy store. On Lafayette Street below Houston Street, a fashionable strip includes shops outside the mainstream, dealing in urban streetwear and vintage 20th-century furniture. Many SoHo stores are open seven days a week.

Chelsea and the Flatiron District

Fifth Avenue south of 23rd Street, along with the streets fanning east and west, is home to a lively downtown shopping scene. In stores here, you'll find a mix of the hip, such as **Emporio Armani, Intermix,** and **Paul Smith,** and the hard-core, such as the mega-discounter **Loehmann's** on 7th Avenue. Broadway has a smattering of stores dear to New Yorkers' hearts, including the richly overstuffed **ABC Carpet & Home** and the comprehensive **Paragon Sporting Goods.** In the teens on 6th Avenue is a cluster of superstores, including the colossal **Bed, Bath & Beyond.** Several blocks west, between 10th and 11th Avenues, a few intrepid retailers, such as the cutting-edge **Comme des Garçons,** are popping up amid the flourishing art galleries in what was until recently the desolate fringe of Chelsea. Further south, the Meatpacking District—an area that until the late 1990s was home primarily to biker bars, after-hours clubs, and suppliers to the city's steak houses—has become newly chic, thanks to high-fashion temple **Jeffrey** and a slew of restaurants-of-the-moment.

Herald Square

Reasonable prices on standard wares prevail at this intersection of West 34th Street, Broadway, and Avenue of the Americas (6th Avenue). Giant **Macy's** has traditionally been the linchpin. Opposite is **Toys R' Us** (✉ 1293 Broadway, at W. 34th St., ☎ 212/594–8697). The newest **H&M** location is at the same intersection. Also on 6th Avenue, the seven-story **Manhattan Mall** is good for bargain browsing, as are **Lechter's** (✉ 10 W. 34th St., between 5th and 6th Aves., ☎ 212/564–3226, and other locations), for housewares, and **HMV,** for its large music selection.

5th Avenue

Fifth Avenue from Rockefeller Center to Central Park South still wavers between the money-is-no-object crowd and an influx of more accessible stores. It seems like the flag-bedecked **Saks Fifth Avenue,** at 50th Street, has always been there. Swedish retailer **H&M** opened its first New York store at 51st Street, adding affordable designer knockoffs to the mix. **Rockefeller Center** harbors smaller specialty shops, both along the outdoor promenade and in the underground marketplace, and big-gun branches of **Sephora, Banana Republic,** and **J. Crew.** The perennial favorites will eat up a lot of shoe leather: **Cartier** jewelers, at 52nd Street; **Takashimaya,** at 54th Street; **Ferragamo** and other various luxury stores in **Trump Tower,** at 56th Street; **Henri Bendel,** across the avenue; **Tiffany** and **Bulgari** jewelers, at 57th Street; and **F.A.O. Schwarz** and **Bergdorf Goodman,** at 58th Street. Exclusive design houses such as **Prada** are a stone's throw from the über-chain **Gap** and a souped-up branch of good old **Brooks Brothers.**

57th Street

The coveted north side of East 57th Street between 5th and Madison Avenues is anchored by the post-modern, white-glass Louis Vuitton Moet Hennesy headquarters. Designed by Christian de Portzamparc, the LVMH Tower's fragmented form lends a light-hearted elegance to the street and houses branches of **Louis Vuitton, Christian Dior,** and **Bliss,** the SoHo-born superspa. These glamazons are surrounded by big-

SoHo Shopping

57th Street/5th Avenue Shopping

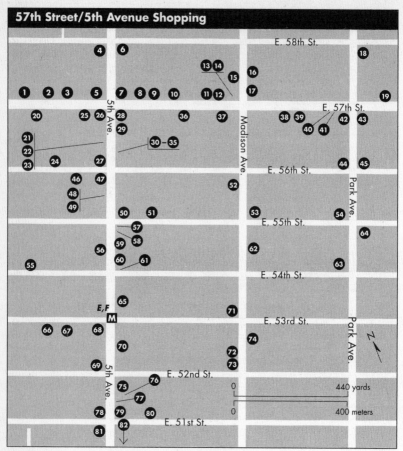

name art galleries and exclusive stores such as **Burberry, Chanel,** and **Escada,** but the block is no longer limited to top-echelon shopping. More affordable (and sizable) stores are an un-missable presence: Giant cartoon characters emblazon a supersize **Warner Bros. Studio Store,** while **NikeTown** and the **Tourneau TimeMachine** use high-tech marketing environments to lure in customers. To the west of 5th Avenue are art galleries and less monolithic shops, such as the scruffily literate **Coliseum Books** and a very oak-paneled branch of **Rizzoli** bookstores.

Columbus Avenue

Between West 66th and West 86th Streets, a former tenement district is home to a decent shopping strip. Stores are mostly modern in design, upscale but not top-of-the-line; many are branches of such familiar chains as **Banana Republic.** Still, you can find some not-too-common places, such as a second **Sean** storefront for quietly dapper menswear, **Nautica** for sport and prepster menswear, and the **Maraolo** factory store for discounted office-worthy shoes. If you venture west at West 80th Street to Broadway, you'll find **Zabar's,** the stuff of urban foodie legend, and the nearby **H&H Bagels** (✉ 2239 Broadway, ☎ 212/595–8003 store; 212/765–7200 mail order), which can ship a dozen just-baked miracles anywhere in the country. A little farther up Broadway is the wonderful **Gryphon** used-book store.

Madison Avenue

Madison Avenue from East 57th to about East 79th Streets can satisfy almost any fashion craving. **Cerruti, Giorgio Armani, Dolce & Gabbana, Valentino,** and **Prada,** are the avenue's Italian compatriots, while New York's hometown designer Donna Karan's first **DKNY** store stands at the corner of East 60th Street and Madison Avenue. British darling **Nicole Farhi** has also set up her fashion camp on East 60th Street, between Madison and 5th Avenues; **Tod's,** of driving-shoe fame, is a stone's throw away on Madison Avenue between East 59th and East 60th Streets. The entire western side of Madison between East 69th and East 70th Streets reinvented itself with the arrival of **Chloé** and branches of **Cartier** jewelers and menswear masters **Alfred Dunhill** and **Sulka.** Many of these occupy much larger spaces than traditional, one-level Madison boutiques; still, some smaller shops, such as **Frédéric Fekkai** (for hair products and accessories), are able to squeeze in. Madison Avenue isn't just a fashion funnel, however; there are several outstanding antiques dealers and numerous art galleries here as well.

Blitz Tours

Get your MetroCard ready and save enough cash for cab fare to lug all your packages home from these shopping itineraries. They're arranged by special interest; addresses, if not included here, can be found in the store listings below.

Antiques

Spend two hours at the **Manhattan Art & Antiques Center,** on 2nd Avenue at East 55th Street; then swing over to East 57th Street for an even posher array of European, American, and Asian treasures. Stroll westward across East 57th Street, stopping at **Israel Sack,** nearby on 5th Avenue, for its superb American antique furniture. Then head up Madison Avenue to **Didier Aaron** and **Barry Friedman** (on E. 67th St.), **Alexander Gallery** (near E. 74th St.), **DeLorenzo** and **Leo Kaplan** (near E. 75th St.), and a block or so further to **Florian Papp** and **Leigh Keno.**

Bargains

Begin by checking for any sample sales—you're bound to find some—and hit them first. Then head down to the lower tip of Manhattan to

discount emporium **Century 21.** Take a cab to Hester and Orchard Streets
and shop north along Orchard Street to Houston Street; be sure to stop
in at **Klein's of Monticello.** (Prowl along Grand Street if you're more
interested in goods for your home than in clothing.) By mid-afternoon
take a cab to Chelsea; check out **Find Outlet** for boutique fashions, then
tackle **Loehmann's** for a range of men's and women's clothing, from
inexpensive basics to designer items. A reminder: On Saturday, many
Lower East Side shops are closed.

Home Furnishings

For a French accent, start at the luscious **La Maison Moderne** (✉ 144
W. 19th St., ☎ 212/691–9603), which has gorgeous bibelots. Walk east
on 19th Street to **ABC Carpet & Home** on Broadway; this phenomenal
emporium could eat up hours on end, so keep an eye on the time and
move on to Greenwich Village to **William–Wayne & Co.** for elegant decorative items, often with an exotic air (or try to stop by the uptown
branches, which are much larger). If your bags aren't too heavy yet,
head down to SoHo, making sure not to miss **Moss** and **Zona.** For cross-
cultural finds, walk east and poke around the pocket-size boutiques
on Elizabeth Street between Houston and Spring streets. Cab it back
uptown to **Crate & Barrel** for great lower-price selections and finally,
if you're looking for basics, head over to **Bloomingdale's,** open late on
Thursday, or to **Macy's,** open late Monday, Thursday, and Friday.

Department Stores

Most of these stores keep regular hours on weekdays and are open late
(until 8 or 9) at least one night a week. Many have personal shoppers
who can walk you through the store at no charge. Some have restaurants or cafés that offer not only a much needed respite from shopping, but a delicious snack or meal.

Barneys New York. Barneys continues to provide the jet set with irre-
sistible objects of desire at its uptown flagship store. The extensive
menswear selection has introduced a handful of edgier designers such
as Alexander McQueen. (Made-to-measure is always available.) The
women's department is a showcase of cachet names such as Armani,
Jil Sander, and Helmut Lang. An expanded version of the successful
(and less expensive) Co-op department now has its own home in Barneys' old Chelsea warehouse (✉ 236 W. 18th St., between 7th and 8th
Aves., ☎ 212/593–7800), also the home of Barneys' legendary warehouse sales (usually held in February and August). ✉ *660 Madison Ave.,
between 60th and 61st Sts.,* ☎ *212/826–8900; World Financial Center,* ☎ *212/945–1600.*

Bergdorf Goodman. Good taste reigns in an elegant and understated
setting; the John Barrett Salon is located in the former Goodman family penthouse apartment. Remember that elegant doesn't necessarily
mean sedate—Bergdorf's carries some brilliant lines, such as John Gal-
liano's sensational couture, Philip Treacy's dramatic hats, and the sexy
Chloe line designed by Beatles offspring Stella McCartney. A recent addition to the basement, The Level of Beauty, is home to an extensive
collection of high-end beauty products as well as spa services. The home
department has rooms full of wonderful linens, tableware, and gifts.
Across the street is another entire store devoted to menswear: made-
to-measure shirts, custom suits, designer lines by the likes of Ralph Lauren and Gucci, and scads of accessories, from hip flasks to silk scarves.
Check out the ground floor atrium and see how dramatically glamorous shopping can be. Bergdorf's has one of the nicest Ladies' Rooms
in town. ✉ *754 5th Ave., at 57th St.; men's store, 745 5th Ave.,* ☎
212/753–7300.

THE FOOD-LOVERS' NONPAREIL MANHATTAN BLITZ TOUR

ATTENTION FOODIES! There's no time to waste, as Manhattan has more destinations for food lovers than ever before. Start early to cover downtown by lunchtime. Begin in Chinatown, at **Kam-Man** (✉ 200 Canal St., ☎ 212/571–0330), packed with dried squid, steamed bread, edible birds' nests, and dried shark fins. Next stop: **Mott Street** (below Grand Street), where markets and stalls sell ginger root, vegetables, meat, and live fish. Egyptian mint leaves, dozens of spices, and Jamaican jerk seasoning perfume **SoHo Provisions** (✉ 518 Broadway, ☎ 212/334–4311). Up the street, brilliantly white **Dean & DeLuca** (✉ 560 Broadway, ☎ 212/431–1691) artfully displays intriguing produce and prepared food such as horned melons and stuffed quail; gleaming racks of cookware are in back. For more affordable kitchen gear, try **Broadway Panhandler** (✉ 477 Broome St., ☎ 212/966–3434), where Calphalon, Le Creuset, and other professional-level makers are priced lower than retail.

Monday, Wednesday, Friday, and Saturday mornings, farmers and other food producers arrive at dawn at the **Union Square Greenmarket** bearing organic produce, flowers, homemade bread, preserves, fish, and seasonal fare. A few blocks away in the West Village, the ceilings of **Balducci's** (✉ 424 6th Ave., ☎ 212/673–2600) are hung with strings of garlic, onions, and woven baskets, while below, pasta, dark green frills of herbs, and hearty prepared dishes beckon. A square block of foodie heaven, **Chelsea Market** (✉ 75 9th Ave., ☎ 212/243–6005) is home to butchers, bakers, and a dozen other specialty food purveyors. For professional-quality equipment, visit nearby **Lamalle Kitchenwares** (✉ 36 W. 25th St., ☎ 212/242–0750).

The next two destinations require a subway or taxi ride. **Macy's Cellar** (✉ Herald Sq., W. 34th St. and 6th Ave., ☎ 212/695–4400) is a great place to rummage through gadgets. Farther uptown, at **Zabar's** (✉ 2245 Broadway, at W. 81st St., ☎ 212/787–2000), grab a loaf of the fabled bread, examine the smoked fish and cheeses, and head upstairs to the well-priced kitchenware section.

If you've still got time, head over to the East Side; these stores also make a fine minitour. On weekdays order an enchanting fruit basket from **Manhattan Fruitier** (✉ 105 E. 29th St., ☎ 212/686–0404). At **Bridge Kitchenware** (✉ 214 E. 52nd St., ☎ 212/688–4220), a dusty, unpretentious hideaway, you can scoop up tiny ramekins and countless doodads. Farther uptown, the **Vinegar Factory** (✉ 431 E. 91st St., ☎ 212/987–0885) carries bread from the *other* Zabar brother, Eli, who sells a great selection of vinegar and oils, plus fresh produce, cheese, kitchenware, and has a loft space for weekend brunch. If you don't want to go quite so far east, hit **Eli's Manhattan** (✉ 1411 3rd Ave., ☎ 212/717–8100), a second, equally well-stocked branch. Nearby, the **Kitchen Arts & Letters** bookstore (✉ 1435 Lexington Ave., ☎ 212/876–5550) has thousands of cookbooks and other titles on food and wine. For a fitting conclusion, head back down to **Payard** (✉ 1032 Lexington Ave., ☎ 212/717–5252), a glossy, Parisian-perfect pâtisserie where you can sample impeccable pastries and pick up elegant chocolates or hard-to-find *pâtes de fruits* (fruit jellies).

— Jennifer Paull

Bloomingdale's. Only a handful of department stores occupy an entire city block; Macy's is one, and this New York institution—a crazy mix of Deco style and '80s glitz—is another. The main floor is a stupefying maze of cosmetic counters, mirrors, and black walls. Get past this, and you'll find some good buys on dependable designers, bedding, and housewares. Don't mind the harried salespeople or none-too-subtle promotions—chalk it up to the Bloomie's experience. ⊠ *1000 3rd Ave., main entrance at E. 59th St. and Lexington Ave.,* ☏ *212/355–5900.*

Henri Bendel. If it's in style, it's at Bendel. This super-trendy, multilevel women's department store boasts not only one of the city's most eclectic cosmetics selections, but a wide array of must-have clothing and accessories. Bendel's showcases its luxurious in-house lines, as well as the styles of designers such as Trina Turk, Catherine, and Robert Cavalli. Most recently, a vintage clothing and accessories section has been added. Shoe lovers should be forewarned that there is no footwear department, just as there is no lingerie department. To console yourself, visit the wonderful tearoom on the second floor; try to get a table near the Lalique windows. ⊠ *712 5th Ave., at W. 56th St.,* ☏ *212/ 247–1100.*

Lord & Taylor. Lord & Taylor is a stronghold of classic American designer clothes. Instead of unpronounceable labels, you'll find Dana Buchman, Jones New York, and a lot of casual wear. It's refined, comfortably conservative, and never overwhelming. ⊠ *424 5th Ave., between W. 38th and W. 39th Sts.,* ☏ *212/391–3344.*

Macy's. Macy's headquarters store claims to be the largest retail store in America. Its ongoing renovation is sprucing up departments one by one—expect to be rerouted at least once and to totally lose your bearings at least twice. Fashion-wise, there's a concentration on the mainstream rather than the luxe; there's no couture, but Macy's has an extensive selection of midprice women's shoes. For cooking gear and housewares, the Cellar nearly outdoes Zabar's. ⊠ *Herald Sq., Broadway at W. 34th St.,* ☏ *212/695–4400.*

Saks Fifth Avenue. A fashion-only department store, Saks sells an astonishing array of apparel. The roster of American and European designers is impressive without being esoteric—the women's selection includes Gucci and Marc Jacobs, plus devastating ball gowns galore. The footwear department is remarkable, with everything from the affordable Nine West to the aspirational Manolo Blahnik. The men's department has a good selection of designer merchandise, including Oxxford Clothes, Alan Flusser, and Helmut Lang. ⊠ *611 5th Ave., between E. 49th and 50th Sts.,* ☏ *212/753–4000.*

Takashimaya New York. This pristine branch of Japan's largest department store carries stylish accessories, beauty products, and fine household items, all of which reflect a combination of Eastern and Western designs. In the Tea Box downstairs, you can have a *bento* box lunch in the serene, softly lighted tearoom or stock up on green tea. The florist-cum-front-window-display provides a mini-botanical garden to stroll through for a shopping respite. ⊠ *693 5th Ave., between E. 54th and E. 55th Sts.,* ☏ *212/350–0100.*

Discount

Century 21. For many New Yorkers, this is the mother lode of discount shopping. Four large floors are crammed with everything from J.P. Tod's driving moccasins to Ralph Lauren bedding—on a good day it may seem to lack nothing but a private dressing room. Men's merchandise is decidedly less exciting than the women's; endless rows of half-price ties from designers such as Gene Meyer and Valentino plus discount Calvin Klein briefs are more appealing than the slim clothing offerings. Scouring the full floor of women's designer clothing can turn up such deals as a Calvin Klein Collection dress for $60 or a Helmut Lang wool overcoat for $350. Don't pass up lingerie, where you can find Valentino silks. The basement linens department has choice buys on pure cotton sheets and wool blankets but watch for IRREGULAR stickers. There's also a collection of name-brand luggage, from gym bags to rolling suitcases. Cosmetics are the only goods not directly discounted, but a purchase elicits coupons good for deductions on other store merchandise. ⊠ *22 Cortlandt St., between Broadway and Church St.,* ☎ *212/227–9092.*

Specialty Shops

Many specialty stores have several branches in the city; in these cases, we have listed the locations in the busier shopping neighborhoods.

Antiques

Antiquing is fine art in Manhattan. Goods include everything from rarefied museum-quality to wacky and affordable. Premier shopping areas are on Madison Avenue north of 57th Street, and East 60th Street between 2nd and 3rd Avenues, where more than 20 shops, dealing in everything from 18th-century French furniture to art deco lighting fixtures, cluster on one block. Around 11th and 12th Streets between University Place and Broadway a tantalizing array of settees, bedsteads, and rocking chairs can be seen in the windows of about two dozen dealers, many of whom have TO THE TRADE signs on their doors; a card from your architect or decorator, however, may get you inside. Finally, for 20th-century furniture and fixtures, head south of Houston Street, especially along Lafayette Street. Most dealers are open on Saturday.

Many small dealers cluster in three antiques "malls."

Chelsea Antiques Building. With a full 12 floors of antiques and collectibles, the options run the gamut from antique books to vintage Georg Jensen silver to lunch boxes. ⊠ *108–110 W. 25th St., between 6th and 7th Aves.,* ☎ *212/929–0909.*

Manhattan Art & Antiques Center. Art Nouveau perfume bottles and samovars, samurai swords, pewter pitchers, and much more fill 100-plus galleries. The level of quality is not, as a rule, up to that of Madison Avenue, but then neither are the prices. ⊠ *1050 2nd Ave., between 55th and 56th Sts.,* ☎ *212/355–4400.*

Metropolitan Arts and Antiques Pavilion. Good for costume jewelry, offbeat bric-a-brac, and '50s kitsch, this antiques mall holds regularly scheduled auctions and specialty shows for rare books, photography, vintage textiles, Victoriana, and other lots. ⊠ *110 W. 19th St., between 6th and 7th Aves.,* ☎ *212/463–0200.*

AMERICAN AND ENGLISH

Florian Papp. The shine of gilt—on ormolu clocks, chaise longues, and marble-top tables—lures casual customers in, but this store has an unassailed reputation among knowledgeable collectors. ⊠ *962 Madison Ave., between E. 75th and E. 76th Sts.,* ☎ *212/288–6770.*

Hyde Park Antiques. This store features English decorative arts from the 18th and 19th centuries, with *objets* ranging from candelabras to tea caddies. ⊠ *836 Broadway, between E. 12th and E. 13th Sts.,* ☎ *212/477–0033.*

Israel Sack Inc. This is widely considered one of the best places in the country for 17th-, 18th-, and early 19th-century American furniture. Although the store is reputed to be very expensive, there's actually plenty of furniture for under $25,000. ⊠ *730 5th Ave., between 56th and 57th Sts.,* ☎ *212/399–6562.*

Kentshire Galleries. Elegant furniture is displayed in room settings on eight floors, with an emphasis on formal English pieces from the early

18th and 19th centuries, particularly the Georgian and Regency periods. ⊠ *37 E. 12th St., between University Pl. and Broadway,* ☎ *212/ 673–6644.*

Leigh Keno American Antiques. Before he was 30, Leigh Keno set an auction record in the American antiques field by paying $2.75 million for a hairy paw–foot Philadelphia wing chair. He has a good eye and an interesting inventory; gaze up at a tall case clock or down at the delicate legs of a tea table. It's best to make an appointment. ⊠ *980 Madison Ave.,* ☎ *212/734–2381.*

Steve Miller American Folk Art. This gallery is run by one of the country's premier folk-art dealers, the author of *The Art of the Weathervane.* ⊠ *17 E. 96th St., between Madison and 5th Aves.,* ☎ *212/348–5219.*

Woodard & Greenstein. Americana, antique quilts and rugs, and 19th-century country furniture are among the specialties of this prestigious dealer. ⊠ *506 E. 74th St., between York Ave. and FDR Dr.,* ☎ *212/ 794–9404.*

ASIAN

Chinese Porcelain Company. This prestigious, high-end shop carries porcelain and ceramics dating from 300 BC to the end of the 18th century, Buddhist and Hindu sculptures from Southeast Asia, and 18th-century Chinese lacquer furniture. ⊠ *475 Park Ave., at E. 58th St.,* ☎ *212/838–7744.*

Flying Cranes Antiques. Here you'll find a well-regarded collection of rare, museum-quality pieces from the Meiji period, the time known as Japan's Golden Age. Items include ceramics, cloisonné, metalwork, carvings, ikebana baskets, and Samurai swords and fittings. ⊠ *Manhattan Art and Antiques Center, 1050 2nd Ave., between E. 55th and E. 56th Sts.,* ☎ *212/223–4600.*

Jacques Carcangues, Inc. Concentrating on antiques from Southeast Asia spanning the entire region from Japan to India, this SoHo gallery offers an eclectic array of objects, from pillboxes to 18th-century Burmese Buddhas. ⊠ *106 Spring St., at Mercer St.,* ☎ *212/925–8110.*

Old Japan. This little West Village shop specializes in antique textiles and kimonos. You'll also find furniture, such as chests and low tables, plus small items such as 100-year-old sake bottles, bamboo baskets, and sewing boxes (which can double as jewelry boxes). Contemporary gift items are also available. ⊠ *382 Bleecker St., between Perry and Charles Sts.,* ☎ *212/633–0922.*

ECLECTIC

Newel Art Galleries. Near the East Side's interior-design district, this is the city's biggest antiques store, with a huge collection that roams from the Renaissance to the 20th century. ⊠ *425 E. 53rd St., between 1st Ave. and Sutton Pl.,* ☎ *212/758–1970.*

EUROPEAN

Barry Friedman Ltd. Wiener Werkstätte, Bauhaus, De Stijl, Russian Constructivist, and other European avant-garde movements star in this collection of contemporary decorative objects. Vintage and contemporary photographs are also available. ⊠ *32 E. 67th St., between Park and Madison Aves.,* ☎ *212/794–8950.*

DeLorenzo. Come here for the sinuous curves and highly polished surfaces of French art deco furniture and accessories. ⊠ *956 Madison Ave., between E. 75th and E. 76th Sts.,* ☎ *212/249–7575.*

Didier Aaron. This esteemed gallery specializes in superb 18th- and 19th-century French furniture and paintings. ⊠ *32 E. 67th St.,* ☎ *212/988– 5248.*

L'Antiquaire & The Connoisseur, Inc. Proprietress Helen Fioratti has written a guide to French antiques, but she is equally knowledgeable about the Italian and Spanish furniture and decorative objects from the 15th through the 18th centuries, as well as the medieval arts, that compose her stock. ✉ *36 E. 73rd St., between Madison and Park Aves.,* ☎ *212/ 517–9176.*

Leo Kaplan Ltd. The impeccable items here include Art Nouveau glass and pottery, porcelain from 18th-century England, antique and modern paperweights, and Russian artwork. ✉ *967 Madison Ave., between E. 75th and E. 76th Sts.,* ☎ *212/249–6766.*

Malmaison Antiques. The country's largest selection of Empire furniture and decorative arts is sold at this gallery. ✉ *253 E. 74th St., between 2nd and 3rd Aves.,* ☎ *212/288–7569.*

Pierre Deux Antiques. The company that brought French Provincial to a provincial America still offers an excellent selection. ✉ *369 Bleecker St., at Charles St.,* ☎ *212/243–7740.*

20TH-CENTURY FURNITURE AND MEMORABILIA

Back Pages Antiques. To acquire a restored antique jukebox or slot machine, just drop in—or rather, down, since this shop is on the basement level. The hours aren't strictly 9–5, so it's best to make an appointment. ✉ *125 Greene St., between W. Houston and Prince Sts.,* ☎ *212/460–5998.*

City Barn Antiques. Come for your fill of the blond-wood Heywood-Wakefield originals (many refinished) and streamlined pieces mostly from the '50s. ✉ *269 Lafayette St., at Prince St.,* ☎ *212/941–5757.*

Darrow's Fun Antiques. A leader among the city's nostalgia shops, the store is full of whimsy: antique toys, animation art, and other collectibles. ✉ *1101 1st Ave., between E. 60th and E. 61st Sts.,* ☎ *212/838–0730.*

Las Venus. Step into these kitsch palaces and you'll feel as though a time machine has zapped you back to the groovy '70s. Look for bubble lamps, lots of brocade, and Knoll knockoffs. ✉ *163 Ludlow St., between Houston and Stanton Sts.,* ☎ *212/982–0608; 113 Stanton St., between Ludlow and Essex Sts.,* ☎ *212/358–8000.*

Lost City Arts. Something between a store and a museum, this place contains swanky modern furniture plus lots of industrial memorabilia, such as neon gas station clocks. A retro-modern line of furniture is designed in-house. ✉ *18 Cooper Sq., at E. 5th St.,* ☎ *212/375–0500.*

Beauty

Aveda. Natural ingredients and plant extracts are the basis of Aveda's shampoos and hair treatments. You can concoct your own perfumes from the impressive selection of essential oils. ✉ *509 Madison Ave., at 53rd St.,* ☎ *212/832–2416; 140 5th Ave., at 19th St.,* ☎ *212/645–4797; 233 Spring St., at 6th Ave.,* ☎ *212/807–1492; 456 W. Broadway, between Prince and Houston Sts.,* ☎ *212/473–0280.*

Creed. Choose from an array of existing fragrances—many of which were named and created for royalty such as Princess Diana and Grace Kelly—or have one custom-made for you. Prices are high at this ancient Anglo-French perfumery, but you will leave the precious and serene shop smelling and feeling better. ✉ *9 Bond St., between Lafayette St. and Broadway,* ☎ *212/228–1940.*

FACE Stockholm. Besides the pretty pastels and neutrals, FACE carries some brazenly colored nail polish (emerald green, sky blue), juicy red glosses, and little pots of jewel-tone glitter. Swabs and tissues at hand make a quick do-it-yourself try-out refreshingly easy. ✉ *110 Prince St., at Greene St.,* ☎ *212/966–9110; 226 Columbus Ave., at W. 70th St.,* ☎ *212/769–1420; 687 Madison Ave., at E. 62nd St.,* ☎ *212/207–8833.*

5S. Color-coded products are designed around five themes: energizing, purifying, calming, adoring, and nurturing. The line is a more experimental offshoot of Japan's beauty giant Shiseido, with affordable prices for its young audience. Interactive computer stations and a rainbow of appealing colors and subtle scents make up for the sappy sentiments. ⊠ *98 Prince St., between Mercer and Greene Sts.,* ☎ *212/925–7880.*

Floris of London. Floral English toiletries beloved of the British royals fill this re-creation of the cozy London original. There's also a nice selection of shaving sets. ⊠ *703 Madison Ave., between E. 62nd and 63rd Sts.,* ☎ *212/935–9100.*

Frédéric Fekkai. After establishing himself with his salon in the Chanel flagship store, celeb-hairdresser Fekkai opened this petite, independent boutique. Hair goodies (from volumizers to an apple-cider rinse) line the walls, as well as softly tinted makeup, leather-bound hair accessories, glamourpuss sunglasses, and even luxe purses to stash it all in. ⊠ *874 Madison Ave., between Madison and 5th Aves.,* ☎ *212/583–3300.*

Fresh. Many of these products sound (and smell) good enough to eat: milk chocolate soap, apple-cranberry body wash, fig-apricot perfume. Florals are hardly neglected though; the rose-scent soap, for instance, comes in Spanish, Turkish, or Bulgarian varieties. ⊠ *1061 Madison Ave., between E. 80th and E. 81st Sts.,* ☎ *212/396–0344; 57 Spring St., between Lafayette and Mulberry Sts.,* ☎ *212/925–0099.*

Helena Rubenstein. This is not your mother's Helena Rubenstein. Ladylike peaches and beiges in the makeup lines have been joined by bold citrine, blue, and glitter. Skincare products line the walls; there are also several skin tests (oil, UV damage). If you are in need of pampering stop at the spa downstairs, once used as a *Sex and the City* location. ⊠ *135 Spring St., between Greene and Wooster Sts.,* ☎ *212/343–9966.*

Kiehl's Since 1851. At this favored haunt of top models and stylists, white-smocked assistants can advise you on the relative merits of the incredibly effective and somewhat expensive skin lotions and hair potions, all packaged in disarmingly simple bottles. The employees dole out generous take-home samples of virtually any product in the store. ⊠ *109 3rd Ave., between E. 13th and E. 14th Sts.,* ☎ *212/677–3171.*

L'Occitane. Extra-mild soaps, shampoos, and creams here pack an olfactory punch with Provençal scents (think almond, thyme, and the ever-present lavender). ⊠ *1046 Madison Ave., at E. 80th St.,* ☎ *212/639–9185; 510 Madison Ave., between E. 52nd and E. 53rd Sts.,* ☎ *212/826–5020; 146 Spring St., at Wooster St.,* ☎ *212/343–0109; 198 Columbus Ave., at W. 69th St.,* ☎ *212/362–5146;* ⊠ *412 Lexington Ave., at E. 43rd St.,* ☎ *212/557–6754.*

M.A.C. Fashion hounds and stylists pile into these boutiques for the basics (foundation and concealer for a huge range of skin tones) and the far-out. Salespeople can offer expert advice—many of them also work as professional makeup artists. ⊠ *113 Spring St., between Mercer and Greene Sts.,* ☎ *212/334–4641; 14 Christopher St., between 6th and 7th Aves.,* ☎ *212/243–4150.*

Make Up For Ever. The makeup from this Paris-based boutique is not for the faint of heart (nor for the mascara-and-lip gloss set). The products are pigment-rich and boldly colored, and many—like aquarelles (small bottles of water-based pigment) and pumps of color cream—can be applied most anywhere on the body. ⊠ *409 W. Broadway, between Prince and Spring Sts.,* ☎ *212/941–9337.*

Ricky's. Shopping at any one of these wacky stores is a uniquely New York experience. The loud and fun drugstores attract an eclectic, mostly young crowd who come just as often for the crazy-color wigs or fishnet stockings as they do for the body glitter and Neutrogena soap. Every fall the stores turn into Halloween central. ⊠ *590 Broadway, at Prince St.,* ☎ *212/226–5552; 718 Broadway, at Astor Pl.,* ☎ *212/ 979–5232; 466 6th Ave., at W. 12th St.,* ☎ *212/924–3401; 44 E. 8th St., at George St.,* ☎ *212/254–5247; 988 8th Ave., at W. 59th St.,* ☎ *212/586–0114.*

Sephora. This black-and-crimson chain has already conquered France, and is now saturating major U.S. cities. A huge, huge roster of perfumes is arranged alphabetically down the walls, and the comprehensive makeup selection ranges from Urban Decay to Stila to Sephora's own mega-brand. Skin-care lines include hard-to-find names such as Peter Thomas Roth. Most important, a scattering of try-on stations, complete with tissues, cotton pads, makeup remover, and disinfectant, make trying on the goods a low-commitment proposition. ⊠ *555 Broadway, between Prince and Spring Sts.,* ☎ *212/625–1309; 119 5th Ave., at 19th St.,* ☎ *212/674–3570; 1500 Broadway, at W. 44th St.,* ☎ *212/944–8168; 636 5th Ave., at 51st St.,* ☎ *212/245–1633; 4 World Financial Center,* ☎ *212/432–1311.*

Shiseido. Both spaces fully embody Shiseido's roots and philosophies. Upon stepping into either there is a feeling of history as well as modernity, and a blending of science and art. At the **Shiseido Studio** (⊠ 155 Spring St., between Wooster St. and W. Broadway, ☎ 212/625–8821) nothing is for sale: products and techniques are there for your experimentation and interactivity. At the Madison Avenue store customers are actually encouraged to make purchases from Shisedo's line of skin-smart products, **Qiora.** The unique line is designed to promote wellness in both the skin and the brain. ⊠ *535 Madison Ave., between E. 54th and E. 55th Sts.,* ☎ *212/527–9933.*

Shu Uemura. One of SoHo's many beauty spots, this is a good place to scoop up top-of-the-line Japanese skin care products, makeup, and tools such as their legendary eyelash curler. One clever touch: there are four light simulators, which allow you to test makeup colors under officelike and simulated outdoor lighting. ⊠ *121 Greene St., between Prince and Houston Sts.,* ☎ *212/979–5500.*

Books

Manhattan supports dozens of bookstores, small and large. All the big national chains are here. **Barnes & Noble** (⊠ 396 Ave. of the Americas, ☎ 212/674–8780; 33 E. 17th St., ☎ 212/253–0810; 4 Astor Pl., ☎ 212/420–1322; 160 E. 54th St., ☎ 212/750–8033; 675 6th Ave., ☎ 212/727–1227; 600 5th Ave., ☎ 212/765–0592; 901 6th Ave., ☎ 212/268–2505; 385 5th Ave., ☎ 212/779–7677; 750 3rd Ave., ☎ 212/ 697–2251; 1972 Broadway, ☎ 212/595–6859; 2289 Broadway, ☎ 212/ 362–8835; 1280 Lexington Ave., ☎ 212/423–9900; 240 E. 86th St., ☎ 212/794–1962), stores are everywhere. **Borders** (⊠ 5 World Trade Center, ☎ 212/839–8049; 461 Park Ave., ☎ 212/980–6785; 550 2nd Ave., ☎ 212/685–3938) are peppered around the city. There is also a wealth of independent bookstores.

CHILDREN'S BOOKS

Books of Wonder. A friendly staff can help select gifts for all reading levels from the extensive stock of children's books here; Oziana is a specialty. ⊠ *16 W. 18th St., between 5th and 6th Aves.,* ☎ *212/989– 3270.*

FOREIGN LANGUAGE

Librairie de France/Libraria Hispanica. This store offers one of the country's largest selections of foreign-language books, videos, and periodicals, mostly in French and Spanish. You'll also find dozens of dictionaries, phrase books, and other learning materials. ⊠ *610 5th Ave., in Rockefeller Center Promenade,* ☎ *212/581–8810.*

GAY AND LESBIAN

A Different Light Bookstore. The city's preeminent gay and lesbian store is also the only chain of its kind in the nation, with a huge selection of fiction, nonfiction, periodicals, calendars, and posters. Free local periodicals and fliers by the door are a great source of information about gay life and happenings citywide. A downstairs gallery (where readings and other events are held nightly—the Sunday-night movie series is popular) is another plus, and it's open daily until midnight. ✉ *151 W. 19th St., between 6th and 7th Aves.,* ☎ *212/989–4850.*

Oscar Wilde Bookshop. Opened in 1967, this was the first gay and lesbian bookstore in the city (and is now the oldest existing one in the country); it's just steps from the site of the Stonewall riots. Choices range from cultural studies and biographies to fiction and erotica collections, plus a large selection of videos and CDs. There are even some rare finds such as Auden first editions. ✉ *15 Christopher St., between 6th and 7th Aves.,* ☎ *212/255–8097.*

GENERAL INTEREST

Archivia. You might see a biography of Dior alongside a guide to English garden design in the narrow window of this shop, which faces the Whitney Museum of Art. There are new, used, and out-of-print books on all sorts of design and decorative arts, particularly architecture, gardening, and interior design. ✉ *944 Madison Ave., between E. 74th and E. 75th Sts.,* ☎ *212/439–9194.*

Biography Bookshop. Published diaries, letters, biographies, and autobiographies fill this neighborly store; there's also a careful selection of general non-fiction, fiction, guidebooks, and children's books. ✉ *400 Bleecker St., at 11th St.,* ☎ *212/807–8655.*

Coliseum Books. This book-lover's dream of a bookstore has a huge, quirky selection of remainders, best-sellers, and scholarly works. ✉ *1771 Broadway, at W. 57th St.,* ☎ *212/757–8381.*

Corner Bookstore. A neighborhood favorite, this shop has a highly knowledgable staff. ✉ *1313 Madison Ave., at E. 93rd St.,* ☎ *212/831–3554.*

Crawford Doyle Booksellers. You're as likely to see the Riverside Shakespeare or an old edition of Czech fairy tales as a best-seller in the window of this shop. There's a thoughtful selection of fiction, non-fiction, biographies, etc., plus some rare books on the tight-fit upstairs balcony. Salespeople offer their opinions *and* ask for yours. ✉ *1082 Madison Ave. between E. 80th and E. 81st Sts.,* ☎ *212/288–6300.*

Gotham Book Mart. The late Frances Steloff opened this store in 1920 with just $200 in her pocket, half of it on loan. But she helped launch James Joyce's *Ulysses,* D. H. Lawrence, and Henry Miller and is now legendary among bibliophiles—as is her bookstore. There's a wealth of signed editions of deliciously macabre Edward Gorey books. ✉ *41 W. 47th St., between 5th and 6th Aves.,* ☎ *212/719–4448.*

Gryphon. This narrow, wonderfully crammed space is a bibliophile's lifesaver in the otherwise sparse Upper West Side. Squeeze in among the stacks of art books and fiction; clamber up the steep stairway and you'll find all sorts of rare books, including original editions of the Oz series. ✉ *2246 Broadway, between W. 80th and W. 81st Sts.,* ☎ *212/362–0706.*

Lenox Hill Bookstore. This tiny shop carries many copies of books signed by their authors. ✉ *1018 Lexington Ave., at E. 73rd St.,* ☎ *212/472–7170.*

Madison Avenue Bookshop. This bona fide neighborhood store bursts with books, which are stacked everywhere—on the floor, on top of bookcases, even on the narrow winding staircase. You can find everything from coffee-table photo books to the latest biographies to a good pulper. ✉ *833 Madison Ave., between E. 69th and E. 70th Sts.,* ☎ *212/535–6130.*

Posman Books. Two of the branches are nestled near a university. The one by NYU specializes in philosophy, literature, and poetry; sale books and remainders are also offered. The branch close to The New School focuses on art and design books. A newer branch that carries mostly best-sellers and new releases is located in Grand Central Terminal. ✉ *1 University Pl.,* ☎ *212/533–2665; 70 5th Ave., at 13th St.,* ☎ *212/633–2525; 9 Grand Central Terminal, at Vanderbilt Pl. and E. 42nd St.,* ☎ *212/983–1111.*

Rizzoli. In midtown, an elegant marble entrance, oak paneling, chandeliers, and classical music surround books and magazines on art, architecture, dance, design, photography, and travel; the downtown stores come with fewer frills. The SoHo location specializes in art and architecture books and is connected to an antique poster shop. ✉ *31 W. 57th St., between 5th and 6th Aves.,* ☎ *212/759–2424; World Financial Center, Vesey St.,* ☎ *212/385–1400.*

St. Mark's Bookshop. Extending far beyond the *New York Times* best-seller list, this store's New Titles section might have a study of post-modernism next to the new Don DeLillo. Cultural and critical theory books are right up front; they've also got a rich store of literature, literary journals, and even a rack of self-published booklets. ✉ *31 3rd Ave., at Stuyvesant St.,* ☎ *212/260–7853.*

Shakespeare & Co. Booksellers. The stock here represents what's happening in just about every field of publishing today: students can grab a last-minute Gertrude Stein for their literature class, then rifle through the homages to cult pop-culture figures. Late hours at the downtown location (till midnight on Friday and Saturday, 11 PM the rest of the week) are a plus. ✉ *939 Lexington Ave., between E. 68th and E. 69th Sts.,* ☎ *212/570–0201; 137 E. 23rd St., at Lexington Ave.,* ☎ *212/ 220–5199; 716 Broadway, at Washington Pl.,* ☎ *212/529–1330; 1 Whitehall St., at Beaver St.,* ☎ *212/742–7025.*

The Strand. The Broadway branch proudly claims to have "8 miles of books;" craning your neck among the tall-as-trees stacks will likely net you something. Rare books are next door, at 826 Broadway, on the third floor. The Fulton Street branch is near South Street Seaport; it's decidedly less overwhelming. ✉ *828 Broadway, at 12th St.,* ☎ *212/ 473–1452; 95 Fulton St., between Gold and Williams Sts.,* ☎ *212/732– 6070.*

Three Lives & Co. On a picture-perfect West Village corner, Three Lives has one of the city's most impeccable selections of books. The display tables and counters highlight the latest literary fiction and serious non-fiction, classics, quirky gift books, and gorgeously illustrated tomes. ✉ *154 W. 10th St., at Waverly Pl.,* ☎ *212/741–2069.*

MUSIC

Joseph Patelson Music House. A huge collection of scores has long made this the heart of the music-lover's New York. ✉ *160 W. 56th St., between 6th and 7th Aves.,* ☎ *212/582–5840.*

MYSTERY AND SUSPENSE

Murder Ink. Mystery lovers have relied on this institution for years; ask the knowledgeable staff for recommendations. ✉ *2486 Broadway, between W. 92nd and W. 93rd Sts.,* ☎ *212/362–8905.*

The Mysterious Bookshop. Come to this atmospheric shop to uncover one of the largest selections of mystery, suspense, and detective fiction in the city—new, used, and out-of-print volumes, as well as first editions. ✉ *129 W. 56th St., between 6th and 7th Aves.,* ☎ *212/765–0900.*

Partners & Crime. Imported British paperbacks, helpful staff, a rental library, and whodunits galore—new, out-of-print, and first editions—make this a must-browse for fans. Revered mystery writers give readings here. Check out the "radio mystery hour" on Saturday evening. ✉ *44 Greenwich Ave., between 6th and 7th Aves.,* ☎ *212/243–0440.*

Academy Book Store. Out-of-print, used, antiquarian, scholarly, and art books overflow here. There's a music Academy next door. ⊠ *10 W. 18th St., between 5th and 6th Aves.,* ☎ *212/242–4848.*

Argosy Bookstore. This sedate landmark, established in 1921, keeps a scholarly stock of books and autographs. It's also a great place to look for low-price maps and prints. ⊠ *116 E. 59th St., between Park and Lexington Aves.,* ☎ *212/753–4455.*

Bauman Rare Books. This successful Philadelphia firm now offers New Yorkers the most impossible-to-get titles, first editions, and fine leather sets. The Madison Avenue store has become their flagship store, eight times the size of their boutique in the Waldorf-Astoria. ⊠ *535 Madison Ave., between E. 54th and E. 55th Sts.,* ☎ *212/751–0011; Waldorf-Astoria, lobby level, 301 Park Ave., at E. 50th St.,* ☎ *212/759–8300.*

Crawford Doyle Booksellers. General Interest, *above.*

Gryphon. General Interest, *above.*

J. N. Bartfield. A legend in the field offers old and antiquarian books distinguished by binding, author, edition, or content. Call ahead for store hours, which tend to be limited. ⊠ *30 W. 57th St., 3rd floor, between 5th and 6th Aves.,* ☎ *212/245–8890.*

Skyline Books and Records, Inc. Come here for out-of-print and unusual books in all fields. The store handles literary first editions, as well as jazz and rock records. ⊠ *13 W. 18th St., between 5th and 6th Aves.,* ☎ *212/675–4773.*

The Strand. General Interest, *above.*

Drama Book Shop. If you're looking for a script, be it a Russian translation or the latest Tom Stoppard, chances are you'll find it here. The range of books spans film, music, dance, TV, and biographies; there are also odds and ends such as sets of preprinted mailing labels for Los Angeles agents or New York theaters. ⊠ *723 7th Ave., between W. 48th and W. 49th Sts., 2nd floor,* ☎ *212/944–0595.*

Cameras and Electronics

Bang & Olufsen. Bang & Olufsen stereos are unmistakable—slim, flat cases, with transparent doors that open when you reach toward them, displaying the whirling CDs inside. In the back of the store is a mock living room, where you can test the impressive surround-sound. ⊠ *952 Madison Ave.,* ☎ *212/879–6161.*

Harvey Electronics. A well-informed staff offers top-of-the-line audiovisual equipment. ⊠ *2 W. 45th St., between 5th and 6th Aves.,* ☎ *212/575–5000; 888 Broadway, at E. 19th St., inside ABC Carpet & Home,* ☎ *212/228–5354.*

J&R Music and Computer World. Just south of City Hall, J&R has emerged as the city's most competitively priced one-stop electronics outlet, with video equipment, stereos, and cameras. Home-office supplies are at No. 17, computers at No. 15, small appliances at No. 27. ⊠ *31 Park Row, between Beekman and Ann Sts.,* ☎ *212/238–9000.*

SONY Style. This equipment and music store comes in a glossy package—window displays are designed by such artists as Kenneth Scharf and Maurice Sendak. Inside, the latest stereo and entertainment systems, video cameras, and portable CD and mp3 players preen on the shelves. Plunge into the blue velvet-swathed downstairs area for a demonstration of the integrated systems. ⊠ *550 Madison Ave., at E. 55th St.,* ☎ *212/833–8800.*

Willoughby's. No longer as immense as it once was, Willoughby's still rates high among amateurs and pros for selection and service. ⊠ *138 W. 32nd St., between 6th and 7th Aves.,* ☎ *212/564–1600.*

CDs, Tapes, and Records

The city's best record stores provide browsers with a window to New York's groovier subcultures. The East Village is especially good for dance tracks and used music.

Academy Records & CDs. You can walk into Academy with just $10 and walk out happy. The new and used CDs, tapes, and records are well organized, low-priced, and in good condition; sometimes they've never even been opened. ⊠ *12 W. 18th St., between 5th and 6th Aves.,* ☎ *212/242–3000.*

Bleecker Bob's Golden Oldies Record Shop. The staff sells punk, new wave, progressive rock, and reggae, plus good old rock on licorice pizza, until the wee hours. ⊠ *118 W. 3rd St., at MacDougal St.,* ☎ *212/475–9677.*

Footlight Records. Stop here to browse through New York's largest selection of old and new musicals and movie sound tracks (hello Judy Garland!), as well as a good choice of jazz and American popular standards. ⊠ *113 E. 12th St., between 3rd and 4th Aves.,* ☎ *212/533–1572.*

Gryphon Record Shop. One of the city's best rare-record stores, it stocks some 90,000 out-of-print and rare LPs. ⊠ *233 W. 72nd St., between Broadway and West End Ave.,* ☎ *212/874–1588.*

HMV. These state-of-the-art record superstores stock hundreds of thousands of discs, tapes, and videos, and provide lots of listening stations to check out what's new. If you're less than enamored with your purchase, don't sweat it—they've got a liberal return policy. ⊠ *57 W. 34th St., at 6th Ave.,* ☎ *212/629–0900; 2081 Broadway, at W. 72nd St.,* ☎ *212/721–5900; 1280 Lexington Ave., at E. 86th St.,* ☎ *212/348–0800; 565 5th Ave., at 46th St.,* ☎ *212/681–6700.*

House of Oldies. The specialty here is records made between 1950 and the late 1980s—45s and 78s, as well as LPs; there are more than a million titles. ⊠ *35 Carmine St., between Bleecker St. and 6th Ave.,* ☎ *212/243–0500.*

Jazz Record Center. The city's well-known jazz-record specialist also stocks collectibles. ⊠ *236 W. 26th St., 8th floor, between 7th and 8th Aves.,* ☎ *212/675–4480.*

J&R Music World. This store offers a huge selection of pop music and videos, with good prices on major releases. Jazz recordings are sold at 25 Park Row, classical at No. 33. You can even buy music by telephone. ⊠ *23 Park Row, between Beekman and Ann Sts.,* ☎ *212/238–9000.*

Kim's Video & Music. Scruffy and eclectic, Kim's is a compact crystallization of the downtown music scene. Their top-20 list is a long, long way from the Top 40; instead, there's a mix of electronica, jazz, lounge, and experimental. ⊠ *6 St. Marks Pl., between 2nd and 3rd Aves.,* ☎ *212/598–9985; 144 Bleecker St., between Thompson St. and La Guardia Pl.,* ☎ *212/260–1010; 350 Bleecker St., at 10th St.,* ☎ *212/675–8996.*

Tower Records. The scene in each branch is pure New York: At the Village location, many customers are multipierced and rainbow-haired, while at the Lincoln Center branch patrons discuss jazz in the store café. The East 4th Street branch features discount selections. ⊠ *692 Broadway, at E. 4th St.,* ☎ *212/505–1500; 1961 Broadway, at W. 66th St.,* ☎ *212/799–2500; 725 5th Ave., basement level of Trump Tower, at E. 56th St.,* ☎ *212/838–8110; 20 E. 4th St., at Lafayette St.,* ☎ *212/228–7317.*

Virgin Megastore. There's a polished Megastore planted in each major square: Times and Union. Despite the rows upon rows of CDs, videos, books, and DVDs, there's plenty of room for live band appearances—and if you're weak in the knees afterward, you can drop into a chair at the in-store café. ⊠ *1540 Broadway, between W. 45th and W. 46th Sts.,* ☎ *212/921–1020; 52 E. 14th St.,* ☎ *212/598–4666.*

Chocolate

Elk Candy Co. This slice of old Yorkville carries European treats such as Mozartkugeln along with specialty chocolates and wonderful marzipan. Bahlsen spice cookies and chocolate advent calendars turn up around the holidays. ⊠ *1628 2nd Ave., between E. 84th and E. 85th Sts.,* ☎ *212/650–1177.*

Fauchon. Stroll into the U.S. branch of the ancient Parisian fine-food chain, and you'll feel transported. The store is full of hard-to-find French imports—tea, chocolate, jam, caviar. For anyone in need of a gift, this is the perfect place to splurge on something extravagant. ⊠ *442 Park Ave., at E. 56th St.,* ☎ *212/308–5919.*

La Maison du Chocolat. Stop in at this chocolatier's small tea salon to dive into a cup of thick, heavenly hot chocolate. The Parisian-based outfit sells handmade truffles, chocolates, and pastries that could lull you into a chocolate stupor. ⊠ *1018 Madison Ave., between 78th and 79th Sts.,* ☎ *212/744–7117; 30 Rockefeller Center, between 5th and 6th Aves.,* ☎ *212/265–9404.*

Li-Lac Chocolates. This charming nook has been feeding the Village's sweet tooth with traditional homemade American treats (such as turtles, bark, and butter crunch) since 1923. ⊠ *120 Christopher St., between Bleecker and Hudson Sts.,* ☎ *212/242–7374.*

Lunettes et Chocolat. The contents of the store may seem random, but when presented in such a harmonious manner they make perfect sense. The brainchild of eyeglass guru Selima and sweets expert Maribel Lieberman, the shop sells only two types of items—eyeglasses and chocolates. If you are in search of the sweetest frames or foods this is the place to go. ⊠ *25 Prince St., between Elizabeth and Mott Sts.,* ☎ *212/925–8800.*

Neuchatel Chocolates. Neuchatel's velvety chocolates, which come in five dozen varieties, are all made in New York to approximate the Swiss chocolates. ⊠ *Plaza Hotel, 2 W. 59th St., between 5th and 6th Aves.,* ☎ *212/751–7742; 60 Wall St., between William and Pearl Sts.,* ☎ *212/480–3766.*

Neuhaus. When they say "Belgian chocolates" they mean it—the treats are flown in from Brussels. Try the pralinés or the flavored crème fraîche–filled chocolates. ⊠ *922 Madison Ave., between 73rd and 74th Sts.,* ☎ *212/861–2800.*

Richart Design et Chocolat. This French shop is worth its weight in cacao beans. Many of the sophisticated chocolates use high percentages of cacao, and all are imprinted with impossibly intricate and colorful patterns. Couturier Sonia Rykiel designed some of the images that glisten on the flat tablets. ⊠ *7 E. 55th St., between 5th and Madison Aves.,* ☎ *212/371–9369.*

Teuscher Chocolates. Fabulous chocolates (try the champagne truffles) made in Switzerland are flown in weekly for sale in these jewel-box shops, newly decorated each season. ⊠ *620 5th Ave., in Rockefeller Center,* ☎ *212/246–4416; 25 E. 61st St., between 5th and Madison Aves.,* ☎ *212/751–8482.*

Clothing

CHILDREN'S CLOTHING

In Manhattan, even children like their styles up-to-the-minute cool. You'll find plenty of mini-me type gear, such as little leopard-print purses and leather jackets, but there are also plenty of cotton T-shirts, sturdy winter coats, and pretty party dresses.

Au Chat Botté. Besides little-princess party dresses, this store has delicate, snowy layettes. ⊠ *1192 Madison Ave., at E. 87th St.,* ☎ *212/722–6474.*

Baby Gap. Granted, this is part of the leave-no-mall-untouched chain, but this branch lives up to its location with an exclusive, luxury line of cashmere, silk, and velvet baby clothes. ✉ *680 5th Ave., at 54th St.,* ☎ *212/977–7023.*

Bellini. One of the world's few children's stores to share the name of a cocktail, Bellini specializes in layettes, furniture, and bedding. ✉ *110 W. 86th St., between Columbus and Amsterdam Aves.,* ☎ *212/580–3801; 1305 2nd Ave., between E. 68th and E. 69th Sts.,* ☎ *212/517–9233.*

Bonpoint. The sophistication here lies in the beautiful designs and impeccable workmanship—jewel-tone cotton-velvet jumpers, linen shifts threaded with velvet ribbon, hand-embroidered sleepwear, and pristine layettes. ✉ *1269 Madison Ave., at E. 91st St.,* ☎ *212/722–7720; 811 Madison Ave., at E. 68th St.,* ☎ *212/879–0900.*

Bu and the Duck. Clothes for the young in an old setting sets this infant and children's clothing shop apart from the rest. Susan Lane, the owner, designs the shop's complete line of clothing and accessories. Everything else in the store is vintage furniture, which is also for sale. ✉ *106 Franklin St., at Church St.,* ☎ *212/431–9226.*

Calypso Enfants. Sailor-stripe tops, plaid schoolgirl jumpers, sophisticated party dresses . . . you may find yourself dressing vicariously through your children. ✉ *284 Mulberry St., between E. Houston and Prince Sts.,* ☎ *212/965–8910.*

Catimini. Petit Bateau underwear, wool coats, velvet dresses printed with snippets of poetry in gold—these European clothes will lend your child a cosmopolitan air. ✉ *1284–86 Madison Ave., between E. 91st and E. 92nd Sts.,* ☎ *212/987–0688.*

Greenstones. Catering to junior yuppies, these stores have a particularly good selection of sweaters, plus some colorfully flowered jumpers. ✉ *442 Columbus Ave., between W. 81st and W. 82nd Sts.,* ☎ *212/580–4322; 1184 Madison Ave., between E. 86th and E. 87th Sts.,* ☎ *212/427–1665.*

Infinity. Mothers gossip near the dressing rooms as their daughters try on slinky Les Tout Petits dresses and snap up the latest hair accessories at the counter. ✉ *1116 Madison Ave., at E. 83rd St.,* ☎ *212/517–4232.*

Jacadi. The classic clothes here, such as toggle coats and appliquéd sweaters, evoke Madeline's "two straight lines." ✉ *787 Madison Ave., at E. 67th St.,* ☎ *212/535–3200; 1281 Madison Ave., at E. 91st St.,* ☎ *212/369–1616.*

La Petite Etoile. These *petit* European imports might cost as much as dinner at one of the neighboring French bistros, but they are unique and very well made. ✉ *746 Madison Ave., between E. 64th and E. 65th Sts.,* ☎ *212/744–0975.*

Lilliput. At both locations, which are across the street from each other, you'll find Curious George T-shirts and toys, as well as retro items such as pint-size Dick Tracy raincoats. The difference is that the shop at No. 265 carries it all up to size 16, whereas the original shop stops at size 8. ✉ *240 Lafayette St., between Prince and Spring Sts.,* ☎ *212/965–9201; 265 Lafayette St., between Prince and Spring Sts.,* ☎ *212/965–9567.*

Little Eric. Hip adult styles—loafers with silver bits, velvet slippers, and brogues—inspire the children's shoes here. Prices can approach grown-up levels, too. ✉ *1331 3rd Ave., at E. 76th St.,* ☎ *212/288–8987; 1118 Madison Ave., at E. 83rd St.,* ☎ *212/717–1513.*

Morris Bros. This gold mine of boys' and girls' active wear carries Bear down jackets, mesh shorts, Quiksilver swim trunks, and stacks of Levi's. ✉ *2322 Broadway, at W. 84th St.,* ☎ *212/724–9000.*

Oilily. Stylized flowers, stripes, and animal shapes splash across the brightly colored play and school clothes sold here. ✉ *870 Madison Ave., between E. 70th and E. 71st Sts.,* ☎ *212/628–0100.*

Shoofly. Children's shoes and accessories range from Mary Janes, moc crocs, and wing tips to hats, socks, tights, and jewelry. ✉ *465 Amsterdam*

Ave., between W. 82nd and W. 83rd Sts., ☎ *212/580–4390; 42 Hudson St., between Thomas and Duane Sts.,* ☎ *212/406–3270.*

Space Kiddets. The funky (Elvis-print rompers) mixes with the tried-and-true (fringed cowboy/cowgirl outfits) at this casual, trendsetting store. ⊠ *46 E. 21st St., between Broadway and Park Ave.,* ☎ *212/420–9878.*

Stork Club. This little store is geared for comfort, not sophistication. Chenille sweaters, painters' pants, and overalls share space with toys. ⊠ *142 Sullivan St., between Prince and W. Houston Sts.,* ☎ *212/505–1927.*

Z'Baby Company. Fun clothes such as Suss Design chenille sweaters are a specialty here. ⊠ *100 W. 72nd St., at Columbus Ave.,* ☎ *212/579–2229; 996 Lexington Ave., at E. 72nd St.,* ☎ *212/472–2229.*

DISCOUNT CLOTHING

Eisenberg and Eisenberg. Bargain hunters have relied on this store for well-priced men's suits for decades. ⊠ *16 W. 17th St., between 5th and 6th Aves.,* ☎ *212/627–1290.*

Find Outlet. These outlets are like samples sales seven days a week. Both locations stock up-and-coming and established designer merchandise for 50%–80% off the original price. It's easy to make finds on a regular basis, as the stock is replenished daily. For a wider selection visit the Chelsea location. ⊠ *229 Mott St.,* ☎ *212/226–5167; 361 W. 17th St., between 8th and 9th Aves.,* ☎ *212/243–3177.*

Forman's. The selection of discounted designer sportswear is particularly good at the Orchard Street store—plenty of conservative clothes by Ralph Lauren, Jones New York, and Liz Claiborne, and lots of merchandise for petite and plus sizes. ⊠ *82 Orchard St., between Broome and Grand Sts.,* ☎ *212/228–2500; 145 E. 42nd St., between Lexington and 3rd Aves.,* ☎ *212/681–9800; 59 John St., at William St.,* ☎ *212/791–4100.*

Klein's of Monticello. One of the most genteel stores in the Lower East Side (no fluorescent lighting!), Klein's has authentic labels—Malo cashmere sweaters, Les Copains separates—normally for 20%–30% off. ⊠ *105 Orchard St., at Delancey St.,* ☎ *212/966–1453.*

Loehmann's. After 75 years of selling exclusively women's clothes, Loehmann's added a men's department, where label searchers can turn up $40 Polo/Ralph Lauren chinos and Donna Karan and Dolce & Gabbana suits. The women's designer section also carries American and European designers, though you may need to make a repeat visit or two before emerging victorious. ⊠ *101 7th Ave., at W. 16th St.,* ☎ *212/352–0856.*

Moe Ginsburg. Come here for a large selection of discounted American and European men's suits and casualwear (chinos, Timberland boots, etc.). ⊠ *162 5th Ave., at 21st St.,* ☎ *212/242–3482.*

Syms. There are some excellent buys to be had for designer suits and separates. Men can flip through racks of Bill Blass and Cerruti, while women can turn up Calvin Klein and Christian Dior without even trying. Nondesigner racks can be uninspiring. ⊠ *400 Park Ave., at 54th St.,* ☎ *212/317–8200; 42 Trinity Pl., at Rector St.,* ☎ *212/797–1199.*

MEN'S AND WOMEN'S CLOTHING

A.P.C. The deceptively simple basics in this hip French boutique are modern and retro at the same time. Picture perfectly cut narrow gabardine suits (for both men and women), plus dark denim jeans and jackets that were around even before Helmut Lang co-opted the look for his collections. The back room holds such odds and ends as a careful selection of CDs, plus A.P.C.'s own scented candles and bottles of olive oil. Watch your step on the uneven wooden floorboards. ⊠ *131 Mercer St., between Prince and Spring Sts.,* ☎ *212/966–9685.*

CHEAP THRILLS

IF A SEASONAL SALE makes New Yorkers' eyes gleam, a sample sale throws the city's shoppers into a frenzy. With so many designer flagships and corporate headquarters in town, merchandise fallout periodically leads to tremendous deals. Sample sales typically comprise leftover, already discounted stock, sample designs, and show models. Location adds a bit of an illicit thrill to the event—sales are held in hotels, warehouses, or loft space. Clothes incredible and unfortunate jam a motley assortment of racks, tables, and bins. Generally, there is a makeshift communal dressing room, and mirrors are scarce. Veteran sample-sale shoppers come prepared for wriggling in the aisles; some wear skirts, tights and tank tops for modest quick-changes. Two rules of thumb: grab first and inspect later, and call in advance to find out what methods of payment are accepted.

The level of publicity and regularity of sales vary; look through local publications (particularly *Time Out New York* and *New York* magazines, which both have a special sections listing sales) for announcements, especially in August/September and February/March, but these days year-round. One of the ultimate experiences is the Barneys Warehouse Sale, held in February and August in the über-stylish department store's Chelsea warehouse. Other luscious sales range from the Vera Wang bridal gown sale (early fall) and TSE (spring and late fall) to the downtown chic of Daryl K (winter). If you're interested in a specific designer, call their shop and inquire—you may get lucky.

— Jennifer Paull

A/X: Armani Exchange. A/X's affordable basics make it possible for most people to own an Armani . . . something. T-shirts and dark-washed jeans abound, but there are also sharp zip-front jackets, pea coats, and stretchy knits. ⊠ *568 Broadway, at Prince St.,* ☎ *212/431–6000; 645 5th Ave., at 51st St.,* ☎ *212/980–3037.*

Brooks Brothers. The clothes at this classic American haberdasher are, as ever, traditional, comfortable, and fairly priced. (There is a modernizing effort underway, but the standards remain.) Seersucker (for summer), navy blue blazers, and the peerless oxford shirts have been staples for generations. The women's selection has variations thereof. ⊠ *666 5th Ave., at 53rd St.,* ☎ *212/261–9440; 346 Madison Ave., at E. 44th St.,* ☎ *212/682–8800; 1 Church St., Liberty Plaza,* ☎ *212/267–2400.*

Burberry. The signature plaid is morphing fast, as kilts, leather pants, and messenger-style bags join the traditional gabardine trench coats. ⊠ *9 E. 57th St., between 5th and Madison Aves.,* ☎ *212/371–5010.*

Calvin Klein. The stark flagship store emphasizes the luxe end of the designer's clothing line. Men's suits tend to be soft around the edges; women's evening gowns are often a fluid pouring of silk. There are also shoes, accessories, housewares, and, yes, underwear. ⊠ *654 Madison Ave., at E. 60th St.,* ☎ *212/292–9000.*

Canal Jean Co. A riotous mix of discounted new and funky old clothes fills this yawning space. Do a 360° and you'll catch sight of name brands (CK, Kenneth Cole, the occasional DKNY), sturdy U.S. Navy–issue wool pea coats, and of course, plenty of jeans (including one of the best selections of Levi's around). Hawaiian shirts, tux shirts, flannels, housedresses, and seasonal apparel fill the vintage racks. Hit the basement for Army-Navy surplus. ⊠ *504 Broadway, between Spring and Broome Sts.,* ☎ *212/226–1130.*

Cerruti. Having earned a sterling reputation for men's suits, Cerruti opened its first American boutique here. Move beyond the tailoring to slink into buttery leather, substantial knits, and even specially designed Manolo Blahnik shoes. ⊠ *789 Madison Ave., at 67th St.,* ☎ *212/327–2222.*

Club Monaco. Having struck the balance between low prices, neutral palettes, and mild designer knockoffs, this chain is shifting into high gear. It's so well priced that you can afford to be trendy, caving in to drawstring trousers or waist pouches. ⊠ *121 Prince St., between Mercer and Greene Sts.,* ☎ *212/533–8930; 2376 Broadway, at W. 87th St.,* ☎ *212/579–2587; 160 5th Ave., at 21st St.,* ☎ *212/352–0936; 699 5th Ave., at 55th St.,* ☎ *646/497–1444; 1111 3rd Ave., at E. 65th St.,* ☎ *212/355–2949; 520 Broadway, between Broome and Spring Sts.,* ☎ *212/941–1511.*

Comme des Garçons. The stark, white, groovy space is filled with men's and women's apparel with an androgynous feel. Clothing is modern and expensive. ⊠ *520 W. 22nd St., at 10th Ave.,* ☎ *212/604–0013.*

Costume National. Men's and women's clothes are done in the same sexy, slim-cut styles here. Velvets, silks, and leathers slink down the racks. ⊠ *108 Wooster St., between Prince and Spring Sts.,* ☎ *212/431–1530.*

DDC Lab. This was the first store on the now heavily trafficked Lower East Side to generate buzz among the traditionally hip SoHo crowd. The store carries its own line of modern, sleek clothing and accessories, as well as Levi's Red Label and Seiko watches. There is a coffee bar in the front for a quick jolt of caffeine. ⊠ *180 Orchard St., at Houston St.,* ☎ *212/375–1647.*

D&G. This was the first U.S. store for the secondary Dolce & Gabbana line, which aims for younger customers addicted to Dolce's over-the-top Sicilian-influenced designs. Look for striped sweaters and skinny pants for men and crocheted dresses and embroidered fabrics for women. Flamboyant accessories, from rhinestone-covered stilettos to logo sunglasses, are also available. ⊠ *434 W. Broadway, between Prince and Spring Sts.,* ☎ *212/965–8000.*

Diesel. The display windows styled like washing machines at the Lexington Avenue superstore will tip you off to Diesel's industrial edge. They've taken their futuristic dabblings from graphic prints to fabric—one line uses cloth made with metal fibers. Some generously sized styles are unisex. **Diesel Style Lab** (⊠ 416 W. Broadway, between Prince and Spring Sts., ☎ 212/343–3863) carries a secondary line with more cutting-edge materials and styles. ⊠ *770 Lexington Ave., at E. 60th St.,* ☎ *212/308–0055.*

DKNY. This three-level flagship store is a must-see. Probably the best example of a complete lifestyle store, this Midtown magnet carries everything from the in-house label's menswear and womenswear to a carefully selected array of complementary electronics, housewares, magazines, and jewelry by outside designers. Feel free to grab a stool at the juice bar, log on to one of the in-store iMacs, or listen to a featured CD. ⊠ *655 Madison Ave., at E. 60th St.,* ☎ *212/223–3569.*

Dolce & Gabbana. It's easy to feel like an Italian movie star amid the extravagant (in every sense) clothes here. Pinstripes are a favorite; for women, they could be paired with something sheer and leopard-print, while for men they elongate the sharp suits. The wine-color, velvet-cloaked dressing rooms make trying on brocades, bustiers, and exaggerated hats a dream, but leave time to peek at the small terrace garden. ⊠ *825 Madison Ave., near E. 68th St.,* ☎ *212/249–4100.*

Emporio Armani. At this "middle child" of the Armani trio, the clothes are dressy without quite being formal, often in muted blues, greens, and the ever-cool shades of soot. ⊠ *601 Madison Ave., 57th and 58th Sts.,* ☎ *212/317–0800; 110 5th Ave., at 16th St.,* ☎ *212/727–3240.*

Etro. There are echoes of 19th-century luxury in Etro's clothing, along with a strong whiff of the exotic and a dash of levity. A man's suit might turn up with horizontal pinstripes, while a tweedy shift might sprout mohair at the hem. The rich fabrics are sometimes saturated with strong color: russet, indigo, or ruby. *720 Madison Ave., between 63rd and 64th Sts.,* ☎ *212/317–9096.*

Gianfranco Ferré. Shiny chrome fixtures, dramatic collars, and deep decolleté for women, studded leather and broad-shouldered suits for men—this Italian designer's exuberance leans toward brashness. ⊠ *845 Madison Ave., between 70th and 71st Sts.,* ☎ *212/717–5430.*

Gianni Versace. The five-story flagship store, in a restored turn-of-the-20th-century landmark building on 5th Avenue, hums with colored neon lights. Although the sometimes outrageous designs and colors of Versace clothes might not be to everyone's taste (or budget), they're never boring. A second five-story store has a steely, modern take; it focuses on higher-end clothes and accessories. ⊠ *647 5th Ave., near 51st St.,* ☎ *212/317–0224; 815 Madison Ave., between 68th and 69th Sts.,* ☎ *212/744–6868.*

Giorgio Armani. Armani managed to beat out Calvin Klein on the exterior-minimalism front; inside, the space has a museumlike quality, reinforced by the refined clothes. Suits for men and women have a telltale perfect drape, and women's might be accessorized with a broad, striking, beaded-collar necklace. ⊠ *760 Madison Ave., between 65th and 66th Sts.,* ☎ *212/988–9191.*

Gucci. The white-hot label shows no signs of cooling off—even the traditional red-and-green ribbon is chic again. The trendiest items inevitably turn up as less-expensive knockoffs for seasons to come, but there are also some subtly modern basics. ⊠ *685 5th Ave., between 53rd and 54th Sts.,* ☎ *212/826–2600.*

Helmut Lang. Lang's men's and women's clothes—mostly in black, white, and gray, plus the less expensive jeans line (which includes more than just denim)—are tough distillations of his skinny-pants aesthetic. Look for Lang's first collection of bags and shoes. Black, mirror-ended walls slice up the space, which is punctuated by the digital ticker-tape designed by artist (and Lang collaborator) Jenny Holzer. ⊠ *80 Greene St., between Spring and Broome Sts.,* ☎ *212/925–7214.*

Hermès. Patterned silk scarves, neckties, and the sacred "Kelly" handbags are hallmarks. The stores carry both the traditional horse-theme merchandise alongside a more current selection. ⊠ *691 Madison Ave., at E. 64th St.,* ☎ *212/751–3181; 745 5th Ave., at 57th St.,* ☎ *212/759–7585.*

H&M. At both locations, crowds of locals and tourists swarm over the racks in search of up-to-the-minute fashions at unbelievably low prices. Fitting room lines are impossibly long and the clothing is rather cheaply made, but at these prices you can afford to indulge your wilder fashion fantasies. Be prepared to fight for your purchases. ⊠ *640 5th Ave., at 51st St.,* ☎ *212/489–8777; 1328 Broadway, at 34th St.,* ☎ *212/564–9922.*

Hugo Boss. All three Hugo Boss lines are sold at this German apparel maker's biggest store so far: The Baldasarini line of hand-tailored luxury items, the Boss line of more mainstream styles and prices, and the Hugo line of hip styles geared younger. While Hugo Boss is known for its menswear, women will have no problems finding classy, yet trendy styles. **Hugo** (⊠ *132 Greene St., between Houston and Prince Sts.,* ☎ *212/965–1300*) carries a spinoff line with more high-tech materials and styles for a younger customer. Pieces of the new women's line are also sold here. ⊠ *717 5th Ave., at 57th St.,* ☎ *212/688–2800.*

Issey Miyake. Pleats of a Fortuny-like tightness are the Miyake signature—but instead of Fortuny's silks, these clothes are in polyester or ultra-high-tech textiles. **Pleats Please** (✉ 128 Wooster St., at Prince St., ☎ 212/226–3600) carries a secondary line with a bolder color palette. ✉ 992 Madison Ave., between 76th and 77th Sts., ☎ 212/439–7822.

J. Crew. At these pristine showcases for apple-cheeked East Coast style, you can get turned out for a job interview or a week in the Adirondacks. Wool crepe suits, rollneck sweaters, chinos, and mix-and-match bikini swimwear tow the basic-but-not-boring line. (Just because you've seen something in the catalog doesn't mean you'll find it in the store–but you may also find items not shown in the catalog.) ✉ 99 Prince St., between Mercer and Greene Sts., ☎ 212/966–2739; 203 Front St., at Fulton St., ☎ 212/385–3500; 91 5th Ave., between 16th and 17th Sts., ☎ 212/255–4848; 230 World Trade Center, ☎ 212/839–8378; 30 Rockefeller Plaza, W. 51st St. between 5th and 6th Aves., ☎ 212/765–4412.

Jeffrey. Manhattan's hot neighborhood du jour, still known as the Meatpacking District, really arrived when this Atlanta-based mini-Barneys opened its doors. You'll find the most incredible array of shoes this side of the Mason Dixon line (Jeffrey also specializes in hard-to-find sizes), plus the ultimate in labels, like Marc Jacobs, Gucci, and the apparel line from Samsonite. ✉ 449 W. 14th St., between 9th and 10th Aves., ☎ 212/206–1272.

Keiko New York. End bathing-suit trauma once and for all by getting your swimsuit customized here—or pick out one of the ready-made, brightly colored numbers (men's and women's). ✉ 62 Greene St., between Spring and Broome Sts., ☎ 212/226–6051.

Marc Jacobs. Next door to a SoHo garage lies Jacobs's sleek boutique displaying piles of perfect (and pricey) cashmere, silk, and wool. But the luscious fabrics aren't always treated with complete gravitas: skirts could have an oversize-scallop hem, or a hidden closure might reveal extra-large snaps. ✉ 163 Mercer St., between Houston and Prince Sts., ☎ 212/343–1490.

Missoni. The signature look weaves stripes and waves of color through knits (often rayon viscose). The fresh color combinations—pink, coral, and pistachio, deep purple, violet, and aqua—show up everywhere from bikinis and dresses to men's sweaters. ✉ 1009 Madison Ave., at 78th St., ☎ 212/517–9339.

Nicole Farhi. The designer's New York flagship store represents the convergence of her many design talents and endeavors—men's and women's apparel, home furnishings, and restaurants. The acclaimed, London-based Farhi's natural yet modern style is carried out throughout the entire store—from bed linens to blouses. For hungry shoppers, the basement level restaurant is a perfect respite for breakfast, lunch, or dinner. ✉ 10 E. 60th St., between 5th and Madison Aves., ☎ 212/223–8811.

Old Navy One Below. The Gap's kissing cousin has quickly garnered legions of fans with its kick-around clothes at terrific prices—but you already know that if you live anywhere near civilization. What you don't know is that Old Navy has an advanced collection of club-oriented styles called One Below (think Diesel on a budget) that's available on the basement level of their Herald Square branch (and in the SoHo store). Also check out the live DJ and the vending machines carrying Japanese candies. ✉ 610 6th Ave., at W. 18th St., ☎ 212/645–0663; 503 Broadway, between Broome and Spring Sts., ☎ 212/226–0838; 150 W. 34th St., at Broadway, ☎ 212/594–0049.

Patricia Field. This shop and its **Hotel Venus** (✉ 382 W. Broadway, near Broome St., ☎ 212/966–4066) offshoot are emporiums of wacky style and bad taste, making them *the* resource for club gear, from shiny vinyl jumpsuits to Hysteric Glamour T-shirts imported from London. Keep an eye out for funky sunglasses, hats, or talking watches that give the time in French or Japanese. At Hotel Venus, there's a far-out beauty salon; be sure to stop by the photo booth outside for some tiny sticker photos. ⊠ *10 E. 8th St., between 5th Ave. and University Pl.,* ☎ *212/254–1699.*

Paul Stuart Inc. The fabric selection is interesting, the tailoring superb, and the look traditional but not stodgy. ⊠ *Madison Ave., at E. 45th St.,* ☎ *212/682–0320.*

Polo/Ralph Lauren. One of New York's most distinctive shopping experiences, Lauren's flagship store is in the turn-of-the-20th-century Rhinelander mansion. Clothes range from summer-in-the-Hamptons madras to exquisite silk gowns and Purple Label men's suits. Across the street and downtown, **Polo Sport** (⊠ 888 Madison Ave., at 72nd St., ☎ 212/434–8000; 381 W. Broadway, near Broome St., ☎ 212/625–1660) carries casual clothes and sports gear, plus a well-groomed lot of vintage pieces such as wool prep-school blazers. ⊠ *867 Madison Ave., at 72nd St.,* ☎ *212/606–2100.*

Prada. Prada's gossamer silks, slick black techno-fabric suits, and ultraluxe shoes and leather goods are among the last great Italian fashion coups of the last millennium. The main stores pulse with pale "verdolino" green walls (remember this if you start questioning your skin tone). The Wooster Street store zeros in on the sport collection (though the parkas may see more club lines than tree lines) and a new location is scheduled to move into a large space on Broadway at Prince Street. ⊠ *724 5th Ave., between 56th and 57th Sts.,* ☎ *212/664–0010; 45 E. 57th St., between 5th and Madison Aves.,* ☎ *212/308–2332; 841 Madison Ave., between 69th and 70th Sts.,* ☎ *212/327–4200; 116 Wooster St., between Prince and Spring Sts.,* ☎ *212/925–2221.*

R by 45rpm. Upon entering the serene store front, you will feel like you have been transported to Japan. The decor is a combination of bamboo, oak, and exposed brick and the store's contents—everything from T-shirts to belts—are made from unique Asian fabrics. Check out the batik scarves that come wrapped in their instructions for tying, and the funky jeans line. ⊠ *169 Mercer St., near Houston St.,* ☎ *917/237–0045.*

Thomas Pink. London's Jermyn Street shirtmaker has hopped the pond with its traditional, impeccably tailored shirts in several styles; besides the British-favored spread collars and French cuffs, there are button-down collars and buttoned cuffs. The eponymous color crops up often, sometimes in brighter shades than Americans are used to. Silk ties, cuff links, and two lines of women's shirts round out the selection at both locations. ⊠ *520 Madison Ave., between 52nd and 53rd Sts.,* ☎ *212/838–1928; 115 6th Ave., at Watts St.,* ☎ *212/840–9663.*

Trash and Vaudeville. Black, white, and electric colors are the focus here—and you never know when you might see Lou Reed buying jeans. ⊠ *4 St. Marks Pl., between 2nd and 3rd Aves.,* ☎ *212/982–3590.*

TSE. The soft delicacy of the cashmere designs here doesn't stop at the fabric; TSE's sweaters are hopelessly refined. ⊠ *827 Madison Ave., between 68th and 69th Sts.,* ☎ *212/472–7790.*

Urban Outfitters. This national hipster chain has been making trends affordable and accessible to the masses for years. It is a mecca for the young and constantly innovating consumer. The apparel can be cheaply made and the home furnishings may not last a lifetime, but you'll be on to something else soon enough. Each location carries similar merchandise in different set-ups. ⊠ *162 2nd Ave., between E. 9th and E. 10th Sts.,* ☎ *212/375–1277; 374 6th Ave., at Waverly Pl.,* ☎ *212/677–9350; 628 Broadway, at Houston St.,* ☎ *212/475–0009; 2081 Broadway, at W. 72nd St.,* ☎ *212/579–3930.*

Valentino. The mix here is at once audacious and beautifully cut; the fur or feather trimmings, low necklines, and opulent fabrics are about as close as you can get to celluloid glamour. ⊠ *747 Madison Ave., between 64th and 65th Sts.,* ☎ *212/772–6969.*

Yohji Yamamoto. Although almost entirely in black and white, these clothes aren't as severe as they seem. Wool sweaters can be so fine they're translucent; necklines, hems, and waists are tweaked imaginatively. ⊠ *103 Grand St., between Mercer and Greene Sts.,* ☎ *212/966–9066.*

Yves Saint Laurent Rive Gauche. The fashion flock has recently renewed their interest in Yves Saint Laurent's theatrical women's styles, sold at the uptown shop. Designer Hedi Slimane's sleek items, sold at the downtown men's shop, are at the top of many wish lists. ⊠ *855 Madison Ave., between 70th and 71st Sts.,* ☎ *212/988–3821; 88 Wooster St., between Spring and Broome Sts.,* ☎ *212/274–0522.*

Zao. A very hip mini-department store, this sleek and modern space is filled with men's and women's apparel and accessories, electronic gadgetry, home decor, and artwork. Shop owners carefully select each item to fit with the 21st century, high-tech lifestyle. ⊠ *175 Orchard St., between E. Houston and Stanton Sts.,* ☎ *212/505–0500.*

Zara. Essentially Spain's version of The Gap, this chain that carries men's and women's clothing and accessories offers its international customers the latest trends at reasonable prices. ⊠ *750 Lexington Ave., between 59th and 60th Sts.,* ☎ *212/754–1120; 101 5th Ave., between 15th and 16th Sts.,* ☎ *212/741–0555; 580 Broadway, between Prince and Spring Sts.,* ☎ *212/343–1725.*

MEN'S CLOTHING

Agnès b. Homme. This French designer's love for the movies makes it easy to come out looking a little Godard around the edges. Turtleneck sweaters, lean black suits, and black leather porkpie hats demand the sangfroid of Belmondo. ⊠ *79 Greene St., between Broome and Spring Sts.,* ☎ *212/431–4339.*

Alfred Dunhill of London. Corporate brass come here for finely tailored clothing, both ready-made and custom-ordered, and smoking accessories; the walk-in humidor stores top-quality tobacco and cigars. ⊠ *450 Park Ave., between 56th and 57th Sts.,* ☎ *212/753–9292.*

Ascot Chang. Perfect tailoring is a given here, from the worsted-wool suits to the ready-made shirts, but the custom-made shirts are truly outstanding. (There's a four-shirt minimum for the first order.) ⊠ *7 W. 57th St., between 5th and 6th Aves.,* ☎ *212/759–3333.*

Façonnable. This French company has a lock on the Euro-conservative look. Their sport coats (about $800) and Italian-made suits may be expensive, but the tailoring and canvas fronting will make them withstand years of dry cleaning. ⊠ *689 5th Ave., at 54th St.,* ☎ *212/319–0111.*

Holland & Holland. This is no Ralph-Lauren-does-country-squire; Holland & Holland provides the Prince of Wales (and wealthy colonials) with country clothing and accessories such as leather falcon hoods. There's a special safari tailoring section and a gun room on the fifth floor. ⊠ *50 E. 57th St., between Madison and Park Aves.,* ☎ *212/752–7755.*

J. Lindeberg. Leathers and shearling are signature fabrics of this high-end, Stockholm-based men's clothing and accessories label. Styles range from trendy to conservative. The quality is high and the prices reflect it. ⊠ *126 Spring St., at Greene St.,* ☎ *212/625–9403.*

J. Press. Oxford-cloth shirts, natural-shoulder suits, madras-patch Bermuda shorts, and amusing club ties will help you join the old boy network—or just look the part. ⊠ *7 E. 44th St., between 5th and Madison Aves.,* ☎ *212/687–7642.*

John Varvatos. Varvatos, who is being hailed as this year's hottest menswear designer, has recently opened these split level digs in Soho.

The store is tastefully filled with everything from ties to shoes, and from outerwear to watches. The in-house line is designed for every lifestyle, featuring casual wear to suiting. ⊠ *149 Mercer St., ☎ 212/965–0700.*

Nautica. Inspired by the nautical lifestyle, the clothing at this store maintains a fairly consistent look. Blue and white stripes are the trademark look of designer David Chu's sporty and classic menswear line. ⊠ *50 Rockefeller Center, between 5th and 6th Aves., ☎ 212/664–9594.*

Paul Smith. Dark mahogany Victorian cases complement the foppish British styles they hold. Embroidered vests, brightly colored socks and shirts, and quirky cuff links and other accessories leaven the classic, dark, double-back-vent suits. (Smith's women's line isn't carried in this boutique, but look for it at Barneys or Bergdorf Goodman.) ⊠ *108 5th Ave., at 16th St., ☎ 212/627–9770.*

Sean. A welcome antidote to the omnipresent minimalist boxes, these snug shops carry low-key, well-priced, and comfortable apparel from France—soft cardigans, very-narrow-wale corduroy pants, and a respectable collection of suits and dress shirts. ⊠ *132 Thompson St., between Houston and Prince Sts., ☎ 212/598–5980; 224 Columbus Ave., between W. 70th and W. 71st Sts., ☎ 212/769–1489.*

Seize sur Vingt. Made-to-order shirts and suits for both the uptown and downtown man are the specialty at this NoLita shop. Be prepared to spend a pretty penny for the handsome, customized patterns and styles. ⊠ *243 Elizabeth St., at Prince St., ☎ 212/343–0476.*

Sulka. Most of the luxurious clothes at these stores are Italian—the silk robes are so swank they've shown up on Broadway, in a Noël Coward play. ⊠ *Waldorf-Astoria, 310 Park Ave., between E. 49th and 50th Sts., ☎ 212/980–5226; 430 Park Ave., between 55th and 56th Sts., ☎ 212/980–5200; 840 Madison Ave., between 69th and 70th Sts., ☎ 212/452–1900.*

WOMEN'S CLOTHING

Agnès b. With this quintessentially French line you can look like a Parisienne schoolgirl—in snap-front tops, slender pants, sweet floral prints— or like her oh-so-chic *maman* in beautifully tailored dark suits. ⊠ *116– 118 Prince St., between 55th and 56th Sts., ☎ 212/925–4649; 13 E. 16th St., between 5th Ave. and Union Sq. W, ☎ 212/741–2585; 1063 Madison Ave., between 80th and 81st Sts., ☎ 212/570–9333.*

Alicia Mugetti. Silks and velvets are layered, softly shaped, and sometimes hand-painted, creating an almost Elizabethan effect. ⊠ *999 Madison Ave., at 77th St., ☎ 212/794–6186.*

Anna Sui. The violet-and-black salon, hung with Beardsley prints and neon alterna-rock posters, is the perfect setting for Sui's flapper- and rocker-influenced designs, which now include bohemian-inspired accessories and cosmetics. ⊠ *113 Greene St., between Prince and Spring Sts., ☎ 212/941–8406.*

Anne Fontaine. The white blouses here might make you swear off plain oxford shirts forever. Rows of snowy blouses (most in cotton poplin or organdy) are jazzed up with lacings, embroidery, or billowing sleeves. There are also a few black shirts. ⊠ *93 Greene St., between Prince and Spring Sts., ☎ 212/343–3154.*

Barbara Bui. Leave it to the French to successfully mix feminine details (jackets with a thin edging of leather or mink, sprays of beading) with a cold, industrial edge (shirts from the secondary line come encased in vacuum-sealed plastic pouches). ⊠ *115–117 Wooster St., between Prince and Spring Sts., ☎ 212/625–1938.*

Betsey Johnson. The SoHo store departs from the traditional (if such a word can be applied) hot pink interior; instead its walls are sunny yellow with painted roses; and there's a bordello-red lounge area in back. Besides the quirkily printed dresses, available in all stores, there's a slinky upscale line. This is not the place for natural fibers—it's ruled by rayon, stretch, and the occasional faux fur. ⊠ *138 Wooster St., at Prince St.,* ☎ *212/995–5048; 251 E. 60th St., between 2nd and 3rd Aves.,* ☎ *212/319–7699; 248 Columbus Ave., between W. 71st and W. 72nd Sts.,* ☎ *212/362–3364; 1060 Madison Ave., between 80th and 81st Sts.,* ☎ *212/734–1257.*

Calypso St. Barth. With feathers, fringe, sequins, and appliqués, Calypso adds a measure of decadence to its flippant clothes. If you are headed to the tropics this is an essential stop for colorful and fun beachwear. ⊠ *280 Mott St., between Prince and Houston Sts.,* ☎ *212/965–0990; 424 Broome St., at Crosby St.,* ☎ *212/274–0449; 935 Madison Ave., at E. 74th St.,* ☎ *212/535–4100.*

Carolina Herrera. The minimalist store is almost as elegant as the women's wear it houses. Devotees of the red carpet-worthy line no longer have to head to high-end department stores to indulge in her finery. ⊠ *954 Madison Ave., at E. 75th St.,* ☎ *212/249–6552.*

Catherine. This store will shake you out of the black habit with lavender leather, powder-blue angora, crocheted dresses, and pink cowboy hats. Designer Catherine Malandrino's line is always cutting-edge, colorful, and decadent. ⊠ *468 Broome St., between Mercer and Greene Sts.,* ☎ *212/925–6765.*

Chanel. The flagship midtown store has often been compared to a classic Chanel suit—slim, elegant, and timeless. The building includes fashion and jewelry boutiques, as well as a five-story, Provence-saturated Frédéric Fekkai salon. The downtown store is designed to attract the younger, hipper Chanel customer. ⊠ *139 Spring St., at Wooster St.,* ☎ *212/334–0055; 15 E. 57th St., between 5th and Madison Aves.,* ☎ *212/355–5050.*

Chloé. Stella McCartney's high-end fashion line features everything from $80 rocker T-shirts to $8,000 beaded dresses. The styles change with the trends, but you can count on the clothing and accessories to be sexy, fun, and expensive. You may have to put your name on a wait list for the coveted sunglasses. ⊠ *850 Madison Ave., at E. 70th St.,* ☎ *212/717–8220.*

Christian Dior. The New York outpost of one of France's most venerable fashion houses now makes its home in the dazzlingly modern LVMH tower, where it continues to offer daytime and evening clothes, plus its signature accessories and perfumes. ⊠ *21 E. 57th St., at Madison Ave.,* ☎ *212/931–2950.*

Daryl K. One of Daryl K's early, no-nonsense design goals was to make her derriere look good in a pair of jeans, and she now doles out the favor with low-rise, skinny-leg denims (about $120–$130) plus cotton-twill versions in shades like olive and black. Leathers, loud T-shirts and slim-fitting jackets have a hard-edged downtown chic. The tiny East 6th Street shop, which features mostly pants, always has a sale going on, while the Bond Street store showcases the full collection, including accessories. ⊠ *208 E. 6th St., between 2nd and 3rd Aves.,* ☎ *212/475–1255; 21 Bond St., between the Bowery and Lafayette St.,* ☎ *212/777–0713.*

Emanuel Ungaro. Ladies-who-lunch daytime suits are matched with grande dame, sometimes bead-encrusted, evening wear. ⊠ *792 Madison Ave., between 66th and 67th Sts.,* ☎ *212/249–4090.*

Escada. Famous for its formalwear—namely, evening gowns and suiting—Escada sells only the finest of finery. The grandiose feel of the six-floor flagship location suits the merchandise. A couture salon recently opened within the store and a Madison Avenue location is set to open in Spring 2001. ⊠ *7 E. 57th St., at 5th Ave.,* ☎ *212/755–2201.*

Geoffrey Beene. Mr. Beene, as he is known even to friends, is revered by fashion followers, and his small but splendid boutique has some curvaceous day and evening wear, which often makes much of the waist. ✉ *783 5th Ave., between 59th and 60th Sts.,* ☎ *212/935–0470.*

Hedra Prue. This funky NoLita boutique houses the clothing and accessory designs of the most up-and-coming young designers, such as Martin and Trosman Churba, displayed among a few more established ones, like Juicy Couture and William B. You will feel like you're in the closet of a downtown hipster. ✉ *281 Mott St., between Houston and Prince Sts.,* ☎ *212/343–9205.*

Intermix. Here, the trend-conscious will find one-stop shopping for upscale items from lines such as Katayone Adeli and D&G. All branches carry higher-end lines like Blumarine, plus shoes and accessories. ✉ *125 5th Ave., between 19th and 20th Sts.,* ☎ *212/533–9720; 210 Columbus Ave., between W. 69th and W. 70th Sts.,* ☎ *212/769–9116; 633 Madison Ave., between E. 77th and E. 78th Sts.,* ☎ *212/249–7858.*

Jade. Aglow with silk and brocade, this little store turns jewel-tone rough silk into dresses, mandarin jackets, and other separates. Prices range from $30 all the way to $500. ✉ *280 Mulberry St., between Houston and Jersey Sts.,* ☎ *212/925–6544.*

Katayone Adeli. Katayone set up her ultrasleek shop on the block that Daryl K made hip. Now you can see the full collection of subtly sexy basics, plus exclusive pieces that are only carried here. The more reasonably priced line, K2, is also available. Pants tend to run very small and the larger sizes sell out fast, so prepare for disappointment. ✉ *25 Bond St., between the Bowery and Lafayette St.,* ☎ *212/260–3500.*

Kirna Zabête. SoHo's store of the moment is full of pieces by hard-to-find designers such as Hussein Chalayan and Eley Kishimoto. There are also coveted e.vil T-shirts (for women, men and dogs), funky-fancy jewels, and even giant gum balls. ✉ *96 Greene St., between Spring and Prince Sts.,* ☎ *212/941–9656.*

Language. The first of the multi-purpose fashion boutiques, this one also offers modern furniture and keeps a library of back issues of cult style–mag *Visionaire* (since some run more than $100 a pop, maybe it's better just to look). ✉ *238 Mulberry St., between Prince and Spring Sts.,* ☎ *212/431–5566.*

Laura Ashley. Laura Ashley's last Manhattan holdout still purveys the hyperfloral look, although some flower prints are nearly abstract and there are simple linen sundresses. ✉ *398 Columbus Ave., at W. 79th St.,* ☎ *212/496–5110.*

Liz Lange Maternity. This is the perfect destination for anyone taking part in the current baby boom. This is modern maternity wear for such modern moms-to-be as Cindy Crawford, who picked up some leather pants here. ✉ *958 Madison Ave., near 75th St.,* ☎ *212/879–2191.*

Malia Mills. Finally, bathing suits for women of every body type. Prices are high, styles are flattering, and pieces are sold separately. The good lighting and sweet salespeople help to make shopping for a bathing suit bearable. ✉ *199 Mulberry St., between Kenmare and Spring St.,* ☎ *212/625–2311.*

Marina Rinaldi. These plus-size tailored suits, cocktail dresses, and sweeping coats know just how to flatter. ✉ *800 Madison Ave., between 67th and 68th Sts.,* ☎ *212/734–4333.*

Max Mara. Think subtle colors and enticing fabrics—photo exhibits lend to the genteel atmosphere. This Italian design house sticks with the classic and avoids the trendy. ✉ *813 Madison Ave., at 68th St.,* ☎ *212/879–6100.*

Mayle. This little shotgun boutique (previously known as Phare) basks in the ineffable vapor of cool. Designer Jane Mayle, who is often found lounging in the store, designs close-fitting knit tops, ultrasuede bags, and retro-style dresses, which are displayed alongside vintage items she culls from flea markets around the world. Word has it she is the hottest young designer around. ✉ *252 Elizabeth St., between Houston and Prince Sts.,* ☎ *212/625–0406.*

Miu Miu. Prada frontwoman Miuccia Prada established a secondary line (bearing her childhood nickname, Miu Miu) to showcase her more experimental ideas, and this boutique was the first she opened in America. Look for Prada-esque styles in more daring colors and fabrics, plus a stable of classic black clothing and accessories. ✉ *100 Prince St., between Mercer and Greene Sts.,* ☎ *212/334–5156.*

Morgane Le Fay. The clothes here borrow from centuries past (swaddlings of silk, high waists); you almost have to be tall and willowy, or French, to carry it off. ✉ *746 Madison Ave., between 64th and 65th Sts.,* ☎ *212/879–9700; 67 Wooster St., between Broome and Spring Sts.,* ☎ *212/219–7672.*

Moschino. IT'S BETTER TO DRESS AS YOU WISH THAN AS YOU SHOULD! proclaims one of the walls of the multi-story Moschino flagship. People with a penchant for comedic couture won't have any trouble finding their wardrobe soul-mate in this whirligig store. ✉ *803 Madison Ave., between 67th and 68th Sts.,* ☎ *212/639–9600.*

Nicole Miller. Known for her silk prints spoofing almost any topic imaginable (French wine, Dalmatians, sports), Nicole Miller also sells some evening dresses that are popular on the bridesmaid circuit. ✉ *780 Madison Ave., between 66th and 67th Sts.,* ☎ *212/288–9779; 134 Prince St., between W. Broadway and Wooster St.,* ☎ *212/343–1362.*

Norma Kamali O.M.O. Dim corners and dislocated stairs characterize this bunkerlike store—an odd setting for evening gowns, long tunics, and resort-ready bathing suits. The store now features a vintage Kamali section. ✉ *11 W. 56th St., between 5th and 6th Aves.,* ☎ *212/957–9797.*

Onward Soho. The airy, two-level space is home to Japanese designer Yoshiki Hishinuma's womenswear lines, ICB apparel, and Moja eyewear. Unusual printing and shrinking techniques produce a unique look in the clothing. ✉ *172 Mercer St., at E. Houston St.,* ☎ *212/274–1255.*

Philosophy di Alberta Ferretti. The designer's eye for delicate detailing is evident in the seaming and sprinklings of beads across gauzy fabrics or soft knits. ✉ *452 W. Broadway, between Houston and Prince Sts.,* ☎ *212/460–5500.*

Searle. Strung along the East Side, these stores have a devoted following for their coats: pea coats, long wool coats, shearlings, leather, or even fluffy Mongolian lamb. In recent years, they've added trendy fashions to their boutiques, in the form of designer labels such as Jill Stuart and Betsey Johnson, plus lots of great accessories. ✉ *1051 3rd Ave., at E. 62nd St.,* ☎ *212/838–5990; 1035 Madison Ave., at E. 79th St.,* ☎ *212/717–4022; 605 Madison Ave., at E. 58th St.,* ☎ *212/753–9021; 1035 Madison Ave., at E. 79th St.,* ☎ *212/717–4022; 1124 Madison Ave., at E. 84th St.,* ☎ *212/988–7318.*

Sonia Rykiel. Paris's "queen of knitwear" sets off strong colors such as fuchsia or orange with, *naturellement,* black. ✉ *849 Madison Ave., between 70th and 71st Sts.,* ☎ *212/396–3060.*

Tocca. You can go into this deliciously girly store and *not* find a stitch of black clothing. Instead there are dozens of dresses, skirts, and sweaters in pastels or deeper hues such as bright pink or mossy green—many embroidered or delicately beaded. Be sure to check out the embroidered bed linens and Tocca's new line of candles and fragrances. ✉ *161 Mercer St., between Houston and Prince Sts.,* ☎ *212/343–3912.*

Tracy Feith. The sexy, frilly dresses (in shades such as pistachio and hot pink) here make it hard to believe that Tracy is actually a tall, lanky, long-haired man who wears a cowboy hat. The clothes are incredibly expensive (blouses can be $350, dresses $500), but it's worth a trip just to swoon. Jewelry is eclectic and can be as low as $40, a relative bargain. The store is starting to carry a surf-inspired menswear line of tops and jams. ⊠ *209 Mulberry St., between Spring and Kenmare Sts.,* ☎ *212/334–3097.*

United Colors of Benetton. Benetton's three-level flagship store is in the old Scribner building on 5th Avenue; among the colorful separates are scores of sweaters. ⊠ *597 5th Ave., at 48th St.,* ☎ *212/317–2501.*

Vera Wang. Sumptuous made-to-order bridal and evening wear is shown here by appointment only. Periodic pret-a-porter sales offer designer dresses for a (relative) song. ⊠ *991 Madison Ave., at 77th St.,* ☎ *212/628–3400.*

Vivienne Tam. Tam is known for her playful take on familiar Asian images: Chinese dragons crawl across T-shirts, embroidered flowers and koi fish spill down shifts, and the Buddha smiles imperturbably from gauzy dresses. Her most recent inspiration is the very-American Empire State Building. ⊠ *99 Greene St., between Prince and Spring Sts.,* ☎ *212/966–2398.*

Vivienne Westwood. Up front, the grande dame of British fashion offers rocker clothes from her Anglomania line; move toward the back for the dandyish fabrics and tongue-in-cheek touches (oversize buttons, elaborate necklines) of the couture line. ⊠ *71 Greene St., between Spring and Broome Sts.,* ☎ *212/334–5200.*

Crystal

Baccarat. "Life is worth Baccarat," say the ads—in other words, the quality of crystal shown here is priceless. ⊠ *625 Madison Ave., at 59th St.,* ☎ *212/826–4100.*

Galleri Orrefors Kosta Boda. Stop here for striking Swedish crystal, including work from the imaginative and often brightly colored Kosta Boda line. ⊠ *685 Madison Ave., between 61st and 62nd Sts.,* ☎ *212/ 752–1095.*

Hoya Crystal Gallery. The stunningly designed vases beg for an exotic bloom or two; the tableware includes everything from hand-etched goblets to a sake set with fish designs at the bottom of the cups. ⊠ *689 Madison Ave., at 62nd St.,* ☎ *212/223–6335.*

Steuben. The adventurous designs on display at this 5th Avenue landmark go beyond the basic vase. You'll find everything from wine goblets to whimsical figurines. ⊠ *667 Madison Ave., at 61st St.,* ☎ *212/ 752–1441.*

Gadgets

Hammacher Schlemmer. The store that offered America its first pop-up toaster still ferrets out the outrageous, the unusual, and the best of home electronics. ⊠ *147 E. 57th St., between 6th and 7th Aves.,* ☎ *212/421–9000.*

Sharper Image. This is the store that launched the "must have" scooter. Each location carries an assortment of things to make the good life even better, including massage chairs, electronics, and whatsits such as miniature replicas of classic cars. ⊠ *Pier 17, South Street Seaport,* ☎ *212/693–0477; 4 W. 57th St., at 5th Ave.,* ☎ *212/265–2550; 900 Madison Ave., at 72nd St.,* ☎ *212/794–4974.*

Home Furnishings

ABC Carpet & Home. Resembling the attic of an eccentric hoarder of decorative things, this immense, crammed emporium sells everything from ornate furniture and rugs to vintage tea sets, linens, and meditation cushions. The in-house restaurants, Chicama and Pipa, offer distinct takes on the Pan-Latino fare of well-known chef Douglas Rodriguez. ⊠ *888 Broadway, at E. 19th St.,* ☎ *212/473–3000.*

The Apartment. It is a real, working, lived-in New York City apartment. Oh, and everything in it is for sale. Most of the contents are European imports. Shopping here is truly an experience. Stroll around the multi-level apartment, lounge on the couch in front of the flat-screen TV, or eat a crêpe in the working kitchen. Anything you see, including the kitchen sink, can be yours. ⊠ *101 Crosby St., near Prince St.,* ☎ *212/219–3661.*

Avventura. Glory in Italian design in all its streamlined beauty here. Tabletop items and handblown glass accessories are all stunning. ⊠ *463 Amsterdam Ave., at W. 82nd St.,* ☎ *212/769–2510.*

Bed, Bath & Beyond. This Chelsea megastore stocks some 80,000 different household items, from bedding to kitchenware, at reasonable prices. Go hungry and feast at the fabulous salad bar. Weekends are mob scenes. ⊠ *620 6th Ave., between W. 18th and W. 19th Sts.,* ☎ *212/255–3550.*

Crate & Barrel. A terrific selection of practically everything imaginable for the home and kitchen, including glassware, kitchen and bath items, and stylish furniture, is the hallmark of this bright blond-wood-lined store. ⊠ *650 Madison Ave., at 60th St.,* ☎ *212/308–0011.*

Eclectic Home. Even after several years, Chelsea's first contemporary home-design store still looks fresh; the lighting and home accessories range from retro to downright silly. ⊠ *224 8th Ave., between W. 21st and W. 22nd Sts.,* ☎ *212/255–2373.*

Felissimo. Spread over four stories of a beaux arts town house are unusual objets d'art and accessories, many handcrafted, that marry classic European and modern Asian sensibilities. Some items (Japanese incense, and aromatherapy and feng shui sets) whisper elegant New Age-iness, while others (Moroccan tagines, lavish glassware, antique silver) celebrate good old-fashioned materialism. A seasonal menu and tarot card readings are offered in the tearoom. ⊠ *10 W. 56th St., between 5th and 6th Aves.,* ☎ *212/247–5656.*

Fishs Eddy. Dish heaven is what you'll find here. They resell the funkiest dishes, china, and glassware from all walks of crockery life—corporate dining rooms, failed restaurants, etc. There are always some cheap new wares, and lots of oddball pieces such as finger bowls and porcelain globe molds. ⊠ *2176 Broadway, at W. 77th St.,* ☎ *212/873–8819; 889 Broadway, at E. 19th St.,* ☎ *212/420–9020; 60 Mercer St., at Broome St.,* ☎ *212/226–4711.*

Gates of Marrakesh. Sharpen your acquisitive streak in this small Moroccan shop, where light filters through henna-painted sheepskin lamps and glistens on the diminutive, gold-painted tea glasses. ⊠ *8 Prince St., between Bowery and Elizabeth St.,* ☎ *212/925–2650.*

Hudson Dry Goods. You'll want to buy everything in these eclectic home furnishings stores, which carry a delightful mix of the old and the new. Uptown is a more cluttered boutique; the downtown store has a wider selection of candles, lamps, dressers, and couches. ⊠ *873 Broadway, between E. 18th and E. 19th Sts.,* ☎ *212/228–7143; 112 W. 72nd St., between Columbus and Amsterdam Aves.,* ☎ *212/579–7397.*

Jonathan Adler. The blunt graphics (stripes, crosses, circles) that emblazon the handmade pottery (ranging from a tiny $30 vase to a stunning $400 lamp), wool pillow covers, throws, and even ponchos are Adler's trademark. If the store is out of stock, place a special order at no extra cost. ⊠ *465 Broome St., at Greene St.,* ☎ *212/941–8950.*

La Maison Moderne. Home accessories with a Gallic flair are a specialty here—to cheer up your mornings, check out the sunny yellow Banania breakfast dishes. ⊠ *144 W. 19th St., between 6th and 7th Aves.,* ☎ *212/691–9603.*

Let There Be Neon. Browse among the terrific collection of new and antique neon signs, clocks, and tabletop accessories. ⊠ *38 White St., between Broadway and Church St.,* ☎ *212/226–4883.*

MacKenzie-Childs Ltd. Fantastical windows and a palatial birdcage, home to elegant live chickens, make this a store unlike any other. Handmade majolica ware, table settings, and trimmings are done with a Victorian exuberance for detail. ⊠ *824 Madison Ave., between 68th and 69th Sts.,* ☎ *212/570–6050.*

McAdoo Rugs. Beautifully crafted hooked rugs display an unfathomable range of designs, from sea creatures to grizzly bears. ⊠ *970 Lexington Ave., between E. 70th and 71st Sts.,* ☎ *212/452–3231.*

Miya Shoji Interiors. This shop offers a superb selection of beautifully crafted Japanese folding screens, plus *tonsu* chests and tatami platforms. ⊠ *109 W. 17th St., between 6th and 7th Aves.,* ☎ *212/243–6774.*

Moss. International designers (many of them Italian or Scandinavian) put a fantastic spin on even the most utilitarian objects, which are carefully brought together by Murray Moss at his store-cum-design museum. Stemware waves as though blown in a high wind; Philippe Starck's citrus juicer perches on tripod legs; and there are several reissued 1960s furniture designs. **More** (⊠ 150 Greene St., between Houston and Prince Sts., ☎ 212/226–2190) is the efficiently named annex. ⊠ *146 Greene St., between Houston and Prince Sts.,* ☎ *212/ 226–2190.*

Mxyplyzyk. Hard to pronounce (*mixyplitsick*) and hard to resist, this is a trove of impulse buys—creative riffs on household standbys such as soap dispensers (here a stylized bird) and nightlights (magic lanterns). ⊠ *125 Greenwich Ave., at 13th St.,* ☎ *212/989–4300.*

Pottery Barn. With its all-occasion glassware, artsy knickknacks, and relatively grounded prices, Pottery Barn has become one of the most visible American purveyors of contemporary interior design. ⊠ *600 Broadway, at Houston St.,* ☎ *212/219–2420; 117 E. 59th St., between Lexington and Park Aves.,* ☎ *917/369–0050; 1965 Broadway, at W. 67th St.,* ☎ *212/579–8477.*

Restoration Hardware. Pottery Barn's industrial little brother offers a selection of life-improving details such as bathroom and cabinet fixtures, tools, a smattering of furniture and lamps, plus little buy-me bar towels and Opinel pocketknives. ⊠ *935 Broadway, at E. 22nd St.,* ☎ *212/260–9479; 103 Prince St., at Greene St.,* ☎ *212/431–3518.*

Room. New Yorkers have welcomed the first freestanding store from the Australian home-product line of the same name. The assortment is random but complete—everything from doormats to bicycles to vases. For a shopping break, grab a seat and check out the TV in the café, Room Service. ⊠ *182 Duane St., between Hudson and Greenwich Sts.,* ☎ *212/226–1045.*

Scully & Scully. Leather footstools in animal shapes and small pieces of reproduction antique furniture exemplify this store's high-WASP style. ⊠ *504 Park Ave., between E. 59th and E. 60th Sts.,* ☎ *212/755–2590.*

Shabby Chic. You've seen the TV show and read the book—now see the store that started it all. You can custom-order any of the furniture styles and fabrics at this little outpost of the L.A. fleamarket-savvy establishment. ⊠ *93 Greene St., between Prince and Spring Sts.,* ☎ *212/ 274–9842.*

Shi. Quirky minimalist design prevails here—whether in the vintage French barroom ashtrays, burnished wooden chopsticks, or a bumpy glass carafe. ⊠ *233 Elizabeth St., between Houston and Prince Sts.,* ☎ *212/334–4330.*

Terence Conran Shop. The British style-monger has made a victorious return to New York City, offering upscale, modern styles at affordable prices. The small glass pavilion beneath the 59th Street Bridge caps a vast underground showroom of kitchen and garden implements, fabrics, furniture, and glassware. ⊠ *415 E. 59th St., at 1st Ave.,* ☎ *212/ 755–9079.*

Totem. This TriBeCa shop, which bills its wares as "objects that evoke meaning," is also a design house. You'll find innovative, avant-garde items that range from the inexpensive (neon-tone plastic dish racks) to the luxurious (glossy red folding screens), not to mention some of the friendliest salespeople in the city. ⊠ *71 Franklin St., between Prince and Spring Sts.,* ☎ *212/925–5506.*

Troy. In this spare space, the clean lines of Lucite, leather, teak, and resin furniture and home accessories may well wreak havoc with your credit card. The store features sleek limited-edition playthings—puzzles, toys, and board games. ⊠ *138 Greene St.,* ☎ *212/941–4777.*

William-Wayne & Co. Ostrich eggs, Viennese playing cards, butler's trays: These whimsical, mildly exotic decorative items are hard to resist. A low-key monkey theme puts smiling simians on dishes, candleholders, wall sconces, and tea towels. ⊠ *40 University Pl., at E. 9th St.,* ☎ *212/ 533–4711; 846 Lexington Ave., at E. 64th St.,* ☎ *212/737–8934; 850 Lexington Ave., at E. 64th St.,* ☎ *212/288–9243.*

Zona. One of the first stores to draw shoppers to SoHo has proved to be much more than a flash in the pan. Homey good-living accoutrements dominate—quilts, sturdy wooden furniture, and handmade *objets* such as glass coasters. ⊠ *97 Greene St.,* ☎ *212/925–6750.*

LINENS

Madison Avenue has an inviting handful of high-end linen shops; move downtown for less expensive—and less conventional—lines. Grand Street on the Lower East Side has a spate of dry-goods merchants.

Ad Hoc Softwares. You'll feel very SoHo as you browse through this stylish stash of natural fibers and nubby textures. Buy cotton or linen sheets and stock up on cushy bath towels. Half the store is devoted to accessories for the kitchen, office, bath, and body. ⊠ *136 Wooster St., at Prince St.,* ☎ *212/982–7703.*

D. Porthault. Porthault's showcase beds are virtual cocoons of pale, crisp linens and pillows. It's no wonder the money-is-no-object crowd covets these sheets. ⊠ *18 E. 69th St., between 5th and Madison Aves.,* ☎ *212/688–1660.*

Frette. Thread counts rise well above 250 here; there are also ultrafine table linens. These are the sheets and towels favored by luxury hotels. ⊠ *799 Madison Ave., between 67th and 68th Sts.,* ☎ *212/988–5221.*

Pratesi. To complement its pristine bedding, Pratesi has layettes, fragrances, and home gift lines, including damask table linens so fine they could almost stand in for the bedding. ⊠ *829 Madison Ave., near 69th St.,* ☎ *212/288–2315.*

Jewelry, Watches, and Silver

Most of the world's premier jewelers have retail outlets in New York, and the nation's wholesale jewelry center is on West 47th Street.

A La Vieille Russie. Stop here to behold bibelots by Fabergé and others, enameled or encrusted with jewels. ⊠ *781 5th Ave., at 59th St.,* ☎ *212/752–1727.*

Asprey & Garrard. The only satellite of the distinguished London jeweler, which holds three royal warrants, this store is just the place for crystal, silver, leather goods, or, perhaps, a brooch fit for a queen. ⊠ *725 5th Ave., between 56th and 57th Sts.,* ☎ *212/688–1811.*

Beads of Paradise. Enjoy a startlingly rich selection of African trade-bead necklaces, earrings, and rare artifacts. You can also create your own designs. ⊠ *16 E. 17th St., between 5th Ave. and Broadway,* ☎ *212/620–0642.*

Bulgari. This Italian company is certainly not shy about its name, which encircles gems, watch faces, even lighters. There are beautiful, weighty rings, pieces mixing gold with stainless steel or porcelain, and Venetian-theme silk neckties and scarves. ⊠ *730 5th Ave., between 56th and 57th Sts.,* ☎ *212/315–9000; 783 Madison Ave., between 66th and 67th Sts.,* ☎ *212/717–2300.*

Cartier. The recently renovated 5th Aveue mansion location was obtained by Pierre Cartier by trading two strands of perfectly matched natural pearls to Mrs. Morton Plant. The jewelry is still incredibly persuasive, from the sparkling precious stones to the riveting Love bracelet. ⊠ *653 5th Ave., near 52nd St.,* ☎ *212/753–0111; 725 5th Ave., in Trump Tower,* ☎ *212/308–0843; 828 Madison Ave., at E. 69th St.,* ☎ *212/472–6400.*

David Webb. The gem-studded pieces sold here are often enameled and in animal forms. Styles and prices have a tendency to go over-the-top. ⊠ *445 Park Ave., between 56th and 57th Sts.,* ☎ *212/421–3030.*

Fortunoff. Good prices on jewelry, flatware, and holloware draw crowds to this large, multilevel store. ⊠ *681 5th Ave., between 53rd and 54th Sts.,* ☎ *212/758–6660.*

Fragments. This SoHo spot glitters with pieces by up-and-coming jewelry designers, whose work is splashed across the pages of glossy fashion magazines. ⊠ *107 Greene St., between Prince and Spring Sts.,* ☎ *212/334–9588.*

Harry Winston. Oversize stones of impeccable quality glitter in Harry Winston's inner sanctum—no wonder the jeweler was immortalized in the song "Diamonds Are a Girl's Best Friend." ⊠ *718 5th Ave., between 55th and 56th Sts.,* ☎ *212/245–2000.*

H. Stern. Sleek designs pose in an equally modern 5th Avenue setting; smooth cabochon-cut stones (most from South America) glow in pale wooden display cases. The designers make notable use of semiprecious stones such as citrine, tourmaline, and topaz. ⊠ *645 5th Ave., between 51st and 52nd Sts.,* ☎ *212/688–0300; Waldorf-Astoria, 301 Park Ave., between 49th and 50th Sts.,* ☎ *212/753–5595.*

James Robinson. This family-owned business sells handmade flatware, antique silver, fine estate jewelry, and 18th- and 19th-century china (mostly in sets, rather than individual pieces). ⊠ *480 Park Ave., at E. 58th St.,* ☎ *212/752–6166.*

Jean's Silversmiths. Where to find a replacement for the butter knife that's missing from your great-aunt's set? Try this dusty, crowded shop. ⊠ *16 W. 45th St., between 5th and 6th Aves.,* ☎ *212/575–0723.*

Me + Ro. The bohemian styles of designers Michele Quan and Robin Renzi (who often hover behind the counter) have gained them an intense cult following. Prices start modestly for silver rings and earrings, and jump for Indian-inspired, hand-finished gold bangles covered with tiny rubies or sapphires. ⊠ *239 Elizabeth St., between Prince and Houston Sts.,* ☎ *917/237–9215.*

Mikimoto. The Japanese originator of the cultured pearl, Mikimoto presents a glowing display of perfectly formed, high-luster pearls. Besides the creamy strands from their own pearl farms, there are dazzlingly colored South Sea pearls and some freshwater varieties. ⊠ *730 5th Ave., between 56th and 57th Sts.,* ☎ *212/664–1800.*

Robert Lee Morris. Striking originals in silver, gold, and gold plate can be discovered at this SoHo jewelry and accessory leader. ⊠ *400 W. Broadway, between Broome and Spring Sts.,* ☎ *212/431–9405.*

Stuart Moore. Many designs here are minimalist or understated, but stunning: the sparkle of a small diamond offset by gold or brushed platinum. Pieces tend to be modest in scale. ⊠ *128 Prince St., between Wooster St. and W. Broadway,* ☎ *212/941–1023.*

Tiffany & Co. The display windows can be elegant, funny, or just plain breathtaking. Alongside the $80,000 platinum-and-diamond bracelets, a lot here is affordable on a whim—and everything comes wrapped in that unmistakable Tiffany blue. ⊠ *727 5th Ave., between 56th and 57th Sts.,* ☎ *212/755–8000.*

Tourneau. Each of these stores stocks a wide range of watches, but the three-level 57th Street TimeMachine, a high-tech merchandising extravaganza, steals the scene. A museum downstairs has timepiece exhibits, both temporary and permanent. The shops carry more than 70 brands, from status symbols such as Patek Philippe, Cartier, and Rolex, to more casual styles by Swatch, Seiko, and Swiss Army. ⊠ *635 Madison Ave., between 59th and 60th Sts.,* ☎ *212/758–6688; 500 Madison Ave., between 52nd and 53rd Sts.,* ☎ *212/758–6098; 12 E. 57th St., between 5th and Madison Aves.,* ☎ *212/758–7300; 200 W. 34th St., at 7th Ave.,* ☎ *212/563–6880; 5 World Trade Center,* ☎ *212/321–1350.*

Van Cleef & Arpels. The jewelry here (lots of classically set diamonds) is sheer perfection. ⊠ *744 5th Ave., at 57th St.,* ☎ *212/644–9500.*

Lingerie

Eres. This high-end Parisian lingerie shop carries the best in simple, but indulgent, bras and panties. It is the ultimate destination. ⊠ *625 Madison Ave., between E. 58th and E. 59th Sts.,* ☎ *212/223–3550.*

Joovay. This tiny store has tempting underwear from floor to ceiling: bras by Rigby & Peller, La Mystère, and Natori, plus chemises and bathrobes. ⊠ *436 W. Broadway, at 57th St.,* ☎ *212/431–6386.*

La Perla. From the Leavers lace, soutache, and embroidery to unadorned tulle, these underthings are so perfect they've inspired a trilogy of books. ⊠ *777 Madison Ave., at 57th St.,* ☎ *212/570–0050.*

La Petite Coquette. Among the signed photos on the walls is one of ultimate authority—from Frederique, longtime Victoria's Secret model. The store's own line of silk slips, camisoles, and other underpinnings comes in a rainbow of colors. ⊠ *51 University Pl., between E. 9th and E. 10th Sts.,* ☎ *212/473–2478.*

Le Corset. This lovely boutique naturally stocks its namesake, plus lacy underwear, nightgowns, and even powder-pink vintage girdles. ⊠ *80 Thompson St., between Spring and Broome Sts.,* ☎ *212/334–4936.*

Luggage, Leather Goods, and Handbags

Altman Luggage. Great bargains (a Samsonite Pullman for a little over $100) are the thing at this discount store, which also stocks tough Timberland and Jansport backpacks. ⊠ *135 Orchard St., between Delancey and Rivington Sts.,* ☎ *212/254–7275.*

Amy Chan. Check the windows of this eccentric downtown shop and you may find one of their trademark tile bags anchored at the bottom of a fish tank. Styles range from disco-reflective silver clutches to hippie-esque leather pouches. ⊠ *247 Mulberry St., between Prince and Spring Sts.,* ☎ *212/966–3417.*

Blue Bag. Affordable and sought-after are the bags at this quaint NoLita shop. The selection of handbags, satchels, and overnight bags is diverse and the styles very trendy. ⊠ *266 Elizabeth St., between Houston and Prince Sts.,* ☎ *212/966–8566.*

Bottega Veneta. Bottega Veneta's signature logo and crosshatch weave grace soigné handbags, satchels, and shoes, in leather and satin. There's also a small selection of leather coats and accessories, not to mention clothing upstairs. ⊠ *635 Madison Ave., between 59th and 60th Sts.,* ☎ *212/371–5511; 108 Wooster St., between Prince and Spring Sts.,* ☎ *212/334–4891.*

Coach. Coach's classic glove-tanned leather goes into handbags, briefcases, wallets, and dozens of other accessories in traditional and modern colors, materials, and styles. Check the 57th Street flagship for the full collection, including furniture. ⊠ *2321 Broadway, at W. 84th St.,*

☎ 212/799–1624; *595 Madison Ave., at E. 57th St.,* ☎ *212/754–0041; 620 5th Ave., at Rockefeller Center,* ☎ *212/245–4148; 342 Madison Ave., at E. 44th St.,* ☎ *212/599–4777; 93 Front St., at Fulton St.,* ☎ *212/425–4350; 143 Prince St., at W. Broadway,* ☎ *212/473–6925.*

Crouch & Fitzgerald. Since 1839 this store has offered a terrific selection in hard- and soft-sided luggage, as well as a huge number of attaché cases. ✉ *400 Madison Ave., at E. 48th St.,* ☎ *212/755–5888.*

Dooney & Bourke. Besides the traditional pebbly-textured leather satchels, handbags, and duffels (often with natural-leather trim), Dooney & Bourke has a line of bags done in a finely perforated leather. Leather sneakers have joined the lineup, as has a collection of denim-and-leather bags. Keep an eye out for this line—it's starting to show up on the fashionistas' radar. ✉ *759 Madison Ave., between E. 9th and E. 10th Sts.,* ☎ *212/439–1657; 725 5th Ave., Trump Tower,* ☎ *212/308–0520.*

Fendi. Come here for the most expensive baguettes and croissants in town—but not if you're looking for baked goods. Fendi's popular styles are named for the French breads they resemble. Each one is beaded, embroidered and fantastically embellished—resulting in prices that skyrocket over $1,000. Fancy leathers, furs, and other accessories are available, too. ✉ *720 5th Ave., at 56th St.,* ☎ *212/767–0100.*

Flight 001. This is one-stop shopping for the contemporary traveller. Travel in style and comfort with any of the chic luggage pieces, foldable maps, eye masks, and pampering kits. The store stocks the latest and greatest in travel technology, plus plenty of aromatherapy products to help with the rigors of jet-setting. ✉ *96 Greenwich Ave., between W. 12th and Jane Sts.,* ☎ *212/691–1001.*

Jamin Peuch. Ravishing beaded and sequined purses and equally decadent scarves and silk flower pins fill this jewel box of a store. Styles range from Belle Epoque to Rhinestone Cowgirl. (And for the record, it's pronounced Zha-min Pwesh.) ✉ *252 Mott St., between Houston and Prince Sts.,* ☎ *212/334–9730.*

Kate Spade. These eminently desirable (and oft-copied) handbags come in various fabrics, from velvet to tweed to the trademark black, satin-finish microfiber. Specialty bags include a dog carrier and a diaper satchel. Kate Spade's original storefront (✉ *59 Thompson St., between Spring and Broome Sts.,* ☎ *212/965–8654*) now carries paper goods, and around the corner at **Jack Spade** (✉ *56 Greene St., between Broome and Spring Sts.,* ☎ *212/625–1820*), Kate's husband peddles his own line of bags and dopp kits for men in a nostalgic setting. ✉ *454 Broome St., between Mercer and Greene Sts.,* ☎ *212/274–1991.*

Lederer Leather Goods. The excellent selection here includes exotic skins such as ostrich, alligator, and lizard. ✉ *457 Madison Ave., between E. 9th and E. 10th Sts.,* ☎ *212/355–5515.*

LeSportsac. This boutique is chock full of the latest in this inexpensive and stylish line of nylon bags. ✉ *176 Spring St., at W. Broadway,* ☎ *212/625–2626.*

Longchamp. Their nylon bags have become an Upper East Side staple and can be spotted everywhere in the Hamptons. The store carries the entire line of classy luggage, wallets, and organizers in a rainbow of understated colors. ✉ *713 Madison Ave., between E. 9th and E. 10th Sts.,* ☎ *212/223–1500.*

Louis Vuitton. Vuitton's famous monogrammed pieces range from purses to extravagant steamer trunks. The shops also offer brightly colored, striated leathers, glossy accessories, and a devastatingly chic line of clothes and shoes designed by Marc Jacobs. ✉ *49 E. 57th St., at Madison Ave.,* ☎ *212/371–6111; 703 5th Ave., between 54th and 55th Sts.,* ☎ *212/758–8877; 116 Greene St., between Prince and Spring Sts.,* ☎ *212/274–9090.*

Manhattan Portage. You know you want one, so visit the source of the messenger-bag fad. Although they're a-dime-a-dozen around these parts, they cost real money—$20–$100—and will impress the folks back home. ⊠ *333 E. 9th St., between 1st and 2nd Aves.,* ☎ *212/995–5490.*

Rugby North America. This Canadian-based store specializes in ultra-simple, unisex calfskin postman's bags, tough backpacks, and sturdy belts, plus unfussy men's and women's jackets. To get into the spirit, cozy into a leather chair. ⊠ *115 Mercer St., between Prince and Spring Sts.,* ☎ *212/431–3069.*

Tardini. For decades this Italian accessories maker has been making handbags from exotic materials such as alligator, lizard, and snakeskin. They've added an equally luxurious line of men's and women's footwear to complement the bags. As if the merchandise itself isn't beautiful enough, the architecture and design of the store is breathtakingly sharp and modern. ⊠ *142 Wooster St., between Houston and Prince Sts.,* ☎ *212/253–7692.*

T. Anthony. The trademark coated-canvas luggage with leather trim can be classic (black or beige) or eye-catching (red, purply-blue). Those who like to carry it all with them can outfit themselves with hatboxes and shirt cases, plus totes, trunks, and hard- and soft-sided suitcases. ⊠ *445 Park Ave, at E. 56th St.,* ☎ *212/750–9797.*

Museum Stores

American Craft Museum. The tie-ins to ongoing exhibits can yield beautiful handmade glassware, unusual jewelry, or enticing textiles. ⊠ *40 W. 53rd St., between 5th and 6th Aves.,* ☎ *212/956–3535.*

Guggenheim Museum SoHo. Among the spin-offs of the museum's collections are Lichtenstein calendars, lamps covered in strips of film, and mugs shaped like the uptown Guggenheim building. Children's art activity books fill several shelves. ⊠ *575 Broadway, between Houston and Prince Sts.,* ☎ *212/423–3500.*

Metropolitan Museum of Art Shop. Of the three locations, the store in the museum has a phenomenal book selection, as well as posters, art videos, and computer programs. Reproductions of jewelry, statuettes, and other *objets* fill the gleaming cases in every branch. ⊠ *5th Ave., at E. 82nd St.,* ☎ *212/879–5500; 113 Prince St., near Greene St.,* ☎ *212/614–3000; 15 W. 49th St., between 5th and 6th Aves., Rockefeller Center,* ☎ *212/332–1360.*

Museum of Modern Art Design Store. Diagonally across the street from the museum is a hoard of good, eye-catching design: Frank Lloyd Wright furniture reproductions, vases designed by Alvar Aalto, and lots of clever trinkets. Posters (from Mondrian to van Gogh's *Starry Night*) and a wide-ranging selection of books are across the street at the museum's bookstore (⊠ 11 W. 53rd St., between 5th and 6th Aves., ☎ 212/708–9700). Although the museum itself will be closed for renovations, scheduled to begin in summer 2002, both shops will remain open for the duration. ⊠ *44 W. 53rd St., between 5th and 6th Aves.,* ☎ *212/767–1050.*

Whitney Museum Store. A funky selection of cards, handmade ceramics and jewelry, and novelty items such as Warhol martini sets are tucked in next door to the hulking museum. Books are for sale in the museum's lobby. ⊠ *945 Madison Ave., between 74th and 75th Sts.,* ☎ *212/570–3676.*

Odds and Ends

Forbidden Planet. The sci-fi stash here is considerable—action figures, videos, and rows and rows of books and magazines (not all of which are for younger children). ⊠ *840 Broadway, at E. 13th St.,* ☎ *212/ 473–1576.*

New York Firefighter's Friend. Appropriately enough, this store is right near a fire station. On sale are firefighter-theme toys, books, and some authentic firefighters' gear, such as the apparently indestructible reflective-stripe jackets. ⊠ *263 Lafayette St., between 74th and 75th Sts.,* ☎ *212/226–3142.*

Pearl River Mart. From the street, the entrance to this sizeable Asian department store looks like a typical Canal Street designer-knockoff handbag shop. Inside, however, are three floors packed with everything from tatami slippers and karate pants to bamboo steamers, parasols, lanterns, porcelain tea sets, and other dishware—and it's all pretty cheap. Rows of noodles, dried seaweed, and Asian gummy candy (in such flavors as Muscat) fill the food section. A second smaller location smack on the border of Little Italy and Chinatown carries the best of the larger branch. ⊠ *277 Canal St., at Broadway,* ☎ *212/431–4770; 200 Grand St., between Mott and Mulberry Sts.,* ☎ *212/966–1010.*

Tender Buttons. Squeeze into this stronghold of clothes fasteners and riffle through the boxes of buttons—mother-of-pearl, novelty-shape plastic, or big, crested bronze numbers. ⊠ *143 E. 62nd St., between Lexington and 3rd Aves.,* ☎ *212/758–7004.*

Paper, Greeting Cards, Stationery

Dempsey & Carroll. Supplying New York's high society for a century, this firm is always correct but seldom straitlaced. ⊠ *110 E. 57th St., between 6th and 7th Aves.,* ☎ *212/486–7526.*

Kate's Paperie. Heaven for paper lovers, Kate's features fabulous wrapping papers, blank books, writing implements of all kinds, paper lamp shades, and more. The 13th Street location carries lots of art supplies. ⊠ *561 Broadway, at Spring St.,* ☎ *212/941–9816; 8 W. 13th St., between 5th and 6th Aves.,* ☎ *212/633–0570; 1282 3rd Ave., between E. 73rd and E. 74th Sts.,* ☎ *212/396–3670.*

Ordning & Reda. These Swedish stores are practically guaranteed to start your organizational synapses buzzing. Handmade, recycled-product notepads, stationery, cloth-bound books, photo albums, and other paper goods are snappily arranged floor to ceiling, color by bright color. ⊠ *253 Columbus Ave., between W. 71st and W. 72nd Sts.,* ☎ *212/799–0828; 1035 3rd Ave., between E. 61st and E. 62nd Sts.,* ☎ *212/421–8199; 1088 Madison Ave., between 81st and 82nd Sts.,* ☎ *212/439–6355.*

Untitled. The stock here includes thousands of tasteful greeting cards and art postcards. ⊠ *159 Prince St., between Thompson St. and W. Broadway,* ☎ *212/982–2088.*

Performing Arts Memorabilia

Drama Book Shop. The comprehensive stock here includes scripts, scores, and librettos. ⊠ *723 7th Ave., between W. 48th and W. 49th Sts.,* ☎ *212/944–0595.*

Motion Picture Arts Gallery. Vintage posters enchant collectors here. ⊠ *133 E. 58th St., 10th floor, between Park and Lexington Aves.,* ☎ *212/223–1009.*

Movie Star News. One look at the walls here and it's hard to doubt their claim that they have the world's largest variety of movie photos and posters. All around you are signed pictures of stars such as Billy Crystal, Lauren Bacall, Anjelica Houston, and even Elvira, TV's Mistress of the Dark. Posters in the outer garage area run $10–$25. ⊠ *134 W. 18th St., between 6th and 7th Aves.,* ☎ *212/620–8160.*

One Shubert Alley. Souvenirs from past and present Broadway hits reign at this theater district shop. ⊠ *311 W. 43rd St., near 8th Ave.,* ☎ *212/944–4133.*

Richard Stoddard Performing Arts Books. This veteran dealer, who offers out-of-print books, also has the largest stock of old Broadway *Play-*

*bill*s in the world. It's closed on Wednesday. ⊠ *18 E. 16th St., Room 305, between 5th and 6th Aves.,* ☎ *212/645–9576.*

Triton Gallery. Theatrical posters large and small can be found here for hits and flops. ⊠ *323 W. 45th St., between 8th and 9th Aves.,* ☎ *212/ 765–2472.*

Salons

If you want to get your hair done before an evening out on the town, you've plenty of choices in New York. Expect top-of-the line talent at prices to match: highlights at a leading salon can run $200 or more, and cuts start around $75. The city's leading hair gurus spend most of their time with celebrity, model, and socialite clients, but when you're in the chair at one of these humming temples of style you'll feel like a bit of a celebrity yourself. Relax and let the pros make you beautiful.

bumble and bumble. Walk into the three-level industrial-looking space, with its high ceilings and metal fixtures, and you'll realize that you've seen these products at a salon or specialty store or, most likely, in a magazine article. The stylists here are known for providing their clients, often runway models, with the trendiest hairstyles and colors. But you can get a reasonably priced cut or coloring, or just stock up on their products. ⊠ *146 E. 56th St., between 3rd and Lexington Aves.,* ☎ *212/ 521–6500.*

Garren New York. Some of the finest colorists and stylists in town work here when they're not jet-setting off to a magazine shoot or runway show, or tending to one of their many model/celebrity clients. Prices run high. ⊠ *Henri Bendel, 712 5th Ave., between 55th and 56th Sts., 2nd floor,* ☎ *212/841–9400.*

Lisa Mitchell Salon. This Lower East Side spot may not look like much, but many finicky fashion types trust no one but Lisa. She specializes in extensions and in straightening black hair (Diana Ross and her three daughters are clients), and gives stylish cuts learned backstage at the Paris fashion shows. ⊠ *90 Rivington St., between Orchard and Ludlow Sts.,* ☎ *212/982–0085.*

Peter Coppola. This small, light-filled salon consistently turns out good, stylishly conservative cuts and color. Kevin Mancuso, who frequently works for top fashion magazines, is the resident star. ⊠ *746 Madison Ave., near E. 65th St.,* ☎ *212/988–9404.*

Pierre Michel. A hive of activity, this salon packs in more than 50 stylists but still manages to remain spacious and airy, thanks to a balcony level and a large back room devoted to color processes (see Stephen Sanna to get a shade better than what Mother Nature gave you). ⊠ *131 E. 57th St., between Park and Lexington Aves.,* ☎ *212/755–9500.*

Privé. Hollywood stylist Laurent D. still jets back to L.A. one week each month to see such clients as Sharon Stone, but if you catch him while he's in town, expect a sexy cut and infectious enthusiasm. Scott Bond produces fantastic color results. ⊠ *SoHo Grand, 310 W. Broadway, between Canal and Grand Sts.,* ☎ *212/274–8888.*

Space. This downtown salon has firmly established itself as *the* place to go for edgy men's and women's cuts. Clients rave about the manicures and pedicures by Ceia Crema. ⊠ *155 6th Ave., at Spring St.,* ☎ *212/647–8588.*

Stephen Knoll. One of the top salons for uptown ladies, from socialites such as Blaine Trump to supermodels such as Cindy Crawford, this shop is housed in the Revlon building (so Cindy can stop in after work). Expect flattering, feminine styles and ultranatural-looking hair color. ⊠ *625 Madison Ave., between E. 58th and E. 59th Sts.,* ☎ *212/ 421–0100.*

Shoes

For dressy, expensive footwear, Madison Avenue is always a good bet, but West 8th Street between 5th and 6th Avenues is what most New Yorkers mean when they refer to Shoe Street; it's crammed with small shoe-storefronts that hawk funky styles, from steel-toe boots to outrageous platforms.

MEN'S AND WOMEN'S SHOES

Bally. This sleek store is full of comfortable, conservative shoes and boots for men and women. Old Bally styles are revived whenever they come back into vogue. ⊠ *628 Madison Ave., at E. 59th St.,* ☎ *212/ 751–9082.*

Camper. Functional and fashionable is the best way to describe the athletic-looking men's and women's shoes at this Spanish export shoe store. Up until now, these must-have kicks could only be found at the rare shoe store. When you see the odd red seat cushions, you'll be dying to sit down and try on the reasonably priced rubber-sole shoes. ⊠ *125 Prince St., at Wooster St.,* ☎ *212/358–1841.*

Cole-Haan. Cole-Haan endlessly varies the basic elements of its woven, moccasin, and loafer styles in brown and black, and it also provides reliably up-to-date styles for a conservative crowd. ⊠ *620 5th Ave., at Rockefeller Center,* ☎ *212/765–9747; 667 Madison Ave., between 60th and 61st Sts.,* ☎ *212/421–8440.*

Hogan. This Italian accessories line features high-end shoes and complementing bags. Prices for their men's and women's bowling-style shoes range from $275 to $600. It costs a lot to look cool and be comfortable. ⊠ *134 Spring St., between Wooster and Greene Sts.,* ☎ *212/343– 3039.*

Jimmy Choo. Pointy toes, low vamps, narrow heels, delicate sling backs—these British-made shoes are undeniably hot to trot, and sometimes more comfortable than they look. While the men's selection is limited (and more sedate), the choices are subtly snazzy. ⊠ *645 5th Ave. (entrance on 51st St.),* ☎ *212/593–0800.*

J. M. Weston. Specially treated calfskin for the soles and carefully handcrafted construction have made these a French favorite; they could also double the price of your outfit. The few women's shoes are made exactly like the men's. ⊠ *812 Madison Ave., at 68th St.,* ☎ *212/ 535–2100.*

Joan & David. Somewhat conservative but never dull, these shoes can complement an all-business suit (the fall wing tips or ankle boots) or a curvy sundress (the strappy-but-not-too-high-heeled sandals). ⊠ *816 Madison Ave., near E. 68th St.,* ☎ *212/772–3970.*

John Fluevog Shoes. The inventor of the Angelic sole (protects against water, acid . . . "and Satan"), Fluevog designs chunky shoes and boots that are much more than Doc Marten copies. He also dives into wackier waters, with Lucite heels and stacked, crepe-sole sneakers. ⊠ *104 Prince St., between Mercer and Greene Sts.,* ☎ *212/431–4484.*

Kerquelen. The West Broadway location was designed to be shoe heaven and it is, both literally and figuratively. The combination of the white, silver, and blue decor and the incredibly eclectic shoe selection makes for a euphoric experience. Men's and women's footwear is carried in both locations with an emphasis on hard-to-find lines such as Callaghan, Jamie Mascaro, and Leere. ⊠ *44 Greene St., between Broome and Grand Sts.,* ☎ *212/431–1771; 430 W. Broadway, between Prince and Spring Sts.,* ☎ *212/226–8313.*

Maraolo. These shoes (monk-straps, wingtips, pumps, ankle boots) are perfect for business meetings; small wonder midtown is full of Maraolo shops. The West 72nd Street location is a factory outlet, where tidy pumps go for less than the cost of a client lunch. ⊠ *782 Lexington*

Ave., between E. 60th and E. 61st Sts., ☎ *212/832–8182; 551 Madison Ave., at E. 55th St.,* ☎ *212/308–8793; 835 Madison Ave., between 69th and 70th Sts.,* ☎ *212/628–5080; 131 W. 72nd St., between Columbus and Amsterdam Aves.,* ☎ *212/787–6550.*

Otto Tootsi Plohound. Downtown New Yorkers swear by this large selection of super-cool shoes. Many, including the store's own line, are Italian-made, and styles jump from vampy Michel Perry pumps to men's wingtips to rubber-sole Prada Sport boots. ⊠ *137 5th Ave., between 20th and 21st Sts.,* ☎ *212/460–8650; 413 W. Broadway, between Prince and Spring Sts.,* ☎ *212/925–8931; 38 E. 57th St., between 5th and Madison Aves.,* ☎ *212/231–3199.*

Rockport. After a day of pounding the sidewalk, a stop here may be just what you need. The comfort-first shoes run from athletic to dressy, and you can be fitted for a customized footbed—after a complimentary reflexology foot massage. ⊠ *160 Columbus Ave., between W. 67th and W. 68th Sts.,* ☎ *212/579–1301; 465 W. Broadway, between Houston and Prince Sts.,* ☎ *212/529–0209.*

MEN'S SHOES

Billy Martin's. Quality hand-tooled and custom-made boots for the Urban Cowboy are carried here. To complete the look, you'll also find everything from suede shirts to turquoise-and-silver belts. ⊠ *220 E. 60th St., between 2nd and 3rd Aves.,* ☎ *212/861–3100.*

Church's English Shoes. Church's has been selling traditionally styled, beautifully made English shoes since 1873. For the conservative dresser, it's especially well located a few blocks from Brooks Brothers and Paul Stuart. ⊠ *428 Madison Ave., at E. 49th St.,* ☎ *212/755–4313.*

Salvatore Ferragamo. This branch has traditional, elegant men's shoes, plus a limited line of suave clothes, patterned silk ties, and accessories. ⊠ *725 5th Ave., at Trump Tower, between E. 56th and 57th Sts.,* ☎ *212/759–7990.*

Santoni. Those who equate Italian with slightly flashy haven't seen these discreet, meticulously finished, handmade shoes. ⊠ *864 Madison Ave., at 71st St.,* ☎ *212/794–3820.*

Stuart Weitzman. The specialty here is hard-to-find sizes and widths. This location carries the designer's entire line. ⊠ *625 Madison Ave., near 59th St.,* ☎ *212/750–2555.*

WOMEN'S SHOES

Christian Louboutin. Bright-red soles are the trademark of Louboutin's delicately sexy couture slippers and stilettos. Look for brocade, mink trim, and tassels. ⊠ *941 Madison Ave., near E. 74th St.,* ☎ *212/396–1884.*

Chuckies. The name may be aw-shucks, but the shoes certainly aren't. Designer pumps by Dolce & Gabbana, Sonia Rykiel, and Jimmy Choo are uptown, while the downtown store stocks more of Chuckies' own cool, slightly lower priced line (check out the knee-high boots). *1073 3rd Ave., between E. 63rd and E. 64th Sts.,* ☎ *212/593–9898; 399 W. Broadway, between Spring and Broome Sts.,* ☎ *212/343–1717.*

Manolo Blahnik. These are, notoriously, some of the most expensive shoes money can buy. They're also devastatingly sexy, with pointed toes, low-cut vamps, and spindly heels. Mercifully, the summer stock includes plenty of flat (but still exquisite) sandals. Pray for a sale. ⊠ *31 W. 54th St., between 5th and 6th Aves.,* ☎ *212/582–3007.*

Peter Fox. Combining old-fashioned lines, such as Louis heels, and such modern touches as thin platforms, these shoes defy categorization. The Thompson Street store has an extensive bridal section. ⊠ *105 Thompson St., between Prince and Spring Sts.,* ☎ *212/431–7426; 806 Madison Ave., between 67th and 68th Sts.,* ☎ *212/744–8340.*

Robert Clergerie. High-priced and highly polished, these shoes are not without their sense of fun. Pick up a pump and you may find an oval or triangular heel. ⊠ *681 Madison Ave., between 61st and 62nd Sts.,* ☎ *212/207–8600.*

Salvatore Ferragamo. Join the ranks of Marilyn Monroe and Audrey Hepburn, who were loyal Ferragamo customers. In addition to scores of ladylike pumps with matching purses and accessories, the company offers revivals of some of their eclectic styles from previous decades. ⊠ *661 5th Ave., between 52nd and 53rd Sts.,* ☎ *212/759–3822.*

Sergio Rossi. The best of Italian shoes, from slinky evening styles to playful daytime styles, can be had here. Save your pennies if you plan on buying more than one pair—prices start around $250 and rapidly climb upwards. *835 Madison Ave., at E. 69th St.,* ☎ *212/396–4814.*

Sigerson Morrison. The details—just-right T-straps, small buckles, interesting two-tones—make these shoes here. Nine West thought so, too—they've been bringing very close adaptations of Sigerson Morrison's shoes to the masses. Prices for the real thing hover around $200. The new location allows more space to display their coveted footwear. ⊠ *28 Prince St., between Mott and Elizabeth Sts.,* ☎ *212/219–3893.*

Tod's. Diego Della Valle's coveted driving moccasins, casual loafers, and boots in colorful leather, suede, and ponyskin are right at home on Madison Avenue. ⊠ *650 Madison Ave., near E. 60th St.,* ☎ *212/644–5945.*

Souvenirs of New York City

Ordinary Big Apple souvenirs can be found all over town. If you're looking for authentic souvenirs of downtown (T-shirts with salty messages, wild sunglasses and jewelry, tattoos), be sure to peruse St. Mark's Place between 2nd and 3rd Avenues in the East Village.

City Books. Discover all kinds of books and pamphlets that on New York City's government and its various departments (building, sanitation, etc.), as well as pocket maps, Big Apple lapel pins, and sweatshirts featuring subway-token motifs. It's closed on weekends. ⊠ *1 Centre St., at Chambers St.,* ☎ *212/669–8246.*

New York City Transit Museum Gift Shop. The Brooklyn shop was built mostly by transit employees and the Manhattan location is in the symbolic heart of NYC's transit system. All the merchandise is somehow linked to the MTA, from "straphanger" ties to skateboards decorated with subway line logos. ⊠ *Grand Central Terminal, at E. 42nd St. and Park Ave.,* ☎ *212/878–0106; Boerum Pl. and Schermerhorn St., Brooklyn Heights,* ☎ *718/243–5068.*

The Pop Shop. Images from the late Keith Haring's unmistakable pop art cover a wealth of paraphernalia, from backpacks to key chains. ⊠ *292 Lafayette St., between Prince and Jersey Sts.,* ☎ *212/219–2784.*

Spas

Stressed-out New Yorkers love luxury, from lavender-scented massages to deep-cleaning facials, so be sure to book well in advance (anywhere from a week to a month or more, depending on the place) if you want to get into any of these soothing spots.

Angel Feet. This little West Village nook offers feet-only massages. It's a perfect way-station after a few days of pavement-pounding. ⊠ *77 Perry St., between W. 4th and Bleecker Sts.,* ☎ *212/924–3576.*

Avon Centre Spa and Salon. The beauty giant's swanky spa in Trump Tower offers the usual services, but it is best known for its world-famous eyebrow guru Eliza Ptrescu. She heads her own division, **Eliza's Eyes,** staffed with three aestheticians. She's booked six months in advance and charges $65 for a 10-minute pluck, so plan ahead and save your pennies. ⊠ *725 5th Ave., between 56th and 57th Sts.,* ☎ *212/ 755–2866.*

Away Spa. This Asian-influenced oasis offers up a full menu of New Age delights. Go for color therapy and have your chakra evaluated (you'll actually see a Polaroid of it), or choose a more traditional full-body mud mask. ⊠ *W Hotel, 541 Lexington Ave., near E. 49th St.,* ☎ *212/ 407–2970.*

Bliss Spa. Ever since word got out a few years back that Uma Thurman comes here for oxygen facials, eager customers have rushed to follow suit. Success spawned an uptown sibling, **Bliss**[57] (⊠ 19 E. 57th St., between 5th and Madison Aves., 3rd floor, ☎ 212/219–8970), which offers concierge services while you're relaxing. Snack on cheese and crackers while awaiting your facial or ginger rub. ⊠ *586 Broadway, at Prince St., 2nd floor (above A/X),* ☎ *212/219–8970.*

Erbe. A little haven just off SoHo's beaten path, this is a good spot for waxing and massages. Breathe in the herbal scents of the house line of Italian-made lotions. ⊠ *196 Prince St., between Sullivan and MacDougal Sts.,* ☎ *212/966–1445.*

The Greenhouse. This full-service spa caters to the affluent man and woman. The clean and serene space is also home to a café, and there's a shop filled with hard-to-find cosmetics and pampering brands. Concierge services are available in addition to the extensive selection of spa and dermatological treatments. ⊠ *127 E. 57th St., between Lexington and Park Aves.,* ☎ *212/644–4449.*

Paul Labreque Salon. Located inside the swank Reebok Sports Club near Lincoln Center, this luxurious salon is known for its top-notch facialist and fantastic and inventive massages. ⊠ *160 Columbus Ave., at W. 67th St.,* ☎ *212/595–0099.*

SoHo Sanctuary. It's women-only at this spa, which somehow makes you feel like you're in Berkeley, California. Housed in a loft, it offers aromatherapy facials, massages, and a eucalyptus steam bath. There's a full yoga schedule. ⊠ *119 Mercer St., between Prince and Spring Sts.,* ☎ *212/334–5550.*

Sporting Goods

Chain stores such as **Eastern Mountain Sports** (⊠ 611 Broadway, near Houston St., ☎ 212/505–9860; 20 W. 61st St., between Central Park W and Columbus Ave., ☎ 212/397–4860), **Speedo Authentic Fitness** (⊠ 5 World Trade Center, ☎ 212/775–0977; 753 Broadway, at E. 8th St., ☎ 212/260–2151; 150 Columbus Ave., between W. 66th and W. 67th Sts., ☎ 212/501–8140; 40 E. 57th St., between Madison and Park Aves., ☎ 212/838–5988; 90 Park Ave., at E. 39th St., ☎ 212/682–3830; 500 5th Ave., at 41st St., ☎ 212/768–7737; 721 Lexington Ave., at E. 58th St., ☎ 212/688–4595), and the **Sports Authority** (⊠ 636 Ave. of the Americas, at W. 19th St., ☎ 212/929–8971; 401 7th Ave., at W. 33rd St., ☎ 212/563–7195; 845 3rd Ave., at E. 51st St., ☎ 212/355–9725; 57 W. 57th St., between 5th and 6th Aves., ☎ 212/355–6430) are reliable, but here are a couple of unique spots to try.

The NBA Store. Push through the bronze-armed door to hit the rows of pro basketball–theme merchandise. The ground floor has stacks of "lifestyle" items; wind down the ramp to score team jerseys, tearaway pants, and even baby clothes. Players grin in the digital-photo station, but they also make live appearances on the store's half-court. ⊠ *666 5th Ave., near 53rd St.,* ☎ *212/515–6221.*

NikeTown. A fusion of fashion and sports arena, Nike's "motivational retail environment" is its largest sports-gear emporium. Inspirational quotes in the floor, computer-driven NGAGE foot sizers, and a heart-pumping movie shown on an enormous screen in the entry atrium make it hard to leave without something in the latest wick-away fabric or footwear design. ⊠ *6 E. 57th St., between 5th and Madison Aves.,* ☎ *212/891–6453.*

Paragon Sporting Goods. Tennis rackets, snowshoes, kayaks, swim goggles, hockey sticks, croquet mallets: Paragon stocks virtually everything any athlete needs, no matter what the sport. They keep up with the trends (snow blades) and don't neglect the old-fashioned (Woolrich shirts). Camping gear includes a wide selection of sleeping bags and tents; Polo sweats and Armani golf shirts attract the label-conscious. ⊠ *867 Broadway, at E. 18th St.,* ☎ *212/255–8036.*

Tent & Trails. New Yorkers who climb Everest outfit themselves at this family-owned survivor from an earlier retail era. Even if you don't need crampons, climbing ropes, or wilderness survival kits, come for the huge selection of outerwear and backpacks and the informed advice. ⊠ *21 Park Pl., between Broadway and Church St.,* ☎ *212/227–1760.*

Toys and Games

Most of these stores are geared towards children, but a few shops that cater to grown-up toy-lovers are mixed in. During February's Toy Week, when out-of-town buyers come to place orders for the next Christmas season, the windows of the Toy Center at 23rd Street and 5th Avenue display the latest thing.

Big City Kite Co. Sport kites, twisters, and technique books are the specialty here. The salespeople can talk winglets and wind windows or suggest a kite that can withstand crashing. ⊠ *1210 Lexington Ave., at E. 82nd St.,* ☎ *212/472–2623.*

Classic Toys. Collectors and children scrutinize the rows of miniature soldiers, toy cars, and other figures. It's a prime source for toy soldiers from Britain's Ltd., the United Kingdom's top manufacturer. ⊠ *218 Sullivan St., between Bleecker and 3rd Sts.,* ☎ *212/674–4434.*

Compleat Strategist. These stores put on a great spread—from board games and classic soldier sets to mah-jongg and even sock monkey kits. ⊠ *11 E. 33rd St., between 5th and Madison Aves.,* ☎ *212/685–3880.*

Disney Store. All branches carry merchandise relating to Disney films and characters—pajamas, toys, figurines, you name it. The flagship 5th Avenue store has the largest collection of Disney animation art in the country. ⊠ *711 5th Ave., between 55th and 56th Sts.,* ☎ *212/702–0702; 210 W. 42nd St., at 7th Ave.,* ☎ *212/302–0595; 39 W. 34th St., between 5th and 6th Aves.,* ☎ *212/279–9890; 141 Columbus Ave., at W. 66th St.,* ☎ *212/362–2386.*

Dollhouse Antics. Besides the rows of miniature furnishings, there are build-your-own dollhouse kits, ready-made houses, and model homes for inspiration. ⊠ *1343 Madison Ave., at E. 94th St.,* ☎ *212/876–2288.*

E.A.T. Piñatas hang from the ceiling, and the shelves are full of toys, gizmos, and knickknacks. Tintin and Babar fans will have a field day. ⊠ *1062 Madison Ave., between 80th and 81st Sts.,* ☎ *212/861–2544.*

Enchanted Forest. Stuffed animals peer out from almost every corner of this fantastic shop. It's packed with all manner of curiosity-provoking gadgets, plus old-fashioned tin toys and a small but choice selection of children's books. ⊠ *85 Mercer St., between Spring and Broome Sts.,* ☎ *212/925–6677.*

F.A.O. Schwarz. Beyond the large mechanical clock at this wonderland are two floors of stuffed animals, dolls (including an inordinate number of Barbies), things with which to build (including blocks by the pound), computer games, and much, much, much, much more. ⊠ *767 5th Ave., between 59th and 60th Sts.,* ☎ *212/644–9400.*

Game Show. From Scrabble and Magic 8 Balls to backgammon and mah-jongg, this game- and puzzle-lover's paradise carries everything to challenge your IQ and tickle your funny bone. Intricate jigsaw puzzles are a specialty, and the ultraknowledgeable staff will help you find exactly what you are looking for. ⊠ *474 6th Ave., between 11th and*

12th Sts., ☎ *212/633–6328; 1240 Lexington Ave., between 83rd and 84th Sts.,* ☎ *212/472–8011.*

Geppetto's Toy Box. Most toys here are handmade. They carry everything from extravagant costumed dolls to tried-and-true rubber duckies. ✉ *10 Christopher St., at Greenwich Ave.,* ☎ *212/620–7511.*

Kidding Around. This unpretentiously smart shop emphasizes old-fashioned wooden toys, fun gadgets, craft and science kits, and a small selection of infant clothes. ✉ *60 W. 15th St., between 5th and 6th Aves.,* ☎ *212/645–6337; 68 Bleecker St., between Broadway and Lafayette St.,* ☎ *212/598–0228.*

Store of Knowledge. This public television–affiliated store caters to the curious, with 3-D puzzles, crafts sets, and science kits. Favorite PBS characters such as Mr. Bean and the Teletubbies are here in droves; grown-ups can riffle through PBS videos, including the *Prime Suspect* series. ✉ *1091 3rd Ave., at E. 64th St.,* ☎ *212/223–0018.*

Tannen Magic Co. This magicians' supply house stocks sword chests, dove-a-matics, magic wands, and crystal balls, not to mention the all-important top hats with rabbits. ✉ *24 W. 25th St., between Broadway and 6th Aves.,* ☎ *212/929–4500.*

Toys R' Us. The name says it all—this place *is* toys. Merchandise ranges from video games to board games and from baby strollers to Barbie dolls. For an extensive selection of toys and gadgets, either location is sure to please. ✉ *1293 Broadway, at 34th St.,* ☎ *212/594–8697; 2432 Union Square E, at E. 15th St.,* ☎ *212/674–8697.*

Warner Bros. Studio Store. Bugs Bunny has a very high 5th Avenue profile. Besides seemingly endless amounts of entertainment-related merchandise and current movie tie-ins, there's a 3-D movie theater. ✉ *1 E. 57th St., at 5th Ave.,* ☎ *212/754–0300.*

West Side Kids. Legos, arts-and-crafts sets, and rubber animal figures share shelf space with multicultural family hand puppets. ✉ *498 Amsterdam Ave., at W. 84th St.,* ☎ *212/496–7282.*

Wine

Acker Merrall & Condit. Known for its selection of red burgundies, this store has knowledgeable, helpful personnel. ✉ *160 W. 72nd St., between Amsterdam and Columbus Aves.,* ☎ *212/787–1700.*

Astor Wines & Spirits. Plain and fluorescent-lit it may be, but this is a key spot for everything from well-priced champagne to Poire William to Riesling. ✉ *12 Astor Pl., at Lafayette St.,* ☎ *212/674–7500.*

Best Cellars. In a novel move, the stock here is organized by the wine's characteristics (sweet, fruity) rather than region—and not only that, the prices are amazingly low. ✉ *1291 Lexington Ave., between E. 86th and E. 87th Sts.,* ☎ *212/426–4200.*

Garnet Wines & Liquors. Its fine selection includes champagne at prices that one wine writer called "almost charitable." ✉ *929 Lexington Ave., between E. 68th and E. 69th Sts.,* ☎ *212/772–3211.*

Morrell & Company. Peter Morrell is a well-regarded and very colorful figure in the wine business; his store reflects his expertise. Next door is his café, where dozens of fine wines are available by the glass. ✉ *1 Rockefeller Plaza, at W. 49th St.,* ☎ *212/688–9370.*

Sherry-Lehmann. This New York institution is a great place to go for good advice and to browse through sales on intriguing vintages. ✉ *679 Madison Ave., between 61st and 62nd Sts.,* ☎ *212/838–7500.*

Union Square Wine & Spirits. The store stocks a great selection and has a regular schedule of wine seminars and special tasting events. ✉ *33 Union Sq. W, near 16th St.,* ☎ *212/675–8100.*

Vintage New York. It is part wine store and part tasting room, and certainly lives up to its hip Soho address. The store sells New York State wines, regional foods, wine accessories, and custom gift baskets. The best part is that they are open for business seven days a week. ✉ *482 Broome St., between Wooster and Greene Sts.,* ☎ *212/226–9463.*

Secondhand Shops

Vintage and Consignment Clothing

A Girl's Habit. In a cozy space, this little-known vintage shop is home to an impressive vintage collection. Garments are affordable and each has a cute tag that gives background on the piece. ✉ *17 Bleeker St., between Bowery and Lafayette Sts.,* ☎ *212/473–8465.*

Alice Underground. Subterranean no longer, Alice now has what almost all vintage-clothing stores lack—elbow room. Staples include cashmere sweaters ($45–$85), jeans, and the store's own line of bowling shirts. ✉ *481 Broadway, between Broome and Grand Sts.,* ☎ *212/431–9067.*

Allan & Suzi. The proprietors, whom you'll no doubt find sitting behind the counter, are the godfather and -mother of fashion collecting. Their wacky shop preserves 1980s shoulder pads and 1940s gowns for posterity (or sale). ✉ *416 Amsterdam Ave., between W. 79th and W. 80th Sts.,* ☎ *212/724–7445.*

Cheap Jack's. Three floors are jammed with almost everything you could wish for: track suits, bomber jackets, early 1980s madras shirts, old prom dresses, and fur-trimmed wool ladies' suits with the eau-de-mothball stamp of authenticity. Often, though, Jack's is not so cheap. ✉ *841 Broadway, between E. 13th and E. 14th Sts.,* ☎ *212/995–0403.*

The 1909 Company. There are excellent picks here, all for women—a special display case holds the Gucci and Pucci, while the racks have 1960s suits in great condition. ✉ *63 Thompson St., between Broome and Spring Sts.,* ☎ *212/343–1658.*

Out of Our Closet. A godsend for couture seekers, this consignment shop is a sure source for real finds for both men and women. Last season's Dolce & Gabbana, Jil Sander suits, Missoni pants (about $250), or a Matsuda men's jacket (around $300) are joined by a small assortment of shoes, accessories, and jewelry. ✉ *136 W. 18th St., between 6th and 7th Aves.,* ☎ *212/633–6965.*

Resurrection. With original Courrèges, Puccis, and foxy boots, this pair of stores is a retro-chic gold mine. The NoLita location is more designer-oriented, while the 7th Street branch is stocked with rock-n-roll leather and such. ✉ *123 E. 7th St., between 1st Ave. and Ave. A,* ☎ *212/228–0063; 217 Mott St., between Houston and Prince Sts.,* ☎ *212/625–1374.*

Screaming Mimi's. Vintage 1960s and 1970s clothes and retro-wear include everything from lingerie to soccer shirts to prom dresses. ✉ *382 Lafayette St., between 4th and Great Jones Sts.,* ☎ *212/677–6464.*

Auctions

New York is one of the world's major auctioning centers, where royal accoutrements, ancient art, and pop-culture memorabilia all have their moment on the block. Look for announcements in the *New York Times,* or in the weekly magazines *Time Out New York* and *New York.* If you plan to raise a paddle, be sure to attend the sale preview and review the catalog for price estimates.

MAJOR HOUSES

Christie's. With more than 200 years of formidable history behind it, British born-and-bred Christie's has presided over the high-profile auctions of the late Princess Diana's gowns and the phenomenal Ganz Collection of 20th-century art. Special departments are devoted to such non-fine-art valuables as wine, cars, and cameras. **Christie's East** (⊠ 219 E. 67th St., between 2nd and 3rd Aves., ☎ 212/606–0400) is a less-extravagant branch. ⊠ *20 Rockefeller Plaza, at W. 49th St. between 5th and 6th Aves.,* ☎ *212/636–2000.*

Sotheby's. Established in London more than 250 years ago, Sotheby's is now American-run. It has sold off the effects of the Duke and Duchess of Windsor, paintings from the Whitney family (one of America's best private art collections), and "Sue," the largest and most complete *Tyrannosaurus rex* skeleton ever unearthed. Collectibles such as wine, vintage cars, animation art, and fashion have their own departments; there's even an Internet auction division. Their **Arcade**, at the same address, handles more affordable selections. ⊠ *1334 York Ave., at E. 72nd St.,* ☎ *212/606–7000.*

Guernsey's. This is a great source for modern memorabilia and collections; one auction put up hundreds of items that belonged to J.F.K. ⊠ *108 E. 73rd St., between Park and Lexington Aves.,* ☎ *212/794–2280.*

Swann Galleries. Swann specializes in works on paper—letters, photographs, antiquarian books, and the like. ⊠ *104 E. 25th St., 6th floor, between Park and Lexington Aves.,* ☎ *212/254–4710.*

Tepper Galleries. General estate collections are sold here every other Saturday, with previews given the Friday before. ⊠ *110 E. 25th St., between Park and Lexington Aves.,* ☎ *212/677–5300.*

Flea Markets

The season runs from March or April through November or December at most of these markets in school playgrounds and parking lots. Certain markets charge a small admission fee.

Annex Antiques Fair and Flea Market. It can be more miss than hit, but it's open weekends year-round. ⊠ *6th Ave. at W. 26th St.,* ☎ *212/243–5343.*

Chelsea Antiques Building. Looking for World War II photographs? Russian samovars? Out-of-print Austrian poetry books? This 12-story building is filled with specialized dealers, though prices can be steep. The best bargaining happens on weekends. ⊠ *110 W. 25th St., between 6th and 7th Aves.,* ☎ *212/929–0909.*

The Garage Antique Shop. This indoor market in a 23,000-square-ft, two-story former parking garage is open weekends year-round. ⊠ *112 W. 25th St., between 6th and 7th Aves.,* ☎ *212/647–0707.*

Green Flea. Green Flea runs the P.S.183 market on Saturday, and the I.S.44 market on Sunday. ⊠ *I.S.44 Market: Columbus Ave. at W. 77th St.; P.S.183 Market: E. 67th St. and York Ave.;* ☎ *212/721–0900 (evening).*

9 BACKGROUND AND ESSENTIALS

Books and Videos

Smart Travel Tips A to Z

WHAT TO READ AND WATCH BEFORE YOU GO

Books

Literary Anthologies and Collections

To sample New York City essays from all the usual suspects—Walt Whitman, Herman Melville, E.B. White (his 1949 classic "Here is New York"), Henry James, Ralph Ellison, Langston Hughes, Elizabeth Bishop, Edna St. Vincent Millay, Jane Jacobs, and Dawn Powell, dip into Phillip Lopate's anthology *Writing New York*. Ably edited by Bill Harris and Mike Marquese, *New York: an Anthology* organizes writing from New Yorkers such as Theodore Dreiser and Kathy Acker around themes such as "mammon," "city of orgies," and "acts of creation." *Mirror for Gotham*, by Bayrd Still, collects the thoughts of visitors since New York was New Amsterdam. Out of print but worth a library visit is *New York Observed* (Cohen, Chwast and Heller, eds.), which compiles writings and illustrations from 1650 to the 1980s. Writers for *The New Yorker* magazine have preserved the texture of 20th-century New York life, and some have published collections of their pieces. *Back Where I Came From*, by A. J. Liebling, is one such collection, as is Mark Singer's *Mr. Personality*, in which he describes the lives of five brothers who are all building superintendents, as well as the activities of court buffs, retired men who meet each day at a courthouse to follow criminal trials. Joseph Mitchell's *Up in the Old Hotel* is a collection of fiction and journalism that he wrote for *The New Yorker* from the 1930s to the 1960s. These stories include a history of the bar that claims to be the oldest in New York, a profile of the self-styled King of the Gypsies, and a description of life along the East River and at South Street Seaport.

History and Journalism

General histories include a witty early account of New York, *Knickerbocker's History of New York*, by Washington Irving; the heavily illustrated *Columbia Historical Portrait of New York*, by John Kouwenhoven; and *The Historical Atlas of New York City*, by Eric Homberger. The Pulitzer Prize-winning *Gotham: A History of New York City to 1898* is by Edwin Burrows and Mike Wallace. Other solid histories are Michael Pye's *Maximum City: The Biography of New York* and Oliver E. Allen's anecdotal volume *New York, New York*, with awe-inspiring accounts of the robber barons of the industrial revolution. *You Must Remember This*, by Jeff Kisseloff, is an oral history of ordinary New Yorkers early in this century. In *The Great Port*, Jan Morris details the origins of New York commerce, while in *Manhattan '45* she reconstructs New York as it greeted returning GIs in 1945. History buffs should also seek out the *Enyclopaedia of New York*, edited by Kenneth T. Jackson, a massive, engrossing, and comprehensive guide to every aspect of city life, from politics to garbage collection.

Many excellent cultural histories of New York have rolled off the presses. Luc Sante writes about the cops, gangs, saloons, and politicians of 19th-century New York in *Low Life*. *Weegee's World*, the catalogue from an exhibition of the legendary photojournalist's work, is a visual equivalent to Sante's history. *New York Intellect* by Thomas Bender is a fascinating history of the emergence of the city's philosophical circles, from the 19th-century founders of the Metropolitan Museum and the New York Public Library to the 20th-century editors of the *Partisan Review*. Christine Stansell's *American Moderns: Bohemian New York and the Creation of a New Century* is a smart, readable, and skeptical account of Manhattan freethinkers and free-lovers; Anne Douglas's *Terrible Honesty: Mongrel Manhattan in the 1920s* captures the Roaring '20s.

Fans of the illicit might seek out Herbert Ashbury's *The Gangs of New York*; Timothy J. Gilfoyle's book on Gotham prostitution, *City of Eros*; or Andrew Roth's crime history, *Infamous Manhattan*. Shaun O'Connell's *Remarkable, Unspeakable New York* is a survey of New York subcultures as represented in fiction. *The Heart of the World*, by Nik Cohn, is a vivid block-by-block account of the high- and lowlife of Broadway, as is David Dunlap's *On Broadway: A Journey Uptown Over Time*. Nathan Glazer documented ethnic change in New York in *Beyond the Melting Pot*. Jill Jonnes' *We're Still Here* is an astonishing account of the fall of the South Bronx. Jane Jacobs' *The Death and Life of Great American Cities* is classic sociology of the contemporary urban center. George Chauncey's *Gay New York* is a hilarious, vivid history of the lively gay world that thrived before 1940—and before identity politics. In *Fame and Obscurity*, Gay Talese profiles Joe DiMaggio and Frank Sinatra while also writing about the anonymous characters and odd occupations that abound in New York. Mitchell Duneier narrates the day-to-day existence of booksellers, panhandlers, and street dwellers on a West Village corner in *Sidewalk*. On the other end of the economic spectrum, *A License to Steal*, by Benjamin J. Stein, concerns Wall Street's Michael Milken, as does *Den of Thieves*, by James B. Stewart. In *Manhattan Passions*, Ron Rosenbaum lunches with the rich, from Donald Trump to Malcolm Forbes.

New York politics has always been colorful, maybe too colorful, and there are dozens of accounts to prove it. *Once Upon a Time in New York*, by longtime *New York Times* writer Herbert Mitgang, narrates the Jazz Age rivalry between New York State governor Franklin Roosevelt and New York City mayor Jimmy Walker. Other political tales can be found in *Fiorello H. LaGuardia and the Making of Modern New York*, a biography of the Depression-era mayor by Thomas Kessner, and Robert Caro's Pulitzer Prize–winning *The Power Broker*, which chronicles the career of parks commissioner Robert Moses. *To Be Mayor of New York* by Christopher McNickle covers ethnic politics and every 20th-century mayoral election and administration through that of David Dinkins. In *Prince of the City*, Robert Daley covers New York police corruption. Critical accounts of city politics in the 1970s and 1980s can be found in *The Streets Were Paved with Gold*, by *New Yorker* writer Ken Auletta; *The Rise and Fall of New York City*, by Roger Starr; *Imperial City*, by Geoffrey Moorhouse; Martin Shefter's *Political Crisis, Fiscal Crisis: The Collapse and Revival of New York City*; and two books by Jack Newfield, *The Abuse of Power* with Paul Du Brul and *City for Sale*, with Wayne Barrett. Diane Ravitch's *The Great School Wars: a History of the New York City Public Schools* is a brilliant exposition of the struggle to educate the unruly crowds (now 1 million strong) of New York schoolchildren. Fred Siegel's *The Future Once Happened Here* is a window into the post-liberal policy and philosophy of New York's last Mayor, Rudy Giuliani.

New York has long taken pride as the capital of ephemeral chic, and Guy Trebay's *In the Place to Be* shows each short-lived beauty for what it was. *Please Kill Me*, edited by Legs McNeil and Gillian McCain, is an astonishing oral history of New York punk rock, while *The Andy Warhol Diaries* covers several decades of celebrity. Grander cultural personalities who recently received biographical treatment include gossip columnist Walter Winchell, magazine publishers Henry Luce, Conde Nast, and Si Newhouse, art director Alexander Liberman, book editors Michael Korda and Bennett Cerf, and *New Yorker* editors Harold Ross and William Shawn. Even the "21" club has a biography; the classic satire of rich Manhattan's foibles is Tom Wolfe's *Radical Chic*.

Art and Architecture

AIA Guide to New York City, by Elliot Willensky and Norval White, is the definitive guide to the city's architectural styles; Paul Goldberger's *The City Observed* describes Manhattan building by building. *Lost New York* by Nathan Silver, documents the famous buildings wiped out by developers before the Landmarks Commission was established. Rem Koolhaas's imaginative *Delirious New York* captures the city's spirit better than many literal histories. *Inside New York* has gorgeous photographs of hard-to-see New York interiors, while Mayer Rus' *Loft* shows a more contemporary Manhattan glamour. Robert A. M. Stern has published a several-volume history of New York architecture for serious scholars. Fans of the mid-20th century New York art movements of Abstract Expressionism and Pop can seek out the intellectual (*How New York Stole the Idea of Modern Art* by Serge Guilbart), the classic (*The New York School: A Cultural Reckoning* by Dore Ashton), or the cynical (Tom Wolfe's *The Painted Word*). Henry Geldzahler's writing on New York art, such as *Making It New,* is always a pleasure.

For Theater Lovers

Theater lovers will want to look at *Act One,* the autobiography of playwright Moss Hart; *The Season,* by William Goldman; David Mamet's *The Cabin;* and Neil Simon's *Rewrites.* Brooks Atkinson's *Broadway* and the oral history *It Happened on Broadway* capture the glory days when the Great White Way debuted playwrights including Eugene O'Neill, Arthur Miller, Edward Albee, and Tennessee Williams, and musical theater figures such as Kauffman and Hart, Rodgers and Hammerstein, David Merrick, Jerome Robbins, and Stephen Sondheim. Walter Kerr's criticism, such as *The Theater in Spite of Itself* and *The Decline of Pleasure,* is worth volumes of academic history. Frank Rich's *Hot Seat* chronicles the more dismal years from 1980 to 1993, which produced David Mamet and Sam Shepard.

Memoirs

American writers and editors often move to New York because it's the center of the publishing industry. Many of these migrants write about the lives they find here, complementing the perspective of native-born authors. Federico Garcia Lorca's *Poet in New York,* written during a nine-month trip just after the Wall Street crash of 1929, records his response to the city's brutality, loneliness, and greed. A great memoir of New York bohemia is Samuel Delany's *The Motion of Light in Water,* while *Brendan Behan's New York* describes the city's underbelly and Mary McCarthy's *Intellectual Memoirs* captures its left-wing circles. Dan Wakefield tells stories about meeting and drinking with such figures as Jack Kerouac and James Baldwin in *New York in the Fifties.* Anatole Broyard writes about that same era in *Kafka Was the Rage,* a description of his coming of age as a literary critic in Greenwich Village. In *New York Days* Willie Morris writes about arriving in town from Mississippi as a young journalist, then describes his stint as editor of *Harper's* magazine during its heyday as a venue for new journalism. Stephen Brook's *New York Days, New York Nights* is a witty and fairly penetrating account of the city in the 1980s. Jerome Charyn's *Metropolis,* written by a Bronx native, dives into the same period, with sharply different results. Other good accounts are *Christopher Morley's New York,* a mid-1920s reminiscence; *Walker in the City,* by Alfred Kazin; *Apple of My Eye,* a memoir of writing a New York guidebook, by Helene Hanff; *Paul Auster's New York*; Eileen Myles' *Chelsea Girls*; and *Manhattan When I Was Young,* by Mary Cantwell.

Fiction

Wonderful Town is a terrific collection of *New Yorker* short stories set in New York, with offerings from Lorrie Moore, Laurie Colwin, John Updike, and Maeve Brennan. *The Time Out Book of New York Short Stories* and *Between C & D* sample younger, trendier writers. *The Bonfire of the Vanities,* by Tom Wolfe, is a sprawling novel set in such divergent precincts as the opulent Upper East Side, the ghettoes of the Bronx, and the labyrinthine criminal justice system. Don DiLillo's *Underworld* is an epic that begins in the Bronx, while recent National Book Award winner *Charming Billy* by Alice McDermott portrays an Irish-American family in Bayside, Queens. Jonathan Ames' hilarious and moving *The Extra Man* spans New York from the world of elegant Upper East Side ladies and their walkers to Times Square transsexual bars. In Jay McInerney's *Bright Lights, Big City*, the young narrator works at a prestigious magazine by day and explores downtown bars and restaurants by night. *The Treatment*, by Dan Menaker, describes the romantic pursuits of a young teacher. In *Manhattan Nocturne*, Colin Harrison tells the story of a tabloid reporter who falls in love with a beautiful woman and investigates a mysterious murder, while his newer novel *Afterburn* features a millionaire in search of a woman to give him an heir, who tangles with a gangster named Christina. The Soho art world and Manhattan real estate market set the scene for *The Third Eye*, an eerie confessional-style novel written by David Knowles. Other recent New York novels include *The Mambo Kings Play Songs of Love*, by Oscar Hijuelos; *The New York Trilogy*, by Paul Auster; and *People Like Us*, by Dominick Dunne. Some of the best new "New York" writing, such as Richard Price's *Clockers* and Junot Diaz's *Drown*, is actually set in cities across the river in New Jersey.

Novels set in 19th-century New York include Henry James's *Washington Square*; Edith Wharton's *The House of Mirth* and *The Age of Innocence*; Stephen Crane's *Maggie, a Girl of the Streets; The Alienist*, by Caleb Carr; and *The Waterworks*, by E. L. Doctorow. The 20th century unfolds in F. Scott Fitzgerald's *The Beautiful and the Damned*, John Dos Passos's *Manhattan Transfer*, John O'Hara's *Butterfield 8*, Mary McCarthy's *The Group*, James Baldwin's *Another Country*, and Chang-rae Lee's *Native Speaker*. New York short stories come from O. Henry, Damon Run-

yon, John Cheever, Bernard Malamud, Grace Paley, and Isaac Bashevis Singer. Incurable romantics might want to revisit the intense New York longing of J. D. Salinger's *The Catcher in the Rye*.

Black, Jewish, and Puerto Rican New York

The black experience in New York City has been fictionalized in Ralph Ellison's *Invisible Man*, James Baldwin's *Go Tell It on the Mountain*, and Claude Brown's *Manchild in the Promised Land*. For a portrait of 1920s Harlem, try *When Harlem Was in Vogue*, by David Levering Lewis. For a look at the experience of black Caribbean women in Brooklyn, turn to Paule Marshall's fiction. Brilliant nonfiction includes Jervis Anderson's *This Was Harlem*, Ralph Ellison's essay "Harlem is Nowhere" in *Shadow and Act*, and Hilton Als' *The Women*. The history of New York's Jews can be traced in such books as *World of Our Fathers*, by Irving Howe; *Call it Sleep*, by Henry Roth; *New York Jew* by Alfred Kazin; *The Promise* and *The Chosen* by Chaim Potok; and *Our Crowd*, by Stephen Birmingham. A classic of New York Puerto Rican (aka "Nuyorican") fiction is Piri Thomas' *Down These Mean Streets*.

Mysteries and Noir

Mysteries set in New York City range from Dashiell Hammett's urbane 1933 novel *The Thin Man* to Rex Stout's series of Nero Wolfe mysteries. More recent picks include *While My Pretty One Sleeps*, by Mary Higgins Clark; *Greenwich Killing Time*, by Kinky Friedman; *The Second Suspect*, by Heather Lewis; *Dead Air*, by Mike Lupica; and *Unorthodox Practices*, by Marissa Piesman.

Videos

Perhaps the quintessential New York City movie is *Breakfast at Tiffany's* (1961), directed by Blake Edwards and based on Truman Capote's 1958 novella. (Brace yourself, however, for Mickey Rooney's shocking yellowface caricature of Holly Golightly's Japanese neighbor.) Another classic,

On the Town, (1949) stars Gene Kelly and Frank Sinatra as sailors on a 24-hour leave.

Filmmaker Woody Allen has filmed almost all his movies in Manhattan. (He says he likes to be able to go home and get a sweater.) *Annie Hall* (1977), *Manhattan* (1979), *Hannah and Her Sisters* (1987), *Crimes and Misdemeanors* (1989), *Alice* (1990), *Manhattan Murder Mystery* (1993), and *Everyone Says I Love You* (1996) are a few.

Director Martin Scorsese has made some of his best films in New York, including *Mean Streets* (1973), *Taxi Driver* (1976), *New York, New York* (1977), *Raging Bull* (1980), *The King of Comedy* (1983), *Goodfellas* (1991), and *The Age of Innocence*(1993).

The late Bronx-born Alan J. Pakula used New York City masterfully in a number of his films. Jane Fonda took home an Oscar for her performance in *Klute* (1971), and Meryl Streep won for *Sophie's Choice* (1982). Other Pakula films featuring New York City are *Rollover* (1981), *Presumed Innocent* (1990), and his final film, *The Devil's Own* (1997). Sidney Lumet's films of misfits and police corruption include *Serpico* (1973) and *Dog Day Afternoon* (1975), both starring Al Pacino.

Some of director Paul Mazursky's most entertaining films have New York settings: *Next Stop, Greenwich Village* (1976), *An Unmarried Woman* (1978), and *Enemies, A Love Story* (1989), based on the novel by Isaac Bashevis Singer.

Neil Simon films with city locations include *Barefoot in the Park* (1967), *The Odd Couple* (1968), *The Goodbye Girl* (1977), and *Brighton Beach Memoirs* (1986).

Joan Micklin Silver portrays the Lower East Side in different eras in *Hester Street* (1975) and *Crossing Delancey* (1988). Spike Lee has perfected his very Brooklyn aesthetic with such films as *Do the Right Thing* (1990) and *Son of Sam* (1999). Jennie Livingston's documentary *Paris Is Burning* (1990) explores a fascinating Harlem subculture. *I Like It Like That* (1994), directed by Darnell Martin, deals with a feisty single mother in the Bronx.

Other New York City–set movies include *The Women* (1939), *The Naked City* (1945), *The Lost Weekend* (1948), *All About Eve* (1950), *Sweet Smell of Success* (1957), *Auntie Mame* (1959), *Love with the Proper Stranger* (1963), *Up the Down Staircase* (1967), *Wait Until Dark* (1967), *The Producers* (1967), *Rosemary's Baby* (1968), *Midnight Cowboy* (1969), *Diary of a Mad Housewife* (1970), *The Way We Were* (1973), *Network* (1976), *Saturday Night Fever* (1978), *Hair* (1979), *Kramer vs. Kramer* (1979), *Dressed to Kill* (1980), *Fame* (1980), *Ghostbusters* (1984), *Moonstruck* (1987), *New York Stories* (1989), *Sea of Love* (1989), *Metropolitan* (1990), *Night and the City* (1992), *A Bronx Tale* (1993), *Household Saints* (1993), *Little Odessa* (1994), *City Hall* (1996), *Smoke* (1996), *Basquiat* (1996), *Donnie Brasco* (1997), *A Perfect Murder* (1998), and *Joe Gould's Secret* (1999).

A great episode of *The Simpsons,* "The City of New York vs. Homer Simpson," is set in the city. While it rehashes some clichés of New York as a crime-ridden cesspool, it has priceless moments—including Bart confusing three Hasidic Jews for the '80s band ZZ Top, and a Broadway musical about the Betty Ford clinic.

ESSENTIAL INFORMATION

ADDRESSES

To locate the cross street that corresponds to a numerical avenue address, or to find the avenue closest to a numerical street address, check the phone book's "Address Locator." This handy chart provides relatively simple calculations for finding Manhattan addresses.

AIR TRAVEL TO AND
FROM NEW YORK

Schedules and fares for air service to New York vary from carrier to carrier and, sometimes, from airport to airport. For the best prices and for nonstop flights, consult several airlines. Generally, more international flights go in and out of Kennedy Airport, more domestic flights go in and out of La Guardia Airport, and Newark Airport serves both domestic and international travelers.

BOOKING

When you book **look for nonstop flights** and **remember that "direct" flights stop at least once.** Try to avoid connecting flights, which require a change of plane. For more booking tips and to check prices and make online flight reservations, log on to www.fodors.com.

CARRIERS

There is an abundance of large and small airlines with flights to and from New York City.

➤ MAJOR AIRLINES: Domestic carriers: **America West** (☎ 800/235–9292, WEB www.americawest.com). **American** (☎ 800/433–7300, WEB www.americanairlines.com). **Continental** (☎ 800/525–0280, WEB www.continental.com). **Delta** (☎ 800/221–1212, WEB www.delta.com). **Northwest/KLM** (☎ 800/225–2525, WEB www.nwa.com). **TWA** (☎ 800/221–2000, WEB www.twa.com). **United** (☎ 800/241–6522, WEB www.united.

com). **US Airways** (☎ 800/428–4322, WEB www.usairways.com).

International carriers: **Alitalia Airlines** (☎ 800/223–5730, WEB www.alitalia.com). **Austrian Airlines** (☎ 800/843–0002, WEB www.aua.com). **British Airways** (☎ 800/247–9297, WEB www.britishairways.com). **Canadian Airlines** (☎ 800/426–7000, WEB www.aircanada.ca). **Virgin Atlantic Airways** (☎ 800/862–8621, WEB www.virgin.com).

➤ SMALLER AIRLINES: **Midway** (☎ 800/446–4392, WEB www.midway.com). **Midwest Express** (☎ 800/452–2022, WEB www.midwestexpress.com).

FLYING TIMES

New York airports welcome incoming flights from all over the world. Some sample flying times are: from Chicago (3½ hours), London (7 hours), Los Angeles (6 hours), Sydney via Los Angeles (21 hours).

HOW TO COMPLAIN

If your baggage goes astray or your flight goes awry, complain right away. Most carriers require that you **file a claim immediately.**

➤ AIRLINE COMPLAINTS: U.S. Department of Transportation Aviation Consumer Protection Division (✉ C-75, Room 4107, Washington, DC 20590, ☎ 202/366–2220, WEB www.dot.gov/airconsumer). Federal Aviation Administration Consumer Hotline (☎ 800/322–7873).

AIRPORTS & TRANSFERS

The major gateways to New York City are LaGuardia Airport and JFK International Airport, in the borough of Queens, and Newark International Airport in New Jersey. It's a bit less expensive to travel between Manhattan and La Guardia or Kennedy than it is to travel between Manhattan and Newark. It's also cheaper to travel to Queens, Brooklyn, or the Bronx from La Guardia or Kennedy.

➤ AIRPORT INFORMATION: **La Guardia Airport** (☎ 718/533–3400). **JFK International Airport** (☎ 718/244–4444). **Newark International Airport** (☎ 973/961–6000).

Air-Ride Transportation Information Service (☎ 800/247–7433) offers detailed, up-to-the-minute recorded information on how to reach your destination from New York's three major airports via car, private bus, shuttle service, or public transportation.

AIRPORT TRANSFERS

➤ TAXIS & SHUTTLES: Outside the baggage-claim area at each of New York's major airports is a taxi stand where a uniformed dispatcher helps passengers find taxis. Cabs are not permitted to pick up fares anywhere else in the arrivals area, so if you want a taxi, take your place in line. Shuttle services generally pick up passengers from a designated spot along the curb, and car services seem to pull up wherever they like (they'll tell you where to meet them when you call for your pickup).

TRANSFERS FROM ALL AIRPORTS

Car services can be a great deal because the driver will often meet you on the concourse or in the baggage-claim area and help you with your luggage. You ride in late-model American-made cars that are usually comfortable, if a bit worn. The flat rates and tolls are often comparable to taxi fares, but some car services will charge for parking and waiting time at the airport. To eliminate these expenses, other car services require that you telephone their dispatcher when you land so they can send the next available car to pick you up. Your wait in this case may be longer than that for a taxi. Inquire about procedures and fees in advance to avoid any unpleasant surprises and to weigh convenience against cost. New York City Taxi and Limousine Commission rules require that all car services be licensed and pick up riders only by prior arrangement. **Call 24 hours in advance for reservations,** or at least a half day before your flight's departure.

➤ CAR RESERVATIONS: **Mirage Limousine Service** (☎ 212/744–9700,

FAX 718/937–9400). **Executive Town Car & Limousines** (☎ 516/538–8551 or 800/716–2799, FAX 516/489–6592). **Greenwich Limousine** (☎ 212/868–4733 or 800/385–1033, FAX 212/736–8733). **London Towncars** (☎ 212/988–9700 or 800/221–4009, FAX 718/786–7625). **Manhattan International Limo** (☎ 718/729–4200 or 800/221–7500, FAX 718/937–6157). **Skyline** (☎ 212/741–3711 or 800/533–6325, FAX 718/937–3711). **Tel Aviv Car and Limousine Service** (☎ 212/777–7777 or 800/222–9888, FAX 212/505–6004).

TRANSFERS FROM JFK INTERNATIONAL AIRPORT

Taxis charge a flat fee of $30 plus tolls (which may be as much as $4) to Manhattan only, and take 35–60 minutes. Prices are $16–$55 for trips to other locations in New York City. You should also tip the driver.

The **Gray Line Air Shuttle** (☎ 212/315–3006 or 800/451–0455, WEB www.graylinenewyork.com) serves major Manhattan hotels directly from the airport; the cost is $14 per person. Make arrangements at the airport's ground transportation counter or use the courtesy phone. Shuttles operate 7 AM–11:30 PM from the airport; between 5 AM and 9 PM going to the airport.

The cheapest but slowest means of getting to Manhattan is to take the Port Authority's free shuttle bus, which stops at all terminals, to the Howard Beach subway station, where you can catch the A train into Manhattan; be sure to take the A train marked **Far Rockaway** or **Rockaway Park**, not Lefferts Blvd. Alternatively, you can take Bus Q-10 (there are no luggage facilities on this bus) to the Union Turnpike–Kew Gardens station, where you can catch the E or F Subway. Or you can take Bus B-15 to New Lots station and catch the 3 Subway. Allow at least two hours for the trip (☞ Bus Travel *and* Subway Travel, *below*).

TRANSFERS FROM LAGUARDIA AIRPORT

Taxis cost $17–$29 plus tip and tolls (which may be as high as $4) to most destinations in New York City, and take at least 20–40 minutes. Group taxi rides to Manhattan are available at taxi dispatch lines just outside the baggage-claim areas during most travel hours (except on Saturday and holidays). Group fares run $9–$10 per person (plus a share of tip and tolls).

The Gray Line Air Shuttle (☎ 212/315–3006 or 800/451–0455, WEB www.graylinenewyork.com) serves major Manhattan hotels directly to and from the airport. The fare is $13 per person; make arrangements at the airport's ground transportation center or use the courtesy phone. Shuttles run 7 AM–11:30 PM from the airport; between 5 AM and 9 PM going to the airport.

The **Delta Water Shuttle** (☎ 800/533–3779, WEB www.nywaterway.com) runs hourly and operates from 7:45 AM to 6:45 PM between La Guardia Airport's Marine Air Terminal and Wall Street (Pier 11). There are stops along the way at 62nd Street and 34th Street on the East Side. The trip from the airport to Wall Street lasts about 45 minutes. The fare is $15, $25 round-trip.

The most economical way to reach Manhattan is to ride the M-60 public bus (there are no luggage facilities on this bus) to 116th Street and Broadway, across from Columbia University. From there, you can transfer to the 1 or 9 subway to Midtown. Alternatively, you can take Bus Q-48 to the Main Street subway station in Flushing, where you can transfer to the 7 train. Allow at least 90 minutes for the entire trip to Midtown (☞ Bus Travel *and* Subway Travel, *below*).

In addition, **Triboro Coach Corp.** (☎ 718/335–1000, WEB www.triborocoach.com) runs its Q-33 line from the airport to the Jackson Heights subway stop in Queens, where you can catch the E or F trains; it also stops at the Roosevelt Avenue–Jackson Heights station, where you can pick up the 7 subway line. The ride costs $1.50.

TRANSFERS FROM NEWARK AIRPORT

Taxis to Manhattan cost $34–$55 plus tolls ($10) and take 20–45 minutes. "Share and Save" group rates are available for up to four passengers between 8 AM and midnight; make arrangements with the airport's taxi dispatcher.

Olympia Trails (☎ 212/964–6233 or 718/622–7700, WEB www.olympiabus.com) buses leave for Grand Central Terminal and Penn Station in Manhattan about every 20 minutes until midnight, and for 1 World Trade Center (WTC) about every 30 minutes until 7:00 PM. The trip takes roughly 45 minutes to Grand Central and Penn Station, 20 minutes to WTC. The fare is $11. Between Port Authority and Newark, buses run every 20 minutes from 7 AM–midnight, every 30 minutes from 5–7 AM. The fare is $11.

The **Gray Line Air Shuttle** (☎ 212/315–3006 or 800/451–0455, WEB www.graylinenewyork.com) serves major Manhattan hotels directly to and from the airport. You pay $14 per passenger; make arrangements at the airport's ground transportation center or use the courtesy phone. Shuttles operate 7 AM–11:30 PM from the airport; between 5 AM and 9 PM going to the airport.

You can also take New Jersey Transit's **Airlink** buses (☎ 973/762–5100, WEB www.njtransit.state.nj.us), which leave every 20 minutes from 6:15 AM to 1:45 AM, to Penn Station in Newark. The ride takes about 20 minutes; the fare is $4. (Be sure to have exact change.) From there, you can catch **PATH Trains** (☎ 800/234–7284, WEB www.pathrail.com), which run to Manhattan 24 hours a day. The trains run every 10 minutes on weekdays, every 15–30 minutes on weeknights, and every 20–30 minutes on weekends. Trains stop at the World Trade Center and at five stops along 6th Avenue—Christopher Street, 9th Street, 14th Street, 23rd Street, and 33rd Street. The fare is $1, and it's easiest to pay with one-dollar bills.

BOAT & FERRY TRAVEL

Ferries run from Battery Park's South Ferry to the Statue of Liberty and Ellis Island. The fare is $7, and tickets are sold at nearby Castle Clinton. NY Waterway's *Yankee Clipper* and *Mets Express* ferries take passengers from Manhattan and New Jersey to Yankee

Stadium and Shea Stadium for $14 round-trip. You can also travel between West 38th Street and 12th Avenue in Manhattan and Weehawken, NJ by ferry for $5; or between the World Financial Center and Hoboken, NJ or Jersey City, NJ for $2. Fares can be paid in cash or with traveler's checks. The Staten Island Ferry runs across New York Harbor between South Ferry and Staten Island. The ride is free.

➤ BOAT & FERRY INFORMATION: **Castle Clinton** (☎ 212/269–5755). **NY Waterway** (☎ 201/902–8700 or 800/533–3779). **Staten Island Ferry** (☎ 718/390–5253).

BUS TRAVEL AROUND NEW YORK CITY

Most city buses follow easy-to-understand routes along the Manhattan street grid. Routes go up or down the north–south avenues, or east and west on the major two-way crosstown streets: 96th, 86th, 79th, 72nd, 57th, 42nd, 34th, 23rd, and 14th. Most bus routes operate 24 hours, but service is infrequent late at night. Buses are great for sightseeing, but traffic jams—a potential threat at any time or place in Manhattan—can make rides maddeningly slow. Certain bus routes offer "Limited-Stop Service," which can save traveling time. Such buses usually run on weekdays during rush hours and stop only at major cross streets and transfer points.

To find a bus stop, **look for a light-blue sign (green for a limited bus)** on a green pole; bus numbers and routes are listed, with the stop's name underneath.

FARES & SCHEDULES

Bus fare is the same as subway fare: $1.50. MetroCards (☞ Public Transportation, *below*) allow you one free transfer between buses or from bus to subway; when using a token or cash, you can **ask the driver for a free transfer coupon,** good for one change to an intersecting route. Legal transfer points are listed on the back of the slip. Transfers have time limits of at least two hours, often longer. You cannot use the transfer to enter the subway system.

Route maps and schedules are posted at many bus stops in Manhattan and at major stops throughout the other boroughs. Each of the five boroughs of New York has a separate bus map, and they are scarcer than hens' teeth. They are available from some subway token booths, but never on buses. The best places to obtain them are the MTA booth in the Times Square Visitors Center, or the information kiosks in Grand Central Terminal and Penn Station.

➤ BUS INFORMATION: **Metropolitan Transit Authority (MTA) Travel Information Center** (☎ 718/330–1234, WEB www.mta.nyc.ny.us). **MTA Status information hot line** (☎ 718/243–7777), updated hourly.

PAYING

Pay your bus fare when you board, with exact change in coins (no pennies, and no change is given), with a subway token, or with a MetroCard.

SMOKING

Smoking is not allowed on New York City buses.

BUS TRAVEL TO AND FROM NEW YORK CITY

Long-haul and commuter bus lines feed into the Port Authority Terminal between 8th and 9th avenues from West 40th to West 42nd streets. Six bus lines, serving northern New Jersey and Rockland County, New York, make daily stops at the George Washington Bridge Bus Station from 5 AM to 1 AM. The station is at Fort Washington Avenue and Broadway between West 178th and West 179th streets in the Washington Heights section of Manhattan. It is connected to the 175th Street Station on the A line of the subway, which travels down the West Side and connects to other subway lines.

FARES & SCHEDULES

Contact the bus companies for information on their routes, fares, and schedules.

➤ BUS INFORMATION: **Greyhound Lines Inc.** (☎ 800/231–2222, WEB www. greyhound.com). **Adirondack, Pine Hill, and New York Trailways** (☎ 800/

225–6815, WEB www.trailways.com) from upstate New York. **Bonanza Bus Lines** (☎ 800/556–3815, WEB www. bonanzabus.com) from New England. **Martz Trailways** (☎ 800/233–8604, WEB www.martztrailways.com) from Philadelphia and northeastern Pennsylvania. **New Jersey Transit** (☎ 973/762–5100, WEB www.njtransit.state.nj. us) from around New Jersey. **Peter Pan Trailways** (☎ 413/781–2900 or 800/343–9999, WEB www.peterpan-bus. com) from New England. **Vermont Transit** (☎ 802/864–6811 or 800/451–3292, WEB www.vermonttransit. com) from New England.

PAYING

Most bus lines accept cash, credit cards, or travelers checks in payment.

➤ BUS TERMINAL INFORMATION: **George Washington Bridge Bus Station** (☎ 212/564–1114). **Port Authority Terminal** (☎ 212/564–8484, WEB www.panynj.gov).

BUSINESS HOURS

New York is very much a 24-hour city. Its subways and buses run around the clock, and plenty of services are available at all hours and on all days of the week.

BANKS & OFFICES

Banks are open weekdays 9–3 or 9–3:30, and some have late hours one day a week or are open Saturday morning.

MUSEUMS & SIGHTS

Museum hours vary greatly, but most of the major ones are open Tuesday–Sunday and keep later hours on Tuesday or Thursday evening.

PHARMACIES

Pharmacy hours vary from store to store. Generally, pharmacies open early in the morning and most remain open until at least 6 PM or 7 PM. Most chain drug stores have at least one pharmacy that is open 24 hours.

SHOPS

Stores are generally open Monday–Saturday from 10 to 5 or 6, but neighborhood peculiarities do exist and many retailers remain open until 8 PM. Some stores on the Lower East Side and in the diamond district on West 47th Street close on Friday afternoon and all day Saturday for the Jewish Sabbath but are open on Sunday. Sunday hours, also common on the West Side and in Greenwich Village and SoHo, are the exception on the Upper East Side.

CAMERAS & PHOTOGRAPHY

There are plenty of photography opportunities in New York. Some people may be sensitive about having their pictures taken without their consent, but if you ask permission first they may happily agree to pose. The *Kodak Guide to Shooting Great Travel Pictures* (available at bookstores everywhere) is loaded with tips.

➤ PHOTO HELP: Kodak Information Center (☎ 800/242–2424).

EQUIPMENT PRECAUTIONS

Don't pack film and equipment in checked luggage, where it is much more susceptible to damage. X-ray machines used to view checked luggage are becoming much more powerful and therefore are much more likely to ruin your film. Always **keep film and tape out of the sun.** Carry an extra supply of batteries, and **be prepared to turn on your camera or camcorder** to prove to security personnel that the device is real. Always **ask for hand inspection of film,** which becomes clouded after repeated exposure to airport X-ray machines, and **keep videotapes away from metal detectors.**

CAR RENTAL

Rates in New York City begin at $85 a day and $350 a week for an economy car with air-conditioning, automatic transmission, and unlimited mileage. This does not include tax on car rentals, which is 13¼%. Rental costs are lower just outside New York City. High-end cars, such as Jaguars and Range Rovers, may be rented from agencies specializing in such vehicles. The Yellow Pages are also filled with a profusion of local car rental agencies, some renting second-hand vehicles.

➤ MAJOR AGENCIES: **Alamo** (☎ 800/327–9633; 020/8759–6200 in the U.K., WEB www.goalamo.com). **Avis** (☎ 800/331–1212; 800/879–2847 in Canada; 02/9353–9000 in Australia; 09/525–1982 in New Zealand; 0870/606–0100 in the U.K., WEB www.avis.com). **Budget** (☎ 800/527–0700; 0144/227–6266 in the U.K., through affiliate Europcar, WEB www.budget.com). **Dollar** (☎ 800/800–4000; 0124/622–0111 in the U.K., where it is known as Sixt Kenning; 02/9223–1444 in Australia, WEB www.dollarcar.com). **Hertz** (☎ 800/654–3131; 800/263–0600 in Canada; 020/8897–2072 in the U.K.; 02/9669–2444 in Australia; 09/256–8690 in New Zealand, WEB www.hertz.com). **National Car Rental** (☎ 800/227–7368; 0845/722–2525 in the U.K., where it is known as National Europe, WEB www.nationalcar.com).

CUTTING COSTS

To get the best deal, **book through a travel agent who will shop around.** Also **price local car-rental companies,** although the service and maintenance may not be as good as those of a major player. Remember to ask about required deposits, cancellation penalties, and drop-off charges if you're planning to pick up the car in one city and leave it in another. If you're traveling during a holiday period, also make sure that a confirmed reservation guarantees you a car.

➤ LOCAL AGENCIES: **Autorent** (☎ 212/315–1555). **New York Rent-A-Car** (☎ 212/799–1100 or 800/697–2227, WEB www.nyrac.com).

INSURANCE

When driving a rented car you are generally responsible for any damage to or loss of the vehicle as well as for any property damage or personal injury that you may cause. Before you rent, see what coverage your personal auto-insurance policy and credit cards provide.

For about $15–$20 per day, rental companies sell protection, known as a collision- or loss-damage waiver (CDW or LDW), that eliminates your liability for damage to the car. New York has outlawed the sale of the CDW and LDW altogether. In New York

you pay for only the first $100 of damage to the rental car.

REQUIREMENTS & RESTRICTIONS

In New York you must be 18 to rent a car. Some agencies in Manhattan require a minimum age of 25. You'll pay extra for child seats (about $5 per day), which are compulsory for children under age five, and for additional drivers (about $5 per day). Non-U.S. residents will need a reservation voucher, a passport, a driver's license, and a travel policy that covers each driver, when picking up a car.

SURCHARGES

Before you pick up a car in one city and leave it in another, **ask about drop-off charges or one-way service fees,** which can be substantial. Note, too, that some rental agencies charge extra if you return the car before the time specified in your contract. To avoid a hefty refueling fee, **fill the tank just before you turn in the car,** but be aware that gas stations near the rental outlet may overcharge.

CAR TRAVEL

If you plan to drive into Manhattan, try to time your arrival for late morning or early afternoon. That way you'll avoid the morning and evening rush hours (a problem at the crossings into Manhattan) and lunch hour.

The deterioration of the bridges to Manhattan, especially those spanning the East River, is a serious problem, and repairs will be ongoing for the next few years. Listen to traffic reports on the radio (☞ Radio & Television, *below*) before you set off and don't be surprised if a bridge is partially or entirely closed.

Driving within Manhattan can be a nightmare of gridlocked streets and predatory motorists. Narrow and one-way streets are common, particularly downtown, and can make driving even more difficult. The most congested streets of the city lie between 14th and 59th Streets and 3rd and 8th avenues.

EMERGENCY SERVICES

If you are in or witness an accident, call 911 to request assistance or report an emergency.

GASOLINE

Fill up your tank when you have a chance—gas stations are few and far between. If you can, **fill up at stations outside of the city,** where prices will be anywhere from 10¢ to 50¢ cheaper per gallon. The average price of a gallon of regular unleaded is $1.59, although prices can vary from station to station. In Manhattan, you can refuel at stations along the West Side Highway and 11th Avenue south of West 57th Street and along East Houston Street. Some gas stations in New York require you to pump your own gas, while others provide attendants. It is customary to give these attendants a small tip if they check your oil or wash your windshield.

PARKING

Free parking is difficult to find in midtown, and violators may be towed away literally within minutes. All over town, parking lots charge exorbitant rates—as much as $15 for two hours in some neighborhoods. If you do drive, **don't plan to use your car much for traveling within Manhattan.** Instead, try to park it in a guarded parking garage for at least several hours; the sting of hourly rates lessens if a car is left for a significant amount of time. If you find a spot on the street, be sure to **check parking signs carefully,** as rules differ from block to block.

ROAD CONDITIONS

New York City streets are in generally good condition, although there are enough potholes and bad patch jobs to make driving a little rough at times. Road and bridge repair seems to go on constantly, so you may encounter the occasional detour or a bottle-neck where a three-lane street narrows to one lane. Heavy rains can cause street flooding in some areas, most notoriously on the Franklin Delano Roosevelt Drive (known as the FDR and sometimes as the East River Drive), where the heavy traffic can grind to a halt when lakes suddenly appear on the road. Traffic can be very heavy anywhere in the city at any time, made worse by the bad habits—double-parking, sudden lane changes, etc.—of some drivers. The best solution to the problem of driving in the city is too do

as little of it as possible, and to remain alert when you do drive.

RULES OF THE ROAD

On city streets the speed limit is 30 mph, unless otherwise posted. In the front and back seats, the law requires that seat belts should be worn at all times. There is no right turn on red within the city limits.

In 1999 Mayor Giuliani and the NYPD introduced a harsh and controversial law intended to discourage drunk driving in the city. All DWI offenders in New York City, first-timers included, will have the car they are driving immediately seized by the police department. Keep this in mind if you're taking your car out for a night on the town.

Always **strap children under age four into approved child-safety seats.**

CHILDREN IN NEW YORK

If you are renting a car, don't forget to **arrange for a car seat** when you reserve.

For calendars of children's events, consult *New York* magazine, *Time Out New York,* and the weekly *Village Voice* newspaper, available free at Manhattan newsstands and bookstores. The Friday *New York Times* "Weekend" section also provides a good listing of children's activities. Other good sources of information on happenings for youngsters are the monthly magazines *New York Family* and the *Big Apple Parents' Paper,* which are available free at toy stores, children's museums, and clothing stores, and other places around town where parents and children are found. If your accommodations provide access to cable television, check the local all-news channel, NY1, where you'll find a spot—conveniently aired several times daily—that covers current and noteworthy children's events.

Fodor's Around New York City with Kids (available in bookstores everywhere) can help you plan your days together. For general advice about traveling with children, consult *Fodor's FYI: Travel with Your Baby* (available in bookstores everywhere).

► PUBLICATIONS: **Big Apple Parents' Paper** (☎ 212/889–6400, WEB www.parentsknow.com). **Fodor's Travel Publications** (☎ 800/533–6478, WEB www.fodors.com). **New York Family** (☎ 914/381–7474, WEB www.parenthoodweb.com).

BABY-SITTING

The **Avalon Registry** is prepared to take very young children off your hands—at least for the day. Rates are $16 an hour for one to two children of any age, and there is a flat fee of $17.50 an hour to care for three or more children. There is also a $3 transportation charge ($8 after 8 PM). The **Baby Sitters' Guild** can take your children on sightseeing tours. Rates are $15 an hour for one or two children over age two, and $17 for one or two children under two, plus a $4.50 transportation charge ($7 after midnight); There is an additional fee of $2 for foreign-language tours (over a dozen languages are spoken among the staff). Minimum booking is for four hours.

► AGENCIES: **Avalon Registry** (☎ 212/245–0250). **Baby Sitters' Guild** (☎ 212/682–0227).

LODGING

Most hotels in New York allow children under a certain age to stay in their parents' room at no extra charge, but others charge for them as adults; be sure to **find out the cutoff age for children's discounts.**

SIGHTS & ATTRACTIONS

Places that are especially appealing to children are indicated by a rubber-duckie icon (☺) in the margin.

COMPUTERS ON THE ROAD

Some hotels in New York offer access to data ports and Web TV. For specific information inquire before making reservations.

CONCIERGES

Concierges, found in many hotels, can help you with theater tickets and dinner reservations: a good one with connections may be able to get you seats for a hot show or prime-time dinner reservations at the restaurant of the moment. You can also turn to your hotel's concierge for help with travel arrangements, sightseeing plans, services ranging from aromatherapy to zipper repair, and emergencies. Always, **always tip** a concierge who has been of assistance (☞ Tipping, *below*).

New York has always had a reputation for being *the* city when it comes to getting whatever you need or want whenever you need or want it. While this reputation is deserved, the problem for visitor and resident alike has always been just how to perform this legendary New York magic trick without burning a hole in your pocketbook or shoe leather. For a fee, **New York Concierge Services, Inc.** can help. The cost begins with a $35 single-service charge and hourly rates of $50 for concierge assistance. Whether your need is dire or whimsical, the sky's the limit. But costs can soar, too, though they will generally correspond with the size of your imagination.

► CONTACT: **New York Concierge Services, Inc.** (☎ 212/590–2530, WEB www.nyconcierge.com).

CONSUMER PROTECTION

Whenever shopping or buying travel services in New York, **pay with a major credit card,** if possible, so you can cancel payment or get reimbursed if there's a problem. If you're doing business with a particular company for the first time, **contact your local Better Business Bureau and the attorney general's offices** in your state and (for U.S. businesses) the company's home state as well. Have any complaints been filed? Finally, if you're buying a package or tour, always **consider travel insurance** that includes default coverage.

► BBBs: **Council of Better Business Bureaus** (✉ 4200 Wilson Blvd., Suite 800, Arlington, VA 22203, ☎ 703/276–0100, FAX 703/525–8277, WEB www.bbb.org).

CUSTOMS & DUTIES

IN AUSTRALIA

Australian residents who are 18 or older may bring home $A400 worth of souvenirs and gifts (including jewelry), 250 cigarettes or 250 grams of tobacco, and 1,125 ml of alcohol (including wine, beer, and spirits). Residents under 18 may bring back $A200 worth of goods. Prohibited items include meat products. Seeds, plants, and fruits need to be declared upon arrival.

➤ INFORMATION: **Australian Customs Service** (Regional Director, ✉ Box 8, Sydney, NSW 2001, Australia, ☎ 02/9213–2000, FAX 02/9213–4000, WEB www.customs.gov.au).

IN CANADA

Canadian residents who have been out of Canada for at least seven days may bring home C$750 worth of goods duty-free. If you've been away less than seven days but more than 48 hours, the duty-free allowance drops to C$200; if your trip lasts 24–48 hours, the allowance is C$50. You may not pool allowances with family members. Goods claimed under the C$750 exemption may follow you by mail; those claimed under the lesser exemptions must accompany you. Alcohol and tobacco products may be included in the 7-day and 48-hour exemptions but not in the 24-hour exemption. If you meet the age requirements of the province or territory through which you reenter Canada, you may bring in, duty-free, 1.5 liters of wine, 1.14 liters of liquor *or* 24 355-ml cans or bottles of beer or ale. If you are 16 or older you may bring in, duty-free, 200 cigarettes and 50 cigars. Check ahead of time with Revenue Canada or the Department of Agriculture for policies regarding meat products, seeds, plants, and fruits.

You may send an unlimited number of gifts worth up to C$60 each duty-free to Canada. Label the package UNSOLICITED GIFT—VALUE UNDER $60. Alcohol and tobacco are excluded.

➤ INFORMATION: **Revenue Canada** (✉ 2265 St. Laurent Blvd. S, Ottawa, Ontario K1G 4K3, Canada, ☎ 613/993–0534; 800/461–9999 in Canada, FAX 613/991–4126, WEB www.ccra-adrc.gc.ca).

IN NEW ZEALAND

Homeward-bound residents 17 or older may bring back $700 worth of souvenirs and gifts. Your duty-free allowance also includes 4.5 liters of wine or beer; one 1,125-ml bottle of spirits; and either 200 cigarettes, 250 grams of tobacco, 50 cigars, or a combination of the three up to 250 grams. Prohibited items include meat products, seeds, plants, and fruits.

➤ INFORMATION: **New Zealand Customs** (Custom House, ✉ 50 Anzac Ave., Box 29, Auckland, New Zealand, ☎ 09/300–5399, FAX 09/359–6730), WEB www.customs.govt.nz.

IN THE U.K.

From countries outside the EU, including the United States, you may bring home, duty-free, 200 cigarettes or 50 cigars; 1 liter of spirits or 2 liters of fortified or sparkling wine or liqueurs; 2 liters of still table wine; 60 ml of perfume; 250 ml of toilet water; plus £145 worth of other goods, including gifts and souvenirs. If returning from outside the EU, prohibited items include meat products, seeds, plants, and fruits.

➤ INFORMATION: **HM Customs and Excise** (✉ Dorset House, Stamford St., Bromley, Kent BR1 1XX, U.K., ☎ 020/7202–4227, WEB www.hmce.gov.uk).

DINING

The restaurants we list are the cream of the crop in each price category.

MEALTIMES

New Yorkers seem ready to eat at any hour. Many restaurants serve dinner up to midnight and some serve food much later. Restaurants in SoHo, Tribeca, and in the West and East Villages are likely to remain open late, while midtown restaurants and those in the theater and financial districts generally close earlier.

PAYING

Credit cards are widely accepted, but many restaurants, particularly smaller ones, or ones downtown, accept only cash. Our restaurant reviews indicate acceptable forms of payment for each establishment, but if you plan to pay by card double-check its acceptability while making reservations or before sitting down to eat.

RESERVATIONS & DRESS

Reservations are always a good idea: we mention them only when they're essential or not accepted. Book as far ahead as you can, and reconfirm as soon as you arrive. We mention dress only when men are required to wear a jacket or a jacket and tie.

WINE, BEER & SPIRITS

Although some restaurants and bars serve only wine and beer, most also serve spirits. Bars and restaurants with liquor licenses are permitted to serve alcohol until 4 AM, but many close earlier. Bottles of wine and liquor may be purchased only at liquor and wine stores. Beer can be bought at delis, groceries, and supermarkets, as well as from stores that specialize in distributing beer by the case and keg.

DISABILITIES & ACCESSIBILITY

New York has come a long way in making life here easier for people with disabilities. At most street corners, curbs dip to allow wheelchairs to roll along unimpeded. Many restaurants, shops, and movie theaters with step-up entrances have wheelchair ramps. And while some New Yorkers may rush past someone in need of assistance, you'll find plenty of people who are more than happy to help you get around.

➤ LOCAL RESOURCES: The **Mayor's Office for People with Disabilities** (☎ 212/788–2830; 212/788–2858 TTY, WEB www.nyc.gov) has brochures and helpful information. The **Andrew Heiskell Library for the Blind and Physically Handicapped** (✉ 40 W. 20th St., ☎ 212/206–5400, WEB www.nypl.org/branch) has a large collection of Braille, large-print, and recorded books, housed in a layout specially designed for easy access for people with vision impairments. Hospital Audiences, Inc. staffs the **HAI Hotline** (☎ 888/424–4685) weekdays 9–5, offering information on transportation, hotels, restaurants and cultural venues. **Big Apple Greeters** (✉ 1 Center St., Suite 2035, ☎ 212/669–8159, WEB www.bigapplegreeter.org) offers tours of New York City tailored to visitors' personal preferences.

LODGING

Most hotels in New York comply with the Americans with Disabilities Act. When you call to make reservations, specify your needs and make sure the hotel can accommodate them.

PUBLICATIONS

The bible for New York visitors with disabilities is **Access for All** ($5), published by Hospital Audiences, Inc. (✉ 538 Broadway, 3rd floor, ☎ 212/575–7676; TDD 212/575–7673, WEB www.hospaud.org). It lists theaters, museums and other cultural institutions that offer wheelchair access and services for people with hearing or vision impairments.

RESERVATIONS

When discussing accessibility with an operator or reservations agent, **ask hard questions.** Are there any stairs, inside *or* out? Are there grab bars next to the toilet *and* in the shower/tub? How wide is the doorway to the room? To the bathroom? For the most extensive facilities meeting the latest legal specifications, **opt for newer accommodations.**

SIGHTS & ATTRACTIONS

Most public facilities in New York City, whether museums, parks, or theaters, are wheelchair-accessible. Some attractions offer tours or programs for people with mobility, sight, or hearing impairments.

TRANSPORTATION

The subway is still all but impossible to navigate; people in wheelchairs should stick to public buses, most of which have wheelchair lifts at the rear door and "kneel" at the front to facilitate getting on and off.

➤ COMPLAINTS: **Aviation Consumer Protection Division** (☞ Air Travel, *above*) for airline-related problems. **Civil Rights Office** (✉ U.S. Department of Transportation, Departmental Office of Civil Rights, S-30, 400 7th St. SW, Room 10215, Washington, DC 20590, ☎ 202/366–4648, FAX 202/366–9371, WEB www.dot.gov/ost/docr/index.htm) for problems with surface transportation. **Disability Rights Section** (✉ U.S. Department of Justice, Civil Rights Division, Box

66738, Washington, DC 20035-6738,
☎ 202/514–0301 or 800/514–0301;
202/514–0383 TTY; 800/514–0383
TTY, ⅋⅋ 202/307–1198, ⅋⅋ www.
usdoj.gov/crt/ada/adahom1.htm) for
general complaints.

TRAVEL AGENCIES

In the United States, the Americans
with Disabilities Act requires that
travel firms serve the needs of all
travelers. Some agencies specialize in
working with people with disabilities.

➤ TRAVELERS WITH MOBILITY PROB-
LEMS: **Access Adventures** (✉ 206
Chestnut Ridge Rd., Scottsville, NY
14624, ☎ 716/889–9096, dltravel@
prodigy.net), is run by a former phys-
ical-rehabilitation counselor. **Accessible Vans of America** (✉ 9 Spielman
Rd., Fairfield, NJ 07004, ☎ 877/282–
8267, ⅋⅋ 973/808–9713, ⅋⅋ www.
accessiblevans.com). **CareVacations**
(✉ 5-5110 50th Ave., Leduc, Alberta
T9E 6V4, Canada, ☎ 780/986–6404
or 877/478–7827, ⅋⅋ 780/986–8332,
⅋⅋ www.carevacations.com), for
group tours and cruise vacations.
Flying Wheels Travel (✉ 143 W.
Bridge St., Box 382, Owatonna, MN
55060, ☎ 507/451–5005 or 800/535–
6790, ⅋⅋ 507/451–1685, ⅋⅋ www.
flyingwheelstravel.com).

➤ TRAVELERS WITH DEVELOPMENTAL
DISABILITIES: **Sprout** (✉ 893 Amsterdam Ave., New York, NY 10025,
☎ 212/222–9575 or 888/222–9575,
⅋⅋ 212/222–9768, ⅋⅋ www.
gosprout.org).

DISCOUNTS & DEALS

In the numerous tourist-oriented
publications that you can pick up at
hotels and attractions you'll find
coupons good for discounts of all
kinds, from dining and shopping to
sightseeing and sporting activities.
Among the city's especially good
deals are the cut-rate theater tickets
available at TKTS (☞ Performing
Arts *in* Chapter 3) in Times Square
and at the World Trade Center, and
free-admission evenings at major
museums.

Be a smart shopper and **compare all
your options** before making decisions.
A plane ticket bought with a promotional coupon from travel clubs,
coupon books, and direct-mail offers

or on the Internet may not be cheaper
than the least expensive fare from a
discount ticket agency. And always
keep in mind that what you get is just
as important as what you save.

DISCOUNT RESERVATIONS

To save money, **look into discount
reservations services** with toll-free
numbers, which use their buying
power to get a better price on hotels,
airline tickets, even car rentals. When
booking a room, always **call the
hotel's local toll-free number** (if one is
available) rather than the central
reservations number—you'll often get
a better price. Always ask about
special packages or corporate rates.

➤ AIRLINE TICKETS: ☎ 800/359–
2727.

➤ HOTEL ROOMS: **Accommodations Express** (☎ 800/444–7666,
⅋⅋ ww.accommodationsexpress.com).
Central Reservation Service (CRS)
(☎ 800/548–3311, ⅋⅋ www.
reservation-services.com). **Hotel
Reservations Network** (☎ 800/964–
6835, ⅋⅋ www.hoteldiscount.com).
Players Express Vacations (☎ 800/
458–6161, ⅋⅋ www.playersexpress.
com). **Quikbook** (☎ 800/789–9887,
⅋⅋ www.quikbook.com). **RMC
Travel** (☎ 800/245–5738, ⅋⅋ www.
rmcwebtravel.com). **Steigenberger
Reservation Service** (☎ 800/223–
5652, ⅋⅋ www.srs-worldhotels.com).
Travel Interlink (☎ 800/888–5898,
⅋⅋ www.travelinterlink.com). **Turbo-
trip.com** (☎ 800/473–7829, ⅋⅋ www.
turbotrip.com).

PACKAGE DEALS

Don't confuse packages and guided
tours. When you buy a package, you
travel on your own, just as though
you had planned the trip yourself.
Fly/drive packages, which combine
airfare and car rental, are often a
good deal. In cities, ask the local
visitors' bureau about hotel packages
that include tickets to major museum
exhibits or other special events.

SIGHTSEEING

If you're planning to sightsee, **consider purchasing a CityPass.** CityPass
is a packet of tickets to top-notch
sights in New York—the Empire State
Building, Guggenheim Museum, the

American Museum of Natural History, the Museum of Modern Art, the *Intrepid* Sea Air Space Museum, and the World Trade Center observation deck—for half of what they cost if you purchase each one separately. The packet is good for nine days from first use, and will allow you to beat long ticket lines at some attractions. You can buy a CityPass at any of the six attractions.

➤ CONTACT: **CityPass** (☎ 707/256–0490, WEB www.citypass.net).

EMERGENCIES

➤ EMERGENCY SERVICES: **Dial 911** for police, fire, or ambulance in an emergency (TTY is available for persons with hearing impairments).

➤ DOCTORS & DENTISTS: **Doctors Management Service** (☎ 212/737–2333), a house-call service, operates in Brooklyn, Queens, and Staten Island only, from 8 AM to midnight. Most large hospitals have 24-hour emergency rooms. **Emergency Dental Service** (☎ 212/972–9299 or 800/439–9299) will make a referral.

➤ HOSPITALS: **Beekman Downtown Hospital** (✉ 170 William St., between Beekman and Spruce Sts., ☎ 212/312–5070). **Bellevue** (✉ 462 1st Ave., at E. 27th St., ☎ 212/562–4141). **Beth Israel Medical Center** (✉ 1st Ave. at E. 16th St., ☎ 212/420–2840). **Cabrini Medical Center** (✉ 227 E. 19th St., between 2nd and 3rd Aves., ☎ 212/995–6620). **Columbia Presbyterian Medical Center** (✉ 622 W. 168th St., at Ft. Washington Ave., ☎ 212/305–2255). **Lenox Hill Hospital** (✉ 100 E. 77th St., between Lexington and Park Aves., ☎ 212/434–3030). **Mount Sinai Hospital** (✉ 5th Ave. at 100th St., ☎ 212/241–7171). **New York Hospital–Cornell Medical Center** (✉ 525 E. 68th St., at York Ave., ☎ 212/746–5454). **New York University Medical Center** (✉ 550 1st Ave., at 32nd St., ☎ 212/263–5550). **St. Luke's–Roosevelt Hospital** (✉ 1000 10th Ave., at W. 59th St., ☎ 212/523–6800). **St. Vincent's Hospital** (✉ 7th Ave. and W. 12th St., ☎ 212/604–7997).

➤ HOT LINES: **Mental Health** (☎ 212/219–5599 or 800/527–7474). **Sex Crimes Report Line** (☎ 212/267–7273). **Special Victims Liaison Unit** (☎ 212/267–7273). **Victims Services** (☎ 212/577–7777).

➤ 24-HOUR PHARMACIES: **CVS** (✉ E. 23rd St. at 1st Ave., ☎ 212/505–1555, WEB www.cvs.com). **Duane Reade** (✉ E. 47th St., at Lexington Ave., ☎ 212/682–5338, WEB www.duanereade.com). **Genovese** (✉ 1299–1301 2nd Ave., at E. 68th St., ☎ 212/772–0104, WEB www.genovese.com) has reasonable prices. **Rite Aid** (✉ 303 W. 50th St., at 8th Ave., ☎ 212/247–8736, WEB www.riteaid.com) is just one of the chain's many 24-hour stores.

GAY & LESBIAN TRAVEL

Local attitudes toward same-sex couples are very tolerant in Manhattan, perhaps less so in parts of the outer boroughs. Chelsea and the West Village are the most prominently gay neighborhoods, but gay men and lesbians feel right at home almost everywhere, especially in areas south of 14th Street. The world's biggest gay pride parade takes place in Manhattan each June.

➤ LOCAL INFORMATION: For advice on gay and lesbian life and organizations in New York, call the **Gay and Lesbian National Hotline** (☎ 212/989–0999, WEB www.glnh.org) or stop by the **Lesbian and Gay Community Services Center** (✉ 208 W. 13th St., ☎ 212/620–7310, WEB www.gaycenter.org).

➤ PUBLICATIONS: For listings of gay events and places, check out **Homo Xtra (HX)**, **MetroSource**, **Next**, **New York Blade**, and the **Village Voice**, distributed free in many shops and clubs throughout Manhattan. At the newsstand, pick up the magazines **Paper** and **Time Out New York** for a gay-friendly take on what's happening in the city. For details about the gay and lesbian scene, consult *Fodor's Gay Guide to the USA* (available in bookstores everywhere).

➤ GAY- & LESBIAN-FRIENDLY TRAVEL AGENCIES: **Different Roads Travel** (✉ 8383 Wilshire Blvd., Suite 902, Beverly Hills, CA 90211, ☎ 323/651–5557 or 800/429–8747, FAX 323/651–3678, lgernert@tzell.com). **Kennedy Travel** (✉ 314 Jericho Tpke., Floral Park, NY 11001, ☎ 516/352–

4888 or 800/237–7433, FAX 516/354–8849, WEB www.kennedytravel.com). **Now Voyager** (⊠ 4406 18th St., San Francisco, CA 94114, ☎ 415/626–1169 or 800/255–6951, FAX 415/626–8626, WEB www.nowvoyager.com). **Skylink Travel and Tour** (⊠ 1006 Mendocino Ave., Santa Rosa, CA 95401, ☎ 707/546–9888 or 800/225–5759, FAX 707/546–9891, WEB www.skylinktravel.com), serving lesbian travelers.

HOLIDAYS

Major national holidays include New Year's Day (Jan. 1); Martin Luther King, Jr., Day (3rd Mon. in Jan.); President's Day (3rd Mon. in Feb.); Memorial Day (last Mon. in May); Independence Day (July 4); Labor Day (1st Mon. in Sept.); Thanksgiving Day (4th Thurs. in Nov.); Christmas Eve and Christmas Day (Dec. 24 and 25); and New Year's Eve (Dec. 31).

FOR INTERNATIONAL TRAVELERS

CONSULATES & EMBASSIES

➤ AUSTRALIA: **The Australian Consulate General** (⊠ 150 E. 42nd St., 34th floor, 10017, ☎ 212/351–6500, FAX 212/351–6501, WEB www.australianyc.org).

➤ CANADA: **Canadian Consulate General** (⊠ 1251 Ave. of the Americas, 10020, ☎ 212/596–1628, FAX 212/596–1790, WEB www.canada-ny.org).

➤ NEW ZEALAND: **New Zealand Consulate-General** (⊠ 780 3rd Ave., Suite 1904, 10017, ☎ 212/832–4038, FAX 212/832–7602, WEB www.un.int/newzealand).

➤ UNITED KINGDOM: **British Consulate-General** (⊠ 845 3rd Ave., 10022, ☎ 212/745–0200, FAX 212/745–3062, WEB www.britain-info.org/consular/ny/).

CURRENCY

The dollar is the basic unit of U.S. currency. It has 100 cents. Coins include the copper penny (1¢); the silvery nickel (5¢), dime (10¢), quarter (25¢), and half-dollar (50¢); and the golden $1 coin, replacing a now-rare silver dollar. Bills are denominated $1, $5, $10, $20, $50, and $100, all green and identical in size;

designs vary. The exchange rate at press time was US$1.46 per British pound, 65¢ per Canadian dollar, 53¢ per Australian dollar, and 43¢ per New Zealand dollar.

CURRENCY EXCHANGES

Currency-exchange booths are located throughout Manhattan, especially in touristy areas such as South Street Seaport and Times Square. Banks will also exchange money, but they have shorter hours (many banks close at 3 PM on weekdays and shut down entirely on weekends).

➤ EXCHANGE OFFICES: **Chase Foreign Currency Department** (☎ 212/935–9935). **Chequepoint USA** (☎ 212/750–2400). **Thomas Cook Currency Services** (☎ 800/287–7362).

INSURANCE

Britons and Australians need extra medical coverage when traveling overseas.

➤ INSURANCE INFORMATION: In the U.K.: **Association of British Insurers** (⊠ 51–55 Gresham St., London EC2V 7HQ, U.K., ☎ 020/7600–3333, FAX 020/7696–8999, WEB www.abi.org.uk). In Australia: **Insurance Council of Australia** (⊠ Level 3, 56 Pitt St., Sydney NSW 2000, ☎ 03/9614–1077, FAX 03/9614–7924). In Canada: **RBC Insurance** (⊠ 6880 Financial Dr., Mississauga, Ontario L5N 7Y5, Canada, ☎ 905/816–2400; 800/668–4342 in Canada, FAX 905/816–2498, WEB www.royalbank.com). In New Zealand: **Insurance Council of New Zealand** (⊠ Box 474, Wellington, New Zealand, ☎ 04/472–5230, FAX 04/473–3011, WEB www.icnz.org.nz).

PASSPORTS & VISAS

When traveling internationally, **carry your passport** even if you don't need one (it's always the best form of I.D.) and **make two photocopies of the data page** (one for someone at home and another for you, carried separately from your passport). If you lose your passport, promptly call the nearest embassy or consulate and the local police.

Visitor visas are not necessary for Canadian citizens, or for citizens of Australia and the United Kingdom who are staying fewer than 90 days.

➤ AUSTRALIAN CITIZENS: **Australian Passport Office** (☎ 131–232). **U.S. Office of Australia Affairs** (✉ MLC Centre, 19-29 Martin Pl., 59th floor, Sydney NSW 2000, Australia).

➤ CANADIAN CITIZENS: **Passport Office** (☎ 819/994–3500; 800/567–6868 in Canada).

➤ NEW ZEALAND CITIZENS: **New Zealand Passport Office** (☎ 04/494–0700 for application procedures; 0800/225–050 in New Zealand for application-status updates). **U.S. Office of New Zealand Affairs** (✉ 29 Fitzherbert Terr., Thorndon, Wellington, New Zealand).

➤ U.K. CITIZENS: **London Passport Office** (☎ 0870/521–0410) for application procedures and emergency passports. **U.S. Embassy Visa Information Line** (☎ 01891/200–290). **U.S. Embassy Visa Branch** (✉ 5 Upper Grosvenor Sq., London W1A 1AE, U.K.); send a self-addressed, stamped envelope. **U.S. Consulate General** (✉ Queen's House, Queen St., Belfast BTI 6EO, Northern Ireland).

TELEPHONES

All U.S. telephone numbers consist of a three-digit area code and a seven-digit local number. Within most local calling areas, dial only the seven-digit number. Within the same area code, dial "1" first. To call between area-code regions, dial "1" then all 10 digits; the same goes for calls to numbers prefixed by "800," "888," and "877"—all toll-free. For calls to numbers preceded by "900" you must pay—usually dearly.

For international calls, dial "011" followed by the country code and the local number. For help, dial "0" and ask for an overseas operator. The country code is 61 for Australia, 64 for New Zealand, 44 for the United Kingdom. Calling Canada is the same as calling within the United States. Most local phone books list country codes and U.S. area codes. The country code for the United States is 1.

For operator assistance, dial "0". To obtain someone's phone number, call directory assistance, 555–1212 or occasionally 411 (free at Bell Atlantic

public phones). To have the person you're calling foot the bill, phone collect; dial "0" instead of "1" before the 10-digit number.

At pay phones, instructions are usually posted. Usually you insert coins in a slot (25¢ for local calls) and wait for a steady tone before dialing. When you call long-distance, the operator will tell you how much to insert; prepaid phone cards, widely available in various denominations, are easier. Call the number on the back, punch in the card's personal identification number when prompted, then dial your number.

LIMOUSINES

If you want to ride around Manhattan in style, **rent a chauffeur-driven car** from one of many limousine services. Companies usually charge by the hour or offer a flat fee for sightseeing excursions.

➤ LIMOUSINE SERVICES: **All State Car and Limousine Service** (☎ 212/741–7440). **Bermuda Limousine International** (☎ 212/249–8400). **Carey Limousines** (☎ 212/599–1122). **Chris Limousines** (☎ 718/356–3232 or 800/542–1584). **Concord Limousine Inc.** (☎ 212/230–1600 or 800/255–7255). **Mirage Limousine** (☎ 212/744–9700). **Greenwich Limousine** (☎ 212/868–4733 or 800/385–1033). **London Towncars** (☎ 212/988–9700 or 800/221–4009).

LODGING

The lodgings we list are the cream of the crop in each price category. We always list the facilities that are available—but we don't specify whether they cost extra: when pricing accommodations, always **ask what's included and what costs extra.**

CATEGORY	COST*
$$$$	over $400
$$$	$275–$400
$$	$150–$275
$	under $150

*All prices are for a standard double room, excluding 13¼% city and state taxes.

APARTMENT RENTALS

If you want a home base that's roomy enough for a family and comes with cooking facilities, **consider a furnished rental.** These can save you money, especially if you're traveling with a group. Home-exchange directories sometimes list rentals as well as exchanges.

In New York City, short-term apartment rentals are often available through organizations that call themselves bed-and-breakfast services.

➤ INTERNATIONAL AGENTS: **Hideaways International** (⊠ 767 Islington St., Portsmouth, NH 03801, ☎ 603/430–4433 or 800/843–4433, FAX 603/430–4444, WEB www.hideaways.com; membership $129). **Hometours International** (⊠ Box 11503, Knoxville, TN 37939, ☎ 865/690–8484 or 800/367–4668, WEB http://thor.he.net/ ãhometour).

B&BS

Most of the bed-and-breakfasts in New York City are residential apartments with some (or all) of their rooms reserved for guests. These are booked through services that don't charge a fee, but often require a deposit equal to 25% of the total cost.

HOME EXCHANGES

If you would like to exchange your home for someone else's, **join a home-exchange organization,** which will send you its updated listings of available exchanges for a year and will include your own listing in at least one of them. It's up to you to make specific arrangements.

➤ EXCHANGE CLUBS: **HomeLink International** (⊠ Box 47747, Tampa, FL 33647, ☎ 813/975–9825 or 800/638–3841, FAX 813/910–8144, WEB www. homelink.org; $98 per year). **Intervac U.S.** (⊠ Box 590504, San Francisco, CA 94159, ☎ 800/756–4663, FAX 415/435–7440, WEB www.intervacus.com; $93 yearly fee includes one catalogue and on-line access).

HOSTELS

No matter what your age, you can **save on lodging costs by staying at hostels.** In some 5,000 locations in more than 70 countries around the world, Hostelling International (HI), the umbrella group for a number of national youth-hostel associations,

offers single-sex, dorm-style beds and, at many hostels, rooms for couples and family accommodations. Membership in any HI national hostel association, open to travelers of all ages, allows you to stay in HI-affiliated hostels at member rates; one-year membership is about $25 for adults (C$26.75 in Canada, £9.30 in the U.K., $30 in Australia, and $30 in New Zealand); hostels in New York City run about $25–$35 per night for shared rooms. Members have priority if the hostel is full; they're also eligible for discounts around the world, even on rail and bus travel in some countries.

➤ BEST OPTIONS: **Big Apple Hostel** (⊠ 119 W. 45th St., between 6th and 7th Aves., ☎ 212/302–2603). **Chelsea International Hostel** (⊠ 251 W. 20th St., between 7th and 8th Aves., ☎ 212/647–0010). **New York International AYH Hostel** (⊠ 891 Amsterdam Ave., at W. 104th At., ☎ 212/932–2300).

➤ ORGANIZATIONS: **Hostelling International—American Youth Hostels** (⊠ 733 15th St. NW, Suite 840, Washington, DC 20005, ☎ 202/783–6161, FAX 202/783–6171, WEB www. hiayh.org). **Hostelling International—Canada** (⊠ 400–205 Catherine St., Ottawa, Ontario K2P 1C3, Canada, ☎ 613/237–7884, FAX 613/237–7868, WEB www.hostellingintl.ca). **Youth Hostel Association of England and Wales** (⊠ Trevelyan House, 8 St. Stephen's Hill, St. Albans, Hertfordshire AL1 2DY, U.K., ☎ 0870/8708808, FAX 01727/844126, WEB www. yha.org.uk). **Australian Youth Hostel Association** (⊠ 10 Mallett St., Camperdown, NSW 2050, Australia, ☎ 02/9565–1699, FAX 02/9565–1325, WEB www.yha.com.au). **Youth Hostels Association of New Zealand** (⊠ Box 436, Christchurch, New Zealand, ☎ 03/379–9970, FAX 03/365–4476, WEB www.yha.org.nz).

HOTELS

Assume that hotels operate on the **European Plan** (EP, with no meals) unless we specify that they use the **Continental Plan** (CP, with a Continental breakfast), **Modified American Plan** (MAP, with breakfast and dinner), or the **Full American Plan** (FAP, with all meals).

All hotels listed have private bathrooms unless otherwise noted. In addition to the lodgings recommended in this guide, many hotel chains have properties in Manhattan or near the airports.

➤ TOLL-FREE NUMBERS: **Best Western** (☎ 800/528–1234, WEB www.bestwestern.com). **Choice** (☎ 800/221–2222, WEB www.hotelchoice.com). **Clarion** (☎ 800/252–7466, WEB www.hotelchoice.com). **Colony** (☎ 800/777–1700, WEB www.colony.com). **Comfort** (☎ 800/228–5150, WEB www.comfortinn.com). **Days Inn** (☎ 800/325–2525, WEB www.daysinn.com). **Doubletree and Red Lion Hotels** (☎ 800/222–8733, WEB www.doubletree.com). **Embassy Suites** (☎ 800/362–2779, WEB www.embassysuites.com). **Fairfield Inn** (☎ 800/228–2800, WEB www.marriott.com). **Forte** (☎ 800/225–5843, WEB www.forte-hotels.com). **Four Seasons** (☎ 800/332–3442, WEB www.fourseasons.com). **Hilton** (☎ 800/445–8667, WEB www.hilton.com). **Holiday Inn** (☎ 800/465–4329, WEB www.basshotels.com). **Howard Johnson** (☎ 800/654–4656, WEB www.hojo.com). **Hyatt Hotels & Resorts** (☎ 800/233–1234, WEB www.hyatt.com). **Inter-Continental** (☎ 800/327–0200, WEB www.interconti.com). **La Quinta** (☎ 800/531–5900, WEB www.laquinta.com). **Marriott** (☎ 800/228–9290, WEB www.marriott.com). **Le Meridien** (☎ 800/543–4300, WEB www.lemeridien-hotels.com). **Omni** (☎ 800/843–6664, WEB www.omnihotels.com). **Quality Inn** (☎ 800/228–5151, WEB www.qualityinn.com). **Radisson** (☎ 800/333–3333, WEB www.radisson.com). **Ramada** (☎ 800/228–2828, WEB www.ramada.com). **Renaissance Hotels & Resorts** (☎ 800/468–3571, WEB www.renaissancehotels.com). **Ritz-Carlton** (☎ 800/241–3333, WEB www.ritzcarlton.com). **Sheraton** (☎ 800/325–3535, WEB www.starwood.com). **Sleep Inn** (☎ 800/753–3746, WEB www.sleepinn.com). **Westin Hotels & Resorts** (☎ 800/228–3000, WEB www.westin.com).

MAIL & SHIPPING

Post offices are open weekdays 8–5 or 8–6 and Saturdays until 1 pm. There are dozens of branches in New York, many of which offer abbreviated

Saturday hours as well. You'll usually find the shortest lines at the smaller branches. The main post office on 8th Avenue is open daily 24 hours.

➤ POST OFFICES: **J.A. Farley General Post Office** (⊠ 8th Ave. at W. 33rd St., ☎ 212/967–8585).

MEDIA

NEWSPAPERS & MAGAZINES

The major newspapers in New York are the *Daily News,* the *New York Post,* the *New York Times,* the *Wall Street Journal,* and the *Village Voice,* a free publication. All of these are widely available at newsstands and shops around town.

RADIO & TELEVISION

Some of the major radio stations include **WBGO-FM** (88.3; jazz), **WBLS-FM** (107.5; R&B), **WKTU-FM** (103.5; urban), **WPLJ** (95.5; pop and rock), **WQXR-FM** (96.3; classical), and **WXRK-FM** (92.3; rock). Talk stations include **WNEW-FM** (102.7), **WNYC-AM** (820; National Public Radio), **WNYE-FM** (91.5), and **WOR-AM** (710). News stations include **WABC-AM** (770), **WCBS-AM** (880), and **WINS-AM** (1010).

The city has its own 24-hour cable TV news station, **New York 1** (Channel 1), with local and international news announcements around the clock. Weather forecasts are broadcast "on the ones" (1:01, 1:11, 1:21, etc.).

MONEY MATTERS

In New York, it's easy to get swept up in a debt-inducing cyclone of $50 per-person dinners, $80 theater tickets, $25 nightclub covers, $10 cab rides, and $300 hotel rooms. But one of the good things about all the boroughs is that they offer such a wide variety of options that you can spend in some areas and save in others as you see fit. Generally prices in the outer boroughs are lower than those in Manhattan. Within Manhattan a cup of coffee can range from $1 to $5; a glass of beer from $3 to $7; a sandwich from $3 to $10.

Prices throughout this guide are given for adults. Substantially reduced fees are almost always available for children, students, and senior citizens.

For information on taxes, *see* Taxes, *below*.

ATMS

Cash machines are abundant throughout all the boroughs and can be found not only in banks, but in some grocery stores, laundromats, delis, and hotels. But beware, many bank ATMs charge users a fee of up to $1.75, and the commercial ATMs in retail establishments often charge even more. Be careful to remain at the ATM until you complete your transaction, which may require an extra step after receiving your money.

CREDIT CARDS

Throughout this guide, the following abbreviations are used: **AE**, American Express; **D**, Discover; **DC**, Diner's Club; **MC**, MasterCard; and **V**, Visa.

➤ REPORTING LOST CARDS: **American Express** (☎ 800/528–4800). **Discover** (☎ 800/347–2683). **MasterCard** (☎ 800/307–7309). **Visa** (☎ 800/847–2911).

PACKING

In New York, jackets and ties are required for men in a number of restaurants—and in general, New Yorkers tend to dress a bit more formally than their west coast counterparts for special events such as the theater. Jeans and sneakers are acceptable for casual dining and sightseeing just about anywhere in the city. Always **come with sneakers or other flat-heeled walking shoes** for pounding the New York pavement. In winter, you will need a warm coat, hat, scarf, and gloves. In summer, when temperatures in New York sometimes approach 100 degrees, shorts are advisable. In the spring and fall, travelers should bring at least one warm jacket and sweater, since moderate daytime temperatures can drop after nightfall.

Do **pack light**, because porters and luggage trolleys can be hard to find at New York airports. And **bring a fistful of quarters to rent a trolley.** Check *Fodor's How to Pack* (available in bookstores everywhere) for more tips.

PUBLIC TRANSPORTATION

When it comes to getting around New York, you'll have your pick of transportation in almost every neighborhood. The subway and bus networks are thorough, although getting across town can take some extra maneuvering. If you're not pressed for time, **take a public bus** (☞ Bus Travel, *above*); they make more stops than subways, but you can also see the city as you travel. You'll see as many yellow cabs (☞ Taxis, *below*) as private cars, and while taking a taxi costs more than a subway or bus ride, the convenience can make it worthwhile. However, the subway (☞ Subway Travel, *below*) is often the quickest way to get around, plus, a subway ride is an only–in–New York experience. But New York's a walking town, and depending on the time of day and your destination, walking might be the easiest and most enjoyable option. During weekday rush hours (from 7:30 to 9:30 AM and 5 to 7 PM, **avoid the jammed midtown area, both in the subways and on the streets**; travel time can easily double.

Once you've decided how to get there, you'll need to determine how best to pay for your trip. Subway and bus fares are $1.50, although reduced fares are available for senior citizens and people with disabilities during non-rush hours. If you're just taking a few trips, you should pay with tokens; they are sold at token booths that are *usually* open at the main entrance of each station. It is advisable to **buy several tokens at one time** to avoid having to wait in line later.

You might find it easier to use a MetroCard, a thin, plastic card with a magnetic strip; swipe it through the reader at the turnstile, and the cost of the fare is automatically deducted. You can **transfer free from bus to subway or subway to bus with the MetroCard.** You must start with the MetroCard and use it again within two hours to complete your trip. MetroCards are sold at all subway stations and at some stores—look for an "Authorized Sales Agent" sign. The MTA sells two kinds of Metro-Card: unlimited-ride and pay-per-ride. Seven-day unlimited-ride MetroCards ($17) allow bus and subway travel for a week. If you will ride more than 12 times, this is the card to get. If you won't be in town for a week, the one-day unlimited-ride Fun Pass ($4) may better suit you. This card is good from the day of purchase through 3 AM the following day. Another option is the pay-per-ride MetroCard, available in any denomination between $3 and $80. When you purchase a pay-per-ride card worth $15 or more, a 10% free-ride credit is added to the card, and you **get eleven rides for the price of ten.** The advantage of pay-per-ride over unlimited ride is that the card can be shared; unlimited-ride Metro-Cards can only be used by one person at a time.

➤ SCHEDULE AND ROUTE INFORMA-TION: Metropolitan Transit Authority (MTA) Travel Information Center (☎ 718/330–1234, WEB www.mta.nyc.ny.us). MTA Status information hot line (☎ 718/243–7777), updated hourly.

REST ROOMS

Public rest rooms in New York are few and far between, and they run the gamut when it comes to cleanliness. Facilities in Penn Station and Grand Central Terminal have shed their formerly notorious reputations, and are now not only safe but surprisingly clean and well-maintained. Unfortunately, the same cannot be said for rest rooms in subway stations. They remain largely sealed off because of vandalism and safety concerns.

As a rule, **head for midtown department stores, museums, or the lobbies of large hotels to find the cleanest bathrooms.** Public atriums, such as the Citicorp Center and Trump Tower, also provide good public facilities, as does the newly renovated Bryant Park and the many Barnes & Noble bookstores. Restaurants usually reserve their rest rooms just for patrons, but if you're dressed well and look as if you belong, you can often just sail right in. Be aware that cinemas, Broadway theaters, and concert halls have limited amenities, and there are often long lines before performances, as well as during intermissions.

SAFETY

New York has become a much safer city in recent years, so you should not let its old reputation dissuade you from visiting. At the same time you should not let its newer, safer reputation lull you into a false sense of security. As in any large city, travelers in New York remain particularly easy marks for pickpockets and hustlers, so **be cautious.**

Do **ignore the panhandlers** on the streets (some aggressive, many homeless), people who offer to hail you a cab (they often appear at Penn Station, Port Authority, and Grand Central Terminal), and limousine and gypsy cab drivers who (illegally) offer you a ride.

Keep jewelry out of sight on the street; better yet, **leave valuables at home.** Don't wear gold chains or gaudy jewelry, even if it's fake. Men are advised to **carry wallets in front pants pockets** rather than in their hip pockets.

Be sure to **avoid deserted blocks in out-of-the-way neighborhoods.** If you end up in an empty area or a side street that feels unsafe, it probably is. A brisk, purposeful pace helps deter trouble wherever you go.

Although the subway runs round-the-clock, it is usually safest during the day and evening. Many residents of the city have a rough cut-off time— 10 or 11 PM—past which they try to avoid riding the subway trains. Nonetheless, the subway system is generally well-trafficked until midnight (even later on Friday and Saturday nights) and overall it is much safer than it once was. But to **err on the side of caution,** you may want to travel by bus or taxi after the theater or a concert. If you do take the subway at night, ride in the center car, with the conductor, and wait among the crowds on the center of the platform or right in front of the token clerk. Watch out for unsavory characters lurking around the inside or outside of stations, particularly at night, and if a fellow passenger makes you nervous while on the train, trust your gut and change cars. When you're waiting for a train, **stand away from the edge of the subway platform,** especially when trains are entering or leaving the station. Once the train pulls into the station, **avoid empty cars.** When disembarking from a train, **stick with the crowd** until you reach the comparative safety of the street.

LOCAL SCAMS

Someone who appears to have had an accident at the exit door of a bus may flee with your wallet or purse if you attempt to give aid; the individual who approaches you with a complicated story is probably playing a confidence game and hopes to get something from you. Also **beware of strangers jostling you in crowds,** or someone tapping your shoulder from behind. Never play or place a bet on a sidewalk card game, shell game, or guessing game—they are all rigged to get your cash—and they're illegal.

WOMEN IN NEW YORK

Women should **never hang a purse on a chair in a restaurant** or on a hook in a rest-room stall. At times, usually while alone or in bars, female travelers may attract unwanted attention. In order to deflect this attention, you should be polite, but firm, about your desire to be left alone.

SENIOR-CITIZEN TRAVEL

The Metropolitan Transit Authority (MTA) offers lower fares for passengers 65 and over, but an extensive application process for the reduced-fare card makes it impractical for tourists to seek the discount. Without the MTA card, you can still receive a reduced fare on New York City subway trains and buses as long as you have a Medicare identification card. **Show your Medicare card to the bus driver or token-booth clerk** and, for the standard fare ($1.50), you will be issued a token and a return-trip ticket.

To qualify for age-related discounts, **mention your senior-citizen status up front** when booking hotel reservations (not when checking out) and before you're seated in restaurants (not when paying the bill). When renting a car, ask about promotional car-rental discounts, which can be cheaper than senior-citizen rates.

➤ CONTACTS: **MTA Reduced Fare hotline** (☎ 718/243–4999).

➤ EDUCATIONAL PROGRAMS: **Elderhostel** (✉ 11 Ave. de Lafayette, Boston, MA 02111-1746, ☎ 877/426–8056, FAX 877/426–2166, WEB www.elderhostel.org).

SIGHTSEEING TOURS

A guided tour can be a good way to get a handle on this sometimes overwhelming city, or to explore out-of-the-way areas to which you might not want to venture on your own.

BOAT TOURS

A **Circle Line Cruise** is one of the best ways to get a crash orientation to Manhattan. Once you've finished the three-hour, 35-mi circumnavigation of the island, you'll have a good idea of where things are and what you want to see next. Narrations are as interesting and individualized as the guides who deliver them. The Circle Line operates daily, and the price is $24; Semi-Circle cruises, a limited tour, also run daily, and the price is $20.

NY Waterway offers a harbor cruise; the 90-minute ride costs $19. The 70-minute Twilight Cruise follows a similar route (for the same price) at night, providing excellent views of the lit-up skyline. The harbor cruise runs year-round, dates and times vary; the Twilight Cruise operates from May through late December, dates and times vary.

At South Street Seaport's Pier 16 you can take 1½- or 3-hour voyages to New York's past aboard the cargo schooner *Pioneer;* cruises depart daily May–September.

Seaport Liberty Cruises offers daily, hour-long sightseeing tours of New York Harbor and Lower Manhattan; there are also two-hour cruises with live jazz and blues on Wednesday and Thursday nights, from April through September.

The Spirit of New York sails on lunch ($35–$45) and dinner ($64–$78) cruises; the meal is accompanied by live music and dancing. There are also occasional moonlight cocktail ($20) cruises. All can be scheduled year-round.

World Yacht Cruises serves Sunday brunch ($39) on two-hour cruises, and dinner (Sun.–Fri. $70; Sat. $83; drinks extra) on three-hour cruises. The Continental cuisine is restaurant quality, and there's music and dancing on board. The cruises run daily,

April through December; weekends only, January through March (weather permitting).

➤ CONTACT INFORMATION: **Circle Line Cruise** (✉ Pier 83, west end of 42nd St., ☎ 212/563–3200, WEB www.circleline. com). **NY Waterway** (✉ Pier 78, W. 38th St. and 12th Ave., ☎ 800/533–3779, WEB www.nywaterway.com). *Pioneer* (✉ Pier 16, South Street Seaport, ☎ 212/748–8786, WEB www. southstseaport.org). **Seaport Liberty Cruises** (✉ Pier 16, South Street Seaport, ☎ 212/630–8888, WEB www. circleline.com). *The Spirit of New York* (✉ Pier 61, at W. 23rd St. and 12th Ave. on the Hudson River, ☎ 212/742–7278, WEB www. annabellee.com). **World Yacht Cruises** (✉ Pier 81, W. 41st St. at the Hudson River, ☎ 212/630–8100, WEB www.worldyacht.com).

BUS TOURS

Gray Line New York offers a number of "hop-on, hop-off" city bus tours in various languages, including a downtown Manhattan loop, upper Manhattan loop, Harlem gospel tour and evening tours of the city. The company also has available sightseeing cruises, as well as day trips to Atlantic City, West Point and other locations in the New York area.

New York Doubledecker Bus Tours runs authentic London double-deck buses year-round, 9–6 in summer, 9–3 in winter, making stops every 15–30 minutes. Tickets, which are valid for boarding and reboarding all day for five days, cost $26 for a downtown loop, $26 for the uptown loop, and $40 for a combination ticket. For all tours, you can hop on and off to visit attractions as often as you like.

➤ CONTACT INFORMATION: **Gray Line New York** (✉ Port Authority Bus Terminal, 625 8th Ave. at W. 42nd St., ☎ 212/397–2620, WEB www. graylinenewyork.com). **New York Doubledecker Bus Tours** (✉ 52-15 11th St., Queens, ☎ 718/361–5788, WEB www.nydecker.com).

HELICOPTER TOURS

Liberty Helicopter Tours has three pilot-narrated tours ranging from $48 to $180 per person.

➤ CONTACT INFORMATION: **Liberty Helicopter Tours** (✉ Heliport at W. 30th St. and the Hudson River, ☎ 212/465–8905, WEB www. libertyhelicopter.com).

PRIVATE GUIDES

Arthur Marks (☎ 212/673–0477) creates customized tours on which he sings about the city.

SPECIAL-INTEREST TOURS

Art Tours of Manhattan (☎ 609/921–2647) custom-designs walking tours of museum and gallery exhibits as well as artists' studios and lofts.

Bite of the Apple Central Park Bicycle Tour (☎ 212/541–8759) organizes two-hour bicycle trips through Central Park with stops along the way, including Strawberry Fields and the Belvedere Castle.

Gracie Mansion Conservancy Tour (☎ 212/570–4751) will show you the 1799 house, official residence of New York City mayors since 1942. The mansion is open to the public on Wednesday; the tours run late March–mid-November, and reservations are mandatory. There is a suggested $4 donation.

Grand Central Station (☎ 212/340–3404, WEB www.grandcentralterminal. com) provides the setting for architectural tours that take you high above the crowds and into the beaux arts building's rafters. There is no charge and reservations are not accepted.

Harlem Spirituals, Inc. (☎ 212/757–0425) offers bus and walking tours and Sunday gospel trips to Harlem. Also in Harlem, you can trace the history of jazz backstage at the **Apollo Theatre** (☎ 212/531–5305).

The Lower East Side Tenement Museum (☎ 212/431–0233, WEB www. tenement.org) offers a tour of the Lower East Side, retracing its history as an immigrant community; available Saturday and Sunday, April through December.

Madison Square Garden (☎ 212/465–5800, WEB www.thegarden.com) has tours of the sports mecca's inner workings.

The Metropolitan Opera House Backstage (☎ 212/769–7020) offers a tour of the scenery and costume shops and the stage area.

Quintessential New York (☎ 212/501–0827) has over a dozen specialty tours for groups of six or more; the trump card is the behind-the-scenes take. For example, during "The Artist Colony: SoHo" tour, guests visit an artist's studio and an antique dealer's workshop. Another plus is the chauffeured car.

Radio City Music Hall Productions (☎ 212/632–4000) schedules behind-the-scenes tours of the theater.

Ellen Sax Tours & Events (☎ 212/832–0350, esax@erols.com) offers architectural sightseeing, visits to museums, galleries, the theater district, the financial district, and other neighborhoods in Manhattan for groups of six or more only.

The **South Street Seaport Museum** (☎ 212/748–8590, WEB www.southst-seaport.com) has tours of historic ships and the waterfront, as well as predawn forays through the bustling Fulton Fish Market.

WALKING TOURS: GUIDED

Adventure on a Shoestring (☎ 212/265–2663) is an organization dating from 1963 that explores New York neighborhoods, including Greenwich Village, Chinatown, and Gramercy Park. Weekend tours run year-round, rain or shine, and cost $5 per person; reservations are a must.

Big Onion Walking Tours (☎ 212/439–1090, WEB www.bigonion.com) has year-round tours on weekdays and weekends. Try "From Naples to Bialystock to Beijing: A Multi-Ethnic Eating Tour."

Citywalks (☎ 212/989–2456, jn-wilwalk@aol.com) offers two-hour private walking tours exploring various neighborhoods in depth; reservations are required.

The **Municipal Art Society** (☎ 212/935–3960, WEB www.mas.org) operates a series of walking tours on weekdays and both bus and walking tours on weekends. Tours highlight the city's architecture and history.

The **Museum of the City of New York** (☎ 212/534–1672) sponsors primar-

ily historical and architectural walking tours on Sunday afternoon from April to early October.

New York City Cultural Walking Tours (☎ 212/979–2388, WEB www.nycwalk.com) focuses on the city's architecture and history, including landmarks; memorials; outdoor art; and other sites, such as 5th Avenue's "Millionaires' Mile." Public tours are offered every Sunday March–December, while private tours can be scheduled throughout the week.

River to River Downtown Walking Tours (☎ 212/321–2823, WEB www.river2river.freeyellow.com) specializes in lower Manhattan on its 2½-hour walking tours.

Urban Explorations (☎ 718/721–5254) runs tours with an emphasis on architecture and landscape design; Chinatown is a specialty.

The **Urban Park Rangers** (☎ 212/628–2345, WEB www.nycparks.org) offer free weekend walks and workshops in city parks.

Walks of the Town (☎ 212/222–5343) will tailor a tour to your interests; special themes include "Cops, Crooks, and the Courts." Tours are available by appointment only.

Among other knowledgeable walking-tour guides is **Joyce Gold** (☎ 212/242–5762), whose history tours include "The Vital Heart of Harlem," "The Women of Washington Square," and "When China and Italy Moved to New York."

WALKING TOURS: SELF-GUIDED

A free "Walking Tour of Rockefeller Center" pamphlet is available from the information desk in the lobby of the **GE Building** (✉ 30 Rockefeller Plaza).

Pop one of the **Talk-a-Walk** cassettes ($9.95 per tape, plus $2.90 packing and shipping for up to four tapes) into your Walkman and start strolling to an in-your-ear history of lower Manhattan or the Brooklyn Bridge.

➤ CONTACT INFORMATION: **Talk-a-Walk** (✉ Sound Publishers, 30 Waterside Plaza, Suite 10D, New York, NY 10010, ☎ 212/686–0356).

STUDENTS IN NEW YORK

New York is a college town, home to major schools from Columbia University to the City College of New York and from New York University to Fordham University. With big schools like these—and many others—plus a huge population of public and private high-schoolers, it's no wonder the city is rife with discounts and programs for students.

Wherever you go, especially museums, sightseeing attractions, and performances, identify yourself as a student up front and ask if a student discount is available. **Be prepared to show your I.D.,** as New York is not a take-your-word-for-it kind of town.

➤ I.D.s & SERVICES: **Council Travel** (CIEE; ✉ 205 E. 42nd St., 15th floor, New York, NY 10017, ☎ 212/822–2700 or 888/268–6245, FAX 212/822–2699, WEB www.councilexchanges.org) for mail orders only, in the U.S. **Travel Cuts** (✉ 187 College St., Toronto, Ontario M5T 1P7, Canada, ☎ 416/979–2406; 800/667–2887 in Canada, FAX 416/979–8167, WEB www.travelcuts.com).

SUBWAY TRAVEL

The 714-mi subway system operates 24 hours a day and, especially within Manhattan, serves most of the places you'll want to visit. It's cheaper than a cab and, during the workweek, often faster than either cabs or buses. The trains have been rid of their graffiti (some New Yorkers, of course, miss the colorful old trains), and air-conditioned cars predominate on every line. Still, the New York subway is not problem-free. Many trains are crowded, and all are noisy. Homeless people sometimes take refuge from the elements by riding the trains, and panhandlers abound. Although trains usually run frequently, especially during rush hours, you never know when some incident somewhere on the line may stall traffic. Don't write off the subway—some 3.5 million passengers ride it every day without incident—but stay alert.

Most subway entrances are at street corners and are marked by lampposts with an illuminated MTA logo or globe-shape green or red lights (green means open and red means closed). Subway lines are designated by numbers and letters, such as the 3 line or the A line. Some lines run "express" and skip lots of stops; others are "locals" and make all stops. Each station entrance has a sign indicating the lines that run through the station; some entrances are also marked "uptown only" or "downtown only." Before entering subway stations, **read the signs carefully.** One of the most frequent mistakes visitors make is taking the train in the wrong direction—although this can be an adventure, it can also be frustrating if you're in a hurry. Maps of the full subway system are posted in stations and on trains, near the doors. You can usually pick up free maps at token booths, too.

For route information, **ask the token clerk, a transit policeman, or a fellow rider.** Once New Yorkers realize you're harmless, most bend over backward to be helpful.

FARES & TRANSFERS

Subway fare is the same as bus fare: $1.50. You can transfer between subway lines an unlimited number of times at any of the numerous stations where lines intersect. If you use a MetroCard (☞ Public Transportation, *above*) to pay your fare, you can also transfer to intersecting MTA bus routes for free. Transfers have time limits of generally two hours.

PAYING

Pay your subway fare at the turnstile as you head for the platform, using a subway token or a MetroCard that you can purchase at the token booth or from a vending machine.

SMOKING

Smoking is not allowed on New York City subways or in subway stations.

➤ SUBWAY INFORMATION: **Metropolitan Transit Authority (MTA) Travel Information Center** (☎ 718/330–1234). **MTA Status information hot line** (☎ 718/243–7777), updated hourly.

TAXES

The city charges tax on hotel rooms (13.25%), rental cars (13.25%), and parking in commercial lots or garages (18.25%).

SALES TAX

New York City's 8.25% sales tax applies to almost everything you can buy retail, including restaurant meals. Clothing under $110, prescription drugs, and non-prepared food bought in grocery stores are exempt from sales tax.

TAXIS & CAR SERVICES

There are several difference between taxis and car services, the main one being that a taxi is yellow and a car-service sedan is not. In addition, taxis run on a meter, while car services charge a flat fee. And by law, car services are not allowed to pick up passengers unless you call for one first. Always **determine the fee** beforehand when using a car service sedan.

Yellow cabs are in abundance almost everywhere in Manhattan, cruising the streets looking for fares. They are usually easy to hail on the street or from a taxi rank in front of major hotels, though finding one at rush hour or in the rain can take some time. Even if you're stuck in a downpour or at the airport, **do not accept a ride from a gypsy cab.** If a cab is not yellow and does not have an aqua-color plastic medallion riveted to the hood, you could be putting yourself in danger by getting into the car.

You can check **if a taxi is available by checking its rooftop light;** if the center panel is lit and the side panels are dark, the driver is ready to take passengers. Taxi fares cost $2 for the first ⅕ mi, 30¢ for each ⅕ mi thereafter, and 20¢ for each minute not in motion. A 50¢ surcharge is added to rides begun between 8 PM and 6 AM. There is no charge for extra passengers, but you must pay any bridge or tunnel tolls incurred during your trip (sometimes a driver will personally pay a toll to keep moving quickly, but that amount will be added to the fare when the ride is over). Taxi drivers expect a 15% tip.

To avoid unhappy taxi experiences, **try to know where you want to go and how to get there before you hail a cab.** A few cab drivers are dishonest, some speak less-than-perfect English, and not all know the city as well as they should. Direct your cab driver by the cross streets of your destination (for instance, "5th Avenue and 42nd Street"), rather than simply the numerical address, which means nothing to most drivers. Also, speak simply and clearly to make sure the driver has heard you correctly—this will save you time, money, and aggravation. A quick pre-call to your destination will give you cross-street information, as will a quick glance at a map marked with address numbers. You can also find the cross street of many Manhattan addresses using the conversion chart found in the front section of the Yellow Pages. A little preparation is well worth the effort—if you have no idea of the proper route, you may be taken for a long and costly ride.

➤ CAR SERVICES: A few reliable services include **Carmel** (☎ 212/666–6666), **Highbridge Car Service** (☎ 212/927–4600), and **Tel-Aviv** (☎ 212/777–7777).

TELEPHONES

Avoid making calls from your hotel room, because you may be charged a higher rate than usual for direct-dial calls or a surcharge on credit-card calls. Telephone calls can be made from public pay phones, both on the street and in hotels, bars, and restaurants.

The area codes for Manhattan are 212, 646, and 917. For Brooklyn, Queens, the Bronx, and Staten Island, the area codes are 718 and 347. The 917 area code is also used for many cellular phones and pagers in all five boroughs.

Make sure that the pay phone is labeled as a Verizon telephone; the unmarked variety are notorious change-eaters. There are also public credit-card phones scattered around the city. If you want to consult a directory or make a more leisurely call, pay phones in the lobbies of office buildings or hotels (some of which take credit cards) are a better choice.

TIME

New York operates on Eastern Standard Time. When it is noon in New

York it is 9 AM in Los Angeles, 11 AM in Chicago, 5 PM in London, and 3 AM the following day in Sydney.

TIPPING

The customary tipping rate is 15%–20% for taxi drivers and waiters; bellhops are usually given $2 per bag in luxury hotels, $1 per bag elsewhere. Hotel maids should be tipped at least $2 per day of your stay. You should always tip your hotel concierge for services rendered; the size of the tip depends on the difficulty of your request and the quality of the concierge's work. For an ordinary dinner reservation or tour arrangements, $3–$5 should do; if the concierge scores seats at an impossible-to-get-into restaurant or show or performs unusual services (getting your laptop repaired, finding a good allergist, etc.), $10 or more is appropriate.

TRAIN TRAVEL TO AND FROM NEW YORK

For information about traveling by subway within New York City, *see* Subway Travel, *above*.

Amtrak trains from points across the United States arrive at **Penn Station** (⊠ W. 31st to W. 33rd Sts., between 7th and 8th Aves.). For trains from New York City to Long Island and New Jersey, take the Long Island Railroad and New Jersey Transit, respectively; both operate from Penn Station. Metro-North Commuter Railroad trains take passengers from **Grand Central Terminal** (⊠ E. 42nd St. at Park Ave.) to points north of New York City, both in New York State and Connecticut. All of these trains generally run on schedule, although occasional delays occur. Smoking is not permitted on any of these trains. If you are taking a trip that necessitates switching trains, call ahead of time to ask how much time you should allow for that change.

➤ TRAIN INFORMATION: **Amtrak** (☎ 800/872-7245). **Long Island Railroad** (☎ 718/217-5477). **Metro-North Commuter Railroad** (☎ 212/532-4900). **New Jersey Transit** (☎ 973/762-5100). **PATH** (☎ 800/234-7284).

TRANSPORTATION AROUND NEW YORK

See Bus Travel, Public Transportation, Subway Travel, *and* Taxis, *above*.

VISITOR INFORMATION

Contact the New York City visitors information offices below for brochures, subway and bus maps, Metro-Cards (☞ Public Transportation, *above*), a calendar of events, listings of hotels and weekend hotel packages, and discount coupons for Broadway shows. For a free booklet listing New York City attractions and tour packages, contact the New York State Division of Tourism.

➤ CITY INFORMATION: **NYC & Company–the Convention & Visitors Bureau** (⊠ 810 7th Ave., 3rd floor, between W. 52nd and W. 53rd Sts., ☎ 212/484-1222, 212/397-8200, or 212/484-1200; 212/397-8222 to order printed or audiovisual materials, FAX 212/582-8765, WEB www.nycvisit.com) weekdays 8:30-6, weekends 9-5. **Times Square Visitors Center** (⊠ 1560 Broadway, between W. 46th and W. 47th Sts., ☎ no phone, WEB www.timessquarebid.com), daily 8-8.

➤ STATEWIDE INFORMATION: **New York State Division of Tourism** (⊠ Box 2603, Albany, NY 12220, ☎ 518/474-4116 or 800/225-5697, WEB www.iloveny.state.ny.us).

WALKING

The cheapest, sometimes the fastest, and usually the most interesting way to explore this city is by walking. Because New Yorkers by and large live in apartments rather than in houses, and travel by cab, bus, or subway rather than by private car, they end up walking quite a lot. As a result, street life is a vital part of the local culture. On crowded sidewalks, people gossip, snack, browse, cement business deals, make romantic rendezvous, encounter long-lost friends, and fly into irrational quarrels with strangers. It's a wonderfully democratic hubbub.

A typical New Yorker, if there is such an animal, walks quickly and focuses intently on dodging cars, buses, bicycle messengers, construction sites, and other pedestrians. Although this might make natives seem hurried and rude, they will often cheerfully come to the aid of a lost pedestrian, so **don't hesitate to ask a passerby for directions.**

WEB SITES

Do check out the World Wide Web when planning your trip. You'll find everything from weather forecasts to virtual tours of famous cities. Be sure to **visit Fodors.com** (WEB www.fodors.com), a complete travel-planning site. You can research prices and book plane tickets, hotel rooms, rental cars, vacation packages, and more. In addition, you can post your pressing questions in the Travel Talk section and, in the site's Rants & Raves section, read comments about some of the restaurants and hotels in this book—and chime in yourself. Other planning tools include a currency converter and weather reports, and there are loads of links to other travel resources

To learn about the city in greater depth, go to the **New York Public Library** at WEB www.nypl.org for wonderful historical information. For more on traveling to New York City, **NYC & Company–the Convention & Visitors Bureau** at WEB www.nycvisit.com is a good source of basic sightseeing and lodging information, and a good place to find out about special offers. If you want to find out what's going on around town, **Movielink 777–FILM Online** at WEB www.777film.com delivers one-stop shopping for movie previews and tickets; **New York CitySearch** at WEB newyork.sidewalk.citysearch.com supplies comprehensive, searchable events listings; the *New York Times* at WEB www.nytimes.com has reviews of current movies and theater or at www.nytoday.com for music, dance, and art listings, and show times; and the *Village Voice* at WEB www.villagevoice.com gives thorough events listings. To figure out how to get around the city, consult the **New York Subway Finder** at WEB www.krusch.com/nysf.html for subway directions to any New York address.

WHEN TO GO

At one time, it seemed New York's cultural life was limited to the months between October and May, when new Broadway shows opened, museums mounted major exhibitions, and formal seasons for opera, ballet, and concerts held sway. Today, however, there are Broadway openings even in mid-July, and a number of touring orchestras and opera and ballet companies visit the city in summer. In late spring and summer, the streets and parks are filled with ethnic parades, impromptu sidewalk concerts, and free performances under the stars. Except for regular closing days and a few holidays (such as Christmas, New Year's Day, and Thanksgiving), the city's museums are open year-round.

CLIMATE

Although there's an occasional bone-chilling winter day, with winds blasting in off the Hudson, snow only occasionally accumulates in the city. Summer is the only unpleasant time of year, especially the humid, hot days of August, when many Manhattanites vacate the island for summer homes. Most hotels are air-conditioned, but if you're traveling in the summer and choosing budget accommodations, it's a good idea to **ask whether your room has an air conditioner.** Air-conditioned stores, restaurants, theaters, and museums provide respite from the heat; so do the many green expanses of parks. Subways and buses are usually air-conditioned, but subway stations can be as hot as saunas.

When September arrives—with its dry "champagnelike" weather—the city shakes off its summer sluggishness. Mild and comfortable, autumn shows the city off at its best, with yellow and bronze foliage displays in the parks.

The following table shows each month's average daily highs and lows:

➤ FORECASTS: **Weather Channel Connection** (☎ 900/932–8437), 95¢ per minute from a Touch-Tone phone.

Jan.	38F	3C	May	72F	22C	Sept.	76F	24C
	25	–4		54	12		60	16
Feb.	40F	4C	June	80F	27C	Oct.	65F	18C
	27	–3		63	17		50	10
Mar.	50F	10C	July	85F	29C	Nov.	54F	12C
	35	2		68	20		41	5
Apr.	61F	16C	Aug.	84F	29C	Dec.	43F	6C
	44	7		67	19		31	–1

FESTIVALS AND SEASONAL EVENTS

NYC & Company–the Convention and Visitors Bureau (☎ 212/484–1222), open weekdays 8:30–6 and weekends 9–5, has exact dates and times for many of the annual events listed below, and the bureau's Web site (WEB www.nycvisit.com) has yet more information on free activities.

➤ EARLY JAN.: The nine-day **New York National Boat Show,** at the Jacob K. Javits Convention Center (☎ 212/216–2000), exhibits the latest in pleasure craft (power- and sail-boats), yachts, and other nautical equipment.

➤ LATE JAN.: Leading dealers in the field of visionary art—also sometimes called naïve art or art of the self-taught—exhibit their wares at the **Outsider Art Fair,** at the Puck Building in SoHo (☎ 212/777–5218).

➤ LATE JAN.–EARLY FEB.: The **Chinese New Year** (☎ 212/373–1800), celebrated over two weeks, includes a barrage of fireworks, extravagant banquets, and a colorful paper-dragon dance that snakes through the narrow streets of Chinatown.

➤ EARLY FEB.: In the invitational **Annual Empire State Building Run-Up** (☎ 212/860–4455), runners scramble up the 1,576 stairs from the lobby of the Empire State Building to the 86th-floor observation deck. Nearly 3,000 well-bred canines and their human overseers take over Madison Square Garden for the **Westminster Kennel Club Dog Show** (☎ 212/465–6741 or 800/455–3647, WEB www.thegarden.com), the nation's second-longest-running animal event (after the Kentucky Derby).

➤ FEB. 14: During the **Valentine's Day Marriage Marathon,** couples marry atop the Empire State Building (☎ 212/736–3100 ext. 377).

➤ EARLY MAR.: The gargantuan **Art Expo** (☎ 888/322–5226), at the Jacob K. Javits Convention Center, includes cultural performances from around the world.

➤ MAR. 17: New York's first **St. Patrick's Day Parade** (☎ 212/484–1222) took place in 1762, making this boisterous tradition one of the city's oldest annual events. The parade heads up 5th Avenue, starting at 44th Street at 11 AM and finishing at 86th Street.

➤ LATE MAR.: At the **International Asian Art Fair** (☎ 212/642–8572, WEB www.haughton.com), 60 dealers from around the world exhibit furniture, sculptures, bronzes, ceramics, carpets, jewelry, and more from the Middle East, Southeast Asia, and the Far East.

➤ LATE MAR.–EARLY APR.: Every spring the world-famous three-ring **Ringling Bros. and Barnum & Bailey Circus** (☎ 212/465–6741 for information; WEB www.ringling.com) comes to town. Just before opening night the Animal Walk takes the show's four-legged stars from their train at Penn Station along 34th Street to the Garden; it happens around midnight but is well worth the effort. The **Triple Pier Expo** (☎ 212/255–0020) lures more than 600 antiques dealers to Piers 88, 90, and 92, offering everything from art glass to furniture. There's a reprise of the event in November, as well.

➤ APR.: The week before Easter, the **Macy's Flower Show** (☎ 212/494–5432) creates lush displays in its flagship emporium and sets its Broadway windows abloom. Exquisite flower arrangements are also on display in Rockefeller Center.

➤ EASTER SUNDAY: As in the classic Fred Astaire movie, you can don an extravagant hat and join the **Easter Promenade** up 5th Avenue. The excitement centers around St. Patrick's Cathedral, at 51st Street.

➤ MID-APR.: The 41st annual **Antiquarian Book Fair** (☎ 212/777–5218 or 212/944–8291), held at the Seventh Regiment Armory on the Upper East Side, is a book-lover's jackpot with 185 book exhibitors displaying first editions, rare volumes, manuscripts, autographs, letters, atlases, drawings, prints, and maps, with prices ranging from $25 to more than $25,000.

➤ APR.–SEPT.: The **Major League baseball season** sees the New York Yankees (☎ 718/293–6000, www.yankees.com) drawing large crowds to Yankee Stadium, in the Bronx, while the Mets (☎ 718/507–8499, WEB www.mets.com) play at Shea Stadium, in Queens.

➤ LATE APRIL: The **Cherry Blossom Festival** (☎ 718/623–7200, WEB www.bbg.org) is held at the Brooklyn Botanic Garden.

➤ EARLY MAY: At last count, about 30,000 cyclists turn out for the annual **Bike New York: The Great Five Boro Bike Tour** (☎ 212/932–2453, WEB www.bikenewyork.org). The 42-mi tour begins in Battery Park and ends with a ride across the Verrazano-Narrows Bridge (which doesn't otherwise allow bikes). A free ferry brings cyclists back to Manhattan. The **International Fine Art Fair** (☎ 212/642–8572, WEB www.haughton.com) brings dealers from all over the country to the Seventh Regiment Armory, where they show off exceptional paintings, drawings, and sculptures from the Renaissance to the 20th century.

➤ MID-MAY: Congregation Shearith Israel (the Spanish and Portuguese Synagogue—the landmark home of America's oldest Orthodox Jewish congregation) sponsors a one-day **Sephardic Fair** (☎ 212/873–0300, WEB www.shearith-israel.org), where you can watch artists making prayer shawls and crafting jewelry, potters throwing wine cups, and scribes penning marriage contracts.

➤ SECOND OR THIRD SATURDAY IN MAY: During the **Ninth Avenue Food Festival** (☎ 212/484–1222) booths lining 20 blocks of 9th Avenue (from West 37th Street to West 57th Street) offer every conceivable type of food, from obscure ethnic taste treats to American classics. Most of 9th Avenue's many food stores and restaurants also participate, offering samples of their wares as well as specially prepared delicacies.

➤ LATE MAY: Navy ships from the United States and abroad are joined by Coast Guard ships during **Fleet Week** (☎ 212/245–0072), for a parade up the Hudson River, then a docking in Manhattan during which ships are open to the public. It all happens at the *Intrepid* Air, Sea and Space Museum during the week before Memorial Day. For more than half a century, Memorial Day has marked the start of the **Washington Square Outdoor Art Exhibit** (☎ 212/982–6255), an open-air arts-and-crafts fair with some 600 exhibitors who set up in the park and on surrounding streets. The action continues for two weekends, from noon to sundown.

➤ EARLY JUNE: The **Belmont Stakes** (☎ 718/641–4700), New York's thoroughbred of horse races, and a jewel in the Triple Crown, comes to Long Island's Belmont Park Racetrack.

➤ EARLY–MID-JUNE: The **Bell Atlantic New York Jazz Festival** (☎ 212/219–3006, WEB www.jazfest.com), which began more than 10 years ago as an alternative to the JVC Jazz Festival, sponsors 350 performances of classic, acid, Latin, and avant-garde jazz at clubs and public spaces around town. **The Knitting Factory** (✉ 74 Leonard St.) is a main venue.

➤ MID-JUNE: During the **National Puerto Rican Day Parade** (☎ 718/401–0404 or 212/374–5176, WEB www.nationalpuertoricanparade.org), dozens of energetic bands send their loud rhythms reverberating down 5th Avenue as huge crowds cheer them on. However, past events have been marred by problems due to unruly crowds.

➤ LATE JUNE: **Lesbian and Gay Pride Week** (☎ 212/807–7433, WEB www.nycpride.org) includes the world's biggest annual gay pride parade, a film festival, and hundreds of other activities. **JVC Jazz Festival New York** (☎ 212/501–1390, WEB festivalproductions.net/jvc/ny) brings giants of jazz and new faces alike to Carnegie Hall, Lincoln Center, the Beacon Theater, Bryant Park, and other theaters and clubs about town.

➤ LATE JUNE–EARLY JULY: The **Washington Square Music Festival** (☎ 212/431–1088) is a series of Tuesday evening free outdoor classical, jazz, and big band concerts.

➤ JUNE–AUG.: Every Monday night filmgoers throng glorious Bryant Park, the backyard of the New York Public Library's Humanities Center, for the **Bryant Park Film Festival** (☎ 212/512–5700 film hot line); the lawn turns into a picnic ground as fans of classic films claim space hours before show time, which is at dusk. In Central Park **Summer Stage** (☎ 212/360–2777, WEB www.summerstage.org) presents free weekday-evening and weekend-afternoon blues, Latin, pop, African, and country music, dance, opera, and readings. **Shakespeare in the Park** (☎ 212/539–8500; 212/539–8750 [seasonal phone at the Delacorte], WEB www.publictheater.org), sponsored by the Joseph Papp Public Theater at Central Park's Delacorte Theater, tackles the Bard and other classics, often with a star performer or two from the big or small screen. The **New York Philharmonic** (☎ 212/875–5656, WEB www.newyorkphilharmonic. org) chips in with free concerts in various city parks. **Celebrate Brooklyn** (☎ 718/855–7882 ext. 52), New York's longest-running free performing arts festival, brings pop, jazz, rock, classical, klezmer, African, Latin, Caribbean multicultural music, as well as spoken-word and theatrical performances, to the band shell in Brooklyn's Prospect Park.

➤ JULY: **Midsummer Night Swing** (☎ 212/875–5766, WEB www. lincolncenter.org) transforms Lincoln Center's Fountain Plaza into an enormous open-air dance hall. Top big bands provide jazz, Dixieland, R&B, calypso, and Latin rhythms for dancers of all ages; dance lessons are offered each night.

➤ JULY 4: Lower Manhattan celebrates **Independence Day** (☎ 212/484–1222) with the Great 4th of July Festival, which includes arts, crafts, ethnic food and live entertainment. South Street Seaport also puts on a celebration. **Macy's 4th of July Fireworks** fill the night sky over the East River. The best viewing points are FDR Drive from 14th to 41st streets (access via 23rd, 34th, and 48th streets) and the Brooklyn Heights Promenade. The FDR Drive is closed to traffic, but arrive early, as police sometimes restrict even pedestrian traffic.

➤ JULY: **Lincoln Center Festival** (☎ 212/875–5928, WEB www. lincolncenter.org), under the direction of an international summer performance event lasting several weeks, includes classical music concerts, contemporary music and dance presentations, stage works, and non-Western arts.

➤ AUG.: **Lincoln Center Out-of-Doors** (☎ 212/875–5108, WEB www. lincolncenter.org) is a series of music, dance, and family-oriented events lasting almost the entire month. **Harlem Week** (☎ 212/862–7200), the world's largest black and Hispanic festival, runs throughout the month. Come for the food, concerts, gospel events, a film festival, children's festival, auto show, and historic bike tour. The music of Mozart and his peers wafts through Lincoln Center during the **Mostly Mozart** (☎ 212/875–5030, WEB www.lincolncenter. org) festival, whose orchestra plays under the inspired baton of the Seattle Symphony's Gerard Schwarz. Afternoon and evening concerts are offered at reasonable prices.

➤ LATE AUG.–EARLY SEPT.: The **U.S. Open Tennis Tournament** (☎ 888/673–6849, WEB www.usopen.org), in Flushing Meadows–Corona Park, Queens, is one of the city's premiere annual sport events.

➤ LABOR DAY WEEKEND: A Caribbean revel modeled after the harvest carnival of Trinidad and Tobago, the **West Indian American Day Parade** (☎ 718/

625–1515, WEB www.nyccarnival.org), on Labor Day in Brooklyn, is the centerpiece of a week's worth of festivities. Celebrations include salsa, reggae, and calypso music performances, as well as Monday's gigantic Mardi Gras–style parade of floats, elaborately costumed dancers, stilt walkers, and West Indian food and music.

➤ EARLY SEPT.: **Broadway on Broadway** (☎ 212/563–2929) brings some of the best current musical theater to the streets for a free two-hour outdoor concert held in Times Square in early September.

➤ SEPT.: Garlands and lights bedeck Little Italy's Mulberry Street and environs for the **Feast of San Gennaro** (☎ 212/764–6330,) the city's oldest, grandest, largest, and most crowded *festa,* held in honor of the patron saint of Naples. Every other September, Jim Henson Productions brings the **International Festival of Puppet Theater** (☎ 212/794–2400, WEB www.henson.com) to Manhattan. The next festival will take place in 2002. This festival delights children and adults alike; it's impressed critics, too, winning both Obie and Drama Desk awards. The festival is always spectacular, in part because performances change yearly and are held at a number of venues throughout the city. Call for more information.

➤ MID-SEPT.: Some 200 publishers of all stripes set up displays along 5th Avenue from 48th to 57th Streets for **New York Is Book Country** (☎ 212/207–7242, WEB www.nyisbookcountry.com), where you can buy new Fall releases, meet authors, admire beautiful book jackets, and enjoy live entertainment and bookbinding demonstrations. Bring the children.

➤ LATE SEPT.–EARLY OCT.: Begun in 1963, the **New York Film Festival** (☎ 212/875–5610, WEB www.filmlinc.com) is the city's most prestigious annual film event. Cinephiles pack various Lincoln Center venues; advance tickets to afternoon and evening screenings are essential to guarantee a seat.

➤ OCTOBER THROUGH DECEMBER: The Brooklyn Academy of Music (BAM)

Next Wave Festival (☎ 718/636–4100, WEB www.bam.org) attracts crowds from throughout the Metropolitan area. Next Wave was begun in 1983 to introduce local and international cutting-edge dance, opera, theater, and music. You can see such "regulars" as Phillip Glass, John Cale, Lou Reed, and the German dance troupe of Pina Bausch at the festival.

➤ OCT.: The **Columbus Day Parade** (☎ 212/249–9923) is held each year around Oct. 12, normally on 5th Avenue between 44th and 86th Streets. Considered one of the world's top art fairs, the **International Fine Art and Antique Dealers Show** (☎ 212/642–8572, WEB www.haughton.com) brings dealers from the U.S. and Europe, who show treasures dating from antiquity to the 20th century at the Seventh Regiment Armory.

➤ OCT. 31: Fifty thousand revelers, many in bizarre but brilliant costumes, march up 6th Avenue (from Spring to W. 23rd Sts.) in the **Greenwich Village Halloween Parade** (☎ 914/758–5519, WEB www.halloween-nyc.com).

➤ OCT.–APR.: **New York Rangers Hockey** (☎ 212/465–6741, WEB www.newyorkrangers.com) attracts passionate fans at Madison Square Garden. The ever-popular **New York Knickerbockers** (☎ 212/465–5867, WEB www.nba.com/knicks) basketball team continues to fill up Madison Square Garden during their home games.

➤ EARLY NOV.: The **New York City Marathon** (☎ 212/860–4455, WEB www.nyrrc.org), the world's largest, begins on the Staten Island side of the Verrazano-Narrows Bridge and snakes through all five boroughs before finishing at Tavern on the Green in Central Park.

➤ VETERAN'S DAY: On **Veteran's Day** an annual parade marches down 5th Avenue to Madison Square Park. Following the parade, there is a service held at the Eternal Light Memorial in the park.

➤ MID-NOV.: The annual **Fall Antiques Show** (☎ 212/777–5218), sponsored by the Museum of American Folk Art, is the foremost American-antiques show in the country and a bonanza for collectors of Americana. It attracts 65 dealers from all over the United States to the Seventh Regiment Armory.

➤ THANKSGIVING DAY: The **Macy's Thanksgiving Day Parade** (☎ 212/494–4495) is a New York tradition; huge balloons float down Central Park West from West 77th Street to Broadway and Herald Square. The day-before inflating of the balloons has become an event in its own right.

➤ NOV.–JAN.: The **Radio City Christmas Spectacular** features the famed Rockettes at Radio City Music Hall (☎ 212/247–4777, WEB www.radiocity.com).

➤ LATE NOV.: One of the tallest Christmas trees in the country is mounted in Rockefeller Center, just above the golden Prometheus statue. Thousands of people gather to watch the ceremonial **tree lighting** (☎ 212/632–3975).

➤ LATE NOV.–EARLY JAN.: Every year the **Christmas window displays** on view at **Saks Fifth Avenue** (✉ 611 5th Ave., between 49th and 50th Sts.) and **Lord & Taylor** (✉ 424 5th Ave., between 38th and 39th Sts.) are more inventive and festive than ever.

➤ LATE DEC.: A **Giant Hanukkah Menorah** is lighted at Grand Army Plaza (✉ 5th Ave. and 59th St., ☎ 212/736–8400).

➤ NEW YEAR'S EVE: The famous **balldrop in Times Square** (☎ 212/768–1560, WEB www.timessquarebid.org) is televised all over the world. **First Night** (☎ 212/676–2000, WEB www.nycmillennium.org), a city-sponsored event that takes place in all five boroughs, includes dancing, live music, magicians, jugglers, arts and crafts, and other entertainment in a variety of alcohol-free venues. In Central Park, a festive **Midnight Run** sponsored by the New York Road Runners Club (☎ 212/860–4455, WEB www.nyrrc.org) begins at Tavern on the Green.

INDEX

NOTES

NOTES

FODOR'S NEW YORK CITY 2002

EDITOR: Constance Jones

Editorial Contributors: Mitchell Davis, Karen Deaver, John J. Donohue, Amanda Freeman, Joshua Greenwald, Lynda Hammes, Elise Harris, Jennifer Levitsky Kasoff, Jane Miller, Margaret Mittelbach, Emmanuelle Morgen, Mark Sullivan, Michael B. de Zayas

Editorial Production: Taryn Luciani

Maps: David Lindroth, *cartographer;* Steven Amsterdam and Bob Blake, *map editors*

Design: Fabrizio La Rocca, *creative director;* Guido Caroti, *art director;* Jolie Novak, *senior picture editor;* Melanie Marin, *photo editor*

Cover Design: Pentagram

Production/Manufacturing: Robert B. Shields

COPYRIGHT

ISBN 0–679–00856–X

ISSN 0736-9395

IMPORTANT TIP

Although all prices, opening times, and other details in this book are based on information supplied to us at press time, changes occur all the time in the travel world, and Fodor's cannot accept responsibility for facts that become outdated or for inadvertent errors or omissions. So always confirm information when it matters, especially if you're making a detour to visit a specific place.

SPECIAL SALES

Fodor's Travel Publications are available at special discounts for bulk purchases for sales promotions or premiums. Special editions, including personalized covers, excerpts of existing guides, and corporate imprints, can be created in large quantities for special needs. For more information, contact your local bookseller or write to Special Markets, Fodor's Travel Publications, 280 Park Avenue, New York, NY 10017. Inquiries from Canada should be directed to your local Canadian bookseller or sent to Random House of Canada, Ltd., Marketing Department, 2775 Matheson Boulevard East, Mississauga, Ontario L4W 4P7. Inquiries from the United Kingdom should be sent to Fodor's Travel Publications, 20 Vauxhall Bridge Road, London SW1V 2SA, England.

PRINTED IN THE UNITED STATES OF AMERICA

10 9 8 7 6 5 4 3 2 1

PHOTOGRAPHY

Poul Lange, *cover.*

Catherine Ashmore, *3 top right.*

Brooklyn Academy of Music Press: *Hermann & Clarchen Baus, 2 top left.*

Daniel, *16A.*

Digital Stock, *30E.*

© Disney: *Joan Marcus, 20C.*

Duomo: *Steven E. Sutton, 22B. Chris Trotman, 22C.*

Four Seasons Hotel New York, *30A.*

Frick Collection, *19F.*

Gramercy Tavern, *2 top right.*

A. Perry Heller, *16B.*

The Image Bank: *Murray Alcosser, 19D. Steve McAlister, 16 top. Andy Caulfield, 9C, 10B, 28C. Color Day, 8A. Wiliam H. Edwards, 24B. Michael Funk, 27B. David W. Hamilton, 12C. Anthony Johnson, 18C. Patti McConville, 7D, 10A, 11D, 15D, 19E, 23E. Joe McNally, 18A. Benn Mitchell, 30F. Marvin E. Newman, 11E, 12A. Andrea Pistolesi, 25 bottom left, 26A. Marc Romanelli, 13 bottom. Antonio Rosario, 17E, 21D. Guido Alberto Rossi, 7E, 11F. Joseph Szkodzinski, 18B. Santi Visalli, 10C.*

Catherine Karnow, *6A, 9D, 14 bottom, 17C, 17D, 25E, 32.*

Kelly/Mooney, *24A, 24C.*

James Lemass, *1, 6B, 12B, 13D, 14B, 15C, 15E, 21E, 21F, 22A, 23D, 23F.*

Liaison Agency, Inc.: *E. Kafka, 25D.*

Livent, Inc., *20A.*

The Lowell, *30C.*

Macy's, *14A.*

Joan Marcus, *20B.*

Charles McKinney, *3 bottom left.*

Scott Murphy, *3 top left, 4-5, 6C.*

NY Mets: *Marc S. Levine, 2 bottom right.*

The New York Palace Hotel, *30B.*

Peter Paige, *30G.*

Don Perdue, *3 bottom right.*

Sony Theaters Lincoln Square, *29D.*

Staten Island Institute of Arts & Sciences: *Ray Erickson, 2 bottom center.*

Trinity Church: *Leo Sorel, 9B.*

Wildlife Conservation Society, *2 bottom left.*

Roy J. Wright, *30D.*

ABOUT OUR WRITERS

The more you know before you go, the better your trip will be. New York's most fascinating small museum, or its cushiest day spa, or its slickest Korean spot could be just around the corner from your hotel, but if you don't know it's there, it might as well be on the other side of the globe. That's where this book comes in. It's a great step toward making sure your next trip lives up to your expectations. As you plan, check out the Web as well. Guidebooks have been helping smart travelers find the special places for years; the Web is one more tool. Whatever reference you consult, be savvy about what you read, and always consider the source. Images and language can be massaged to make places appear better than they are. And one traveler's quaint is another's grimy. Here at Fodor's, and at our on-line arm, Fodors. com, our focus is on providing you with information that's not only useful but accurate and on target. Every day Fodor's editors put enormous effort into getting things right, beginning with the search for the right contributors—people who have objective judgment, broad travel experience, and the writing ability to put their insights into words. There's no substitute for advice from a like-minded friend who has just come back from where you're going, but our writers, having seen all corners of New York, are the next best thing. They're the kind of people you'd poll for tips yourself if you knew them.

From their vantage point at The James Beard Foundation, Dining chapter writers **Mitchell Davis** and **Jane Miller** keep their eyes (and palates) peeled on New York's ever-changing restaurant scene. They have worked together on numerous cookbooks and articles for magazines such as *Fine Cooking* and *Food & Wine*. Jane also brought her good taste to bear on the update of the Lodging chapter.

Karen Deaver, who updated the downtown sections of Exploring Manhattan, also keeps tabs on the social dance scene for our Nightlife chapter. Karen thrives on a Big Apple diet of tango on Thursday, swing on Friday, and salsa on Saturday, and is forever shopping for comfortable shoes.

John J. Donohue is the nightlife editor of the "Goings On About Town" section at *The New Yorker*. His intimate knowledge of the city proved invaluable as he updated our Nightlife chapter and parts of Exploring Manhattan.

Amanda Freeman, who updated the shopping chapter, is a full-time trendhunter who considers New York City her favorite hunting grounds. Obsessed with being "in-the-know," she is always on the look out for something new. She is a former style columnist for *The Daily News,* who is ecstatic that she was able to turn her passion into her profession.

Freelance food writer and part-time chef **Josh Greenwald** updated Smart Travel Tips A to Z. He's cooked for top NYC restaurants such as Danube and Eleven Madison Park.

Lynda Hammes, a former editor at *Art & Auction* magazine, updated the Arts chapter. She is a freelance writer and runs a nonprofit gallery in Brooklyn.

A native New Yorker and decade-long Brooklyn resident, **Elise Harris,** our Exploring the Outer Boroughs and Books and Videos updater, has never lived farther from the city than Princeton, NJ. She recently traded in her gig as an editor at *Out* magazine for a daily schlepp to the New York Public Library, where she does freelance journalism.

Outdoors and sports updater **Jennifer Levitsky Kasoff,** a former Fodor's staff editor, has walked, bowled, and climbed her way around New York City since 1995.

Margaret Mittelbach has written about all aspects of the city, including the uptown sections of our Exploring Manhattan chapter.

Since earning a Master of Fine Arts degree from Sarah Lawrence College, **Michael de Zayas,** updater of the midtown sections of Exploring Manhattan, has lived in the East Village, Midtown, and on the Upper West Side. He has worked at two of the city's more venerable institutions: the Metropolitan Museum of Art and the *New York Post*.

Don't Forget to Write

Your experiences—positive and negative—matter to us. If we have missed or misstated something, we want to hear about it. We follow up on all suggestions. Contact the New York editor at editors@ fodors.com or c/o Fodor's, 280 Park Avenue, New York, New York 10017. And have a fabulous trip!

Karen Cure
Editorial Director